Peter Norton's
Complete Guide to
Windows XP

John Paul Mueller

SAMS

201 West 103rd Street, Indianapolis, Indiana 46290 USA

International Standard Book Number: 0-672-32291-9

Library of Congress Catalog Card Number: 2001093497

Printed in the United States of America

First Printing: November, 2001

04   03   02   4   3   2

Trademarks

Warning and Disclaimer

Associate Publisher
Jeff Koch

Executive Editor
Terry Neal

Development Editor
Steve Rowe

Managing Editor
Matt Purcell

Book Packaging
Justak Literary Services

Indexer
Sharon Hilgenberg

Proofreader
Lara SerVaas

Technical Editor
Greg Guntle

Interior Designer
Gary Adair

Cover Designer
Aren Howell

Page Layout
William Hartman

Overview

Contents

Dedication

This book is dedicated to Uncle Bob on his birthday; may he have many more!

Acknowledgments

Thanks to my wife, Rebecca, for working with me to get this book completed. I really don't know what I would have done without her help in proofreading my rough draft. She also helped research, compile, and edit some of the information that appears in this book.

Greg Guntle and Russ Mullen deserve thanks for their technical edit of this book. Both technical editors greatly added to the accuracy and depth of the material you see here. I also feel they added a lot to the flavor of the book by making many suggestions for additional content. This is well above their duties as technical editor.

This book required a lot of discussion with other people. A special thanks goes to Russ Mullen. Chapters 8 and 9 wouldn't exist without his help. Many of the development staff at Microsoft assisted with this book by providing answers to my never-ending questions. The members of the various Microsoft newsgroups were also a source of constant aid.

I would like to thank Scott Clark for his help and direction. His input was instrumental in helping this book achieve the depth of information it required.

Matt Wagner, my agent, deserves credit for helping me get the contract in the first place and taking care of all the details that most authors don't really think about. I always appreciate his help. It's good to know that someone wants to help.

Finally, I'd like to thank Terry Neal, Steve Rowe, Marta Justak, Becky Whitney, Jason Burita, and other members of the Sams staff for their assistance in bringing this book to print. Writing this Windows XP book presented many logistical challenges and I appreciate their willingness to give me the time required to put a good book together. I especially appreciate Terry's aid in obtaining some of the software required to write the book.

About the Author

John Mueller is a freelance author and technical editor. He has writing in his blood, having produced 52 books and over 200 articles to-date. The topics range from networking to artificial intelligence and from database management to heads-down programming. Some of his current books include a SOAP developer guide, a small-business and home office networking guide, and a Windows 2000 performance, tuning, and optimization book. His technical editing skills have helped over 25 authors refine the content of their manuscripts. John has provided technical editing services to both *Data Based Advisor* and *Coast Compute* magazines. He has also contributed articles to magazines like *SQL Server Professional*, *Visual C++ Developer*, and *Visual Basic Developer*. He is currently the editor of the .NET electronic newsletter for Pinnacle Publishing.

When John isn't working at the computer, you can find him in his workshop. He's an avid woodworker and candle maker. On any given afternoon, you can find him working at a lathe or putting the finishing touches on a bookcase. One of his newest craft projects is glycerin soap making, which comes in handy for gift baskets. You can reach John on the Internet at JMueller@mwt.net. John is also setting up a Web site at http://www.mwt.net/~jmueller/; feel free to look and make suggestions on how he can improve it. One of his current projects is creating book FAQ sheets that should help you find the book information you need much faster.

Tell Us What You Think!

As the reader of this book, *you* are our most important critic and commentator. We value your opinion and want to know what we're doing right, what we could do better, what areas you'd like to see us publish in, and any other words of wisdom you're willing to pass our way.

As an Associate Publisher for Sams, I welcome your comments. You can fax, email, or write me directly to let me know what you did or didn't like about this book—as well as what we can do to make our books stronger.

Please note that I cannot help you with technical problems related to the topic of this book, and that due to the high volume of mail I receive, I might not be able to reply to every message.

When you write, please be sure to include this book's title and author as well as your name and phone or fax number. I will carefully review your comments and share them with the author and editors who worked on the book.

Fax: 317-581-4770

Email: feedback@samspublishing.com

Mail: Jeff Koch
          Sams Publishing
          201 West 103rd Street
          Indianapolis, IN 46290 USA

Introduction

What is Windows XP all about? Everyone is asking this question, and you'll find there are more than a few opinions about the answer. Windows XP has generated more than a little press and for more than a few reasons. With Windows XP, Microsoft has combined two long-standing product lines. People wonder if Windows XP is up to the task of providing services for all of the Windows markets; home, small business, and enterprise alike. In fact, that's one of the topics we discuss in this book—you'll learn just how well Windows XP can meet your needs. In many cases, the answers will surprise you. Windows XP is one of those products that looks like a simple upgrade, but provides more than many people think that it will.

Microsoft is always fiddling with the Windows interface, and Windows XP is no exception. Windows XP sports a new, brighter interface that reduces the complexity of using Windows. Fortunately, for those of us who like all of our power close, you can modify the default interface to gain better access to all of the features that Windows XP supports. You can also use the Windows 2000 interface if you prefer. This book shows you how to manage all of the interface options.

Multimedia is another big win for Windows XP users. Never has Windows provided more accessibility to multimedia features than you see in this version. Windows XP not only includes a wealth of multimedia, but it also enables you to use more software than ever. You gain the protection of a Windows NT/2000–based operating system, but with none of the limitations of past offerings. A special chapter in this book tells you how to overcome every major obstacle to enjoying your favorite piece of educational software or game with Windows XP.

You've probably heard conflicting stories about the privacy issues surrounding Windows XP. Some reports say that Windows XP is full of potential privacy problems, and other people feel that the privacy issues are minor. We discuss these issues so that you can make a decision yourself. Interestingly enough, many of these issues are in your own hands. The options you choose during installation and the features you choose to use determine how much or how little personal information you expose. Of course, you need to know your options and learn how to exercise them, two important topics discussed in this book.

Windows XP is also about networking and securing your data. We discuss many new networking and security options throughout the book. You'll learn about the new version of

NTFS and see what it has to offer. The book covers new connectivity options and shows you how to use them. If you're moving from Windows 9x, you'll learn about the Microsoft Management Console and see how it helps you manage your system. You'll learn about local security policies and understand their place in the networking scenario.

The bottom line is that Windows XP is a great new product that also contains many features you've come to expect from Windows. It's safe to say that you'll view Windows XP as the best of Windows 9x and the best of Windows NT/2000 combined in one package that's accessible to everyone. This book is your key to understanding how all of these new features can help you become more productive using the new Windows XP features.

Who Should Read This Book?

I wrote this book for the intermediate-to-advanced Windows XP users who need to get the last ounce of computing power from their machines. To use this book, you should know how to use a mouse and have some familiarity with graphical user interfaces (GUIs). You should also know the basic parts of your machine and understand basic computer terms, such as central processing unit (CPU). If you have just turned on your computer for the first time, you might find some concepts in this book difficult to understand.

This book also targets anyone who needs to learn how to perform Windows XP tasks. I'll provide you with tips and techniques to make Windows XP easier to use, enhance overall system performance, and improve system stability. You'll learn advanced usage techniques and how command-line programs can help you perform tasks faster. I'll also show you how to fix Windows XP problems and troubleshoot your equipment when it fails.

Of course, every Windows XP user can gain something from this book, even if it's only a better understanding of how Windows XP works. We'll also spend some time looking at the internal workings of Windows XP. Not only will you learn about where Windows XP is today, but I'll also help you understand how Windows XP differs from its predecessors and how these differences help you become more productive.

What You Will Learn

It's difficult to summarize the content of an entire book in a few sentences. However, some topics are more important than others are. Here are some of the more important topics I cover in this book:

- Learning about all of the new Windows XP interface options
- Getting the most from the Internet
- Installation tips that everyone can use
- Working with Microsoft Management Console (MMC) and network management tools
- Exploiting the new utilities that Windows XP provides

- Getting your games and multimedia applications running quickly
- Understanding the purpose of the files in the \SYSTEM folder
- Learning to install and manage Windows XP fonts and discovering ways to make them easier to use
- Performance tips to turn your machine into a speed demon
- Overcoming certain types of application support problems, especially problems with network clients
- Using Outlook Express for all your communication needs
- Navigating the Explorer interface
- Discovering the object-oriented approach to using resources on your machine
- Enhancing battery life and reducing power costs using Advanced Power Management (APM) and Advanced Configuration and Power Interface (ACPI) features.
- Compatibility tips about what works and what doesn't under Windows XP
- Learning about the objects available on the context menu and discovering how you can modify it to meet your needs
- Modifying your system setup to meet your needs fully
- Diagnosing, troubleshooting, and fixing hardware and software failures
- Work-arounds for potential Windows XP problems

I spend a great deal of time talking about the Windows XP architecture in various chapters. There are two reasons for this extensive exposure. First, you, as a user, really *do* need to know how the operating system works—or at least get an overview—so that you can maximize the way you use its features. Second, you need to know what Windows XP provides that older versions of Windows didn't. Exploring the architecture is one of the best ways to meet this goal.

How This Book Is Organized

This book divides Windows XP into functional and task-oriented areas. These parts of the book break each piece of Windows XP apart to see how it ticks and what you can use it for. Of course, many chapters help you understand what's going on under the hood, too. Without this information, it would be difficult at best to make full use of the new features that Windows XP offers.

I'd like to offer one final piece of advice. Windows XP is a very user- and data-oriented operating system. It's probably the most user-tuned product available right now for the PC. This doesn't mean that Windows XP is perfect, nor does it mean that everything is as it seems. Sometimes, you'll find something that's so difficult to use that you'll wonder why Microsoft did it that way. For example, I found the Registry difficult to work with until I discovered all of the tools that Microsoft provides to make the job easier. You should take the time to explore this product fully and figure out which techniques work best for you. Windows XP offers more than one way to do every task. You need to find the one that's best for you.

Introducing the Windows eXPerience (XP)

This book begins with an overview of the Windows XP interface. You'll learn how this interface can help you complete tasks quickly. Chapter 1 tells you about all of the new and updated features that Windows XP provides. It also helps you understand the combined code base and how the changes in Windows XP affect features you might have used in the past.

Chapters 2 and 3 are a complete description of the Explorer interface. You'll learn about both the new Windows XP interface and the Windows 2000 interface you can use as an alternative. Chapter 2 shows how to use some of the standard utilities that Windows XP provides. Chapter 3 concentrates on advanced user features and helps you customize the Windows XP environment to meet your specific needs.

Power Primers

This section of the book has three chapters. Chapter 4 helps you get a good start with Windows XP by showing how to perform several types of installation. Of course, I also offer a few tips on actually getting the installation done, based on real-world experience rather than on what should theoretically happen. Sometimes, you want to do the opposite of what the Microsoft documentation says to do, just to get a more efficient setup. This section of the book looks at some tips and techniques I've accumulated over months of testing Windows XP.

Chapter 5 deals with tuning tips. Getting the best performance and highest reliability is the concern of everyone who's just starting to use a new operating system. Windows XP offers many ways to tune your system. It would seem that all these controls could help you get a tuned system with a minimal amount of effort. Actually, the exact opposite is true. All of these controls interact—and you have to take these interactions into account as you change settings. Optimizing one area usually means detuning another area by an equal amount.

This section of the book helps you determine what type of tuning you need to perform and shows how tuning affects your system. A little turn here and a bump there can really make a big difference in how your system performs. The idea is to tune each area of Windows XP in moderation. You also need to consider your special needs. Even the type of network you use affects the way you tune your system.

One thing is certain: Windows XP offers more in the way of reliability and performance features than previous versions of Windows did. Your job now is to decide how to use those features to your benefit. Getting that high-performance system together is the first goal you want to achieve under Windows XP. After that, the datacentric approach to managing your system should make operating it a breeze.

Chapter 7 answers the question of how you can get the best performance from your applications. I'll show you techniques for interacting with Windows faster and show how you can use Windows features to your advantage when working with data. Some readers have asked that I show a few more keyboard tricks, so there's a special keyboard shortcut section in this chapter. You'll be amazed at how much you can accomplish using simple keyboard tricks.

Advanced Windows XP Usage Techniques

Some people learn to use a computer but never learn to use it well. The problem, in many cases, is that they lack knowledge of some of the hidden features a product provides. In other cases, a lack of system optimization is to blame. Still other people have problems understanding the documentation that comes with the product.

I've filled this section of the book with tips and techniques that are so often missing from the vendor documentation. You'll find a big difference between the way things should work and the way they really do. We'll look at everything from general printing techniques to the latest in multimonitor displays.

Chapter 7 is the place to look for configuration needs, especially using the Microsoft Management Console (MMC). You'll learn how to work with applications in Chapter 8. This chapter includes everything from getting applications installed to optimizing their use within Windows XP. I've also included a special section on scripting. Chapter 9 provides hardware installation and usage techniques. Finally, Chapter 10 contains everything you need to know to play games and use multimedia in Windows XP. You'll want to pay special attention to the DirectX diagnostic section in this chapter if you've ever had a problem getting a game to work under Windows XP.

The Windows XP Anatomy

Learning how to use an operating system often means learning a bit about how it works inside. For some people, a quick overview of Windows XP's internals is enough, especially if you plan to use Windows XP in a single-user mode and don't need to get every ounce of power from your machine.

However, if you do have to manage a large number of machines or need to get inside and learn how things work from a programmer's point of view, you'll really appreciate this section of the book. I don't go into a bits-and-bytes, blow-by-blow description, but this section blows the lid off all the architectural aspects of Windows XP (see Chapter 11). We'll examine every major component of Windows XP, from the file system (see Chapter 13) to the API. I'll even include some information about the Registry (see Chapter 12).

Windows and the Underlying Hardware

This is the section where you will learn about the mechanics of working with Windows XP. You'll begin with a view of fonts and printing. This chapter includes new material on working with network printers. We'll also discuss new font technologies, such as ClearType.

Chapter 15 discusses your mouse and keyboard. We'll begin with a look at multilingual support. A special section tells you how to handle keyboards with special features. The mouse section includes special mouse types, including both USB mouse tips and those used with laptop computers. The chapter ends with a discussion of special accessibility features provided with Windows XP.

You'll find a complete discussion of your video adapter in Chapter 16. The chapter begins with information about graphics standards and the Windows XP graphics architecture. You'll also learn how to install and configure both display adapters and monitors. Finally, we will discuss multiple display scenarios, graphics technologies, such as AGP, and troubleshooting techniques for display adapters.

The final chapter in this section discusses mobile computing needs. Chapter 17 tells you about both laptops and PDAs. You will learn about technologies such as ACPI and creating some types of remote user connections. I'll also show you how to solve some of the problems of using Microsoft ActiveSync on Windows XP.

Making the Right Connections

Getting online doesn't have to be difficult. We'll begin this section by looking at how Windows helps you get online in a variety of ways, not just the Internet. Of course, the first thing you need to know how to do is make a connection, and that's what Chapter 18 is all about. You'll also learn some details about how Windows XP implements various communication features, like Dial-Up Networking.

Chapter 19 focuses on network connectivity. You'll learn about Internet Connection Sharing (ICS) and Virtual Private Networks (VPNs). This chapter also contains sections that describe Universal Plug and Play (UPnP), Web Based Enterprise Management (WBEM), and using HyperTerminal to create a Telnet connection.

Chapter 20 is the Internet Explorer and Outlook Express chapter. You'll learn the details of using both these applications to create online connections. We'll also discuss issues such as how URLs and protocols work.

Networking with Windows XP

Very few companies do without the benefits provided by networks these days. The smallest office usually has a network setup of some kind if for no other reason than simple e-mail and file sharing. The surprising thing is how many home networks are popping up. Not only are these networks used for obvious applications, like allowing a child to access some of the files on their parent's machine, but also new applications, like game playing. It's surprising to see just how many new games allow two or more people to play a game using a simple network setup.

All of these new applications work with home and small-business networks, where the need for network-specific information becomes greater every day. Although Chapter 21 can't fully explore every networking solution available to you, it does fully explore the solutions supported by Windows XP. This chapter also discusses some special client issues, especially those attached to using NetWare with Windows XP.

Given the networking environments in which you use Windows XP, security doesn't seem like it would be that big of an issue. However, even a small company has to protect its data. Needless to say, we'll spend some time looking at security issues in Chapter 22.

Troubleshooting Windows XP

One of the big issues for Windows XP users upgrading from Windows 9x is the loss of DOS. Chapter 23 contains information on working around problems with older applications, especially those that rely on DOS to get the job done. We'll also discuss how to create boot disks.

Have you ever installed something and gotten it to work right the first time? That's what I thought. I usually have some problems, too. Unlike the Macintosh, the PC contains parts that come from a myriad of vendors. All these parts are supposed to work together, but sometimes they don't.

Many hardware (see Chapter 24) and software (see Chapter 25) installation-related problems have nothing to do with hidden agendas or vendor ineptitude. Some problems occur because of a poorly written specification. One vendor interprets a specification one way, and another uses a very different interpretation. The result is hardware and software that really don't work together. Each one follows the "standard," but each one follows it differently.

At other times, a user shoots himself in the foot. How many times have you thought that you did something according to the instructions, only to find out that you really didn't? It happens to everyone. Even a bad keystroke can kill an installation. Take the Windows registry. It's all too easy to take a misstep when editing it and end up with an operating system that doesn't boot.

Even if you do manage to get a fully functional system the first time through and you keep from shooting yourself in the foot, what are the chances that the installation will stay stable forever? It's unlikely. Your system configuration changes daily as you optimize applications and perform various tasks.

As you can see, the typical computer has many failure points, so things fall apart from time to time. This section of the book helps you quickly diagnose and fix most major problems you'll run into with Windows XP. We'll even look at a few undocumented ways to determine what's going on and how to interpret the information you get.

Conventions Used in This Book

It's important to know what I mean when you see certain types of information in the book. For example, I use special fonts to set aside Web site URLs. I've used the following conventions in this book:

File | Open   Menus and the selections on them are separated by a vertical bar. File | Open means "Access the File menu and choose Open."

`http:\\URL`   You'll find lots of Web sites listed in the book. I use this special font to make them easier to find them in the text. Web sites contain additional information, specifications, or other helpful tips that I feel you might like to know about.

`monospace`   It's important to differentiate the text that you use in a macro or that you type at the command line from the text that explains it. I've used monospace type to make this differentiation. Whenever you see something in monospace, you know that this information appears in a macro, within a system file, such as CONFIG.SYS or AUTOEXEC.BAT, or as something you'll type at the command line. You'll even see the switches used with Windows commands in monospace.

`italic monospace`   Sometimes, you need to supply a value for a Windows or DOS command. For example, when you use the DIR command, you might need to supply a filename. It's convenient to use a variable name—essentially a placeholder—to describe the kind of value you need to supply. The same holds true for any other kind of entry, from macro commands to dialog box fields. Whenever you see a word in italic monospace, you know that the word is a placeholder that you need to replace with a value. The placeholder simply tells you what kind of value you need to provide.

`<Filename>`   A variable name between angle brackets is a value you need to replace with something else. The variable name I use usually provides a clue to what kind of information you need to supply. In this case, I'm asking for a filename. Never type the angle brackets when you type the value.

`[<Filename>]`   When you see square brackets around a value, switch, or command, it means that this component is optional. You don't have to include it as part of the command line or dialog box field unless you want the additional functionality that the value, switch, or command provides.

italic   I use italic wherever the actual value of something is unknown. I also use italic where more than one value might be correct. For example, you might see FILE*xxxx* in text. This means that the value could be anywhere between FILE0000 and FILE9999. I also use italic to introduce new terms in text.

ALL CAPS   Commands use all capital letters. Some registry entries also use all caps, even though they aren't commands. Normally, you'll type a command at the command prompt, within a PIF file field, or within the Run dialog box field. If you see all caps somewhere else, it's safe to assume that the item is a case-sensitive registry entry or some other value. Filenames also appear in all caps.

Icons

This book contains many icons that help you identify certain types of information. The following paragraphs describe the purpose of each icon.

Note: Notes tell you about interesting facts that don't necessarily affect your ability to use the other information in the book. I'll use note boxes to give you bits of information I've picked up while using Windows XP.

Tip: Everyone likes tips because they tell you new ways of doing things that you might not have thought about. Tip boxes also provide an alternative way of doing something that you might like better than the first approach I provided. Many tips also contain URLs for Web sites or newsgroups you might want to visit for additional information.

Warning: This means watch out! Warnings almost always tell you about some kind of system or data damage that will occur if you perform a certain action (or fail to perform others). Make sure you understand a warning thoroughly before you follow any instructions that come after it.

Peter's Principle:

I'll usually include a Peter's Principle to tell you how to manage your Windows environment more efficiently. I base these recommendations on my personal experience with different ways of doing the same thing. Boxes with this icon might also include ideas on where to find additional information or even telephone numbers you can call. You also find the names of shareware and freeware utility programs here.

PART I

Introducing the Windows eXPerience

The Updater's Guide to Windows XP

Windows XP promises to provide the next big thing in Windows computing. The problem is that no one is sure what the "next big thing" means in this situation. Microsoft's marketing machine is working overtime to bring people the good news about Windows XP, but all that they've managed to do is confuse many users who would normally update their systems. Although Windows XP has some clear benefits to offer, some in the trade press wonder aloud whether the vast majority of users will update their systems.

The problem, in short, is one of cost in an economy where slowdowns are the rule of the day. One big question that users have today is whether they really need a new version of Windows. After all, Windows 9x makes a great gaming platform, and Windows 2000 is a stable business platform. More than a few users feel that they could spend the money they'd normally spend on a Windows upgrade in other places. Microsoft's first marketing pitch is that Windows XP is a platform that can do both tasks well, but it's an argument that many people don't buy. Most people need one or the other, not both, so an upgrade that allows them to perform two tasks well doesn't have a lot of appeal. Windows XP does work equally well for games and business needs. It has freed my system from having to support multiple versions of Windows.

Viewing Windows XP in light of current technological requirements is important. Microsoft designed Windows 9x to work at the desktop, not on the Internet. Security is a problem when working with Windows 9x, especially if you have a permanent connection, such as a cable modem or digital subscriber line (DSL). Although Microsoft designed Windows 2000 to work on the Internet, the rigid Windows 2000 environment doesn't allow you to run a full suite of applications, which frustrates users who need to use a combination of both new and old applications. The most important Windows XP feature is that it provides the security of Windows 2000 with the flexibility of Windows 9x.

Of course, Windows XP does improve the system environment in other ways. For example, you now have access to three user interfaces. The first, a Windows XP–specific interface, keeps novice users from shooting themselves in the foot by reducing the number of potentially damaging choices. The second, also a Windows XP interface, allows more access to low-level operating system functionality for intermediate users. Finally, power users can still access the classic Windows 2000 interface and gain full access to the operating system functionality. Therefore, another big issue with Windows XP is that it allows you to control your environment better.

The saying "There's no such thing as a free lunch" is true with operating systems as much as with anything else. Windows XP does provide a flexible work environment, but you still lose access to some Windows 9x functionality. In addition, some people have already complained that Microsoft made poor decisions in some security areas with Windows XP. As we'll see later, many of these poor choices are due to the increased flexibility in the user environment.

For better or worse, Windows XP is Microsoft's latest operating system offering. It has a lot to offer users, and I consider it one of the best operating systems Microsoft has ever put together. Not that I'm saying that Windows XP is perfect—far from it. Microsoft has made plenty of mistakes with this operating system, and I'll show you how to get around them as the book progresses. However, from an initial release perspective, you'll find that Microsoft has come a long way with Windows XP.

Understanding the Combined Code Base

One term you hear associated with Windows XP is combined code base. From the 50,000-foot-overview perspective, the combined code base means that you'll find only one version of Windows on your store shelf from now on. You don't have to worry whether you're getting a Windows 9x version or a Windows 2000 version; they're all essentially the same operating system.

However, Windows XP does come in different editions. For some people, the term *editions* is another way of saying *versions*. What Microsoft is trying to say is that it has released products that have different levels of functionality. The base operating system is the same, but your ability to interact with and augment the operating system is different. The two editions we'll discuss in this book are the Home Edition and the Professional Edition:

- *Home Edition*   Microsoft designed this edition for people who want to play games or install educational software for their children. It has some odd limitations, especially in the area of security, which makes it a poor choice for business use. Some beta testers complained about the security decisions Microsoft made because they're artificial limits imposed by additional software. We'll discuss the whole issue of security in Chapter 22, "Setting Up Security." Suffice it to say that some people will buy the less expensive Home Edition and then express surprise at its security limitations.

- *Professional Edition*   This edition is the direct successor to Windows 2000 Professional. You'll find that the Professional Edition includes robust security and other business-oriented features. In fact, as we'll discuss in the "New Windows XP Features," section, later in this chapter, Microsoft has added some new features you'll really like. The big area of change (besides the obvious interface changes) is security. All the bad press Microsoft has received recently must have had an effect on the Windows XP design team. Security is still a problem, but it should be less of a problem than with past versions of Windows.

A combined code base doesn't mean that Microsoft literally combined Windows 9x and Windows 2000. The improved flexibility of Windows XP might make it feel like you're using a true combination of Windows XP, but this product uses the same kernel (core operating system elements) as Windows 2000. You gain access to the security provided by NTFS, along with features such as file compression. The added flexibility you see is a measure of the changes that Microsoft made to the Windows 2000 code. Its programmers wanted to create an environment where users would feel completely comfortable and become productive quickly.

Of course, Windows XP still comes with limitations because of its Windows 2000 kernel roots. I've tested many of my games on Windows XP. They have a few problems, but I can honestly say that this version of Windows runs more games than Windows 2000 ever thought of allowing, although some older Windows 9x games don't run no matter what you do. I still have to maintain a separate DOS partition for my DOS games and my hardware diagnostics programs. Unlike Windows 9x, you can't choose to boot into a DOS session when you start Windows XP, which means that you need to boot DOS separately to gain full access to all your system hardware for testing.

Microsoft has tried to ease some compatibility problems for both Windows 9x and Windows NT users alike. One feature we'll discuss later in the book allows you to place an application in compatibility mode. You can choose to make it appear as though the application is running under either Windows 9x or Windows NT. I found that this feature works to a certain extent, although it's not completely effective. Some applications just don't run if you're moving from the Windows 9x or Windows NT environments.

The bottom line on the combined code base is that the Windows XP operating system is based on the Windows 2000 kernel, but with some additional flexibility built in. Windows XP represents an effort on the part of Microsoft to ease users' transition from the world of a DOS-based operating system to a secure environment. This move is justified given the realities of computing today. Windows 9x just can't provide the level of security, reliability, performance, and stability that users want.

New Windows XP Features

Windows XP comes with a wealth of new features. Just how new these features are depends on whether you're moving from Windows 9x or Windows 2000 to Windows XP. Many new features are upgrades from Windows 2000. They look new to Windows 9x users because they haven't used Windows 2000 in the past. Even if you're a Windows

2000 Professional user, you'll want to look at the features of utilities you've seen in the past. Microsoft has made many changes to the Windows 2000 utilities to make them more flexible and easier to learn.

In some cases, Microsoft tries to convince you that a feature is new or noteworthy, when it's really a standard feature you need in today's computing environment. For example, Windows XP comes with the same Windows Installer you'll find in Windows 2000. The feature isn't new; it's not even unusual. Windows Installer is something you need in order to install modern applications. Of course, it's a vast improvement over the installation methods used in Windows 9x, so from that perspective you're getting something better.

Other features, such as Windows File Protection, appeared in limited form in Windows Millennium Edition (Me). This feature automatically restores a DLL if an older application overwrites it during the installation process. In other words, you don't have to worry about having applications fail because you suddenly have an older version of a DLL on your system. You also gain access to the Side-by-Side DLL feature from Windows 2000. This particular feature helps prevent DLL Hell by allowing more than one version of a DLL to reside on your system.

Now that I've piqued your curiosity, let's talk about the new features. The following sections provide an overview of important new Windows XP features, some of which are simply improvements over Windows 2000 counterparts. These sections don't include small changes, such as the personalized welcome screen feature, because we'll cover these features later in the book. Make sure that you look at the "Improvements to Existing Features," section, later in this chapter. Any changes to features that existed in Windows 9x appear in that section.

> **Note:** I've taken every precaution to ensure the accuracy of this material. However, errors can and do creep in. Please feel free to contact me at JMueller@mwt.net if you find any errors in this book. I'm also available to answer any questions you might have about my book. As people write in, I'll post updates to my Web site at http://www.mwt.net/~jmueller/.

New User Interface

As previously mentioned, one big news item for Windows XP is the user interface changes. Microsoft is trying to create a user interface that everyone can use. What it created is, in reality, three user interfaces that should appeal to specific groups of users. The first is a simple interface that most novices will like, but will make power users feel claustrophobic. Figure 1.1 shows what this interface looks like.

The second interface is a little more powerful. It looks like the Windows XP interface shown in Figure 1.1, but contains many power-user features found in the Windows 2000 interface. I consider it a good choice for average users. Microsoft is also calling it the Classic Start Menu interface. We'll see how to set up this interface in the "Switching to the Standard Interface" section in Chapter 3, "Advanced User Features."

FIGURE 1.1
The new Windows XP interface is extremely easy to work with, but limited in functionality.

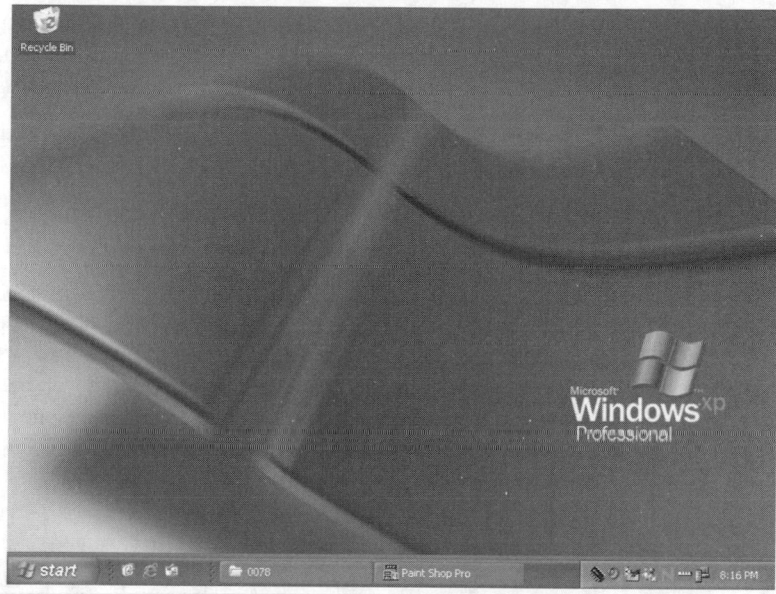

Finally, you can choose to go back to the Windows 2000 interface, as shown in Figure 1.2. As you can see in the figure, the interface still has a few changes, but they aren't nearly as noticeable. Power users who don't like gizmos will probably use this interface most often. This third interface allows you to get work done quickly, but also offers a bit less in the way of help. I'll show you how to enable this interface in the "Switching to the Windows 2000 Interface" section in Chapter 3.

FIGURE 1.2
Power users may want to try the Windows 2000 interface for Windows XP to gain maximum flexibility.

Note: Figures 1.1 and 1.2 show the user interface if you install Windows XP and don't perform any customization. Normally, you want to customize the interface to meet your specific needs. For example, you might not want to see the taskbar unless you're selecting something from it. Many users change the appearance of the desktop as well.

Task-Based Work Environment

Another new Windows Explorer feature is a task-based work environment, which is an extension of the Web content that appeared in Windows Explorer in previous versions. However, rather than just show you the statistics for a file, the new feature shows which tasks you can perform with the file. For example, if you're working with a Word document, Windows Explorer tells you that you can copy, rename, move, publish, e-mail, print, or throw away the file. Figure 1.3 shows a typical task-based work environment for a single-pane view.

FIGURE 1.3
Windows XP stresses a task-based work environment.

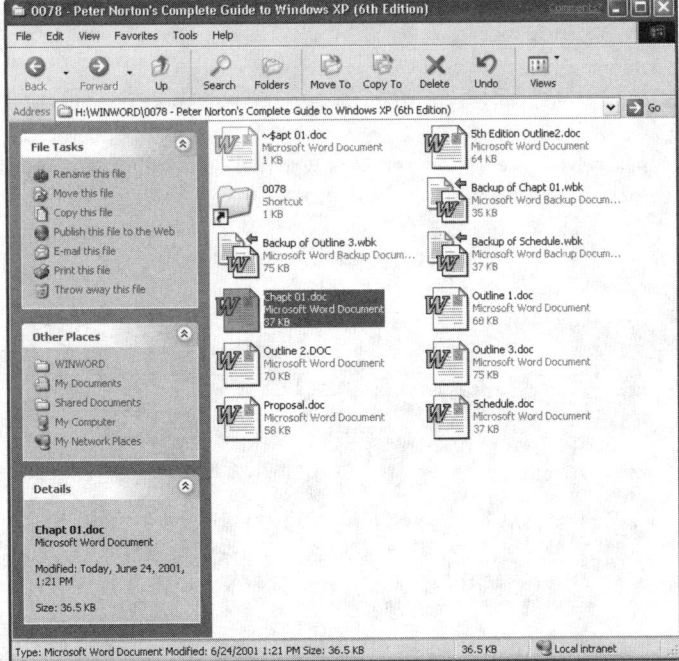

Search Companion

Finding information is hard, and it is getting harder all the time. Yet, the need to gain access to just the right information is becoming more important all the time, as well. Users don't have time now to spend an afternoon in the library researching important data—they need it in a few minutes (and sooner, if possible). Even Microsoft is getting into the *data mining* business, which is an effort to make it easier to find the information you need quickly. In short, faster and easier searching techniques are the name of the game.

Windows XP comes with many features that make searching faster. For example, it indexes your drives if you ask it to do so. An indexed drive is faster to search than one where you have to perform comparisons at search time.

Windows 2000 users will remember the painful experience of finding information on their drives. Even when a user knew that a piece of data existed, Windows 2000 would often refuse to return any search results on the topic. Windows XP does a better job in this area. Not only are searches more likely to succeed, but Search Companion (see Figure 1.4) also makes it easier to find what you need.

FIGURE 1.4

Search Companion is an essential part of the Windows XP search strategy.

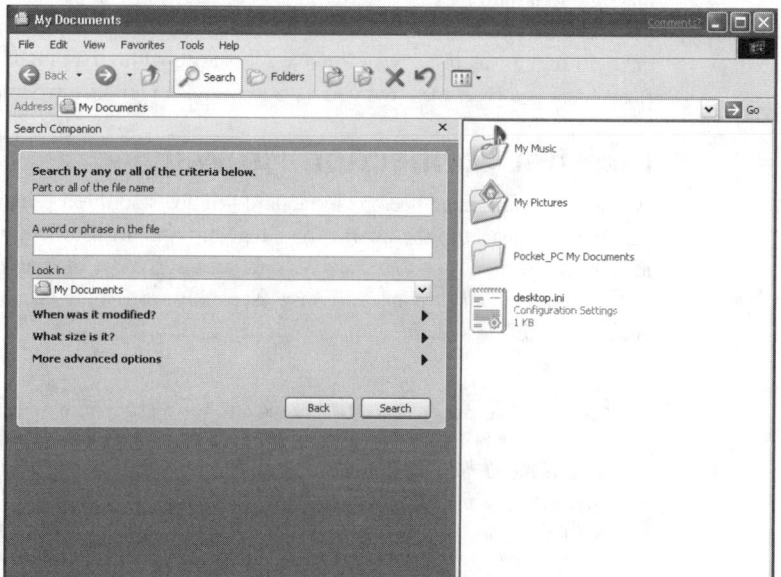

Search Companion is *task based*, which means that it changes its appearance based on the type of search you're conducting. Figure 1.4 shows the dialog box for searching all files. You could also search for music, graphics, or other specialty file types. As you can see, this dialog box is simpler than the one in Windows 2000, although it contains many of the same features.

In addition to using the task-based approach to searching for files, you can request help by using Search Companion. An animated help figure appears onscreen, as requested, to provide helpful hints. Although many novice users will find this feature useful, power users will probably keep it turned off to maintain an efficient work environment.

Remote Assistance

Good help is hard to find—at least, that's what many people say. Remote Assistance is a way to make good help easier to find. It allows users to communicate using a peer connection. The connection can occur on a local network or over the network. One machine is the target, and the other is the helper. The *helper* machine is the one that has the user who knows how to perform a given task.

Remote Assistance is a good idea in one way because it allows you to gain hands-on help as needed. Not only can fellow users help you, but Remote Assistance also provides the means for network administrators to help users without leaving their desks. The Remote Assistance feature uses several levels of security to ensure that your helpers don't gain more access to your machine than you want them to, but security can only go so far.

This statement brings us to the negative part of this feature. Whenever you open your machine to a third party, you take the risk of allowing that person to damage your machine. Given Microsoft's security problems over the years, it's conceivable that someone will find a way to activate Remote Assistance without an invitation. In short, Remote Assistance is a great idea, but you have to exercise vigilance when using it.

Internet Connection Firewall

Personal firewalls have become a standard Windows addition because more people than ever before connect to the Internet on a regular basis. In addition, many people use a permanent connection (one that's always on), such as a cable modem or a digital subscriber line (DSL). Permanent connections are especially worrisome because someone could use your computer's resources without your permission.

> **Note:** For the purposes of this book, the term *cracker* always refers to an individual who's breaking in to a system on an unauthorized basis. This includes any form of illegal activity on the system. On the other hand, a *hacker* refers to someone who performs low-level system activities, including testing system security. In some cases, you need to employ the services of a good hacker to test the security measures you have in place, or else suffer the consequences of a break-in. This book uses the term *hacker* to refer to someone who performs these legal forms of service.

The availability of "free" resources make Internet-related computer disasters, such as distributed-denial-of-service (DDOS) attacks, possible. Crackers often break in to your system, install DDOS software, and then go away before you notice anything. You may not even know that you have a problem until a cracker uses your system as part of an attack on someone's Web site. Windows XP adds a personal firewall as standard equipment. Now, when you create a connection to the Internet, you can at least monitor the connection to ensure that it's safe.

Warning: Many users have a false sense of security after they install a combination of a firewall and virus protection on their machines. The fact is that crackers are adept at breaking in to systems. If someone really wants to break your security, they will. Tools such as virus scanners and firewalls help you monitor your system for unusual activity. Constant vigilance is your most important tool in maintaining a secure system. Of course, you'll also want to install vendor-supplied patches and perform regular audits. The important consideration is that you know the limitations of the software installed on your system. Although it doesn't protect you from determined crackers, it can alert you to their presence and slow their access. These two deterrents often make the difference because a cracker often moves on to an easier system rather than waste time breaking in to a system with good security.

Smart Card Support

A *smart card*, which looks like a credit card, is a low-cost, alternative password device. Rather than type a password at the Windows password screen, you swipe your smart card in a reader.

The use of smart cards allows network administrators to assign secure passwords to users without worrying that they will either write down the passwords or forget them. Secure passwords have no discernable pattern—they're a series of random numbers and letters. Using a secure password still doesn't prevent someone from guessing it eventually, but a secure password is a lot harder to guess. It usually requires a "brute force" method of trying every possible combination.

Don't get the idea that smart cards are the ultimate in security, however. Users can still lose their smart cards, or someone can steal them. Smart cards are a physical security device, which means that they'll eventually wear out. The most secure passwords still come from scanning the human body in a process known as *biometrics*. Although iris and fingerprint scanners are becoming more popular, smart cards still cost considerably less and do offer increased security potential.

Application Compatibility

Windows XP is the first version of Windows based on the Windows NT and 2000 kernel that I can recommend for game playing and educational software. During testing, I found that some of my games would run without any changes at all. For those games that don't run in the normal Windows XP environment, I could use the Compatibility Mode Wizard, as shown in Figure 1.5. Note that you select an application and tell Windows XP which version of Windows to use to run the application.

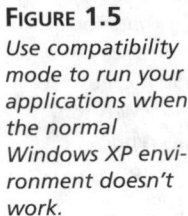

FIGURE 1.5

Use compatibility mode to run your applications when the normal Windows XP environment doesn't work.

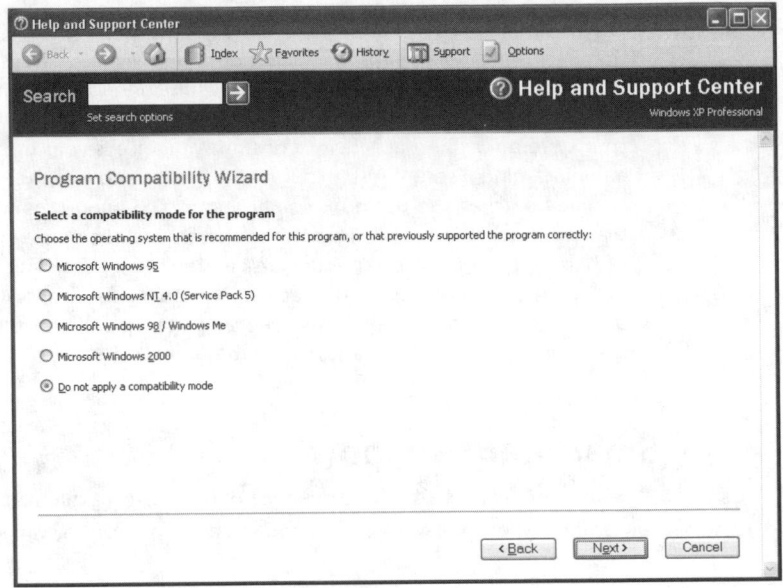

Between the higher level of compatibility provided by Windows XP and compatibility mode, I was able to run 19 out of 21 test Windows games on a singe processor machine. A dual processor machine requires a further tweak that we'll discuss in the "Tips for Working with Dual Processor Machines" section in Chapter 10, "Exploiting Multimedia and Games." I found that slower games, such as strategy or role-playing games, were the most likely to run. Action games ran, in many cases, but presented anomalies that I found unacceptable.

I had a lot more problems running DOS games. Only 7 out of 11 test games ran. All other games required a DOS partition on my machine. I didn't find this requirement limiting because I already maintain a DOS partition for diagnostics purposes.

Every piece of educational software I tried ran without a hitch as long as I selected the Windows 95 or Windows 98 compatibility modes. Despite Microsoft's best efforts, educational software remains one of the harder applications to install and run on a Windows XP system. The bottom line is that Windows XP offers a protected environment you won't find in Windows 9x and still manages to run applications that you'd never get to work in Windows NT or Windows 2000.

Resultant Set of Policy (RSoP)

Microsoft is trying to make it easier to manage an entire network of users using policies. *Resultant Set of Policy* (*RSoP*) is a group policy management tool that allows you to see the effect of a new policy on either a computer or a user. Using this tool removes the guesswork out of making changes to the system as a whole. You can also use this tool to verify changes during user downtime. This means that you can make changes without going to the user's machine to visually check the change results.

Windows XP also supports a wealth of new local and group policies. These policies determine how the system interacts with users. It also determines which actions a user can take. Unlike previous versions of Windows, group policies now override local policies. In addition, setting a local policy limits a user's access to resources.

Integrated CD Burning

Anyone who has tried to get third-party CD-burning software to work in Windows knows the frustration that this software can create. In many cases, you end up calling technical support to find out that you have to manually copy files to the Windows System32 directory in order to get the product to work. This is one reason that I'm so happy to see CD-burning support built into Windows XP. You not only save time installing a third-party product, but can also be sure that the program will work the first time.

DualView Monitor Support

Imagine that you're giving a presentation. Normally, you have to choose between allowing your audience to see the display, looking at it yourself, or investing in expensive third-party products to allow both of you to see the display at one time. Windows XP now allows you to connect two monitors to your system. Both monitors present the same desktop display.

> **Tip:** Some users are almost certain to confuse DualView with multimonitor support. A *multimonitor* setup allows you to extend your desktop across more than one monitor. Each monitor presents a different piece of the overall desktop mosaic. You use this setup for individual needs. The two features are distinct.

Remote Desktop

The Remote Desktop feature allows you to grab control of your desktop from a remote location. You could use this feature to access your work machine from home, for example. No longer do you need products (such as pcAnywhere) to perform this task. Of course, the third-party products are almost certain to provide some level of additional functionality, but at least you now have a choice.

ClearType

Yes, Microsoft has *yet another* new and improved font technology for you to use. The ClearType technology doesn't replace TrueType; instead, ClearType triples the number of horizontal lines of resolution using software. We'll explore this feature in the "Understanding ClearType" section in Chapter 14, "Fonts and Printing."

Improvements to Existing Features

As I said earlier in this chapter, Microsoft hasn't completely changed everything in Windows XP. You still see lots of old friends from previous versions of the product, and they work, for the most part, the same as before. Fortunately, Microsoft has been busy fixing up some of these utilities and enhancing others. They're not older—just better. The following sections give you an overview of the changes you'll find in your old friends.

Device Driver Support

The Professional Edition supports two important device driver features. The first is the ability to verify device driver functionality. The Device Driver Verifier runs a stress test on your device driver so that you can check it for failures before you're in the middle of an important task.

The Device Driver Rollback feature allows you to remove an errant driver and replace it with one that you know works. This means you can test the compatibility of a new driver, and easily get rid of it if you discover it won't work properly on your system.

File Association Handling

Older versions of Windows had a problem with file associations. If you installed an application that handled a default file association, such as TXT or BMP files, Windows lost control of that file association. Uninstalling the application meant that a user no longer could open the file, even though the system provided default applications to handle the file association.

Windows XP fixes this problem by monitoring the file associations on your system. When it sees that you've uninstalled a third-party application that handles default file associations, the program automatically restores the system application association. If you uninstall the program that handles BMP files, Windows XP uses a default editor, such as Paint.

Help and Support Center

Anyone who has had to work with the Microsoft online help system knows that finding help, even when it's available, is never easy. A user can spend hours scouring Microsoft Knowledge Base looking for the one piece of information they need in order to fix a problem. When a search of Microsoft's resources fail, the user often relies on peer assistance to fix the problem. In short, the help you need is probably available, but don't depend on it.

You'll find that the Help and Support Center is a big improvement over previous versions of Windows. Rather than provide help files and HTML-based help, the Help and Support Center is a one-stop place for Windows information. The Help and Support Center consolidates many sources of information to make it a lot easier to find the information you need. You'll find that it uses both local and Web resources equally well.

The Help and Support Center is more than just an extended help file. If you can't find what you need, the Help and Support center provides the means to ask a professional. It also provides access to Microsoft Remote Assistant, newsgroups, MSN communities, and Microsoft Assisted Support.

> **Note:** In some cases, a Microsoft support representative asks to take over your machine to help diagnose a problem. A separate Microsoft Support account allows lower-level access to your machine than the normal Remote Assistance account.

Improved NTFS Support

Windows XP supports a new version of the NT File System (NTFS). I didn't define the NT part of the acronym because no one at Microsoft can decide what NT means any more. If you have been around for a while, it means New Technology from a time when Windows NT was a new technology.

The big new feature you gain access to is multiuser Encrypted File Support (EFS). Windows 9x didn't include a feature even remotely similar to this one. Windows 2000 has included this feature, but only one user can encrypt the file and access it, so you give up multiple user support when you encrypt a file.

Anyone familiar with Microsoft's way of providing upgrades should be concerned about now. That's right—the new version of NTFS is incompatible with the version in Windows 2000. If you run a dual boot setup, you need to format both partitions with Windows 2000 before you install Windows XP.

Another problem with this support is that Home Edition users don't get it. Microsoft has installed additional software to disable this support under the Home Edition. It's still there—you just can't use it. I imagine that some bright entrepreneur will discover a way around this problem and make millions selling a third-party product that allows you to encrypt your files when using the Home Edition.

> **Tip:** You'll find many differences between the Professional Edition and Home Edition. For example, the Professional Edition supports dual processors and as much as 4GB of RAM. You can find a tabular view of Home Edition features at http://www.microsoft.com/windowsxp/home/guide/featurecomp.asp. The Professional Edition version of the same table is at http://www.microsoft.com/windowsxp/pro/guide/featurecomp.asp.

Installation Features

Windows XP has four updated installation features you need to know about. The first is a dynamic check of system files as part of the installation process. Windows XP checks the Microsoft Web site for updates before it completes your installation. What this means to you is that you won't have to update your system manually any more after an installation.

You'll find that unattended installations are easier than ever before. Previous versions of Windows allowed you to control only a subset of installation features using an unattended install. In most cases, you had to modify the install after it was complete. Windows XP allows you to control all installation features during an unattended installation so that the installation is perfect the first time.

The System Preparation (SysPrep) Tool provides better cloning support. You can use this tool to clone a machine's configuration and its settings and application suite. For example, you might want all machines to have Microsoft Office installed on them. The SysPrep tool allows you to clone a single Microsoft Office installation across all machines on the network, which reduces configuration and installation time.

Finally, the Remote OS Installation feature allows you to install Windows XP on a client machine from any other computer with sufficient rights on the network. You can even use this feature with SysPrep. You could install all the required upgrades on your network directly from your office rather than travel to each user machine individually.

Internet Connection Sharing

Many small-business and home users rely on Internet Connection Sharing (ICS) to allow users to share one high-speed connection rather than rely on individual dial-up connections. Because you can now disconnect an ICS connection from a remote location, you can use the phone for a voice conversation. Otherwise, ICS works much the same as it did for Windows 9x.

Microsoft Management Console

Windows 2000 users are already familiar with the Microsoft Management Console (MMC), although it's a new feature for Windows 9x users. MMC is a container application that accepts snap-ins that you use to manage your system or perform other tasks. Think of MMC as a socket wrench and the snap-ins as sockets you add onto it. MMC looks the same in Windows XP as it does in Windows 2000. The only major difference is that you have more configuration options in many cases.

My Documents Folder Update

Two of the My Documents default folders, My Music and My Pictures, have changed in Windows XP. The My Music folder uses a thumbnail view that allows you to organize your music more easily. This view shows the album cover for each piece of music you place in the folder. (Of course, you have to supply the album cover art if you can't obtain it online.)

The My Pictures folder includes a wealth of new features, including the ability to order pictures in the folder directly from an online site. You can, for example, take pictures with your digital camera this afternoon and send an order to get them printed without going to the photo store first. Microsoft has also enhanced My Pictures, with direct links to your camera and scanner, and improved file-manipulation features, such as compression and the ability to upload your files to a Web site. You can also view your pictures as a slideshow.

Recovery Console

The Recovery Console command-line utility allows you to recover if the graphical user interface (GUI) becomes inaccessible. Some administrators even prefer to use the command line at all times. They feel that it's faster than using the GUI tools. You can use the Recovery Console to perform these tasks:

- Format drives.
- Start and stop services.
- Read and write data from a local drive.
- Perform other administrative services.

System File Protection and Update

You'll find that Windows XP provides support for two important file-related features. Windows 2000 already supports both these features, but you'll find that the support is either lacking in Windows 9x or significantly upgraded in Windows XP. The first feature is system file protection. Whenever an older application tries to overwrite a system file, Windows XP restores the newer version automatically.

The second feature is side-by-side DLL support. This feature allows network administrators to get around the problems of DLL Hell where Application A requires one version of a DLL and Application B requires a second version.

System Restore

Windows XP includes the same System Restore feature found in Windows Me. Some changes to the interface make this feature easier to use. In addition, the feature doesn't seem quite as aggressive as in Windows Me, where it occasionally interferes with application upgrades.

Windows Explorer

Windows XP includes several updates to the standard Windows Explorer interface. You can now access Tiles view, which shows a detailed view of the files on your system, as shown in Figure 1.6. The problem is that the tiles are so large that they make seeing an entire directory of files at the same time nearly impossible. You use this view at those times when an extended view of your data is required and you don't mind lots of scrolling to see all the files.

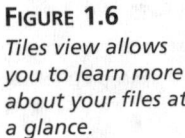

FIGURE 1.6
Tiles view allows you to learn more about your files at a glance.

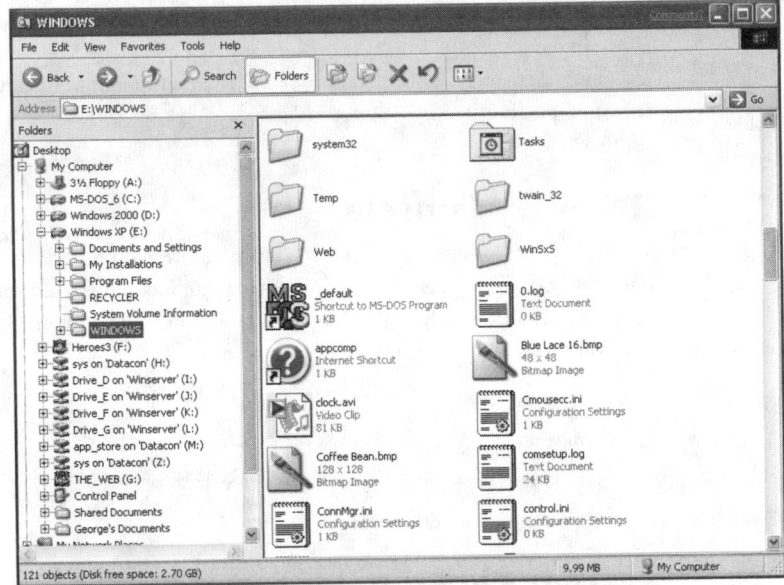

You can also group like files together. The groups look similar to the entries in a glossary. You can group them by name, type, size, and modification date. Look for third parties to add extensions that allow you to group files in other ways. For example, you might group Word documents by author or music files by musician.

Wizards

Windows XP contains the same networking features as found in Windows Millennium Edition. You can use the Home Networking Wizard to create a home network setup. The Web Publishing Wizard allows you to publish documents online. Finally, the Scanner and Camera Wizard allows you to create connections to your favorite device. All three of these features include some minor improvements. For example, you'll find that the Scanner and Camera Wizard include more devices in the list.

Windows Update

Windows Update has also experienced some changes, not all of which are for the better. For example, you'll find that this feature is extremely aggressive now. Windows Update automatically nags you to install changes whenever it detects that they're available online. Some users may find the pop-up request to install an update helpful; many power users will simply find it annoying.

This feature does include a few positive changes. For example, any change you download applies to all users of the computer, not just to the person downloading the update. This feature alone should save considerable time for network administrators.

Another new feature automatically searches for driver updates whenever you install a new device on your system. This means that you'll no longer have to suffer with the default Microsoft driver if there's a better driver available. Unfortunately, this feature will likely rely on vendor support, so you may still find that some driver updates are much the same as they were in the past.

Windows 9x Features Not Found Here

Windows XP is the upgrade for Windows Me and 9x users, but it isn't a direct upgrade. You'll find that some Windows 9x elements are gone, and you won't get them back. In some cases, the reasons for the missing features are obvious. For example, you can't boot into DOS because DOS no longer exists. Games and other applications that required a reboot to DOS in the past won't run now without a DOS partition in many cases.

Windows 9x came with a slew of little utility programs for managing the system. If you wanted to scan the drive, you needed one utility; defragmenting the drive required something else. In most cases, these older utilities don't run under Windows XP because it's a new operating system. I consider the MMC interface a vast improvement because it offers a consistent interface for every utility. In addition, you can combine utilities into custom consoles that allow you to perform all your maintenance tasks without opening another application. This is one area where a lost feature is replaced by something better—you won't want to keep the old Windows 9x utilities around after you work with MMC for a while.

Some Windows 9x features are simply missing, and there isn't any obvious reason for their demise (and Microsoft isn't saying much about them either). For example, Windows 9x supported the Multilink Aggregation feature as part of Dial-up Networking. This feature allowed you to use multiple devices to create the connection and therefore speed it up. Someone at Microsoft probably assumed that few users require Multilink Aggregation and those that did have moved on to cable modems or DSL by now. They might be correct, but this was a nice feature to have when you had to make a long download over a dial-up connection.

In a few cases, Microsoft made a change because some new study showed that there was a better way to do things or its marketing department simply decided that it was time for a change. For example, the Windows XP interface is similar to the one in Windows 9x, although it's not a direct substitute. In fact, even Windows 2000 users will notice some changes. For example, I prefer the search mechanism provided by Windows 9x. It was easy to use and provides consistent results. The search mechanism provided by Windows 2000 is nearly unusable—I seldom received usable results from it. Windows XP seems to be a mix between the two with the Search Companion thrown in for good measure.

On Your Own

This chapter provided a whirlwind tour of features you need to know about before you upgrade to Windows XP from Windows 9x, Windows Me, or Windows 2000. The first thing you need to do is decide which new features appeal to you. Then make up a list of features you want to try out before you perform the Windows XP installation. That way, you can get your new setup put together before you start experimenting.

Since this chapter is only an overview, make sure that you check out the full description of each item you want to use in other parts of the book. After all, you want to know the full capability of each Windows XP feature before you install it.

Make sure that you try out at least some of the Internet-related features, even if you don't think that you'll use them right away. Windows XP really is an Internet-oriented operating system. You need to explore some of this capability to get the most from the upgrade.

Of course, the big question you need to answer after you read this chapter is whether Windows XP is the operating system for you. You probably have something to gain by making the move, and even if you're using Windows 2000 now, Windows XP offers more in the way of security. However, you also need to consider what you'll lose. If you're still running mainly DOS applications from the Windows shell, Windows XP might be a questionable choice. (I'd also be willing to bet that users of DOS applications are a finite minority of users reading this book.)

Introducing Windows XP

The most noticeable change in Windows XP is the new user interface. Compared to other versions of Windows, this interface is almost dazzling when you start it the first time. The dramatic wallpaper, updated colors, and lack of 3D buttons all serve to set this version of Windows apart from its predecessors. A friend of mine calls it a "poke in the eye" interface, indicating the effect of all those colors the first time you see it.

Fortunately, many of the same Windows 9x and Windows 2000 interface features are in Windows XP. You'll still see a Start Menu on the left side of the display and the Taskbar tray on the right. Windows Explorer is still your window to the world of Windows, and you'll still use the Taskbar to choose open files. In short, many familiar features exist in Windows XP.

However, Microsoft has also changed the interface for the better by simplifying the way users interact with the operating system. When you first start Windows XP, your system uses a simple interface designed to minimize choices and make it easy to move from one point to another. I call this interface the simplified Windows XP interface, for the lack of a better term. This chapter helps you understand the significance of this new interface and details how it can allow you to work faster.

We'll also look at one of the essentials of working with Windows—Windows Explorer. I'll use the term *Explorer* throughout this chapter because the division between Windows Explorer and Internet Explorer is largely artificial at this stage. You can use Windows Explorer to view sites online, and Internet Explorer is adept at looking at your local drives. The main difference is one of application interface. Windows Explorer has a different feel from Internet Explorer (which still looks like a browser).

This chapter also introduces some standard Windows applications, such as Paint and Character Map. These utilities can make it easier to use Windows and some utilities are essential to getting work completed quickly. Most important, these applications provide default handling of some application data types. For example, if you don't install a graphics application or you decide to uninstall the graphics application you normally use, a default application handles your graphics file needs (within limits).

Using the Simplified Interface

As previously mentioned, Windows XP supports three user interfaces, which may seem like overkill at the outset. For many users, learning to use just one interface is more than sufficient. The fact is that you need to learn to use only one of the three interfaces, so the user learning curve isn't any higher than it was in the past. The difference now is flexibility. You gain access to an interface that meets your needs rather than depend on Microsoft to make the choice for you.

Most people immediately think that Microsoft intended the simplified Windows XP interface for only novice users. After all, the interface hides away much of the power of Windows XP and keeps only a small subset of commonly used features within easy reach. I would agree that the simplified interface is a great place for novice users to start. However, this interface can also be a great timesaver for advanced users who don't want to look at lots of clutter.

I was thinking about this issue the other day while I searched for an application I use all the time. I download lots of software for testing purposes, so my Start Menu contains numerous product entries. Although I reconfigure the Start Menu on a regular basis to keep it organized, finding what I need becomes time consuming because so many submenus pop up and get in the way. Normally, I use five or six of my applications for common tasks, and the rest are available as needed. Using the simplified interface still allows access to these other applications, but only the ones I use most often appear on the Start Menu (as you will see in Figure 2.1, in the following section). Look at the lower-left corner, and you'll see an All Programs icon that lets you choose from other installed applications, although the main Start Menu remains clean. (We'll discuss the Start Menu in detail in the section "The Start Menu," later in this chapter.)

Tip: Interestingly enough, Windows XP doesn't automatically place some Windows-specific applications, such as Windows Explorer, on the main Start Menu. This feature is designed to save space for non-Windows applications. The best way to overcome this problem is to place Windows applications that you use regularly on the Quick Launch toolbar. The "Customizing the Quick Launch Toolbar" section in Chapter 3, "Advanced User Features," fills you in on the details of changing this essential toolbar.

The simplified interface can help advanced users in other ways as well. For example, trying to figure out which applications you use most often by reading entries in the Add/Remove Programs applet of the Control Panel is time consuming. The simplified interface shows only the applications you use regularly and automatically changes its configuration as you use certain applications more often. If you want to determine which applications to remove from your system to make room for that new game, for example, checking the Start Menu of the simplified interface is a good place to begin.

One new feature you should notice about Windows XP is that it's constantly cleaning things up. For example, you'll eventually see a dialog box that asks whether you want to clean up your Taskbar icons. Getting rid of these icons clears the display so that you have more room to work. However, an unexpected side effect of all this cleaning is that Windows XP doesn't bog down as quickly. It uses resources more efficiently than its predecessors, which means that you can work faster. Using the simplified interface increases both the work- and performance-enhancing effects of using the simplified interface.

There's one potential negative for advanced users who transition from older versions of Windows. Microsoft has determined that you need to change the way you work with Windows XP. Everything I have read about this product emphasizes its task-based menus and its task-oriented ways of working. The simplified interface tends to reinforce the task perspective because of the way it optimizes the menus and displays. You don't have to work this way, though. Using a data-oriented approach still works as well with Windows XP as it did with Windows 9x and with Windows NT and Windows 2000. It's all a matter of how you want to organize your work. So, while Windows XP is furiously trying to organize your work by task, you can ignore it and do things the way you see fit.

The Start Menu

One noticeable feature of the Windows XP simplified interface is the Start Menu (or lack thereof). Figure 2.1 shows a typical Start Menu after you've used Windows XP for a while. The default Start Menu is Spartan; it doesn't contain any application entries on the left side because you haven't started to work with Windows XP yet. As you use Windows XP, the left side of the Start Menu fills with applications, as shown in the figure.

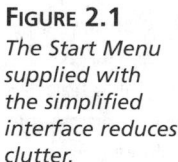

FIGURE 2.1
The Start Menu supplied with the simplified interface reduces clutter.

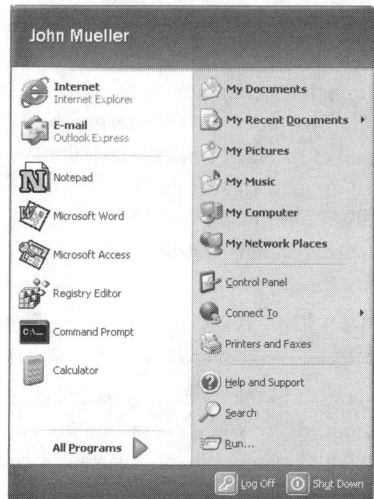

Usage Details

It's time to take a closer look at how you use this new Start Menu. As mentioned earlier, the left side of the Start Menu shows the applications you use most often. A user must select an application more often than others installed on the system for the application to appear on—and stay on—the Start Menu. Applications you use for a while, and then stop using, disappear from the Start Menu. Therefore, if you normally open applications before you access data, the Start Menu reflects the list of applications you use most often. It shows how you use your computer for the most part and can help you work more efficiently.

The right side of the menu display always shows the same icons, no matter how you work with Windows XP. You can divide these icons into three major areas:

- *Data processing*   Windows XP displays data locations in descending order of accessibility. The list begins with your personal data, which includes My Documents, My Pictures, and My Music. Local data comes next, in the form of My Computer. Finally, you can access remote data using My Network Places.

- *System control*   The Control Panel is the only entry in the center section on the right side of the Start Menu. Click this icon, and you'll see a listing of applets that allow you to control system functionality. For example, one applet allows you to install new hardware and another allows you to install new software. We discuss the Control Panel in detail in the "Control Panel" section in Chapter 7, " Windows XP Configuration."

- *Other resources*   These three icons are Help and Support, Search, and Run. Help and Support is the new Microsoft help system we discussed in the "Help and Support Center" section in Chapter 1, "The Updater's Guide to Windows XP." Search allows you to find resources on your system. For example, you can use the applet to look for files, other computers, or even other people. It also allows you to search the Internet through a hidden browser interface. Finally, the Run icon allows you to start a command prompt. A *command prompt* allows you to type commands in a text-based environment and see a result. For example, you use this prompt to start low-level utilities, such as the Registry Editor, in many cases (although it isn't the only way). Anyone who's used DOS or other early operating systems knows the value of a command prompt. Some network administrators still use the command prompt extensively, although it's fallen out of use with most users. We'll discuss the few uses for the command prompt that you need to know about as this book progresses.

You also see two icons at the bottom of the Start Menu. The Log Off icon shows all options for *logging off* the system, where you leave the system running and allow someone else to log in to it. Click Shut Down Computer, and you'll see various options for shutting down Windows XP. Only one of those options turns the computer off. You may also see options for restarting the computer and for placing it in Suspend mode, which is a type of sleep cycle.

Customization

The Start Menu is highly customizable. Figure 2.1 shows the appearance of the Start Menu if you simply leave it as is. Let's begin with the various application entries on the Start Menu. If you right-click either Internet Explorer or E-mail, Windows XP asks whether you want to work with that application (to browse the Internet or retrieve e-mail, for example), remove the application from the Start Menu, or change the Internet properties. We discuss how to change the Internet properties in the "Changing the Internet Properties" section in Chapter 20, "Internet Connections."

Standard applications present various options for working with that application. The two customization options are what you need to worry about for now. The Pin to Start Menu option allows you to keep an application entry on the Start Menu, even if you don't use it often. You could use this feature for applications you have to find quickly, such as a monitoring or administrative application. The Remove from This List option removes the entry from the main Start Menu, although you can still find it on the All Programs list. Use this feature to clear space on your Start Menu for an application you use more often. I often use this feature with demonstration programs I'm evaluating.

> **Tip:** Look carefully at Figure 2.1, and you see a thin separator line between the E-mail and Microsoft Word options. This line separates applications that are pinned to the Start Menu from those that appear on the main Start Menu because you use them regularly. Use the Unpin from Start Menu option on the context menu to remove an application from the pinned list.

The data processing icons on the right side of the Start Menu behave the same as if you right-clicked them on the desktop. For example, they all allow you to open, explore, and search the resource. The Control Panel icon context menu has options for opening and exploring the Control Panel. Opening the Control Panel presents the single-pane Explorer view, which we're all used to seeing. Exploring the Control Panel presents a two-pane view. We'll discuss these views in the section "Explorer: The Familiar Interface," later in this chapter. The remaining three icons on the context menu contain only the single task for which they're designed. You can't pin or unpin any of these entries—they always appear on the Start Menu.

Let's discuss customization of the Start Menu itself. If you right-click the name area of the Start Menu and select Properties, you'll see a Taskbar and Start Menu Properties dialog box, similar to the one shown in Figure 2.2. Notice that the Customize button near the middle of the dialog box is highlighted, which means that you can use it. The button near the bottom of the dialog box is grayed out because you use it with the Classic Start Menu, discussed in Chapter 3.

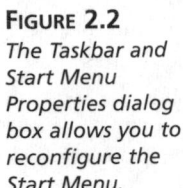

FIGURE 2.2

The Taskbar and Start Menu Properties dialog box allows you to reconfigure the Start Menu.

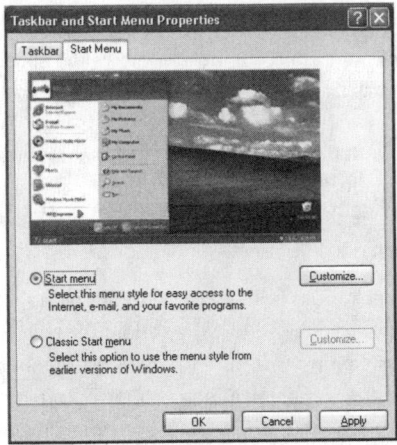

Click Customize, and you'll see a Customize Start Menu dialog box, like the one shown in Figure 2.3. The General tab of this dialog box allows you to choose between large and small icons. The tab also allows you to set the size of the list on the main Start Menu and determines whether you'll see the Internet and E-mail icons. Notice that you can choose something other than Internet Explorer and Outlook Express as your Internet and e-mail applications.

Setting the number of programs on the Start Menu is important. I normally set it to one or two higher than the number of applications I'm currently using on a regular basis. For example, when I'm performing lots of word and graphics processing, I set the number to six to allow space for six applications: Word, Corel Draw, Paint Shop Pro, Bookshelf Basics, and two other applications. I go back and pin the four common applications, leaving two blanks below the applications I use often. In this way, I ensure a maximum of flexibility with a minimum of clutter.

Click Advanced, and you'll see a dialog box similar to the one shown in Figure 2.3. The main purpose of this dialog box is to allow you to control the content of the right side of the menu. The dialog box also allows you to optimize the way the Start Menu works.

You might think it unfair that the Start Menu contains entries such as the Control Panel if you never use them. Notice that this dialog box allows you to set the Control Panel entry to act as a menu or a link, or you can remove it from the Start Menu. The list of items you can display on the Start Menu includes items I find essential. For example, if you spend time looking for items on your network, you might want to include a Network Connections entry on the Start Menu. I also like to include the Printers menu so that I can access printers quickly when I need to stop a print job or rearrange print priorities.

The Advanced tab also contains some efficiency and performance settings. For example, checking Open Submenus on Hover might unnecessarily clutter the display if you only want to see the top-level menus. Selecting Highlight Newly Installed Applications might make them easier to see, but could also cause problems if you have vision problems. In short, you need to customize these options for your specific needs and tastes.

FIGURE 2.3
The Advanced tab allows you to configure, among other things, the right side of the Start Menu.

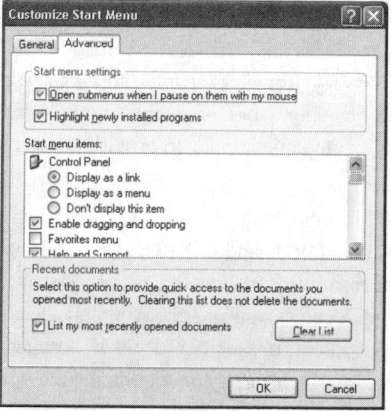

Explorer: The Familiar Interface

Let's begin your tour of Explorer by examining how it's organized. Figure 2.4 shows the two-pane configuration of Explorer and Icons view. The left side of the display contains the directory tree. You need to take note of several features of this directory tree.

FIGURE 2.4
The Explorer display is easier to understand when you break it into its components.

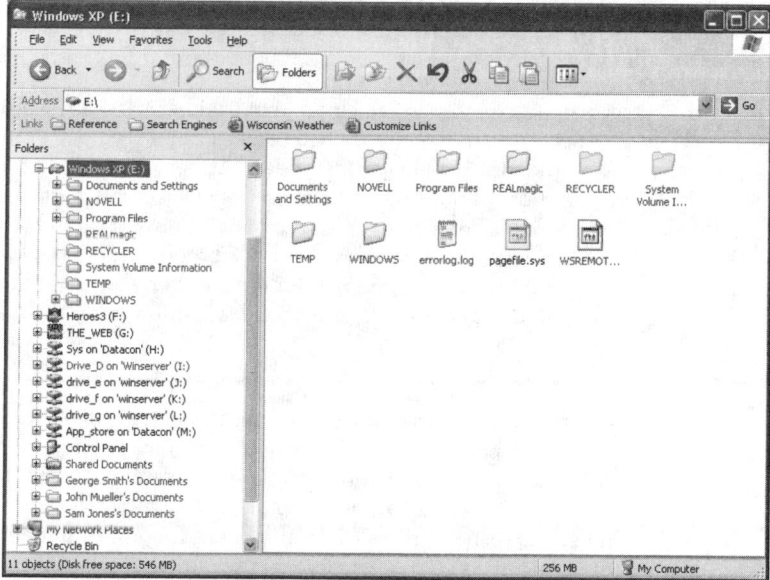

The first thing you'll notice is that the tree doesn't represent a single drive or even the contents of all the drives; it's more of a "machine tree" than anything else. This machine tree is divided into these elements:

- *The document section*   This section includes your personal local data contained in My Documents, My Pictures, and My Music. Whether you see this section depends on company policy. Some companies prefer to store all user data on the network drive for easy backup. My Documents is a nice feature for smaller companies, but many large companies prefer to provide a place that's easy to back up and maintain for users.

- *The drive section*   This area displays the contents of all your local data drives, including devices such as DVDs and CD-ROMs. It also includes all mapped drives that point to network resources, such as the sys on DataCon drive shown in Figure 2.4. Any mobile devices appear here. You can access the local representation of mobile device content, not the device itself. Applications such as Microsoft ActiveSync allow you to synchronize the mobile device with your local drive. Finally, you'll see the contents of any local shared drives.

- *The network section*   This section contains all network drives and locations. At the top of the list, you'll see an Entire Network icon. Below this icon is a list of network shortcuts. Windows XP often detects network connections for you and creates a shortcut automatically. If you don't see a location you need, you can always look through the hierarchical Entire Network folder.

- *The Recycle Bin*   This icon provides access to the Recycle Bin. You can use this icon to view the contents of the Recycle Bin, empty it, or set its properties. We'll discuss this icon further in the "Recycle Bin" section, later in this chapter.

> **Note:** It's essential to remember that Explorer has many configuration options. You can view it in a one- or two-pane view. The left pane can contain any of the Explorer bars, including folders, search screen, and favorites list. Although the content of the right pane varies, you can view it in a number of ways, including tiles, icons, a detailed list, or a thumbnail. This section of the chapter shows you the default Explorer view. As this book progresses, I'll show you many of these other configuration options. Learning one step at a time about the features that Windows XP provides is a good idea—this section is a first step.

> **Note:** Windows Explorer also features the special Tip of the Day option, which you can display in addition to any other options. It appears at the bottom of the right pane rather than in the left pane. Activate the Tip of the Day feature using the View | Explorer Bar | Tip of the Day command. Every day, you'll receive a new tip on how to use Explorer more efficiently. A special link within this pane allows you to read additional tips.

Let's look at the right pane. Generally, you'll use the left and right panes together. For example, if you're using the Search Explorer bar, the right pane shows the results of the search. When you use the Folders Explorer bar, the right pane shows the details of the selected object. If you click a drive icon, you see in the right pane the folders and files the drive contains.

You can use the icons in the right pane to work with detail objects. For example, you can use the icons to open a file or folder. Double-click a folder, and you see what it contains. Double-click a file, and you perform the default action associated with that file.

Context Menus

There are a number of ways to use Explorer to organize your data. Each tool provides a different method of viewing and working with your data. Let's begin with one of the first tools you'll need to use under Windows XP: the context menu. Figure 2.5 shows a typical context menu, although each type of object has some differences from the one that is shown.

FIGURE 2.5
Context menus contain an organized list of actions you can perform on an object.

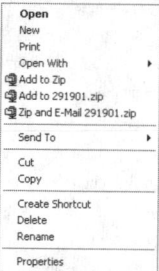

Open
New
Print
Open With ▶
Add to Zip
Add to 291901.zip
Zip and E-Mail 291901.zip
Send To ▶
Cut
Copy
Create Shortcut
Delete
Rename
Properties

Every object you use in Windows XP provides a context menu. If you're not sure what something is or how to configure it, or if you're unsure about anything else you can do with that object, a simple right-click answers your question.

Every context menu for a file or folder contains five or six major sections. Each section tells you something about the object associated with that menu. The following list outlines each section and describes its purpose.

- *Actions*   The first section of the context menu tells you what kinds of actions you can perform with the object. The default action—Open, usually—appears in bold print. In addition to seeing the Open action, you're likely to see a Print Data File action. Folders normally include an Explore action and a Search action.

  You might see one special entry in the list of actions. The Open With action allows you to choose an alternative application for opening the file. In some cases, when Windows XP doesn't know how to work with the file, the Open With action is the only one you'll see. In other cases, such as with executable files, you won't see an Open With entry because Explorer assumes that you don't want to interact with the file as data.

- *Network* This optional section normally contains a single entry—Sharing and Security. Some objects support sharing and others don't, depending on how your network is set up. Normally, peer-to-peer networks enable this option only for folders. Larger networks, such as those from Novell, provide this entry for both files and folders.

- *Send To* Use this special entry if you want to send the object to another location. Windows XP supports sending to a floppy disk, a compressed folder, the Briefcase, the desktop, a mail recipient, removable drives, My Documents, and the Web Publishing Wizard. If a mobile device is attached to your system, you might see an entry for sending the file there.

Tip: Creating additional destinations for the Send To menu, such as project folders and network drives, is handy. All you need to do is place a shortcut to the new destination in your \Documents and Settings\<User Name>\SendTo directory. Every user has a separate SendTo directory—it's one item you can't share across all users using a \Documents and Settings\All Users entry. (You might find that Windows XP hides this folder initially. If so, unhide the directory using the Show hidden files and folders option on the View tab of the Folder Options dialog box.) Always make these destinations practical. In other words, don't add another directory listing to this rather important list. All you need to do is add destinations you use on a daily basis. One object missing from the previous editions of Windows is the Briefcase. The "Briefcase" section, later in this chapter, shows you how to add a briefcase to your desktop. After you add a new briefcase, you can create a shortcut to it in the SendTo directory, which makes placing files in your briefcase a lot easier.

- *Editing* Believe it or not, you can edit an object just like everything else under Windows XP. This section contains entries for Cut, Copy, and Paste. You can place a copy of the object on the Clipboard and then paste as many copies as needed on other objects. These objects are full-fledged copies, not the shortcuts (object links) we'll examine in the next section. If you cut an object, Windows XP doesn't remove the icon from the display. It grays out the icon and waits until you paste it somewhere else before removing it permanently, which prevents you from accidentally erasing objects. Cutting a new object before you paste the first one leaves the first object in its original location.

- *Manipulation* This section usually contains three entries, but it can contain more. The Create Shortcut option enables you to place a link to the file or folder somewhere else. Chapter 5, "Windows Performance Primer," shows how you can use this feature to make your desktop a friendlier place. The Delete option sends the file to the Recycle Bin. You still can recover the file later, if necessary. The Rename option enables you to change the long filename associated with the file.

Tip: You don't have to send deleted objects to the Recycle Bin. Simply select the object you want to delete and then press Shift+Delete to erase it permanently. Deleting an object permanently means that you won't find it in the Recycle Bin later; make sure that you really want to delete a file before using the Shift+Delete method.

- *Properties* Every object, no matter what type, contains a Properties entry on its context menu. Clicking this entry always displays a dialog box that enables you to view and configure the properties of the object. For example, the Properties dialog box for a file shows the full filename, any attributes associated with the file, and some statistical information. Folder properties usually contain about the same information as files but also provide some additional statistics. Disk properties, on the other hand, contain a wealth of information about the drive as a whole. This dialog box even provides access to the three maintenance tools that Windows XP provides to manage disk drives. The Properties dialog boxes for other objects contain a wealth of information as well. For example, the Desktop Properties dialog box allows you to change the system colors and display resolution. You can even use the dialog box to change your wallpaper.

Some objects on your system include some specialized context menu entries. For example, if you right-click the Recycle Bin, you'll see an option to empty it. Right-clicking the desktop provides a New option you can use to create new files. (You see the same menu option if you right-click a blank area of Explorer.)

Explorer Toolbars

The Windows XP version of Explorer provides three toolbars: Standard, Address, and Links. You can choose any or all of the toolbars. Figure 2.4 shows all three toolbars. Normally, Explorer appears without the Links toolbar in place. In addition, Explorer normally locks the toolbars in place. Notice the dots on the left side of each toolbar in Figure 2.4. The dots indicate that the toolbars are unlocked and you can move them around. Use the View, Toolbars, Lock the Toolbars command to lock the toolbars in place after you change their position and size.

Standard Toolbar

The Standard toolbar contains all the buttons required in order to move around in Explorer. The first three buttons are Back, Forward, and Up. You'll use the first two buttons to move from one location you've already visited to another. The Up button takes you up one level in the directory structure.

The Search and Folders buttons control the view in the left pane. As previously explained, Search displays a form you can use to find resources on your drive, and Folders provides the hierarchical view of your system shown back in Figure 2.4. Clicking one of these buttons automatically deselects the other. You can also clear both buttons so that you see just the middle (when Web view is enabled) and right panes.

The Views button allows you to see another view in Explorer. Explorer has five standard views: Thumbnails, Tiles, Icons, List, and Details. They control how Explorer displays the objects you see in the right pane. Thumbnail view enables you to see a small version of a file rather than the standard icon.

Explorer allows you to customize the Standard toolbar to meet specific needs. Use the View | Toolbars | Customize command (or right-click the Standard toolbar and select Customize) to display the Customize Toolbar dialog box, as shown in Figure 2.6.

FIGURE 2.6
Use the Customize Toolbar dialog box to change the appearance of the Standard toolbar.

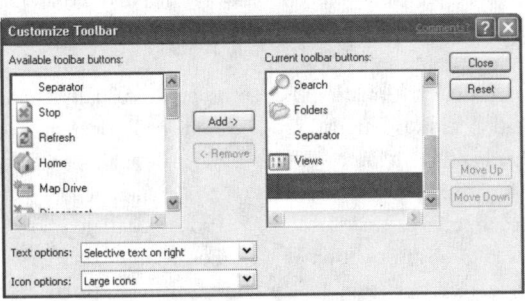

Moving a command from the left pane to the right adds that entry to the toolbar. The dialog box also includes special entries, such as Separator, that help you to organize your data. Here's a list of the Standard toolbar additions:

- *Stop* Stops the current action. For example, if you try to find resources on a Web site, clicking Stop stops the current search.

- *Refresh* Obtains a new copy of the data displayed in the right pane. Servers often retain a copy of data in memory to enhance performance. Using this button forces the server to update the information.

- *Home* Displays the default Web page. The home page could be your company Web site or a blank page. The "Changing the Internet Properties" section in Chapter 20 discusses this option in detail.

- *Map Drive and Disconnect* Creates a new connection between a local system drive letter and a network drive or removes an older connection. Using local drive letters for commonly used network drives makes it easier to work with the data these drives contain. Drive mapping can also make users aware of new network resources.

- *Favorites* Displays your list of favorite places in the left pane. The hierarchical display uses the same arrangement as the menu version of Favorites in Internet Explorer.

- *History* Displays a list of places you've visited in the left pane. Explorer arranges the list hierarchically by date and location. Clicking a link takes you to that location.

- *Full Screen*   Places Explorer in a kiosk mode that uses the entire screen to display Explorer content. Users often employ this mode to view Web sites. You can also use it when you're organizing local or network drives that contain numerous data files.

- *Delete*   Moves a file or folder from its current location to the Recycle Bin. Use the Properties button to display a file's or folder's Properties dialog box.

- *Undo*   Undoes the preceding action you performed in Explorer. For example, if you renamed a file and then clicked the Undo button, the original name returns.

- *Properties*   Displays the Properties dialog box for the selected object or objects. When you select multiple objects, the Properties dialog box displays only properties common to all objects. If the objects have no common properties, Explorer ignores the button press (unless an error occurs and it displays a blank Properties dialog box).

- *Move To*, *Copy To*, *Cut*, *Copy*, and *Paste*   Moves files or folders from one location to another. Simply cut or copy the file or folder in one location, and paste it in another. The Move To and Copy To buttons incorporate the functionality of Cut and Paste or Copy and Paste into a single button.

- *Folder Options*   Displays the Folder Options dialog box so that you can change the method Explorer uses to display data, file associations, and offline file-viewing options. This button performs the same task as the Tools | Folder Options command.

Note that the Customize Toolbar dialog box contains other options. For example, you can select an entry in the right list and then use the Move Up and Move Down buttons to change the entry's position on the Standard toolbar. The Text Options list box changes the way Explorer displays text on the Standard toolbar. You can choose to display text below every button, text to the right of certain buttons, or no text. Finally, the Icon Options list box determines the size (large or small) of the icons the Standard toolbar uses.

Address Toolbar

The Address toolbar might look extremely simple, but it's a powerful feature. If you place the cursor on this toolbar, you can type a path to a local or network directory or to a location on the Internet. After you type the location and press Enter, the location appears in the right Explorer pane. You also can type the name of an application or file. Explorer automatically opens the file or starts the application after it finds what you're looking for. Finally, you can use the drop-down list box to browse within the current context. If you're looking at local or network drives, you see a directory tree. If you're looking on the Internet, you see a history listing of Web sites you've recently visited.

Links Toolbar

You'll use the Links toolbar often if you set it up the right way. A single click on any icon takes you to that location. The Links folder in your Favorites folder controls the contents of this toolbar. You get a choice of four Microsoft-specific Web sites to begin with. However, nothing stops you from adding your ISP's home page, the location of your company's Intranet site, or any other link you care to add.

> **Tip:** You can add folders to the Links folder in addition to shortcuts. (You can create a new folder in the Links folder when you add a new Favorite or you can go directly to the \Documents and Settings\<User Name>\Favorites\Links folder on your hard drive and add the folder that way.) I normally set up two folders, named Search and Reference. The Search folder contains shortcuts to all my favorite search sites, along with unusual search sites I might not use every day. The Reference folder contains shortcuts to my favorite reference sites online, such as Acronym Finder and Webopedia (see the Glossary for detailed descriptions of both). By placing these two folders on my Links toolbar, I make the sites they contain more accessible and reduce the time required to find information quickly.

My Network Places

Think of My Network Places as a dynamic extension of Explorer for a network. My Network Places usually appears near the bottom of the directory tree in the left pane of Explorer, as shown back in Figure 2.4. When you open My Network Places, My Computer is replaced by the Entire Network icon. No longer are you looking at the local machine, but, rather, at all the resources you can access on the network as a whole. Figure 2.7 shows a typical example of My Network Places. This figure includes icons for computers, printers, and file server drives.

FIGURE 2.7
My Network Places allows you to see the network resources available to your machine.

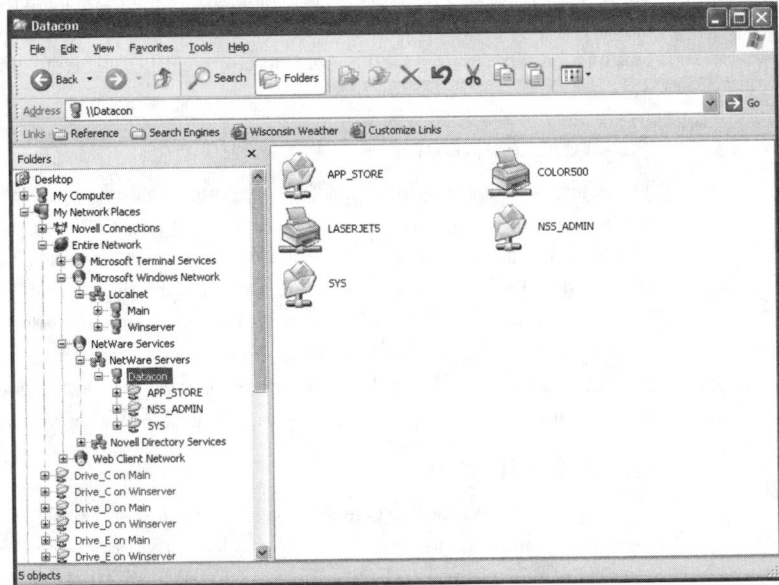

Note: Novell Client 32 handles My Network Places entries differently from its Microsoft NDS client counterpart. I cover Novell Client 32 differences in the "Using Novell Client 32" section in Chapter 21, "Networks." Fortunately, the idea behind using the entries is the same, so you can still follow along in this section and learn what My Network Places can do for you.

Notice in Figure 2.7 that drive resources appear in both the left and right panes, but that printer resources appear only in the right pane. Be sure to keep this fact in mind as you work with My Network Places because you might not see all the resources by looking at the hierarchical view. Remember that the left pane shows only container resources, such as machines and drives. A printer connected to a server is a noncontainer resource. However, if you connect a printer directly to the network (it has its own Ethernet card), a representation of the printer connection appears in the left pane. Windows XP views the printer connection as another machine node. What you're seeing is the network card, not the printer itself. You still have to click on the printer connection entry in the left pane to see the printer in the right pane.

Tip: At first glance, listing your machine along with everything else in My Network Places might seem like a waste of effort. However, you have one good reason to do so: You can see at a glance every resource you're sharing with the rest of the network. Rather than force you to look through the directory tree for these elements, Microsoft has thoughtfully placed them in My Network Places.

You need to know a few interesting things that make My Network Places different from the rest of Explorer. For one thing, you can't access the properties using the Entire Network icon. A Properties entry is in the context menu for this object, but selecting the entry displays an error message. Entire Network is simply a placeholder for My Network Places and doesn't exist as a concrete object.

Below the Entire Network option are entries for each network connection you have mapped. In most cases, you'll see the workgroup or domain name, not the name of the network vendor or product. This list changes as your connections change. Looking there tells you whether a problem is application or network related. An application error, such as the inability to open a file, might look like a network error for a variety of reasons. However, if you look in the Entire Network folder and see the connection, the connection is unlikely to be the problem. Chapter 24, "Software Problems," and Chapter 25, "Hardware Problems," contain tips to help you locate and fix other problems with the hardware or software on your machine.

Recycle Bin

The Recycle Bin works the same in Explorer as it does on the desktop. You can drop things into the Recycle Bin, examine its contents, empty it, or restore a file it holds to its original (or another) location. The Explorer copy of the Recycle Bin comes in handy if you see a file you want to erase and the desktop copy is covered by another application. Figure 2.8 shows what this area of Explorer looks like.

FIGURE 2.8
The Recycle Bin holds all temporarily deleted files, but not those you delete permanently.

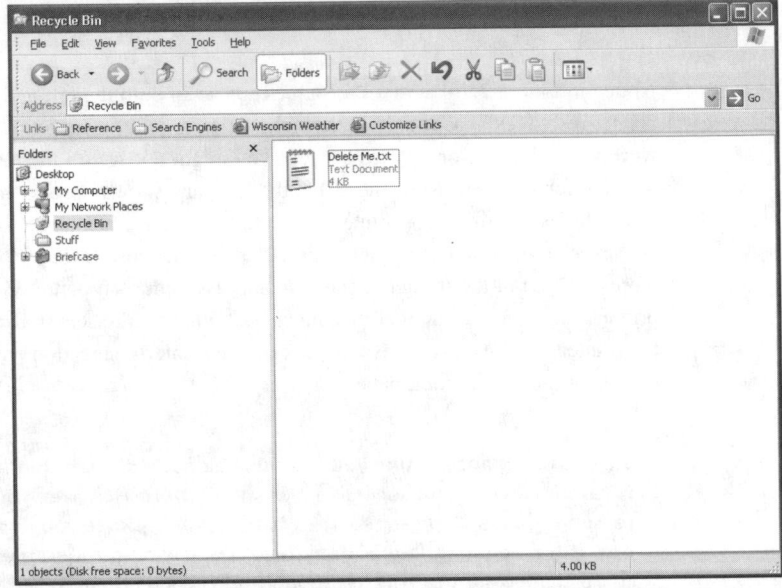

> **Tip:** Files in the Recycle Bin continue to take up space on the drive. Windows XP moves deleted files to the Recycle Bin—a special folder—until you erase them for good. (Windows XP changes short filenames to allow multiple files of the same name in the Recycle Bin.) If you're short on hard drive space, you might want to see whether you can get rid of anything in the Recycle Bin.

In most cases, your Recycle Bin doesn't contain anything. Files in the Recycle Bin look just like files anywhere else. You can move objects in the Recycle Bin to other areas of Explorer to "unerase" them. Until you do, the Properties dialog box doesn't tell you much except the filename and the date you deleted it, as shown in Figure 2.8.

One interesting phenomenon about the Recycle Bin is that you can't open any files for editing. This situation makes sense because you've theoretically deleted the file. However, this also makes it hard to check the file again for valuable data before you erase it permanently. I usually move the file to a temporary folder for examination if I need to check it again before deleting it.

Briefcase

Briefcase is one of the best Windows XP features for mobile users. It allows you to pack everything you need for a project into one folder and then move that folder around, just like the briefcase you carry to and from work. Chapter 17, "Mobile Computing," takes a look at how you can use Briefcase. You might want to read this material even if you aren't a mobile computer user, because I discuss a few techniques for using Briefcase that you will want to know about.

Briefcase adds one option to the context menu of items it holds. The Update All option enables you to update a file from its original copy on your network hard drive or send the modified Briefcase contents to the network hard drive. You need to perform this task before you take Briefcase on the road, and again when you return. If you want to update individual files, you need to open Briefcase and work with the individual files.

Previous versions of Windows automatically assumed that you wanted Briefcase on your desktop if you installed the required support. Windows XP comes with the support installed by default, but doesn't provide a Briefcase icon. Adding one is easy: right-click the desktop (not an Explorer folder or any other location) and choose New, Briefcase from the context menu. You can create as many instances of Briefcase on the Desktop as you want, as long as each instance has a different name.

Compressed (Zipped) Folders

Let me make a special mention about folder and file compression. Using compression can save considerable space on your hard drive, especially if you work with many graphics or text files. (Application files don't compress well.) Of course, compressing and decompressing the files incurs a performance hit, so you need to consider the tradeoff in performance versus disk space in a world where disk space is cheap.

> **Note:** Windows XP compression and encryption features work on only drives formatted under the NT File System (NTFS). In addition, you might find this functionality severely limited when using the Home Edition of Windows XP. Current Microsoft plans call for purposely removing encrypting functionality and removing file compression as well for the Home Edition.

You'll never notice the performance difference when working with relatively small files, including anything that measures 1MB and smaller. I always use compression with files of that size. However, some files incur a penalty. For example, I don't compress a large, 20MB graphics file that I use regularly because it would take too much time to load when I'm in a hurry. On the other hand, I compress many of my other large graphics files because I don't load them often and I want to save some of the space they consume. Because Windows doesn't know how to optimize your system in this case, you'll need to decide how to use compression wisely.

Enabling compression is easy: right-click any file or file storage object, such as a disk drive, and choose Properties from the context menu. You see a compression option you can check on the General tab of a disk drive Properties dialog box. When you check the Compress Drive to Save Disk Space option, Explorer asks whether you want to compress just the root directory of the drive or the entire drive. File objects show an Advanced button. Click the button, and you'll see a compression attribute. Checking the attribute compresses just that file, and clearing the attribute decompresses it.

After you compress a drive or individual file, you have no way to know that it's compressed. You don't know, therefore, whether a delay in retrieving a file is because of Windows, compression, or an error of some kind. Fortunately, Windows XP provides an option to display compressed drives and files in a second color. Use the Tools | Folder Options command to display the Folder Options dialog box. Click View. Near the bottom of the Advanced Setting list is the Show Encrypted or Compressed NTFS Files in Color option. Checking this option displays the drive or file in a different color so that you can determine its state just by looking.

Standard Windows XP Applications

We explore many applications together throughout this book. A few are generic in nature. Just about everyone uses them at one time or another, and they provide essential functionality. The following sections describe these generic applications.

Calculator

The Calculator looks and acts similar to the handheld devices many people own. The initial Calculator display replicates the four-function calculator many people use when they go to the store or when they perform easier tasks at home. The Calculator includes memory keys and the ability to calculate both percentages and square root.

You can use the View | Scientific command to transform the Calculator into the full-featured device shown in Figure 2.9. Notice that one new feature adds commas (or other separation characters) between groups of numbers to make the display easier to read. You can turn this feature on by using the View | Digit Grouping command.

FIGURE 2.9
Calculator is a handy tool for both simple and complex calculations at the computer.

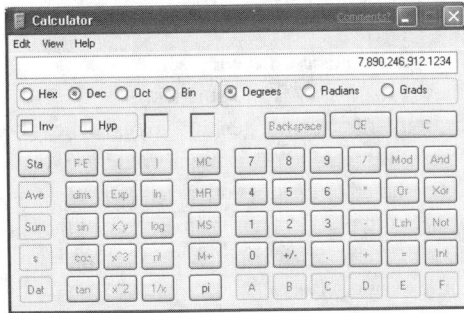

As you can see, Microsoft packed its scientific calculator with features. You can work with binary, octal, decimal, or hexadecimal numbers. Choosing each number system enables some buttons and disables others, depending on how users normally work with the number system. At first, I found this structure cumbersome, but eventually realized that it reduces the number of entry errors I make.

Of course, a calculator doesn't exist in a vacuum; you use it with other applications. The Calculator has an Edit | Copy command to copy the result of any calculation to the Clipboard so that you can paste the result into another application. Likewise, you can retrieve a value from the Clipboard using the Edit | Paste command.

> **Tip:** You can employ the Clipboard as a second memory by using the Copy and Paste commands. This feature comes in quite handy when you're working with complex calculations where a second memory is helpful. Of course, using the built-in memory is always faster and safer.

Character Map

Many users wrongly assume that the characters they see in a particular font are all the characters the font file contains. In most cases, font files contain a wealth of characters. I'm often surprised at the number of special characters I find tucked away in font files— characters I can use for special purposes in my work. Of course, accessing these special characters is the hard part, and that's where Character Map comes in. Figure 2.10 shows an example of Character Map in action.

FIGURE 2.10
Character Map can help you find the hidden characters in the fonts on your machine.

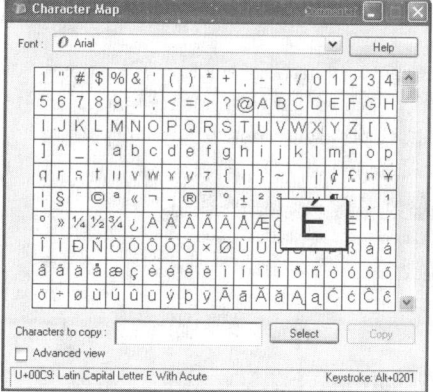

You should notice several small things about Figure 2.10. First, if you click on a character, Character Map shows a large view of it, as shown in the figure. Clicking again reduces the size of the character to normal size. In the bottom lower-left corner, you'll see a description of the character, including its hexadecimal position within the file. You can get this same information by hovering the mouse over the character and waiting for balloon help to appear. In the lower-right corner, you might see instructions for reproducing the character without using Character Map. (Many special characters lack a keyboard combination.) In this case, you press Alt and then type **0201** on the numeric keypad.

Users make some common mistakes in typing those special characters into their favorite applications. First, when Character Map shows Alt+0201, it means that you must type the first zero. Typing Alt+201 results in a different character. Second, make sure that the Num Lock key is turned on. Many keyboards default to the Num Lock off position so that users can use the numeric keypad for cursor movement. Third, don't use the numbers across the top of the keyboard—strange things happen, none of which has anything to do with special characters.

Creating a string of characters with Character Map can be time consuming. Choose the character you want by clicking it. Click Select to place it in the Characters to Copy edit box. Then, move on to the next character. When you find all the characters you need, click Copy, which places the characters on the Clipboard. Just paste the characters into your favorite application.

Some fonts are so large that you could spend the rest of your life looking for a particular character. When this situation happens, click Advanced View. An additional set of list boxes and an edit box appear. These options allow you to reorder the font, group it in a different way, and even search for a specific font. For example, I chose the Arial font, typed **Euro** in the Search For field, and clicked Search. Character Map listed the Euro font for me. Given the size of the Arial font, finding the Euro would have taken considerable time otherwise. Another method to find the Euro font quickly is to choose Unicode Subrange in the Group By field and then select Currency in the Group By dialog box that appears. This method has the advantage of finding the Euro font without typing anything.

Paint

Some form of Paint has appeared in every version of Windows, for one reason: It's any easy way to create quick drawings and view images you get from someone else. Figure 2.11 shows a basic Paint window with some of my fancy art in it.

FIGURE 2.11

Paint is a simple program for creating and manipulating graphics.

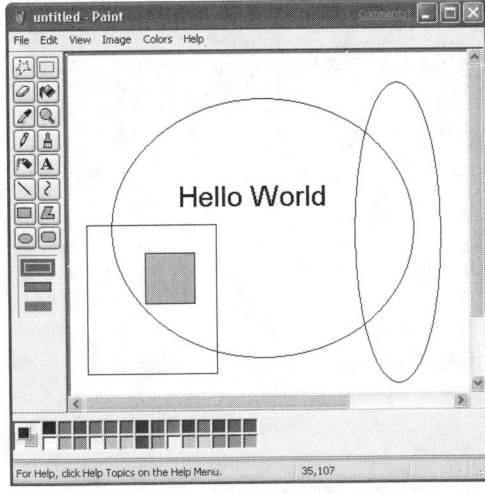

The form of this application has changed little over the years. On the left is a set of drawing tools, and colors appear across the bottom of the display. The application has the usual menu structure across the top, and the rest of the display is your drawing area.

Paint is easy to operate because it includes only a few drawing commands. The Edit menu contains commands for selecting an image, copying an image selection to the Clipboard, and pasting an image from the Clipboard. You can also import and export images. The View menu allows you to change window options and zoom in to or out of the drawing. You can perform tasks such as flipping and rotating the image using commands on the Image menu. Finally, the Colors menu allows you to change the colors shown at the bottom of the window. You can also double-click a color to change it.

The current version of Paint does include a few new features, mostly associated with the way you open and save files. The oldest versions of Paint supported both PCX and BMP files, but Microsoft dropped PCX support some time ago because of incompatibilities in different versions of the PCX specification. BMP support was all that Paint provided until recent versions of Windows. The Windows XP version includes support for BMP, DIB, GIF, ICO, JPEG, PNG, and TIF file formats. In addition, you can save the file in various color depths, including monochrome, 16-color, 256-color, and 24-bit color. Interestingly enough, you can't save a 16-bit or 32-bit color image.

Another new feature is the ability to work with peripherals, such as cameras and scanners. That's right—you can grab an image from one of these devices, place it in Paint, make a few modifications, and send the image off to a friend. In short, this simple utility of yesterday is still simple to operate, but now contains lots of nice, new features.

Screen Savers

A healthy third-party market exists for screen savers. Some Windows users buy screen savers in bulk. You can find them in stores and on every online service in existence. Unless you own an older system, using a screen saver probably isn't necessary—just fun. I own a *Star Trek* screen saver for its fun element. One interesting thing about Windows XP is that it runs this screen saver. Windows 2000 simply shut it down all the time, without giving it much of a chance. A good Web site for all kinds of screen savers is http://www.ratloaf.com/, provided by Screensavers A to Z.

> **Tip:** You don't have to spend lots of money to get some interesting screen savers. At the Ratloaf Web site, for example, you can find a screen saver for displaying your favorite JPEG, PIC, and KQP files. If you happen to be a gardener, this site enables you to build your own virtual garden onscreen. Many screen savers are at this site; look for something that interests you.

Windows XP also provides screen saver options. They aren't as much fun as some screen savers on the market, but they do the job. Of course, they include the OpenGL screen savers, such as the 3D pipes I've seen on many desktops. You find these options on the Screen Saver page of the Display Properties dialog box, as shown in Figure 2.12.

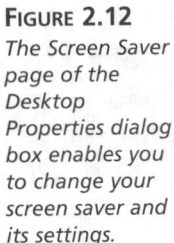

FIGURE 2.12
The Screen Saver page of the Desktop Properties dialog box enables you to change your screen saver and its settings.

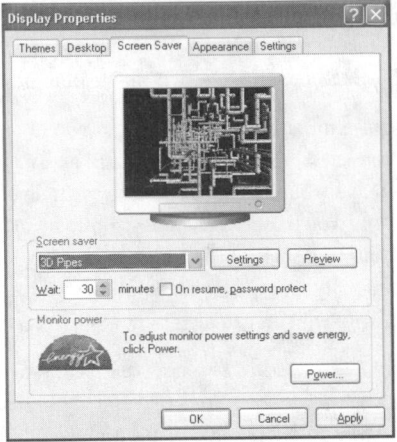

The Screen Saver page contains a miniature view of your monitor. The page displays a thumbnail sketch of what the screen will look like when you configure the screen saver. The Screen Saver field enables you to choose from the screen savers (files with an SCR extension) in the System32 folder. If you decide to use a third-party screen saver that uses the Windows format, you need to place the file in the same directory as the others, or else Windows doesn't see it.

After you select a screen saver, you can use the Settings button to change its settings. In most cases, the settings affect how Windows XP displays the screen saver. For example, you might change the number of lines you see or the number of colors.

The Wait field enables you to change the number of minutes Windows XP waits before it activates the screen saver. To turn the screen saver off, move the mouse cursor or press a key.

The final option on the Screen Saver page, Preview, enables you to see what changes to the screen saver look like. I've also used this as a quick way to hide my display when someone walks into my office and I don't want that person to see what I'm working on.

This dialog box also contains a special Power button that enables you to set up your system's energy-saving features. Click Power to display the Power Schemes tab in the Power Options Properties dialog box. I discuss this dialog box in detail in the "Power Management Strategies" section in Chapter 17.

On Your Own

The simple interface shown in this chapter isn't for everyone. In fact, many power users will find the interface too confining to be of much use. However, try out this new interface to see whether it allows you to work faster without any loss of flexibility—it pays.

Some users find that they don't want to switch back to the cumbersome Windows 2000 interface after they've tried the new Windows XP interface for a while.

Explorer, one cornerstone of the Windows XP interface, enables you to move around your machine—and the network, for that matter. You can also use Explorer to get on the Internet or view file specifics, such as compression state. Spend some time getting used to the Explorer interface and trying out its various display modes. Click the column headings in Detail view to see how Explorer rearranges filenames.

Context menus are an important part of Windows XP. Try right-clicking all the objects you see. See how the context menus vary from object to object. Don't forget that even the desktop is an object with a context menu. Make sure that you click the desktop to close its context menu without selecting anything.

Try some of the utility programs that ship with Windows XP. For example, the Calculator allows you to perform math-related tasks, both simple and scientific. I find the Character Map utility indispensable. Not only does it allow me to add control and special characters to my documents, but I can also use it to verify the content of a particular font. In some cases, you can find, without much effort, unique characters that add pizzazz to documents.

Advanced User Features

Windows XP comes with more ways to modify your interface than any previous version of Windows. Not only can you use the new Windows interface, but many of the features of the Windows 2000 interface are available as well. All of this flexibility means that you can have the interface you really want—the one that will make you most productive. Unfortunately, all of this flexibility can also mean confusion on the part of the user. That's why I placed what I consider advanced user features in a separate chapter.

In the preceding chapter, we looked at the simplified Windows XP interface. This interface is easy to use, but doesn't provide much in the way of flexibility. Windows XP also supports what I call a standard interface, the kind of interface that most Windows users have come to expect. This chapter will show you how to convert from the simplified interface to the standard interface that many power users will want. In addition, we'll discuss how to obtain the Windows 2000 interface. Just because you're using Windows XP doesn't mean that you have to settle for an interface that doesn't suit your tastes.

Part of using the standard interface is negotiating the Classic Start Menu, the one found in previous versions of Windows. Chapter 2 discussed the new, simplified Start Menu that you'll see when you start Windows XP. This chapter concentrates on the standard menu components as well as on the standard toolbars. In fact, I'll show you how to create your own toolbars to make working with Windows more efficient.

One issue we really didn't discuss in the preceding chapter is the Desktop—the part of the display where you place icons, applications, and data files. Windows XP has two different Desktops. The first is the standard desktop found in even the old versions of Windows 9x. The second is the relatively new Active Desktop. We'll discuss both desktops, and you'll discover how to make maximum use of the Active Desktop if you decide to take the plunge and use it.

You learned in Chapter 2 that Explorer is one of the first tools you should learn how to use, and everyone should learn to use it fully. We only scratched the surface in Chapter 2. This chapter discusses advanced Explorer techniques. You'll learn how to configure Explorer to suit your needs and use it to reconfigure your system, and you'll even get some customization tricks that no one should be without. Most importantly, you'll learn why this tool is so essential for novice and expert alike.

This chapter ends with a discussion of some important but miscellaneous interface configuration issues. You'll learn about the Startup folder and how to use it to make your system self-configuring (at least to an extent). Anyone who has read Chapter 2 will see the effects of using Web content in folders. You can change the appearance of the Web content to suit your needs, so the effects in Chapter 2 are only the beginning. These sections will also tell you about screen savers and themes. If you used themes under Windows 9x and liked them, you really need to see how Microsoft has improved theme support for Windows XP.

Switching to the Standard Interface

The simplified Windows XP interface has many appealing features, but it also hides some of the power of Windows. If you perform the same tasks every day, the hidden features may not make much of a difference. An accountant who uses the same application all day to compute someone's tax bill won't worry much if he or she doesn't see the Administrative Tools folder. However, many power users will find the hunt for their favorite administrative tool frustrating. Speed is of the essence for the power user.

The standard interface is one that reflects the power of the original Windows 9x interface and the functionality of the Windows XP feature set. It allows a power user to find what he needs quickly. The same interface that confuses the novice and thwarts someone who performs the same task every day makes the power user more efficient. I'm making these distinctions because the myth of the perfect interface seems to pervade the media. The perfect interface is a myth. There's only the interface that works best for you, which is why I'm happy to see that Microsoft is adding much-needed flexibility to Windows XP.

Enabling the standard interface is as simple as making a few changes to your environment. Begin by right-clicking the Start Menu and selecting Properties. You'll see the Start Menu tab of the Taskbar and Start Menu Properties dialog box, shown in Figure 3.1. Select Classic Start Menu, as shown in the figure. (I'll show you how to customize this menu in the "Start Menu Customization" section of this chapter.) You'll find that the Classic Start Menu has most of the same features of the Windows 2000 Start Menu, but that the look and feel of the Start Menu differs slightly.

You'll also need to consider other features for the standard interface, such as Taskbar configuration. Power users will often hide the Taskbar to free screen real estate for application use. In addition, power users will often add standard and custom toolbars to their Taskbars. For example, I keep a list of folders on my desktops for all my current projects. I make those folders instantly available, even with applications open, by adding the Desktop toolbar to my Taskbar. We'll discuss enhancements to the standard Taskbar in the "Using Toolbars" section of this chapter.

FIGURE 3.1
Switching to the standard interface means using the Classic Menu setup.

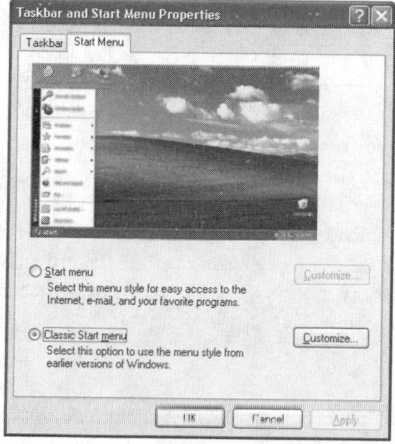

A final user interface adjustment for the standard interface is to modify Windows Explorer. Power users have many ways of using Windows Explorer. Most prefer a clean environment that's fast to use. Often, this means disabling Web content or at least creating customized Web content. As you saw in the preceding chapter, the default Web content, although helpful, is space consuming and not particularly helpful to someone who already knows how to perform basic tasks with Windows.

Switching to the Windows 2000 Interface

As nice as you can make the Windows XP interface, it differs from the one in Windows 2000. Some power users won't want to take the time to learn the new interface. At least a few companies will shy away from the Windows XP interface in any form because it means training support staff and then all users in the organization.

Interestingly enough, some users have also complained that the new interface is a case of too much of a good thing. Some have complained that the new interface gives them headaches or is too difficult to see. During the beta process, complaints ran from too many colors to the wrong color selection. Still other users miss the 3D look of Windows 2000. The point is that Windows XP is too bright and cheerful for some users—they want things quiet and mundane, which is just fine. Microsoft provides the means for users to select the older Windows 2000 interface.

Tip: At least a few users have claimed that the source of headaches (at least for them) when using Windows XP is the new Clear Type font smoothing. The new font-smoothing technique could cause problems when coupled with the new

continues

interface colors and flat appearance. At least one Microsoft representative commented that the company designed Clear Type for liquid crystal display (LCD) use, the kinds of displays provided with laptop computers. Windows XP still includes the standard font smoothing found in Windows 2000, so you can choose to use standard font smoothing or no font smoothing to see if your headaches go away. Right-click the Desktop, and choose Properties. Select the Appearance tab of the Display Properties dialog box. Click Effects, and you'll see an Effects dialog box. Choose something other than Clear Type for the font-smoothing option. Click OK twice to close the Effects and Display Properties dialog boxes. We'll discuss how Windows works with fonts in detail in the "Windows and Fonts" section of Chapter 14.

To obtain the Windows XP version of the Windows 2000 interface, you'll need to switch to the Classic Start Menu, as we did in the preceding section. After you make that change, you'll need to change the Windows theme. As we'll see in the "Themes" section of this chapter, themes are more than simple window dressing in Windows XP. Changing a theme requires that you right-click the Desktop and choose Properties. Select the Themes tab of the Display Properties dialog box, as shown in Figure 3.2. Choose the Windows Classic theme from the Theme drop-down list box.

FIGURE 3.2

The Windows Classic theme is all you need to see a Windows 2000 view of Windows XP.

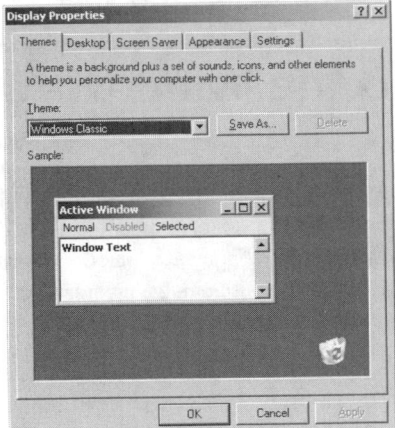

Don't get the idea that this interface is precisely like the one you used in Windows 2000. It looks like the Windows 2000 interface and has many of the same features, but you'll still find Windows XP features mixed in. For example, none of the Properties dialog boxes will change simply because you change the theme. Although the Windows Classic theme does make more changes than a theme under Windows 2000, it can't change basic operating system functionality.

Note: Some of you who have used Windows 3.x will eventually notice that the System32 folder contains a copy of Program Manager (Progman.EXE). Yes, this is the same program that Windows 3.x used as an interface, and you can still start it if you want. Going back to that interface during testing showed me just how far Windows has come—the latest Windows interfaces have so much more to offer. Although you can run Program Manager if you wish, installing it as the main interface is nearly impossible. Microsoft provides Program Manager as a means for supporting older applications. Some of these older applications won't install unless they can start a copy of Program Manager to store their icons. You can move the icons (when necessary) from Program Manager to the Start Menu. However, you should ignore Program Manager for the most part; it's simply a piece of an old version of Windows that we still need for a while longer.

What can you expect from the Windows Classic theme? Anything that deals specifically with the Windows interface will change. The colors, icons, text, and basic look will all change. Some items, such as the Start Menu, will take on a decidedly Windows 2000 look. Some of the tabs of property pages will change. For example, the Appearance tab of the Display Properties dialog box will contain Windows 2000 options instead of their Windows XP equivalents. However, the way you use the tab will remain the same as it did under Windows XP. In short, you end up with a partial change that will feel much like Windows 2000, but won't go all the way.

The Classic Start Menu

The Classic Start Menu is the one that Windows has used since Windows 95 first appeared on the scene. Over the years, Microsoft has made slight changes to the Classic Start Menu, but it's essentially the same as that early version. Figure 3.3 shows the Classic Start Menu for Windows XP. The Windows 2000 version is the same except for color choices. Windows 2000 also has the chiseled 3D look that Windows XP lacks.

FIGURE 3.3
The Classic Start Menu provides full access to Windows XP features.

As you can see, the Classic Start Menu is quite a departure from the Start Menu described in Chapter 2. The following sections describe two important aspects of the Start Menu. I'll tell you how to use this important part of Windows, and then we'll look at methods for customizing it.

> **Note:** We have viewed several versions of the Windows XP interface and there are more to consider. However, the vast majority of this book will use the Windows XP theme and the classic Start Menu. An informal poll of users during the writing of this book shows that most Windows XP users prefer this combination. You might find that some of your dialog boxes differ slightly from the ones shown in the book if you use some other theme or the Windows XP Start Menu configuration. The appearance will definitely differ if you choose the Windows Classic theme.

Usage

The Classic Start Menu provides optimum access to Windows XP features for many power users. The cascading menus hide detail you don't want, yet allow full access to features you do want to use. In addition, the Classic Start Menu doesn't hide anything. The following sections discuss the standard Classic Start Menu entries. We'll discuss the special Time Check folder that appears in Figure 3.3 in the "Start Menu Customization" section of this chapter.

> **Note:** The following sections describe a basic setup. You can customize the Start Menu to include other settings. In addition, Start Menu configuration options and local security settings will affect the availability of certain items. You'll want to spend some time working with the configuration options that we discuss in this chapter to create a complete understanding of the Start Menu and learn how you can change it to meet your needs.

Windows Update

Windows XP is proactive about checking for operating system updates. It automatically checks for device driver and other updates for you on a regular basis. However, if you're having a problem with Windows XP, you might want to check for an update manually. That's where the Windows Update entry comes into play. Selecting this option will take you to the Microsoft Windows Update Web site, where you can check for new files. We'll discuss this feature in detail in the "Using Windows Update" section of Chapter 4.

Programs

Every application you install in Windows XP that provides application icons will place them under this menu. Windows XP also places under this menu the icons for the applications it provides. You'll use the program icons to start applications. Of course, most applications also provide file associations that automatically start the application when you double-click a file icon. The Programs folder is the one that users organize most often because you end up with an unwieldy list of icons otherwise.

> **Tip:** You can save yourself some reorganization time by installing application icons in the correct location. Most modern applications ask where to place the application icons in the Start Menu. Many people accept the default location, which is normally under the Programs menu. This choice leads to the excessive number of program icons that most of us have to battle. You can always install the application icons in a custom folder with other icons of the same type. Of course, this means that the installation program lumps your application icons together, which still leads to clutter. Another alternative is to use the default name, but to prepend a common folder name. For example, if you're installing Corel Draw and you use Graphics as a common folder, the icon installation location might look like \Graphics\Corel Draw instead of Corel Draw alone. This little tip also ensures that the uninstall program can find the application icons later and remove them when you remove the application from your system.

Documents

This menu contains a list of the ten documents you've accessed most recently. Some people find that the Documents menu contains everything they need. It works well if you spend most of your time working on just a few documents. However, most of us are working on more than one project at a time and a list of ten files is pretty much useless. I'll show you how to get around this problem in the "Folders: A Real Organizational Tool" section of Chapter 6.

Settings

The Settings menu allows you to access most of the settings for your Windows setup. It contains a minimum of four entries, each of which appears in this list:

- *Control Panel* Depending on how you set this entry up, you'll either create a separate window or see a menu of additional entries. Each entry is an applet that controls a particular element of your system. For example, one applet allows you to add or remove applications, and another applet allows you to add or remove hardware. We discuss the Control Panel in detail in the "Control Panel" section of Chapter 7.

- *Network Connections* This menu contains a list of your network connections. It contains entries for not only the local area network (LAN), but also any dial-up connections you have. The Make New Connection applet allows you to add connections to your system as needed. We'll discuss dial-up connections in detail in the "Creating a Connection" section of Chapter 20. Network connectivity issues appear in Chapter 21, "Networks."

- *Printers and Faxes* Every printer or fax you can access will appear on this menu. Interestingly enough, the menu often fails to show the fax support for a local modem. Both local and remote printers will appear, however, allowing you to change their configuration if you have sufficient rights. An Add Printer applet will allow you to add new printers, but not faxes. We'll discuss printer connectivity in the "Installing a Printer" section of Chapter 14.

- *Taskbar and Start Menu* Displays the Taskbar and Start Menu dialog box, shown in Figure 3.1. We'll discuss the Start Menu features of this dialog box in the "Start Menu Customization" section of this chapter. Taskbar customization tips appear in the "Using Toolbars" and "Customizing Your Desktop" sections, later in this chapter.

Search

Windows XP makes it easy for you to find what you need. Not only does it provide the Search buttons in both Windows Explorer and Internet Explorer, but you can also use the options on this Search menu. The following list tells about each option:

- *For Files or Folders* Select this option to display a copy of Windows Explorer with the Search Explorer Bar selected. In this case, Explorer optimizes the Search Explorer Bar for local searches using the Index Server when available. We'll discuss the Search Explorer Bar in the section "Using the Explorer Bars" of this chapter.

- *On the Internet* Select this option to display a copy of Internet Explorer with the Search Explorer Bar selected. In this case, Explorer optimizes the Search Explorer Bar for Internet searches using the online search engines you select. We'll discuss some ways to get around limitations of this search feature in the "Using the Explorer Bars" section of this chapter.

- *For People* Select this option to display the special Find People dialog box, shown in Figure 3.4. We'll discuss this dialog box later in this section.

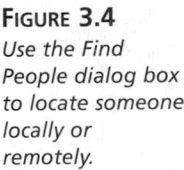

FIGURE 3.4
Use the Find People dialog box to locate someone locally or remotely.

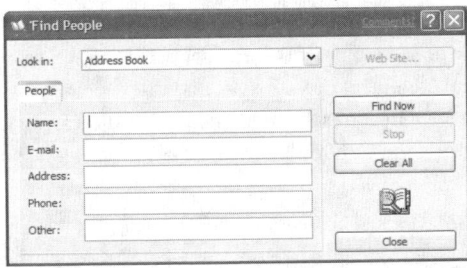

When you first start using Windows, you'll see the Search Companion display. You can also set Windows to use the Search dialog box that appeared in Windows 2000. All you need to do is use the Tools | Folder Options command in Windows Explorer to display the Folder Options dialog box. Select the View tab and clear the Use Search Companion for Searching option (found in the Advanced Settings list). Click OK, and Windows will use the Search dialog box found in Windows 2000. Unfortunate as it may seem, there isn't any way to access the Search dialog box found in Windows 9x.

The only dialog box not affected by the Use Search Companion for Searching option is the For People menu entry. You'll always see the dialog box shown in Figure 3.4. Notice that you can use a number of criteria to find people, including their name, e-mail address, street address, telephone number, or other criteria when working with your address book.

The number of entries on the People tab of the Find People dialog box will change when you select other locations. For example, when you select Yahoo! People Search, the People tab contains only the Name and E-mail fields. However, this online search option exposes the Advanced tab shown in Figure 3.5. As you can see, the Find People dialog box now allows you to specify a freeform search to reduce online search time.

FIGURE 3.5

Certain Look In field options activate the Advanced tab that allows you to perform freeform searches.

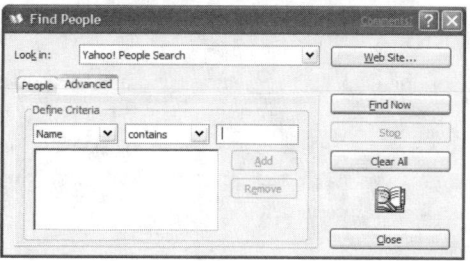

Notice that the Web Site button is no longer grayed out in Figure 3.5, as it was in Figure 3.4. Click Web Site if you want to open a copy of Internet Explorer. Search will send you directly to the Web site listed in the Look In field. The Web site will often support more search options than the Find People dialog box does, allowing you to extend your search in other ways.

After you enter the search criteria, click Find Now. The Find People dialog box will extend, as shown in Figure 3.6. Highlight any of the names, and select Properties to find out more about the person you've selected. The Properties dialog box contains all of the same entries that you'd find in the Address Book Properties dialog box. You may also see a General tab containing search-site-specific information about the person. The Add to Address Book button allows you to add to your Address book someone found on a Web site or within Active Directory, and the Delete button allows you to remove the person's name from your Address Book.

Note: The screen shot shown in Figure 3.6 purposely has the names found during the search blanked out for privacy reasons. Normally, you'd see a list of names in the dialog box.

FIGURE 3.6

Finding a person's name allows you to contact him via e-mail or perform other tasks.

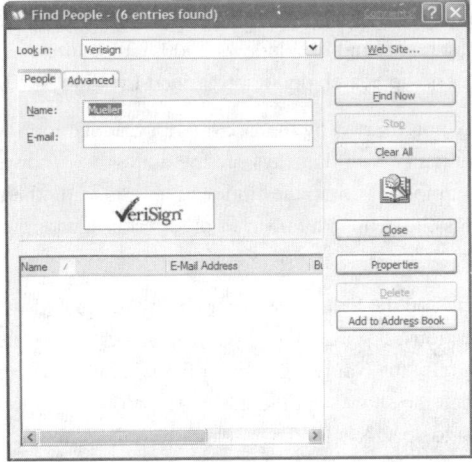

Help and Support

Selecting this menu option displays the general Help and Support Services dialog box, shown in Figure 3.7. This is a new approach to an age-old problem for Windows XP. Help and Support Services provides access to all of the latest information about Windows XP. It also provides access to support tools you use to repair or maintain your system. We'll discuss this feature in detail in the "A Look at Help and Support " section of Chapter 25.

FIGURE 3.7

Help and Support Services is the centralized location to find out more about Windows XP.

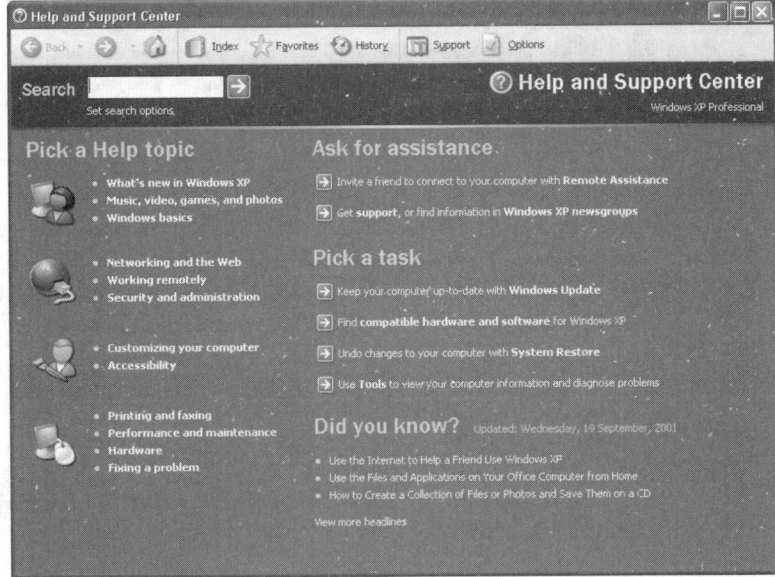

Run

You'll use the Run menu entry to start applications without using the Programs menu on the Start Menu. Not every utility provided with Windows has an icon in the Start Menu. Microsoft doesn't provide direct icon access for some utilities because it feels that average users won't need to use the utilities or that they are too dangerous to expose to novice users. For example, if you want to use the Registry Editor (RegEdit), you'll need to know how to access it outside the normal Start Menu entries.

The Run option displays a Run dialog box, where you can type of the name of an application to run. You can also use the Browse button in this dialog box to find utilities on your hard drive. The Run option works best for GUI- (graphical user interface) based applications, such as the Registry Editor. Some character-mode applications, such as Telnet, will also work using the Run dialog box. You need to create a command prompt for character mode applications, such as IPConfig.

Don't worry if this option doesn't make much sense to you right now. All you need to know is that it allows you to run certain types of applications. We'll explore both the Run dialog box and the command prompt in detail as this book progresses.

Log Off

Use this option to log off your system without shutting it down. You'll see a Log Off Windows dialog box with two buttons when you select this option. (Note that you might not see this button when using Windows XP Professional Edition; you must check the Display Log Off option in the Customize Classic Start Menu dialog box.)

The Switch Users button allows you to close your current session and open a new one under a different name. This option allows you to keep your application active while someone else works on your system for a few minutes.

The Log Off button allows you to log off without shutting down, but it closes all your applications. This option is the one to choose if you plan to leave your desk for a while or if you want to provide remote access without using any local resources.

Shut Down

Select the Shut Down menu option when you want to turn your computer off or restart it. You'll see a Turn Off Computer dialog box containing three buttons:

- *Stand By* Places the system in a standby, or reduced power, state. The system still has power applied to it, but uses much less power. Just how much power the system uses depends on the system design, but it's in the neighborhood of 7 watts—the equivalent of burning a nightlight. The main advantage of using standby is that it increases system longevity by reducing the shock of turning the system completely off and on. However, this mode does bring more dust into some machines and does consume a small amount of power.

- *Shut Down* Turns the system completely off. All of the fans stop running, and no power is applied to the system. This mode is the one to choose if you plan to leave for a while, when you need to maintain the inside of the machine, or if you need to move the machine to another location. This is also your only option for shutting the machine down if your system doesn't support the Advanced Power Control Interface (ACPI). We'll discuss ACPI in the "Advanced Configuration and Power Interface (ACPI)" section of Chapter 9.

- *Restart* Shuts Windows completely down and performs a soft boot of the system. Your machine will appear to turn itself on and then restart automatically. This is the option to use if you need to restart your system for some reason. For example, many application installation programs require that you restart the machine immediately after the installation completes.

Start Menu Customization

Customizing the Classic Start Menu is different from the simplified Start Menu described in Chapter 2. You'll begin the same way, by clicking Customize in the Taskbar and Start Menu Properties dialog box. (You access this dialog box by right clicking the Taskbar and choosing Properties from the context menu.) Windows will display the Customize Classic Start Menu dialog box, shown in Figure 3.8.

FIGURE 3.8
The Customize Classic Start Menu dialog box enables you to change your Start Menu appearance.

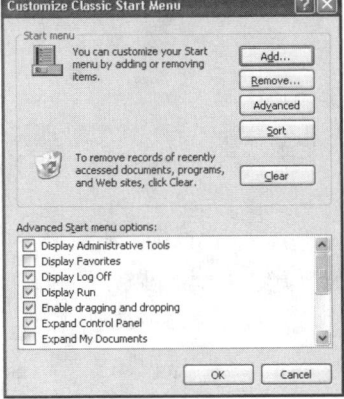

Notice that the list of advanced Start Menu options appears on the same dialog box as the other options. Along the right side of the dialog box, you'll see options for adding, removing, and sorting the Start Menu entries. Clicking the Advanced button displays a copy of Windows Explorer with the Start Menu directory selected. This allows you to perform tasks such as organizing your Start Menu for efficient use. Click the Clear button, and Windows XP will remove the entries from your Documents list, along with the application and Web site lists.

It pays to try the entries in the Advanced Start Menu options list. For example, I like to see the Control Panel applets displayed as a submenu below the Start | Settings | Control Panel menu, so I check the Expand Control Panel option. If you're an administrator, you might find it more convenient to display the Administrative Tools folder within the Programs menu. This allows you to select applications without searching for them in the Control Panel.

Customizing the Start Menu content is also something you should consider. For example, Figure 3.3 shows a Time Check entry. I have an application I use to track the time I spend on various projects. This application also tells me how many hours of "up time" the computer has had for maintenance purposes. It's an application I use all the time, but it's not important enough to place on the Quick Launch toolbar. Still, I don't want to spend time digging for it.

Adding new entries to the Start Menu is relatively easy, but you should take time to consider the placement of these new entries. I placed the Time Check folder at the root level because I use it so often. You may want to place other folders at other levels because they aren't as important. To see your current Start Menu structure, right-click Start and choose Explore from the context menu. Figure 3.9 shows a typical Windows Explorer view of the Start Menu.

FIGURE 3.9
Use this Windows Explorer view to modify your personal Start Menu entries.

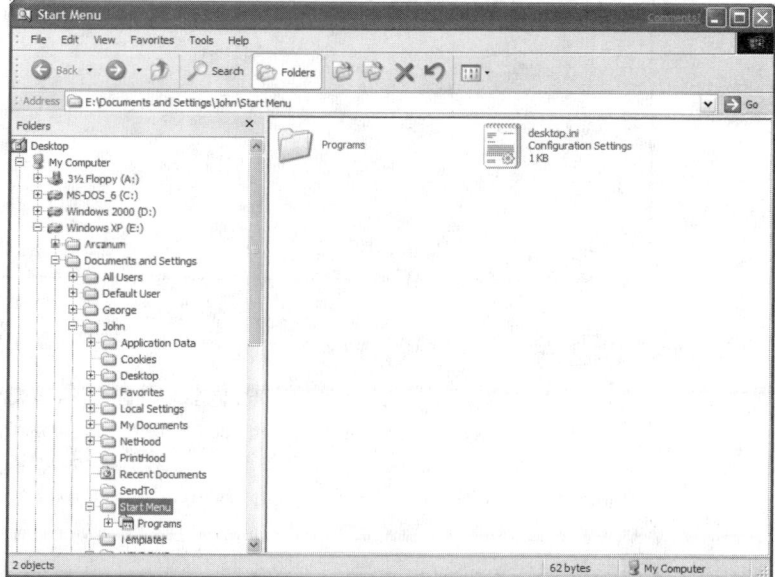

The first thing you should notice is the Programs folder, which contains all of my private applications. The second thing you should notice is that the Time Check folder is missing. This brings up another issue. You need to consider whether you want everyone, or just one or two people, to access this folder. If you right-click Start and choose Explore All Users, you'll see a Windows Explorer view similar to the one shown in Figure 3.9, but this time it affects every user of your machine.

Figure 3.10 shows the All Users\Start Menu entry. Notice that this folder contains the Time Check folder. I placed the Time Check folder here because everyone who uses my machine will need to track the time they use. In short, because Time Check is a common application that everyone uses regularly, it appears above the Programs folder in the All Users\Start Menu folder. As you can see, changing the content of your Start Menu is easy, but deciding how to change it requires some amount of experimentation.

FIGURE 3.10
It's important to decide on common versus individual applications.

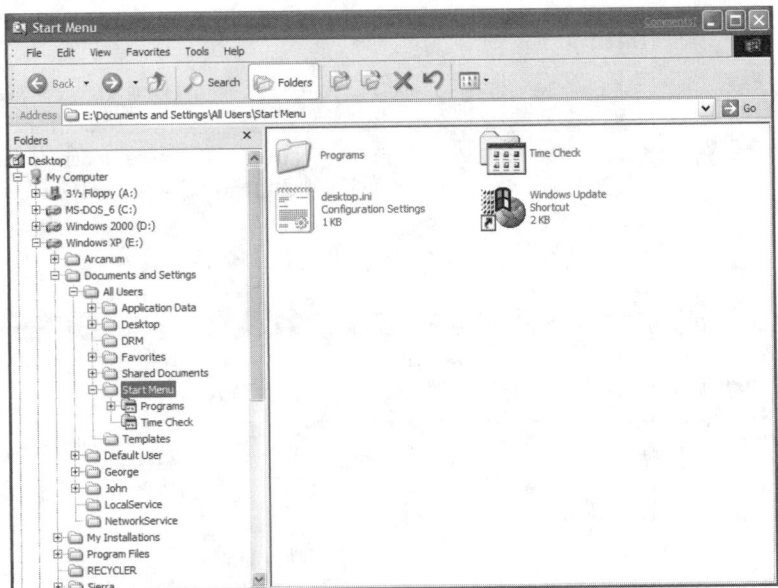

Using Toolbars

Windows XP is bristling with toolbars of all shapes and sizes. Even the Taskbar has several toolbars you can use. What's the purpose of all these toolbars? They make it easier for you to move around Windows XP. The toolbars in Windows XP reflect a continuing effort on Microsoft's part to enable you to customize every part of an application as you see fit.

As with most toolbars, you can move these around and resize them as necessary. Unlike most toolbars, those provided with the Taskbar aren't free floating. You can't move them off the Taskbar and have them sitting around like a dialog box. This makes sense. Consider all the confusion that would occur when a user tries to figure out where a free-floating toolbar belongs.

> **Peter's Principle:** Don't Bury Windows XP in a Pile of Toolbars
>
> Some people will most likely go crazy with the toolbars Microsoft provides. After all, if one toolbar can increase efficiency a little, and two toolbars a little more, why not have a toolbar for every purpose? If you look at toolbars as the sole method for improving your Windows XP efficiency, such logic might actually look good.
>
> The problem is that you can end up cluttering your screen with more toolbars than you'll ever use. Think what will happen to the Taskbar if you add four or five toolbars and have that many applications open besides. Will you really be able to figure out what's going on without checking each icon individually? When a toolbar begins to get in the way of the work you're doing, it's no longer a method of improving efficiency, but rather a hindrance to that efficiency.
>
> The trick to using toolbars is to look for a few tasks you perform regularly. I'm not talking about once a day; I'm talking about tasks you perform hourly or perhaps even more frequently. An efficiency-enhancing toolbar is one that makes getting the most from Windows XP a matter of a single click.

The next few sections will help you learn more about the Taskbar toolbars. I'll show you how to add, create, remove, and destroy toolbars.

Standard

Windows XP comes with four standard toolbars (although your toolbars may not necessarily appear in the same order mine did). The first is the Quick Launch toolbar, which enables you to view the desktop, to launch Internet Explorer, or to check out the channels to which you've subscribed. The second toolbar, Desktop, replicates all the icons on your desktop so that you can access them without minimizing your current application. Just select the Desktop icon you want to see from the toolbar, and Windows XP displays it. The third toolbar, Address, displays a list box in which you can type an address of something you want to see. (You also can type the name of a file on your local or network drive as a location on the Internet.) The list box keeps track of your most recent requests so that you can select them rather than type them. The fourth toolbar, Links, displays a list of the links you've defined for Internet Explorer. A single click takes you to one of your favorite locations.

You can access any of these toolbars by right-clicking the Taskbar and then selecting Toolbars from the context menu. To place a standard toolbar on the Taskbar, add a check to its context menu entry.

Custom

Just because Windows XP comes with standard toolbars doesn't mean that you have to keep things that way. You can create your own toolbars to meet specific needs. For example, you might want to create a toolbar that gives you access to the various projects you're working on. Another toolbar might contain the applications you use on a daily basis. The list could be endless.

It's a good idea to keep the number of items on your toolbar as low as possible. I usually keep the number of items to 10 or fewer. A toolbar can really start to clog things up when you get past that level. If your toolbar starts to reach 10 items, you should consider alternatives to listing every item. For example, you could place the items you use less often in a folder and then place that folder on the toolbar.

Creating a toolbar is easy. All you need to do to start the process is create a folder containing shortcuts to the items you want to access using the toolbar. For example, you might create a folder named Common Applications that contains shortcuts to your favorite applications. After the folder is completed, right-click the Taskbar. Select the Toolbars | New Toolbar option from the context menu. You'll see a New Toolbar dialog box containing a field for the link name or Internet address and an Explorer-style directory listing you can use to choose the folder containing the shortcuts.

The capability to use an Internet address means that you can create a toolbar of the Web sites you visit on a daily basis. You even can include your company intranet as a potential toolbar item. You can get only one site per toolbar when specifying an Internet or intranet location, so you should use toolbars for only the most important sites.

After you type a folder name or URL, Windows XP displays it on the Taskbar. Figure 3.11 shows an example of both types of toolbars. The toolbar on the left points to a local folder. The one on the right points to Microsoft's home page on the Internet.

> **Tip:** You might find it a bit difficult to view Web sites on the Taskbar, especially if you have more than one. To see the Web site in a window, right-click the toolbar you want to see and select Open in Window from the context menu. You also can save room on the toolbar by right-clicking it and removing the check from the Show Title option in the toolbar. This removes the Web site title from the toolbar and creates more space for actually viewing the Web site.

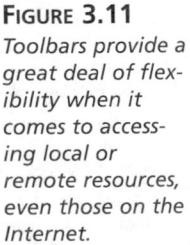

FIGURE 3.11
Toolbars provide a great deal of flexibility when it comes to accessing local or remote resources, even those on the Internet.

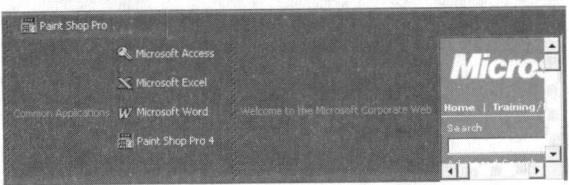

Getting Rid of a Toolbar You Don't Need

After a while, you might find that all those toolbars you created really don't do as much as you'd like, or you may find that you want to get rid of some old toolbars to make room for new ones. Whatever the reason, getting rid of an old toolbar is easy. Simply right-click the Taskbar and then select Toolbars from the context menu. Find the toolbar you want to remove, and then remove the check next to its name by selecting it.

Customizing the Quick Launch Toolbar

I consider the Quick Launch Toolbar a substitute for the simplified Start Menu, discussed in Chapter 2, for the advanced user. It can hold all of the applications you use regularly, but doesn't change dynamically. You should include all of the applications you use daily, but not those that you start by double-clicking application files.

To give you a better idea of how the Quick Launch Toolbar should work, consider the way I use Microsoft Office. I almost never open Access as an application; it's common for me to double-click one of the database file shortcuts in my work folder. Likewise, I seldom open Word as an application because I usually open an established file, such as an outline or existing manuscript file first. Neither of these applications is a good candidate for the Quick Launch toolbar. On the other hand, I always open Excel as an application because I use it to modify so many files. It's easier to open the application and load the data files I need using the File | Open command. Excel is one of the applications on my Quick Launch toolbar because I use the program almost daily and usually open it by using the application icon.

There are many ways to modify your Quick Launch toolbar. For example, you could open a copy of Windows Explorer and locate \Documents and Settings\<User Name>\Application Data\Microsoft\Internet Explorer\Quick Launch. Personally, I prefer not to dig that many layers down the drive hierarchy if I don't have to.

An alternative to using Windows Explorer is to locate in the Programs folder of the Start Menu the application you want to place in the Quick Launch toolbar. Right-click the application icon and drag it to the Quick Launch toolbar. You'll see a context menu with Copy Here, Move Here, and Cancel in it. Notice that Move Here is the default option, which is why you don't want to use a standard drag to move the application icon. Choose Copy Here from the context menu, and you'll see the application icon appear in the Quick Launch toolbar.

If you later decide that the application doesn't really belong in the Quick Launch toolbar, you can right-click it and choose Delete. The icon will still appear with your programs under the Start Menu. However, if you had used the normal drag method, the icon would now be gone for good. In short, always create copies of icons you move to one of the toolbars.

Customizing Your Desktop

You probably don't have a "formal" physical desktop at work. I'll bet that you customize it to meet every need you have. Your desk reflects the way you work. No one, for example, forced you to place the stapler in the upper-right corner.

The Windows XP desktop has some features you might not think about right away. If you right-click the desktop, for example, it has a context menu, just like everything else in Windows XP. (We discussed the context menu in the "Using Context Menus" section of Chapter 2.) Suffice it to say that there are plenty of nice surprises when it comes to arranging items under Windows XP.

The entries under the Arrange Icons By menu work just like the same entries under Explorer. (See how everything seems to have a bit of Explorer in it?) You can rearrange your icons by name, type, size, or modified date). Personally, I find the type and name orders the most convenient. You can use the Auto Arrange option to automatically keep your icons aligned and in order.

Some people detest the standard arrangements, so they put the icons in the order they want them. If you're one of these people, the Align to Grid option is custom tailored for you. It enables you to keep the icons in a specific order, but arranges them into neat rows and columns. This option provides a grid effect that enables you to keep your desktop neat yet still arranged in the order you want.

Another method for arranging icons is to use the Show in Groups option. This feature will group your icons using the chosen sorting criteria. For example, if you choose to arrange your icons by name, you'll see alphabetical groupings.

You'll find two entries in the Arrange Icons By menu that don't appear on the standard Explorer menu. The first is Show Desktop Icons. Clearing this option will remove all the icons from your desktop so that you can enjoy your wallpaper. The Lock Web Items on Desktop option, which is part of Active Desktop, prevents users from moving any Web content. This is a nice feature because it's possible to move things around without really meaning to do so.

The following sections look at the desktop as a whole. They discuss different options to make your desktop more usable, but they don't stop there. These sections are a guide to the most common tricks people use to optimize their Windows XP environment. This is an unofficial "must do" checklist you should look at when trying to get the most from your setup.

Taskbar

A major part of the Windows XP interface is the Taskbar, which appears as a horizontal bar at the bottom of the display (or on one of the sides or at the top if you decide to move the Taskbar there). The *Taskbar* is the central control area for most actions you'll take under Windows XP. The Taskbar contains three major elements: the Start menu, the

Task List, and the Notification Area (known as the Taskbar Tray and various other names in the past). You also might see one or more toolbars. We've already discussed many of these elements in this chapter, so you should have a good feel for the Taskbar components.

It's time to discuss the Taskbar as an entity. Here are a few ways you can configure it. The Taskbar starts out at the bottom of the display, but you don't have to leave it there. With Windows XP, you can place the Taskbar on any side of the desktop. Simply drag the Taskbar where you'd like it to go. Of course, moving the Taskbar by accident would disrupt the setup you tried to hard to achieve. The Taskbar content menu contains a Lock the Taskbar entry that allows you to lock the Taskbar content and location so that you don't have to worry about inadvertent changes.

Like other objects under Windows XP, the Taskbar provides a properties dialog box. To display it, right-click the Taskbar and select Properties from the context menu. Figure 3.12 shows what the Taskbar tab of the Taskbar and Start Menu properties dialog box looks like.

FIGURE 3.12
Use the Taskbar tab to change your Taskbar settings.

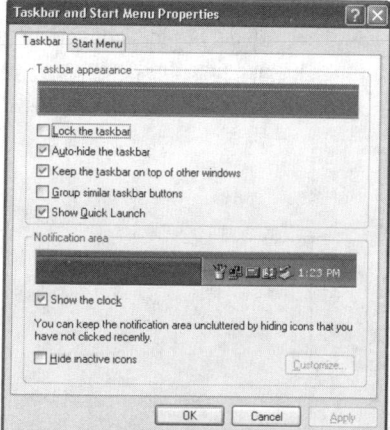

The seven settings on the Taskbar Options tab enable you to change how it reacts. We've already discussed the Lock the Taskbar option. My personal favorite is the Auto-hide the Taskbar option. When you select this option, the Taskbar appears as a thin line at the bottom of the display (or on one of the sides or at the top if you decide to move the Taskbar there). Whenever the mouse cursor touches this line, the Taskbar resumes its normal size. This feature enables you to minimize the Taskbar to clear space for application windows, yet the Taskbar stays handy when you need it.

You should always select the Keep the Taskbar on Top of Other Windows option. Otherwise, the applications you have running at the time could hide the Taskbar, making it hard to work with. To access a hidden Taskbar, you'd have to minimize most of the running applications—a time-consuming and unnecessary process.

Some people run many applications at the same time. Normally, the Taskbar displays applications in the same order that you start them. The Group similar Taskbar buttons option places the icons in alphabetical order, making them easier to find in some cases.

The Show Quick Launch option displays the Quick Launch toolbar on the Taskbar when selected. We discussed the Quick Launch toolbar in the "Customizing the Quick Launch Toolbar" section of the chapter, so I won't discuss it again here.

The Show the Clock field enables you to clear more space for applications. Simply clear this option to hide the clock from view. You can normally add one more application to the Taskbar and see it clearly by removing the clock.

The Notification Area normally contains a wealth of icons. As you install more vendor-specific drivers, the number of icons seems to increase. Eventually, the Notification Area consumes a great deal of space on the Taskbar—space that's wasted if you don't use the icon. Use the Hide inactive icons option to hide these icons until you actually need them.

Windows XP will always hide inactive icons if you use the default settings. However, if you click Customize, you'll see the Customize Notifications dialog box, as shown in Figure 3.13. This dialog box shows the current and past icons. The list box next to each item allows you to always show, always hide, or hide icons when inactive. In short, you can keep the icons you use all the time and hide those you never use.

FIGURE 3.13

The Customize Notifications dialog box allows you to choose which icons always appear in the Notification Area.

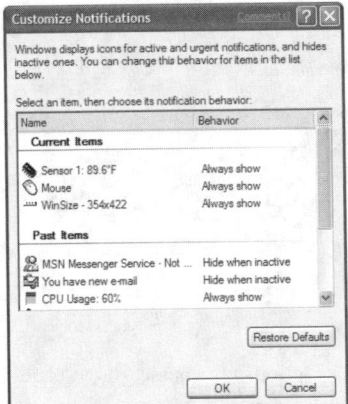

Right-clicking the Taskbar displays a few other object-specific options, all of which affect the way Windows XP organizes the applications displayed on the Taskbar:

- *Toolbars* This option contains a list of toolbar options for the Taskbar. We already discussed this feature in the "Using Toolbars" section of this chapter, so I won't discuss it again here.

- *Cascade Windows* When you select this option, all application windows are resized to the same size. Windows XP arranges them diagonally, much like the display in a spreadsheet when you open more than one file. You can select any application in the list by clicking its title bar (the area at the top of the application window that contains the application's name).

- *Tile Windows Horizontally* or *Tile Windows Vertically* Use either of these options if you want to see the window areas of all your applications at one time. Windows XP uses every available inch of desktop space to place the applications side by side, either horizontally or vertically. Each application receives about the same amount of space.

- *Show the Desktop* If your screen is so cluttered that you can't tell what's open and what's not, use this option to clean up the mess. The Show the Desktop option minimizes every application you have running on the desktop.

- *Task Manager* This option displays the Windows Task Manager, which provides a quick way to check your system's performance. We'll discuss this feature in detail in the "Using Task Manager" section of Chapter 5.

Desktop Settings

Most people look to desktop settings as the means to improve the appearance of their computers. Just changing an object's color won't make it work better, but it'll affect the way you view your system. A new piece of wallpaper or a change of color can produce a subtle performance increase. Any positive change in attitude usually translates into improved efficiency. I find that changing my wallpaper and display colors from time to time gives my computer that "new" feel everyone needs occasionally.

Other reasons can necessitate a change of configuration. For example, wallpaper, although attractive to the eye, chews up valuable memory. You might run into a situation in which memory is at a premium. Giving up your wallpaper is one way to increase memory to complete a specific task.

Eyestrain is also a common problem among computer users. Sitting for eight hours in front of a monitor doesn't do anyone's eyes much good. If you're like me, however, you probably spend more than eight hours a day staring at the screen. Somewhere along the way, you might want to make your icons and text bigger to reduce eye fatigue. Changing your desktop settings to improve readability is a very practical use of this feature.

Themes

We already discussed one use for Windows XP themes in the "Switching to the Windows 2000 Interface" section of this chapter. When you select the Windows Classic theme, you also change the interface to look like Windows 2000. The Windows XP theme reverts the display to the one we've used in most of the chapters.

Note: Even though Windows 2000 shipped without the Desktop Themes icon in the Control Panel, you can still use themes with it. The Microsoft Knowledge Base article "Q257841 – How to Configure Desktop Themes in Windows 2000" (http://support.microsoft.com/support/kb/articles/Q257/8/41.ASP) tells how to start the Desktop Themes dialog box so that you can use themes under Windows 2000. Another Knowledge Base article, "Q258478 – Windows 2000 Desktop Themes Compatibility" (http://support.microsoft.com/support/kb/articles/Q258/4/78.ASP), tells about compatibility problems you may have with certain themes. These compatibility problems also appear in Windows XP.

Fortunately, with Windows XP, you can still use all of the themes with a .THEME extension that you used under Windows 9x and Windows 2000. When you use a theme with Windows XP, the interface reverts to the Windows Classic form. Microsoft has opted not to publish the application programming interface (API) for Windows XP themes. (An API makes it easier for people to develop add-ons to a product.) A Windows XP theme contains more information than one used with Windows 9x or Windows 2000.

Tip: One of the more interesting places to find help with Windows themes is ThemeDoctor.com. Desktop Architect (http://www.themedoctor.com/cafe_pg.shtml) provides better support for themes than you'll find in Windows. It not only allows you full control over the installed themes, but also provides more theme settings than Microsoft does. In addition, you can download (among other things) additional wallpaper and screensavers from this site.

The problem is that Microsoft uses a new technique for handling themes, and your old theme files may require a few changes. For example, you'll find that there's no Plus folder under the Programs folder—themes are stored in individual user directories when working with Windows XP. You'll add at least the .THEME file to your \Documents and Settings\<User Name>\Application Data\Microsoft\Windows\Themes folder.

The one change that most themes will require is some means of handling the %ThemeDir% entry they all contain. You can take care of this requirement by adding an environment variable to your Windows XP setup. This variable tells Windows XP what ThemeDir means. You add environment variables by right-clicking My Computer and selecting Properties. You'll see a System Properties dialog box. Select Advanced and click Environment Variables. Figure 3.14 shows the Environment Variables dialog box.

You have two choices at this point. Placing the ThemeDir environment variable in the User variables list will make it accessible for only the current user; placing it in the System variables list will make it accessible to all users. Go the User variable route if you want everyone to have a separate set of themes. This method uses more hard drive space, but ensures that changes made by one person won't affect anyone else. If you're running a business and want everyone to use the same set of themes, you can place in a common directory all of the files required to support the themes and place in the user's directory just the .THEME files. This technique uses less disk storage and tends to enforce a consistent look.

FIGURE 3.14

The Environment Variables dialog box allows you to set the ThemeDir environment variable.

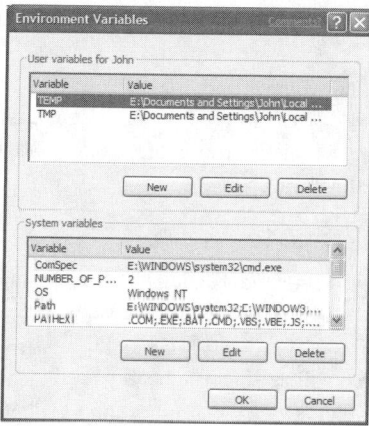

When you decide which technique to use, click New under the appropriate list. Type **ThemeDir** in the Variable Name field and the location of the theme files in the Variable Value field. Click OK, and your themes should be ready to test.

In some cases, poorly written themes may still refuse to work. This means editing the .THEME file by hand. A .THEME file is simple text, so you can use Notepad to edit the file. Look for entries with specific directories that don't point to the resource's actual location. For example, if you placed all the cursor (.CUR) files in the D:\Themes\My Theme directory with the rest of the theme files, yet the entry in the .THEME file says that the cursor files reside in C:\Temp, then .THEME file won't work. Earlier versions of Windows overcame problems like this by placing all of the theme files in one directory and then looking at that directory before checking the file path. Because Windows XP places themes in individual user directories, you'll find that this old technique won't work. It's best to place all theme files in a single directory and then point to them using the %ThemeDir% environment variable, like this:

```
empty=%ThemeDir%\MyTheme\MyTheme_Empty.ico,0
```

Let's discuss the centralized method of handling themes in a little more detail. Create a central directory for all of the themes for your system. Using a network drive ensures that everyone in a small company can access company-approved themes and that you have to change only a single set of theme files to change everyone's system setup. I create a separate subdirectory for each theme. That way, if you need to remove a theme, you can do so without having to wade through all of the other themes on the system. For example, the first theme for your company might be located in the F:\My Company\Theme 1\ network drive.

Create the theme and place all of the supporting files in the directory you set up on the network drive. Edit the .THEME file so that it reflects the current location of the theme files. For this example, you'd change the entries for every resource in the .THEME file to read like this:

```
empty=%ThemeDir%\Theme 1\MyTheme_Empty.ico,0
```

Notice that the %ThemeDir% environment variable isolates the .THEME file from change. It would point to the F:\My Company directory in this case. However, you could easily change the environment variable later to reflect a new storage location and not have to change any of the .THEME files.

Wallpaper and Desktop Items

The Desktop page of the Display Properties dialog box has two major sections. The top half of the page shows a monitor. Changing any of the wallpaper or pattern settings immediately affects the contents of this display. The monitor gives you a thumbnail sketch of how your background will appear. The bottom section contains a list of available bitmaps and Web pages. Windows XP doesn't support the patterns found in previous versions of the product—a real loss because using patterns could dress up your display without using lots of memory.

The Wallpaper list defaults to files found in your main Windows folder. You don't have to use these files, however. Click the Browse button to look in other folders on your drive. To display wallpaper, you can center it on the background (the best choice for pictures) or tile it (the best choice for patterns). You also can choose the Stretch option, which changes the dimensions of a bitmap to fill the entire desktop area.

If you want to change the items on your Desktop, click Customize Desktop. You'll see a Desktop Items dialog box. The General tab of this dialog box allows you to set which standard icons appear on the Desktop, including My Documents, My Computer, My Network Places, and Internet Explorer. The middle of this dialog box contains a list of the standard icons and allows you to change their appearance. Finally, the bottom of the General tab contains an option that allows you to run the Desktop Cleanup Wizard. This new wizard helps you keep desktop clutter under control by moving to a folder any items you haven't used very often.

The Web tab of the Desktop Items dialog box allows you to set the Active Desktop features. We'll discuss Active Desktop in the "Active Desktop: A View of the Internet" section of this chapter.

Screen Saver

A very healthy third-party market exists for screen savers. Some Windows users buy screen savers in bulk. You can find them in stores and on every online service in existence. Unless you own an older system, using a screen saver probably isn't necessary—just fun. A good Web site for all kinds of screen savers is http://www.ratloaf.com/, provided by Screensavers A to Z. This includes a screen saver for displaying your favorite JPEG, PIC, and KQP files. If you happen to be a gardener, this site enables you to build your own virtual garden onscreen. There are many screen savers at this site; look for something that interests you.

Windows XP also provides screen saver options. They aren't as much fun as some screen savers on the market, but they do the job. You'll find these options on the Screen Saver tab of the Display Properties dialog box.

Just as with the Background page, the Screen Saver page contains a miniature view of your monitor. It displays a thumbnail sketch of what the screen will look like when you configure the screen saver. The Screen Saver field enables you to choose from the screen savers in the SYSTEM32 folder. (Screen savers have an SCR extension.) If you decide to use a third-party screen saver that uses the Windows format, you need to place the file in the same directory as the others, or else Windows won't see it.

After you select a screen saver, you can use the Settings button to change its settings. In most cases, the settings affect how Windows XP displays the screen saver. For example, the settings might change the number of lines you see or the number of colors. Click Preview to see the results of any changes you make.

Check the On Resume, Password Protect option if you want to return to the Welcome (or other logon) screen every time the screen saver starts. This option forces you to log back in when the screen saver stops, but also enhances system security. This feature enables you to leave the room without fear that someone will use your machine while you're gone.

The Wait field enables you to change the number of minutes Windows XP waits before it activates the screen saver. To turn the screen saver off, move the mouse cursor or press a key.

This dialog box also contains a special Power button that enables you to set up the energy-saving features of your system. Click this button to display the Power Schemes tab of the Power Options Properties dialog box. I'll discuss this dialog box in detail in the "Power Management Strategies" section of Chapter 17, "Mobile Computing."

Appearance

The Appearance tab of the Display Properties dialog box enables you to change the actual appearance of your display, not just the Desktop. As previously mentioned, this dialog box allows you to choose between the Windows XP and Classic Windows styles using the Windows and Buttons field. The Color Scheme field allows you to choose which color scheme Windows will use. The selections change to match the current display style. Likewise, the Font Size field chooses the generic font size. When working with the Classic Windows style, you can choose from Normal, Large, and Extra Large.

Click Effects, and you'll see the Effects dialog box. The options in this dialog box remain the same no matter which display style you use. The first option allows you to choose either a fade effect or a scroll effect for menus and tooltips. The next option determines the method used to smooth the font edges. We already discussed this option, in the "Switching to the Windows 2000 Interface" section of this chapter. The last four options determine if you'll use large fonts, display shadows beneath the menus, show window content while dragging, and hide the underlined letters for keyboard navigation.

Click Advanced to display the Advanced Appearance dialog box, shown in Figure 3.15. Users of previous versions of Windows will recognize this dialog box immediately as the one used to change the appearance under Windows 9x and Windows 2000. To change the appearance of an item, click the picture of the display. (You have to select some items manually from the list because they don't appear in the picture.)

FIGURE 3.15

The settings on the Advanced Appearance dialog box enable you to change the colors and fonts used by your display.

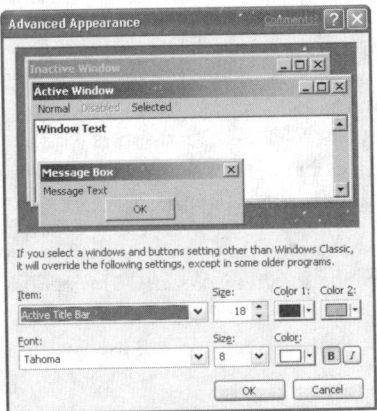

Windows XP provides a great deal of flexibility when it comes to selecting fonts for your display. I have several configurations with "tired eye"–size text settings. You can change individually the size of the menu and title bar text. Everything else with text also has a setting here for font and type sizes.

Changing an entry consists of making list box selections. This dialog box contains seven list boxes. The first four affect the item itself and include Item Name, Size, and Color (two selections, in many cases). Size refers to the size of the window or other display element. For example, you could change the width of a menu bar using this option. The first color selection normally affects the top or left side of an item, such as a title bar. The second color affects the bottom or right side of an item. The second set of three list boxes controls the text within a display element. These settings include Font, Size, and Color. You can select any installed font as your display font, but most people find that MS Serif or MS Sans Serif works best on displays. I occasionally use Arial and find that it works quite well. You can also choose bold or italics text (or both), if you want.

Resolution

The Settings page of the Display Properties dialog box enables you to change your display resolution and number of colors. You usually can change the settings without rebooting your machine. Note that Windows XP forces you to use a minimum of 16-bit color resolution, which differs from previous versions of Windows that allowed you to use 256 colors.

This dialog box also allows you to change the font size. Click Advanced to display the General tab of the Display Adapter Properties dialog box. The DPI Setting drop-down list box contains two standard sizes: Normal Size (96 DPI) and Large Size (120 DPI), which are nebulous definitions. Choose the Custom Setting option to display the Custom DPI Setting dialog box. This dialog box enables you to create a custom-size system font. This feature is very handy if you need a font that's either very large or very small. Normally, however, you'll use the standard sizes that come with Windows.

Click Troubleshoot if you're having problems with your display. Help and Support Services will start and ask you some questions about the problems. In at least some cases, you'll receive a list of the most common problems affecting your display.

Clock

We discussed the clock previously in this chapter, when talking about the Taskbar. The clock isn't just a means to keep time. You can use the clock to change the computer's hardware storage (CMOS) and, therefore, the time stamps on all your files. The clock also affects any events you schedule and anything else that relies on the clock.

The clock's properties consist of a single check box—Show the Clock—on the Taskbar Properties dialog box. All this entry does is display or hide the clock. In most cases, you'll want to display the clock because you gain nothing from shutting it off.

Double-clicking the Clock icon displays the Date and Time Properties dialog box. This dialog box is the same one used during the installation process to set the clock. The Date & Time tab contains a calendar and a clock, which you can use to change the system settings.

> **Note:** Some network operating system and client combinations will thwart any effort on your part to change the system time. For example, the Novell client will automatically synchronize the time on your machine with the time on the server. This is actually an advantage because the entire company can remain synchronized this way.

The Time Zone tab enables you to change the time zone to match the current area of the world. Simply select the time zone for the area of the world in which you live. The Daylight Savings Time check box enables the computer to adjust the time for you automatically.

Windows XP includes a new Internet Time tab. Check the Automatically Synchronize with an Internet Time Server option if you want to update your system's time automatically. Windows provides several default time servers, or you can type one of your own. Any time server you select must support the Simple Network Time Protocol (SNTP).

Businesses that rely on a shared Internet connection should automatically synchronize the communications server with the Internet and then use other methods to synchronize workstations and other servers to communication server time.

Working with Desktop Objects

Making your desktop more efficient is easy in Windows XP. First, you need to learn to work with objects, types of which are data containers. After all, what's more important— the tool that creates an object or the object itself?

Second, you need to learn how to manage objects. You'll start by looking at methods of moving objects around. Remember that everything is an object of some sort, and objects are easy to copy, cut, and paste. You can move them around just like any object in the physical world.

Third, you'll learn to organize objects. Keeping your data organized makes it easier to find, easier to manipulate, and easier to secure. Organizing your data now pays large dividends in efficiency later.

Creating New Objects

One of the first tasks you need to learn is creating a new object. New objects are empty containers you can fill with data. The desktop, Explorer, and most Windows XP folders have a New option in the context menu. This option displays a list of file types that Windows XP can produce automatically. The content of this list will vary according to the applications and operating system features installed on your machine.

Look at the context menu now by right-clicking on the Desktop and highlighting the New option. Note that one of the entries is a folder. You always can place a folder within another object normally used for storage (even another folder). Using folders helps you organize your data into more efficient units.

Manipulating Objects

Many people use cut-and-paste to move data around within applications, such as Word. You just cut the data from where you no longer need it and paste it to a new location. Windows XP also supports cut-and-paste for objects. To move a file from one location to another, cut and then paste it using the commands on the Windows Explorer Edit menu. The beauty of this approach is that a copy of the file is now in memory. This means that you can make as many copies of it as you want.

Windows XP also allows you to copy objects. Anything you can cut, you can copy. Copying the object means that you leave the original in place and create copies where needed. The copy resides in memory, where you can paste it to as many new locations as you'd like.

You can't paste a file on top of another file. If you attempt to do this, Windows XP will create a copy of the file using a different name (normally beginning with the word *copy* or by adding a number to the end of the filename). However, you can paste a copy of a file on the desktop or within a folder. If you take a logical, real-world approach to moving objects under Windows XP, you'll never run into problems getting objects to work.

Most people find the cut, copy, and paste technique easy to use because that's how they work with data in their applications. Windows Explorer doesn't provide these options on the Standard Buttons toolbar by default, so you'll need to add them. Right-click the Standard Buttons toolbar and choose Customize from the context menu. You'll see a Customize Toolbar dialog box, like the one shown in Figure 3.16. Notice the Cut button highlighted in the figure. Simply click Add to place it on the Standard Buttons toolbar. Highlight the Copy and Paste buttons in turn to place them on the Standard Buttons toolbar as well.

FIGURE 3.16

Use the Customize Toolbar dialog box to add the Cut, Copy, and Paste buttons to the Standard Buttons toolbar.

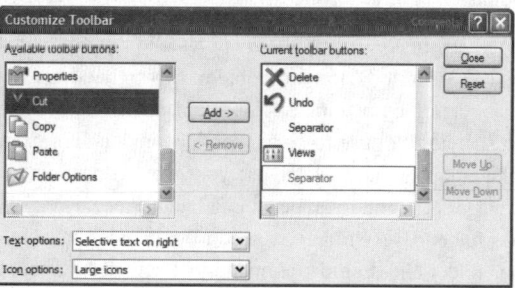

Microsoft does place four object management buttons on the Standard Buttons toolbar for you. The following list describes each button and tells how you can use it to manage objects on your system:

- *Move To*   Highlight one or more objects and then click this button. Windows Explorer will display a Move Items dialog box that contains a hierarchical view of the folders on your system. Choose a folder from the list and then click Move to move the file from the current location to a new location.

- *Copy To*   Works like the Move To button, except that Windows Explorer will copy the file instead of moving it. This means that the original copy of the file stays in place and that you'll make another copy in the new location.

- *Delete*   Places the highlighted files into the Recycle Bin. Windows Explorer doesn't actually delete the files; it merely marks them for deletion. You can recover the files from the Recycle Bin for a limited amount of time. Use Shift+Delete to remove files permanently without moving them to the Recycle Bin first.

- *Undo*   Undoes the previous action. For example, if you created a copy of a file, Windows Explorer will remove the copy. Undoing a delete will place the file back in the original directory. However, you can't undo permanent actions, such as permanently deleting a file using the Shift+Delete key combination.

Using a Template

One problem with the New menu is that it creates objects of a default type. For example, if you have a graphics program, like Paint Shop Pro, installed on your machine, you might get a new BMP image rather than a new TIF image. Even though Paint Shop Pro handles both file types, it defaults to a specific file type.

Some applications get around this problem by using New menu entry extensions. For example, if you create a new Word for Windows object using the selection on the context menu, it uses the Normal style sheet. What you really wanted was the Letters style sheet, but there isn't a fast way to create that document using the direct New | Microsoft Word Document entry on the context menu. However, in the case of Microsoft Office, you'll see an entry for Other Office Documents. Selecting this option displays a dialog box that contains a complete list of all of the Microsoft Office templates you've defined.

Unfortunately, Microsoft is about the only application that provides a method for you to get around the new default document problem, so you need another way of doing things. I got around this problem by placing a folder named Templates on my Desktop. Inside are copies of each sample file I use to create new documents. For example, if you write many letters using the same format, you can use your word processor to create a document containing everything that normally appears in a letter. Place a copy of the letter template in your Templates folder. Every time you need to write a letter, right-click the template in your Templates folder and drag the template to a new destination, such as a project folder. When the context menu appears, select Copy to create a copy of your template.

This approach to creating new documents can reduce the time necessary to start a task. You can create enough copies of a template to satisfy project needs in a few seconds. Using the template also means that all of your settings are correct when you enter the document for the first time.

Creating Work Areas

Now that you have an idea how to move and copy data, let's look at a more efficient way to work with it. I've started using a new method of organizing information because of the way Windows XP works. You can follow several easy steps to start a project:

1. Create a main project folder on the Desktop.
2. Open the folder and place one folder inside for each type of data you plan to work with. When writing this chapter, for example, I created one folder for the word-processed document, another for the electronic research information, and a third for the graphics files.
3. Open the first data folder, create a copy of your template, and then make as many copies of that template as you'll need within the data folder.
4. Rename the data files to match what they'll contain.
5. Close this data folder, and repeat steps 3 and 4 for each of your other data folders.
6. Complete your project by filling each data folder.

Tip: Using the same method of creating new data files for all your data might not be possible because of the way an application is designed. In some cases, as with the screen shots in this book, the data file is created in a different way. My screen shots are all captured from a display buffer. I don't need to create a blank file to hold them because the screen capture program does this for me. Always use the data-creation technique that works best with the applications you use.

You might wonder about the benefits of using a datacentric approach to work with Windows. The old application-based method of managing your data may appear to provide the same results as the method I've outlined. However, the new technique offers advantages you just don't get using the application-centric approach:

- *Data transmittal* Giving someone else access to a group project means sending him a folder, not a bunch of individual files. How many times have you thought that you had gathered all the files for a project, only to find that you didn't send an important file? This method of organizing data prevents such problems.

- *Application independence* It doesn't matter which application you need to use in order to modify a file. If everyone in your office uses the same applications, modifying a file means double-clicking it and nothing else. You no longer need to worry about which application to open; all that matters is the data.

- *Location* Where's your data? Do you ever find yourself searching for hours to find a file you thought you'd lost? This method enables you to place all project data in one place. Its physical location no longer matters because the pieces are together. Of course, you still need to know the data location when you organize the project folder, but would you rather look for a file once or a hundred times? Using desktop folders means that you'll find the data once and never worry about it again.

- *Ease of storage* When I finish a project in Windows XP, I don't worry about putting all the bits and pieces together. I send one folder to storage. When I need to work on the project again, I know that I need to load only that one folder back on my local drive.

Active Desktop: A View of the Internet

Active Desktop allows you to place content from the Internet or an intranet on your Desktop. It enables you to get work done quickly and with much less effort. However, I find that Active Desktop comes in handiest in handling information overload.

The following sections look at the Active Desktop approach to working with Windows. You'll learn what sets Active Desktop apart from the Explorer interface. You'll also encounter tips and techniques for making Active Desktop work for you.

What Is an Active Desktop?

All the desktops you've used to-date are *static*—in other words, they don't change. Active Desktop does change. The desktop you used today won't be the same desktop you see tomorrow. When you arrive at work or start up your machine at home tomorrow, the contents of your desktop will change to reflect the new day.

Here's another way to look at Active Desktop. Think, for a second, about the newspaper. You receive a newspaper every day and place it on your desk. The one from yesterday gets thrown in the trash. Your desktop has changed—it contains new content that reflects what you're doing today. Likewise, Windows XP will change the content of your desktop each day to reflect changing events when you use Active Desktop. If you subscribe to a news channel and display it on your desktop, the display will change each day to reflect the changes in the news.

Active Desktop does more than change content. Consider what happens when you go to look for something on your local machine, the network, or the Internet. In the past, you used three different procedures to get the data you needed. Your local machine required one procedure, the network required another, and the Internet something different. Windows XP allows you to keep all your resources in one place. You'll be able to find the data you need without really thinking about where it came from.

Let's expand your horizons a little bit. Consider the role of a supervisor. If you want to direct people's attention to a specific event, a bit of data, or another company-related matter, you usually have to write a memo and distribute it to everyone. Wouldn't it be nicer if you could just place this information on the person's Windows Desktop? Windows XP permits you to do this. A company intranet can easily supply everything necessary for a supervisor to direct what an employee is doing. In addition, you can monitor employee progress without looking over his shoulder by looking at his desktop on the company intranet.

The following sections will help you get started using Active Desktop. After you understand its principles, how you use it is really a matter of how much imagination you have. Active Desktop, unlike the static desktop of old, has very few limitations.

Active Desktop Usage Tips

If you decide to use Active Desktop, you need to use it efficiently to get the maximum benefit. Some people stuff their Desktop with every folder available, making it just as cluttered as their actual office desk. What happens now that you can also fill the Windows XP Desktop with additional information from the Internet? This could cause some people to have real problems using Windows XP; the Desktop could become cluttered to the point of being unusable. The following points should help you keep the clutter to a minimum:

- *Avoid excess* When using Active Desktop, decide what you need and what you don't need. After all, do you really need that folder containing last year's financial report? Determine the contents of your Desktop by frequency of access; this keeps your desktop uncluttered and makes you more efficient. If you visit the same Web site every day, it pays to place it on your desktop.

- *Create a filing cabinet* Active Desktop is designed to give you the Internet on your desktop. The Internet uses links and pages to organize information, much as you'd use drawers and file folders to organize information in a filing cabinet. We've all seen Web pages that are really nothing more than links to other places. You could create pages of this sort to help organize and cross-reference information that you need every once in a while, but not on a daily basis.

- *Consolidate as necessary* Some people work on many different projects at the same time and need access to many sources of information. Trying to keep these desktops uncluttered might seem like a losing proposition. You can avoid this problem, however, by consolidating what you need into folders. For example, you might have on your Desktop right now four or five folders that contain information for the same project. Consolidating that information into one master folder would make life easier.

- *Use a Taskbar toolbar* You can save space on your desktop and make it easier to access your projects in the process. Create a toolbar for the Taskbar and point it to a local or network directory. Pointing your toolbar to a network directory can be more efficient than using the Desktop, which is an added bonus for people in a workgroup. That way, everyone has the same list of folders with the same names and shortcuts. Because everyone has the same project list, there's less confusion when talking to other people. In addition, the manager can keep the project folder list up-to-date by managing a single directory rather than trying to keep track of many employee desktops. We discussed toolbar usage in the "Using Toolbars" section of this chapter.

- *Minimize your Web pages* In most cases, you don't need to view in their entirety the Web pages you frequent. A small view is usually sufficient until you need the information the page contains. I normally reduce the size of a Web page to the minimum possible, but large enough that I can still see any changes as Windows XP automatically updates the page content for me. You can always resize the page later to get a full view of the content it provides.

Customizing the Active Desktop

Previous versions of Windows allowed you to perform extensive customization of Active Desktop. Microsoft has stepped back from this technology after realizing that not everyone used it. You can perform all of the customization required for Active Desktop using the Web tab of the Desktop Items dialog box. Access this dialog box by right-clicking the Desktop, choosing Properties, selecting Desktop, and, finally, clicking Customize Desktop.

The default view shows the Web Pages field on the left side of the Desktop Items dialog box and four buttons on the right side. The Web Pages field usually contains two entries: Internet Explorer Channel Bar (optional) and My Current Home Page. Checking either of these options will display it on the Desktop.

Click New if you want to add a new Web page. The New Active Desktop Item dialog box will allow you to browse Favorites, manually type a uniform resource location (URL), or visit Microsoft's gallery to add a new URL to the Web Pages field. Click OK, and you'll see an Add Item to Active Desktop dialog box. Click OK again, and Windows XP will download the new page from the Internet.

Use Delete to remove an URL from the Web Pages field. Windows XP won't allow you to remove your home page from the list.

Highlight an URL and click Properties to display the Web Page Properties dialog box. The General tab of this dialog box contains statistics, such as the last time you visited the site and the number of visits. The Make This Page Available Offline option allows you to store the page on your hard drive rather than download a new copy every time you want to view it. The settings on the Schedule tab of the Web Page Properties dialog box determine when and how Windows XP downloads the Web page. The Download tab determines how Windows XP handles the Web page. For example, you can specify the number of link layers to download and the amount of disk space the Web page can use. This is also the tab where you enter your name and password information.

Web pages require updates from time to time if you want to keep the content fresh. Windows XP allows you to set individual pages for automatic or manual updates. Automatic updates occur on a predefined schedule. Manual updates require that you highlight the affected URL and click Synchronize.

The final option on the Web tab of the Desktop Items dialog box is Lock Desktop Items. Checking this option prevents users from moving Active Desktop content around. This feature is nice to use once you have your Active Desktop arranged and don't want to change it by accident.

Advanced Windows Explorer Usage Techniques

As mentioned in Chapter 2, Windows Explorer is the one Windows XP tool that everyone should know about. Chapter 2 presented an overview of the most important and easily used parts of Windows Explorer. The following sections show you some advanced usage methods and tell you more about Windows Explorer configuration.

Setting the Folder Options

Windows XP provides lots of flexibility in the way you present data onscreen. The default Windows Explorer configuration represents Microsoft's best guess at what you might like to see. Use the Tools | Folder Options command in Explorer to change the way you view data. You'll see a Folder Options dialog box.

The General tab of the Folder Options contains three main entries. First, you select classic Windows folders or common tasks in folders. You saw the results of using Web-enabled folders in Chapter 2. Although the additional information is nice, it reduces system performance and clutters the display. Second, you choose between opening each folder in the current window or a new window. Choosing a new window allows you to compare two folders without opening two copies of Explorer manually. On the other hand, using the current window reduces screen clutter. The final option allows you to choose between a single- and double-click to open items. The double-click is the traditional Windows method of performing this task. I find that the single-click is faster and a little less error prone for users who spend lots of time on the Internet. Longtime users tend to find the single-click method confusing because they're used to a double-click.

The View tab contains two main sections. The first section contains options for automatically setting your folders. Use Apply to All Folders if you want all folders to look like the one you just configured. Use Reset All Folders to set all of your folders to the Windows default settings. The second section contains advanced folder settings. We've already discussed some of these settings. For example, you'll clear the Use Search Companion for Searching option if you want to use the standard search dialog box. I'll tell you about more of the options as this book progresses; it's best to learn about them in the context in which they're used.

The File Types tab contains a list of all the file types on your machine. The majority of these file types are associated with one or more applications. This association allows you to open that file automatically by double-clicking on it within Explorer. We'll discuss this tab in more detail in the "Creating File Associations" section of this chapter.

Working with Offline Content

The Offline Files tab, shown in Figure 3.17, determines how Windows XP works with files you download from another location (mainly the Internet or an intranet). Offline files allow you to view remote content without having a connection to that location. Of course, the data is static, so you don't see any changes to the remote location unless you synchronize the data.

> **Note:** Windows XP might not allow you to use offline content if you have Fast User Switching enabled. To turn this feature off, open the User Accounts applet in the Control Panel. Click Change the way users log on or off. Clear the Use Fast User Switching option and then click Apply Options.

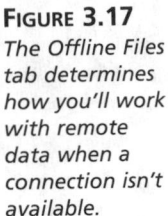

FIGURE 3.17
The Offline Files tab determines how you'll work with remote data when a connection isn't available.

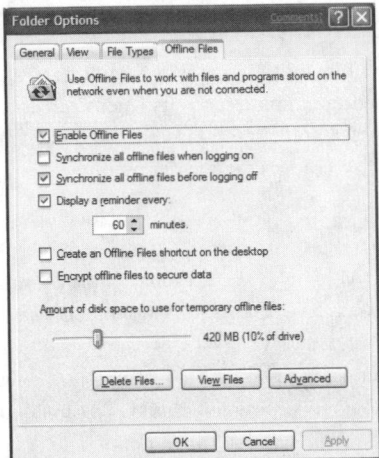

Before you can create offline files, you need to check Enable Offline Files. The next two options on the Offline Files tab determine when Windows XP synchronizes content. You'll use the Display a Reminder Every option to remind yourself when the computer goes offline so that you know when the data you're viewing is static. You can use the next option to create a shortcut to your offline files on the Desktop to allow for easier management. Because security is now such a major issue, you'll likely want to encrypt the offline files. However, encrypting the files increases the space they consume and increases the time required to open them. Finally, you can choose how much disk space to allocate to offline file use. This setting is especially important because you also need to consider Recycle Bin and swap file requirements along with all of the other data that your drive needs to store.

Click Delete Files if you want to remove offline content from the Offline Files folder. You can choose to delete just the temporary offline version of the file or both the temporary and permanent versions of the file. If you want to see what the Offline Files folder contains, click View Files. Finally, clicking Advanced displays the Offline Folders-Advanced Settings dialog box. The settings in this dialog box determine what Windows XP will do when you lose a network connection. The first option simply notifies you that the connection is lost and that you're using the offline file. The second option tells Windows XP that you want to try to reestablish a connection to the remote system continuously. You can also create exception lists that select a specific behavior for a particular system.

Using Views

Explorer supports more than one view of your data. A *view* is a method of presentation. For example, you may want to know what the content of the file looks like versus the file statistics, such as the last modification date. Graphics folders may require a thumbnail view, and the System32 folder requires a detailed view. The following list tells you about the five data views supported by Windows XP and describes how you might use them:

- *Thumbnails* This view displays the content of the individual files. This view works best in data directories where you're more concerned about finding specific content than learning file details. Many people use this view for folders containing graphics files. Note that Thumbnails view incurs a performance penalty because Explorer has to create a picture of each file's content onscreen. In addition, this view requires additional hard drive space for the thumbnail database.

- *Tiles* The default Explorer view displays a relatively large icon coupled with the filename, data type, and file size. Use this view when you need to know more than just the filename, but less than Details view provides. This is an inefficient way to view folders with large numbers of files.

- *Icons* Some people consider this the best overall view for any folder. It presents a medium-size icon and a filename. The larger icon makes it easy to determine the file type (or at least the associated application).

- *List* This view presents a list of small icons and a filename. This is the best choice when you know the name of the file you want to find and there are a large number of files to scan. Some people also consider this the least confusing Explorer display.

- *Details* This view displays a list of files using small icons. It also presents a wealth of information about each file. The default settings include the filename, size, type, and modification date. As we'll see in the "Customizing the Details View" section of this chapter, you have many other details to choose from for this view. This is the best view to use when you're concerned about the technical details of the file. Some users also consider it one of the best choices for data mining because you can learn so much about the file without opening it.

Customizing the Details View

Details View is the most comprehensive data view that Explorer provides. The data you see when using the default settings is just the tip of the data iceberg. Right-click the columns above the Details view, and you'll see a list of the most common additions for this view. Choose More from the list, and you'll see the Choose Details dialog box.

Click any entry in the columns list, and you can change its width and position within the list using Move Up or Move Down. Use Show and Hide to either add or remove the column from the list. Many column entries, such as attributes, work with any file. However, some columns won't work with some types of files. For example, the Album column won't contain any information when you work with word processing files.

Creating File Associations

Most applications you work with will add file associations to Windows XP for you. For example, when you install Microsoft Office, the installation program automatically creates an association between Word and the .DOC file type. However, in some cases, you need to work with file associations to ensure that you can access files in the way you want to access them.

You can create and edit files associations in a number of ways. The easiest way to create a file association is to double-click on a file of the correct type. Windows XP will display the Windows Cannot Open File dialog box, which gives you an option of automatically looking for an application that opens the file or selecting an application from a list of those installed on your machine. As soon as you select an application, Windows XP creates a file association for you.

A more common way to create file associations is to open the Folder Options dialog within Explorer using the Tools | Folder Options command. The File Types tab contains a list of all predefined file types for Windows XP, along with file types that applications add when you install them. Select any file extension, and you'll see information about the main application associated with that file type.

Explorer provides two methods for creating a new file association. The easy method is to click Change. Explorer will display an Open With dialog box that lists applications you can use to open the file. You can also choose to browse for an application that the Open With dialog box doesn't list.

The harder method is to click Advanced. You'll see an Edit File Type dialog box, like the one shown in Figure 3.18. At the top of this dialog box are an icon, the text description of the file type, and the Change Icon button. You can modify the text description of the file type, but normally you won't need to do so. However, you might want to change the icon associated with a file type if you change the main application used to modify it.

FIGURE 3.18
The Edit File Type dialog box contains options for changing the context menu entries for a specific file type.

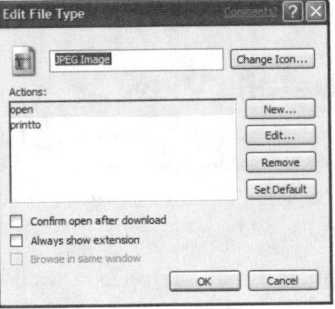

You can associate more than one action with a file. However, only one action is the default that occurs when the user double-clicks the file. Otherwise, the user right-clicks and chooses the desired action from the context menu. You set the default action by highlighting its entry and clicking Set Default. Click Remove to remove an action from the list.

Explorer allows you to add new actions to the list or edit existing actions. Clicking New or Edit displays an Action dialog box containing an Action and an "Application used to perform action" field. When adding a new action, just type the action name and the name of the action you want to use. The Browse button allows you to find an application with relative ease.

A few applications still require the use of Dynamic Data Exchange (DDE) to create a proper file association. This is an old technology left over from previous versions of Windows. If you run into an application that requires DDE, it's a good idea to use another file type as a template for creating the entries you'll need. Simply check DDE, and fill out the four new fields that show up.

> **Tip:** You can create low-level file associations as well as associations strictly for applications. One of the most useful low-level files associations I've used is to create an instant command line for Windows XP folders. Locate the Folders entry and click Advanced. Click New to create a new action. Type **Command Prompt Here** in the Action field and **cmd.exe /k "cd %1"** (include the quotes) in the Application Used to Perform Action field. Click OK twice to create the new action. Now you can create a command prompt wherever you need it by right-clicking any file folder and choosing Command Prompt Here from the context menu.

Modifying the Startup Folder

Think of the Startup folder as a means for automatically configuring your desktop. Windows looks in this file during the boot process and launches anything it finds there, including everything from starting applications to opening files and folders.

> **Peter's Principle:** Getting a Great Start in the Morning
>
> Many people are under the impression that the Startup folder is only for loading applications. Other people feel that you should place only certain classes of applications there, such as screen savers or Microsoft Office Startup. Although putting a background application in the Startup folder is a good idea, using the Startup folder for this purpose alone doesn't make full use of the resource.
>
> Placing a shortcut to the Startup folder on your desktop is a great idea because you can put things in there that you'll need the next morning. (Microsoft buried this folder so far in the directory tree that you'll quickly tire of trying to use it if you don't take this step.) For example, if I'm working on a proposal over the course of a few days, I'll stick a shortcut to the master file in Startup. That way, it will automatically open when I start my machine the next day.
>
> Adding objects to the Startup folder can really boost your productivity. Instead of spending the first 15 minutes of the morning getting set up, you can start your machine, go get a cup of coffee, and be ready to work when you return. Making Windows XP more efficient is largely up to the user now. Most of the tools are there; all you need to do is use them.

Like everything else in Windows XP, you'll find the Startup folder in Explorer. Unfortunately, Microsoft buried it deep in the directory tree. If you look in the \Documents and Settings\<User Name>\Start Menu\Programs folder, you'll see the Startup folder. A faster way to access the folder is to right-click Start and select Explore from the context menu. This starts Explorer at the Start Menu folder for your configuration.

On Your Own

Try using the Active Desktop features to enhance your productivity. For example, try placing your favorite Web page on the desktop for a week to see how this feature works. You also might want to try creating one or more toolbars to consolidate the icons that are on your desktop.

Open Explorer and check out each of the special sections discussed in this chapter. Try to identify each section and its purpose without referring back to this book. Examine some of the unique capabilities provided by your machine. For example, see if Windows XP provides special file associations you didn't know about.

Spend some time customizing your desktop for optimum efficiency. See which wall-papers or other aesthetics you can change. Try out the screen saver options.

Learn how to organize your data using a datacentric approach. Set up project folders and use them to manage the data objects required for your business. Try using different techniques to move data. Create a shortcut to the Startup folder on your Desktop so that you set up Windows to open your projects automatically.

PART II

Power Primers

4

Setup Primer

I'm often surprised at just how little emphasis some people put on the installation of their software. Many people—including me—got the idea somewhere along the way that you should be able to stick a CD-ROM in the drive, type a command (or double-click an icon), and then forget about anything other than waiting for the software to install. For the most part, software installation should work this way, but it doesn't.

Unlike early versions of Windows where you had to enter settings manually, or even Windows 95, where hardware detection was far from perfect, Windows XP is easy to install. It can detect most types of hardware automatically. In fact, this version does a better job than Windows 9x or Windows NT/2000 in detecting what settings to use. Is Windows XP perfect? No. You'll still find a few situations in which you need to give it an assist. The one caveat to remember is that Microsoft has started getting rid of installation problems by getting rid of support for old or nonstandard hardware.

> **Tip:** Windows XP does a great job when it comes to detecting your hardware. However, it's still likely that you're going to run into problems if Windows XP doesn't support your hardware and you don't have a driver disk handy at the time of installation. It always pays to check which hardware Microsoft supports for a particular version of its operating system. You can check most versions for Windows at http://www.microsoft.com/hcl/default.asp.

This chapter will help you install Windows XP with a minimum of problems. You'll check your hardware, make an installation disk, perform a preinstallation backup if necessary, and decide on which type of installation to perform. We'll also discuss some things you can do when the installation doesn't go as expected. For example, we'll discuss some ways to get around Plug and Play installation problems. You'll also learn how to modify or create your own INF (information) files. In some cases, creating a modified INF file can change a bad installation into a good one.

Installing Windows XP

You might want to spend a little time preparing for your Windows XP installation, especially if you want to maximize its capabilities or if you're planning to reverse the installation later. Of course, the first piece of preparation is to make a complete backup of each system before you start the installation. Trying to back out of a failed installation can prove to be quite a problem sometimes.

Getting all the required equipment together to perform the installation is only the first step. You need to do other things before you perform the installation. The following sections give you the inside scoop on all the preinstallation steps you should take. Then you'll see several different installation methods.

Peter's Principle: Boot Disks: The Cheap Form of Insurance

Some people consider the boot disk outdated because you can boot Windows XP from the CD-ROM for installation purposes and you can't see an NTFS formatted partition when using DOS. However, what happens if you have a problem with the machine that you can't fix by using the Windows XP boot disk or if the CD-ROM decides not to read the CD-ROM for some reason? Your installation stalls until you can fix the problem or get someone else to do it.

A boot disk is still a nice piece of insurance because it allows you to access your system when everything fails. A boot disk contains all of the DOS drivers needed to start your machine for troubleshooting purposes and allows you to create a clean environment for performing other kinds of tasks. I never start anything as involved as an operating system installation without making a boot disk first.

Just what does a boot disk contain? It must contain the operating system (normally, DOS). To format a floppy with the DOS operating system, use the FORMAT /S command.

This disk will include CONFIG.SYS and AUTOEXEC.BAT files (found in the root directory for Windows 9x systems). CONFIG.SYS contains all of the commands required to install my device drivers, along with HIGHMEM.SYS. Here's a typical CONFIG.SYS file for starting DOS with a CD-ROM driver:

```
DEVICE=C:\DOS\HIMEM.SYS /TESTMEM:OFF /VERBOSE
DOS=HIGH
FILES=30
DEVICE=TEAC_CDI.SYS /D:CD_DRIVE
```

The AUTOEXEC.BAT file should contain the commands required to start utilities and set the DOS environment variables. Here's a typical AUTOEXEC.BAT file for the same system; notice the use of MSCDEX to install support for the CD-ROM drive:

```
C:\DOS\SMARTDRV.EXE /X
PROMPT $p$g
```

```
PATH C:\DOS
SET TEMP=C:\DOS
MSCDEX /V /D:CD_DRIVE
```

A boot disk needs utility programs. I include FDISK, and FORMAT. DEBUG usually makes an appearance also. The disk has to include any files required to activate your disk compression (if the drive is compressed). A disk editor usually comes in handy, as does a small text editor. You also should include a disk-scanning program, such as CHKDSK, because a disk crash will require the services of such a diagnostic program.

Minimum Hardware Requirements

Before we go much further, you'll want to do a quick check of your hardware. Microsoft has published hardware specifications, but I don't think you'll want to use them. The problem is that the "minimum" system the specifications describe is too minimal to get any kind of performance. If you want a system that'll really work with Windows XP, use the following parameters:

- *450 MHz Pentium II/Pentium III processor or AMD equivalent* You can try to use one of the faster Pentium systems, but the performance you receive won't be all that useful, especially if you plan to make use of the new features of Windows XP. Graphics and multimedia require fast processors. Some games are CPU cycle eaters that won't be happy with anything less than the fastest processor. In fact, newer games require a 450 MHz processor as a minimum—vendors usually recommend something faster.

Tip: The Pentium IV processor might be the newest kid on the block, but tests show that it won't provide additional processing power unless the vendor specifically designs the application to use the new features that the Pentium IV provides. You may want to look at other performance enhancements, such as a faster hard drive or more memory, instead of buying a system with a Pentium IV installed.

- *256MB memory minimum* I'd really think about increasing your memory to 512MB to get the best performance, but a 256MB system will perform adequately when using Windows XP. Windows XP uses the same memory-management techniques as Windows NT and Windows 2000. No longer do you have to worry about the 512MB memory limit of Windows 9x. In addition, memory is inexpensive right now, so this is an easy purchasing decision to make.

- *5GB of free hard disk space* The Microsoft minimum just isn't realistic, unless you want to install a stripped-down version of Windows XP with no room to run any applications. In fact, given the relatively low cost of hard drives, you may want to get a hard drive in the 20GB to 80GB range.

- *High-density 3½-inch floppy drive* The need for a floppy drive is diminishing all the time. At one time, you needed a floppy drive in order to create an emergency boot disk for Windows 9x, but that's not a consideration for Windows XP. A floppy drive does come in handy for older games, file exchange, a DOS boot floppy, and other purposes, but you can theoretically get by without one in today's computing environment.

- *1024×768 or higher display adapter* You can get by using a Super Video Graphics Array (SVGA) display (800×600 resolution) with Windows XP, but that doesn't really provide enough space to get any work done. In addition, you'll find that some dialog boxes no longer fit in an 800×600 display area. You should get a high-speed adapter capable of 32-bit color display at your preferred resolution if you plan to play games or work with graphics under Windows XP. This means getting an adapter with a minimum of 64MB of Double Data Rate Synchronous Dynamic Access Memory (DDR SDRAM) for higher-end uses.

- *Mouse (pointing device)* Someone will try to tell you that you can work efficiently in Windows XP using just the keyboard. You can get around; there's no doubt about it. But a mouse makes Windows XP so much more efficient that I can't understand why anyone would want to go without one. Windows XP also works very well with the mouse wheel found on many "rodents" today.

- *CD/DVD drive* Don't slow down your system by getting a slow CD-ROM drive. I'd suggest a 40× CD-ROM drive as a minimum. In fact, if you plan to use the CD-ROM a lot, make sure that you get something a little faster, such as one of the newer 50× (or even 56× if you can afford it) drives on the market. If you're getting a new machine, check into getting a DVD drive because they can read CD-ROMs as well. Getting a DVD-RAM drives means that you'll be able to make system backups without investing in an expensive tape drive. Some of the newer CD-RW drives are also a good deal because you can use special read/write media with them (making your CD-ROM almost like a hard drive), burn new CD-ROMs, and read existing CD-ROMs, all with one drive. However, check the specifications for the CD-RW drive you get. In many cases, the extra flexibility comes at the price of reduced performance.

- *Optional devices* You also can install any number of optional peripheral devices. I strongly recommend that you install a modem as a minimum. Windows XP provides much better multimedia capabilities as well. You'll probably want to install a sound board somewhere along the way. A Zip drive (or a similar removable media device) would also be a good addition because you may want to use one for backup purposes. If you don't get a Zip drive, at least consider getting a tape drive for backup purposes.

The new installation used by Windows XP is the best I've seen, but I still experienced a few problems. For example, some hardware was detected fine during one installation, but not during another. Most notorious in this category was the inability of Windows XP to detect the hardware decoders used with DVD drives.

Some of the worst failings of one installation routine were the highlights in another. For example, during one installation I found it nearly impossible to get through the procedure and end up with a functional network card installed in my machine.

Windows XP is better than previous versions of Windows. I tested Windows XP on the same machines I used for my original Windows 2000 installation tests and found that the detection process is nearly perfect as long as Windows XP actually supports the hardware you're using. Having third-party drivers on hand does increase the probability of a successful installation, so make sure that you have drivers for any nonsupported hardware on your machine.

Check Your Hardware

Windows XP automatically detects the vast majority of hardware out there. It even includes information files that allow it to detect older hardware (the term *older* is relative in this case). However, the detection capabilities that Windows XP provides are less than perfect, so you'll want to spend a little time checking your system hardware for potential problems.

> **Note:** Microsoft cheated in some ways when it comes to hardware detection. The company made it appear that Windows XP does a better job of detecting hardware, by shortening the hardware compatibility list (HCL). Yes, Windows XP does a better job of detecting the hardware it supports, so you'll experience few problems as long as your hardware appears on the HCL. The bad news is that Windows XP supports fewer devices, making it possible that the sound board you bought two or three years ago won't appear on the HCL. You can find the HCL at http://www.microsoft.com/hcl/default.asp.

Certain types of older hardware almost guarantee problems under Windows XP. It's unlikely that you'll have any of this hardware on your machine, especially if you bought it within the past two years. If you have hardware with the following characteristics, you might want to take a second look at it before you install Windows XP. Of course, you can always try to install it, but I've run into more than my share of problems with these hardware types:

- *Machines that use a clone BIOS* Some older machines use what I call a "clone BIOS." [The Basic Input/Output System (BIOS) enables the computer to boot and performs some low-level functions.] These machines boot with some strange logo from a company you've never heard of. A machine containing a BIOS from one of the mainstream companies—such as Award, AMI, or Phoenix—is usually a better bet than a clone BIOS machine. Fortunately, the clone BIOS affects Windows XP to a much smaller degree than in Windows 9x because it doesn't rely on the BIOS once you boot the system.

- *Nonstandard peripheral devices* Standards evolve as users and companies gain knowledge about a particular area of technology. A standards organization meets after enough companies produce a product to iron out implementation details so that one version of the product works the same as every other version. Unfortunate as it might seem, some of the hardware that appeared before the standard just isn't compatible with that standard. Without a standard way to access the hardware, it's very difficult to talk to it and determine what capabilities it provides.

- *PCI devices that won't share* PCI devices are routinely called on to share resources such as IRQs. (An *IRQ* is an interrupt request and is the peripheral device's method of asking the CPU to do some work on its behalf.) However, some vendors just haven't figured this out yet, and, as a result, you'll have problems installing the hardware they provide. For example, I recently purchased a DVD decoder board for my system. Installing the board and DVD was a snap. However, on starting the system up, Windows XP thought that the DVD-ROM drive was actually a CD-ROM drive. The reason was quite simple: Windows XP didn't recognize the DVD decoder board. Imagine my amazement when the technical support person suggested that I remove all of the other PCI boards in the machine, restart the computer, and see if the board would work. The result: My DVD-ROM drive then worked as expected. To make a long troubleshooting scenario short, I ended up reserving resources for the PCI DVD decoder board to ensure that it would work in the future. (I also returned the board the next day for a full refund.) In many cases, you can get around this problem by reading reviews about the hardware you want to buy before you make the purchase.

- *Peripherals that almost emulate something else* IBM and other vendors are to blame for this problem. They started placing their company names in the BIOS of some hardware types. When someone would try to use a piece of generic software developed by those companies, the software would check the BIOS for the correct company name. Clone makers aren't stupid; they started putting the IBM (or other) company name in their BIOS chips, too. This isn't a problem as long as the device in question completely emulates the hardware it replaces. However, if the clone maker took shortcuts, Windows might think that the peripheral device includes features it doesn't include.

You can fix some marginal hardware after the initial installation is over. A sound board is one big item that falls into this category. Windows XP does a good job of detecting sound boards, considering that one sound board emulates the qualities of another. Trying to detect this hardware is a nightmare. In some cases, you'll just have to install the hardware manually later. You'll see the procedure for performing a manual installation later in this chapter.

Some hardware still uses jumpers for configuration purposes. (The manual that comes with your hardware will tell you about the jumpers and show where they're located.) The one big item that just about everyone will need to consider is the NIC (network interface card). Some NICs have one or more address settings and an IRQ setting. You need to write down the settings of any boards that use jumpers before you start your Windows XP installation. This list will come in handy later, as you try to resolve any IRQ or address conflicts that arise during installation.

> **Peter's Principle:** Replacing Old Hardware to Save Money
>
> Sometimes, you'll save money by spending a little on new hardware. Whenever you choose to keep an old piece of hardware to save money, but introduce some type of instability into your system, you're actually wasting more money than you're saving.
>
> Windows XP provides an opportunity to rid your system of all the old hardware that makes it inefficient. Not only will you get your work done faster, but you'll also get it done with fewer problems. Think about the last time you spent days trying to find a problem with your system, only to discover that it was a bad driver or some other hardware-related problem. The hardware still works, so it's very difficult to give it up. But doing so when you upgrade might mean that you spend fewer hours trying to find those mysterious problems related to the real-mode drivers that the hardware requires to work.

Getting Ready to Install

By this point in the chapter, you should have created a boot disk and inventoried your hardware. It's time to look at the setup program. You can start by using the Setup program that appears in the root directory of the Windows XP distribution disk, but this is just a front-end for the real setup programs that appear in the \I386 directory. The real setup programs are WINNT.EXE and WINNT32.EXE.

Let's look at some of the Setup command-line switches. They'll help you get around any problems you might experience while installing Windows XP. For example, you'll need to use a combination of the /s and /u switches to perform an unattended installation. The following is a complete list of these switches. The list tells you which switches to use with each setup program.

> **Note:** The following list uses some special notation. When you see something between angle brackets (< >), it means that you have to supply a value of some kind. The description will tell you what to provide. Don't type the angle brackets when you type the switch. Square brackets ([ ]) tell you that the value is optional. You don't have to use the value with the switch, but normally Setup expects to see the value.

- **/? (WINNT and WINNT32)** Use this switch to display a list of currently documented command-line switches.
- **/A (WINNT)** Use this switch to enable the accessibility options.
- **/CheckUpgradeOnly (WINNT32)** Starts the setup process and checks for upgrade compatibility only. When using the /Unattend switch, Setup stores the data from the update screen to the UPDATE.TXT file in the <System Root> folder, which is normally \WINNT.

- **/Cmd:<Command>** **(WINNT32)** Tells Setup to execute a command after Setup completes the configuration process, but before it completes. You could use this command to perform additional configuration or to check on the status of a device before completing the setup process.

- **/CmdCons (WINNT32)** Installs the Recovery Console, which is one of the items you don't normally see during a GUI setup. You can use the Recovery Console start and stop services, reformat a drive, or perform other low-level tasks.

- **/CopyDir:I386[:<Folder>] (WINNT32)** Tells Setup to install an optional folder. The folder remains in place after the installation completes.

- **/CopySource[:<Folder>] (WINNT32)** Tells Setup to install an optional folder. Setup removes the folder after the installation completes.

- **/Debug[<Level>][:<Filename>] (WINNT32)** Creates during the installation process a debug log that helps you find errors more quickly. The default debugging level is 2, and the default filename is C:\<System Root>\WINNT32.LOG. Setup supports five levels of debugging: 0 for severe errors, 1 for errors, 2 for warnings, 3 for general information, and 4 for detailed information. Each level is cumulative, so the default debugging level checks for severe errors, errors, and warnings.

- **/DUDisable (WINNT32)** Disables Dynamic Update, which prevents Setup from looking for new setup files. This switch will override any settings in your answer file during an unattended installation.

- **/DUPrepare:<Pathname> (WINNT32)** Creates a sharable directory for Dynamic Update to use in storing the files it downloads from Windows Update. You can then use the shared directory when installing other clients. This reduces setup time by reducing the time required to download files from the Internet.

- **/DUShare:<Pathname> (WINNT32)** Tells Setup to perform Dynamic Update using a shared directory rather than download files from Windows Update. You must prepare the directory in advance using /DUPrepare.

- **/E (WINNT)** Tells Setup to execute a command at the end of the GUI portion of the setup process.

- **/M:<Folder> (WINNT32)** Tells Setup to copy replacement files from an alternative directory. Any time Setup needs a file, it will look in the alternative directory first and then in the normal directory.

- **/MakeLocalSource (WINNT32)** Tells Setup to copy all installation files to the local hard drive. This allows an installation to continue even if the normal file source becomes unavailable.

- **/NoReboot (WINNT32)** Tells Setup to stop after it finishes copying the files to the hard drive during the installation process. This allows you to execute a command after the file copy process is complete.

- **/R[:<Folder>] (WINNT)** Tells Setup to install an optional folder. The folder remains in place after the installation completes.

- **/RX[:<Folder>] (WINNT)** Tells Setup to install an optional folder. Setup removes the folder after the installation completes.

- **/S[:<Source Path>] (WINNT and WINNT32)** You can include between one and eight source paths. Each source path requires a separate switch. The source path tells Setup where to look for files. For example, you might include a source path for an answer file when performing an unattended installation.

- **/SysPart:<Drive Letter> (WINNT32)** Allows you to perform the system setup part of the installation and then move the drive to another machine. The second phase of Setup will continue on the second machine. You must use the /TempDrive switch with this switch.

- **/T[:<Temporary Drive>] (WINNT)** This switch enables you to tell Setup which drive to use as a temporary directory. It normally tries to use the drive you're using for installation. If that drive is short on space, however, you can use this switch to redirect installation-specific items to another drive.

- **/TempDrive[:<Temporary Drive>] (WINNT32)** Same as the /T switch.

- **/U[:<Answer File>] (WINNT)** You need to provide an answer file when performing an unattended install. This switch tells Setup which file to use. If the file doesn't appear within the current directory, you must use the /S switch to tell Setup where to locate the file. Microsoft supplies a sample unattended installation file (UNATTEND.TXT) in the \I386 directory of the distribution disk.

- **/UDF:<Identifier>[:<Uniqueness Database File>] (WINNT and WINNT32)** A UDF file contains answers to setup questions that override the contents of the answer file you supply. For example, the user name and computer name will be different for every installation. You'd supply an answer file that contains all of the standard answers and then provide a UDF that contains the unique answers. Setup merges the content of the UDF file with the answer file to provide the final answer file. This is the file that Setup uses to answer all of the questions during an unattended installation. The Identifier entry on the command line tells which Identifier to use within the UDF file for special answers.

- **/Unattend[:<Answer File>] (WINNT32)** Same as the /U switch.

You're finally ready to install Windows XP. The following section, "Installing Windows XP from a CD-ROM," tells you how to complete the installation process.

Installing Windows XP from a CD-ROM

Microsoft provides several ways to install Windows XP directly from the CD-ROM. The two major methods are the graphical user interface (GUI) and the character mode installation. In most cases, you'll use the GUI method when updating a system that already has Windows on it. Use the character mode installation when working with a new system or one that won't work with the GUI installation. The following steps tell you how to perform a GUI installation:

1. Click Install Windows XP. Windows XP will ask what type of installation you'd like to perform.

> **Tip:** If you want the quickest possible installation, choose the Upgrade option. Choosing the New Installation option will remove all your old settings and optionally reformat your drive, which means installing and configuring all of your applications. However, this method also presents the fewest compatibility problems when you complete the installation.

2. Choose Upgrade (Recommended) and then click Next. You'll see a License Agreement dialog box.

3. Read the agreement, choose I Accept this Agreement, and then click Next. You'll see a Your Product Key dialog box.

4. Type the product key that appears on your CD-ROM sleeve and then click Next. Setup will ask if you want to perform an upgrade check of your system.

5. Check for system updates (precisely what this entails depends on your system configuration). After Windows XP checks for problems with your system, it will display a Report System Compatibility dialog box. If you perform the compatibility precheck, this dialog box should be blank.

6. Click Next. Windows XP will copy some files to your hard drive. Setup will reboot Windows XP several times as it examines the system, copies files, and performs configuration tasks. Eventually, you'll see the product activation screen.

7. Activate Windows, if desired. If you don't activate Windows XP now, it will remind you to activate the product every few days. You have a limited time to activate your product before it stops functioning.

8. Click Next. Windows XP will ask if you want to register your product. You can skip this step and perform it later, just like with product activation.

9. Register Windows, if desired. Click Next. You'll see a success screen.

10. Click Finish to the complete the process.

There are also two types of character mode installation. Most modern computers will automatically detect the Windows XP operating system on the CD-ROM and give you the opportunity to boot from it. If your system is one of the few that won't boot from the CD-ROM, you'll need to boot a simple operating system, such as DOS, to begin the process. Make sure that you have a device driver for the CD-ROM and a copy of MSCDEX on the boot floppy when working with DOS. (Microsoft provides MSCDEX with both DOS and Windows.) The following steps take you through a typical character mode installation.

Note: After you start Setup, you'll see prompts that allow you to install small computer systems interface (SCSI) support and automated system repair. If you have a system with a special SCSI driver, select the driver installation when prompted by pressing F6. However, most SCSI systems for workstations don't require a special driver. Windows XP will continue to load all of its support files during this time, so don't worry when it doesn't stop immediately after you press F6. Follow the prompts to install SCSI support, if necessary, and allow Windows XP to continue to load.

1. Execute WINNT in the \I386 directory of the distribution disk. Eventually, you'll see a Welcome to Setup window. This window has three options. Press F3 if you want to exit Setup (you'll see a restart window that automatically restarts your system). Press R if you want to repair your system.

2. Press Enter to continue the installation. Setup will display a licensing screen.

3. Click F8 if you agree with the terms. Setup will search your system for drives that can hold the new operating system. Once it searches all the drives, you'll see a list of them, along with the partitions on each drive.

4. Select a partition or unpartitioned space to install Windows XP and click Enter. If you select unpartitioned space, Setup will ask how you want the partition formatted. Using the File Allocation Table (FAT) format will provide better compatibility with existing operating systems. Using the NT File System (NTFS) format will provide you with better security, data compression, and data access. Use the quick formatting method only if you're certain about the quality of the hard drive.

Note: Be careful about selecting a partition. Setup will erase anything in a partition as part of the installation process if the content of the partition isn't compatible with Windows XP.

5. Select a formatting technique and press Enter. After Setup finishes formatting the drive, it will reboot the system. You'll see the first screen of the GUI setup. Click Customize if you want to change the language used as a basis for regional settings within Windows. Click Details to change the keyboard settings for Windows.

6. Perform any required regional and language setup tasks and then click Next. Windows will ask you to enter your name and company name.

7. Type your name and company name; then click Next. Windows will ask you to enter your product key. This key appears on the back of the CD cover. It pays to make a copy of this cover and place it in a safe location in case the original gets lost.

8. Type the key code and then click Next. Windows will ask you to enter a computer name and an administrator password.

Tip: Give your computer a friendly yet descriptive name, especially when working on a network. The default name provided by Setup is usually hard to remember. Also, be careful about the comment you provide for the machine. Windows XP displays the comment first and the machine name second within Windows Explorer. Therefore, if you create a long and nondescriptive comment, the machine name is still obscured and difficult to see. Don't leave the administrator password blank. Otherwise, your system will be easy to attack. Using a complex password is your best defense again crackers.

9. Type a computer name and administrator password. Click Next. Setup will ask for modem and telephone information.

10. Type any information required in order to use the modem and telephone. Make sure that you include any information required to dial out in addition to the area code for your location. Click Next. Windows will ask about the date and time.

11. Enter the date and time; then click Next. Setup will begin installing network components. You'll see a Network Settings window. Use the Typical settings if you have a pure Microsoft network. Select Custom to install NetWare or third-party components.

12. Choose the Typical or Custom network installation and then click Next. If you choose a custom network installation, add and remove any required components. Setup will ask if you want to make this computer part of a workgroup or a domain.

13. Choose between a workgroup and domain connection. Type a name for the connection (use the same name as every other computer on the network). Click Next. After copying some files and performing configuration, Windows will reboot. You'll see a Welcome to Windows screen.

14. Click Next. Windows XP will check your Internet connectivity. You can choose to configure the Internet now or skip it and configure it later using the Internet Connection Wizard.

15. Set up your Internet Connection, if desired. Click Next. Windows XP will ask if you want to activate Windows now or wait until later.

16. Activate Windows, if desired. Click Next. Windows XP will ask if you want to register your product.

17. Register Windows, if desired. Click Next. Windows XP will ask if you want to set up some user accounts. A default account with your name will appear, but you can add other users to the list.

18. Add users, if desired. Click Next. You'll see a success screen.

19. Click Finish to the complete the process.

Tip: It's best to create user accounts after installation because Windows won't assign security or make other changes if you add users at this screen.

Plug and Play Installation Tips

I'm a great fan of automation that works. In my book, anything that makes my job easier or faster is a good idea. Using Plug and Play to install any hardware it recognizes automatically is that kind of automation. It makes sense that a computer can figure out port and interrupt settings faster and with greater accuracy than the average human. One reason that this level of automation is possible in Windows XP is that the computer has all the statistics it needs to do the job.

Windows XP does a good job of detecting non–Plug and Play hardware, even when mixed with Plug and Play–compatible hardware. All the configuration information for the hardware that Windows XP supports is stored on the hard disk. If you look in the \WINDOWS\INF directory, you'll see some of these files. (They all have an .INF extension.) Besides storing the required configuration information on disk, Windows XP gives older hardware its first choice of ports and interrupts. This enables older hardware to work most of the time (at least when Windows XP provides the required support).

Windows XP support isn't perfect. Some hardware can look like other pieces of hardware, so Windows XP installs the wrong driver. If two pieces of hardware need the same ports and interrupts and won't use anything else, Windows XP often enables one and fails to recognize the other. Windows XP won't recognize hardware that doesn't appear on the HCL. In short, although you'll experience far fewer problems with Windows XP Plug and Play support than with past versions of Windows, the support is far from perfect.

Quick Fixes

So, now that you have some idea of what the problem is, let's take a quick look at ways you can fix it. This list isn't exhaustive, but it'll help you with the majority of the problems you're likely to run into:

- Ensure that all boards in your system are on the Windows XP HCL or that you can obtain bona fide Windows XP drivers from the vendor. A lack of drivers and INF file support will always cause problems.

- Avoid interrupt and port address conflicts whenever possible. This is probably the number-one reason that Windows XP fails to recognize the board. If two devices use the same address, there's no way that Windows XP can test for the presence of the second board.

- Whenever possible, plug your older boards into the slots next to the power supply. Windows XP checks the slots in order during startup. Placing older, less flexible boards first ensures that Windows XP will allocate resources for them first. This, in turn, improves the probability that all boards work as anticipated.

- Try different board configurations to see whether Windows XP recognizes one of them. In some situations, the INF files used by Windows XP to check for the older boards contain only the default board settings. A good rule of thumb is to try the best setting first and then the default setting if that doesn't work.

- Check the INF files to see whether they contain all the settings for your boards. There's an INF directory directly below the main Windows XP directory. It contains ASCII text files used by Windows XP to search for these older boards. Modifying these files is a tricky proposition, but it could help Windows XP find the peripherals on your machine.

Manual Installation

It always seems to come down to the same old procedure. You finally get everything working using the automated procedures—except for that old CD-ROM drive or an especially difficult sound card. There are a few situations in which you'll have to help Windows XP install an older device in your machine. Usually, a new device uses a resource that the older device needs. The following example shows how to complete a manual installation. Let me warn you ahead of time that installing the device might not make it work. You might have to perform some troubleshooting to get this older device to work (see Chapter 25).

1. Use the Start | Settings | Control Panel command to open the Control Panel. Double-click the Add Hardware icon. You should see the Add Hardware Wizard.

2. Click Next. You'll see a dialog box saying that Windows is checking your system. Don't worry if the screen goes blank during this process—Windows also checks for display adapters (the reason for the blank screen).

3. Wait until Windows completes the detection process. The wizard will ask if you connected the hardware to your system. Generally, you must connect the hardware before Windows XP will detect it. A very few pieces of hardware insist that you install the drivers first and then add the hardware, but that won't be the situation in this case.

4. Select Yes, I Have Already Connected the Hardware, and then click Next. You'll see a list of hardware that Windows XP detected. Sometimes the hardware is marked as non-operational, using a yellow exclamation mark, as shown in Figure 4.1. You'll learn how to resolve this situation in the "Installing and Deleting Devices" section of Chapter 9. You can also add hardware that doesn't appear in the list by using the Add New Hardware Device option at the end of the list. This example assumes that Windows didn't detect the device, so we'll use the Add a New Hardware Device option.

5. Select the Add a New Hardware Device option and click Next. The Add Hardware Wizard will ask if you want Windows XP to search for the hardware automatically or choose the hardware from a list manually. The detection software performs a check of your hardware using the INF files I talked about previously. At this point, I'm assuming that you tried the automatic installation procedure and it didn't work.

FIGURE 4.1

Look for marked entries in the list first and then use the Add a New Hardware Device option if necessary.

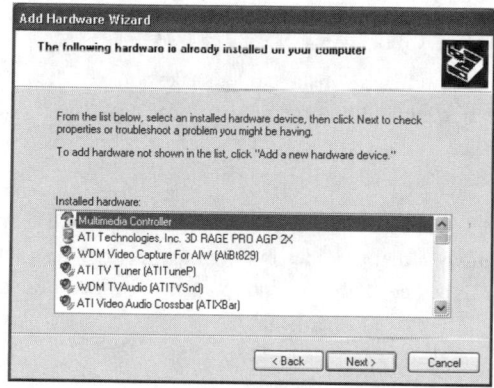

6. Select Install the Hardware That I Manually Select from the list (Advanced) and then click Next. Highlight one of the entries in the Common Hardware Types field and then click Next. You'll see an alphabetical list of vendors, as shown in Figure 4.2. In this case, I selected the Show All Devices option, so your list will be shorter. The Manufacturers and Models lists in this dialog box allow you to scroll with ease through the list of devices supported by Windows XP. If the device installed on the current machine doesn't appear in the list, the dialog box also affords the opportunity to use a third-party disk. This dialog box appears every time you select a device from the previous dialog box. The Manufacturers list changes to match the selected device type.

FIGURE 4.2

Select a vendor and then a device that Windows XP supports from that vendor.

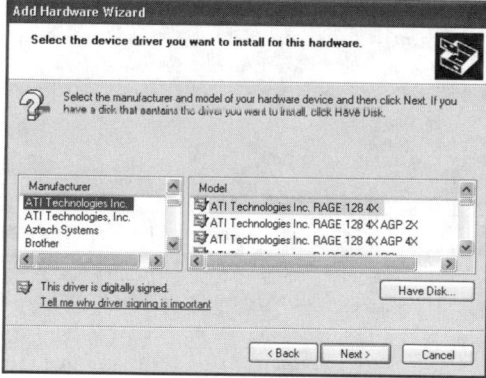

7. Select the device connected to your machine and then click Next. Clicking the Next button again installs the device drivers required for this device. Windows XP might prompt you for a disk if the driver doesn't appear on the hard drive and the appropriate disk doesn't appear in the CD-ROM drive. It displays a dialog box showing the file copy progress.

Creating Your Own INF Files

Now that you have Windows XP installed, let's take some of the magic out of the new Windows XP detection capability. Look in the \WINDOWS\INF directory, and you'll see a set of INF files. The INF file is part of the database of information that Windows XP uses to recognize hardware. These files contain a description of the hardware.

As good as these INF files are, you might want to modify them. For example, you might have a piece of hardware that provides interrupt and port address settings in addition to those found in the INF file. Modifying the INF file to reflect these additional capabilities could help you install a piece of hardware in some cases. The following sections describe the INF file format and show how to create your own INF files.

Understanding INF Files

Let's look at some of the general characteristics shared by INF files. You might find all or only some of these sections in a given file; it depends on what kind of hardware the INF file is trying to define. An INF file contains only the information required to define the characteristics of the hardware fully. A display adapter, for example, needs to define the resolutions it supports. A multiscanning monitor, such as the NEC MultiSync series, needs to define the precise frequency ranges it supports. Table 4.1 lists the generic sections and tells you what they mean. You might want to open an INF file to see whether you can identify each section.

> **Warning:** Don't save the INF file or change its contents in any way. Any change you make could result in unpredictable Windows behavior. Windows XP relies on the INF files for hardware identification and if you change the file Windows XP might misidentify the hardware on your system.

Table 4.1 INF File Generic Sections

Heading	Description
Version	Provides version-specific information, such as the operating system, vendor name, and device class supported by the INF file. It also provides the name of the general setup file. The *general setup file* contains the definitions common to all devices of that type. You might see some additional entries in this section. One special entry enables the vendor to link a new INF file to the list of files for a specific device type. Never change the contents of this section.

Heading	Description
Manufacturer	Contains a list of all the manufacturers for devices of this class. Not every INF file contains this section. The only time you need to change this section is when you want to add a new vendor. The list might seem incomplete if more than one INF file is required in order to describe a specific class of device. There are several monitor files; each one contains only the vendors that appear in that particular file. You need to check all the INF files for a particular device class before you resort to adding a new vendor. Make sure that you add the new vendor in alphabetical order in the correct INF file. A subsection after this one provides specifics about each device the vendor supports. If the vendor already appears in the Manufacturer list, adding a new device consists of adding an entry in the subsection, in the Install section, and in the Strings section.
Install	Describes the hardware characteristics and the device drivers necessary to activate the hardware. It also contains macro commands that install support in the Registry. Follow the example of other entries in this section when adding a new device. When modifying an existing entry, change only physical characteristics, such as the port address and interrupt.
Miscellaneous Control	Describes how a device works with the Windows XP interface. If you see this section, you need to use other entries as an example for creating your own entries. Most INF files don't contain this section.
Strings	Contains descriptive strings that tell the user about the hardware. This section contains user-friendly strings. It identifies the device in human-readable form.

Modifying an INF File

I was looking through my list of available displays the other day and noticed that one of my displays—a Samsung CQ-4551 monitor—wasn't supported. It's easy to add support for this new device to the Monitor7.INF file, so I made a copy and placed it in a backup folder right below the .INF folder. That way, I wouldn't erase the original file by accident. We can go through this exercise together to make the process for adding a new device a little clearer. Before we begin, though, I'll outline a few guidelines I used during the modification process.

Warning: Always modify a copy of an INF file after making a backup. Place the original in a backup directory, using a different extension. Your modified version of the original file must appear in the INF directory for Windows XP to recognize it. Keeping a copy of the original version in a temporary directory enables you to restore the file later.

- Always print a copy of the original INF file. You then can scan through the listing quickly as you make a new entry. Some entries depend on the contents of other entries in the file. A mistyped or misinterpreted entry makes the INF file useless.

- Use the other entries in the file as a guideline for new entries. Windows XP performs a strict interpretation of the contents of the INF file. Adding "enhancements" to what seems like an inadequate entry might make the INF file unusable.

- Follow punctuation marks, spelling, and capitalization carefully when making a new entry. Windows XP is extremely sensitive when it comes to how you format entries in an INF file.

- Never change the Version section of the file.

- Make your entries to an existing file. That way, you can be sure that your entries look like the other entries in the file.

Let's go through the procedure for modifying an INF file. You can use the same set of steps to modify any of the files in the INF folder. The only thing that changes from file to file is the precise format of the entries and the sections the file supports.

Note: This procedure should work with any version of Windows. However, I used Windows XP when writing the procedure. The filename will differ from the one I listed in the procedure. You can use the Search utility provided with Explorer to locate the exact MONITORxx.INF file for your machine.

1. Use Notepad to open MONITOR7.INF. There are four sections in the .INF file that you need to change (refer to Table 4.1). The first section we'll modify contains the manufacturer information. Because I wanted to add an entry for a Samsung monitor, I used Notepad's Edit | Find command to see whether I could find the vendor name. Samsung is already in the vendor list, so I didn't need to add it.

2. After I found the vendor name entry, I searched for the device subsection containing the list of devices from the vendor that Windows XP supports. I added the following text (shown in bold) to this section so that Windows XP would know to add a new device:

```
 [Samsung]
%CQ-4551%=CQ-4551, Monitor\CQ-4551
%SAM-3Ne%=SAM-3Ne, Monitor\SAM0000
```

As you can see, I formatted my entry to look exactly like the existing entry. This is a very important part of the process for adding an unsupported device to Windows XP. This entry tells Windows XP that Samsung produces a model CQ-4551 monitor and that it can find further details about that monitor in the CQ-4551 section of the .INF file.

3. Now use the Find command to locate the SAM-3Ne entry. This entry appears in the Install section of the .INF file. I added the following bold text to tell Windows XP how to install this new monitor. Notice that these instructions look much like the macros you might have created with applications in the past—which they should because that's exactly what this section contains:

```
; ------------- Samsung
[CQ-4551]
DelReg=DCR
AddReg=CQ-4551.AddReg, 640

[SAM-3Ne]
DelReg=DCR
AddReg=SAM-3Ne.AddReg, 1024, DPMS
```

I added a heading that identifies the macro code that follows as the Samsung model CQ-4551 installation procedure. An .INF file always encloses its headings between left and right brackets. I also added two macro entries to the section. The first one tells Windows XP to delete the current Registry entry. You need to delete the old entry to avoid confusion when Windows XP tries to configure the display adapter to match the monitor. The second entry tells Windows XP to add a new Registry entry following the instructions located in the CQ-4551.AddReg section of the .INF file. The 640 after the AddReg tells Windows XP to use the 640 display mode as the default.

4. Use the Find command to find the SAM-3Ne entry in the next section of the file. I added the following bold text to tell Windows XP how to modify the Registry to support this new monitor. We're still in the Install section of the file:

```
; ------------- Samsung
[CQ-4551.AddReg]
HKR,"MODES\640,480",Mode1,,"31.5,60.0-70.0,-,-"

[SAM-3Ne.AddReg]
HKR,"MODES\1024,768",Mode1,,"31.5-48.0,43.5-75.0,+,+"
```

The Registry entry section of any .INF file requires some detective work on your part. Knowing how the existing device modified the Registry can help you to determine how to add support for a new device. (See Chapter 12 for a complete description of the Registry.) Check the device specification sheet for "common" characteristics. Any change you make to an .INF file will ultimately require this type of detective work. In this case, the first important component is "MODES\640,480". This describes the operational resolution for that monitor mode. The second component, Mode1, tells Windows XP that this is the first mode supported by the monitor.

Looking at other entries in this .INF file shows that some monitors support multiple modes. The final component, "31.5,60.0–70.0,–,–", looks a bit mysterious until you check a monitor manual. The first number, 31.5, is the horizontal scanning frequency. You could supply a numeric range here as well. The second numeric range, 60.0–70.0, is the vertical scanning frequency. The two minus signs tell you that this isn't a multiscanning monitor.

5. Let's get to the final section of the .INF file—the Strings section. You'll describe the monitor in terms the user can understand. To do this, use the Find command to search for the last occurrence of the SAM-3Ne string. When I found this entry, I added this bold text:

```
CQ-4551 ="Samsung CQ-4551"
SAM-3Ne="Samsung SyncMaster 3Ne"
```

Well, that's all there is to it. When you get the hang of it, you can add support to Windows XP for just about any unsupported device. Of course, that won't solve some problems, such as the lack of protected-mode drivers and some of the incompatibilities you'll experience. If you want to see how the new entry looks, save the MONITOR7.INF file. You can use this quick procedure to display the monitor entries:

1. Right-click My Computer, choose Properties, and then select the Hardware tab.

2. Click Device Manager to display the Device Manager dialog box.

3. Open the Monitors folder, right-click your current monitor, and then choose Properties to display the Monitor Properties dialog box.

4. Select the Driver tab and click Update Driver. You'll see the Hardware Update Wizard dialog box.

5. Choose Install from a list or specific location (Advanced) and then click Next. Select Don't Search, I Will Choose the Driver to Install; then click Next. You'll see a list of monitor models that are compatible with your current selection.

6. Clear Show Compatible Hardware to display a list of all of the monitors that Windows XP supports. This is a two-pane list that has the vendor name on the left side and the models the vendor supports on the right side.

7. Scroll through the list of vendors until you find Samsung. You should see the new monitor selection, as shown in Figure 4.3.

8. Click Cancel three times to exit the Display Settings dialog box without changing the monitor type.

Adding a new device to an .INF file can prove time-consuming and even frustrating at times. However, the benefits in reduced maintenance time are well worth the effort.

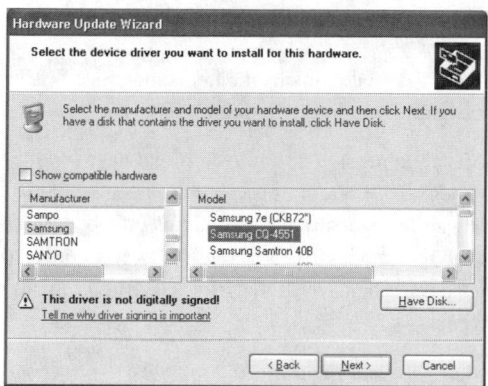

Figure 4.3
Modifications to the MONITOR7.INF file appear in the Hardware Update Wizard dialog box.

Using Windows Update

Windows Update allows you to check the status of updates and patches for your system. The shortcut appears at the top of the Start Menu. When you start Windows Update, a copy of Internet Explorer opens and goes to the Windows Update site.

Windows Update will begin by checking the Windows Update control on your system. If your copy of the control is outdated, Windows Update will ask to download a new copy. Click Scan for Updates to begin the scanning process. Windows Update will begin the process of comparing your system state to the update list online.

Eventually, Windows XP will show you a list of updates for your system. Microsoft groups these updates by criticality. To install an update, select it from the list. Microsoft offers you the chance to obtain detailed information about the update, and you'll want to read that information before you make a commitment.

After you create an update list, click Install and follow the directions. The update process does vary from update to update; but normally you'll download the update, watch Windows install it automatically, and then reboot your machine if needed. A few updates may require manual installation or configuration.

> **Tip:** Maintain a directory containing uninstall instructions for all updates to ensure that you can remove them later. The uninstall instructions appear with the detailed information you should read about the update. You never know when Microsoft will remove an update from the list.

On Your Own

Create your own boot disk that contains the items mentioned earlier in this chapter. Be sure to test the disk before you install Windows XP.

Make a list of all the equipment you think you might have problems with. Include all the items for which Windows XP doesn't provide entries in the existing INF files. Do you see any entries you can fix by using the procedures provided in this chapter? Are there ways to eliminate the real-mode drivers you might need in order to keep older equipment running? Develop a comprehensive strategy for handling problem areas before you begin the installation process.

Use Windows Update to check the status of your system after you install Windows XP. Make sure that you apply any required updates before you install any applications. Creating a stable Windows XP platform ensures that you'll have a trouble free environment in which to work.

Windows Performance Primer

Once they install a new operating system, the first thing that many people think about is tuning it for optimum performance. After users install applications, they want to see how fast they can make their new toy work. Performance is everything for many people, and vendors know that. Just look at the ads for computers—they all tell you how fast the computer will run.

However, there are different types of tuning. Tuning could mean getting every ounce of power out of a system to perform one specific task. It also could mean enabling a system to perform a variety of tasks simultaneously. In fact, tuning could involve making the system easier to use, making the human using it more efficient in the process. General tuning could be used to provide the best performance in a variety of situations. In fact, tuning doesn't have to involve high speed at all. It might simply mean configuring all your applications to work with older hardware that's well past its prime.

This chapter doesn't tell you how to tune your specific machine. It's impossible to provide step-by-step tuning instructions without knowing individual situations. This chapter provides guidelines and tips you can use to create your own solution.

You'll find a wealth of tips in this chapter, but you probably won't find everything you need the first time. It takes time and patience to tune a system for optimum performance. For example, mechanics tune a racecar to fit its particular "personality." The mechanic and the driver work together to discover the best configuration for that particular car. The mechanic also tunes the car to fit an individual track and even the current weather conditions. Actually, tuning the car is the easy part of the process. Planning how to tune it requires more effort.

You don't need to worry about the weather when tuning your system, but many other principles do apply. Planning how to tune your system is always a good idea. Just like any other endeavor, tuning your system requires that you create a few goals and consider a few potholes. Your machine contains hardware from a variety of sources. It probably contains a combination of components unique to your company. You need to consider how that hardware will react. Your applications are unique. Even if your job isn't unique, your way of doing that job probably is. A system perfectly tuned for the way I work probably won't do much for you.

After you finish your hardware configuration, consider your software configuration. Windows XP does a much better job of managing resources than previous versions of Windows, but it's not perfect. Microsoft makes assumptions about a generic system that may not fit your specific system. For example, you may find that you want to give higher priority to background tasks to ensure that your spreadsheet applications run quickly. Tuning the swap file is also a concern. Windows 9x users will have to learn about the Windows NT/2000/XP way of handling large amounts of memory.

By now, you should see where all this preliminary checking is headed. A mechanic would never tune a car before checking it over. Likewise, you should never tune your system before you know what type of system you have and learn how to use it. It's not enough to say that you have 128MB of RAM installed. The way you use that RAM determines whether it's sufficient. A 5GB hard drive might sound impressive—unless you're trying to create multimedia presentations with it. Then it sounds like a rather paltry amount. (I've seen some multimedia systems that start out with 40GB of storage and read about those that work up into the terabyte (TB) range.)

Getting the Best Performance from Low-End Systems

Tuning is a matter of knowing what your system can do, what you need it to do, and what conditions the system experience. Low-end systems can perform many tasks just as well as the high-performance monster machine on your neighbor's desk. It's all a matter of tuning.

Keeping your personal needs in mind, consider the following components before you start tuning your machine. Sometimes a simple upgrade is all you need to get a large boost in performance. These items all affect the performance of your system in a big way. You can often upgrade a system to gain the extra performance benefits that these components provide at a fraction of the cost of a new system:

- *Memory* The amount of real memory your system contains is a big factor in how well Windows XP operates. You shouldn't start to tune until you have a minimum of 128MB of real RAM (although with the low cost of memory today, I strongly recommend getting 256MB). You should tailor this number to meet the demands of the applications you plan to run. For example, a spreadsheet requires lots of memory, and a database needs even more. A word processor, however, is relatively light when it comes to memory consumption. The number of applications you plan to run simultaneously also affects the point at which you start to tune your system. My system has 512MB of RAM because I often run a word processor, a spreadsheet, and a communications program simultaneously. Virtual memory helps cover the difference between real memory and what you need, but you can't count on it to assume the full burden.

- *Hard disk size* Windows XP runs best when you give it a large swap area to work with. You need space for the application itself and for data files. One factor many people underestimate is the size of their data files. Recently, I translated a small Word for Windows file from 1.0 format to 2000. The 2000 version consumed almost twice as much space, although the amount of data hadn't changed one iota. The Word 2000 format provides many features that 1.0 doesn't. The extra space used by Word 2000 provides added functionality—an important tradeoff to consider. When figuring how much hard disk space I need, I add up the space required for installed configurations of my applications and then triple it. This is a very coarse calculation, but it works for me.

- *Hard disk speed* Older operating systems are much less disk intensive than Windows XP is. Not only do you have the swap file that Windows XP creates, but applications also make greater use of the hard drive today for temporary storage. To see what I mean, open just about any application and check for the number of TMP files on your drive. What you see will surprise you. This additional disk access means one thing: You need a fast drive to make Windows XP run quickly. Professionals measure drive access speed in several ways. First, you need to have a drive with high rotational speed. Good drives provide 7,200 revolutions per minute (RPM) or higher. However, many drives have perfectly acceptable rotational speeds in the 5,000 RPM to 5,500 RPM range. Second, you need to consider the access time in milliseconds (ms); 11 ms is average, and 8 ms is good. Third, you want to consider the data-transfer speed. This figure varies by drive type, but you should look for the highest transfer speed you can.

- *DVD-ROM/CD-ROM drive speed* Many of you will install a program to the hard drive and expect that everything the program needs will get copied there. The truth is sometimes different, especially when it comes to game and graphics programs. There are many games today that store both sound and graphics files on the CD-ROM drive only. In some cases, programs that allow you to create graphics output will store files on the CD-ROM as well. This means that the speed of your CD-ROM or DVD-ROM drive directly affects the performance of the application. You'll want to get a CD-ROM or DVD-ROM drive that supports a minimum of 40× speed to get the most out of today's applications. In fact, get a 56× drive, if at all possible because game vendors are constantly pushing the hardware envelope in an attempt to stick just one more feature in a game.

- *Processor speed* Processor speed affects the way your computer runs. After you meet the basic storage requirements, no other factor so greatly affects your system. Therein lies the rub. Many people opt for a high-speed processor and then choke it with limited memory and hard drive space. Remember, the processor makes an impact on system throughput only after you meet the basic storage requirements. A thrashing hard drive can eat up every ounce of extra speed you might add to a system.

- *Motherboard features* The size of the motherboard's static random access memory (SRAM) cache might seem a bit on the technical side, but this feature isn't just for technicians. An optimized system starts with an optimized motherboard. Get a motherboard that offers plenty of room to grow and the capability to tune. Make sure that you have plenty of room for memory expansion and that the processor has the full amount of cache (private local memory) available. Swapping a motherboard could also provide you with enhanced BIOS functionality, larger memory capacity, and updated peripheral support such as faster hard drive bus speeds.

- *Peripheral devices* Input/Output (I/O) has always been a bottleneck in PCs. The number-one device you can change to optimize Windows is the graphics adapter. Faster is always better in this area. Windows is a graphical user interface (GUI); it consumes huge amounts of time drawing the images on the display. A display adapter that uses processor cycles efficiently (or even unloads some processing tasks) can greatly affect the perceived speed of your system. The less time Windows spends drawing icons and other graphics, the more time it'll have to service your application.

Note: Many motherboards come with the I/O devices you need built in. For example, at one time you needed to buy a separate disk controller, but now you'll find this item on the motherboard in many cases. Likewise, many motherboards include a built-in network interface card (NIC). When you do need to buy any of these add-ons, get the highest speed you can afford. I/O performance bottlenecks only get worse as processing speed increases.

- *Bus speed* You might not think about the little connectors you stick cards into, but your system does. The system bus has been a source of major concern for many years, and I don't see this situation changing any time soon. Make sure that you get the fastest possible bus for your machine. In addition, a wider bus is better because it moves more bits at once.

Tuning Windows As a Whole

Let's face it, Windows XP consumes more resources than any previous version of Windows. It seems every new release of Windows raises the hardware requirement bar a little higher than the one before. In this case, the cost is significant because Microsoft has stuffed so many new features into Windows XP, such as instant messaging. Needless to say, many of you will want to tune Windows just so that you can get rid of the extras and use your current machine a little longer.

This section of the chapter divides performance between those tips you can use with any version of Windows and those you can use with Windows XP alone. The following section, "General Tuning Tips for Windows," contains tips that will work with everything from Windows 9x to Windows NT/2000. The section "Windows XP–Specific Tuning

Tips," later in this chapter, contains tips that will definitely work with Windows XP. You may find that a few of the tips also work with Windows NT and a few more with Windows 2000, but I tested them only with Windows XP.

General Tuning Tips for Windows

When you're trying to improve performance, I recommend that you first try a few general tuning methods. Although anyone can use these methods, they always involve some level of compromise that you might not be willing to make. The following list shows my quick fixes to memory problems:

- *Wallpaper* Did you know that it costs memory and processing time to keep wallpaper on your system? If you have a memory-constrained system and can do without some bells and whistles, here's one item to get rid of.

- *Colors* The number of colors in your display directly affects the amount of memory it uses and the processing power required to move bits around. The 16-bit color display mode uses roughly half the memory of a 32-bit color display. In addition, it can have a noticeable effect on processing speed. You probably won't notice much of a difference in appearance if the programs on your machine are mainly word processors and spreadsheets. In fact, you may not even notice a difference for other purposes, such as light graphics editing.

- *Screen resolution* The resolution at which you set your display affects processing speed and, to a much smaller degree, memory. The problem with changing your display resolution isn't hard to figure out. Although you can get by with fewer colors, using fewer pixels is a different matter. Changing the screen resolution should be a final effort to get that last bit of needed performance. You have to consider application requirements before taking this step to tune Windows. Microsoft assumes that most users have a 1024×768 display as a minimum. Their use of large dialog boxes within Windows XP demonstrates this fact. If you use a smaller 800×600 display resolution, you may find that some dialog boxes won't fit completely (they do fit enough to make changes) and some applications will provide marginal performance.

- *Doodads* Many utility programs fit into the "doodad" category. For example, some people also keep a small game program running (such as Solitaire). Other people constantly fiddle with appointment schedulers, instant messaging, and other tool-type applications that do serve a purpose, but not at the time they're using them. These small applications might serve a purpose, but you don't need to keep them active all the time. If you insist on playing a game—keep it open when you play it, and then close it before you get back to work. Likewise, use productivity applications only when needed.

- *Notification Area clutter* Look for icons in the Notification Area. You'll find that these icons connect to applications that you may not use very often, but start automatically when you start Windows. See if you can turn the application off and start it manually when you need to. I'll show you how to disable these applications permanently in the section "Using the System Configuration Utility (MSCON-FIG)," later in this chapter.

- *Icons and other graphics* Every icon on your desktop consumes memory. The same is true for any other form of graphical image or window. Interestingly enough, Microsoft has included in Windows XP a new feature, called Clean Desktop Now, that offers to clean up your desktop icons. Windows XP usually adds this application to the Scheduled Tasks folder automatically. Another feature cleans up the icons in the Notification Area. You enable this feature by checking the Hide Inactive Icons option on the Taskbar tab of the Taskbar and Start Menu Properties dialog box. In addition, to saving a little memory, optimizing your use of icons and folders also makes you more efficient.

- *Leaky applications* Some programs *leak* memory: They receive memory from Windows but never give it back, even after they terminate. After a while, you won't have enough memory to run programs, even though you should. The Windows XP datacentric interface tends to accelerate the rate at which memory dissipates if you open and close an application for each data file. You can alleviate this situation by keeping leaky applications open until you know that you won't need them again. You can find a leaky application by checking system resources and memory before you open it. Open and close the application a few times (make sure that you also open some documents while inside), and then check the amount of memory again after the last time you close it. If you find that you have less memory—I mean a measurable amount, not a few bytes—the application is leaky.

Note: Windows XP includes a new feature called the .NET Framework. Many of the features of this framework are appealing only to developers. However, one new feature, called *garbage collection,* prevents leaky applications. The operating system collects unused memory (the garbage) after applications finish with it. This means that an application can no longer leave the operating system in such a state that it loses track of memory, and your system should work better. The result of .NET Framework is a system that will stay online longer without the need for a reboot. Unfortunately, developers have already created thousands of traditional Windows applications, so don't expect to see this feature in full use for quite some time to come.

- *Extra drivers* Windows 9x and Windows NT/2000/XP do a good job of cleaning old drivers out of the Registry. Even so, after you remove an application, you'll want to see whether the uninstall program removed all the drivers from the system. Microsoft keeps designing new and exciting methods of installing and uninstalling applications. So far, none of them provides absolute reliability. It's true that recent installation program advances do a better job than any technology in the past, but you'll still want to exercise care. We'll explore one tool for checking on old drivers in the section "Using the System Configuration Utility (MSCON-FIG)," later in this chapter. I'll also show you some techniques in the "Care and Cleaning of the Registry" section of Chapter 12, "The Windows XP Registry."

- *DOS applications* Nothing grabs memory and holds it like a DOS application under Windows. Unlike other applications, Windows can't move around the memory used by a DOS application to free space. You might have lots of memory on your system, but Windows won't be able to use it because it's all too fragmented. If your system has so little memory that it can't tolerate even the smallest amount of memory fragmentation, avoid using DOS applications.

> **Tip:** Always look for applications that bear the Windows logo. This logo assures you that Microsoft has tested the application and that it should perform reasonably well on your machine. The Windows 2000 and Windows XP logo require the most stringent support of Windows features and is the logo you should look for first on an application. You can find out more about the Windows XP logo program at http://www.microsoft.com/WINLOGO/Software/SWprograms.asp. There's also a logo program for hardware and other computing elements. Links on this Web page can help you locate the other logo requirements.

Windows XP–Specific Tuning Tips

Now that we've gotten past the generic tips, let's look at a few Windows XP–specific ways to enhance overall system performance and the amount of memory you have available. All these tips are Windows XP–specific, but they may work with earlier versions of Windows, such as Windows NT/2000.

> **Tip:** One of the most interesting performance-tuning Web sites you'll find is TweakXP.com (http://www.tweakxp.com/). The site contains a wealth of well-documented tips that will make your system run faster. Of course, there are tradeoffs when you adjust your system. Although the site doesn't always list every potential drawback of a tuning tip, it does list enough that you shouldn't run into problems. Note that many of these tuning tips aren't for the faint of heart because they involve registry edits.

- *Use an efficient hard drive format* Hard drive format affects system performance in several ways. The most obvious is direct file access; you'll get the best level of performance using an NT File System (NTFS) partition. (However, you'll give up some flexibility to get this speed boost.) The second area is a little less obvious. Placing your pagefile on an NTFS partition can actually improve performance because NTFS is an optimized disk-formatting technology. I wouldn't count on a large speed improvement; however, moving your pagefile is more in the line of an incremental improvement.

- *Create the hard drive partition with Windows XP*   Every version of the Windows NT–based operating system seems to bring a new version of NTFS as well. Windows XP is no exception. The latest update provides subtle reliability, security, and performance benefits. The biggest change is the organization of data on the hard drive. Microsoft has made the data arrangement more efficient.

- *Increase the number of processors*   One of the most common ways to add more performance to a Windows XP system is to add more than one processor. Vendors design some machines to move from one to two or four processors. In most cases, workstation-class machines limit you to two processors, which still provides a significant performance increase. Windows XP Home Edition will work with only one processor, and the Professional Edition supports up to two processors. You'll need one of the server products if you want to use more than two processors.

Warning: Windows XP and Windows 2000 handle multiprocessor machines differently than Windows NT did, in part because of the Plug and Play features they provide. Windows XP also provides additional features that include compatibility support for older applications. In some situations, Windows 2000/XP may not recognize that your machine has more than one processor due to BIOS or configuration problems. Make certain that your multiprocessor machine is on the Hardware Compatibility Layer (HCL) before you buy it. If you have an existing machine and find that Windows 2000/XP can't see the multiple processors it contains, start with a BIOS upgrade to see if that fixes the problem. In most cases, you should also contact the motherboard manufacturer to determine if you need to make other Windows 2000/XP changes.

- *The single-pane folder window is more streamlined and more efficient than the two-pane Explorer window*   This might seem like a contradiction in terms because folders use the Explorer interface. However, a folder displays just the interface, not the full Explorer. Opening a copy of Explorer eats up many more system resources than opening a folder. The idea is that you place all your data in folders and then place a shortcut to those folders on the desktop. You can still get to all your important files without opening a copy of Explorer.

  The memory savings you get by using this tip are hard to quantify. To see how Explorer uses memory, look at Task Manager's Processes display (right-click the Taskbar, and then choose Task Manager). Click the Processes tab, locate the explorer.exe process, and watch what happens to memory usage when you open Windows Explorer instead of merely opening a folder. If you look carefully, you can actually see the numbers increase as Windows Explorer searches the network and adds icons for any mapped network drives. On my system, opening Explorer exacts a memory penalty of 1,048 KB or more, and opening a folder costs at least 68KB, but less than the 1,048KB used by Windows Explorer.

  Explorer is always active and caches the results of using either a folder or a full copy of Windows Explorer. The caching costs vary as a function of object count.

Because Windows Explorer usually has a higher object count, the caching cost for it is higher. Windows XP eventually returns cached memory, but you can't use it in the short term.

- *Use context menus in place of the Control Panel* I find that I occasionally need to adjust the properties of system elements during a session. You don't have to open the Control Panel to make these adjustments. Simply right-click the object in question and choose Properties from the context menu. Using the context menu isn't only an efficient way to access information about the object, but it uses less memory as well. This is something to consider if you need to keep an object Properties dialog box open for any length of time.

- *Set your printer for RAW printing* Windows XP automatically installs support for Enhanced Metafile Format (EMF) printing on systems that it thinks will use it. This feature enables Windows XP to print faster by translating the output to generic commands in the foreground and then creating printer-specific output in the background. Creating generic commands requires much less processing time than writing printer-specific output. The tradeoff of using RAW printing is longer foreground print times, but you use less memory and make your system more efficient in the end. To set your printer for RAW printing, open the printer Properties dialog box, select the Advanced tab, and click Print Processor. Select the RAW printing option on the Print Processor dialog box and click OK twice to make the change permanent.

- *Keep your disk defragmented* Even NTFS drives experience file fragmentation problems. As you read and write files on your drive, the size of each file changes. A file that used to fit in one spot grows so that it can no longer fit there, so Windows XP retains the original area and adds to it. The file now resides in two or more areas on the hard drive. Your system experiences a performance hit every time the drive has to move the read/write head to another location on the disk. Defragmenting the drive places all of the files into one area again, reducing read/write head movement.

- *Simulate a permanent swap file* Earlier versions of Windows enabled you to create a permanent pagefile. Using a permanent pagefile improves performance by reducing hard disk head movement to read pagefile data. It doesn't matter how fragmented your drive gets after you set up the swap file, because the swap file always resides in the same contiguous disk sectors. Windows XP doesn't provide the permanent swap file option; it always uses a temporary file. Fortunately, you can simulate a permanent pagefile under Windows XP. Right-click My Computer and choose Properties from the context menu. Select the Advanced tab and click Settings in the Performance area. You'll see a Performance Options dialog box. Select the Advanced tab and click Change. You'll see a Virtual Memory dialog box. Highlight the drive you want to use for a swap file. Set the minimum and maximum pagefile sizes to the same value. You can incrementally enhance the performance of your system if you have a two-disk setup. Move the pagefile to the first drive while you completely defragment the second. After you've defrag-

mented the second drive, move the pagefile from the first drive to the second
drive. You'll create a simulated swap file that resides in one contiguous section of
the hard drive, which will improve system performance.

- *Place your swap file on the fastest drive*   Windows XP usually places the swap
  file on the drive with the largest amount of available memory. In most cases, the
  drive it selects doesn't make a big difference. However, if you have a system with
  one large, slow drive and a second small, fast drive, you should probably change
  the virtual memory settings. See the previous bullet for instructions on accessing
  the swap file settings.

- *Eliminate 16-bit applications, drivers, and DLLs*   Windows XP is a 32-bit operating system, so there's never a good reason to use 16-bit applications, drivers, or
  DLLs with it. It runs every 32-bit application in a separate session. Doing this
  allows Windows XP to perform some very intense memory management on the
  resources needed by that application. The 16-bit applications also run in separate
  sessions, but share resources. The amount of management Windows XP can perform on these shared resources is much less than what it can do for the individual
  32-bit sessions because it can't make certain assumptions about how that memory
  is being used. In addition, the 32-bit memory space is flat, reducing the number of
  clock cycles required to make a function call or look at something in memory. On
  the other hand, the segmented address space used by 16-bit components requires
  two to three times the number of clock cycles to process. I'll show you some techniques for finding 16-bit leftovers in the section "Using the System Configuration
  Utility (MSCONFIG)," later in this chapter.

- *Get rid of nonessentials*   Some parts of Windows XP make you more efficient,
  but at a fairly large cost in memory. For example, enabling the International
  Settings feature makes you more efficient if you work with several languages, but
  costs you memory. Unfortunately, after you activate this feature, you can't get rid
  of it until you reboot the machine. The same holds true for many other icons that
  appear in the Notification Area with the clock.

Finding Unneeded Hidden Drivers

At times, Windows XP does a less-than-perfect job of setting up your machine. Earlier in
this chapter, I mentioned that you should remove any unneeded drivers. What would happen if you had some hidden drivers you didn't need installed on your system? Figure 5.1
shows a dialog box that illustrates this point perfectly. I installed Windows XP on a network with both a Windows XP server and a Novell NetWare file server. Notice that it
installed both NetBIOS and IPX/SPX support. In fact, because this is a NetWare 5 system, I don't need either protocol—running TCP/IP is enough. Unchecking these two protocol options won't remove them from My Network Places (which means that the files
are still on disk), but it does prevent them from starting, which saves memory and processing cycles.

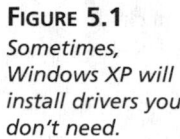

FIGURE 5.1
Sometimes, Windows XP will install drivers you don't need.

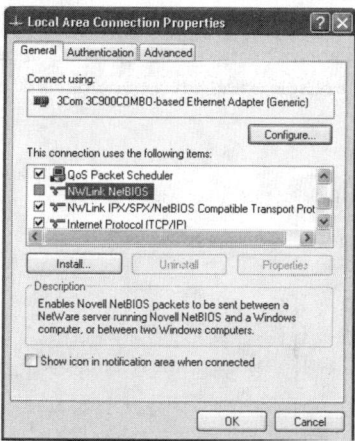

Obviously, not every driver will be this easy to spot, but with patience you can find most of the extra drivers on your system. If you find yourself in this particular situation, follow these three steps:

1. Eliminate additional network support. You need to install support for only one network if you're using a peer-to-peer setup. In most cases, this means that you'll retain the Microsoft network and discard NetWare support. Likewise, if you don't plan to set up a peer-to-peer network, remove the Microsoft network support in a NetWare environment.

2. Reduce the number of protocols you have installed. I typically maintain TCP/IP support for a peer-to-peer setup. Of course, the protocol you choose must reflect the capabilities of the network you install. (You'll find a list of installed protocols in the Connection Properties dialog box, such as the one shown in Figure 5.1, for a local area connection.)

3. Install the fewest possible network services. Installing sharing support for a floppy drive is a waste of memory because it's unlikely that someone will need it. If someone does need it, you can always add the support later. Try starting out with the lowest level of support possible. You'll also want to think about which workstation printers you really want to share. If a workstation has an older printer attached, you probably won't want to install print sharing support for it.

Using Windows XP Automatic Tuning Features

Windows XP includes a few methods for automatically tuning your system. It still doesn't provide as many methods as you found under Windows 9x, but in many ways it provides superior performance tuning capabilities. You just have to spend a little more time tweaking than you did before.

The automatic tuning options appear on the Performance Options dialog box, shown in Figure 5.2. You access this dialog box by right-clicking My Computer and choosing Properties from the context menu. Select the Advanced tab, and then click Settings in the Performance area.

FIGURE 5.2

The automatic tuning features appear on the Performance Options dialog box.

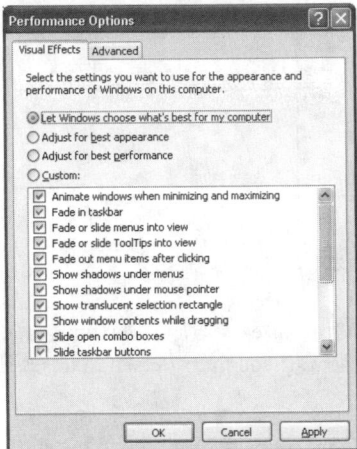

The Visual Effects tab, shown in Figure 5.2, allows you to choose between several preset options. Notice that you can set the visual effects to maximum performance. Although these settings do work well, you may find that tuning the individual settings that appear in the list on the bottom half of the dialog box works better. For example, some people prefer to have the shadow under the mouse cursor to make it easier to see. You have to balance the cost of visual effects against any personal performance benefits they provide.

Note: If you want to retain the Windows XP appearance of your display, you must check the Use Visual Styles on Windows and Buttons option as a minimum. Even so, you'll lose some of the new visual effects by clearing the other options.

Select the Advanced tab, and you'll see three general tuning areas. The Processor Scheduling area determines how Windows XP uses processing time. Select Programs if you want your foreground applications to run faster. However, some users actually have more background processes to run on their system and would benefit from setting this option to Background Services. For example, a friend who uses graphics extensively found that she was actually waiting too long for print jobs to complete. Changing this setting allowed the print jobs to complete faster, and she became more productive. You can also temporarily change this setting. For example, you might have a large download from the Internet. Using the Background Services option will speed up the process at a slight cost of foreground application responsiveness.

The Memory Usage area determines how Windows XP uses memory. Use the Programs option if you run large, memory-intensive applications on your machine. For cxample, a spreadsheet consumes large amounts of both processor cycles and memory. Use the System Cache setting if you want to increase Windows XP responsiveness when using smaller or less memory-intensive applications. For example, I find that this settings affects the time required to perform system backups. It also speeds file searches on the network and has even helped with some types of Internet access.

The final area, Virtual Memory, changes the allocation of disk space for a swap file. Click Change, and you'll see a Virtual Memory dialog box. The top of the Virtual Memory dialog box contains a list of your drives. The section below it allows you to set the swap file size for each drive. To change the settings for a particular drive, highlight the drive in the list box, set an initial and a maximum value, and then click Set. You can also choose a system-managed size or choose to use no page file at all. Any change in this dialog box requires a system reboot. The bottom part of this dialog box contains Microsoft's recommendations for a swap file, which is usually huge. Generally, your system will find it hard to use even a portion of the swap file that Microsoft recommends, unless you have exceptionally small hard drives or use incredibly large applications.

Using the System Configuration Utility (MSCONFIG)

I've known some users to scour the countryside looking for some deep, dark, secret way to tune Windows performance. They'll seek obscure registry changes and file modifications to satiate their need for more speed. In some cases, these folks are fully qualified to use low-level techniques, but many of them are simply looking for trouble. MSCONFIG provides a means to perform some low-level tuning tricks in a safe manner and in an easy-to-understand way. You get the treat without the trick.

You won't find MSCONFIG on the Start Menu; it's another of those utilities that Microsoft considers too dangerous for the average user to understand. To start MSCONFIG, select Run from the Start Menu, type **MSCONFIG** in the Open field, and then click OK. You'll see a System Configuration Utility dialog box, as shown in Figure 5.3.

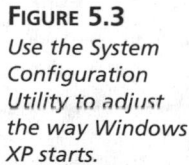

FIGURE 5.3

Use the System Configuration Utility to adjust the way Windows XP starts.

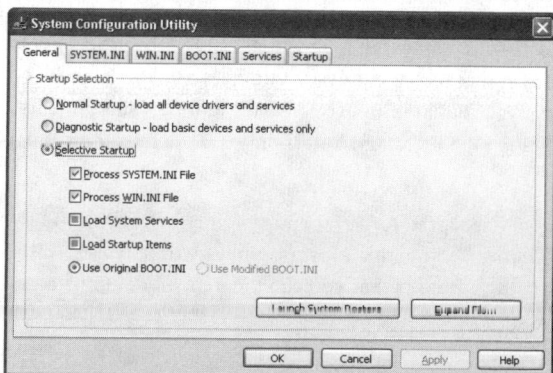

The General tab controls the way Windows XP will launch the next time you start it. You can choose a normal, diagnostic, or selective install. The Normal Startup option is the one that you'll use most often. It loads all the drivers and applications configured for your machine. The Diagnostic Startup option starts Windows XP with only the essentials so that you can check for problems with the operating system. (Don't worry about the Expand File and Launch System Restore buttons for now; we'll cover them in the "Using the System Restore Utility" section of Chapter 24, "Software Problems.")

> **Warning:** This section of the chapter discusses the boot options for your system. Enabling or disabling boot options is always risky because you can cause your system to freeze during the boot process by disabling a needed driver, service, DLL, or other part of the operating system. Use the content of this section carefully. Disable or enable entries one at a time so that you can see what effect the single entry will have on the system. Using MSCONFIG does offer safety because you can always boot in safe mode and enable an option you need—the option isn't gone forever.

The Selective Startup option is the one that you'll use for performance purposes. However, you won't normally change the boot options from this tab. You need to select files more carefully than simply telling Windows not to process an entire portion of the normal boot process. It's important to use a logical approach to working with this utility, or you won't garner any information from it. With that in mind, let's look at the various tabs and learn how they can affect machine performance.

> **Note:** We won't cover the BOOT.INI file in this chapter because you can use it better for diagnostic purposes. Look in the "Changing the BOOT.INI Options" section of Chapter 24 for details on this tab.

SYSTEM.INI and WIN.INI

The SYSTEM.INI and WIN.INI tabs are leftovers from previous versions of Windows. Figure 5.4 shows a typical example of this tab. However, these are the two tabs to check first for old 16-bit drivers and applications. Both tabs have an entry marked ";for 16-bit app support." If this entry contains anything at all, you have 16-bit applications on your machine that you should retire. (Note that Figure 5.4 has an ";msconfig" preceding the ";for 16-bit app support" entry. You'll only see the ;msconfig entry if you disable the option.)

It also pays to look at the [drivers] entry on the SYSTEM.INI tab because these are normally 16-bit drivers. Note that most machines will have a 16-bit wave and timer driver for compatibility purposes that you can theoretically eliminate unless you play DOS games on your system.

FIGURE 5.4

The SYSTEM.INI and WIN.INI tabs allow you to view and change the content of these files.

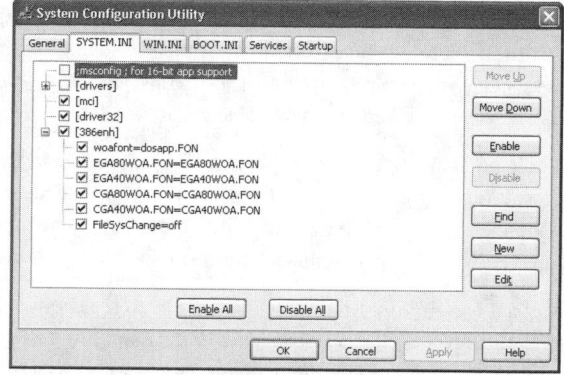

Entries in the [driver32] section of the SYSTEM.INI tab are safe, but suspect. Only older 32-bit drivers use this section, so you might want to look for updates. Likewise, take a close look at the [386enh] section for potential problems.

Notice in Figure 5.4 that you can change the position of entries and enable or disable them. The check box next to each entry indicates its enabled or disabled state. Click Find if you want to locate a particular entry. You can also create new entries and edit existing entries.

Services

The Services tab, shown in Figure 5.5, contains a complete list of the services that Windows XP will load during the boot process. As you can see, this tab uses the same check box indicator to show the service's enabled or disabled state. Notice the Disable All button on this dialog box. I'm not certain why Microsoft provided it, but you won't want to use it. Disabling all services just about ensures that your system will have difficulty restarting.

FIGURE 5.5

Make changes on the Services tab carefully.

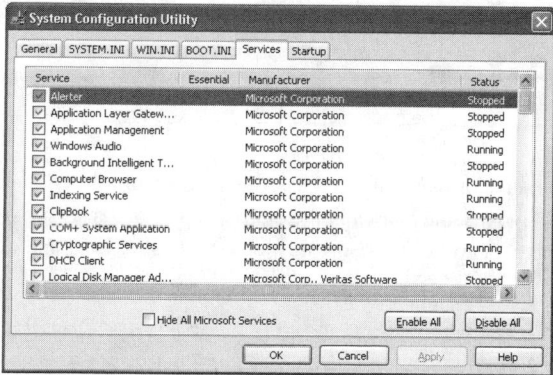

Let's discuss some important aspects of the entries on this tab. First, notice the Essential column. Don't rely on this column to tell you if the service is essential. If a service is marked as essential, you can be certain that it is. However, many essential services aren't marked, so exercise care when you make changes to this tab.

The Status column is also important. A service that's marked Stopped is loaded into the system, but isn't running at the time. This means disabling the server may not have much of an effect on the system. You may save a little memory, but because the service is stopped, you won't see any performance improvement.

The best way to know if you can disable a service is to research it first. Sometimes, you can tell a great deal by just the service name. For example, if you see an entry marked NetMeeting Remote Desktop Sharing and you never use NetMeeting, you can probably save some memory by not loading that service. However, no matter what you think you know about the services listed in this dialog box, always disable them one at a time, reboot, and test your theory before you make any other changes.

Startup

The Startup tab, shown in Figure 5.6, is one of the safest choices for performance changes. You can disable all of the entries in this list and still expect the system to boot properly. Of course, you may notice the loss of some functionality, but the operating system will work as intended.

FIGURE 5.6

The Startup tab is a safe place to begin looking for applications to trim.

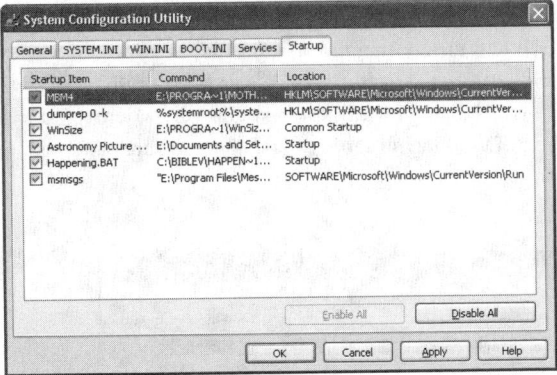

Notice that some of these entries appear in the Startup folder. That's right—you can use MSCONFIG to disable entries in the Startup folder rather than move them to another location on the Start Menu. Using this feature can save time and effort.

Some of the entries appear in the registry. Unlike the other tabs we've looked at so far, this one tells you where to find the entry in the registry. Disabling an entry allows you to see its effect on the system. If the system runs well for a week or two without the application, you can probably remove it from its location, even if that location is in the registry. As with any other registry editing, make sure that you back up the key before you delete it. We'll discuss this process in more detail in Chapter 12.

Automating Tune-ups with Task Scheduler

Task Scheduler enables you to perform automated tasks by using different criteria. For example, you can configure the computer to run ScanDisk at 7 p.m. every Sunday, your disk defragmenter at 5 p.m. every Friday, and your antivirus program at 9 a.m. the first Monday of every month. In short, Task Scheduler allows you to automate any task that you normally start and let run by itself.

> **Tip:** You can use Task Scheduler to run more than just disk utility programs. It also works with applications designed for Windows 95/98/NT/2000, Windows 3.*x*, OS/2, MS-DOS, batch files (*.bat), command files (*.cmd), or any properly registered file type. For example, you could use Task Scheduler to send out a fax in the middle of the night when telephone rates are lower. You could also use it to print database reports after business hours so that it doesn't tie up your computer during the day.

A task can have more than one trigger to determine when Windows should execute it. A *trigger* is a set of criteria that, when met, activates and causes a task to execute. There are two types of triggers: time-based and event-based.

A time-based trigger activates at a specified time. You can not only set the time it activates, but also activate it at intervals. Activation scenarios include once, daily, weekly, monthly, on a specified day of the month (the third day of the month), or on a specified day of the week of a month (the second Tuesday of the month).

An event-based trigger activates in response to certain system events. Some event-based triggers activate when the system starts up, when a user logs on to the local computer, or when the system becomes idle. The last of these is an idle trigger. An *idle* trigger becomes active a specified amount of time after the computer becomes idle. When you set idle-related flags for a task, you create an idle trigger.

Starting Task Scheduler

You can start Task Scheduler using the Start | Programs | Accessories | System Tools | Scheduled Tasks command. You also can start Task Scheduler by double-clicking the Task Scheduler icon in the Notification Area. Figure 5.7 shows the Scheduled Tasks window you'll see when you start the program.

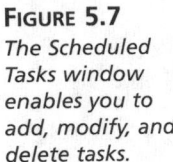

FIGURE 5.7
The Scheduled Tasks window enables you to add, modify, and delete tasks.

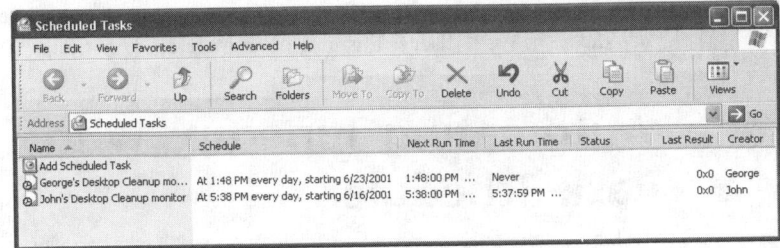

Scheduling a New Task

Before you can use Task Scheduler, you have to schedule specific tasks you want done. (If you ever need to delete a task, just click it and then click the Delete icon in the Task Scheduler toolbar.) The following procedure shows you how do this:

1. Double-click the Add Scheduled Task icon, which is shown in Figure 5.7. As soon as you double-click this icon, the Scheduled Task Wizard appears.

2. Click Next. The next dialog box enables you to choose the application you want to run. You can use the Browse button to find an application that doesn't appear in the list.

> **Tip:** Some of the utilities you need for general use are different from those used for automated use. For example, you'll use the DFRG.MSC program for interactive disk defragmenting, but the DEFRAG.EXE program for automated use. Always remember to check for a command-line version of any application you want to automate. The command-line version will always work better than the interactive version of the same utility. In addition, remember to add any command-line parameters for the utility. For example, DEFRAG.EXE requires that you supply a drive letter or mount point. You may need to add the parameters using the Advanced Parameters dialog box after completing the wizard.

3. Select the application you want to run and then click Next. The Scheduled Task Wizard asks for a specific time to run the task—daily, weekly, monthly, one time only, at when the computer starts, or when you log on. You also can change the name automatically provided for the task if it isn't descriptive enough.

4. Select the scheduling option you want to use. Click Next. Depending on the time you choose (daily, weekly, monthly, and so on), you'll see another list of options asking you to specify the exact time and date to run your chosen task.

5. Choose a time and date, and then click Next. The Scheduled Task Wizard asks for the name and password of the person running the application. Make sure that this person has enough rights to perform the task.

6. Type a name and password; then click Next. The Scheduled Task Wizard shows the application you chose to run and the time you selected. You'll also see a check

box that enables you to display the application's Advanced Properties dialog box after the Scheduled Task Wizard is complete. The Advanced Properties dialog box enables you to add a command-line parameter, to check the schedule for the application, and to choose additional settings, such as running the application during idle time or stopping it after a specific interval. This feature is discussed more in the following section, "Customizing a Scheduled Task."

7. Click Finish if you're ready to schedule the task.

> **Tip:** After scheduling a task, right-click the task and choose Run. This gives you a chance to see how your scheduled task actually runs. That way, you can see whether the task hangs or needs additional input before running.

Customizing a Scheduled Task

After you create a task, Task Scheduler continues running it until you either delete it or specify a time to stop running it. In addition to specifying when to stop running a task, there are other reasons to customize your tasks. You might want Task Scheduler to delete a scheduled task automatically after a certain date. If you're running Task Scheduler on a laptop, you might not want to run tasks automatically, especially if your batteries are running low. You also might want to run a task only when the computer is idle. After all, you wouldn't want Task Scheduler suddenly to interfere with your work at the computer.

> **Tip:** Sometimes, you need to pause Task Scheduler so that it won't run any tasks. For example, you might be in the middle of a download and not want your system distributed. Use the Advanced | Pause Task Scheduler command if you want to pause Task Schedule for a short time. Use the Advanced | Stop Using Task Schedule command if you want to make the pause a little more permanent.

Customizing a scheduled task involves changing a task's properties. To view a task's properties, right-click the task and choose Properties. The Task tab enables you to change the Run (the application's command line), Start In (the working directory), and Comments fields. Unchecking the Enable check box lets you retain a task but keep it from running. You can use the Browse button to find a new copy of the application. Finally, you can change the name and password used to run the application.

The Schedule tab enables you to define the date and time to run a task. Click the Advanced button to display the Advanced Schedule Options dialog box. You can specify an ending date for your task or direct it to repeat.

The Settings tab enables you to specify whether to delete a task after it's done, if it's not scheduled to run again. It also permits you to stop a task if it's still running after a certain time, determine whether to run the task on a laptop using its battery power, and run the task when the computer is idle.

Checking Performance

It doesn't pay to optimize your system if you can't quantify the results. Knowing that you succeeded in creating a faster system is the reason to tune it. Of course, we've discussed several levels of performance gain. For example, you can optimize your system to provide better memory handling. You can optimize it for speed. Finally, you can optimize it to make it easier to use and make you more efficient. Only you can determine the success of this third level of performance tuning. The following sections show two methods of checking your work in the other areas.

Using Task Manager

The Task Manager can provide you with a quick view of system performance. Using this utility is simple. All you need to do is right-click the Taskbar and choose Task Manager from the context menu. Select the Performance or Networking tabs, and you'll see a graphic display of processing, memory, and network performance, as shown in Figure 5.8. It's an overview at best, but adequate in many cases.

FIGURE 5.8

The Performance tab shows a view of CPU and memory usage.

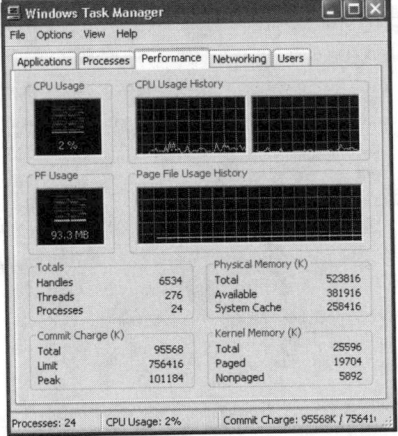

Figure 5.8 shows the default view of the Performance tab. You can change this view in several ways. For example, I have a dual processor machine, so Windows XP shows one window for each processor. You can use the View I CPU History options to change it to a single view. Task Manager also allows you to control the speed of display using the View I Update Speed options. Finally, you can add the kernel processing times to the display by using the View I Show Kernel Times command. The Networking tab provides similar options. However, instead of processor options, you can change the network adapter display using the View I Network Adapter History options.

Many people bypass the Processes tab when it comes to performance, yet this is the most powerful option the Task Manager offers. The initial display is a little anemic; it shows only the memory usage and CPU processing time. However, you can easily beef up this display using the View | Select Columns command to display the Select Columns dialog box, shown in Figure 5.9.

FIGURE 5.9
The Select Columns dialog box allows you to choose new additions for the Processes tab.

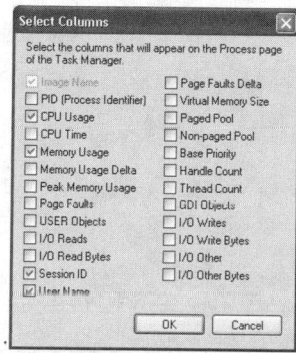

The list isn't exhaustive, but it does provide more information than the graphic displays shown in Figure 5.8. You can choose a wealth of overview information to display in a tabular format based on a particular process. This is a fast way to see how changes you make in configuration affect an individual process.

System Monitor Usage

Windows XP installs the Performance console by default. This console contains two Microsoft Management Console (MMC) snap-ins: System Monitor and Performance Logs and Alerts. The Performance console is a very worthwhile tool because it enables you to track a variety of system statistics, including CPU usage and actual memory allocation. Monitoring these statistics tells you whether a certain optimization strategy was successful. Performance Monitor also provides a means of detecting performance-robbing hardware and software errors on the system.

Understanding the Views

When you start Performance Monitor for the first time, you see a blank screen. This screen will show a typical graph view of system statistics. Before you can do anything, you need to select some events to monitor. Figure 5.10 shows a display containing four processor counters. A *counter* tracks an individual object statistic, such as the time the processor spends answering user requests.

Five buttons on the toolbar change the way you track information: View Current Activity, View Log Data, View Graph, View Histogram, and View Report. The first two view options determine whether you view current system activity or the contents of a log you've created. Some types of system configuration changes will require the log file approach because you'll need to see how the change affects system performance over an entire day, or even longer.

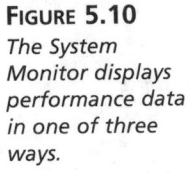

FIGURE 5.10

The System Monitor displays performance data in one of three ways.

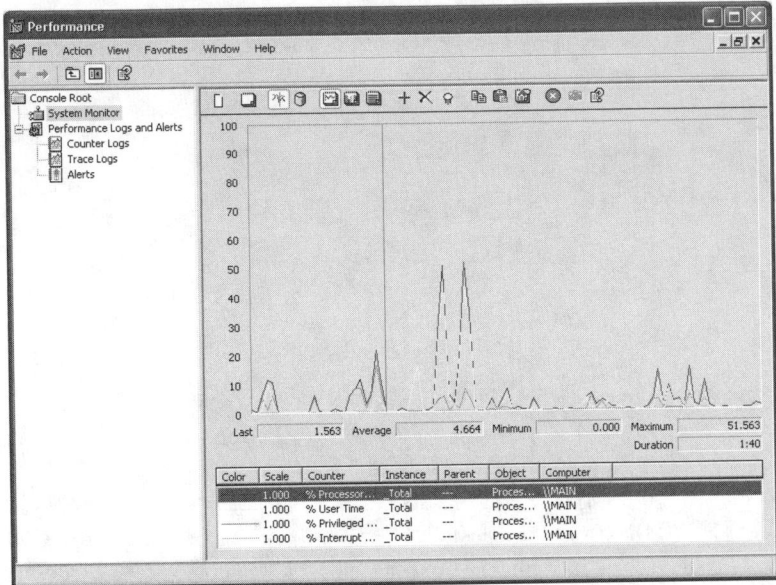

The other three buttons affect the actual presentation of information onscreen. I find that the View Graph presentation is the most helpful when I need to monitor system performance over a long interval. This view also helps me to see the interaction of various statistics.

The View Histogram option provides the best method for performing instantaneous comparisons of system data. In this view, you see vertical bar graphs that change at the interval you select. I can use this view to make quick comparisons of two statistics when I'm adjusting a configuration option that makes a large change in system performance.

The third button, View Report, is very useful when you need to compare large quantities of data or save the information to an application that normally requires text input, such as a spreadsheet. This view is a table. It contains numbers that tell you about the system statistics at any given instant. This view is the least likely to provide quick counter comparisons, but does provide precision not found in the other two views.

Performance Monitor uses a default-monitoring period of one second, which is great if you're troubleshooting a bad NIC or want instant feedback on a configuration change. However, this might be too fast in certain situations. For example, if you're performing long-term monitoring, you might want to set the monitoring period to a high value. Click the Properties button within any of the views to change this setting. Select the General tab of the System Monitor Properties dialog box.

You'll also use this dialog box to embellish the default Performance Monitor views. For example, you can use options on the Graph tab to add both a horizontal and a vertical grid to either the chart or histogram views. Options on the Appearance tab enable you to change the chart colors, font, and other display features. Using the Source tab, you can choose between current system data or logged data. This tab also allows you to select a source of logged data.

Adding and Removing Counters

Next to the view buttons we talked about in the previous section are three buttons that affect the "counters" used to display information for Performance Monitor. A counter is a special kind of program that keeps track of a system statistic for a specified time and then passes the count (the amount of that statistic) to Performance Monitor for display. These three buttons enable you to change and highlight the items that Performance Monitor displays.

Use the Add button to add new items to the list. Click this button, and you'll see the Add Counters dialog box, which contains entries for the computer, the performance object, a counter within that object, and instances of a particular counter. A counter requires instances when there's more than one of an item to count, such as dual processors or multiple hard drives.

You select an object, such as the processor, to monitor and then select an instance of that object. In the case of a processor, you may have only one instance, but disk drives usually provide several instances. After you select an instance of an object, you can select one of the counters (the items that Performance Monitor will track). Special radio buttons add all counters for a specific object or all instances of a specific counter to the display. You can also monitor statistics from more than one computer by selecting another in the Select Counters from Computer field.

> **Tip:** Clicking the Explain button in the Add Counters dialog box provides a full description of the selected counter. This makes it easier for you to determine which counters to monitor.

Use the Delete button to remove an item from the monitoring list. Remember that the more items you display onscreen, the less screen area each item receives. Small views limit the accuracy of the readings you'll take. Make sure that you monitor only the essentials. For that matter, you might want to break the items into groups and monitor a single group at a time.

Finally, the Highlight button allows you to highlight a specific item in the monitoring list. This feature is available only in chart view, where highlighting a line will help you see it better. The highlighted line defaults to an extra-wide white line that you can see with ease compared to other lines on a chart.

What types of things will Performance Monitor track for you? You can track everything from the number of bytes the disk writes per second to the number of times someone tries to access your machine from the network. Performance Monitor tracks more items than I have room to talk about, and Microsoft keeps adding more items with every version of Windows.

Creating Performance Logs

As mentioned earlier in this chapter, you can create log files of counters that you plan to monitor over a long period. Obviously, the first thing you need to do is create the log before you can view the results. The following steps show you how to create a new log:

1. Open the Performance Logs and Alerts folder, and then choose the Counter Logs entry.

2. Right-click in the right pane and then choose New Log Settings from the context menu. You'll see the New Log Settings dialog box.

3. Type a name for the new log setting (the example uses Temp) and click OK. You'll see a Log Settings dialog box, like the one shown in Figure 5.11. This is where you'll add counters and perform any required setups for the log. The one requirement for every log is selecting one or more counters to track.

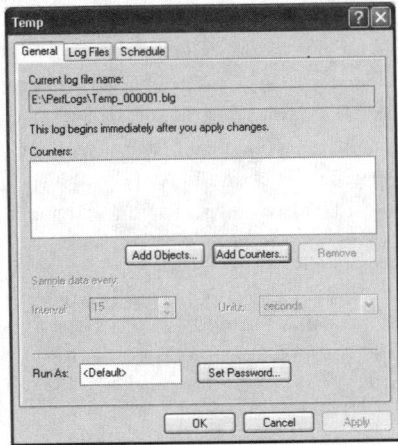

FIGURE 5.11

This dialog box allows you to define what Windows will record in the log file for you.

4. Click Add Counters. You'll see a Select Counters dialog box.

5. Select one or more counters to track. (Highlight the counter and instance information you want, and then click Add.) Click Close in the Add Counters dialog box when you've finished adding new counters. At this point, your counters are ready to go, but you haven't decided when to record the log.

6. Click the Schedule tab. You can start the log at a specific time, or you can manually start it using a shortcut menu command. Likewise, stopping the log can be automatic or manual. Special considerations also come into play when stopping the log. For example, you can stop the current log at the end of a specific time interval and automatically begin a new one.

7. Choose the starting and ending time for your log, and then click OK. The log settings are now ready to use.

Depending on how you've set up your log, Windows may start recording it automatically. You can also right-click the log entry in the Counter Logs folder and choose Start from the context menu. Stopping the log recording process is just as easy: Just select Stop from the context menu when you right-click the log settings icon. Log file icons are red when stopped and green when started, making it easy to see what Windows is currently logging for you.

Viewing Performance Logs

You recorded a log, and you want to view the results in Performance monitor. Click the View Log Data button on the System Monitor toolbar, select a filename in the Select Log File dialog box, and then click Open. System Monitor opens the log file and shows you any of the counters you select using the Add Counter dialog box. Note that when you open the Add Counters dialog box, instead of seeing all the available counters, you'll see only those that are recorded in the log.

Let's discuss another important feature of Performance Monitor. If you're recording data for days or even weeks, you won't want to look at all the data in one big lump. Wouldn't it be nice if you could look at just a small piece of it? Performance Monitor enables you to do just that.

Right-click the chart and choose Properties from the context menu. Click the Source tab. Notice the Total Range bar at the bottom of the dialog box. In the upper-left corner is the starting time for the log, and the upper-right corner shows the stopping time. In the lower-left corner is the starting view time, and the bottom-right corner shows the stopping view time. You can move the two thumbs on this bar to change the starting and stopping view times, which will then affect the display you see in the chart.

On Your Own

Survey your hardware to see if any components might be holding back your system's performance. Consider replacing that old CD-ROM drive or adding more memory if necessary to enhance system throughput. A whole new machine might be in your future if the current one is completely out of date—don't waste money replacing all the components in your machine one at a time.

Check out the section "General Tuning Tips for Windows," earlier in this chapter, to see if you can get rid of any memory- or performance-wasting features. You might want to consider spending a week without wallpaper. The performance improvement you get might be worth the sacrifice. Look at some of the doodads you have loaded as well. I'm often surprised at how many little utility programs get loaded on my machine and then never get used.

Hunt for any unnecessary drivers on your machine (only if you suspect that there are any—new machines usually don't have unnecessary drivers lurking around). Make sure that you look for some of the inconspicuous sources of wasted device drivers, such as network protocols you don't use.

Spend some time learning to use the Event Viewer. What kinds of events does your system appear to monitor as a default? Do you see any events that require your immediate attention? How do the Event Viewer entries help you diagnose problems?

Learn to use the Performance Monitor as both a diagnostic aid and a tuning tool. What type of setup helps you most when it comes time to tune your system? Make sure that you try various setups to perform specific kinds of tuning. You'll want to monitor disk statistics when tuning your hard drive, for example, and monitor network statistics when monitoring your connection efficiency. Likewise, what setup works best for various types of diagnostic situations?

6

Application Performance Primer

An efficient machine is only as fast as the operator using it is. In days gone by, users spent time waiting for their machines to complete tasks. The hardware wasn't capable of performing even one task quickly, much less three or four. Today, even a low-end machine can perform several tasks quickly. In many cases, the machine waits for the user, not the other way around. To a certain extent, that's how things should work. However, it also means that some machine resources go to waste. Making the user more efficient without adding stress is an important goal.

This chapter looks at some ways you can make yourself a little more efficient so that you can get the full benefit of using Windows XP as an operating system. This means every-thing from the way you start your applications to the way you arrange your desktop. Windows XP provides many new tools you can use to make each step a little faster.

So, why is this chapter called "Application Performance Primer" rather than "User Performance Primer?" Over the years, I've found that most users work at a constant speed. No amount of jumping up and down by a supervisor is going to make them work any faster. In fact, even though users are moving faster, they may accomplish less because they make more mistakes. Initial performance improvements occur as users gain knowl-edge and reduce the number of missteps they make. Later performance gains occur in other ways. Optimizing the work environment, the application, and the operating system all serve to reduce the number of steps users must perform to accomplish a task. Fewer steps mean increased productivity, so it appears that users are working faster. Therefore, this chapter shows how to optimize the application, not the user.

Windows XP Shortcuts and OLE

At one time, Windows used a technology known as object linking and embedding (OLE). It's a simple concept. Microsoft needed some method for creating complex documents. Someone there decided that everything should appear as an object and then proceeded to create two methods for handling objects.

The first object-handling method is to create a pointer to the object—sort of a sign that tells where the object resides. The second method is to embed the object within the document. The original object still resides on the hard drive; Windows creates a copy of it and places it within a container document. This principle is still with us. Applications such as Microsoft Word still rely on OLE to create complex documents where objects reside within the document through links or as embedded copies. I don't go into all the details here. You can find out more about OLE at `http://www.microsoft.com/Office/ORK/034/034.htm`, `http://www.microsoft.com/Office/ORK/2000/Four/68t2_2.htm`, and `http://www.tvchannel.co.uk/knowledge/tutorials/masterclass/word/linking_and_embedding.htm`.

Let's take some time to look at a unique way Windows XP uses OLE. Every shortcut you create is a form of OLE. It's an actual link to another object on your machine. Windows XP provides some special handling for these objects.

Unlike an application that can create compound documents to hold all the linking information, Windows XP has to store that information somewhere on the drive. After all, the drive is the container that Windows XP uses to store information. The LNK file, which is Windows XP's answer to this problem, contains all the linking information needed to keep the shortcuts on your desktop current with the real object.

You can easily test this solution by creating a shortcut to a folder on your desktop. Every change you make to the real folder appears in the linked copy. Likewise, every change you make in the linked copy appears in the real thing. OLE and the desktop are a part of Windows XP.

Faster Startups

Starting an application might not seem like a big deal. After all, how many ways can you double-click an application icon? Windows XP provides more than just one or two ways to start your applications (even more than Windows 9x did). In fact, here's a whole list of ways:

- Right-click the application's icon in Explorer and then click Open in the context menu.
- Double-click the application's icon in Explorer. (If you have the single-click interface enabled, just single-click on the application's link.)

Tip: Some of you may be wondering what this "single-click" interface is all about. Microsoft made it possible for you to single-click on Windows objects just as you would single-click links on a Web page. Although some people consider single-clicking more efficient (we're talking milliseconds here), other people find it confusing. It pays to check out this feature, and enabling and disabling it is

continues

easy. However, you probably want to try it out on a single folder first. Use the Tools | Folder Options command to display the General tab of the Folder Options dialog box. Select the Single-click to Open an Item (Point to Select) option. You can also choose how Explorer underlines the filenames. Click OK. You can now use the single-click method to work with files in that folder.

- Double-click a data file associated with the application in Explorer. *File associations* make it possible for you to open both the data file and the application at the same time. Using file associations also means you don't need to care where the application program is located—Windows automatically finds it for you.

Note: Using a file association requires that you create a file association or that the application create it for you. To change file associations, open Windows Explorer, choose Tools | Folder Options, click the File Types tab, and click the Change button to define which application should open the selected file type.

- Choose Start | Run and then type the application's path and filename in the Open field. Click OK to start the application.
- Select the application's entry in the Start Menu.
- Create a shortcut icon on the desktop. You can start the application by double-clicking the icon.
- Set up your desktop to use the single-click interface, which allows you to start applications or select files more quickly.
- Assign a shortcut key to the application, and then start it by using the keyboard shortcut. (You must create an LNK file to do this. We look at the process for doing this in the "Using Shortcuts " section of Chapter 13.)
- Place the application's icon or associated data file in the Startup folder to run it automatically the next time you start Windows. Placing a data file in the Startup folder automatically opens it for you.
- Use the Search Results dialog box to find your application, and then double-click it.
- Type a data filename and path in the Explorer Address bar, and then press Enter. In many cases, you see the file open within Explorer; in other cases, Windows starts a separate application for you. Of course, this assumes that you have a file association set up for the file.
- Embed or link the application's data in an OLE compound document. The user can start the application by double-clicking the object embedded in the document. (The application must support OLE for this to work.)

At this point, you should have the basic idea. You aren't limited to performing a task in any given way under Windows XP. The only thing that limits your ability to perform a task in a new way is imagination. Even if Microsoft's help file tells you one way to perform a task and this book tells you another way, you aren't limited to those two methods. You can choose a third method, if you like.

The following sections discuss two important productivity topics. First, we discuss ways to perform Windows tasks using the keyboard. (We discuss application shortcuts in the "Application Keyboard Shortcuts" section of this chapter.) There's no doubt about it: Most users suffer a loss of efficiency in having to move their hand from the keyboard to the mouse. Using the keyboard helps you work more efficiently and with less stress when the key combination isn't something designed for contortionists.

The second important topic is using your mouse efficiently. When I create a drawing, it's actually less efficient to use the keyboard because my hand rests on the mouse most of the time. If you spend much time using the mouse, you should learn how to use it efficiently.

Startups from the Keyboard

Microsoft has actually improved keyboard use over the years—some users just don't know about it. Some keyboard shortcuts require a special keyboard (the one with the Windows key), some work for all keyboards, and still others require a special application, such as one of the Accessibility features. Table 6.1 provides a list of keystrokes and the actions they perform.

Table 6.1 Windows XP Shortcut Keys

Key Combination	Purpose
Alt+F4	Ends the selected application. You can also use this key combination to end Windows if you're at the desktop.
Alt+Shift+Tab	Switches to the previous window.
Alt+Spacebar	Displays the Control menu of the active window.
Alt+Tab	Switches to the next window.
Ctrl+Esc	Opens the Start Menu on the taskbar. You can use the arrow keys to select an application. Press Enter to start the selected application.
Esc	Cancels the last action in most cases.
sF1	Displays online help. In most cases, this help is general in nature but is application specific.
F2	Allows you to change the object name after you highlight an icon.

Key Combination	Purpose
F3	Accesses the Search Results dialog box. In most cases, you get better results if you press F3 while at the desktop. You can also use this key at the Taskbar and the Start Menu.
Left Alt+Left Shift+Num Lock	Turns on the MouseKeys feature of the Accessibility options.
Left Alt+Left Shift+Print Screen	Turns on the High Contrast feature of the Accessibility options.
Menu	A special key found on some keyboards. The key has a picture of a context menu with one item selected and a mouse pointer. Press this key to display a context menu for the selected object.
Num Lock	Held down for five seconds, this key turns on the ToggleKeys feature of the Accessibility options.
Right Shift	Held down for eight seconds, turns on the FilterKeys feature of the Accessibility options. Make sure you use the Right Shift key.
Shift five times	Turns on the StickyKeys feature of the Accessibility options when pressed five times.
Shift+F1	Displays context-sensitive help when the application supports it.
Shift+F10	Displays a context menu for the selected object.
Tab	Switches between the desktop, Taskbar, and Start Menu while you're at the desktop. You also can use Ctrl+Esc to bring up the Start Menu and then press Tab to switch between applications.
Windows	A special key found on some keyboards. The key has a flying Windows flag on it. Press this key to display the Start Menu.
Windows+F1	Starts the Help and Support Center.
Windows+B	Places the cursor in the Notification Area on the Toolbar.
Windows+D	Shows the desktop; restores minimized applications when pressed a second time.

continues

Table 6.1 Continued

Key Combination	Purpose
Windows+E	Displays a two-pane copy of Windows Explorer with My Computer selected.
Windows+F	Displays Windows Explorer with the Search Explorer Bar open.
Windows+L	Locks Windows and goes back to the Login screen.
Windows+M	Minimizes all windows.
Windows+R	Displays the Run dialog box.
Windows+Shift+M	Undoes the effect of the Windows+M combination and restores all windows.
Windows+U	Starts the Utility Manager for the Accessibility options.

Tip: Table 6.1 contains some of the most common keyboard shortcuts for Windows. However, if you need to find some of the more esoteric combinations, check out the Technophile Windows Keyboard Shortcut List at http://www.twcny.rr.com/technofile/texts/bkkeys97.html. Another list of shortcuts appears at the In Cube site at http://www.commandcorp.com/cci/keystrok.html.

If you find that you need to perform complex setups for your applications and you really need the efficiency of the keyboard, you can always try writing a script to do the job. We look at using Windows Scripting Host (WSH) in the "Using Windows Scripting Host (WSH)" section of Chapter 8. This powerful feature of Windows XP allows you to extend the capabilities of your keyboard immensely. Obviously, you have to be willing to write a script that performs the tasks you want and then assign a shortcut key to that script to allow execution from the keyboard.

Undocumented Parameters

The first program you need to learn about in order to use this section of the book is START. I started playing with it and, with the undocumented parameters that most Windows applications provide, figured out a few ways to use this program. Note that Windows 9x provides this program, but doesn't include all of the switches that the Windows XP version provides. Let's look at some documented parameters that START provides:

- *<path>* Starting directory for the program. Normally, this directory contains any data you want to work with.

- *<program name>* The name of the program you want to run and any parameters it needs in order to execute. You must place this entry last on the command line; all other START switches must appear first. START passes any switches that appear after the program name to the program you want to execute.

- <*"title"*> The title to display in the window title bar. Include the double quotes with the title.
- */ABOVENORMAL* Starts the application and runs it in the above-normal priority class.
- */B* Starts character mode applications without opening a new window. GUI applications normally create their own window as part of the startup process. Character mode applications also ignore Ctrl+C unless they implement it as part of their startup sequence. You can still use Ctrl+Break to stop the application.
- */BELOWNORMAL* Starts the application and runs it in the below-normal priority class.
- */HIGH* Starts the application and runs it in the high priority class.
- */I* Tells START to use the initial environment passed to CMD.EXE to start the application and to ignore any environment changes you might have made. This setting applies only to character mode applications.
- */LOW* Starts the application and runs it in the idle priority class. Avoid using this setting unless you don't care when the application completes its task. The only time the application receives processing cycles is if the system isn't doing anything else.
- /MAX Runs a maximized application in the background.
- /MIN Enables you to run the application minimized in the background.
- */NORMAL* Starts the application and runs it in the normal priority class. This setting is standard for all applications. It provides the application with a standard share of the background or foreground processing cycles, depending on the application status.
- */REALTIME* Starts the application and runs it in the real-time priority class. Use this setting with extreme care because it can cause the application to interfere with normal system operation. In addition, using this setting virtually guarantees that background applications will either stall or receive few processing cycles.
- */SEPARATE* Starts a 16-bit Windows application in a separate memory space.
- */SHARED* Starts a 16-bit Windows application in the shared memory space.
- /W Use this switch if you want to start a Windows application, work with it for a while, and return to the DOS prompt when you're done.
- */WAIT* Starts the application and waits for it to terminate.

All this information is fine if you want to run a Windows application from DOS. However, this information doesn't really become useful until you can get some work done in Windows without leaving the DOS prompt. What would happen if you wanted the advantage of Windows background printing while performing other work at the DOS prompt? You could switch back to Windows, start Notepad or some other appropriate application, load your file, and print, but that would disrupt what you were doing. The following line shows an easier, faster, and much better method:

```
START /MAX NOTEPAD /P SOMEFILE.TXT
```

You need to look at the specifics of this command line. The first is the /P parameter, right after NOTEPAD. Where did I get it? It isn't documented anywhere. All you have to do is look in Explorer.

Let's look at the use of parameters within Explorer now. Open Explorer. It doesn't matter what directory you're looking at. Use the Tools | Folder Options command to display the Folder Options dialog box. Click the File Types tab. Scroll through the file types until you come across an entry for Text Document. Highlight it and click Advanced. You see an Edit File Type dialog box. Highlight Print and then Edit. You should see an Edit Action dialog box. Look at the Application Used to Perform This Action field.

Now you can see where I came up with the /P parameter. Notice also that the field contains a %1 argument that passes the filename to Notepad. Press Cancel three times to get back to the main Explorer display. Every other registered application provides the same types of information. Some of them are a little too complex to use from the DOS prompt, but you can use them if you want. The whole idea of this shortcut is that you get to stay at the DOS prompt and still use the new features that Windows provides.

> **Tip:** Just about every Windows application provides undocumented command-line switches. Although you can only guess at what those switches are, in most cases you can usually count on them supporting one or two switches. The /P parameter usually allows you to print by using that application. Some applications also provide a /W parameter that suppresses the display of any opening screens. Looking through the Explorer file listings provides you with additional ideas.

There are a few other caveats you need to consider. Notice how I formatted my command line. You have to place the START program command-line switches first and then the application name, the application switches, and any filenames. If you change this order, the application usually starts, but it reports some type of error in opening your file.

Shortcut Keys

Windows XP is more user friendly than its predecessors. I find that I spend much less time at the DOS prompt now because I can get everything accomplished without it. Microsoft has enhanced the Address Bar so much in Windows that you can use it in place of a command prompt for executing commands. However, that still doesn't make me happy about moving my hand from the keyboard to the mouse to start a new application.

Remember the first section of this chapter, where I talked about the desktop and OLE? Using shortcut keys is one of those times when that fact comes into play. To use one of the keyboard shortcuts Windows XP provides, you have to create an application shortcut. It doesn't matter where the shortcut is, but it does matter that it's a shortcut.

> **Tip:** Every entry on the Start Menu is a shortcut. If your application appears on the Start Menu, you already have a shortcut to use. If the application doesn't appear on the Start Menu, you should add it there or on the desktop.

To get the ball rolling, let's look at the Notepad shortcut on the Start Menu. All you need to do is open the Start Menu (press Ctrl+Esc and then Esc), open the context menu (Shift+F10), and select Explore. Use a combination of the arrow keys (the right arrow opens new levels in the hierarchy) and Tab to get to the Notepad shortcut. Press Shift+F10 to display Notepad's context menu. Select Properties and press Enter. You need to select the Shortcut tab.

The Shortcut Key field of this dialog box is where you enter the shortcut key combination you want to use. Select the field now and press the Ctrl+Shift+N keys. The key combination will show up in the field. To save the setting, just close the dialog box as usual. The next time you press that key combination, Windows XP opens the application for you.

Startups from the Desktop

Windows used to come installed with several applications already on the desktop. Windows XP comes with a clean desktop because Microsoft studies concluded that desktop icons confused users. In many cases, applications still install an icon on the desktop to make them easier to access. Just like the Start Menu, none of these icons represents the actual application. You create a shortcut to the application, as you would for the Start Menu.

Of course, the big question is why you would even consider adding an application shortcut to the desktop. The big reason is convenience: It's faster to grab an application on the desktop than to burrow through several layers of menu to find it. On the other hand, your desktop has only so much space, so placing all your applications there would lead to a cluttered environment very quickly. In addition, remember from Chapter 5, "Performance Primer," that each icon uses memory, so you need to consider whether the efficiency you gain is worth the memory you use by adding an icon.

However, placing one or two icons on the desktop or Quick Launch toolbar for applications you use regularly could mean an increase in efficiency. Just think how nice it would be if your word processor and communications program were just a double-click away. You could open them as needed and close them immediately after you finished using them. This would mean that the applications you used most would still be handy, but would be out of the way and wouldn't use up precious memory.

> **Tip:** Keyboard users will probably get the same response time by using shortcut keys instead of placing their applications on the desktop. This gives you a neater-looking desktop and reduces the number of redundant links your computer has to maintain.

Placing a shortcut to your application on the desktop can provide an increase in efficiency, but double-clicking isn't the only way to open an application. The next few sections describe other ways you can access your applications faster by placing shortcuts to them on the desktop. The section "The Data-Oriented Approach to Applications," later in this chapter, also looks at something new for Windows XP. You really owe it to yourself to get out of application-centric mode and take the new datacentric approach.

Click Starts

Right-clicking displays a context menu for Windows XP objects. Previous chapters took a quick look at the context menu. However, it's such an important concept that I feel we need to take a special look at right-clicking for applications.

To start an application this way, all you need to do is select the Open option from the context menu. This has the same effect as double-clicking, but it might be more convenient if you have slower fingers. Some people really do have a hard time getting the double-click to work. This new method of starting an application has the advantage of requiring only a single click.

> **Tip:** Try setting up your desktop to use single clicks rather than double-clicks if you have trouble double-clicking fast enough to start applications or open files. All you need to do to enable single-clicking is use the Tools | Folder Options command in Windows Explorer to display the Folder Options dialog box. Choose the Single-Click to Open an Item option, and then click OK to make the change complete.

Auto Starts

Windows XP provides a Startup folder to run specific applications every time you start your machine. All you need to do is add an application to the Startup folder to allow it to run automatically. I always start a copy of Explorer this way so that my machine is ready for use the instant Windows completes the boot process.

The Startup folder comes in handy for other tasks as well. I usually drag the data files I'm going to be working on for the next few days into my Startup folder. The reason is simple: I not only automatically start the application associated with that data file, but also automatically load the file itself. This makes morning startups extremely efficient. When I get back to Windows after starting it, my machine is completely set up for use. Every application I need is already loaded with the files I want to edit.

Peter's Principle: Becoming Too Efficient for Your Own Good

Have you ever seen the "ransom note" effect produced by someone who's just discovered the joy of using multiple fonts in a document? To that person, it looks like the most incredible document he has ever produced. The rest of us think the document is incredible too, but not for the same reason.

You can get into the same kind of habit with Windows XP and its advanced features. Consider the Startup folder. It would be very easy for people to load every document they think they'll use for the entire week so that the documents would be ready when they booted the machine the next morning.

The best way to use this feature is to think about what you plan to do first thing the next morning or perhaps for the majority of the day. Don't open more than two or three documents unless they all use the same application. Someone who works on the same document, such as a writer, can really benefit from this feature. People who create presentations or work on other documents for long intervals can also benefit. However, if you work a little bit on one document and then a little bit on another, you might be better off starting the main application you use and letting it go at that.

So, how do you add entries to the Startup folder? Just as you would with any other folder. Anything you place in the Startup folder executes or opens the next time you start Windows. I recommend two methods for getting the "objects" placed in the Startup folder.

The first technique is for those who have good manual dexterity. Right-click a data or executable file and then drag it to the Start Menu. Don't release the file when the Start Menu opens. Continue to drag the file to the Programs folder, which opens, and then to the Startup folder. Release the right mouse button. You see a context menu asking what you want to do. Select Create Shortcuts Here from the list. If you make a mistake at any time during this process, simply select Cancel from the context menu. The reason you use a right-drag versus a left-drag is to gain the ability to cancel the action.

The second technique is to place a shortcut to the Startup Folder on the Desktop. Locate the Startup folder in the Start Menu. Right-click the folder and then drag it to the desktop. Release the right mouse button. Select Create Shortcuts Here from the context menu, and you see a copy of the Startup folder on your desktop. Open this folder and add anything you want to start automatically the next morning. You can use any of the other techniques we discussed in this book for accomplishing this task if dragging the folder isn't appealing. For example, you could right-click the Start Menu, select Explore from the context menu, and then drag a copy of the Startup folder from Explorer to the desktop.

After you complete this task, the application or data file you added to the Startup folder loads automatically each time you start Windows XP. Getting your system set up efficiently means that you can do a little extra reading or perform some other task while you wait for everything to load. Of course, adding a file to the load sequence doesn't make it load faster, but it gives you a bigger block of time.

Controlled Starts

We don't spend much time on the controlled-starts method of starting your application because you're already familiar with most of what you can do. Everyone is familiar with double-clicking an application to start it. The fact that Windows XP provides so many places to double-click doesn't change the mechanics one iota. It might be useful, though, to take a quick look at the number of ways you can double-click to start an application. The following list does just that:

- *Explorer* You can double-click an application or its associated data files. This interface also supports dynamic data exchange (DDE). DDE is an ancient (Windows 3.x and earlier) method of transferring information between applications. You need to know something about the application to use it. DDE requires the application name and path as usual. It also requires the Registry application name (for example, WinWord for Word), the topic of conversation (normally, System), and the DDE message. The message part is difficult to figure out in some cases. For example, if you want to open a document in Word, you would send the [FileOpen("%1")] DDE message (including the square brackets).
- *Search Results* The Search Results dialog box comes in very handy. You can look for a data file and then double-click it to bring up the application associated with it. I've also used this dialog box as a quick method of finding the program I need.
- *Desktop* Any data file or application on the desktop follows the same rules as Explorer.
- *My Network Places* You can double-click any application or file on someone else's machine.

Well, that's the long and short of double-clicking. You can always use the old controlled-start method (that we all know and love) to start an application. I hope this section provided some food for thought on other—perhaps better—ways of using the Windows XP interface.

Tuning the Start Menu

Organizing your Start Menu is probably the best time you'll ever invest in making yourself more efficient. You need to overcome two problems when organizing your Start Menu.

First, Microsoft sets Windows XP up with a Start Menu it finds most efficient. I don't find that setup particularly convenient, so I adjust it as needed for my purposes. For example, I like to play games during my spare time, so the Games menu appears right under Programs in the hierarchy, rather than getting buried several levels deep. I also create a Maintenance folder. It contains all of the tools that Microsoft provides, plus the third-party tools, such as the test application for my network interface card (NIC). I also stuff important diagnostic programs and anything else that helps me troubleshoot my machine in this folder.

Second, every third-party vendor I know of places its application folder right under the Programs folder. As you add applications to your system, the number of folders under the Programs folder increases. Eventually, the Programs folder starts to scroll because your screen can no longer hold all the application folders. Finding anything is problematic because you can't even see the entire Start Menu any more.

I solve the organization problem by using several approaches. The first is to create folders in the Start Menu that fulfill my needs. For example, the Maintenance folder is one item I always add. The Games folder already exists, but I move it to a new location to ensure that I can find it when I want to play a game. In both cases, you can move any applications that fit within the folder category to the new location. This move alone helps keep the Start Menu organized, or at least easy to see.

To create a new folder in the Start Menu, right-click Start and select Explore from the context menu. Find the location for the new folder in the details pane. Right-click the details pane and choose New | Folder from the context menu. Type the folder name you want to see within the Start Menu.

> **Tip:** Moving files and folders around in the Start Menu is as easy as dragging the object where you want to see it. Using a right-drag doesn't allow you to cancel the action, in this case, so make sure that you place the file or folder where you want it the first time.

If you think ahead and the application cooperates, you don't even have to move the application folders. Many installation programs allow you to specify something other than the default location for the application folder. Unfortunately, the installation instructions don't normally tell you how to do this. All you need to do is add the name of the top-level folder and a backslash in front of the default folder name. For example, if your NIC maintenance program installs in the 3COM folder, you might type Maintenance\3COM rather than use the default of 3COM. Some older installation programs don't allow you to use this technique, but it's worth a try.

Getting the files and folders organized is a good first step, but it isn't the only one you should take. Sorting the entries makes them easier to find. You can perform this task in one of two ways. First, you can right-click the menu and then select Sort By Name from the context menu. This sorts only the current menu. If you want to sort all the menus, right-click the Taskbar and choose Properties from the context menu. Select the Start Menu tab on the Taskbar and Start Menu Properties dialog box. Click Customize. Click Sort. Click OK twice to close the dialog boxes. Unfortunately, this second approach works on only the classic Start Menu.

The Data-Oriented Approach to Applications

Windows XP shines when it comes to data. In fact, the whole interface is oriented toward datacentric access. The next few sections discuss some of the tools Windows XP provides to make a data-oriented approach easier.

Using Explorer to Get the Job Done

We've taken a look at Explorer in several sections of this book already. However, we haven't looked at one important feature. Windows XP no longer ties you to one action when it comes to data on your machine. If you've looked at the various context menus presented so far, you've noticed that there's always more than one thing you can do to a particular file. What you might not have realized is that the actions you saw are all under your control. You don't have to do things the Windows XP way; you can do them any way that feels comfortable and enables you to get your work done faster.

> **Tip:** The first time you double-click a file that lacks a file association, Windows XP asks which application you want to use to open it. You can choose an application that's already on the list or use the Browse feature to find a new one. Windows XP defines only one action for this new association—Open. Always take the time to modify that file association and add options for all the ways you plan to work with it. That way, the context menu associated with it is completely set up the next time you right-click the file or any others like it.

Let's look at how you can add a new file extension and then define a set of actions associated with that file:

1. Open a copy of Windows Explorer.

2. Use the Tools | Folder Options command to open the Folder Options dialog box. Click the File Types tab.

3. Click New to display the Create New Extension dialog box.

4. Type **ASCII** in the File Extension field and then click OK. Windows Explorer displays the new file extension in the Registered File Types list.

5. Highlight the ASCII entry and then click Advanced. You see an Edit File Type dialog box. Notice the field at the top along with the "blank" icon space and the Change Icon button. These three elements describe your file type.

6. Type **ASCII Text File** as the file type description. Click Change Icon. Windows Explorer displays a Change Icon dialog box with SHELL32.DLL loaded. This is the default icon file. You use the Browse button to locate executable files associated with a new file type. For now, locate the star icon used for the Favorites folder and then click OK. You've defined the file type description; now it's time to create some actions for it.

7. Click the New button. Fill in the fields in the New Action dialog box, as shown in Figure 6.1. (This is just one way to fill in this dialog box.) Notepad uses a command-line interface, so you just need to fill out the Application Used to Perform Action section of the dialog box. Click OK.

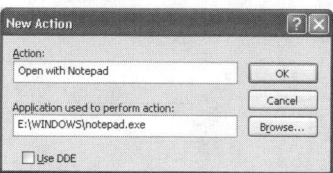

FIGURE 6.1
Many applications require only a command-line interface when using them for a file association.

8. Create the same kind of entry for WordPad. Be sure to substitute WORDPAD.EXE for the location and change the path as necessary. (WordPad normally resides in the \Program Files\Windows NT\Accessories\wordpad.exe directory.) Also, change the Action field to read Open with WordPad.

9. Click the New button. Fill out the information as shown in Figure 6.2. This second type of association might look overly complicated, but it isn't really. It's the DDE format of a file association and an extremely powerful way to manage your data files. The DDE instructions form what equates to macros. They actually force the application to perform the same types of tasks you would accomplish by using a menu or built-in macro capability. You should try to use DDE macros if your application provides the required support. Most Microsoft Office products provide DDE support, and Microsoft documents the DDE interface in the Office help files.

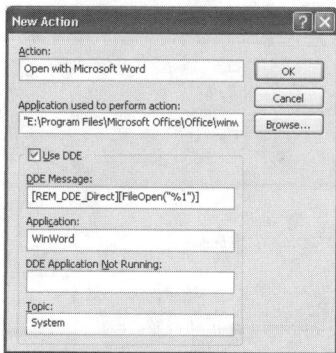

FIGURE 6.2
This DDE entry enables you to include macro-like instructions that control the way the application works with the file.

10. Click OK. After you finish this entry, you should see in the Edit File Type dialog box three entries like the ones shown in Figure 6.3. Notice the three check boxes near the bottom of the dialog box. The first, Confirm Open After Download, tells Windows to display a dialog box asking whether you want to open the file after you download it from the Internet. The second check box, Always Show

Extension, enables you to display file extensions at all times. Normally, you'd leave this cleared to make it easier to rename files in Explorer without accidentally changing their extensions. However, I set this option for any file type that someone might send me over the Internet so that I can verify the extension within the e-mail attachment. The third check box, Browse in Same Window, enables you to view the file without opening a new copy of the browser.

FIGURE 6.3

A completed Edit File Type dialog box contains a file type description and set of actions.

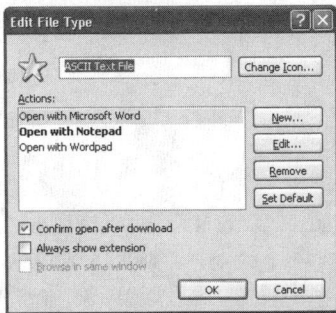

11. Highlight Open with Notepad and click Set Default. This sets the double-click action for the file type. You can right-click to display the full context menu and use a different application to open the file, but this is the default action. Click OK to complete the process. Click Close to close the Folder Options dialog box.

12. Create a new file with an ASCII extension. I placed my copy in Windows Explorer for sample purposes, but you can put your copy anywhere.

13. Right-click the file. You should see a list of opening options similar to the ones shown in Figure 6.4. Note that Explorer highlights the Open with Notepad entry, indicating that it's the default setting.

FIGURE 6.4

The result of the new file association is an extended context menu that enables any of three applications to open the file.

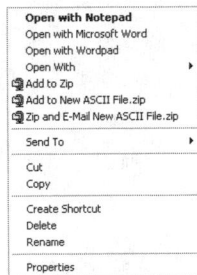

You can do a few other things to extend this new file association. Because you just added a new text-file entry to the list of file associations, you can use the Registry to add a ShellEx entry as well. That way, when you right-click the desktop or within Explorer, you see the new file extension as one of the file types you can create using the New option of the context menu.

Here's an experiment to try if you want to see the New menu in action. (Only expert users should attempt to add this temporary ShellEx entry to the Registry.) You find the required key at HKEY_CURRENT_USER\Software\Microsoft\Windows\CurrentVersion \Explorer\Discardable\PostSetup\ShellNew. You need to add a new entry for the ASCII file type we created earlier. Right-click in the right pane and select New | Binary Value from the context menu. For a value name, I used ASCII File in this case. For a value, I usually copy the value from another entry and then modify it for my needs. Using the Text Document entry is a good idea because it's a simple entry without any added information.

You find three areas you need to modify using the Edit Binary Value dialog box. The first value determines the name of the file you'll create. I replaced Text Document with ASCII File. If you make this substitution, you'll notice that ASCII File is shorter than Text Document. You must replace the remaining letters with 00 on the left side of the editor. The value must remain the same length.

The next entry is the file extension. You replace .txt with .ASCII in this case. The value must match the entry in the Registry exactly or else the shell extension doesn't work.

The final entry is the file association value. This varies by extension, but you can find it by looking at the extension in HKEY_CLASSES_ROOT. The text document entry uses an easy-to-remember value of txtfile. The .ASCII association I created uses a relatively hard-to-remember value of ft000001. At this point, you can save the new entry.

We're not done yet. You need to find the file extension entry in the Registry. For the .ASCII extension, it's HKEY_CLASSES_ROOT\.ASCII. You need to add a new key, at this point, called ShellNew. Look at the .txt entry as an example. You must add a string value named NullFile to this key, but don't assign it any value. At this point, you can right-click in Windows Explorer and see ASCII File listed as one of the types under the New menu, as shown in Figure 6.5. Select this entry, and you create a new file of the .ASCII type.

FIGURE 6.5
The results of adding the ASCII file type to the New menu.

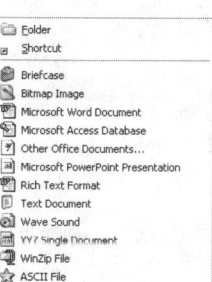

Although this example isn't permanent (it lasts for only one file creation), it shows the mechanism in place for creating new files using the New menu. This example also shows you something else: Productivity under Windows XP depends as much as anything else on how you configure the desktop and file associations. Being able to use the speed of your machine is what this datacentric approach to computing allows.

Folders: A Real Organizational Tool

Folders are essentially the containers of the Windows world. So how do folders help you work efficiently? Folders support a context menu. As with most objects in Windows XP, you can open and explore them. This isn't surprising by now. I was a little surprised when I saw that you could copy and paste folders just like you can with any other object. Putting a group of files in a folder enables you to move an entire project from place to place or make a copy of the data for someone else to use.

The Sharing and Security option of the context menu enables you to share the folder with other folks on the network. Chapter 21, "Networks," covers this feature in detail.

You'll find the Send To option very useful. This option enables you to place the folder somewhere else. Default locations include the floppy drives and Briefcase. You even can send the folder to Microsoft Exchange. Imagine using e-mail to send the folder to a partner or coworker who needs to see the information you've put together. Unlike past experiences in which I had to get all the files together and zip them up, this option is convenient and really makes the workflow smoother.

I use the Create Shortcut option to create a link to the existing file. Then I move the shortcut to my desktop or another convenient location. Each shortcut uses about 1KB of memory, a small price to pay for the convenience that shortcuts provide.

Chapter 21 covers the Properties option in detail. For right now, all you need to know is that the files and folders share many of the same characteristics. The Properties dialog box reflects this fact.

Desktop Tips and Techniques

I've gone to a totally datacentric approach on my desktop when it comes to projects. All I do is create a folder, give it a project name, and then gather shortcuts to everything I need for that project in that folder. It doesn't matter any more where the data resides or what application I need to use to open the file. The only important element is that I have a data file that needs editing, so I open the project folder and double-click its icon.

This datacentric approach is important for managers. Think about the time you save by putting together one folder and then mailing that folder to all the people who have to work on it. You control the location of the data and the type of access these people have to it. They need to know only that the data exists and that they can access it as needed.

You'll experience some problems with the totally datacentric approach. At times, you need to open an application rather than a piece of data. For example, I keep NetMeeting handy on the desktop. I can't access any of its data from outside the application. My database manager sits on the desktop too, but that's for a different reason. I use Access to design databases more often than I use it for data entry, so for me it's more important to work with the application.

You'll probably run into situations in which working with the application is more important than working with the data. The bottom line is that you should try to work with the data first. If this solution proves to be inconvenient, the datacentric approach probably isn't correct for that situation. The following is a list of some of the types of data I work with, using the project folder approach I just described. You probably have some of these applications, too:

- *Word processing* Every word processor is designed to work primarily with data, so it makes a perfect candidate for the datacentric approach. Microsoft Word even appears on the New submenu of the context menu; this icon shows that there isn't any problem with creating new files without entering the word processor first. There's one minor inconvenience: Word always creates a new document using the Normal template. This means that if I use the context menu to create a new file, I'll probably have to change the template after I open the file. It's a minor flaw, but an irritating one. (Microsoft has fixed this problem with later versions of Microsoft Office—you now find an Other Office Documents option on your New submenu that displays a New Office Document dialog box containing all of the templates in your Office Templates folder. Just choose a template to create a document of that type.)

- *Spreadsheets* I seldom open just one spreadsheet. If I open one at all, I use the program for hours. Therefore, I stick all my major files in a folder and place it on my desktop. That way, I can at least open a data file that stays open throughout most of the editing session. I usually end up opening the other files I need using File | Open.

- *Graphics* I work with quite a few different types of graphics, each of which requires its own application. Keeping the graphic files in a folder and opening them that way makes perfect sense. Graphics are one application type that made me see the value of a datacentric approach.

Application Keyboard Shortcuts

We've already covered the Windows keyboard shortcuts you can use. Some of these shortcuts also work in applications. For example, press Alt+F4 and your application exits. If you press Shift+F1, you normally receive context-sensitive help.

Tip: Many Web sites provide lists of keyboard shortcuts. One of the best places to find keyboard shortcuts for Microsoft applications is http://www.microsoft.com/enable/products/keyboard/keyboardsearch.asp. The Bud's Troubleshooter site at http://www.geocities.com/~budallen/hotkeys.html also offers some unique keyboarding advice. You can find the documented Microsoft keyboard shortcuts at http://support.microsoft.com/support/kb/articles/q126/4/49.asp.

So which application keyboard shortcuts do you need to know about? Table 6.2 contains a list of shortcuts that I find work with many applications. They don't work with every application, but trying them doesn't hurt. The point is that these key combinations are undocumented, in some cases, so knowing that they exist is the only way you can use them.

Table 6.2 Common Application Keyboard Shortcuts

Key Combination	Purpose
Ctrl+Arrow	Moves the cursor across the document one word or object at a time.
Ctrl+A	Selects the entire document.
Ctrl+B	Toggles bold text mode.
Ctrl+C	Copies the highlighted data to the Clipboard.
Ctrl+D	Toggles between monospace and proportional fonts for some applications. In other cases, it displays the Font dialog box.
Ctrl+E	Centers the object within the document area.
Ctrl+F	Displays the Find or Search dialog box.
Ctrl+G	Displays the Goto dialog box when available.
Ctrl+H	Displays the Replace dialog box.
Ctrl+I	Toggles italics text mode. Also acts as an insert function for some applications.
Ctrl+J	Justifies text within the current or selected document. This key combination has no effect on other object types.
Ctrl+K	Varies by application. For example, this key combination creates a hyperlink in some versions of Word.
Ctrl+L	Places the object on the left side of the document area.
Ctrl+M	Varies by application. In Word, the key combination acts as a formatting tool. In other applications, it performs functions such as sending a file to another location via e-mail.
Ctrl+N	Creates a new document.
Ctrl+O	Displays the Open dialog box so that you can select a file.
Ctrl+P	Prints the selected document. In most cases, the application displays a Print dialog box.
Ctrl+Q	Quits the application in most cases.
Ctrl+R	Places the object on the right side of the document area.
Ctrl+S	Saves the current document or displays a Save dialog box.

Key Combination	Purpose
Ctrl+T	Varies by application. In Word, the key combination acts as a formatting tool. Most applications don't assign a task to this key combination.
Ctrl+U	Toggles underline text mode.
Ctrl+V	Pastes the selected (highlighted) data in the Clipboard.
Ctrl+W	Varies by application. This key combination toggles word wrap in many text editors.
Ctrl+X	Cuts the highlighted data to the Clipboard.
Ctrl+Y	Varies by application. In Word, the key combination acts as a formatting tool. In other applications, it performs a delete function, such as deleting a line of text or the highlighted object.
Ctrl+Z	Undoes the last action.
Shift+Arrow	Selects text in the direction of arrow movement.

Tip: Although not a keyboard shortcut, this mouse shortcut has saved me many hours. Press Alt and then drag the mouse cursor. Some applications allow you to perform a column select.

On Your Own

Try adding a shortcut to the Startup folder on your desktop. Tonight, place in that folder any work you need to do tomorrow. Watch what happens when you start your machine tomorrow morning. You should get a desktop that has automatically loaded all the work you need to do.

Start separating your work into projects, if possible. Place each project in a separate folder on the desktop. Use separate folders, if necessary, to make it easier to find a particular kind of data. For example, you might need to place your graphics files in one sub-folder to keep them from crowding the text files.

Look through your drives for data files that Windows XP can't associate with a particular application. In Explorer, add any new file extensions you might need, using the procedure discussed earlier. Check out each new association as you add it. Does the new addition work as anticipated? After a few weeks, evaluate the results you get to see if you need to add more options to the data file context menu.

Try using both Windows and application keyboard shortcuts. See which shortcuts save time and determine which simply cause frustration. The point of using a new method is to save time and effort. A keyboard shortcut can help by keeping your hands on the keyboard. On the other hand, some keyboard shortcuts require the services of a contortionist and don't do much to help you out.

PART III

Advanced Windows XP Usage Techniques

Windows XP Configuration

Some people install Windows and immediately begin installing applications. The reasons vary from not knowing there's anything else to do to not having time to do much else. The ideal setup sequence is to install Windows, install any required patches, check for hardware problems, and configure the system. If you do all this before you begin installing applications, you'll find that your system experiences fewer problems, runs faster, and is more reliable and more stable.

However, unlike installation, configuration is an ongoing process. You need to change the configuration of your machine every time the hardware or application set changes. In some cases, you may want to change the configuration of your machine as you gain experience or your needs change.

This chapter helps you understand how to configure your system. We may not look at every nuance of configuration, but you'll know about the tools required to perform the task. I continue to discuss configuration requirements as this book progresses. For example, the hardware chapters show you how to configure your hardware, while the networking chapters discuss network configuration issues.

The two most important configuration tools are the applets in the Control Panel and the Microsoft Management Console (MMC) snap-ins. We discuss both of these tools in this chapter. As part of working with the Control Panel, you learn about the purpose of each applet it contains and see how that applet can help you configure your system. The MMC section shows you how to create your own consoles as well as use the default consoles that Microsoft provides.

You'll also learn how to install new features, an important part of the configuration process. For example, you'll learn what to do when you need a new networking or printing component. The discussion also includes a section on working with power. We look into what you need to do when installing a UPS because this part of the Windows configuration process is far from automatic.

Configuring the Windows XP Applets

One topic we haven't covered yet is the process of installing and removing applets on your system. Part of the installation process always involves configuring an applet before you use it.

When you install Dial-Up Networking, for example, Windows XP automatically asks you for information regarding your computer setup. You can't network without a telephone number, so it makes sense that Windows XP would ask about this information before it completes the installation process.

The same reasoning holds true the first time you start Backup. Although Windows XP automatically takes care of the configuration, it displays a dialog box telling you that it got the job done (in this case, creating a set of backup files for you). You can use the sample file as the basis for your own configuration sets. That's one of the reasons that Backup creates it for you. The other is that you can't perform a backup without at least some idea of what to do. This sample file can help you learn how Backup works. The following list outlines the methods of installing applets on your system, as described in the following four sections:

- The standard method I cover initially is the one you're probably most familiar with. It enables you to install or remove standard Windows XP features.

- The section "Special Utility Installation" tells you how to install some of the extra utilities Windows XP provides. You use this procedure to install the Windows XP Resource Kit and other utilities the standard user probably shouldn't know about. Make sure that you read any text files provided with these utilities because you're unlikely to find sufficient documentation elsewhere.

- Many third-party vendors provide printer utilities that help you manage this resource better when using certain types of printers. Most of those utilities come with a standard Setup application now, so you don't have to worry about any special installation technique. However, a few vendors still supply utilities that rely on the older installation method, or you may have an older printer that still uses this technique. I tell you how to install them in the "Special Printer Installation" section.

- Finally, some third-party vendors provide network-management tools with their products. You'll find the installation procedure for them in the "Special Network Installation section. The only time you'll use this section is if you have a special client, service, or protocol to install for your network. Some management tools fall into the service category or require the installation of a special client. You use this procedure in those instances.

Part of the reasoning behind this four-layered approach to installation is the nature of the applets themselves: They aren't all necessarily applets in the full sense of the word. You can't really execute them and expect something useful to happen. Some of them are halfway between a driver and an applet. Other types of applets work almost as TSRs, helping Windows XP to monitor specific items of information in the background.

Standard Installation and Removal

You start the standard installation in the Control Panel. Just double-click the Add or Remove Programs applet and click Add/Remove Windows Components. You see a Windows Component Wizard dialog box. If you look through the list of applications you can install, you see all the familiar utility programs Windows provides.

> **Note:** Older versions of Windows required you to jump through hoops to install some types of network management tools. Windows XP installs most network management tools by default, supplies them through the Windows XP Resource Kit, or places them in one of the Windows Component Wizard folders, such as Management and Monitoring tools or Networking Services. We discuss how to access common network management tools in the "Working with Microsoft Management Console" section of this chapter.

Completing this particular installation process is easy. Just check the items you want to install and click Next. The Add/Remove Programs applet takes care of the rest. You might need to supply a disk or two if you aren't using the CD-ROM installation. Otherwise, Windows XP automates the rest of the process.

Most Windows XP applets wait until you run them the first time to detect the required configuration information automatically or to ask you to supply it. Some of them, however, ask for this information immediately if they provide a system service. For example, installing modem support requires an immediate answer because the system never knows when it'll need that information.

Special Utility Installation

The CD-ROM contains some utilities that don't appear in the Add/Remove Programs Properties dialog box. Many of these utilities appear in either the \SUPPORT or the \VALUEADD directories of the distribution disk. You need to know they exist, so read about them in one of the README files on the CD-ROM or do a little exploring, as I did. It's surprising to see just how many different utilities the CD-ROM contains.

To check your CD-ROM, just use Explorer's Search Explorer Bar to look for INF, MSI, or SETUP.EXE files. Only the INF files require a special setup. MSI and SETUP.EXE files allow you to perform a standard application setup. Ignore any INF files you find in the \I386 directory because Windows XP uses those files directly or you use them as part of a standard installation. It's usually safe to assume that any INF files you see in other areas on the CD-ROM have something to do with an applet's installation routine.

The CD-ROM has many INF files, and it's difficult to tell which ones you want to have installed on your machine. Knowing that the files exist provides some information, however. Many INF files contain notes about the application they're supposed to work with. The CD folders that hold INF files and their associated applications might provide README files as well.

After you decide that an applet will meet your needs, the first thing you need to do is decide what type of installation to perform. You'll find that some of these applets are general-purpose utilities; use the following procedure to install them. Other applets require special installation. Use the procedure in the "Special Printer Installation" section to install printer-specific applets. Likewise, use the procedure in the "Special Network Installation" section for any network-related applets. Using the correct installation procedure ensures that you'll get a useable utility when you finish. When in doubt, use this general-purpose installation and test the application to see whether it works.

To perform a special utility installation, right-click the INF file and choose Install from the context menu. In some cases, the utility installs without any outward sign that something has happened. You need to check for the utility in the Control Panel, the Start Menu, MMC, or other specialized areas. Most utilities display a splash screen telling you that they're ready to install. You might see a progress indicator for longer installations. Finally, the installer will tell you that the installation process is complete.

Note: Unlike previous versions of Windows, special utilities normally appear in the standard Add or Remove Programs dialog box rather than in the Windows Component Wizard. You can remove the utility by highlighting it and clicking Remove. Follow any special instructions the uninstall routine may provide.

Special Printer Installation

Windows XP provides some special printer support. It would seem that you should use the standard installation methods to install these applets, but Microsoft decided to take a different path. The printer applet installation looks almost the same as a printer installation, with a few important differences.

To begin the installation process, open the Printers and Faxes folder and double-click the Add Printer icon. You should see the Add Printer Wizard opening display. Click Next to get past the opening display. Select Local printer attached to this computer, clear the automatic-detection option, and click Next to get to the next screen. When working with a Plug and Play–compatible local printer, you have the option of allowing Windows XP to detect it automatically. Select a port for the printer and click Next to get to the next screen. Note that you can create special port types, like a TCP/IP port, on this dialog box. You'll now see a list of standard printers that Windows XP supports.

Tip: Microsoft is constantly updating the drivers for existing printers and adding new ones to the list. Clicking the Windows Update button when you see the list of supported printers allows your machine to connect to the Windows Update Web site on the Internet. This site may contain additional print drivers you can use when setting up a new printer.

Click the Have Disk button to display the Install from Disk dialog box. Click the Browse button and use the Open dialog box to find the applet's INF file. Double-click this file to add its name to the Copy Manufacturer's Files From field of the Install from Disk dialog box. Click OK to complete the selection process. Windows XP displays a dialog box. Use the Add Printer Wizard dialog box to select the applets you want to install. Notice that the method of listing the potential resource has changed.

Windows XP copies some files to disk and then asks some additional questions based on the type of resource you want to install. Following the prompts is easy, and adding the applet should resemble the process of adding a printer.

Special Network Installation

Third-party vendors might provide special network administration tools for your hardware or network application. As with the printer-specific resources, you don't use the standard installation routine to add these applets to your system. The following procedure helps you perform a special network installation:

1. Right-click My Network Places and choose Properties from the context menu. You see a Network Connections dialog box.

2. Right-click the Local Area Connection icon and then choose Properties from the context menu. You see a Local Area Connection Properties dialog box.

3. Click Install. Highlight the type of network component you want to install (service, in most cases) and then click Add. If you've chosen to install a service, you see a Select Network Service dialog box.

4. Click Have Disk to display the Install from Disk dialog box.

5. Click Browse and use the Open dialog box to find the applet's INF file. Double-click this file to add its name to the Copy Manufacturer's Files From field of the Install from Disk dialog box.

6. Click OK to complete the selection process. Use the Select Network Service dialog box to select the applets you want to install. Notice that the method of listing the potential resource has changed.

7. Click OK. Windows XP copies some files to disk and then displays the Network dialog box with a new entry added.

Control Panel

Few people ever get comfortable with the Control Panel. You access it to change a major hardware or software configuration item; then you leave and you don't come back to it until your system needs adjustment again. In other words, you don't visit the Control Panel on a daily basis.

The reason I bring up this point is simple: This lack of contact with the Control Panel is probably the reason that some people seem to forget it's there. I've spent hours trying to figure out how to change certain settings in the Control Panel. It's not just that the Control Panel is difficult to use or illogically laid out, but rather that too few people have experience with it.

> **Tip:** You can "expand" the Start | Settings | Control Panel option so that you can pick an applet rather than open the full window. Select the Expand Control Panel option on the Customize Classic Start Menu dialog box (accessible from the Start Menu tab of the Taskbar and Start Menu Properties dialog box).

The following sections introduce you to the Control Panel. They help you see the significance of this portion of Windows in the overall configuration scheme. You also learn about new Windows XP features that make the Control Panel easier to use.

Standard versus Advanced Control Panel View

One of the goals of Windows XP is to simplify the user interface, including the Control Panel. This means using descriptive text, adding help, and reducing the number of visual options for the typical user. For example, Windows XP ships with the "clean desktop" in an effort to reduce user confusion.

Figure 7.1 shows a typical view of the standard Control Panel folder (also known as Category view). Notice the simplified interface compared to the advanced Control Panel (also known as Classic view) that appears in Figure 7.2. Category view always presents the same icons, so the learning curve for this setup is minimal. No two classic Control Panels are alike, however. The classic Control Panel usually contains a set of default icons and a series of icons related to your particular system configuration.

FIGURE 7.1
The standard Control Panel offers a simplified view that allows access to common configuration needs.

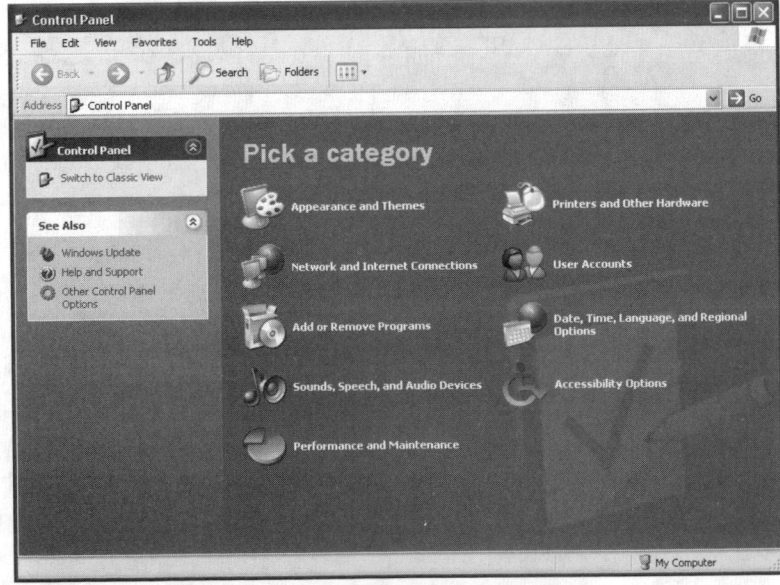

FIGURE 7.2

The advanced Control Panel offers better access to all Windows XP configuration features, but at the cost of complexity.

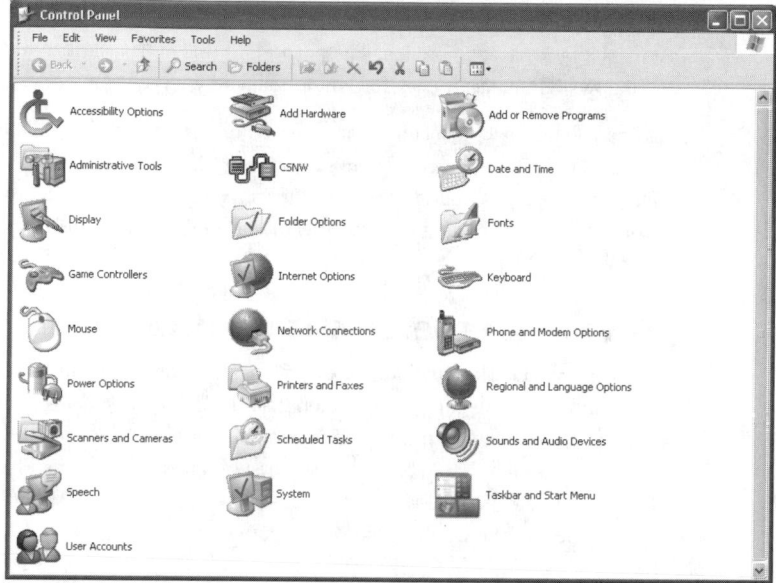

Using the category Control Panel differs from the classic Control Panel. When you use the classic Control Panel, you'll see dialog boxes that allow you to configure system resources directly. You receive little help from the operating system when making decisions.

The category Control Panel simplifies the entire process. The operating system continues to hide direct system settings and prompts you for input instead. Figure 7.3 is a typical view of a task-based category Control Panel.

FIGURE 7.3

The category Control Panel uses a task-based approach to managing system configuration needs.

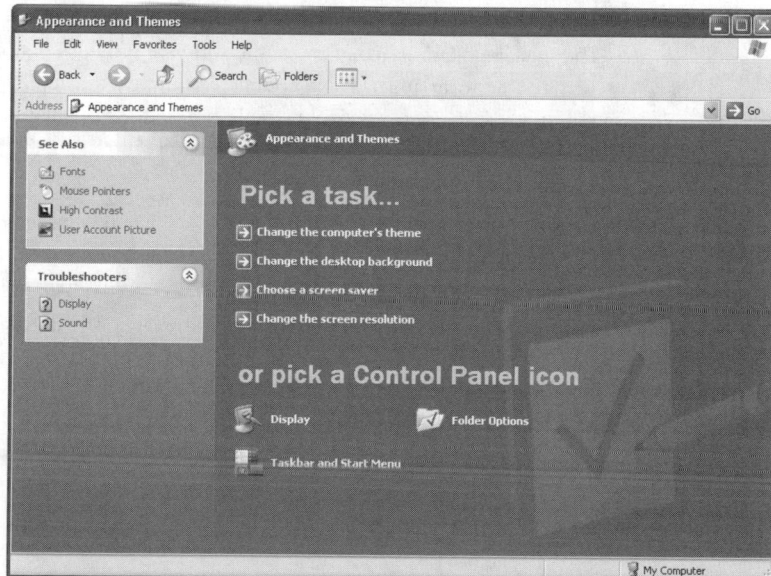

Notice that you can still choose a Control Panel icon, although the interface definitely favors a task-based approach. The purpose of this approach is to hide complexity. Windows XP makes it easy for you to manage your system.

After you do select a specific option based on task choices, the dialog boxes look the same as the ones you access using the classic Control Panel. The Themes tab of the Display Properties dialog box looks the same as the one you access with the classic Control Panel. The main difference is one of understanding how you get to the dialog box you need.

A View of the Classic Control Panel

As mentioned earlier, the classic Control Panel offers a variable number of applets depending on which applications you install and which Windows XP features you use. Now might be a good time to check out some of the applets in the Control Panel. Some of them seem familiar because we've already talked about them elsewhere in this book. Others are new because we haven't really covered them yet. The following list provides an overview of the Control Panel's primary contents:

- *Accessibility Options* We visit the shortcuts for this particular applet in the "Access for Users with Disabilities" section of Chapter 15. These options enable you to change some Windows XP features to make them easier to operate for people challenged in various ways. For example, this applet helps you to enable the StickyKeys option for the keyboard.

- *Add Hardware* Use this icon to add hardware to your system. Windows XP can automatically detect most modern hardware. You can also manually install the hardware when Windows XP can't detect it. We discuss this applet more in the "Installing and Deleting Devices" section of Chapter 9.

- *Add or Remove Programs* Use this applet to check the status of your applications and manage them. In many cases, the software provides options to add or remove features, perform updates, and completely remove the application. Adding and removing software is relatively simple in Windows XP, but probably not as easy as it could be. We discuss this applet in detail in the "Using the Add/Remove Programs Utility" section of Chapter 8.

- *Administrative Tools* This is a folder, not just a single utility. It's now the repository of other utilities that, in some cases (Data Sources, for example), used to be in the main Control Panel folder. I tell you more about this folder at the end of this list.

- *Client Service for NetWare* Provides additional configuration options for your NetWare connection. For example, you use this applet to set the default tree and context. See the "Using the Client Service for NetWare (CSNW) Applet" section of Chapter 21 for more details.

- *Date and Time* Keeping the date and time current on your machine becomes more important as your machine makes more connections to other resources. Older installations worry about the date and time only to time-stamp files. New users rely on the clock to schedule automated tasks, keep track of appointments, schedule automatic downloads from the Internet, and carry out a variety of other responsibilities.

- *Display* This applet enables you to perform tasks such as changing the display resolution and colors. You can also use the applet to enlarge the display fonts and change the wallpaper on the desktop. All these features add up to an incredibly flexible and easy-to-modify display system.

- *Folder Options* This feature displays the same properties dialog box you see when you choose Tools | Folder Options in Windows Explorer. These options define the way Windows Explorer looks and acts. We discuss this topic more in the "Setting the Folder Options" section of Chapter 3.

- *Fonts* Use this applet to manage the fonts on your system. Some applications include hundreds of fonts and most include at least a few, so your system can quickly fill with unwanted fonts. Learn more about this applet in the "Windows and Fonts" section of Chapter 14.

- *Game Controllers* This relatively simple utility lets you test and configure joysticks and similar input devices. Learn more about this applet in the "Installing and Configuring Game Controllers" section of Chapter 10.

- *Internet Options* Click this icon, and you see the same properties dialog box you get when you choose Tools | Options in Internet Explorer. We discuss this applet in detail in the "Changing the Internet Properties" section of Chapter 20.

- *Keyboard* A simple click of the International icon on the taskbar enables you to choose from any of the installed keyboard layouts. This applet not only installs support for these languages, but also provides other forms of keyboard support, such as repeat-rate adjustment. Learn more about this feature in the "Multilingual Support" section of Chapter 15.

- *Mouse* The purpose of the Windows XP Mouse applet is to help you configure the mouse. This doesn't mean just the double click speed and other mouse-specific features; it also includes the actual pointers the mouse uses and whether Windows XP displays mouse trails. You can learn more about this feature in the "Configuring Your Mouse" section of Chapter 15.

- *Network Connections* We spend a great deal of time with this particular applet in Chapter 21. This applet enables you to install new network components or get rid of old ones. It's where you set how the network controls access to your resources as well as where you see dial-up connections. TCP/IP users use this applet to configure the various addresses needed to make their network functional.

- *Phone and Modem Options* Use this applet to create and modify dialing locations. You can also defeat call waiting. The Modems tab is where you can add, remove, or change the properties of modems attached to your system. You learn more about this applet in the "Working with Modems" section of Chapter 9.

- *Power Options* This utility helps conserve power by turning off system components after a period of inactivity. The suggested settings determine the time interval before Windows XP turns off system components, such as the monitor and hard drives. The Hibernate feature is similar to the sleep feature found on some portables—it stores the current contents of RAM to your hard drive and then shuts down. When you restart the machine, Windows restores the saved contents to RAM, thus restoring your desktop. You can learn more about this feature in the "Setting Power Options" section of this chapter.

- *Printers and Faxes* This applet enables you to configure existing printers and faxes or add new ones. It also enables you to maintain control over any print jobs the printer is processing. You can learn more about this applet in Chapter 14. Also look at the "Working with Faxes" section of Chapter 9.

- *Regional and Language Options* This applet manages all the text-formatting information required to make the output of an application correct. It includes the actual time zone. You also use this applet to change the numeric, currency, time, date, and regional settings. Read the "Multilingual Support" section of Chapter 15 for details.

- *Scanners and Cameras* Click this icon to add or troubleshoot those devices.

- *Scheduled Tasks* You can tell Windows XP to run applications or utilities at scheduled times automatically. Click the Add Scheduled Task button and the Scheduled Task Wizard opens up, guiding you through the process of choosing a program and then telling Windows XP how often, or when, to run it. Learn more about this applet in the "Automating Tune-ups with Task Scheduler" section of Chapter 5.

- *Sounds and Audio Devices* This applet controls everything relating to the sound features supported by Windows XP. The applet not only controls the actual drivers and their settings, but also helps you configure the interface. We discuss this applet in detail in the "Multimedia Hardware" section of Chapter 10.

- *Speech* Controls the settings for the text reader provided with Windows XP. We discuss this feature in detail in the "Access for Users with Disabilities" section of Chapter 15.

- *System* This applet enables you to maintain your computer as a whole. It enables you to select hardware profiles and configure the system environment. You also use the applet to select some shutdown features and determine which operating system appears as the default on the boot menu. We discuss this applet several times throughout this book.

- *Taskbar and Start Menu* Use this applet to configure your Start Menu and Taskbar options. We discuss this applet throughout Chapter 3.

- *Users Accounts* Use this applet as a simple method to create, configure, and maintain user accounts. We discuss this feature in detail in the "Working with the User Accounts" section of Chapter 21.

Your Control Panel might have more or fewer applets than mine, but this list should give you a good idea of what the common applets do. If you have a few additional icons, the vendor documentation should tell you how to use them.

Let's talk a little more about the Administrative Tools folder. Figure 7.4 shows the contents of this folder if you're using Windows XP Professional. Windows server products usually contain more tools because servers require more configuration and management. I discuss most of the utilities shown in this folder elsewhere in this book. All of the utilities, except Data Sources (ODBC), rely on the Microsoft Management Console (MMC) described in the "Working with Microsoft Management Console" section of this chapter.

FIGURE 7.4
The Administrative Tools folder contains all of the icons needed to manage your system.

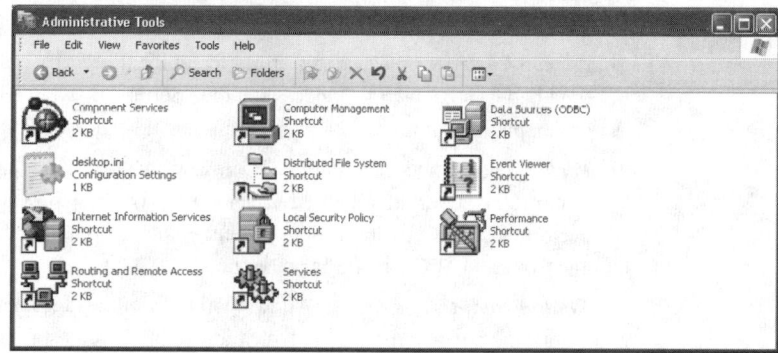

The following list provides a quick summary of the icons within this folder.

- *Component Services* Manages COM+ applications. This and other administrative tools are part of the new MMC (Microsoft Management Console) snap-ins set. MMC hosts administrative tools for managing individual computers, networks, and other system components.

- *Computer Management* Embraces many somewhat unrelated utilities. It performs disk drive management (such as defragmentation), but also includes a variety of disparate utilities, such as the new Indexing Service, IIS (Internet Information Service), Hardware Resources, Components, and others. You can reach many of these utilities via other paths.

- *Data Sources (ODBC)* Anyone who works with database management systems for very long understands the importance of this applet. It enables you to create new table connections and modify old ones. You can also see which drivers your system has available.

- *Distributed File System* Enables you to organize and manage multiple network shares in a logical namespace. What this means is that you can keep track of a file system that extends over more than one machine. This distributed file system (DFS) promises to reduce network administrator workload. However, you can't use this system unless you have a DFS-capable server that's properly configured to manage such a system. This is an optional feature and you might not see it in your Professional Edition installation.

- *Event Viewer* Use the Event Viewer to learn about system events. The Event Viewer provides three types of messages: information, warning, and error. The

information messages tell you about a noncritical condition. You find these messages in three folders when using the Professional Edition. The Application folder
contains messages generated by applications and high-level operating system
tasks. The System folder contains messages from the operating system and low-
level background tasks. Finally, the Security folder contains messages from the
security system.

- *Internet Information Services* Allows you to host Internet and intranet sites—and
  also to test Web pages on your own machine without having to involve a server.

- *Local Security Policy* Use this utility to set local security policies, such as the
  time between password changes. See the "Setting Local Security Policies" section
  of Chapter 22 for more details on setting local security policies.

- *Performance* Includes both the Performance Monitor (displaying graphs of your
  system's behavior) and the Performance Log. Both snap-ins allow you to monitor
  performance as you tune various system elements. See the "Checking Performance" section of Chapter 5 for more details.

- *Routing and Remote Access* Allows you to create bridges between network seg-
  ments and create remote communication setups, such as a virtual private network
  (VPN). See the "Understanding Virtual Private Networking (VPN)" section of
  Chapter 19 for details. This is an optional feature and you might not see it in your
  Professional Edition installation.

- *Services* Allows you to stop, pause, or start various services (Event Log, Indexing,
  Fax, and many others) on a local or remote machine. You can also use the Services
  snap-in to specify what should happen if a service fails. Standard actions include
  restart the machine or restart the service. .

Warning: Some applications insist on installing a custom applet in the Control
Panel. In most cases, Windows XP ignores incompatible applets that it doesn't
need in order to work with hardware or software you install. If you do get into
a situation where the old driver gets loaded and affects system stability, call
the vendor to see whether there's an easy way to remove the applet. In most
cases, you can eliminate the problem by deleting the required CPL file in the
/SYSTEM32 directory. However, if possible, you should use the Add or Remove
Programs utility in the Control Panel to delete the applet.

What other kinds of applets can you expect to see in the Control Panel? The only limitation is the types of applications and hardware you install. A few less-common examples
include a digitizer pad, a CAS-compliant fax, and data-capture boards. You probably see
special applets for non-Microsoft network connections, such as the CSNW applet used
with NetWare. Most mail packages also require an entry in the Control Panel.

Customizing Icon Displays

Some people fail to realize that the Control Panel is just another incarnation of Explorer, albeit in a specialized form. You saw how to access the Control Panel from Explorer earlier in this chapter. The display even looks the same as the other displays. There's nothing strange about Explorer's capability to interact with the Control Panel.

The earlier section really showed you all the similarities. There are a few differences between a standard Explorer interface and the Control Panel, too. I think the most obvious difference is that you can't manipulate Control Panel objects the same way you can other objects. The context menu reveals this fact. The only tasks you can perform with a Control Panel object are to open it or create a shortcut. Even the Properties option is missing, and it's nearly always available when you're working with objects.

You see other display differences, too. When it comes to arranging these objects, you have only two choices: by name and by comment. (Comments is a new field displayed if you're in Details view). In actuality, you'll probably never even rearrange these icons. There are so few to look at, most people leave them just the way they are. Figure 7.5 shows the Comment view for the Control Panel. As you can see, the descriptions help you understand the purpose of each applet.

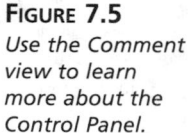

FIGURE 7.5

Use the Comment view to learn more about the Control Panel.

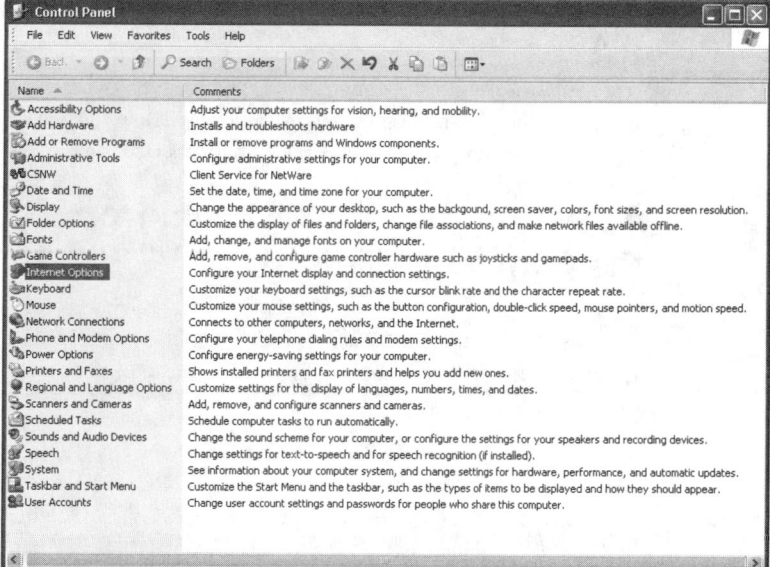

If you open a context menu in the Control Panel itself (right-click the Control Panel background rather than one of its applet icons), you notice a Refresh option. Every time you add a new application or piece of hardware and want to see whether it added a new Control Panel icon, you can use this command to refresh the display. Unlike Explorer, closing Control Panel might not force it to display any new icons you add. Using this command ensures that you get an accurate picture.

> **Tip:** You can always refresh Control Panel (or Explorer, Outlook Express, and Internet Explorer, for that matter) by pressing F5.

I never thought I'd use the Control Panel's shortcut option, but I did. After reading the past few pages, you've probably figured out that there's no fast method to access all the applets in the Control Panel. You can right-click the desktop and change your display settings, and right-clicking the My Computer icon grabs the System applet for you. However, what if you want to change your system sounds? You have to go to the Start menu or use some other method to bring up the Control Panel and then the appropriate applet.

Placing a shortcut to the applet on the desktop or Quick Launch toolbar is one of the best ways to optimize your setup. Any time you want to change your system sounds (or any other configuration item), you can click the icon on the desktop. The problem is how to create the shortcut. If you use the context menu entry (right-click an applet's icon in the Control Panel and then choose Create Shortcut), Windows displays an error message saying that it can't create the shortcut in the Control Panel. However, it does offer to create one on the desktop.

You can also right-click the applet's icon and drag it to wherever you want the shortcut to appear. After you release the mouse button, Windows displays a brief context menu. All you need to do is choose the Create Shortcuts Here option.

Accessing the Control Panel from the Command Line

The *Control Panel* is a container that holds a set of objects some people call applets. If you understand this fact, you also realize that the Control Panel is one object and that each of the applets it contains are other objects. Each of these entities resides in a separate file.

When you want to open the Control Panel, execute CONTROL.EXE, found in the /SYSTEM32 directory. As soon as you execute CONTROL.EXE, the Control Panel loads. It then loads all of the CPL files it can find in the /SYSTEM32 directory. What you see is the Control Panel display we used for discussion purposes earlier in this chapter.

It may interest you to know that you can also access every CPL file directly. Type ACCESS.CPL at the command prompt and press Enter, and you'll see just the Accessibility Options applet. You can also access the CPL files in scripts or the Scheduled Tasks utility. Table 7.1 equates the common applets with their CPL counterparts.

Table 7.1 Common-Applet-to-CPL File Comparison

Applet Name	CPL File
Accessibility Options	ACCESS.CPL
Add Hardware Wizard	HDWWIZ.CPL
Add or Remove Programs	APPWIZ.CPL
Client Service for NetWare	NWC.CPL
Date and Time Properties	TIMEDATE.CPL
Display Properties	DESK.CPL
Game Controllers	JOY.CPL
Internet Properties	INETCPL.CPL
Mouse Properties	MAIN.CPL
Network Connections	NCPA.CPL
ODBC Data Source Administrator	ODBCCP32.CPL
Phone and Modem Options	TELEPHON.CPL
Power Options Properties	POWERCFG.CPL
Regional and Language Options	INTL.CPL
Sound and Audio Devices Properties	MMSYS.CPL
System Properties	SYSDM.CPL
User Accounts	NUSRMGR.CPL

Working with Microsoft Management Console

The *Microsoft Management Console* (*MMC*) is the central management tool for Windows XP. MMC is a container application. It doesn't provide any services on its own. You have to add special applications, called *snap-ins*, to the container before MMC can do anything for you. The combination of MMC and one or more snap-ins is a *console*. Microsoft provides several default consoles for you as part of the Windows XP setup. We discussed these default consoles as part of the Administrative Tools folder discussion in the "A View of the Classic Control Panel" section of this chapter.

Learning to use MMC is an important part of the configuration of Windows XP. You use MMC to manage and maintain all of the major system elements. The following sections show basic usage techniques, how to add snap-ins to an existing console, and how to create your own console. When you complete these sections, you'll know how to use the flexibility that MMC provides to create your own management tools.

Using a Console

Starting a console is as easy as selecting its entry in the Administrative Tools folder. Figure 7.6 shows the Computer Management console. Notice that this tool has several major sections. By this point in the book, you should know that you can also access several of these sections individually. For example, the Event Viewer also opens as a separate MMC console. The Computer Management console is an excellent example of how you can bolt a number of snap-ins together to create your own management tool.

Figure 7.6

The Computer Management console uses several snap-ins that also appear as standalone consoles.

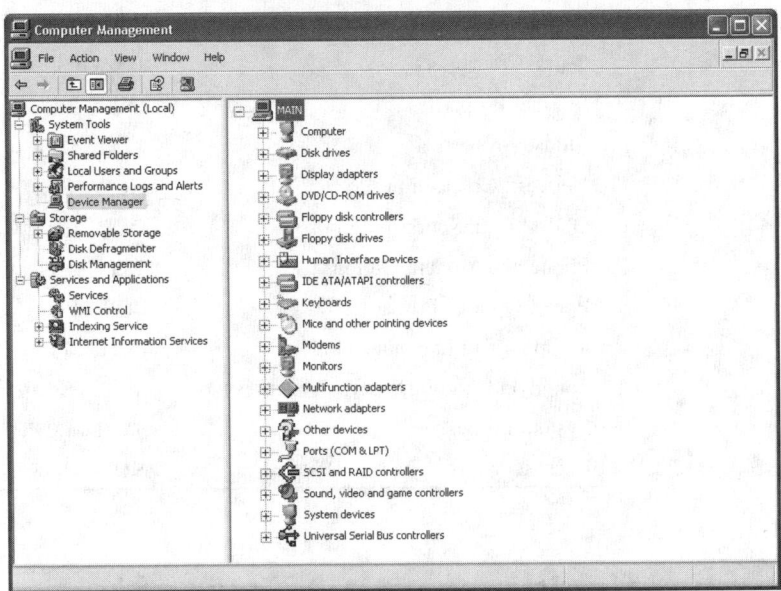

Every layer of the MMC console has a context menu associated with it. The context menus contain some common and some special entries. For example, every level of the hierarchy includes a Help entry that should provide context-sensitive help for that entry. In some cases, the help is generic, but it's usually pertinent to the entry you selected.

Some entries allow you to perform specific tasks. For example, if you right-click the Computer Management level, you see an All Tasks entry on the context menu. The options within this menu allow you to send a console message to another computer or to connect to another computer in order to maintain it. The Action menu also contains the tasks you can perform with a level of the hierarchy.

You immediately notice some similarities between MMC and Windows Explorer. For example, the View menu allows you to change the way MMC displays the entries in the details pane. The difference is that MMC provides fewer options than Windows Explorer because the snap-ins usually display in only one or two ways. Trying to display the data in other ways doesn't make sense for the type of data in question.

MMC also allows you to export the data you see. Click the Export List button on the toolbar or select it from the context menu, and you see an Export List dialog box. Type a name for the exported list, and MMC saves it for you. The exported data appears in tab-delimited form. This makes it easy to import into a database application for analysis.

As with Windows Explorer, you can customize the columns shown in the details pane when you select Details view. However, unlike in Windows Explorer, the columns vary by snap-in. This means you can't assume anything about the columns you see; the snap-in may provide additional columns of information you'd find helpful in diagnosing a problem or configuring the system. You can access the Customize View dialog box using the View | Customize command.

The final tidbit of useful information is a special command you'll see on some context menus, but not on all of them. The New Window from Here option allows you to separate one snap-in from the rest. Say you're working with the Computer Management console and decide that you want to see only Device Manager. You can right-click Device Manager and choose New Window from Here from the context menu. The display changes to show only the Device Manager.

Creating Your Own Consoles

At some point, you might decide that the tools Microsoft provides are nice but you want to create your own consoles out of the snap-ins you use in combination most often. This means starting with an empty MMC container. All you need to do is use the Start | Run command to display the Run dialog box. Type **MMC** in the Open field and then click OK. You see an empty MMC window.

To start creating your MMC console, you need to add some snap-ins. Use the File | Add/Remove Snap-In command to display the Add/Remove Snap-in dialog box. Notice that this dialog box contains a Snap-ins Added To field, a list box, a description field, and three buttons (Add, Remove, and About). Everything is empty at this point, and the only thing you can do is click Add. We'll see later that this is a temporary condition.

Click Add, and you'll see an Add Standalone Snap-in dialog box, like the one shown in Figure 7.7. Notice that I've selected the Disk Defragmenter snap-in. The short description for this snap-in appears in the Description field.

> **Tip:** If you look through the list of available snap-ins, you'll notice many that appear out of place in a workstation environment. You can't use the administration tools that come with Windows 2000 Server, but you can build your own version of those tools using these snap-ins. It pays to spend some time looking through the list because you'll find some interesting additions to make to your own consoles.

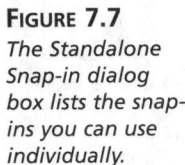

FIGURE 7.7
The Standalone Snap-in dialog box lists the snap-ins you can use individually.

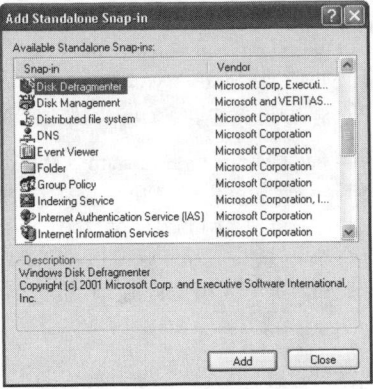

Click Add. If you have the dialog boxes positioned correctly, you see the snap-in added to the list in the Add/Remove Snap-in dialog box. You can select all the snap-ins you want to see in your new console. I'm creating a console that contains the Disk Defragmenter, Disk Management, and Distributed File System snap-ins.

This brings up an interesting point. When you select some snap-ins, such as the Disk Management snap-in, you'll see a configuration dialog box. The Disk Management snap-in asks which computer you want to manage. This may seem like a silly question, considering that you can connect to another computer later. One of the things I haven't mentioned yet is that you can add multiple copies of the same snap-in. Let's say you want to monitor all of the hard drives on your network simultaneously. You can build a console to do that by adding multiple copies of the appropriate snap-in and configuring each of them to monitor a different machine.

After you finish adding new snap-ins, click Close in the Add Standalone Snap-in dialog box. You should see an Add/Remove Snap-in dialog box filled with snap-ins, like the one shown in Figure 7.8. Notice that the Description field contains the same short description of the highlighted snap-in we saw earlier in this chapter.

Sometimes the short description you see in the Add Standalone Snap-in dialog box isn't enough; you may want more information than it can provide. Highlight the snap-in and click About. You see an About dialog box for the snap-in that provides more information than the short description. You still don't receive a help manual this way.

Snap-ins actually come in two sizes. The first type you work with is the *standalone* snap-in. A standalone snap-in can literally appear by itself in a console. A second type of snap-in is the extension. An *extension* provides additional behavior for a standalone snap-in. You can see if a standalone snap-in provides extensions by clicking Extensions in the Add/Remove Snap-in dialog box. Figure 7.9 shows an example of how extension snap-ins work.

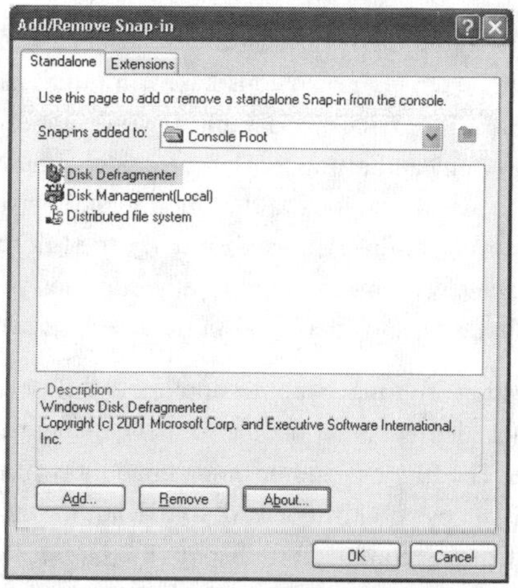

Figure 7.8

The Add Standalone Snap-in dialog box shows the snap-ins you've added to your console.

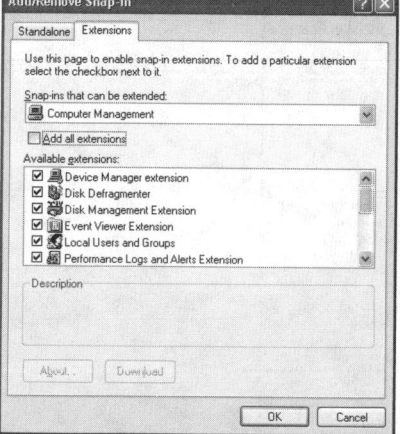

Figure 7.9

Extension snap-ins allow you to modify the behavior of a standalone snap-in.

The reason I chose the Computer Management snap-in is that it shows that standalone snap-ins can also act as extensions to other snap-ins. MMC snap-ins are extremely flexible. When you build a console, you need to check all of the possibilities. Notice that you can check the Add All Extensions option if you want to create a snap-in with all extensions in place.

At this point, we've added all the snap-ins we want to add to this console. Click OK, and you see the results of the console you created. All you need to do now is save the console so that you can access it later. Use the File | Save command to display the Save As dialog box. Notice that MMC defaults to saving new consoles in your Administrative Tools folder. This console appears only in your Administrative Tools folder unless you place it in the All Users version of the same folder. If you take this approach, make sure you set strict security for the new console so that users don't gain access to operating system features they shouldn't use.

Adding Snap-ins to Existing Consoles

Now that you know how to create your own consoles, you might ask what you can do to enhance the consoles Microsoft provides by default. If you want to change a console, you need to have access to it in "author mode." Unfortunately, the Microsoft-supplied consoles aren't in author mode. If you look at the File menu, you see there isn't any option for adding and remove snap-ins. You can't modify the Microsoft consoles supplied with Windows XP. However, you can modify any consoles you create using the File | Add/Remove Snap-in command, as we did in the previous section.

This leads to another question. You may want to retain the ability to modify your own consoles, but may not want to allow other people to make changes. This means saving two copies of the console. The first has author mode enabled, while the second uses a restrictive mode. MMC assumes you always want to use author mode unless you tell it otherwise. Use the File | Options command to display the Options dialog box shown in Figure 7.10.

FIGURE 7.10

The Options dialog box allows you to change the mode of the console.

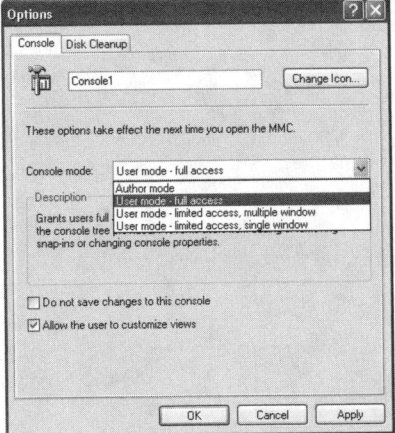

Notice that MMC supports four levels of access. Author Mode gives you full access to all features. User Mode – Full Access allows the user to access all MMC functions, but doesn't allow the user to add or remove snap-ins. User Mode – Limited Access, Multiple Window mode limits the user view to those elements that were visible at the time you saved the console. The user can open additional windows, but is restricted in all other ways. The most limited option, User Mode – Limited Access, Single Window prevents the user from doing anything other than use the console.

Note: Don't rely on the level of access setting alone to protect your consoles—use security settings as well. Ensuring that your custom-designed consoles stay in the hands of those you want to use them is an essential part of making custom consoles work.

This dialog box also contains two options that further limit user access. Select Do Not Save Changes to This Console if you want to limit a user's ability to change a console to that session. The Allow User to Customize Views option allows users to modify the display to their specific needs.

Setting Power Options

The Power Options applet helps you control the way your system uses power. You can use this applet to change everything from the system inactivity shutdown times to the UPS configuration. The following sections describe the various options of the Power Options Properties dialog box.

Working with Schemes

One of the most important elements of the Power Options Properties dialog box is the Schemes tab shown in Figure 7.11. This dialog box determines when your system will shut down after various systems after periods of inactivity. Figure 7.11 shows just the monitor and hard disk options. Some machines allow you to tune the system in other ways. For example, you can determine how long the system waits before it enters standby mode.

FIGURE 7.11

The Schemes tab allows you to configure your system for various power-saving scenarios.

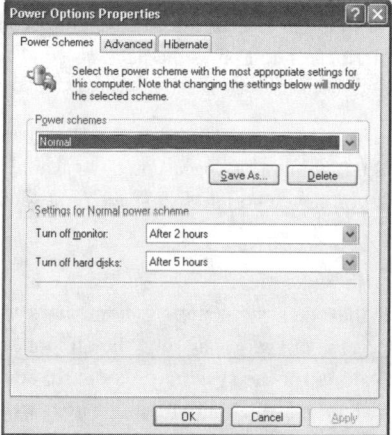

The Power Schemes drop-down list box of this dialog box allows you to select from several predefined schemes. Microsoft provides several predefined schemes that work well for common applications. Select a scheme from the Power Schemes drop-down list box and then click OK to put it in effect.

You may want to create your own schemes to go with those that Microsoft provides. For example, I created an Always On scheme that doesn't allow the system to shut anything down. I use this scheme during computer maintenance and diagnostics. Another special scheme is Read Mode. It allows extra time to shut the monitor down for those times I'm reading something online. Simply select the times you want for each system element, click Save As, type a scheme name, and then click OK.

Using the Advanced Features

The options on the Advanced tab vary by motherboard vendor. Most vendors don't provide any additional capabilities. You'll see an Always Show icon on the taskbar option on this tab. It's a good idea to check this option if you're working with a laptop computer. Doing so allows you to track battery time by looking in the Notification Area of the Taskbar.

Enabling Hibernate Support

The Hibernate tab contains the hibernate options. When your computer goes into Hibernate mode, it copies the content of RAM to the hard drive and then shuts itself down. The next time you start the computer, it loads the saved state information from the hard drive into RAM. Theoretically, you'll return to the same setup you left before the system went into Hibernate mode.

The first problem people run into is that the system doesn't have enough disk space to go into Hibernate mode. Windows XP requires enough hard drive space to store the entire content of RAM, even if you aren't using all of the available RAM space at the time. This means I need 512MB of hard drive space on my system because I have 512MB of RAM installed. Windows XP doesn't compress the data, so you can't cheat even a little on the disk space requirement.

You'll find the hibernation disk space requirement on the Hibernate tab. Two entries show the required space and the amount of space you have available. If you plan to use Hibernate mode, ensure that you have enough disk space (and some to spare) to hold the contents of RAM.

Some people also find that Hibernate mode is less impressive in practice than it is in theory. Many people tell me that the system starts to come back to life, only to freeze. They end up starting from scratch anyway. The time they might have saved using Hibernate mode is wasted waiting for the system to reboot. In addition, they often lose data or see corruption on the hard drive. Hibernate mode does work—it just doesn't work reliably on some systems. Make sure you test Hibernate mode before you rely on it to work unmonitored.

> **Tip:** Hibernate is a safer alternative to stand by for laptop machines. A laptop continues to use power from the battery while in standby mode. Sure, it's less than when the system is powered up and ready for action, but the power drain is real and the loss of power could leave the battery in the critical state. Hibernate mode requires nothing from the battery. You can leave a laptop in Hibernate mode as long as you want.

Given the less-than-stellar reputation of Hibernate mode, I normally save and close all my data files before I use it. That way, if Hibernate fails to work as anticipated, all I lose is a system setup. If it does work, I save setup time, and all I need to do is reload the data files.

Working with a UPS

An uninterruptible power supply (UPS) is the number-one add-on for your system, yet most people don't have one because they consider it an unnecessary expense. I view a UPS as more important than any other peripheral because it enables your computer to keep running when the power shuts off and provides better protection than any surge suppressor. Most high-quality UPSs completely disconnect your system from the power line. They supply power to your system through the battery. The power company supply recharges the battery.

The fact that a UPS keeps your system running when a power outage occurs is important. The extra run time gives you the chance to save your data and gracefully shut your machine down. Nothing is harder on your computer than the instantaneous loss of power that a power outage can provide (some experts say a brownout is even harder on the system).

> **Tip:** Get your UPS from a reputable vendor, such as American Power Conversion (http://www.apcc.com/) or Best Power (http://www.bestpower.com/). Make sure you get the right size for your system and computing needs. Many UPS vendors include calculators you can use to obtain the right size UPS for your system. The calculator works by asking questions about your computing needs.

Installing the UPS means shutting your system down and plugging the UPS into the wall and all of your computer equipment into the UPS. Make sure you charge the UPS first. The UPS usually communicates with the computer through a serial cable. Some vendors supply different cables for different versions of Windows, so make sure you get the right cable.

Windows XP offers a generic UPS tab as part of the Power Options Properties dialog box. However, many UPS vendors provide software that takes the place of this tab. This special UPS software normally includes a diagnostic test you can use to test the UPS for faults, such as a bad battery.

Make sure you maintain your UPS. I test mine at least once a week; more often if we've had a storm with lightning. The UPS circuitry may decide to sacrifice itself to protect your system. In addition, the UPS battery lasts only so long. You'll eventually have to replace the battery to continue getting the protection the UPS can provide.

Although a UPS isn't as glamorous as a new sound system, it's an essential part of your computer. A UPS helps you enjoy the other parts of your computer and keep your data in good shape.

On Your Own

Spend some time working with the Control Panel applets. It's important to know which applet to use in a given situation, especially when time is short. Learn how to open them from the command line when necessary. This feature can help you configure a system faster using scripts or other forms of automation.

Look at the MMC consoles supplied by Microsoft. Make a list of your favorite consoles and learn how to use them completely. It also helps if you make a list of favorite snap-ins. Sometimes, a custom console works better than the ones Microsoft supplies. As an experiment, try creating your own consoles and test them.

Create a power strategy for your system. Discover the optimal times for turning off various devices during periods of system inactivity. Try using the hibernate feature on your system to see how well it works. Install and configure a UPS for your system. The data you save may be your own.

Get a UPS and install it on your system. Make sure you get a UPS that is sized correctly for your system components and computing needs. Don't forget to install any vendor-supplied software after you install the UPS so that you can monitor the UPS state and test it for faults.

Exploiting Your Software

You may find this chapter's title somewhat confusing, but it best expresses the way most users manage their systems in today's world. In fact, if you're not exploiting your software, I hope you will be after reading this chapter. To help you understand what I mean by the title, I take a few minutes of your reading time to explain just what I mean by "exploiting your software."

Exploiting every possible feature in today's bloated software is nearly impossible for the average user. The fact that some power users continue to have difficulty doing it says plenty about current software comprehensiveness. Word XP is a good example, but there are others that would fit the bill. Even if you don't install all the options, you'll have more application features at your fingertips than you're likely to use in a lifetime. Microsoft's Word development team has included nearly every conceivable feature you'd ever want, let alone use. So, exploiting your software doesn't always mean using every feature the software manufacturer has included in the product.

What do I mean by exploiting your software so that it exercises every feature to its fullest potential? I use four basic criteria to measure my level of software exploitation. They're all interrelated, so you'll find that changing one element affects all the other elements. For me, it's kind of a game to see just how well I can get all these elements to work together. A fully exploited piece of software does the following:

- *Accomplishes the job at hand with a minimum of effort* Everyone knows that learning to use a computer is both expensive and time consuming. Add to that the cost of buying the equipment itself, and you have a major investment before you see any kind of return. A fully exploited piece of software enables you to accomplish the same job as before, but with less effort. Concentrating on the task rather than on the means of performing it allows you to be more creative in your work. I've always felt that computers should provide a way to remove the burden of work and leave the "fun" parts for us to accomplish. A fully exploited piece of software can do just that.

- *Produces results in a modicum of time* It wasn't too long ago that people wondered why it was faster to do something by hand rather than use a computer. I frequently saw this problem. What people were forgetting was that to use that older software to its fullest potential, you needed to set up the application only once. The computer could then automate the task for you so that it would take less time to perform the task the second time. If you didn't set up your computer for rapid duplication of routine work (such as using macros), you weren't exploiting it. Fortunately, spending that much time to create an original document is no longer a problem. I can use a variety of packages to write an application in a fraction of the time it used to take. Templates and other software add-ons make it faster to produce the first copy of a document, in addition to variations of that document later. The wizards provided with many software packages give you a built-in ease of use that was unheard of only five years ago. A fully exploited piece of software today enables you to produce results faster than you could by hand in many cases.

- *Produces output that requires the least amount of system resources* The amount of system resources you have is relative. Much of it has to do with the technology you have at your disposal. Some other considerations include the money you have to spend on upgrades. However, I'll concentrate on the relative aspect of this picture. A fully exploited piece of software is optimized so that it uses a minimum of system resources and the least memory-intensive yet fastest way to accomplish a task. Optimizing the way you use the software features usually results in reduced system resource requirements.

- *Produces the best results possible* Optimizing your software to reduce system requirements, improving your techniques to reduce the time it takes to get the job done, and reducing the effort required to complete the task are all fine goals. It's the result of all this effort, however, that everyone sees. The boss doesn't care that it took you half the time to get something done if the final result isn't up to par. That's a problem for many people: They look for a quick fix to a problem, which isn't the route they really need to pursue. The test of whether you've successfully exploited your software is in the results you produce. Using the software and hardware available today should enable you to produce a product superior in every way to what you could do yesterday. If you aren't getting that result, it's time to take another look at how you're exploiting your software.

Exploiting your software also means that you use the right tool for the task you're trying to accomplish. Many people use a spreadsheet as a word processor; but is that really exploiting your software, or is the software exploiting you? Of course, few people can afford to buy every application on the market. There are limitations to what you can realistically use. If an inexpensive tool does the job, that's the one you should select. It's a matter of defining the parameters of the job. Just how much work do you need to do? If I need to dig a small hole, I get a spade. A really big hole requires a backhoe. Perhaps your job requires only a spade.

To summarize, then, exploiting your software means that you spend your hard-earned money on an application that's the right size and type for the job. You optimize its operation and environment. Then you sit back and watch the application do its job in the most efficient manner possible.

If this sounds impossible, read on. Many things seem impossible until you take the time to analyze the situation, break it into its component parts, and solve the small problems. Trying to solve an entire project with one answer doesn't do much, if anything, to make you efficient. Of course, you probably do all this with your current business. Most successful businesses take the time to get the most out of their employees and the resources they have available. Now what you need to do is apply these same principles to your computer's software.

Using the Add or Remove Programs Utility

Have you seen the immense size of some applications today? I'm often amazed at how fast the applications I install can eat up a major piece of the 4GB drive on my first partition, the C: drive. Installing Visual Studio—the full install—demands almost 2GB for itself! And if you include the MSDN Visual Studio Library, it adds more than another 1GB. If you have an older, smaller drive, you may need to remove one or more less frequently used applications to make room for the applications you use often. A few years back (I'm telling my age now), a 10MB drive was more than one could hope to ever fill with software. The $5\frac{1}{4}$-inch floppy disk held not only the complete word processor, but also all your DOC files with room to spare.

Fortunately, Windows XP enables you to install and remove most applications with ease. The Add or Remove Programs feature keeps track of the DLLs, Registry or INI entries, support files, miscellaneous debris, menu icons, satellite utilities, and folders occupied during the original installation. Then, if you decide to uninstall, all the unique dependencies (files and data used only by the application in question and not shared with other applications) can be cleanly removed from the places they reside.

The Windows XP Add or Remove Programs feature doesn't handle earlier Windows NT–specific products—those designed for versions 3.5 and earlier. It also doesn't work with any Windows 3.x applications. To install and then later uninstall these products, you still need to use a third-party utility or try to delete things by hand.

Using the Add or Remove Programs feature ensures that proper Registry entries are made (or removed) by Windows XP. You need to decide between using the capability to easily remove a legacy application later and performing a little more work to get the application installed correctly or getting the best possible installation up front, but perhaps doing a great deal of work later to remove it. Using the correct installation utility helps you get rid of those old applications quickly.

Adding an Application

Click the Add New Programs button on the left pane of the Add or Remove Programs applet in the Control Panel to try to install a new application. Put the application CD in your CD-ROM drive. Click the CD or Floppy button and then, when the wizard appears, click Next. The install utility searches for an installation program (Setup.Exe or Install.Exe). If it doesn't find one on your floppy or CD drive, it permits you to use the Browse These Devices option to manually locate the Setup or Install programs sometimes hidden in folders on the CD or floppy drive. Double-click the name of one of these programs and then click Finish to begin the installation process.

Removing an Application

What's involved in removing an application after you've installed it? Uninstall programs should consider the following five application elements. These programs handle each criterion to a different degree:

- *Application directory* Every uninstall program handles this element with the same efficiency. For that matter, it would probably take you even less time to delete the application directory yourself when it's no longer needed. The problem is the application's data. Some uninstall programs leave it in place so that you can recover it later; others just remove the entire directory without giving much thought to the data it contains. I prefer the first approach because it keeps me from shooting myself in the foot and losing something I might later find valuable. The second approach is a little too thorough, in my opinion.

- *Windows directory* Most older applications place an INI file in the Windows directory so that they can find it easily (rather than use the Registry, as newer programs do). Some applications place two, or even three INI files, there. I had one application place three different INI files in this directory. Each managed a different aspect of the product. I was surprised by the number of uninstall programs that don't take these files into account.

Note: Although all your older applications probably use one or more INI files, Microsoft discourages their use in newer applications. In most cases, an application uses the Registry to store settings that once appeared in an INI file. Even if an application does use an INI file, you'll probably find it in the application's directory rather than in the Windows directory. The same principle holds true for many of the other bullets in this section. A new application, for example, is supposed to use its own directory for file storage rather than the Windows SYSTEM folder.

- *Windows system file modification* It's a sure bet that Windows XP will have the same problem previous versions of Windows did when it comes to spurious entries in WIN.INI and SYSTEM.INI. Even though Windows XP provides only compatibility support for these files, it does read them when you boot. Suffice it to say that some problems you had in the past will still appear when you try to uninstall 16-bit applications.

- *SYSTEM and SYSTEM32 directories* Your SYSTEM directories have a ton of files, and there's no way of knowing which ones belong to your application. Even if an uninstall program tracks these files, it has no way of knowing how many applications use a particular file. This is especially true of DLLs. An application might install a copy of VB6DB.DLL in your SYSTEM32 directory, for example. When you install another application that also requires the same file, the second application might not add the file because it sees that the latest version of that file is already present. If an uninstall program removed VB6DB.DLL along with all the other files for the first application, any other application using that DLL would also cease to work. How do you handle this situation? I don't know, and neither does your uninstall program. Some programs make a valiant effort to remove the less common files. When it comes to removing one, you're on your own—deleting files from the SYSTEM32 directory by hand. Sometimes, an uninstall program reports that a DLL isn't in use by any other application. In that case, it's safe to assume that the DLL is application specific and isn't shared by other applications. Go ahead and agree to have it removed.

Note: Windows XP maintains a \SYSTEM directory only for compatibility with 16-bit applications; all 32-bit applications use the \SYSTEM32 directory.

- *Common application directories* Many applications try to reduce the number of files on your hard drive by placing files that more than one application could use in a separate directory the. You'll find an MSAPPS directory on your machine if you use Microsoft applications, for example. The positive side of such directories is that they do reduce the load on your hard drive. The negative aspect is that you really don't know which files to remove if you use multiple products from the same vendor and you want to remove only one product. In fact, I found that this common directory can actually confuse your uninstall program.

Tip: Windows doesn't let you remove a file that's in use. Even if you close an application, Windows might not unload all its associated DLLs right away. Whenever you want to remove an application from your drive, shut everything down, reboot, and perform the uninstall routine with all applications closed. This technique ensures that the uninstall program can actually remove all the files it identifies as part of the application.

Windows XP uses the same technique that Windows 2000/95/98 do to ensure that you can add and remove applications with ease. All this happens because the install program gives the operating system more information about what it installs, and why, than previous versions of Windows did. That allows you to uninstall only Windows XP, 2000, NT 4, or Windows 95/98-specific applications with the new install/uninstall capability.

Newer applications actually make Registry entries that tell the operating system what to remove later. This also allows Windows XP to look for common files and perform other types of analysis. When you finally upgrade each application on your machine to a newer (Windows 95 or later) version, the Install/Uninstall program should work perfectly—theoretically, at least. The following steps tell you how to use the Install/Uninstall program:

1. Open the Control Panel using the Start | Control Panel menu.

2. Double-click the Add or Remove Programs icon. You should see a dialog box like the one shown in Figure 8.1.

FIGURE 8.1

This utility has been redesigned slightly for Windows XP.

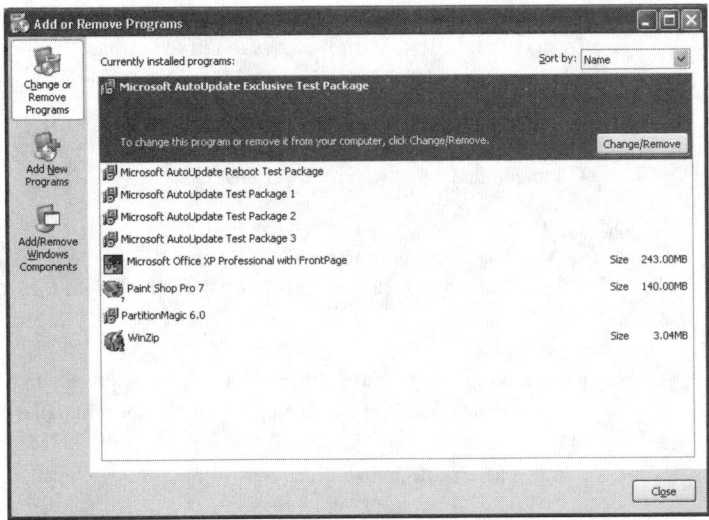

3. Click the Add New Programs button. The utility then searches the network, or you can specify that it should look on a CD or floppy diskette. In addition, you can choose Windows Update, which looks on the Internet for any bug fixes, or features updates, to Windows XP. If you select that option, you go to http://v4.windowsupdate.microsoft.com/en/default.asp and see a screen like the one in Figure 8.2.

> **Tip:** Interestingly, Internet Explorer 6 boasts a similar feature (Tools | Windows Update). It takes you to the same site that displays a list of updates to Windows XP, at http://v4.windowsupdate.microsoft.com/en/default.asp.

Fortunately, the previous confusion caused by blending Windows components and accessories into the same list as all other applications has now been cleared up. When you use the Windows XP Add or Remove Programs utility, you have buttons that clearly indicate what they do.

FIGURE 8.2
Here's where you can have Windows XP automatically update itself.

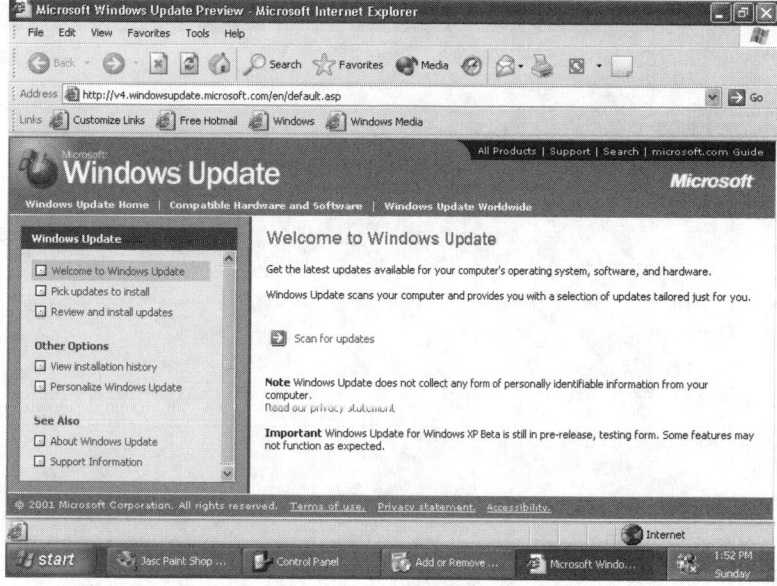

4. Click the Add or Remove Windows Components on the left side of the Add or Remove Programs dialog box. This step launches the Windows Components Wizard, as shown in Figure 8.3:

5. Close the Add or Remove Windows Components dialog box and in the Add or Remove Programs dialog box choose Change or Remove Programs. Then try an intriguing new feature: Click the Sort By ListBox option and choose Frequency of Use, as shown in Figure 8.4.

FIGURE 8.3
Use this wizard to add Windows XP features (or remove them).

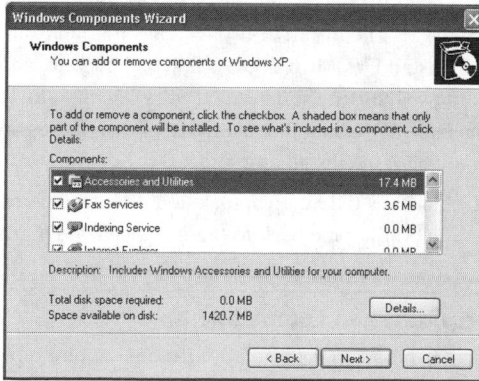

FIGURE 8.4
*The Add or
Remove dialog
box sorted by fre-
quency of use.*

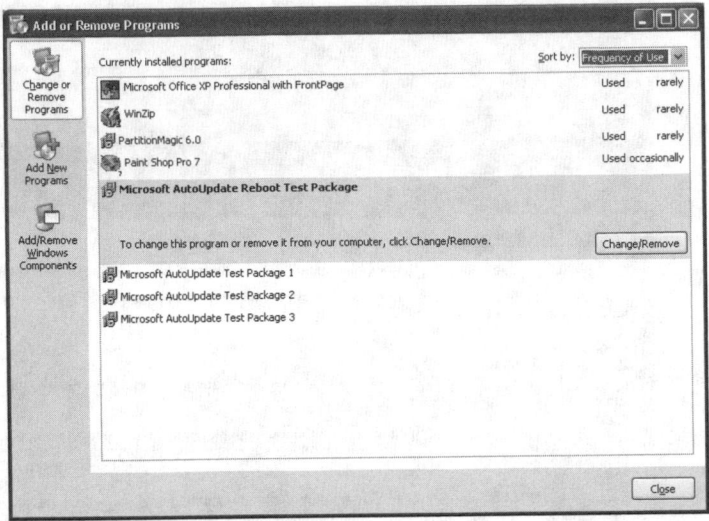

Warning: You probably know how often you use your various utilities and
applications. However, if you need to free up disk space for some reason, it
would be helpful to see your programs listed by frequency of use. Good idea,
and finally more accurate with Windows XP. My programs are listed in Figure
8.4, and I can tell you that one item in this list isn't accurate. I use WinZip quite
a bit, although this report says that I rarely use it. The others are fairly accurate.

6. Click the Add New Programs button on the left pane of the Add or Remove
   Programs dialog box to try installing a new application. Put the application's CD
   in your CD-ROM drive. Click the CD or Floppy button; then, when the Wizard
   appears, click Next. The install utility searches for an installation program
   (Setup.Exe or Install.Exe). If it doesn't find one on your floppy or CD drive, it
   permits you to use the Browse These Devices option to locate the Setup or Install
   programs manually. Double-click the name of one of these programs and then
   click Finish to begin the installation process.

7. Windows XP launches the Setup application. Follow the vendor instructions for
   installing it. You don't come back to the Install Wizard when you're done.

Peter's Principle: When Compatible Isn't

Microsoft has determined that some applications require a higher level of compatibility than others when it comes to Windows XP. I'm not sure that I can say I
blame Microsoft for wanting applications such as disk management utilities and
firewalls to provide the highest level of compatibility. After all, these applications do change the way the operating system works.

However, some industry pundits are already saying that this measure is another way for Microsoft to force its will on the unsuspecting public. Some have already mentioned the compatibility messages Microsoft included with Windows in the past for products such as DR DOS (the compatibility problems didn't exist). In many minds, it's also a means for forcing users to pay to upgrade products they could get free within Windows XP (making the free software more attractive). Fortunately, the authors of products such as Zone Alarm and Black Ice (both firewalls) are already working on products that will address the product-blocking Microsoft put in place. It isn't known whether products such as Voice Express and Web Booster Ninja have compatible versions on the way.

The question, then, is how do you know if an installation problem is product-blocking-induced or a real problem with the application? If you look in the \WINDOWS\AppPatch directory, you'll see a file with the name APPHELP.SDB. This file contains a list of the applications that don't run with Windows XP because of product blocking. Open the file using a hexadecimal editor, such as WinVI (http://www.winvi.de/en/) and you see a list of applications starting about a third of the way through the file. At the time of this writing, each of these entries also included a Web page containing test information. I hope that they include an explanation of the incompatibility further down the road.

Uninstalling an application is just as easy, if not easier, as installing one. The following procedure shows you the steps you'll follow in most cases. Remember that you also have the option of using the application's Uninstall utility. Of course, the trade-off is that the application might not remove all the Registry entries that Windows XP made when you installed it. To uninstall an application, follow these steps:

1. Open the Control Panel using the Start menu or Explorer.
2. Double-click Add or Remove Programs. You should see a dialog box like the one shown in Figure 8.1.
3. Select the application you want to uninstall and click the Change/Remove button. You're asked whether you want to remove the application.
4. Click Yes. If the Uninstall utility can't remove all the files, it provides you with a list and suggests that you later remove them by hand.
5. The utility doesn't inform you that it has uninstalled the application—it only shows a list of installed applications, with one of them (the one you just uninstalled) no longer listed.

If you open the Add or Remove Programs dialog box and see an item in the list that doesn't uninstall, you should remove the item from the list. Run Regedit and locate this Registry entry: HKEY_LOCAL_MACHINE\SOFTWARE\Microsoft\Windows\CurrentVersion\Uninstall. Then remove the key from the Registry. In Figure 8.5, you'll see that the Add or Remove Programs applet contains new features that you might find useful.

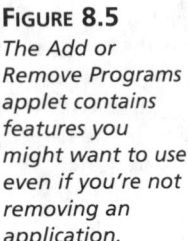

FIGURE 8.5
The Add or Remove Programs applet contains features you might want to use even if you're not removing an application.

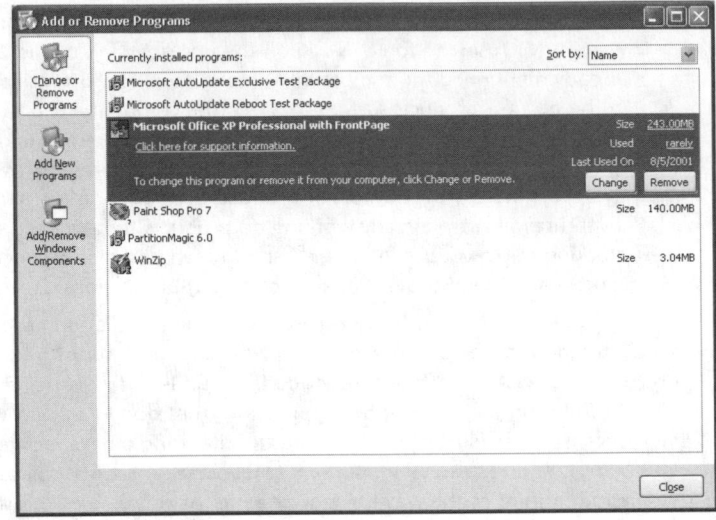

As you can see, the entry contains much more information than a simple application removal. One of the most important features is the Click Here for Support Information link. Figure 8.6 shows a typical Support Info dialog box.

FIGURE 8.6
The Support Info dialog box tells you where to get help with an application.

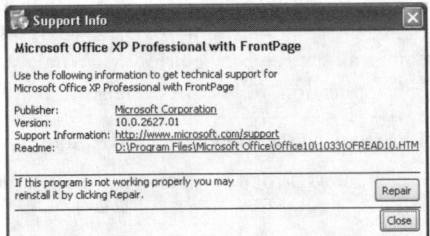

Cleaning Up Application Remnants

As you can see, trying to remove a Windows application from your machine isn't an easy task. A Windows application spreads files all over the place and makes entries in system files you might need, even if you do remove the application. (Multiple applications might need the same entry to run.) It's not surprising, then, that Windows uninstall programs usually do a partial, not a complete, job of removing old programs from your system. Of course, a partial removal is better than nothing.

Even if an uninstall program tracks all these files, it has no way of knowing how many applications use a particular file. This is especially true of DLLs. An application might install a copy of VB6DB.DLL in your SYSTEM32 directory, for example. When you install another application that also requires the same file, the second application might not add the file because it sees that the latest version of that file is already present. If an

uninstall program removed VB6DB.DLL along with all the other files for the first application, any other application using that DLL would also cease to work. How do you
handle this situation? I don't know, and neither does your uninstall program. Some
programs make a valiant effort to remove the less common files. When it comes to
removing one, you're on your own—deleting files from the SYSTEM32 directory by
hand. An uninstall program sometimes reports that a DLL isn't in use by any other
application. In that case, it's safe to assume that the DLL is application specific and isn't
shared by other applications. Go ahead and agree to have it removed.

Using the Microsoft Windows Installer

Windows Installer is an installation and configuration service that ships as part of
Windows XP. It's used for corporate software deployment and provides a standard
format for component management. A listing of Windows Installer features can be found
in the MSDN section of the Microsoft Web site: http://msdn.microsoft.com/library/
default.asp?url=/library/en-us/msi/hh/msi/over_8wtv.asp.

An installation package contains all the information the Windows Installer requires to
install or uninstall an application or product and to run the setup user interface. Each
installation package includes an .msi file, containing an installation database, a summary
information stream, and data streams for various parts of the installation. The .msi file
can also contain one or more transforms, internal source files, and external source files or
cabinet files required by the installation.

Understanding the MSI Advantage

Windows Installer reduces the total cost of ownership (TCO) for corporations by efficiently installing and configuring products and applications. The installer can also
provide a product with new capabilities to advertise features without installing them,
to install products on demand, and to add user customizations.

Getting Support for Your Application

Click the URL in the dialog box shown in Figure 8.6 and Internet Explorer will display
the support site for that application. This dialog box also contains the vendor name and
the product build information. A support person will likely require the build information,
so it's nice to have this information handy.

Repairing an Application

Notice the Repair button in this dialog box. Click this button and the application begins a
repair installation. For some vendors, this means performing the last installation over
again, so you need to have your application CD handy. At least a few vendors perform a

check on the application and associated DLLs and update only those that don't match the installed conditions.

Some applications also have a Change/Remove button or separate Change and Remove buttons. In some cases, you may find that you don't use all of the features an application has to offer. The unused features can waste processing cycles and definitely waste hard drive space. Click Change if you want to remove these extra features or add features you may have removed in the past.

Optimizing Windows Applications

After you get a new application installed, you need to optimize it for your use. Notice that I said "for your use." The difference between an optimized and an exploited application is simple: The optimized application might run fast, but the exploited application is more efficient for you. Windows applications provide a wealth of settings that enable you to tune the way they work. These tuning steps affect the application's speed and memory requirements. They also affect the user interface. I look at both elements in the following sections because they're both important for fully exploiting your applications. Make sure that you read the entire section before you start tuning your applications. Some elements involve a trade-off: You need to select one or the other. I cover the most common choices, but you might need to make some decisions based on your application's specific setup.

Installing your new application is an important part of the tuning process. The decisions you make here will affect the way you view the application in the future as well as determine how the application performs. The following list should help you make some of the difficult decisions that will come up during installation:

- *Hard disk space* If hard disk space is at a premium, you might need to limit the number of installation features you choose. For example, very few applications come without a fully functional tutorial now. Generally, the tutorial makes use of the multimedia features Windows provides to reduce the time it takes to learn the product. All of these features come at a price, however. Learning to use the product from the manual may not seem as efficient as using the interactive tutorial. In fact, I'll tell you right out that it isn't. The disk space you save, though, could make room for another option you use long after the need for the tutorial is gone. Theoretically, you could install the tutorial and remove it later; some people invariably forget to do this, however, making the resulting loss of disk space permanent. If you install the tutorial, make sure that you remove it when it's no longer needed. Also, if the application comes with a large collection of fonts, clip art, graphics, or other such files, consider leaving these off your hard drive. Graphics, in particular, are disk hogs. Software manufacturers are aware of this, and most applications allow you to use the CD for clip art and graphics as needed while running the application.

Nowadays, many larger applications permit you to select which portions of their software should be loaded into your hard drive (for speed and easy access) and which should be accessed from the CD (you're asked to insert the CD if you choose one of these features). Use your own judgment about which items you need frequently and which you can use off the CD.

- *Uninstall capability* Some applications provide a custom uninstall capability. Even if your application provides only a stock uninstall capability, you could install it fully once to learn how to use the product, uninstall it, and then install it partially a second time to get what you really want.

- *Memory* This particular item of concern applies to graphics programs, for the most part, because they're the biggest users of memory. Some other applications are equally guilty, though. Have you ever noticed that some applications seem to gobble every spare bit of memory on your system? The problem might be your installation choices and not the way the application works. Graphics programs (and, to a smaller degree, other categories) often ask what types of filters and other "utility" elements you want to install. A graphics application might include a laundry list of application files it imports from and exports to. Or a graphics program might have many MB of sample photos and such.

  A database manager might include an autodial feature, and spreadsheets are rife with background problem solvers. It might seem like a good idea to select them all. After all, you may need them sometime. From a memory standpoint, however, this decision could be problematic. Some badly behaved applications load all those fancy utilities and filters whenever you start them. Each filter or other add-on costs memory that you could use for some other purpose. If you need that product element, fine; but why pay a memory and performance penalty for something you don't need? The bottom line is that you should install only the filters and utilities you'll actually use later.

- *Interapplication communication* I used to absolutely hate packaged applications. These suites of products contained things no one wanted—mini word processors with limited capabilities and a spreadsheet that could barely track your checkbook. Bundled applications suffer much less from this problem now and have improved in one other area as well. If you install a suite of products, such as Microsoft Office XP, rather than separate applications, there's a much better chance that the separate parts will communicate seamlessly or offer other efficiencies, such as sharing a spell checker between them.

I used to use products from different companies to get the best that each category had to provide. With today's huge applications, however, getting enough features is no longer a consideration, for the most part. Unless there's a very good reason to do so, you'll probably want to go with a "one-stop-shop" solution to fulfill the better part of your applications needs. Also, some of the docucentricity and ActiveX technologies built in to Windows XP make interapplication communication far simpler that it used to be.

Getting Application Settings Right

Although similar applications (such as word processors) might have a few settings in common, very few applications use the exact same settings. This section discusses some general principles for customizing your applications.

> **Tip:** Your first inclination might be to get into the application and complete this part of the setup immediately. That would probably be the worst mistake you could make. Software settings change as you learn how to use the application more efficiently. A little change here and there can make a big difference in how well the application works for you. Take the time to go through the tutorial first, and then make any setting changes you think will help. I usually keep Notepad handy to record any ideas I come up with while running the tutorial.

Changing your settings is largely a matter of personal preference. Even a small change, however, can make a big difference in the way you use an application. Simply customizing a toolbar, for example, can reap a fairly large increase in efficiency. Disabling an application's autocorrect feature might help you run background tasks more efficiently. The following tips can help you get the most out of your applications:

- *Toolbars* A toolbar is one way you can greatly increase your efficiency for a small increase in memory usage. Every icon you allocate uses additional system resources, but the amount of *memory* an icon uses is very small—usually less than 1KB. When setting up a toolbar, don't assume that the vendor provides the most commonly used icons. I try to track which commands I use the most; then I add them to the toolbar because it takes less time to access a command from the toolbar than from a menu. Seven icons should appear on every toolbar: Open, Close, New, Print, Cut, Copy, and Paste. Be sure to remove any standard toolbar buttons you don't use to save memory.

- *Printer settings* In most applications, you can set the printer configuration separately from the Windows general configuration. I usually set my printer configuration to match my use of an application. I use my word processor for final output, for example, so I use the best letter-quality resolution available. On the other hand, I never use my graphics programs for final output, so I select draft quality there. A draft printout might not seem acceptable, but it's more efficient than letter quality when you just want a quick look at your document. (Another benefit of using draft output, whenever possible, is that you use less ink, making those expensive toner cartridges last longer.) You also can vary the print resolution. A low-resolution, letter-quality printout might work fine for workgroup presentations, but you should use the highest available quality when making the same presentation to a larger audience. The resolution you use affects the amount of memory and time required for completing the printout.

- *Macros* A *macro* is a shortcut created to represent keystrokes you repeat frequently. I create macros for every repetitive task I perform with my main applications. For example, I always set up word processing files using a macro. It makes more sense for the computer to do the work than for me to do it. In fact, I use this macro so often that I attached it to my toolbar as an icon. Other tasks, however, don't work well as macros. I always thought changing a document from one format to another would make a great macro, but implementing it proved frustrating. Sometimes it takes a human mind to perform certain tasks.

- *Style sheets and templates* You can never have too many custom style sheets and templates. I always use a style sheet or template for documents if the application supports it. The reason is simple: Style sheets and templates don't take more than a few minutes to create, but they can save lots of time later. Templates and style sheets also provide another benefit: They enforce uniformity in the format of your documents. This is important whether you're part of a group or working as an individual. I view consistent output as the mark of a professional—most other people do, too.

- *Autocorrect* The autocorrect features provided by many applications can be a source of much consternation. On one hand, they provide a valuable service in automatically correcting misspelled words. On the other hand, they can chew up valuable memory and processor cycles—resources you could use to run a task in the background. I usually turn off autocorrect features and rely on a spelling checker (or other tools) to find mistakes at one time.

> **Tip:** You can also use Autocorrect to substitute short phrases for long ones. Suppose you often have to type your company name; for example, Jackson Consolidated Freight Company. You can add an acronym, such as JCFC, to your autocorrect dictionary. Then, every time you need to type your company name, you can just type **JCFC**. Your application automatically substitutes the long name in its place.

You need to work with an application long enough to build a rapport with it. After you figure out how you want to work with the application, you can start changing some personal settings to meet your specific requirements. Some of your settings might end up working for the group as well. Experimentation is a prime ingredient in finding the settings that work best for you.

Running 16-Bit Windows Applications

You'll find that your network probably has a few 16-bit applications hanging around. I have a special application I wrote that I use for printing labels; I could recompile that application in a 32-bit format (because I wrote it, I've got the source code), but most of you don't have that option. What do you do with those old applications? After you see the ease with which your new Windows XP applications install and remove, holding on to these hard-to-manage applications takes more than a little self control. Let's face it: The new applications you install definitely make those old (but necessary) applications look completely out-of-date, in various ways.

The best way to resolve the situation is to see whether a new, 32-bit version of the product will work with Microsoft's Add or Remove Programs utility. You'll probably find that some applications just don't fall into that category, however; custom software is especially prone to this problem. Another way to resolve the problem is to find an update or patch that includes its own uninstall program. You could remove most of the program, if not the entire program, that way (the actual capabilities of these uninstall programs vary widely).

How can you guard against wasting disk space when you try to remove a legacy application? One way is to look through the vendor documentation to see whether it provides a list of files an application requires. Make a note of which files you installed. You can also make notes on the state of your machine before and after the install.

You'll need to protect your installation by looking for odd entries in both WIN.INI and SYSTEM.INI. If an older, 16-bit application relies on device drivers or DLLs to get the job done, you'll probably have problems getting the application to work properly. I had a problem application that relied on a replaceable graphics driver to get the job done. You can imagine the mess it created when it replaced the 32-bit driver used by Windows XP with its own 16-bit driver.

Tip: If you do want to run 16-bit applications, you'll find that some of them like to cause problems—crashes and system instability. (Technically, misbehaving 16-bit applications don't actually crash Windows XP itself; they disrupt other 16-bit applications.) You can greatly improve things by preventing these rogue applications from wandering clumsily into the memory in a shared address space or the shared memory heaps (system resources) used by other 16-bit applications. How? Force the rogue application to run in its own, separate memory space. (You can also do this with DOS applications.) Right-click the application's icon and then select Properties. Click the check box that says Run in Separate Memory Space. This creates a unique process for the application, where it can do little damage to the community of applications.

Running 32-Bit Windows Applications

I tested a number of 32-bit applications and discovered a few interesting facts. Overall, a 32-bit application is larger and just a tad slower (when you view a single section of code) than its 16-bit counterpart. It's larger because you're using 32 bits for everything—even structures that might not require 32 bits. In addition, 32-bit code is typically larger than its 16-bit counterpart. Does this mean that 32-bit applications are memory hogs you shouldn't use? Not by a long shot.

I want to explain the slower part of 32-bit application performance a little better. A 32-bit application starts out a little slower than its 16-bit equivalent, but ends up faster for a number of reasons. Most of these reasons have come from using a flat address space and the other architectural benefits of a 32-bit format. Yes, it takes more time to process 32-bit code than the equivalent sections of 16-bit code because the 32-bit code is larger. There's still a big speed benefit in the long run, however, because of the way a 32-bit application executes.

Running a 32-bit application has definite benefits in terms of speed. For one thing, it supports true multitasking. I found that background repagination in the 16-bit version of Word usually meant that I had to wait anyway until the application finished the task. Under the 32-bit version, Word spawns a task that really does run in the background. I seldom notice that anything is happening; the document just gets repaginated without my thinking about it. This is how multitasking should work from a user perspective. E-mail should download, Active Desktop items should update, and other background tasks should silently and invisibly activate while you remain unaware that they're even taking place.

Multitasking also helps you perform some tasks, such as printing, much faster than you could using a 16-bit application. For one thing, Windows can make better use of idle time with a 32-bit application. You'll notice that you regain control of the system faster. After a 32-bit application spawns a print task, it can return control of the computer immediately. It doesn't even need to slow you down as it checks on the status of the "background" print job like a 16-bit application does.

> **Warning:** Every time a 32-bit application spawns a new task (called a *thread*), it uses some system resources. Some applications can create so many threads that your system begins to slow to a crawl and Windows runs out of resources. The second you run completely out of resources, the machine usually freezes. Although Microsoft did increase the size of some memory areas and moved others to the 32-bit area, Windows XP still isn't perfect when it comes to managing 32-bit resources. The best thing to do is avoid the situation altogether. Don't try to run every feature a 32-bit application can provide at one time. Limit the number of tasks you ask an application to perform in the background to a reasonable level. Finally, run the Resource Monitor from time to time, just to see how you're doing on system resources. You might find that you need to adjust some of your techniques to compensate for limitations in the Windows XP design. It's good multitasking, but the tasks are, at base, happening serially. Your computer hasn't broken the laws of macro-level physics and started operating simultaneously in multiple states. It's still switching between operations, but gracefully.

The big performance-tuning tip for Windows XP and 32-bit applications is to use as many automatic settings as possible. The more room you give Windows XP to compensate for changing system conditions, the better. Chapter 5 contains quite a few tips you can follow to optimize the environment. I discuss the need to monitor the swap file size to ensure that you don't end up wasting processor cycles in thrashing, for example. After you optimize the environment for a 32-bit application, you've essentially optimized the application itself. All you need to do is check out the "Settings" section later in this chapter, to make the application as efficient as possible during use.

Optimizing DOS Applications

I haven't found many gray areas when running DOS applications under Windows XP. Either it works or it doesn't; there's not much middle ground. Unlike 16-bit Windows applications, a DOS application doesn't interfere with the operation of Windows itself when you install or remove it. In fact, removing a DOS application usually consists of a single step: removing the directory that holds the application. If you use a separate directory for your data, you shouldn't run into any problems if you decide to reinstall the application later.

MS-DOS Emulation

You use MS-DOS under Windows XP through the MS-DOS emulation mode. What actually happens when you run a DOS application is that Windows XP makes a copy of the phantom DOS session stored in memory, spawns a new Virtual 86 session (a "virtual machine"), and places the copy it made in the new session. What you see is a windowed DOS emulation. See the "Creating a DOS Session" section later in this chapter.

As with almost everything else under Windows XP, right-clicking on the DOS cmd.exe title bar produces a context menu. In this case, it contains three entries that are important to you as a user: Close, Edit, and Properties. The Close option enables you to close the DOS window without typing Exit and pressing Enter at the DOS prompt. The Edit option enables you to mark, copy, or paste text from the DOS screen to the Clipboard. The Properties option displays the Properties dialog box shown in Figure 8.7.

As you can see, this dialog box contains four pages. I provide a bit more information in the "Settings" section of this chapter. The following list provides a quick rundown of the more important features you find on these four pages (features you normally use as part of an active DOS window versus application configuration).

Options

Use the Options tab shown in Figure 8.7 to select the cursor size, such as Small, Medium, or Large. The Display Options section contains options to run the session in a window or full screen. You use the Command History option to set the buffer size and number of buffers with an option to discard old duplicates. This tab also contains Edit options for Quick Edit mode, and Insert mode.

FIGURE 8.7
The Properties dialog box for cmd.exe.

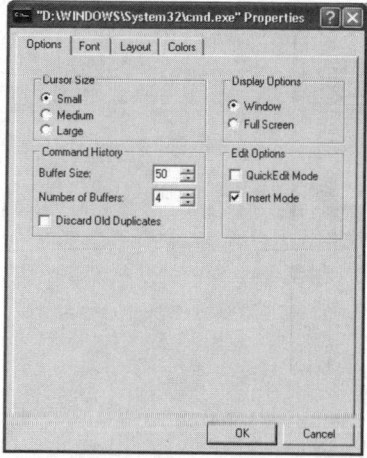

Font

Use the Font tab shown in Figure 8.8 to set the Window Preview size, ranging from 4X6 to 10X18. You can select the font you want to use from the listings available on your computer. At the bottom, the selected font is shown with some additional information about the font, including its location and its width and height in pixels.

FIGURE 8.8
The Font tab, where you select window size and font.

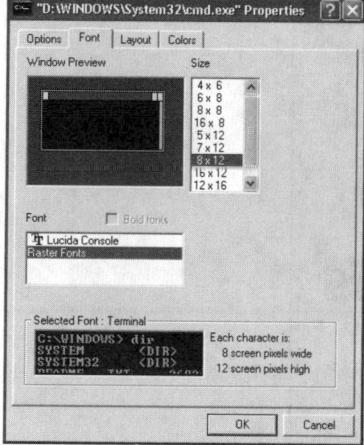

Layout

Using the Layout tab shown in Figure 8.9, you can select the screen buffer size, window size, and window position. Notice that you can also choose to let the system position the window.

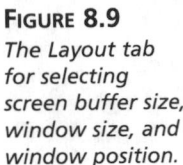

FIGURE 8.9
The Layout tab for selecting screen buffer size, window size, and window position.

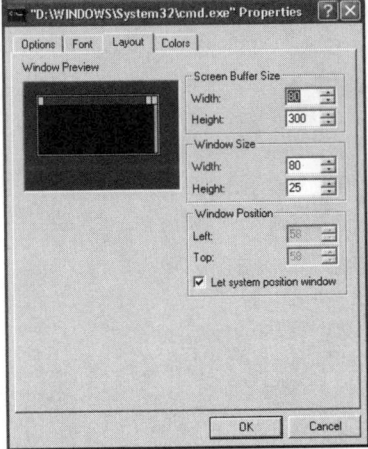

Colors

Using the Colors tab shown in Figure 8.10, you can select colors for the screen text, the screen background, the pop-up text, and the pop-up background. You may set the Red, Green, and Blue values or select a color from the color patches shown in the middle of the page.

FIGURE 8.10
The Colors tab is where you select colors for screen text, screen background, pop-up text, and pop-up background.

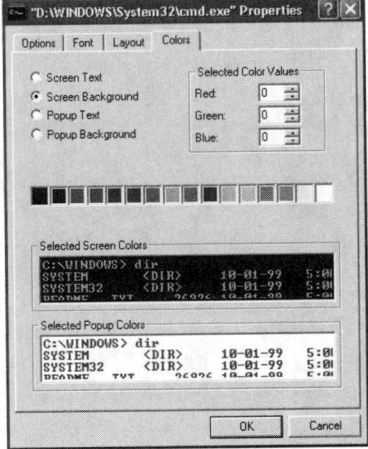

Creating a DOS Session

Windows XP uses a command shell program that provides direct communication between you and the operating system. This program doesn't have a GUI interface. The command shell uses a command interpreter called CMD.EXE. To run the command shell, use the Run command from the start menu. This brings up the DOS-like window you're familiar with if you've ever run DOS from a Windows operating system. Figure 8.11 shows a typical command shell after running the DIR (directory) command.

> **Tip:** You can also use long filenames when typing commands. The only requirement is that, in a few cases, you might be required to use quotation marks to enclose the long filename or directory, as in this example:
>
> DIR "Some Long Directory Name"

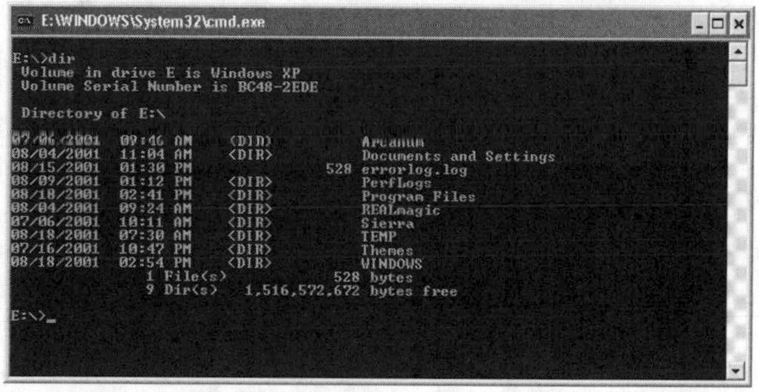

FIGURE 8.11
A typical command prompt that shows the results of a character-based command.

DOS Objects

As with any other object in Windows XP, right-clicking a DOS object displays a context menu from which you can cut, copy, and paste the object. The Properties option opens the Properties dialog box, which is described in the next section. This is one major area in which DOS applications are treated differently from Windows applications.

Settings

A DOS application's Properties dialog box contains much more than most Windows applications' Properties dialog boxes. The Properties dialog box shown in Figure 8.7 enables you to change every setting involving the DOS application. In fact, Windows XP provides several new features for DOS applications that make running them a snap.

> **Tip:** If you want to increase the environment size, edit CONFIG.NT using Notepad. Either create or modify an existing SHELL line within CONFIG.NT so that it looks like this (assuming your Windows XP resides in the WINDOWS directory):
>
> SHELL=C:\WINDOWS\SYSTEM32\COMMAND.COM /e:512
>
> This line effectively doubles the default 256 bytes allocated for the environment; you can, however, set it as large as 32KB.

Using Windows Scripting Host (WSH)

Windows Scripting Host is available in two versions: A Windows version (WScript.exe) and a command-prompt version (CScript.exe). The Windows version provides a property sheet for setting your script properties. The command prompt version lets you use command-line switches for setting the script properties. To run either version, use Start | Run and type either **WScript.exe or CScript.exe** at the prompt.

This feature is new with Windows XP; in the past, it supported only the MS-DOS command language. WSH supports scripts written in VBScript or Jscript. The scripting engine uses filename extensions to identify the correct scripting language, such as .vbs for VBScript and .js for Jscript. WSH uses the appropriate engine based on the file extension, so you don't need to be concerned with the programmatic identifier of the script engine needed.

Running Your Script

Running a script at the command prompt or from the Run dialog box is easy. Using the start | Run menu, type the following at the command prompt if you're using a CScript:

```
use cscript [script name] [host options] [script arguments].
```

The script name must include the filename extension. The host options are the command-line switches that enable or disable various WSH features. Always precede host options with two slashes (//). *Script arguments* are switches passed to the script and must be preceded with a slash (/). The command-line bases script supports the options described in Table 8.1.

Table 8.1 Command-line Script Options

Parameter	Action
//B	Specifies batch mode, which doesn't display alerts, scripting errors, or input prompts.
//D	Turns on the debugger.
//E:engine	Specifies the scripting language used to run the script.
//H:cscript or //H:wscript	Registers either CScript.exe or WScript.exe as the default script host for running scripts. If neither is specified, the default is WScript.exe.
//I	Specifies interactive mode, which displays alerts, scripting errors, and input prompts. This is the default and the opposite of //B.
//Job:xxxx	Runs the job identified by *xxxx* in a .wsf script file.
//Logo	Specifies that the Windows Script Host banner is displayed in the console window before the script runs. This is the default and the opposite of //Nologo.

Parameter	Action
//Nologo	Specifies that the Windows Script Host banner isn't displayed before the script runs.
//S	Saves the current command-prompt options for the current user.
//T:*nnnnn*	Specifies the maximum length of time the script can run (in seconds). You can specify up to 32,767 seconds. The default is no time limit.
//U	Specifies that CScript should use Unicode characters for redirected output from the console.
//X	Starts the script in the debugger.
//?	Displays available command parameters and provides help for using them (this is the same as typing CScript.exe with no parameters and no script).

WScript

WScripts can be run in several ways, by browsing in Windows, using the Run command, or running the script from a command prompt window. Here's how you would run a script each way.

Browsing in Windows

Browse to the folder that houses your script and double-click it. You can use My Computer, Windows Explorer, or even a script you've placed on your desktop.

Using the Run command

Use Start | Run and enter WScript.exe followed by a space and then the complete pathname, including the extension of the script you want to run. Click OK to run the script.

Using the Command Prompt

At the command prompt, type **WScript.exe** and then a space, followed by the full path to your script, including the file extension. Pressing Enter starts your script.

At some point, you might want to set global properties for all scripts run using WSCRIPT.EXE. Let's take a minute, then, and look at how this is accomplished. Using the Start | Run menu item, enter WSCRIPT in the dialog box and click OK. The Windows Script Host Settings dialog box, shown in Figure 8.12, should appear.

In this dialog box, you can set your script to stop after a specified number of seconds. Remember that this is applied to every script run with this host.

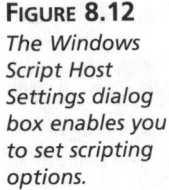

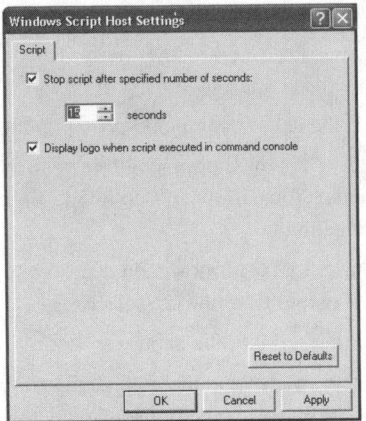

Using The Script Debugger

The Microsoft Script Debugger must be downloaded and installed; it's not included with a normal installation of Windows XP. You can obtain the Script Debugger directly from Microsoft at http://msdn.microsoft.com/scripting/. Select Script Debugger from the left side menu and then Downloads. A wealth of information about the Script Debugger is available from the same menu, such as documentation and a complete overview of the program.

The Script Debugger can be started in two ways. From Internet Explorer, choose View | Script Debugger. The Debugger opens with the current HTML source file loaded. To use the debugger, load a document, choose Break at Next Statement from the Edit menu, and execute a script. The debugger window opens and stops at the first statement in the current script.

In response to an error if the browser or server encounters a syntax or run-time error in a script, the browser or server displays a message that asks if you want to debug. If you choose to use the debugger, the debugger opens and starts at the line where the error occurred.

The help file included with the Script Debugger contains useful information should you need any additional help. Figure 8.13 shows the Script Debugger.

If at any time you prefer to return to the original Internet Explorer minus the debugger, use the Add or Remove Programs option in the Control Panel. The Script Debugger is listed there.

Understanding the Dangers of Script Support

Caution is the best way to describe how to use the debugger. This section describes several typical dangers to be aware of when using the debugger.

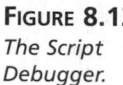

FIGURE 8.13
The Script Debugger.

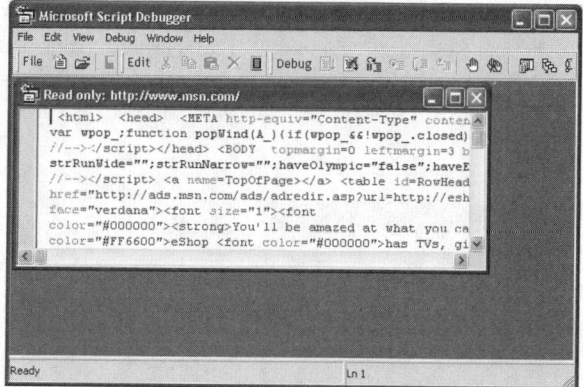

If you're debugging a client script generated by an ASP file, the line numbers reported in error messages refer to lines in the HTML document currently displayed in the browser. These lines usually don't correspond to line numbers in the original ASP file because the server script doesn't appear in the HTML output of an ASP file.

A syntax error, reported by the debugger, might not always reflect the exact error. In that case, you have to research the error on your own.

When the Script Debugger is enabled for one or more ASP applications, all server errors are passed to the debugger. Therefore, you shouldn't enable the Script Debugger for an ASP application unless you can work on the server itself.

Using the Event Viewer Console

To use the Event Viewer, open the Control Panel and select Administrative Tools. Double-click the Event Viewer applet. You see the Event Viewer dialog box, shown in Figure 8.14.

FIGURE 8.14
The Event Viewer contains event entries for applications, the system, and security.

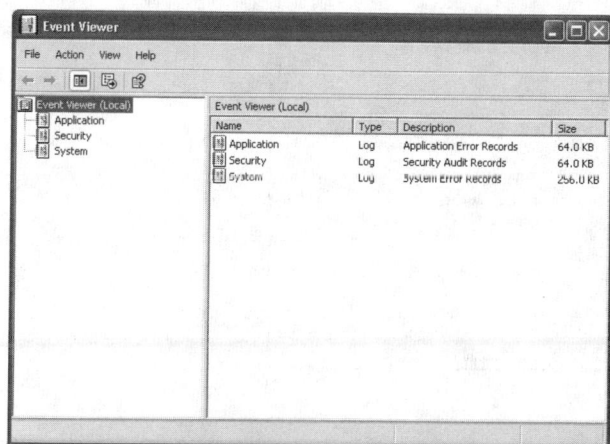

As you can see, the Event Viewer contains lots of information about Application, Security, and your System. In Figure 8.14, I've selected System and then the first event item listed. Whenever you double-click an Event Viewer entry, you view the Event Properties dialog box for that entry. Figure 8.15 shows a typical event log entry for the Event Viewer.

FIGURE 8.15
The Event Properties dialog box contains a single event from the Event Viewer.

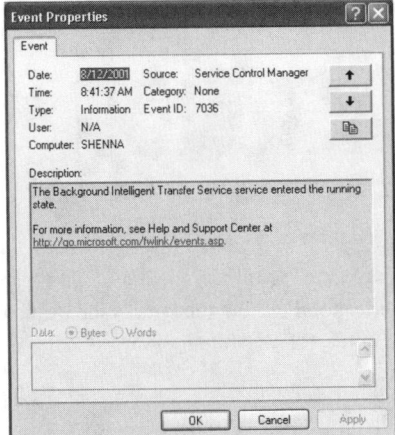

By selecting the Application listing under Event Viewer, you can discover a great deal about application events. For example, applications often generate an informational message to tell you they're starting a task, a warning message to indicate a noncritical problem, and an error message to tell you about a critical problem. Figure 8.16 shows an application event on my system with a Warning type. Double-clicking the warning brings up the Event Properties page.

FIGURE 8.16
The Event properties for an application event.

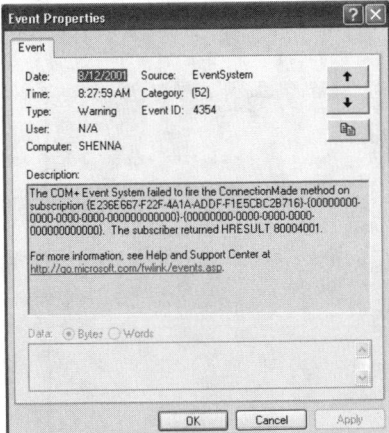

On Your Own

Make a list of tasks that are repetitive and that you must frequently accomplish. Then see if you can record macros for any of them.

Find a DLL for one of the smaller applications installed on your machine. Use the procedure in Chapter 13 for viewing the contents of the files to determine which DLLs and other system files this application needs to work. After you make the list, see whether other applications require the same files. You might be surprised by what you find. Windows XP reuses a number of the same files.

Open two DOS windows and then use the DOS Title command to change their names to something more meaningful than Command Prompt.

Try running an ill-behaved DOS application, such as a game, under Windows XP, Windows 2000, and Windows 98. What happens if the application causes system problems under Windows XP? Does Windows 98 or Windows 2000 respond in the same way? How does the application perform? Is it faster under Windows 98, Windows 2000, or Windows XP? It pays to look at marginal applications to see what you can expect from an operating system. Try the same tests for an older 16-bit application.

9

Exploiting Your Hardware

Hardware and software work together in today's PCs to create a computing environment in which users can perform tasks literally unheard of just a few years ago. However, before users can gain the benefits a PC can provide, they have to tune the system to work at its peak efficiency (or have someone do it for them). That means optimizing the system in its entirety as well as optimizing individual components.

We've already discussed the software part of the picture in detail. Chapter 8, "Exploiting Your Software," looked into some things you can do to maximize the effectiveness of your software. This chapter shows how to get the most out of your computer hardware.

Installing and Deleting Devices

Windows XP usually detects all of the hardware on your machine during setup. Windows XP provides the same support for Plug and Play devices as Windows 2000/95/98/Me for some time. The "Installing Windows XP" section of Chapter 4 covers this entire process. It also covers some of the things you can do if Windows XP doesn't detect your hardware, so I don't repeat that discussion here.

However, you need to answer some other device-related questions while using Windows XP, such as "What happens if you install a new piece of hardware after installing Windows XP?" and "What do you do with old devices?" This section of the chapter covers both these topics. I also outline troubleshooting procedures you can follow if Windows doesn't act as expected.

Installing Hardware

Your first clue that there's a problem with your new hardware is when you start the machine and you don't see it listed with the Plug and Play hardware during the BIOS check. Of course, this statement assumes that you can read fast enough to see the chart containing this information. If the chart passes you by and Windows starts, you still have another clue that there's a problem. If Windows supports a piece of hardware you install on your machine, yet doesn't automatically detect it during startup, it's likely that you have a configuration problem.

Tip: Make sure that you read the entire user guide for your new piece of hardware. Vendors often place the one piece of information you need in the most inconspicuous place in the manual. Check the disks that accompany the hardware and read the README files as well. The README files contain last-minute information that doesn't appear in the manual. Look on the vendor Web site for new drivers and updated information. Never assume that the manuals and drivers you have are up-to-date. Finally, see if the vendor offers support through a newsgroup and ask any questions you have. Peer support is often better than the information you get from support personnel on the telephone. If the vendor doesn't provide support through a newsgroup, try one of the generic newsgroups, such as `alt.ibm.pc.hardware`, `alt.computer.hardware`, `alt.comp.hardware`, or `microsoft.public.win2000.hardware` (or a Windows XP alternative when it becomes available). You can find all Microsoft newsgroups on the `news.microsoft.com` server if your ISP doesn't carry them.

The fact is that Windows XP should always detect your hardware. It should ask you to install a driver for the new hardware except under two conditions. The first condition is if you install an older, but simple, device, such as an extra serial (COM) or parallel (LPT) port. My machine came equipped with one parallel port, and I have two printers, so I installed a second port. The second is if the device is newer than Windows XP. In most cases, Windows XP should still detect the new device, but you have to supply a driver for it.

What happens if the device doesn't fit into these two categories and you still can't get Windows XP to recognize it? First, remember that kicking your machine isn't an option. The following list contains some fixes I've used in the past—they work most of the time, and you find that you get much less frustrated if you try them first:

- Verify that the hardware doesn't require any setup. If you see any jumpers on the board, spend some time reading the manual and figuring out what they do. If the manual doesn't document the jumpers, try to find an answer online. Jumpers always perform some function, even if it's vendor-specific testing.

- Ensure that you connect all cables to the right location and that the cables are firmly seated on their posts. If you can place the cable in more than one place, check the manual to ensure that you've connected them to the correct place.

- Try exchanging this board with another board in your system. The BIOS reads boards nearest the power supply first. In addition, rearranging the boards forces the BIOS to update the system configuration. Finally, this technique reveals "dead," or non-operational, expansion slots on the motherboard. Be extremely careful when doing this because the boards are somewhat fragile, and you don't want to break any of the "fingers" within the expansion slots. The boards require a firm push into the expansion slots—just don't force the board and break it.

- Check all boards to make sure that you fully seat them in the correct expansion slots. A properly seated board makes good contact with the expansion slot fingers, which allows good contact with the motherboard.

- Remove any boards you don't need in order to start the system. For example, your system does require a hard drive controller and a display adapter, but it doesn't require a soundboard. Sometimes, starting the system with the minimum number of boards plus the problem board forces Windows to recognize it. After Windows recognizes the board, you can add the other boards back into the system.

- Try installing the device driver anyway. If you've tried everything else, this is the option of last resort. It generally doesn't work because Windows doesn't know which piece of hardware you're trying to install. The recognition process is important.

At this point, a call to the vendor is in order. You've tried installing the board according to vendor instructions without success. The process we just tried eliminated common causes of setup failure, such as a board that requires setup. You've eliminated the motherboard, interactions with other boards, and bad expansion slots.

You have only three possibilities to consider. First, the board requires some "magical" setup that the vendor will tell you about for this system. For example, some CD-RW drives require special assistance before the recording application will work. Second, the board is incompatible with your system and will never work with it. This scenario is rare, but it does happen. Third, the board is non-operational. In some cases, a board gets jostled just enough during transit to cause it to fail.

Removing Hardware

Removing hardware—at least the driver—is usually easier than installing it. In most cases, you should remove the drivers for a device first and then remove the device. Reversing this process could prevent Windows XP from booting properly. Fortunately, Windows XP at least boots in safe mode even if you leave the device in place. I always like to take the safest route possible, however, when it comes to the configuration of my machine. Removing the driver first is the safest route. The following steps show you the procedure for removing a driver from your machine:

1. Right-click My Computer from the Start menu and select the Properties option. Click the Hardware tab and then the Device Manager button in the System Properties dialog box. Select the device category you want to remove and click the plus sign next to it. Right-click the device you want to change. The dialog box should look similar to the one shown in Figure 9.1. Notice the context menu options for this device; some devices include additional options.

2. Highlight the device you want to remove. Click the Properties button to display the Device Properties dialog box and select the Driver tab. Click the Driver File Details button (if it's present). You should see a list of device drivers. Make a copy of the driver list so that you can verify later that Windows XP removed them. Otherwise, you end up with additional disk clutter after installing and removing a few devices.

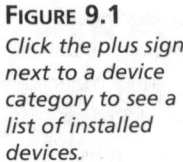
FIGURE 9.1

Click the plus sign next to a device category to see a list of installed devices.

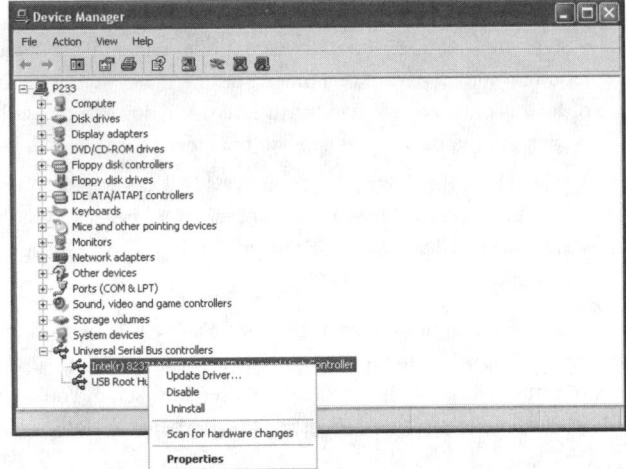

Note: Some adapters contain more than one real device. For example, the Diamond Monster sound board in my machine contains devices for Sound Blaster Pro emulation, MIDI device, game port, and standard PCI audio. Each device has a separate entry in the Device Manager. The only way you know which devices are related is to look at the vendor documentation and see what support an individual card provides. (In some cases, the vendor also adds its name to every entry it makes in Device Manager.) To remove the device, you must find the main entry and remove it. Windows XP automatically removes all supporting entries. Make sure you record the drivers used by each entry because the main entry doesn't provide a master list.

3. After you finish recording the driver names, click Cancel to clear the Device Properties dialog box.

4. Highlight the device you want to remove and then click the Uninstall button. (You can also right-click the device and choose Uninstall from the context menu.) Windows XP removes the device and all its supporting entries.

5. Shut down Windows.

6. Remove the device so that Windows doesn't reinstall support for it.

7. Restart Windows so that the changes can take effect.

Configuring Ports

Windows XP provides three different port-configuration methods, depending on the type of hardware you want to configure. Most hardware uses the first method, which I present in the sections that follow. The second and third methods apply to your parallel and serial ports. The last two configuration methods provide more of a performance boost than a means of conflict resolution. They tune your ports for maximum application and network compatibility.

Standard Port Configuration

Communication is the name of the game in your computer. For communication to occur, there must be some way to exchange information. In the PC, the physical part of the communications path is an input/output (I/O) port. If you want to send data from one area of the machine to another, your application must first tell the computer what I/O port (or address) to send it to. The following procedure takes you through the process of changing a COM port on your machine:

1. Click Phone and Modem Options in Control Panel.
2. On the Modems tab, click the modem you want to configure and then click Properties.
3. On the Advanced tab, click Advanced Port Settings. If this option doesn't appear, the modem doesn't support changing the assigned COM port.
4. In the COM Port Number field, click the port you want to use.

Serial Port Configuration

The serial port offers a variety of configuration options that go beyond address conflict resolution. Several options control both the port speed and its compatibility with software. In the Ports tab, you select the port you want to change. You access it through the Print Server Properties dialog box. Choose Start | Printers and Faxes and then select Server Properties from the File menu. Choose the Ports tab. Select the port you want to change and then click the Configure Port button. Windows XP displays a Properties dialog box for that port.

There's another way to set the serial port parameters. When you're using the Direct Cable Connection program provided with Windows XP, you want to set these settings to Maximum. Some users miss this particular bit of irony because the utility never asks to set the port settings. Users assume that the Direct Cable Connection program uses the maximum settings available. Experience says otherwise, however. You can actually slow data transfers from your notebook to a crawl by failing to observe this little "gotcha."

One area where Windows XP rises above its predecessors is in the way it handles advanced universal asynchronous receiver transmitter (UART) chips. Let's discuss the differences between certain UARTs. Earlier UARTs could store only one character at a time. This meant that the CPU had to retrieve that character immediately, or else the next character the UART received would overwrite it. This is what people mean when they say that their port "dropped a character." It means that the CPU couldn't respond fast enough and the UART overwrote a character in its buffer.

Forcing the CPU to attend to the needs of the UART is fine in a single-tasking system, such as DOS, but it isn't that efficient in a multitasking environment, such as Windows.

After UART vendors realized that the older UARTs were a bottleneck when used in a multitasking environment, they started making new UARTs with a FIFO (first in, first out) buffer. The FIFO buffer can store up to 16 characters, giving the CPU time to complete whatever it was doing and then respond to the needs of the UART.

Parallel Port Configuration

The parallel port offers just one configuration setting as far as Windows XP is concerned, the Configure LPT Port dialog box. You access it through the Print Server Properties dialog box. Choose Start | Printers and Faxes, and then select Server Properties from the File menu. Select your LPT port and click the Configure Port button.

Parallel port configuration consists of setting a timeout interval. I usually maintain the default setting unless the port captures a network connection that needs more time to react. This transmission-retry specification defines how long, in seconds, Windows XP waits to notify you that the printer isn't responding. You might want to set this to a delay longer than the default 90 seconds if you normally leave the printer off and need to wait for it to warm up for printing.

Using Fonts

Fonts are an essential part of the Windows experience. You'll probably find a font for every need preinstalled during the Windows XP installation. However, you probably won't find all of them on your hard drive. At some time or another, you need to install a new font on your system. Of course, that means knowing the location and name of the font before you begin.

Once you know which font to load, open the Fonts applet in the Control Panel. You see a list of fonts your system contains. Use the File | Install New Font command to display the Add Fonts dialog box. The Folders and Drives fields help you find the location of the fonts you want to install. As soon as you locate a drive with fonts, the List of Fonts field begins to fill with font names. Highlight the font you want to use and then click OK. Windows XP displays an Install Font Progress dialog box. When the copying is complete, both the Install Font Progress and the Add Font dialog boxes go away.

Windows XP makes removing Fonts easy. Simply locate the fonts you want to remove and press Delete. Note that this form of deletion is permanent. Unlike other areas of Windows, deleting a font removes it from your hard drive and doesn't place it in your Recycle Bin, so you have to exercise some care in pruning your font burden.

At some time, you'll want to view a selected font. Double-click any of the font icons, and you see a dialog box similar to the one shown in Figure 9.2. This dialog box doesn't show every character in the font. To see all of the characters, you need a utility such as Character Map. However, this view does show what the font looks like at various sizes and tells you something about the font creator.

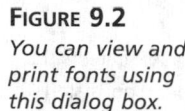

FIGURE 9.2

You can view and print fonts using this dialog box.

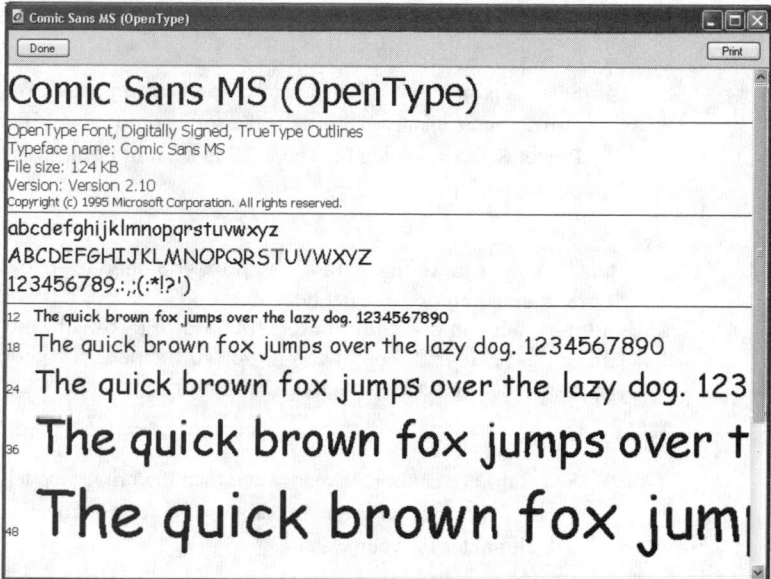

Notice the Print button in the upper-right corner of the dialog box. Click Print, and you see a Print dialog box. Select the printer and options you want to use, and then click Print to send a copy of the window to your printer.

Working with Printers

Before you can use a local printer, you have to install and configure it. I used to hate doing this because it seemed as if every printer was just different enough to make life difficult. It was a nice surprise to see how easy things were under Windows 2000 and now with Windows XP. This section of the chapter provides details for installing a printer. It also includes some productivity tips.

Even if you don't have any printers installed on your system, you have a Printers and Faxes folder in the Control Panel. At a minimum, this folder contains an applet that enables you to install a new printer or local fax printer. This is the applet you use to add a new printer to your system. I show you how to install printers in Chapter 14; for now, here's a brief summary.:

1. Choose the Start | Printers and Faxes icon to open the Printers and Faxes folder. You might see one or more printers already installed in the folder along with an Add Printer icon.

2. Double-click Add Printer. Click Next to pass the Welcome screen. You see the Network or Local Printer dialog box. In this dialog box, you have the choice to connect to an existing printer on the network or to use a local printer. We'll discuss the local printer connection in this case.

3. Select Local printer attached to this computer. Click Next. You see the Select a Printer Port dialog box.

4. Select a printer port and then click Next. In many cases, Windows XP detects the printer automatically and installs the software for you. If not, you see an Install Printer Software dialog box, containing a list of printer vendors and associated printer models.

> **Note:** If you choose to create a new port, you need to follow a few additional steps, depending on the port type. You don't use this option for most local printers, but you use it for printers that attach directly to the network. If your printer has a direct Ethernet connection to the network, choose Create a New Port and then select the Standard TCP/IP Port option.

5. Select the correct printer vendor and then the printer model. Click Next. Windows XP asks for a printer name. In addition, you can optionally set this printer as the default printer for your system.

6. Type a printer name and set the printer as your default printer (if desired). Click Next. You see a Printer Sharing dialog box.

7. Choose a printer sharing option. If you choose to share your printer, you also need to type a share name for it. Click Next. You see a Print Test Page dialog box.

8. Select a test page option. Generally, you should print a test page to verify that your printer is working as anticipated. Click Next. You see a Completion dialog box.

9. Click Finish. Windows XP installs the required software. It optionally prints a test page to verify that your printer is working as expected.

> **Tip:** Sometimes, you might need an updated driver for your printer. Inside the Printers and Faxes folder, select Get Help with Printing to go to the Microsoft Support Services site at http://support.microsoft.com/support/printing/. Using this site helps you solve many printer problems. You can also download the latest printer drivers for all the Windows operating systems from this site.

Sometimes, you don't want to waste much time opening a document to print it. Windows XP offers several shortcuts you can use to avoid opening an application to print a document using the default settings. For example, you can right-click the document and choose the Print option from the context menu. This first method has the disadvantage of limiting you to one printer, the one you set as the default.

Another technique is to place a shortcut to the printer on the Desktop. You can drag any documents you want to print to the printer shortcut. In this case, the document goes to the selected printer rather than to the default printer. However, you have to drag the document to the printer, which isn't quite as automatic as right-clicking, but is faster than opening the application, in some cases.

Working with Modems

Communication is a major part of the job these days. It used to be that you could take care of everything with the office fax and a few telephone calls. Today, many people can't take the time to use the office fax; they need one nearby to take care of their needs. The amount of electronic "paper" people send is amazing. Many people are busy in other ways, too. Playing telephone tag isn't fun, especially when you can leave a message for the person by e-mail and receive a response later that day.

The Internet has become the premier source of information for many people. I can usually get an answer to a networking- or application-related question far more quickly by going online than I could if I called a vendor support line. The difference is the fast search engines and by now measureless amount of knowledge that the Internet provides.

We've all gotten used to downloading data in the background while using an application in the foreground. Configuring your machine for optimum communication performance isn't hard; it just takes time. You can try a setting, communicate a little to see its effect, and then tune more as necessary. Unlike other tuning tips I present in this chapter, there's no quick and easy way to tune your communications programs. The problem is that every machine is slightly different, as is every modem and every communications program that uses the modem.

Tuning Your Modem

To tune your modem settings, open the Control Panel and double-click the Phone and Modem Options icon. Click the Modems tab. Right-click your modem and choose Properties from the context menu. (You could also click the Properties button.) You see a dialog box similar to the one shown in Figure 9.3. (Some modems provide additional tabs that we won't discuss in this chapter.)

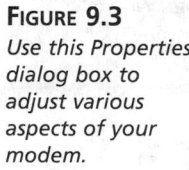

FIGURE 9.3

Use this Properties dialog box to adjust various aspects of your modem.

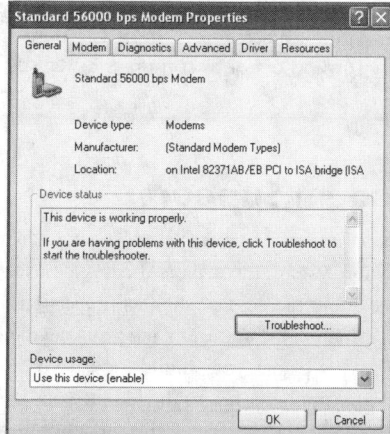

In the Modem tab, you can adjust the speaker volume and specify the maximum speed at which your modem is capable of accepting data from applications (not sending or getting data over the telephone, for example). If your modem has trouble recognizing the dial tone, try turning that option off.

> **Tip:** The Maximum Port Speed list displays the highest speed your modem can achieve when interacting with your computer. (This isn't the maximum speed at which it communicates over the Internet or over other modem-to-modem connections—many factors can retard that speed.) Choose the highest speed that doesn't cause problems to gain the best performance.

Click the Diagnostics tab to get technical information about (and test) the modem. If you're experiencing problems with your modem and you contact the manufacturer, someone might ask you to use this page.

Finally, the Advanced tab allows you to manually specify initialization commands (see your modem manual), or you can click the Change Default Preferences button to adjust the port speed, protocol, compression, and flow control. Furthermore, you can set the length of time to wait before canceling a call if it's not connected or before disconnecting after a period of idleness (no activity). If your modem supports data compression, you should use it; it can boost your effective transfer rate as much as four times the usual rate. The Advanced Port Settings buttons permit you to adjust the transmit and receive buffers. Normally, you leave both at their high settings for maximum speed—but if you're having problems with your connection, you can try lower settings.

> **Tip:** Sometimes, data compression can actually hurt the efficiency of your transmission. Certain types of Telnet connections fall into this category, as do some BBS calls in which the host modem doesn't support your modem's protocols. If you're having trouble maintaining a connection or the data transfer rate isn't as high as you expected, try turning off data compression to see whether there's any improvement.

Using WDM Modem Support

Device Manager provides an overview of your system from a hardware perspective. It lists every major device in your system, the drivers the device uses, the operational state of the device, and other facts about the device, such as the system resources it uses. In some cases, you also find rudimentary diagnostics for your device in the Device Manager, so this is one of the first places you should look if you think you're having a problem with Windows and your modem. Every device on your system provides a Device Properties dialog box. Modems are one of the most common devices installed on any machine, and they make a good device to look at because they include a few uncommon features.

The Diagnostics tab is the most important troubleshooting aid for any device because it contains the vendor-recommended diagnostic routines. Figure 9.4 shows a typical example for a modem. To see this screen, click Query Modem. The list of information you get back from the modem (when it works) tells you a great deal about the capabilities of that modem. For example, you can check the list to see if the modem provides fax capability and the level of capability offered. The returned information also tells you about standards the modem supports and a few unexpected surprises. For example, some modems keep track of the last number you dialed, making it relatively easy for someone to check on your dial-up access habits.

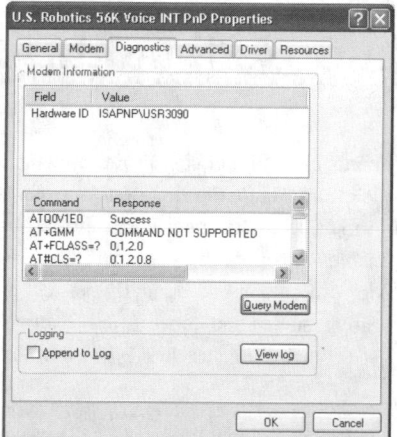

FIGURE 9.4

Use the Diagnostics tab to troubleshoot your modem and find out more about it.

The General tab adjusts the modem-connection settings. It controls how long the modem waits to create a connection and determines how long the modem holds an idle connection. This tab also controls the connection speed and features, such as error correction (EC). You can also use it to enable data compression, a feature that helps the modem work more efficiently, but introduces compatibility problems that may not work with all modems. You also find flow control options on the General tab. The default setting usually works best, but you may need to change it for compatibility reasons as well.

Using USB Modem Support

A USB modem isn't that different from its external counterpart, from a usage perspective. You still communicate at the same speed, and many of the configuration items for standard modems are the same. All you need to do to install a USB modem is plug it into a USB port. Windows XP recognizes the new addition, queries it for information, and installs any drivers required to use it.

USB modems automatically provide WDM support (see the preceding section for details on WDM support). When accessing a USB modem the signal goes through the TAPI, Unimodem, and VCOMM layers as all Windows modems do; then through the WDM layer; and, finally, through two USB object layers. The first of these two USB object layers is modem specific. Your USB modem provides a driver that helps the Windows XP communication system access the USB bus. The second USB object layer is the USB bus object itself. This part of Windows XP transfers data and commands from the communication system to your modem. It also handles the standard USB details, such as determining the presence or absence of the modem at any given time.

You can disconnect USB modems from the port without turning the machine off. Although this may not seem like such a big advantage at first, it really is. Unlike on older systems, where the configuration you started with is the configuration you use, USB allows you to reconfigure your system on the fly. In short, you get greatly improved flexibility.

Understanding TAPI and MAPI Support

Application programming interfaces (APIs) enable programmers to accomplish a great deal of work with only a little effort. That's the first goal of every API. The second goal is to ensure a standardized form of access to specific system resources and capabilities. Using a standard interface enables the operating system vendor to change the implementation details without "breaking" too much code. Finally, an API also standardizes the results of using specific system resources and capabilities. Using the Windows API, for example, ensures that users see some of the standard types of interface components they take for granted.

Windows XP provides two APIs: The Telephony API (TAPI) provides a standardized method of handling telephone services, and the Messaging API (MAPI) provides a standardized method of handling e-mail and other forms of messaging. Both APIs provide standardized methods for using your modem more efficiently to conduct business. It's important to remember that both APIs exist in Windows XP in the form of utilities.

You can see the effects of TAPI in the Phone and Modem Options applet in the Control Panel. The Modem applet enables you to configure your modem in one place. Any Windows XP application that supports TAPI—such as Microsoft Exchange, Microsoft Outlook Express, and Microsoft Network—uses those settings. It doesn't include older, 16-bit Windows applications. If you want the benefits of TAPI, you need to upgrade those applications as the vendors produce new versions.

Microsoft Exchange is an example of a MAPI application. It enables you to access Microsoft Mail using a MAPI driver. A different MAPI driver provides access to CompuServe. Still another driver enables you to send a fax. In fact, you could have a MAPI driver to access each online service you subscribe to. The presence of these drivers enables you to access them all using just one application. The result is reduced training costs and the capability to move information from one service to another with the click of a button.

MAPI and TAPI aren't limited to Windows XP–specific applications. Microsoft Word, for example, provides a Send option on the File menu. This option enables you to send all or part of a document using MAPI to anywhere you can communicate. Using the native capabilities of Windows XP, this means that you could send the document as a fax or an e-mail or to an online service, all without leaving Word.

Accessing the Standard Hardware Support

Windows XP provides a wealth of hardware support that was new just a year or two ago, but that many consider standard today. This includes support for an Accelerated Graphics Port (AGP), an Advanced Configuration and Power Interface (ACPI), and a Digital Video Disk (DVD). Some computers also come equipped with device bay and FireWire (IEEE 1394) support, although these two features aren't commonplace. Just how important these features are to you probably depends on whether you have the required hardware installed on your machine.

> **Tip:** One of the best places to find out about the latest Windows XP hardware developments is the Microsoft hardware site at http://www.microsoft.com/hwdev/. This site has everything you could possibly want to know about Windows XP and hardware, including full technical specifications (when available).

Accelerated Graphics Port (AGP)

Accelerated Graphics Port (AGP) is a bus specification by Intel that gives low-cost 3D graphics cards faster access to main memory on personal computers than the usual PCI bus does. AGP dynamically allocates the PC's normal RAM to store the screen image and to support texture mapping, z-buffering, and alpha blending.

AGP operates at a 66MHz bus speed, which it doubles to 133MHz (compared with 33MHz for PCI) and allows for efficient use of frame buffer memory, thereby helping 2D graphics performance as well. AGP provides a coherent memory management design that allows the system to read scattered data in system memory in rapid bursts. AGP reduces the overall cost of creating high-end graphics subsystems by using existing system memory.

Advanced Configuration and Power Interface (ACPI)

The Advanced Configuration and Power Interface (ACPI) is an open industry specification that defines a flexible and extensible hardware interface for the system board. Software designers use this specification to integrate power management features throughout a computer system, including hardware, the operating system, and application software. This integration enables Windows XP to determine which applications are active and handle all of the power management resources for computer subsystems and peripherals. ACPI enables the operating system to direct power management on a wide range of mobile, desktop, and server computers and peripherals.

ACPI design is essential to take full advantage of power management and Plug and Play in Windows XP. If you aren't sure whether your computer is ACPI compliant, check your manufacturer's documentation. To change power settings that take advantage of the ACPI, use the Power Options applet in the Control Panel.

During setup, Windows installs the ACPI only if all components that are present during setup support power management. Some components, especially legacy components, don't support power management and can cause erratic behavior with Advanced Power Management (APM) or may prevent the ACPI from installing. Examples of such components are Industry Standard Architecture (ISA) components or a BIOS that's out-of-date. I recently found a Web site that can supply your BIOS upgrade needs: http://www. biosupgrades.com/.

To use Plug and Play with ACPI hardware to take full advantage of Plug and Play, you must be using an Advanced Configuration and Power Interface (ACPI) computer and running in ACPI mode, and the hardware devices must be Plug and Play. In an ACPI computer, the operating system, not the hardware, configures and monitors the computer.

For an easy way to see if your computer is using ACPI, open the Power Options applet in the Control Panel. If an APM tab is available, your computer isn't ACPI compliant. ACPI automatically enables Advanced Power Management, which disables the APM tab.

Digital Video Disk (DVD)

If you receive an error message the first time you try to play a DVD, you might not have a decoder installed or your decoder might need to be updated to be Windows XP compatible. To play DVDs, you must have a DVD-ROM drive, player software, and a hardware or software decoder.

A hardware decoder also requires a decoder driver. Decoders and their drivers are available from third-party manufacturers. Here are a few that have Windows XP–compatible decoder drivers: National Semiconductor Corporation (Mediamatics DVD player), MGI Software Corp. (Zoran SoftDVD and MGI SoftDVD Max), Ravisent Technologies (Software CineMaster or CinePlayer 1.0), InterVideo, Inc. (WinDVD), and CyberLink Corp. (PowerDVD).

Device Bay Support

The first question that most of you may have is "What's a Device Bay?" because none of these devices is in production at the time I'm writing this chapter. A *Device Bay* is simply a technique for installing devices, such as hard drives, into your machine.

One Device Bay holds one device of the size it's rated to hold. Therefore, if you have four devices in your machine (hard drive, floppy drive, CD-ROM drive, and tape drive), you'd typically need four Device Bays to store them. Device Bays of one size can hold multiple devices of a smaller size.

Right now, you have to go through a great deal of effort to change a hard drive. A Device Bay makes adding or removing devices about as easy as adding or removing floppies. Obviously, reality is a little more complex than the simplistic view I've just presented. However, it's important to cut away the hype and look at Device Bay as what it really is—a method of holding devices.

Device Bays are unique when compared to other device storage methodologies. They support both USB and the IEEE 1394 High Performance Serial Bus specification (also known as FireWire).

> **Tip:** If you want to learn more about Device Bays or simply want to know who's developing systems that provide this feature, check out Microsoft's Web site at `http://www.microsoft.com/hwdev/devicebay/`. This Web site includes an overview of Device Bay, a list of vendors who've indicated they'll support it, and the current Device Bay specification.

Because Device Bays support USB and IEEE 1394 devices, you don't need to power your machine down any more to swap out devices. You can just unplug the old device and plug in the new one. The Plug and Play support in Windows XP automatically reconfigures your system to reflect the new device configuration.

IEEE 1394 FireWire

Windows XP supports a number of new capabilities for an IEEE 1394 bus. This enhanced support for a variety of audio and video devices includes:

- Stereos and speakers
- SP/DIF (Sony and Philips Digital Interconnect Format) audio
- MPEG-2 streams from digital video systems and digital satellite transmission
- Digital video cameras
- Digital Video Disk (DVD), digital VHS, and Digital Television (DTV)
- Virtual device creation and driver support for connecting to legacy devices that aren't compliant with IEEE 1394

FireWire support enables Windows XP to interoperate with these devices. Windows XP can also send and receive MPEG-2 streams. Like Windows Me, Windows XP supports networking with simple IEEE 1394 connectors, enabling true "walk-up" networking. In addition, Windows XP support for ICS means that PCs connected in the home across IEEE 1394 can share a single Internet connection. Visit the Microsoft Web site at http://www.microsoft.com/hwdev/1394/1394tech.htm#XP for detailed information concerning Windows XP and IEEE 1394.

Understanding the Universal Serial Bus (USB)

Universal Serial Bus (USB) is a connectivity specification developed by the USB Promoter Group. Vendors aim USB at peripherals connected outside the computer to eliminate the need to open the computer case to install cards. USB provides for ease of use, expandability, and speed for users.

USB connections allow data to flow both ways between the PC and the peripheral. This means that you can use your PC to control peripherals in new and creative ways. For example, you can use your PC to automatically manage a telephone call center to maintain voice, fax, and data mailboxes; screen and forward your calls; and even deliver a variety of selected outgoing messages. You can also use your PC to tune a set of USB-compliant stereo speakers to match the acoustics of your listening environment.

Understanding the USB Versions

USB 1.1 is enjoying broad adoption in the marketplace. Over 1,000 devices have passed compliance testing. USB peripherals are the best-selling products in several device categories. Also, according to data from DataQuest, the USB installed base of USB-capable PCs will grow from a mere 6 million PCs in 1996 to over 700 million by the end of 2003.

The next version of USB, dubbed USB 2.0, is a higher-speed version fully compatible with USB 1.1. You can download the USB 2.0 specification from the official USB-IF Web site at http://www.usb.org/developers/usb20. The USB 2.0 specification defines a transfer rate of 480Mbps. That's a 40X increase over the 1.1 specification.

Troubleshooting USB Hardware

USB is located in the Components category in System Information. It displays information about universal serial bus (USB) devices and controllers on your computer. The Device column in the details pane lists each USB device, and the PNP Device ID column lists the ID for the device.

If there's a problem with your USB device, first try unplugging and plugging in the device. If that doesn't fix the problem, you can use the Device Manager to locate and troubleshoot the problem.

Working with USB Hubs

You can connect high-power devices only to self-powered hubs and connect low-power devices to either bus or self-powered hubs. High-power devices draw more than 100mA from the USB power line, and low-power devices draw 100mA or less. High-power devices are typically bus-powered cameras. Low-power devices are typically mice, keyboards, joysticks, and any devices that come with their own power supply (also known as *self-powered* devices). Most general-purpose hubs come with their own power supply as well, and Windows XP considers them self-powered. Bus-powered hubs obtain power from the bus and support only low-power devices.

Understanding USB Alternatives

USB and IEEE 1394(FireWire) are complementary technologies. 1394 is for devices where high performance is a priority, and USB is for devices where price is a priority.

Although the two serial buses seem similar, they're intended to fulfill different bandwidth and cost needs. IEEE 1394 can move more data in a given amount of time, but is considerably more expensive than USB because of its more complex protocol and signaling rate. You normally use IEEE 1394 for disk drives, high-quality video streams, and other high-bandwidth applications, all of which are higher-end consumer devices. USB is appropriate for middle- and low-bandwidth applications, such as audio, scanners, printers, keyboards, and mice.

Understanding How RAM Type Affects Your System

Some people don't fully understand the effect RAM can have on their system. A memory-starved system runs slower than the same system with enough memory installed. In short, memory is the most important performance enhancement you can add to your system.

Memory comes in assorted sizes and shapes. More types of memory are out there than most people care to think about. All of these forms of memory have different operating characteristics. Some types of memory are faster than others are; some provide nearly permanent storage; other types lose their contents as soon as the user removes power.

You need to know about the memory found in your machines. Reading the manuals for your display adapter and motherboard (the places where you find configurable memory) is important. It's also important to understand the meaning behind the memory acronyms you're likely to run into, such as dynamic random access memory (DRAM), synchronous DRAM (SDRAM), double data rate (DDR) SDRAM, synchronous link DRAM (SLDRAM), and Direct Rambus DRAM (RDRAM). When working with display adapters, you may also run into video random access memory (VRAM), processors often require static random access memory (SRAM). These Web sites can help you understand the memory in your machine:

- Enhanced Memory Systems (http://www.edram.com/)
- Fujitsu Microelectronics (http://www.fujitsumicro.com/)
- Hitachi Semiconductor America (http://semiconductor.hitachi.com/)
- Intel (http://www.intel.com/)

- Rambus, Inc. (http://www.rambus.com/)

- SLDRAM Consortium (http://www.sldram.com/)

- Synchronous DRAM: The DRAM of the Future (http://www-3.ibm.com/chips/techlib/techlib.nsf/productfamilies/SDRAM)

- Texas Instruments Memory Reference (http://www.ti.com/sc/docs/products/memory/)

Working with Network Interface Cards (NICs)

Choosing a network interface card (NIC) is one of those decisions you make based on your network usage. If you spend lots of time performing high-bandwidth tasks, such as graphics, on the network, you want a high-capacity NIC. The cost of a 16-bit card compared to 32-bit card makes it easy to buy a PCI 32-bit card. On the other hand, if you're running a home network where the highest bandwidth task is word processing, a 16-bit card still works fine.

Of course, the 32-bit card only benefits from the processor or system communication to network interface. A 10Mbps LAN is still a bottleneck, even with a 16-bit card, so if you get a 32-bit card, you also want to update your network to use 100Mbps cards. This is a good choice if you're working with graphics or even with some video games.

> **Note:** Microsoft discontinued support for the NetBIOS Extended User Interface (NetBEUI) protocol in Windows XP. If your configuration requires the temporary use of NetBEUI for Windows XP, try right-clicking the NETNBF.INF file in the \VALUEADD\MSFT\NET\NETBEUI directory on your Windows XP CD and selecting Install from the context menu. If this doesn't work, you can always copy the files manually. Locate the \VALUEADD\MSFT\NET\NETBEUI directory on your Windows XP CD. Copy NBF.SYS into the \WINDOWS\SYSTEM32\DRIVERS directory. Then copy NETNBF.INF into the \WINDOWS\INF directory. In the Control Panel, click Network and Internet Connections and then click Network Connections. Right-click the connection you want to configure and then click Properties. On the General tab, click Install to add the NetBEUI protocol to your system.

Using the Computer Management Console

The following section discusses a special one-size-fits-all MMC console named Computer Management. It allows you to perform many types of computer maintenance, and this one console may be all you need to perform most of the maintenance tasks on a small network. (You always need other tools, but probably not every day.)

MMC is the central tool in the Windows XP management arsenal. However, it's important to understand that MMC is really a container application. You place snap-ins inside the container. The combination of snap-ins and the container is a console. The MMC console is the actual tool you use to maintain some part of the network.

An Overview of Computer Management

The Computer Management MMC console is the Swiss army knife of the console world. You access it by using Computer Management icon in the Administrative Tools folder found in the Control Panel. As you can see from Figure 9.5, this console contains a little bit of everything needed to maintain your system.

FIGURE 9.5

Use the Computer Management console as your view to system configuration and performance.

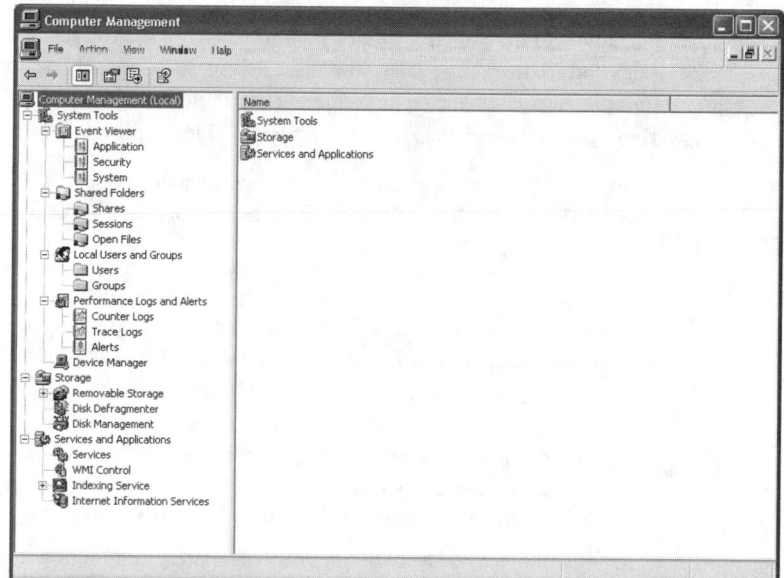

As you can see, this truly is a central repository of tools for the small network. You can manage the three computer system areas: System Tools, Storage, and Services and Applications. In addition, you can manage more than your own system by right-clicking Computer Management and choosing All Tasks | Connect to Another Computer from the context menu. (You can find the Connect to Another Computer option on several other context menus as well.) The Select Computer dialog box contains the Another Computer field you use to select another machine on the network. Use the Browse button if you don't know the other computer name. Click OK, and you see the same information for the other machine. The location information (in parentheses beside the Computer Management entry in Figure 9.5) changes to show the new computer name.

The main entries you see in Figure 9.5 remain the same when you switch to another computer. However, you may see a difference in subentries. For example, if you connect to a server, Event Viewer contains several new logs, including Directory Service, DNS

Server, and File Replication Service. The entries you see depend on the capabilities of the machine you monitor.

Some entries stay intact, but you can't use them. For example, you can't use the Disk Defragmenter on a remote drive. The entry stays in place, but you see an error message instead of the local display. Fortunately, the situations where you can't perform a task on a remote system are rare.

Using the System Tools

The System Tools folder of Computer Management helps you configure and maintain your system. This folder doesn't contain every snap-in you'll ever need, but you find that you can spend most of your time using this folder for system-specific needs. For example, although the System Monitor snap-in doesn't appear in this folder, the Performance Logs and Alerts snap-in does. You need System Monitor only when tuning your system for optimal performance, but you might use Performance Logs and Alerts daily to ensure your system stays in shape. The differentiation in purpose is important.

Now that you know why particular tools appear in the System Tools folder, let's talk about their purpose. The following list provides an overview of each tool and tells why you might use it on a regular basis.

- *Event Viewer* The Event Viewer helps you keep track of special occurrences on your system. The three folders this snap-in contains track Application, Security, and System events. Event Viewer provides three levels of tracking: information, warning, and error. Depending on which machine you're monitoring, you might see more logs. It's also possible (but unlikely) that a vendor uses special message types. You want to check Event Viewer each day because it normally provides the first indication that something is wrong with your system. In fact, a well-written application can alert you to conditions long before they become problems.

- *Shared Folders* Networking involves sharing resources with other people. For example, you might have a project folder on your system that requires the efforts of several people to complete. It's important to share the data, but you also want to monitor access to ensure that no one abuses their privileges. The three folders provided by this snap-in (Shares, Sessions, and Open Files) help you track which resources are available, who's using them, and for how long.

- *Local Users and Groups* This snap-in contains two folders. The Groups folder contains a list of all groups that can access your machine. The Users folder contains a list of all users who can access your machine. You use the groups to define the same level of access for more than one person. In both cases, you want to provide access to other users, but limit that access to ensure that your data remains safe.

- *Performance Logs and Alerts* Some people view performance tuning as a one-time task they'll begrudgingly do someday. Performance tuning begins when you monitor system performance, select a course of corrective action for problem areas, and implement the changes as needed. However, this is just the beginning. If you don't continue to monitor your system, performance eventually declines as the system state changes. This snap-in helps you track system performance on a continuous basis. You can create alerts to tell you when specific events occur, such as a significant drop in disk space or performance. In short, System Monitor is the tuning tool you use occasionally, and Performance Logs and Alerts is your helper for daily performance tuning.

- *Device Manager* The Device Manager contains a complete list of the devices on your system. The Device Manager displays the devices by type, making them easier to find. You can tell if a device has failed because Windows XP marks it for you. This snap-in also allows you to check how Windows XP uses system resources, update device drivers, and perform some device configuration tasks.

Your system has three essential resources you must control in order to get good performance: memory, processing cycles, and hard drive space. A lack of any of these three items results in a system that performs poorly. You can control memory by configuring applications to use only the features you need and by opening only the applications that fit within memory. Of course, you can always take the "add more memory" route because it does work. You can control processing cycles by keeping processor-intensive applications to a minimum.

Managing Storage

The Storage folder contains utilities you need in order to maintain the hard drive space requirement for good performance. You find that this folder provides access to three snap-ins, specifically designed to make managing storage easier. The following list discusses these options and tells you where you can learn more about them:

- *Removable Storage* Computers have many removable storage options today. For example, you can use permanent removable media, such as CD-ROMs and DVDs. Some removable media is semipermanent. The CD-RW and DVD-RAM drive both fall into this category. Still other devices, such as zip drives, look just like hard drives. This snap-in helps you keep track of your removable drives by checking the media they contain and their status.

- *Disk Defragmenter* The Disk Defragmenter snap-in reorganizes the data on your hard drive so that your system can find it faster. Defragmenting your hard drive removes some of the costs of working with physical devices, such as head movement.

- *Disk Management* Use this snap-in to create new partitions, format a drive, change the drive letter, and determine drive status. You also use this utility to create special drive setups, such as using a redundant array of inexpensive disks (RAID) to increase system reliability.

Working with Services and Applications

The Services and Applications folder contains a minimum of one folder, Services. The Services folder contains a list of services on your system plus a status for each service. The Services folder also provides two views: Standard and Extended. The Standard view contains the list of services in a details-type view. The columns include Name, Description, Status, Startup Type, and Log On As. The Extended view contains the same information along with a secondary pane that extends the description so that you can see it. Unfortunately, you can't adjust the size of the secondary pane, which means that you need to move items around to see all of the column entries properly. Figure 9.6 shows a typical example of the Extended view.

FIGURE 9.6

The Extended view of the Services folder allows you to see the entire service description at a glance.

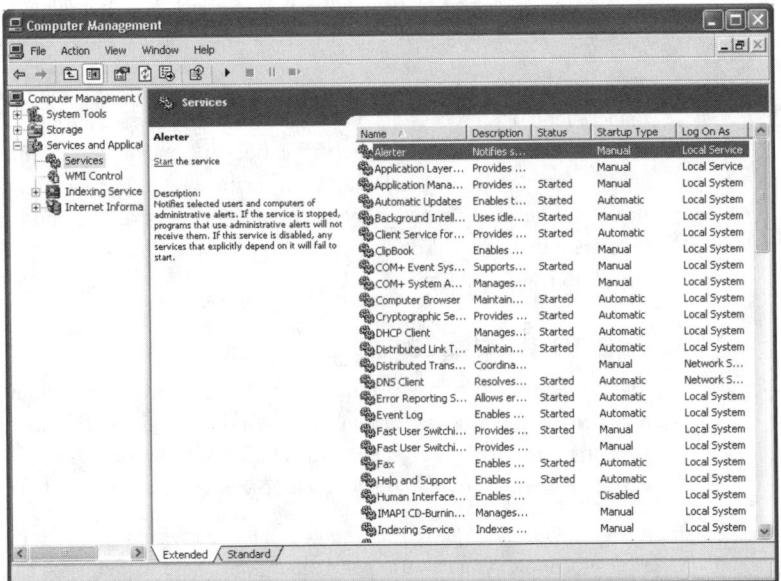

Figure 9.6 shows three applications in addition to the Services folder. Sometimes, these applications show up in the folder even if you haven't activated them. In this case, only the Indexing Service is active. The WMI Control and Internet Information Services entries produce error messages when you click on them.

You should also notice that the applications aren't applications in the standard sense of the word. These are background, service-related applications. For example, the Indexing Service keeps track of your hard drive content in the background. It comes into play when you need to find data on your hard drive. The Indexing Service can provide answers to the search engine much faster than a real-time search can.

Windows XP provides several interfaces for managing users and groups on your machine. The first method is the simplified interface provided by the User Accounts applet. This interface has the advantage of using a task-based approach to user management. You don't need to worry about which menu has the option you need. The disadvantage is one of flexibility and access. This interface is somewhat rigid and doesn't provide full access to user information. In addition, using this technique doesn't allow you to manage groups.

The second method is the Local Users and Groups MMC snap-in. You saw this snap-in loaded in the Computer Management console in Figure 9.5. This method does allow you to manage both users and groups, but at the expense of a more complex interface and increased management time. Problems aside, this is the method you want to use to create users, in most cases, because it allows you to assign a password and group permissions. The following sections discuss both interfaces.

Using the User Accounts Applet

The User Accounts applet helps you manage user accounts without the complexity of an MMC snap-in. In addition, it consolidates several functions, such as changing the way users log in to the system, and uses a task-oriented management approach. Figure 9.7 shows a typical view of the User Accounts dialog box from the network administrator perspective. You see in a few moments that the average user sees something different.

FIGURE 9.7

The User Accounts dialog box provides an easy interface for many of your user management needs.

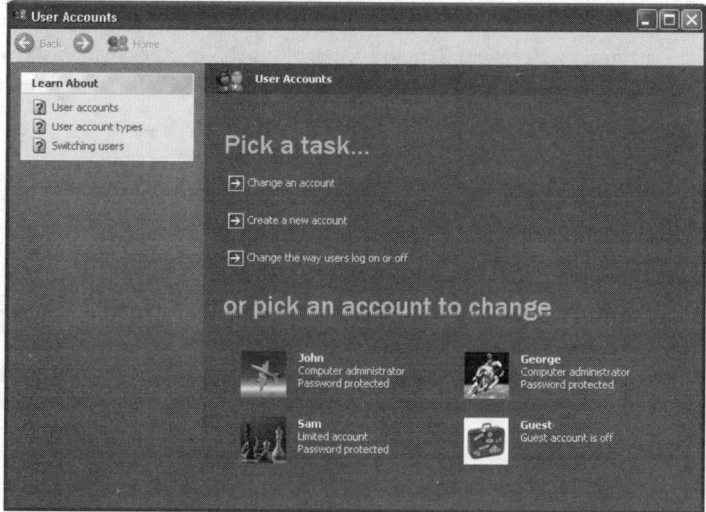

Tip: The User Accounts dialog box doesn't provide access to the Local Users and Groups MMC snap-in. It also limits the tasks you can perform on a user account. Making this applet accessible to users allows them to change some of the characteristics of their account, such as the picture displayed on the Welcome screen without leaving any security holes. This solution is a good one for network administrators who want to give users freedom without leaving the network open for attack. With this applet in place, there's no reason to expose the Local Users and Groups MMC snap-in to anyone but network administrators.

Click Change An Account, and you see a Pick an Account to Change dialog box that lists the accounts the user can access. Select an account, and you see the What Do You Want to Change about Your Account? dialog box. You can also reach this dialog box by clicking the account you want to modify on the Users Accounts dialog box, shown in Figure 9.7. You can also choose other people's accounts. Again, this is the network administrator view of the User Accounts applet. The average user doesn't see any accounts other than the one he normally uses.

When using this dialog box, you can change or remove your password, change your picture, and set your system up to use a .NET Passport. The User Account applet always enables these options. The availability of the other options depends on the rights of the user and the local security policy settings. For example, the average user can't change the network name assigned to him or his account type.

Using the various links is easy. If you change your name, the User Account applet presents your current name and asks for a new one. Changing your password involves typing the old password, the new password twice, and a phrase or word used to provide a password hint. Generally, you're better off enforcing a policy that prohibits the use of hints. Removing your password is almost too easy. All you need to do is type the old password and click Remove Password. Windows XP doesn't complain unless you set the Minimum Password Length policy to something other than 0 (the default). The Change My Account Type setting is also simplistic. You choose between a computer administrator and a limited account.

> **Warning:** The password hint is visible to anyone on the network. Some users will almost certainly try to use their password as a hint. Unfortunately, Windows XP doesn't check for this potential problem. It accepts the user's password as a perfectly acceptable hint. This means that you could have passwords that are completely visible to anyone on the network. The problem is more serious than you might think. No local security policy bans this practice, so you can't enforce the user's password and hint choice. A written policy might help, but it's difficult to enforce, considering that the network administrator doesn't know the user's password.

When you click Change My Picture, Windows XP displays a list of new pictures for your account. Many of the pictures are generic, and you may want something special. Click Browse for more pictures if you want to use your own picture for an icon.

Using the Local Users and Groups MMC Snap-In

The Local Users and Groups MMC snap-in provides you with the greatest flexibility in changing the accounts for a specific machine. In addition, you can use this MMC snap-in on more than one machine by connecting to the machine. You don't find these features in the User Accounts applet.

You can use the Local Users and Groups snap-in in two essential areas: users and groups. The Users folder contains individuals in your company, and the Groups folder contains settings for groups of individuals who perform similar tasks. The following sections help you learn to work with both users and groups and to better define the differences between them.

When you open the Users folder of the Local Users and Groups snap-in, you see a list of users set up for the local machine. This doesn't represent the users for a domain unless you connect to a server. In addition, Active Directory provides another set of snap-ins that you use to manage users and computers. The list includes the name (login), full name, and description for each user.

To create a new user, right-click an open area in the details window and choose New User from the context menu. You can also use the Action | New User command to perform this task. Figure 9.8 shows the New User dialog box you see. It allows you to enter the user's login name, full name, description, and preliminary password. A network administrator should force a user to change his password during login so that he can never say that the administrator used the account for illegal purposes.

FIGURE 9.8

Creating a new user is as easy as opening this dialog box and typing a few basics.

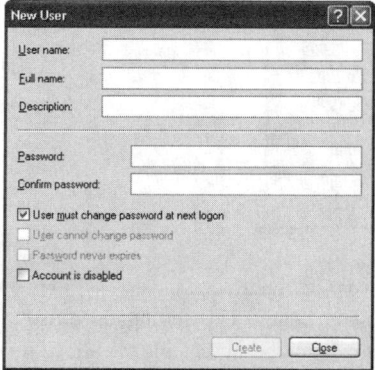

The New User dialog box contains only the essentials for defining a user. If you right-click the New User entry and choose Properties from the context menu, you see a User Properties dialog box with several tabs of information. The General tab contains the information we just defined for the user.

Click the Member Of tab, and you see a list of groups. Click Add if you want to add a new group to the list. You see a blank Select Groups list, which is something that confuses many people. Microsoft listed the groups in previous versions of Windows, but doesn't list them for Windows XP. Click Advanced, and you see a Select Groups dialog box. Click Find Now, and Windows XP provides a list of groups on your local machine. Notice that I've already conducted a search using the entries in this dialog box.

The Profile tab contains login settings for the user. The Profile Path field allows you to assign a profile to the user. (Profiles generally reside on the server.) This allows the user to roam from machine to machine and still use the same setup. Windows XP supports two types of profiles: roaming and mandatory. In both cases, the user downloads a profile from the server when he logs in. In the case of a roaming profile, Windows XP updates the profile settings on the server when the user logs out. The mandatory profile doesn't allow any changes, so Windows XP doesn't update it when the user logs out.

The Dial-in tab shown in Figure 9.9 is active for only server-based accounts. These settings determine if a user can call into the server. They also determine how the user can call into the server. Generally, Windows XP relies on whatever remote access policy you set for dial-up connections. Fortunately, you can override those settings to always deny or allow access.

FIGURE 9.9
The Dial-in tab defines the dial-in connection settings for a particular user.

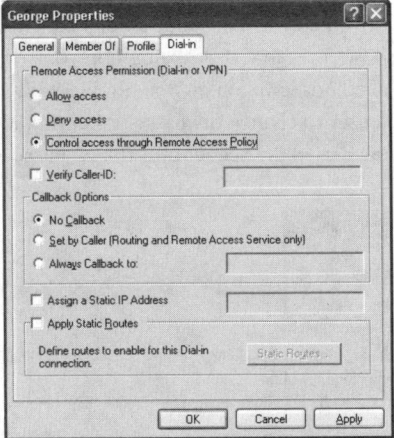

If you check the Verify Caller-ID option, the user must call in from the same number every time he uses the dial-in connection. This setting also sets limits on the features the user can add to his remote connection because some telephone services hide the number.

A more traditional method of checking the remote caller's identity is to use the callback system. In a *callback* system, the user calls the server and provides identification. The server hangs up the telephone, validates the user's identity, and then calls the user back to establish a connection.

You use the Assign a Static IP Address and Apply Static Routes options to access remote networks that call into a main network number. For example, a satellite office might need to call in to the office to establish a connection each morning. Assigning the caller a static IP address enables communication between the two networks and users of the two networks. Using static routes also allows communication between two individual machines by allocating a static route for all machines on the remote network.

Groups are an organizational tool, and you find that they're simpler to understand than the user settings. Click the Groups folder in the Local Users and Groups snap-in, and you see a list of groups for the system. The groups don't contain much in the way of settings.

The Group Properties dialog box contains the group name, a description, a list of users and objects, and buttons for adding and removing members. The New Group dialog box looks similar to the one shown in Figure 8.9. The main difference is that the New Group dialog box allows you to change the group name.

Sharing Hard Drives and Folders

Sharing hard drives and folders is an essential part of networking. It's the basis for every network in existence. In fact, early network operating systems (NOSs) built their reputations on file and print sharing.

Windows XP provides file and drive sharing, just like almost every version of Windows before it. The model used for file and drive sharing is similar to the one used in Windows 2000 rather than the less secure model used in Windows 9x. This means that you set specific levels of security on an individual or group basis.

This section discusses the Shared Folders MMC snap-in. This snap-in helps you keep track of user connections and other information about your drives. We also talk about auditing and quotas, two methods of tracking drive resource usage. *Auditing* creates a record for disk accesses, and *quotas* limit the drive space each user can access.

The Shared Folders snap-in contains three folders: Shares, Sessions, and Open Files. You use each of these folders to monitor drive usage on your system.

The Shares folder, shown in Figure 9.10, shows which drives you've shared and the number of connections people have made to them. Don't assume that this means one person for each connection. The same user can connect to more than one drive, and Windows XP counts each drive connection separately. Notice that this list includes both standard shares and default or administrative shares (those with a "$" in their name). These shares allow you to monitor all system activity.

The Sessions folder contains the name of each person using your system. The entries also include the number of files a person has opened, the time he connected, and the amount of idle time since his last activity. The Guest column tells you if the user logged in using the guest account.

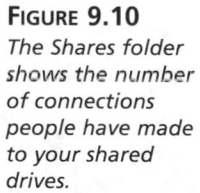

FIGURE 9.10

The Shares folder shows the number of connections people have made to your shared drives.

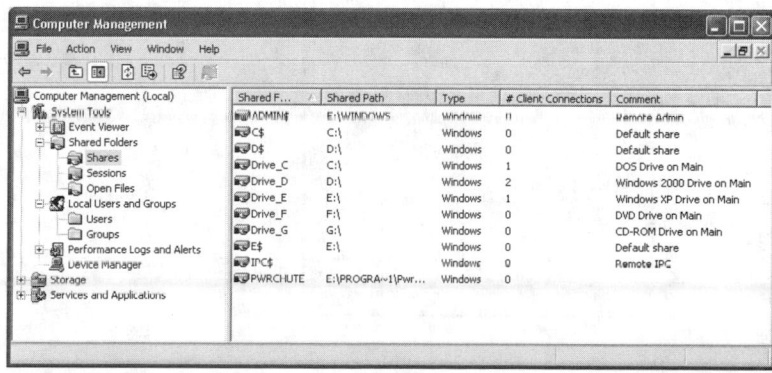

The only task you can perform in this folder is to end the user's session using the Close Session option on the context menu. Using this feature can have undesirable results. For example, the user could lose data because his session ended with a file in an uncertain state. Normally, you want to contact the user first and ask him to disconnect from your system. You do this by right-clicking Computer Management and then selecting All Tasks | Send Console Message from the context menu.

You use the Open Files folder to monitor the files opened by other people on your system. Notice that the columns list the user's name, type of file access, number of locks on the file, and type of access requested. A file lock indicates some type of shared access. For example, two people can share a database file. It's important to use locks in such a case to ensure that one user doesn't infringe on the edits made by another user.

As with the Sessions folder, you can perform only one action on files in the Open Files folder: Close Open File. Closing a file opened for Read access is usually safe. The action might inconvenience the other user, but is unlikely to harm the file. However, closing a file opened for either Write or Write+Read access could damage the file, cause data loss, and definitely do more than irritate the other user. Again, it's always better to send a console message to ask the other party to close the file rather than close the file yourself.

You can enable drive quotas under Windows XP in a number of ways, but one way is easier than all the rest. Open a copy of Windows Explorer, right-click the drive you want to modify, and then select the Quota tab. You see a display similar to the one shown in Figure 9.11. The first step in using drive quotas is to check the Enable Quota Management option, as shown in the figure.

You'll want to decide if new users should have an automatic quota set on their accounts or if you want to set the limit as necessary. You can also choose to log any excessive use of disk space. The log can contain just the users that exceed their limit, or you can include those that reach the warning level.

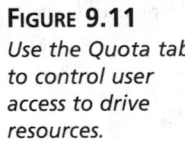

FIGURE 9.11
Use the Quota tab to control user access to drive resources.

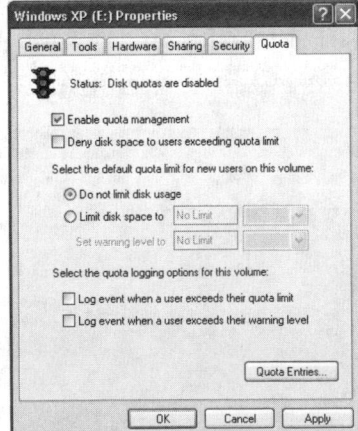

Enabling quotas and setting a default limit isn't enough to ensure good resource management. You also need to review the users who have a quota. To do that, click Quota Entries. You see a Quota Entries dialog box, which contains a list of users who have a quota for this drive. The list indicates their warning level and quota limit. You also see how much space the user has already used and learn if he has exceeded his limit.

To add a new user to the list, click New Quota Entry. You see a Select Users dialog box. Type a user's name or locate it using the Advanced button. Click OK, and you see a New Quote Entry dialog box. Select a quote limit and warning level for the new user and click OK. That name appears in the Quota Entries list.

Auditing, for the purpose of this discussion, is the act of creating a log of user activity on your system. You can audit all kinds of user activity. For example, if you want to know about every time a user successfully deletes a file, you can create an audit entry for it. These logs are useful if you want to monitor user activity or check for illegal actions.

You can enable auditing in a number of ways, but the easiest method is to right-click a drive in Windows Explorer and choose Properties from the context menu. Select the Security tab in the Drive Properties dialog box and then click Advanced. You see an Advanced Security Settings dialog box.

As you can see from the dialog box, you can monitor users for success, failure, or both success and failure in performing certain tasks. Windows XP helps you monitor everything from taking full control of the drive to deleting files to simply changing file attributes.

To add a new entry, click Add. You see a Select User or Group dialog box. Click Advanced and then Find to display a list of local user and group names. Select a user or group from the list and then click OK. You see an Auditing Entry dialog box. Select the tasks you want to monitor and then click OK. Windows XP adds the new auditing entry to the drive. The audit remains in place until you remove it.

Many offices I've set up in the past use multiuser workstation setups. One user has possession of the computer during the day; another, by night. Several users might share the same computer because one user doesn't use it all day. A manager might need access to an employee computer because the one in his office is too far away. The reasons could go on forever, but multiuser workstations are common. The following tips help you set up a multiuser workstation in the most convenient way:

- *Create a default user setup*   The \Documents and Settings\Default User directory contains a complete set of empty folders. Every user you create for a local machine uses this set of folders as a starting point. The user receives input from this folder only during the creation phase. Don't confuse this set of folders with the all users folder.

- *Use the all users folder (\Documents and Settings\All Users) to hold all common elements*   For example, if everyone needs access to the word processor, you want to place the icons for it in this folder rather than duplicate those icons for every user. However, if most, but not all users, require access to an application, you'd place it in the default user setup. This placement allows you to remove the icons from those users who don't need it.

- *Implement Start Menu security*   You might have a machine where all employees need access to some icons, but guest users shouldn't have access. Assigning security to those icons allows you to place them in the all users folder and still restrict access. Icons normally inherit rights from their parents, so you need to click Advanced on the Security tab of the Object Properties dialog box. Clear the Inherit option and then click OK before you begin setting a new security policy. Note that everyone can still see the icon, but only those with the required permissions can use it.

- *Create common desktop elements as needed*   For example, everyone might work on the same project together, so placing the folder for that project in the \Documents and Settings\All Users\Desktop folder makes sense. This way, you can ensure that everyone uses the same folder and that all of the data is changed at the same time.

- *Set security to assume that the user always fails to log out when leaving the area*   For example, you can set the screen saver to log the user out automatically and return to the login screen. This forces the user to log back in to the system and protects it from prying eyes.

On Your Own

Install several versions of your printer, each with different settings. Try each new installation for several weeks and see whether you notice the additional ease of use that several pseudoprinters can provide. Also, try the various print settings to see whether you notice the variations in print speed and output quality.

Place a shortcut to your printer on the Desktop and try the drag-and-drop method of printing. Just drag a file with your mouse pointer to the Printer icon and drop it. This is the easy way of sending output to the printer using the default setup. You might want to experiment to see which printer settings work best as a default setup for you.

Install and remove various fonts to become familiar with the process. Sometimes, you want to install a new font for a special purpose or to remove fonts to gain more system resources.

Exploiting Multimedia and Games

Considering the multimedia orientation the Internet is taking, everyone's use of multimedia will only increase in the future. Everyone seems to be embracing multimedia in a big way. Even Microsoft has a multimedia-specific Web site (`http://windowsmedia.com/mg/home.asp`) that we'll visit later in this chapter. Multimedia on the Internet includes not only visual effects, but also audio effects. I regularly get cards from Blue Mountain (`http://www.bluemountain.com/`) that include a combination of animated effects and audio. In fact, some stores such as CD-Now (`http://www.cdnow.com/`) are using this new method of getting you to buy both CDs and videos.

Another sales technique is to use multimedia for testimonials. Happy clients talk about how they use the vendor's product in a short movie. Although this is still a niche use of multimedia, it will eventually become commonplace online because such movies could offer interactive features.

In addition to using multimedia on the Internet, you can use multimedia for training, education, and games. Many games provide intense graphics and sound presentations meant to thrill users. Both 3D sound and 3D graphics are now commonplace in action games; these technologies are starting to appear in other game types as well. It takes considerable hardware horsepower to play some of these games. When your hardware falls short of providing the needed features, Windows XP can emulate many of these technologies at least partially in software (although game performance suffers when using software emulation). In fact, some of the more robust sales campaigns for multimedia hardware appear in gaming magazines.

This isn't even the tip of the iceberg when it comes to multimedia. As voice-recognition technology improves, more people will use sound applications for feedback, for controlling their computers, and for storing and recording their own sounds. In fact, you'll find rudimentary speech technology in Windows XP in the form of the Microsoft Reader program. Because multimedia requires advanced hardware, this chapter looks at the hardware and a few of the software technologies you might need. By the time you finish this chapter, you'll have a better idea of what multimedia in Windows XP entails and how you can make it easier to use.

Installing and Configuring DirectX

DirectX is one of the most important multimedia features in Windows XP today. The reason is simple; DirectX provides a modicum of safe direct hardware connectivity for multimedia developers. This is especially important for game developers who need every ounce of speed your system can provide. DirectX support will become even more important as developers begin working with Windows XP. Safe hardware access becomes more important when the operating system enforces integrity issues that Windows 9x would allow to pass unnoticed.

DirectX is also the part of your system that will change most often. It seems at times that Microsoft has developed a DirectX version-of-the-month routine. Changes occur so quickly that some users have a hard time keeping up. Some of the reasons for all these changes include advances in multimedia hardware, game developer requirements for better access, and the results of Microsoft's own research. Unfortunately, these changes mean that you'll run into compatibility problems as well as errors that defy a quick fix.

The following sections show you how to work with DirectX. We'll discuss what you need to do to keep DirectX updated. You'll also learn about methods for troubleshooting DirectX problems and the DirectX diagnostic aid, DXDIAG.

Updating DirectX As Needed

Because the DirectX drivers change so often, you need to look for changes on Windows Update regularly. Unfortunately, Windows Update sometimes fails to provide the most current update, so you want to check the DirectX Web site (`http://www.microsoft.com/directx/default.asp`) for changes as well. The DirectX Web site also contains the latest news about Windows media tools and drivers. If you're a gamer, it pays to check this site often. Even if you use multimedia occasionally, you want to keep track of the content on this site.

After you download the latest version of DirectX, you install it as you would any other application. One of the differences you'll notice with DirectX is that it doesn't create any new entries in the Start menu. This is surprising because DirectX does include some applications. We'll talk about these applications in the "Testing Your Hardware" section of this chapter.

Another surprise is that you find you can't remove DirectX from your system once you install it. Theoretically, you shouldn't need to uninstall DirectX, but some people have found they need to downgrade to a previous version because of compatibility problems. It pays to look spend some time learning about the latest version of DirectX from other users in your favorite newsgroup before you install it.

DirectX Troubleshooting Tips

Many people see DirectX as problematic. It's true that early versions of DirectX applications were buggy, to say the least. In addition, people often tried to run an application designed for the latest version of DirectX with an older version of the product. In short, DirectX received lots of bad press because of implementation problems.

You can still run into problems with DirectX if you're not careful. The main issue is to ensure that you have the latest stable version of the product installed on your machine. I emphasize the word *stable* because DirectX has more than its fair share of stability problems. Using a .0 version of DirectX is likely to cause problems for you and your system. Always wait until the "a" version appears on the scene or, better still, the .1 release.

Trying to use DirectX with older hardware is another problem. We'll discuss some of these problems in detail in the "Testing Your Hardware" section of this chapter. However, the main issue is that Microsoft always assumes that you have updated hardware that can make full use of the features DirectX can provide. This means DirectX relies on hardware acceleration in most cases and an onboard processor for graphics. The device also needs to support some of the newer shading and rendering features. You can get around old hardware problems by disabling the DirectX features that don't work with your system. However, you don't know which features are causing problems until you run diagnostics.

Applications designers also have a fair number of problems with DirectX because it's a complex application programming interface (API) to use. Some older applications don't work well with newer versions of DirectX. However, the problem isn't one of backward compatibility—it's one of advanced features. Unfortunately, you can't test for advanced feature compatibility when working with an application. Sometimes it's a matter of trial and error to get an old DirectX application to work.

Testing Your Hardware

DirectX versions since 6.1 include a tool named DXDIAG.EXE. This tool is your main helper in finding problems with DirectX and testing system compatibility. You don't find DXDIAG.EXE in the Start Menu, and Microsoft seems to delight in moving it around on the hard drive as well. The easiest way to access this application is to open the Run dialog box using Start | Run. Type **DXDIAG** in the Open field and then click OK. You'll see a DirectX Diagnostic Tool dialog box, similar to the one shown in Figure 10.1. Notice that the System tab displays lots of useful information about your system.

The main purpose of this tool is to help you diagnose problems with your DirectX setup. Obviously, this means having the right files installed. The DirectX Files tab, shown in Figure 10.2, contains a complete list of all DirectX files on your system. Notice that this list contains everything you need when talking with a support person about your DirectX problem.

Also, notice the "No problems found" entry in the Notes field. This tool is telling you that it couldn't find anything wrong with this page of data. However, it doesn't always means that the page really is free of trouble. For example, it's unlikely that the DirectX Diagnostic Tool will find a file with the wrong version number.

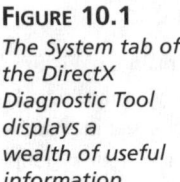

FIGURE 10.1
The System tab of the DirectX Diagnostic Tool displays a wealth of useful information.

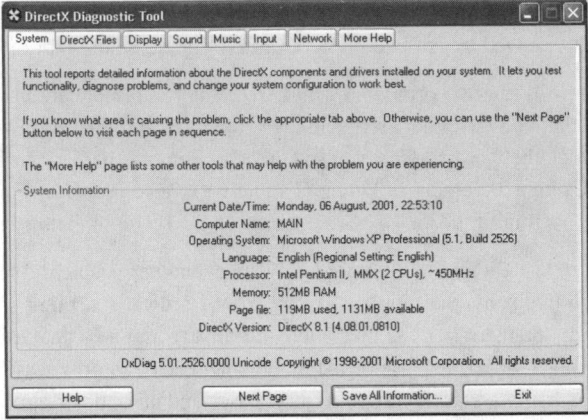

FIGURE 10.2
The DirectX Diagnostic Tool provides the usual list of files and version numbers to help support personnel troubleshoot a setup.

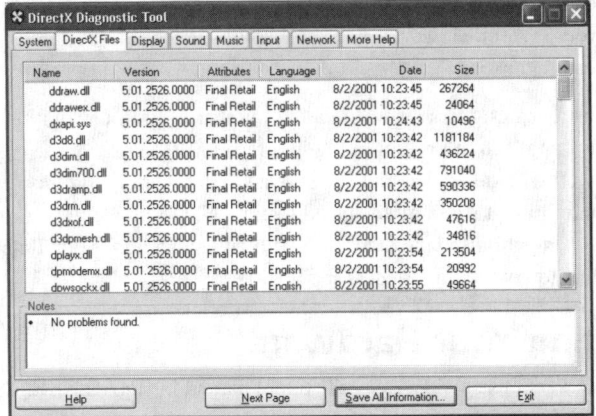

Unlike previous versions of DirectX, the tools provided with the latest version of DirectX can help you diagnose problems with your system. Figure 10.3 shows the Display tab. The buttons on this tab allow you to disable a DirectX feature momentarily to see if your problem clears up. You can also run the diagnostic to see if your display adapter and monitor provide the features required to use a feature.

The diagnostics tabs tend to provide less technical information and more in the way of facts you can check. For example, the Display tab provides a vendor name, the amount of memory installed on the display adapter, the current display resolution, and the type of monitor attached to the system. These all are facts that you can verify and use to determine if there are any problems with your DirectX setup.

Let's say that you haven't gotten enough help from the tools the DirectX Diagnostics Tool supports directly. The More Help tab provides access to additional tools that can help you localize problems. One of the tools, MSInfo, should be familiar to you already.

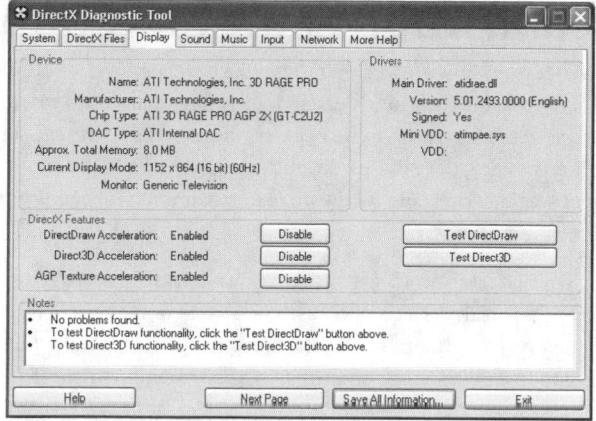

FIGURE 10.3

This tab and others provide access to diagnostic aids you can use to test your system.

You'll also find a tool that allows you to report DirectX bugs to Microsoft. You should use the Override button only with help from a Microsoft technician because you can make your display unusable by entering the wrong value.

Pressing Troubleshoot on the More Help tab displays a Help and Support Center dialog box, like the one shown in Figure 10.4. This is where you can use the experience put together by Microsoft technicians to find a problem on your own. Just answer the questions the Troubleshooter asks, and you can find at least a few common answers. Although this doesn't necessarily guarantee that you'll solve the problem, it does mean you'll exhaust all of the common sources.

FIGURE 10.4

The Help and Support Center dialog box helps you find the most common sources of common problems.

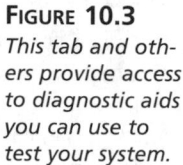

Getting Your Games to Cooperate

Game vendors do lots of tweaking to get the ultimate level of efficiency from their products. It's not too difficult to understand, therefore, that you'll run into some problems when using these products. In most cases, the glitches represent something the vendor couldn't test during the product development cycle. Still, the root of the problem is often the direct screen writes and hardware manipulation that game programs perform to provide dramatic effects.

Getting your game to work with your hardware and software setup can be an exercise in frustration, especially if you purchase games that don't adhere to published standards. Unfortunately, it's difficult to tell much about a game from the outside. In most cases, you have to install the game and try it on your machine to see if it works.

I've actually had a game install perfectly on one machine and not at all on another, even though the two machines used identical hardware and drivers. Sometimes, it's a compatibility problem with DLLs installed by other software on the machine. This particular problem is worse under Windows because many DLLs are common to several pieces of software.

To protect yourself from potential problems when buying games, buy the software from a store that has an exchange policy. Some stores refuse to accept a game back after you've opened it (and for good reason—some buyers don't return all the pieces, making it impossible for the store owner to sell the game to someone else). I make sure that the store offers store credit as a minimum if I return a game that doesn't work on my machine. If possible, I try to buy at a place that offers a full cash refund, especially if there aren't any other games I want at the time of purchase.

Another way to protect yourself is to look at game reviews in magazines. Game reviews often mention potential problems the author saw when installing the game. A bug-filled game will probably receive a poor review. Unfortunately, a game review is also subjective. Your tastes might be completely different from those of the reviewer. In other words, a review can't tell you whether you'll like a game; just look at it for clues to whether the game will play as expected.

The following sections help you further reduce your risk when making a game purchase. They examine some of the more common problems people run into. Because there are many other problems you could run into, such as simple hardware failure, make sure you look for every potential source of a problem before you throw in the towel.

> **Tip:** You don't have to try to conquer gaming problems alone. The Internet has a wealth of game-related newsgroups you can use to try to resolve your problem. You find at least 10 newsgroups to check out under `comp.sys.ibm.pc.games`. For example, `comp.sys.ibm.pc.games.strategic` helps you with strategy games. Make sure that you check your game packaging for any vendor-related Web sites. Although you might find help a little lacking on some Web sites, you can find out about patches and updates to your game.

Windows Games

Windows games have certain advantages over their DOS counterparts. A Windows game requires less setup in most cases, and the setup issues you do run into are easier to resolve. The reason is simple: For the most part, a Windows game uses the same drivers as your other Windows applications. Setting up Windows is enough to ensure that the game has everything it needs to perform a semiautomatic installation. You don't have to worry about which interrupt your soundboard uses or how much memory your display adapter contains. You might still have to worry about whether to install DirectX, however, because many games use DirectX to speed things up.

Most Windows games have fewer compatibility problems because there's at least a little standardization among them. The use of common drivers is a major advantage in the Windows environment. Standards such as DirectX also have gone a long way toward making it easier for game vendors to ensure their products will run on your machine.

Another reason to use Windows games is that they usually have a standard interface. Although there are differences between games (much more so, in fact, than other application types), you'll see evidence of the Windows interface in small tasks, such as saving your files. I can't promise you won't have any problems using Windows games, but in most cases you'll find them less difficult to use than DOS games.

Using Windows as a platform has some problems. For example, Windows games tend to run slower than their DOS counterparts. You'll also find that many Windows games require more hardware resources than their DOS counterparts. There isn't any good rule of thumb for determining how much of a difference there is; you just have to make an educated guess when looking at the game package in the store.

I also have run into many color-depth and resolution problems. This is unique to Windows because of the flexibility of the display configuration. I have run 1024×768 displays in 16-bit color mode. Many older games want 640×480 and 256-color mode, while newer games try to use at least 800×600 resolution and 16-bit color. (At least one game that I read about recently uses 1024×768 mode, so games are finally able to use more of the display area.) You can read how to circumvent these compatibility problems in the "Using Compatibility Mode" section of this chapter.

Looking for the Microsoft Seal of Approval

Most people who use Windows applications wrongly assume that any game in the store is on Microsoft's approved list. You should always look for the Microsoft seal. This is your assurance that someone at Microsoft has at least looked at the game design. There might be nothing wrong with an unapproved game, but you can't be sure.

However, a Microsoft seal isn't a guarantee that you won't run into any problems. All the seal tells you is that the developer created the game in accordance with Microsoft's guidelines. Newer products also go through compatibility testing, but the testing can't check for every possible problem. In other words, the game meets certain minimal requirements. The seal may not be enough to ensure that the game will run on your system.

You should still make sure that you can return a game to the store, even if it has a Microsoft seal on it. I always buy approved games because I've had far fewer problems with them. Not only that, but companies who take the time to go through the certification process usually provide better customer support. Purchasing a game with Microsoft's seal usually ensures that you can get help resolving compatibility problems.

Compatibility Issues

I haven't covered a few Windows compatibility problems in other sections of this chapter. You'll run into most of these only under very specific conditions. One of the most common problems is old drivers. Some game installation programs, for example, don't bother to check which DirectX drivers you're using—they just overwrite your new files with the old ones on the CD. Other game installation programs misread the drivers and assume you have whatever it takes to run the game, when in reality you don't. Windows XP does get around most of these problems by keeping a close watch on your files and preventing installation programs from overwriting your new drivers. If you occasionally ran into this problem in Windows 9x, it's unlikely that you'll run into it with Windows XP.

Another problem is laptop specific. For whatever reason (and I've heard more than a few conflicting reasons), the flat-screen display provided with laptop computers doesn't react as well to DirectX as the displays used with desktop machines. As a result, I've seen many video problems when running games on laptop machines. If you run into this problem, check with the laptop vendor for updated drivers. In many cases, someone else has already run into the problem and the laptop vendor has the fix you require.

> **Tip:** Many game magazines now carry reviews of laptop machines as gaming platforms. The list of laptops that actually pass their tests is short, but you'll find at least one model from most vendors. If you need a laptop for business trips and want to mix a little pleasure with your business, look for a laptop that's capable of performing well with today's games.

Some problems I place into the "Strange" category. One game I liked to play, for example, had a problem with IP addresses. I could contact another party on the Internet only if the first IP number was two digits or fewer. I couldn't enter an IP number beginning with three digits. Fortunately, the vendor came out with a patch that fixed the problem. Many people, however, assumed there was a problem with their machines and went through troubleshooting procedures before contacting the vendor. If you have a problem with a game, try contacting the vendor first (or at least a suitable newsgroup on the Internet) to see if it's a common problem.

DOS Game Issues

Every time I think that DOS is dead in the gaming community, I see a new thread start about someone who has blown the dust off their DOS game and rediscovered how great it is. If this happened once a year, I might consider it a fluke, but it happens regularly on many of the game forums. With this in mind, let's look at a few tips for working with DOS games under Windows XP should nostalgia get you in its grip.

DOS games that use eXtended Memory Specification (XMS) work best under Windows XP. In fact, most of these games run just by double-clicking them in Explorer. (You also can add them to your Start menu or as a shortcut on the desktop.) I recently had a touch of nostalgia myself and tried Darklands. Except for a problem with the sound, the game played better than it ever did under DOS (well, at least it ran faster).

You should be aware of a few things when playing DOS games under Windows. First, try them without any configuration changes at all. In some cases, game vendors have added code to make DOS games Windows friendly. If you change any of the settings in the PIF file associated with the DOS game, you could disable this special code and prevent your game from running.

If you just double-click the game and it doesn't work, you can perform some additional configuration setup. The "Settings" section of Chapter 8, "Exploiting Your Software," discusses various PIF configuration issues. Try working with the settings on the Memory, Screen, and Misc tabs of the Program Properties dialog box.

When It's Time to Shelve that Game

Eventually, you'll get to the point at which a game can no longer keep up with technology. One game I had, for example, wouldn't work with Pentium processors because of an assumption made by the original programmer. In this particular case, the game vendor released a patch to fix the Pentium problem. This situation is the exception, however, rather than the rule. When a game ages sufficiently, the vendor provides a modicum of technical support and that's about it. Technology eventually leaves these games gathering dust on your shelf.

I use a simple rule of thumb when it comes to shelving a game. Playing games is supposed to be fun and relaxing. If a game starts to take more time to set up and fix, you might want to put it on the shelf. It's hard to give up a game that feels as comfortable as an old pair of shoes, but even old shoes have to go by the wayside eventually. You can say the same thing of many games.

Is there a lifespan you can expect for a game? Probably not. I recently rented a copy of Zork III. Despite the old text interface, the game was still fun to play. It even ran under Windows XP. Was the thrill still there? Well, the game was showing its age. Having great graphics to look at is pretty addicting. The point is, I could play this game without problems. Some games aren't quite that lucky. I can't get M1 Tank Platoon to play under Windows XP, no matter what I do. I was able to get this game to work under Windows 9x with the Pentium patch, but I think it has seen its final playing day.

Installing and Configuring Game Controllers

Anyone who plays simulations or action games wants a game controller of some type to make the game more fun to play. A few people I know have quite a few game controllers of different size and shapes. Windows XP doesn't detect your game controller in most cases because it can't detect it through the game port on your machine. This means you have to install support for your joystick or foot pedals separately.

Of course, you'll want to verify that you actually need to install the game controller. You could do that by starting a game and trying your joystick out, but that's not the best way to do things. Open the Game Controllers applet found in the Control Panel. You'll see the Game Controllers dialog box. Check this dialog box to ensure the game controller doesn't appear in the list. If it does, check the Status column. You may find the device is already recognized and functional. Adding a device twice can have undesirable results. After you verify that you need to install the game controller, you can use the following steps to do it:

1. Click Add. You'll see the Add Game Controller dialog box.

> **Tip:** Because vendors have introduced so many game controllers on the market, Microsoft chose not to try to add every one of them to the game controller list. However, if your favorite game controller is missing, you can still use it under Windows XP. Notice the Custom button in this dialog box. If you click this button, you see the Custom Game Controller dialog box. It contains everything you need to configure all of the specifics for the custom game controller. For example, you can differentiate between a joystick, game pad, flight yoke or stick, and racecar controller.

2. Choose a standard game controller or configure a custom game controller. Click OK. Windows XP adds the new game controller to the Installed Game Controllers list on the Game Controllers dialog box. You need to test and adjust the game controller before you can use it.

3. Click Properties. You'll see a Properties dialog box for your game controller. The Test tab helps you check the buttons and the positioning capability of the controller. The Settings tab helps you calibrate the controller. To calibrate the game controller, click Calibrate and follow the prompts provided by the Game Device Calibration Wizard.

4. Test and calibrate your device. Click OK. Click OK a second time to close the Game Controllers dialog box.

Multimedia Hardware

Before you can play games, listen to that streaming radio broadcast, or watch a video, you need properly installed and configured multimedia hardware. This means adjusting sound levels, installing the correct speaker support, and ensuring that your system plays video properly. The following sections look at the multimedia portion of hardware configuration. You'll find most of the multimedia configuration settings in the Sounds and Audio Devices applet in the Control Panel.

Audio Configuration

The Sounds and Audio Devices dialog box contains three tabs that affect audio configuration. The Volume tab, shown in Figure 10.5, configures the volume settings for your machine and helps you configure your speakers. The Device Volume slider, shown in the figure, adjusts the volume for Windows XP as a whole. If you want to adjust individual volume settings, click Advanced and you'll see the Volume Control dialog box, which has sliders for each sound system component.

FIGURE 10.5

The Volume tab adjusts the volume levels for your machine, but also contains speaker settings.

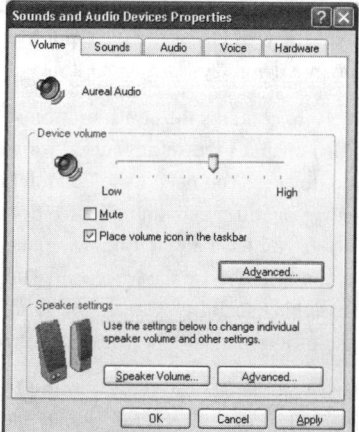

Click Speaker Volume, and you'll see two sliders that allow you to adjust the left and right speaker volume separately. These sliders don't affect the soundboard—they affect the speaker volume directly. Therefore, they don't do anything with standard speakers that plug into the Line Out connection on your soundboard. The speaker has to provide some type of logic connection with the computer.

The Advanced button is another story. Click this button, and you'll see the Advanced Audio Properties dialog box. The Speakers tab of this dialog box contains a Speaker Setup list box. You'll find settings for everything from stereo headphones to 7.1 Surround Sound speakers. Adjusting this property to match your speakers has a definite affect.

The Performance tab of the Advanced Audio Properties dialog box controls the audio performance of your system. The Hardware Acceleration slider controls how many soundboard features Windows XP uses. The more processing you can offload to the soundboard, the more processing time Windows has for other tasks. Of course, the downside is that you also introduce compatibility problems in some cases. A test using DXDIAG.EXE (see the "Testing Your Hardware" section, earlier in this chapter, for details) ensures that the setting you use doesn't interfere with games and other multimedia programs.

The Sample Rate Conversion Quality slider sets the amount of processing power used to convert digital signals to audio output. Select the Best option if possible because the sound-quality difference is dramatic. However, if you notice your system working at a snail's pace, you may need to scale back to Good.

The Sounds tab matches a sound to particular system events. You can change all of the sounds at once by selecting an option in the Sound Scheme field. The Program Events field contains a list of events associated with various parts of Windows. For example, you see the Exit Windows event. You can associate a sound with an individual event by highlighting the event and typing the name of a sound in the Sounds field. Use the Browse button to find a sound if necessary. Clicking the arrow key between the Sounds field and the Browse button plays the sound for you. Once you have put together a sound setup you like, you can save it as a scheme using the Save As button.

The Audio tab, shown in Figure 10.6, contains the configuration settings for wave (WAV) file recording and playback. It also changes the settings used for musical instrument device interface (MIDI) files and devices. You need to select a default device for each of the entries, which normally means selecting your soundboard. Some people install separate MIDI boards in their system. If you have a MIDI board, make sure that you select it in place of the soundboard. You can also choose the Microsoft-supplied software MIDI selection if your soundboard lacks this capability. Check Use Only Default Devices if you want to restrict Windows use of alternatives if a primary device fails.

The Volume buttons open either a Volume Control or Recording Control dialog box. These dialog boxes contain sliders that control each of the playback or record features of your sound card. The Volume Control dialog box contains options to mute individual playback channels, while the Recording Control dialog box allows you to choose a single device for recording purposes.

Click Advanced to display the Advanced Audio Properties dialog box. This is the dialog box you use to adjust your speaker type and performance settings.

Voice Configuration

Microsoft includes several voice applications with Windows XP. All of these applications rely on the same engine and perform about the same tasks. We discuss the most common use of voice technology in Windows right now in the "Access for Users with Disabilities" section of Chapter 15. The Screen Reader application can tell you what is onscreen, and many people find it useful for wading through large amounts of text.

FIGURE 10.6
The Audio tab helps you configure the record and playback levels for your system.

The Voice tab, shown in Figure 10.7, helps you configure your system for use with voice software. You begin by selecting default devices for both playback and record. The next step is to test your hardware to see if it works. The following steps show you how:

1. Click Test Hardware. You'll see a Sound Hardware Test Wizard welcome screen.

2. Click Next. Sound Hardware Test Wizard tests your hardware and then presents you with a Microphone Test dialog box.

3. Test your microphone by reading the supplied text. Adjust the volume as needed. Click Next. The Sound Hardware Test Wizard displays a Speaker Test dialog box.

4. Test the combination of your microphone and speaker by reading the supplied text. Adjust your speaker so that you can hear the text read into the microphone without any feedback. The dialog box contains sliders to adjust both the microphone and speaker settings, but it's normally best to adjust only the speaker settings.

FIGURE 10.7
Use the Voice tab to set your system up to use voice software, such as Screen Reader, included with Windows XP.

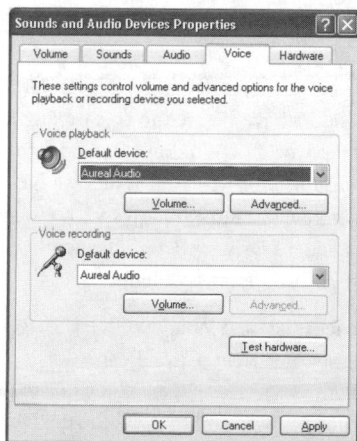

5. Click Next. You'll see a Successful Completion dialog box.

6. Click Finish to complete the test. You'll see the Voice tab of the Sounds and Audio Devices Properties dialog box.

You can make further adjustments to the volume levels for your system by clicking Volume in either the Voice Playback (Volume Control dialog box) or Voice Recording (Recording Control dialog box) sections. Click Advanced if you need to adjust your speakers.

Viewing Hardware Properties

The Hardware tab, shown in Figure 10.8, contains a complete list of all the multimedia hardware on your system that Windows recognizes. The reason I stress this point is that you may find some of your hardware missing. Microsoft significantly cut the size of its supported hardware list in this version of Windows, which means that hardware that worked fine in the past may not work now. Check the hardware compatibility list (HCL) at http://www.microsoft.com/hcl/default.asp.

Figure 10.8

You'll find a complete list of the hardware Windows XP recognizes on the Hardware tab.

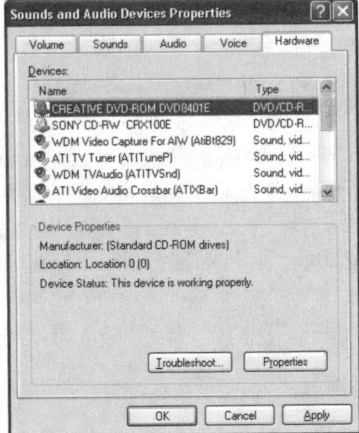

In addition, some third-party vendors have refused to release any new Windows drivers—these vendors are still living in the world of Windows 9x and refuse to see Windows 2000 as a viable platform. Because Microsoft based Windows XP on Windows 2000, you may find that the hardware you counted on in Windows 9x no longer works in Windows XP. Check the Using the "Nonstandard Driver" Peter's Principle in this chapter for some ideas on how to overcome third-party support problems.

Highlight any device in the Devices list, and Windows XP shows you some basic information about it in the Device Properties field. Click Properties if you want to see the Device Properties dialog box from Device Manager. You can use the tabs on this dialog box to make changes to the device settings and to view the device status information.

Click Troubleshoot if you want to see a Help and Support Center window containing helpful hints for working with your hardware. The Troubleshooter in this window leads you through a series of troubleshooting steps for the selected device.

Video Configuration

Microsoft provided a Video tab under Windows 9x that allowed you to select the size for video playback. You could choose a standard size screen, full screen, or variations of the standard screen, such as twice the normal size. However, this tab became useless as soon as Microsoft introduced the Windows Media Player. This tab disappeared from Windows 2000 and you don't see it in Windows XP.

You still have video configuration options to consider. We'll look at the specific Windows Media Player settings in the "Windows Media Player" section of this chapter. The choices you make affect the size of your video and determine how well the video plays.

Of course, a nonflickering display goes only so far. You control the appearance of the video the same way as you control the appearance of Windows in general. Open the Display Properties dialog box by right-clicking the Desktop and selecting Properties from the Context menu. You'll see the majority of the settings that affect video quality. Select the Settings tab and click Advanced to display the Monitor and Display Adapter Properties dialog box (the name of this dialog box will vary according to your machine setup). Note the Screen Refresh Rate setting on the Monitor tab. This setting, more than any other, affects display quality. We discuss this issue more in the "Working with Display Adapters and Monitors" section of Chapter 16.

Peter's Principle: Using the Nonstandard Driver

I have run into many situations where a vendor was less than nimble about providing a new driver for a piece of hardware I own. In at least some of these situations, the hardware was new at the time a new version of Windows appeared on the scene, and the vendor never got around to producing the required driver. To have a piece of hardware in your machine that you can't use because the vendor can't be bothered to write a driver for it is frustrating at best.

In some cases, you'll find that someone else produces an acceptable driver and application software for the device. Sometimes that third party is the vendor who produced the chip on the board you're using. For example, there was a case where I couldn't get a video driver for my system from the original vendor. nVIDIA (http://www.nvidia.com) ended up producing a driver that worked just fine on my and many other people's systems.

Another time, I was having problems obtaining a driver and application for my DVD drive. The DVD part worked just fine, but I lacked software for the hardware decoder, making it impossible to play any movies on my machine. In this situation, Sigma Designs (`http://www.sigmadesigns.com/support/download_hollywood_plus_win2000.htm`), a third party with no personal stake in the DVD or the hardware decoder graciously produced the required software. If you happen to have an orphaned DVD, you might try this driver with Windows XP. The vendor for my DVD still lacks any interest in producing the required driver, but the Sigma Designs driver works fine under both Windows 2000 and Windows XP.

In both these situations, I received help from users with the same problem. Users share their problems and new finds on newsgroups to obtain help and to help other users. The risk you take in using a third-party driver is that it may not work. The third-party product could also cause damage to your system. In addition, the vendor could refuse to provide customer service because you're using a third-party product that its support staff doesn't know anything about. In short, there is no free ride in the world of device drivers.

Windows Game Support

Microsoft is steadily improving the game support provided by Windows. This latest version is another step in the right direction. Not only is DirectX support better, but Microsoft has also included new features, like Compatibility mode.

You may find a new wrinkle in Windows XP, however. Unlike Windows 9x, Windows XP Professional Edition can more than one processor. Unfortunately, most games don't work well with more than one processor.

The following sections tell you that Windows XP provides game support in a new way. First, we'll look at the positive, in the form of Compatibility mode. Second, we'll discuss a potential problem you'll need to overcome: multiple processors.

Using Compatibility Mode

Compatibility problems come in many forms. For example, Windows XP uses a minimum color depth of 16-bit color at an 800×600 resolution. Unfortunately, some education and game programs don't run on anything but 256 colors. You'll also find applications, especially older games, that work only in 640×480 resolution.

The solution to this problem is to open the application shortcut by right-clicking it and selecting Properties from the context menu. Select the Compatibility tab, and you'll see an Application Properties dialog box, like the one shown in Figure 10.9. Notice the Run This Program in Compatibility Mode For list box. It contains four options: Windows 95, Window 98/Windows Me, Windows NT (Service Pack 5), and Windows 2000. These four levels of compatibility assist you in running most applications.

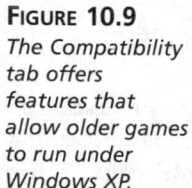

FIGURE 10.9
The Compatibility tab offers features that allow older games to run under Windows XP.

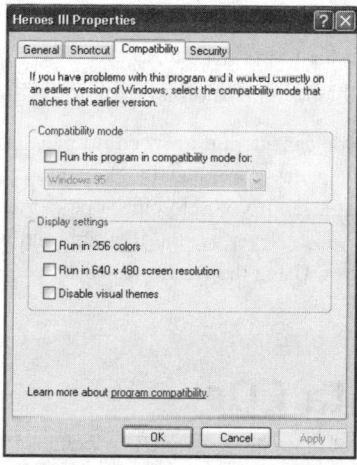

Of course, sometimes just the color or resolution settings create problems. If you're having color problems, check the Run in 256 Colors option. Click OK, and your game or educational program begins running in 256-color compatibility mode. You can also use Compatibility mode to run the game in 640×480 resolution and to disable the visual themes. To prevent further problems, use only the features you actually need.

Tips for Working with Dual Processor Machines

Some games and educational software don't react well to more than one processor. The application depends on certain actions on the part of the processor and may not see those actions if Windows XP spreads the application across two processors. The results you'll see when a conflict occurs vary, but Windows XP generally sees the application as misbehaved and you'll end up back in Windows. Any action taking place when the incident occurs is lost and you'll have to start over again from your last save.

Fortunately, there is a simple way to fix this problem. The following steps show how to create an environment where the game will run and is oblivious to the additional processor in your machine:

1. Start your game. As soon as you get to a menu or other good stopping point, use Alt+Tab to minimize the game and view Windows.

2. Open Task Manager and select the Applications tab. You'll see the Windows Task Manager dialog box.

3. Locate your game in the task list. Right-click the entry and choose Go To Process from the context menu. You'll see the game process in the Processes tab of the Windows Task Manager.

4. Right-click the process entry and choose Set Affinity from the context menu. You'll see a Processor Affinity dialog box.

5. Clear all but one of the processor entries. In most cases, you want to leave the CPU 0 entry checked and clear the rest of the entries.

6. Click OK. Your game will now run as normal.

Now that your game is stable, you can attempt to speed it up, an especially nice addition for action games. Right-click the game process again. Notice the Set Priority menu. Most applications begin at the Normal level. If you set your game to the AboveNormal or High setting, you see a performance boost. Never use the Realtime setting, which is reserved for high-priority system processes. Using the Realtime setting could cause your system to freeze or act strange.

Recording Data CDs

Have you ever tried to get one of those third-party CD programs to work the first time? The ones that come with the CD drive have a less-than-stellar reputation, and the reliable third-party products usually cost something. Windows XP solves this problem by including CD-burning software as part of the product. It even works with CD-RW drives, after a fashion. This is one utility category where it's nice to have the software as part of Windows. If you want something better than the basics, you can always buy it, but at least the basic program works.

As soon as you shove the burnable (blank) CD into the drive, Windows XP will display the dialog box shown in Figure 10.10. As you can see, the CD Drive dialog box gives you the option of burning a CD or ignoring the blank media. There are two problems with this display. First, Windows XP doesn't differentiate between CD and CD-RW media, so you can't tell if it recognizes the media as read/write until after the fact. Second, you can't create audio CDs using this technique. (We'll see in the "Creating an Audio CD" section that you can create an audio CD using the Windows Media Player.) The following steps show you how to create a simple data CD:

FIGURE 10.10
Windows XP finally offers the option to burn a CD.

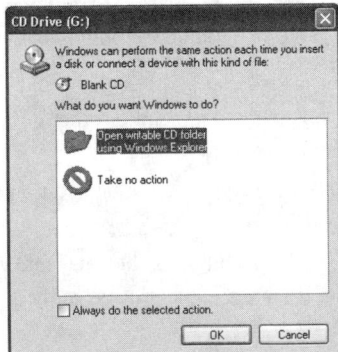

1. Highlight Open writable CD folder using Windows Explorer and then click OK. This is where you place all your data before writing it to the CD. Make certain that you place copies of your data here because Windows XP will erase the contents of the folder after it burns the CD.

2. Place all of the files you want to write into the single-pane view of Explorer. You can create folders to organize the data by right-clicking the folder area and selecting New | Folder from the context menu.

3. Use the File | Write These Files to CD command to start the writing process. You'll see the CD Writing Wizard. The first thing you need to decide on is a name for your CD.

4. Click Next. The writing process will begin. Check your CD drive to ensure that it's actually writing data. (Normally, the light on the front of the CD drive is a different color for reading than for writing.) The progress indicator tells you how long the writing process will take. When the CD Writing Wizard is complete, the drive will open. You'll see an option to write the data files to another CD.

5. Decide if you need to create another CD. If so, check the Yes, Write These Files to Another CD option and wait for Windows XP to complete the process. Repeat this step as often as needed to create all the CDs you need.

6. Click Finish to complete the CD-writing process.

7. Verify the content of the CD by closing the drive door and viewing the contents using Windows Explorer.

8. Close the initial Explorer single-pane view. Windows XP will automatically remove the temporary files from your system.

You'll see one difference when working with CD-RW media. If you place a nonblank CD-RW in the drive, Window XP will display a single-pane view of the CD-RW content. You can use the File | Erase This CD-RW command to remove the content from the CD. If you drag another file to the CD-RW, it will appear grayed out with a plus sign on it. Use the File | Write These Files to CD command to send the new files to the CD-RW. You can keep adding files until the CD-RW is full.

Tip: You can use CD-RW drives with Windows XP, but at the time of this writing, the process is quite painful. Windows XP treats the disk as a multisession CD during the recording process. When you place the disk in the drive later, you'll see an option to erase the entire disk or add more data. The problem with this approach is that most people want to work with individual files on their CD-RW drive. If you want this capability with Windows XP, you'll need a third-party product. One of the best products at this time is Nero's InCD (http://www.ahead.de/en/download.htm). Not only is this product feature-packed, but you can also get it in several languages.

Windows Multimedia Software

Windows XP comes with a wealth of multimedia software. In fact, the amount of multimedia functionality in this version is somewhat staggering. However, unlike previous versions of Windows, you'll find most of the functionality in the three applications described in the following sections, rather than spread across an array of applications.

Sound Recorder

The Sound Recorder application, shown in Figure 10.11, hasn't changed much since ages past. You can still record data from the current recording source for 60 seconds at a time. If you want to record more than 60 seconds, you have to press the Record button more than once.

FIGURE 10.11

The Sound Recorder performs one task well: It records sounds for storage as WAV files.

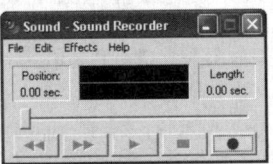

After you record a sound byte, you can manipulate it in a number of ways. Entries on the Effects menu increase or decrease the volume, increase or decrease the recording speed, add echo, or play the recording backward. The Edit menu options allow you to mix the sound with other sounds, delete portions of the sound byte, and insert other files into the current file.

You save the file using the File | Save command. The Change button on the Save As dialog box allows you to convert the sound to a different format before you save it. For example, you can increase or decrease the sampling rate. You can also attempt to convert the file to another format, although Sound Recorder often refuses to perform the requested conversion.

Windows Movie Maker

The Windows Movie Maker is named incorrectly. Many people use this utility for something other than creating movies. One of the best and easiest ways to use this product is to create automated slide shows. You can also use it to create animations or movies, but both of these uses require more effort and perhaps better input tools than the average user can access.

Figure 10.12 shows an example of a short slide show I created using Windows Movie Maker. Creating this presentation was amazingly easy. I was able to complete it in a minimum of time, and the results look somewhat professional.

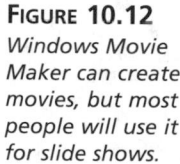

Figure 10.12

Windows Movie Maker can create movies, but most people will use it for slide shows.

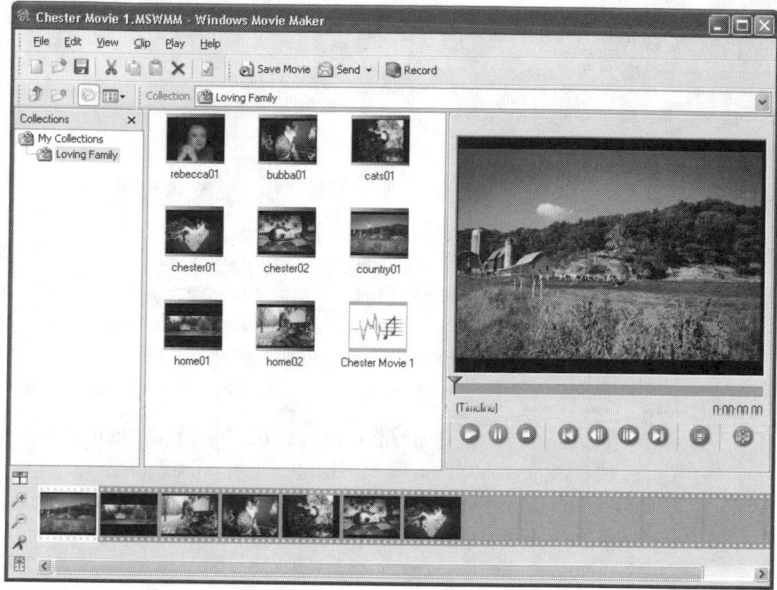

The first thing you'll need to do is obtain the pictures required for the slide show. I used a scanner to create electronic versions of the pictures shown in the figure. You also need to gather any other media you want to use, such as sound bytes. The only media you don't have to gather immediately is any annotation for the "movie."

Once you have the pictures and other media ready, create a folder to hold your presentation by right-clicking My Collections and choosing New Collection from the context menu. Highlight the new collection so that the Windows Movie Player will use it to hold the imported data. Use the File | Import command to import the media you created. You should see any pictures as thumbnails, as shown in Figure 10.12. Of course, you can change this presentation to a details or list view using options on the View menu.

You have all of the data collected, so now you have to place it in order. The movie frames at the bottom of the display hold each picture you want to present. This is the storyboard view of the data as it appears in Figure 10.12. Don't worry about timing or anything else right now—just get the pictures in order.

After you get all of the pictures in order, you'll want to create timing between them. Click the Timeline icon at the bottom of the display area. Your view should look similar to the one shown in Figure 10.13. Notice the timing marks at the top of the display and the two trim points surrounding the home01 picture. The first trim point shows when the slide show will start showing the picture, while the second trim point shows when the slide show will stop showing the picture. You can continue to move these trim points around as needed.

The final task is to record some annotation for your presentation. Use the File | Record Narration command to start the recording process. You'll see a Record Narration Track dialog box appear. The slide show will start. Add the narration as you see each picture appear in the viewing area. Don't worry if the narration doesn't precisely match—you can move the trim points as needed to match your narration later.

At this point, you have most of your slide show put together. You need to synchronize the narration with the pictures. Use the trim points to get rid of timing errors. Click Save Project to save your project to disk. Create the slide show by clicking Save Movie. You see a Save Movie dialog box that sets options such as the movie quality. When you finish changing the movie settings, click OK and Windows Movie Maker will output your latest film.

Windows Media Player

The Windows Media Player is the new way to play all types of media on your system. It allows you to become extremely creative in the way you view your data. The music may sound the same, the video may look the same, but the player is definitely different. Figure 10.14 shows just one of many skins that come with Windows XP. (A *skin* is a way of dressing up the functionality of the Windows Media player. The controls are functional—just the look is different.)

> **Note:** You don't find the CD Player installed on Windows XP. The Windows Media Player consolidates multimedia features that used to appear as part of several utility programs. Instead of forcing you to learn how to use a media application for each media type, the Windows Media Player uses a single interface and makes life much easier for you.

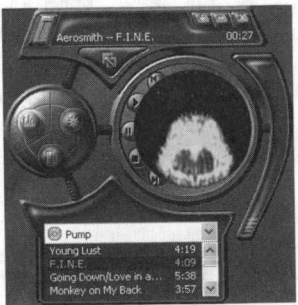

FIGURE 10.14
The Windows Media Player is as fun to use as it is functional.

Although the look of Figure 10.14 is fun, it isn't the easiest way to learn to use the Windows Media Player. When you first open the Windows Media Player, it looks like the view in Figure 10.15. This view is still fun, but not quite as tricky to use as the previous view.

FIGURE 10.15

The standard Windows Media Player View is much easier to use.

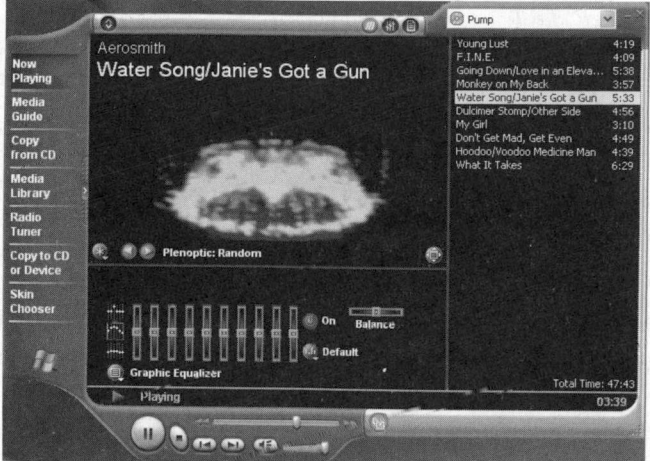

Let's begin with the basics. You'll see a list of the songs for an album in the playlist portion of the Windows Media Player. The visualization area can hold randomized pictures, as shown in Figures 10.14 and 10.15, or an album cover (when available). You need an Internet connection to use the album cover option. The visualization area can also hold tools, including the SRS WOW effect, a graphic equalizer, video settings, media information, captions, and lyrics.

You don't actually see any lyrics unless you type them into the system. To add lyrics, right-click the song in the playlist and choose Properties from the context menu. Select the Lyrics tab of the Properties dialog box. Type the lyrics and click OK, and you'll see them onscreen if you've selected the Lyrics tool.

You'll see a list of buttons along the side of the Windows Media Player. This list describes the purpose of each button:

- *Now Playing* Shows the display shown in Figures 10.14 and 10.15. You see the current media content, a visualization, a tool, and a few controls for making your listening experience more enjoyable. This view is the one most people know.

- *Movie Guide* Takes you to the WindowsMedia.com Web site. You can see highlighted artists, download samples, play some short cuts from albums, and generally immerse yourself in media.

- *Copy from CD* Moves songs or other media from a CD to your hard drive. This button allows you to play the songs from your hard drive or use the files to create audio compilations.

- *Media Library* Displays a hierarchical view of the media library content. The *media library* is an area of the hard drive set aside for storing songs, film clips, WAV files, and other forms of media. The media library organizes the data to make it easier for you to find.

- *Radio Tuner* Takes you to the WindowsMedia.com Web site. You can choose a radio station on the site. The Windows Media Player accepts streaming audio from the Web site, so you can listen to your favorite songs or commentary.

- *Copy to CD or Device* Creates an audio or other media CD. See the "Recording Data CDs" section earlier in this chapter to learn how to create data CDs.

- *Skin Chooser* Creates an interesting presentation for your Windows Media Player. Windows XP ships with a number of skins. You can also create your own skins.

Creating Your Own Skins

You can go crazy creating your own skins for the Windows Media Player. The samples provided with Windows XP are just that—samples. As interesting as some of these examples are, you can find even more examples online.

This is such a popular activity in some groups that you can find lots of information about it online. One of the more important places is the Windows Media Player SDK (http://download.microsoft.com/download/winmediaplayer/wmpsdk7/7/NT5/EN-US/ WMPSDK7.exe) because it contains the tools required to work with the files and the documentation for creating changes. Microsoft has created a special "skins" newsgroup at microsoft.public.windowsmedia.player.skins. In some cases, you'll have to access this server through the news.microsoft.com news server. You'll find some links for articles on the Windows Media Web site (http://msdn.microsoft.com/nhp/ default.asp?contentid=28000411). It's also important to read individual articles on the topic. You'll find excellent articles on the topic of creating skins for the Windows Media Player at http://msdn.microsoft.com/library/en-us/dnwmt/html/ wmpskins.asp and http://www.zdnet.com/zdhelp/stories/main/ 0,5594,2629064,00.html.

Okay, what's the short take on creating skins? It turns out that the Windows Media Zip (WMZ) files found in the \Program Files\Windows Media Player\Skins directory are renamed Zip files. Create a copy of one and rename it to see what I mean.

Inside the Zip file, you'll find several files. The main file that defines the skin is the Windows Media Skin (WMS) file. If you know anything about eXtensible Markup Language (XML), then you have a good idea of how to read this file. Microsoft defines the skin parameters using standard XML tags.

Besides the WMS file, you'll find graphics files. Each of these graphics contributes toward the appearance of the skin. You need to separate changeable elements from those that always appear on screen. For example, if the appearance of a button changes during the course of use, you'll need to define it as a separate graphic.

You'll also find one or more script files in many WMZ files. This optional file determines certain skin behaviors. It's possible to create a basic skin without using scripts, but adding scripts also makes the skin more functional.

Creating an Audio CD

The Windows Media Player can help you create audio CDs. You can use it to record special events, create compilations of CDs you own, or make your own music CDs. The uses for audio CDs increase as people have better access to recording equipment. The following steps tell you how to create a basic audio CD:

1. Compile a list of music, voice recordings, or other audio you want to save on a CD. Place the media in the My Music folder. You can use the Copy from CD option of the Windows Media Player to copy your favorite music to your hard drive. Simply place the CD in the drive, select the Copy from CD option, place a check mark next to each piece you want to copy, and then click Copy Music. The first time you use the Windows Media Player for this task, it will warn you about copying copyrighted music.

2. Select the Media Library option of the Windows Media Player. You'll see a hierarchical view of all the content on your hard drive.

3. Click New Playlist. You'll see a New Playlist dialog box.

4. Type a name for the playlist and click OK. You'll see the playlist appear in the My Playlists folder.

5. Drag any media you want to appear on the CD to the new playlist folder.

6. Open the playlist. Place the media in the order you want it to appear on disk. Simply highlight the media you want to move, and then click the Move Up or Move Down buttons as needed.

7. Select the Copy to CD or Device option of the Windows Media Player.

8. Select the playlist you just created from the Music to Copy list. You should see the list of music appear in the left pane in the order you placed it in the playlist.

9. Select the CD you want to use to create the audio CD from the Music on Device list. Make sure the media list on the right side of the display is blank.

10. Click Copy Music. Windows Media Player will begin converting the files. The formats of the files on disk don't match the CD format, so Windows Media Player must perform the conversion. After Windows Media Player completes the conversion, it will begin copying files to the CD. This process isn't nearly as fast as they make it look on television, so you'll have to be patient.

11. Test the disk on your stereo before you leave for the picnic or party.

Note: After working with this process for a while, I came to the conclusion you must use standard CDs for making audio CDs if you plan to play the CD on a standard player. The standard players refuse to work with CD-RW media. Unfortunately, this makes your copies permanent because you can't erase them as you could when using a CD-RW.

On Your Own

Go to the Microsoft site at `http://www.microsoft.com/directx/default.asp` to see if you have the latest version of DirectX. Making sure you have the latest operating system support is one way to reduce the number of problems you'll encounter. You should also spend some time checking your hardware and associated drivers. Most vendors have Web sites from which you can download updated drivers. Hardware that uses flash ROM technology can benefit from downloads as well.

Try to get an old game running under Windows XP. Some older games are a special challenge because you have to use special settings to get them to run. Make sure you take a close look at the game to see whether it's getting too old to run. As technology advances, it leaves some games behind, making it difficult to install or play them. You also should check game vendor Web sites to see if a patch is available for your game. These patches often fix compatibility problems.

If you have the right type of CD drive, try creating a data or audio CD. Creating your own special mix of audio CDs is especially fun. Using a recorded CD when you go somewhere, like a picnic or other places where damage might occur, is one way to protect your CD investment. The master CD stays at home, while the copy goes with you to have fun. Make sure you copy only CDs you own and only for your own needs.

Work with the Windows Media Player. Try out the various skins and create a few of your own. The Windows Media Player is one of the fun features of Windows XP. It makes using multimedia fun, rather than the chore it used to be.

PART IV

Windows XP Anatomy

The Windows XP Architecture

Learning about a new operating system usually includes knowing a bit about the components that comprise it. Look at it this way. When you go to your auto mechanic, you expect that he'll know something about the engine, electrical system, and computers that make the car work. He may not know everything about every car component, but you expect him to know enough to fix your car given he has the proper tools and reference books to research answers.

In some ways, you're the mechanic for your computer. You need to know the basics of how it's put together. That means knowing something about the operating system. No one is expecting you to know every detail about the operating system, but you should understand enough to recognize certain problems and then know how to find answers to those problems.

With this knowledge requirement in mind, let's look at the Windows XP architecture and some of the components that comprise it. I looked specifically at the Professional Edition of the product while writing this chapter, but later verified that all of the pieces appear in the Home Edition as well. The main architectural differences between the Professional Edition and the Home Edition are in the areas of security and NTFS support. The core operating system is the same in both cases.

We won't go into bits and bytes during this discussion. In fact, we'll barely scratch the surface of what the Windows XP core operating system contains. Still, you'll gain an appreciation of what goes on under the hood of this operating system. Having that knowledge can make it much easier to both configure and use Windows XP effectively. In short, you'll become a better computer mechanic by understanding the contents of this chapter.

A Quick Look Inside

Windows XP is a complex operating system. In fact, every version of Windows seems a little more complex than the one before it. Much of this additional complexity comes in the form of new utilities and additional operating system features. Any time you add new features to a piece of software, you have to pay a price for it.

The following sections discuss Windows XP architecture from an overview perspective. This is the "toe in the water" section of the chapter. You'll learn the basics of the Windows XP architecture so that you can better understand the material that follows.

Architecture

Microsoft based Windows XP on the Windows 2000 operating system, so those of you who are looking for the old Windows 9x files will find them missing. However, you won't find a direct correlation between Windows 2000 and Windows XP either. Windows 2000 provides a rigid operating environment that's ill suited to running many applications, such as games and educational software. If you know Windows 2000 architectural details, you also know those in Windows XP, but only to an extent.

Before you can understand the Windows XP architecture, you have to understand some of the principles on which it's based. The first principle is the Intel processor. Security is a part of most operating system designs. It's important to keep the data and applications that the operating system relies on to function safe from harm. The Intel processor provides four levels of protection, but Windows XP uses only two of them. Applications the operating system trusts run in *kernel mode*, or the highest level of protection. User applications and other pieces of nontrusted code run in *user mode*, or the lowest level of protection. Between these two modes is a wall that neither of them can cross without help. The user code remains outside the wall, and operating system code remains protected inside the wall.

The second principle you must understand is that Windows XP is really a series of inter-related applications. You can't point to a single file in the \SYSTEM32 directory and say that it contains Windows XP. Certain functions are assigned to specific files, but that's about as far as you can go. Windows XP is composed of many files. This approach allows other vendors to "bolt" new features onto the operating system and increase its functionality. Most developers describe Windows XP as *a modular operating system* because it consists of more than one application.

Because Windows XP is modular, just as Windows 2000 is modular, you'll find that Windows XP and Windows 2000 do share some files (the ones in Windows XP are updates of those in Windows 2000). Microsoft didn't have to change every part of Windows 2000 to meet the design goals of Windows XP. That's why someone who knows the Windows 2000 architecture already has some idea of how Windows XP works.

You can divide the Windows XP architecture into four main areas. The following list describes each area:

- *Core* The core files include six fixes we'll explore in detail as this chapter progresses: GDI.EXE, GDI32.DLL, KRNL386.EXE, KERNEL32.DLL, USER.EXE, and USER32.DLL. The core files contain only part of the operating system— they're the files that bolt everything together. Every other part of the operating system calls on these files for services. You'll find these files in the \SYSTEM32 folder.

- *Drivers* Windows XP uses drivers to access the hardware on your system. Drivers provide a safe means to access the devices in a multitasking environment where more than one application might want simultaneous device access. Every device in Device Manager has one or more driver files associated with it. To see the drivers associated with a device, click Driver Details on the Driver tab of the Device Properties dialog box. The Driver File Details dialog box, shown in Figure 11.1, tells you about the driver vendor, file version, signed status, and copyright.

FIGURE 11.1
Every device requires one or more device drivers in order to run correctly.

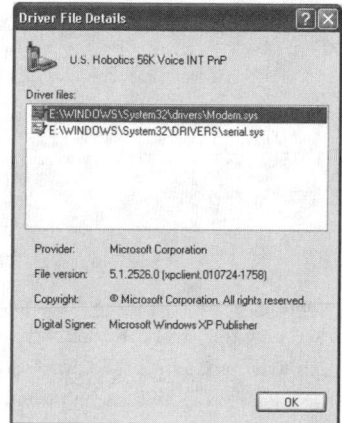

- *Services* A *service* is a background application that enhances the operating system in some way. For example, the Indexing Service creates a searchable index of your hard drive when you aren't using the system for anything else. The Uninterruptible Power Supply (UPS) service shown in Figure 11.2 monitors the state of the UPS attached to your system. A service can interact with the user, but normally works in the background unnoticed. You can obtain a complete list of services on your system by looking at the Services console, found in the Administrative Tools folder. The General tab of the Service Properties dialog box contains a Path to executable field that tells you the name of the application associated with the service.

- *Utilities* An operating system needs some method of interacting with the user. Utilities provide this front end and are usually the only part of the operating system that runs in user mode. Some utilities, such as Packet Internet Groper (PING), run at the command prompt. Microsoft designed them for use by administrators, and these utilities work at a low level of the operating system. Other utilities, such as Microsoft Management Console (MMC), provide a friendlier graphical user interface (GUI). Both administrators and general users have access to GUI utilities. However, administrators normally have access to more application features than general users do.

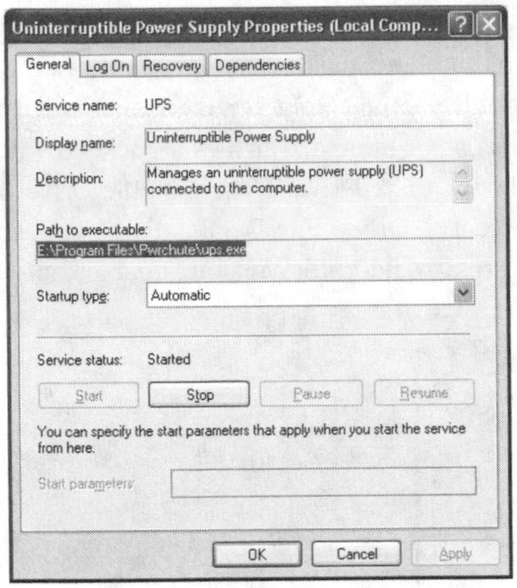

FIGURE **11.2**

Every service has a main executable file; some services require several DLLs as well.

The System Files

Now that you have a better understanding of the Windows XP architecture, let's begin taking some of the pieces apart to see how they work. Remember that Windows XP has two modes for application execution: *user* and *kernel*. The processor actually enforces these modes using two of the four levels of protection it can provide to applications. Protecting the operating system files ensures that the operating system can continue to run even if an application crashes. In short, protection is important to ensure system stability and reliability.

User mode is the lowest level of protection. All user applications and operating system utilities operate at the user-mode level. The operating system doesn't trust user mode applications, and so the user mode applications have to go through an intermediary to contact the operating system.

Kernel mode is the highest level of protection. All of the operating system core and driver files use this mode of operation. In addition, most (if not all) services use this mode of operation. The operating system trusts any file that executes within kernel mode, so these files require additional checks to ensure that it won't crash the system. That's why Microsoft encourages you to use signed drivers for your system.

The following sections examine the concept of user mode and kernel mode in detail. It's important to understand these two concepts and learn how they affect the operating system. Knowing how a file can affect the operating system is important for troubleshooting. If a driver crashes, it can bring the entire operating system down with it. On the other hand, the chances of an application crashing the operating system are slim. When you see the "blue screen of death" in Windows XP, what you're really seeing is the result of a kernel mode application that didn't work as anticipated. When you see a message box from Windows XP saying that it's closing an application because of an error, that's the result of a user mode application that didn't work as anticipated.

User Mode

User mode is all about running applications. When you launch a 32-bit Windows application in Windows XP, the operating system creates a separate memory space for the application to use while running. Applications can use up to 4GB of simulated memory to operate in. That is, each application has up to 4GB available to it. Windows allocates memory to an application based on the amount of code and data it's storing in its memory space, called a *process working set*. Few applications, except for some high-level graphic design and simulation programs, will actually approach the 4GB limit.

This 4GB application work area is *virtual*, which means it doesn't actually exist. Many people don't have 4GB of physical RAM available on their entire system. In some cases, users may not even have 4GB to spare when they combine their physical RAM with the swap file space on the hard drive. The 4GB limit for programs is essentially a theoretical limit today, but it provides a generous specification for possibly much larger future RAM and hard drive space.

We'll discuss the technique Windows XP uses to allocate memory later in the chapter, when we talk about the Virtual Memory Manager. Each 32-bit Windows application plays in its own little sandbox; Windows XP doesn't allow one application to interfere with the memory used by another application. This is quite a divergence from the other Microsoft operating systems, where any program could work with any area of memory it so desired, sometimes with disastrous results. Microsoft built Windows XP to avoid these sometimes not-so-little disasters.

Support for 16-bit Windows applications differs from support for 32-bit applications. Windows XP creates a single memory area for 16-bit applications because that's the way they were originally designed to work. In fact, Windows XP doesn't even launch these applications directly. A special utility program called WOWEXEC.EXE in the /SYSTEM32 folder launches the 16-bit application. We'll see in the section "The Windows XP System (Kernel Mode) Files" that 16-bit support extends to the core of Windows XP. In short, user mode for a 16-bit application is the same as for a 32-bit application, except that it relies on 16-bit support components and executes in a single memory space.

Tip: When Microsoft designed Windows NT, it built the program so that it would integrate with other systems. Microsoft continued this tradition with Windows 2000. Part of that integration is the capability to run programs and scripts from other operating systems, such as Portable Operating System Interface for Unix (POSIX) (a UNIX derivative) OS/2 version 1.0, and Disk Operating System (DOS). When you load Windows XP on your system, you'll notice Microsoft enhanced DOS support, but removed both POSIX and OS/2 support. The official reason for this change is that the support is outmoded and no one needs it any more. Unfortunately, this means that none of the POSIX tools found in the Windows 2000 Resource Kit will work in Windows XP and that

continues

some government sites may find it difficult to find suitable alternatives. One
potential solution for this problem is using Microsoft Interix (`http://www.`
`microsoft.com/WINDOWS2000/interix/`) to replace POSIX. Interix is yet another
UNIX alternative.

Windows XP also provides support for DOS applications. In this case, however, we're no
longer simulating an older version of Windows using built-in support. DOS is another
operating system, one that's very different from Windows XP.

Microsoft provides a way for DOS programs to believe they're running on the original
development machine. The use of an environment subsystem creates an environment
that simulates the older operating system. Microsoft calls this environment the *DOS
Virtual Machine.* In this case, the application is unaware of user mode, Windows XP, or
anything else, for that matter. The DOS application believes that it's running on a
machine all by itself.

Windows XP has to maintain this illusion because many DOS programs try to grab all
available memory, consistently work with the system using odd techniques, and generally
violate all of the rules they can. Considering Microsoft designed DOS as a single-tasking
operating system, it's little wonder that these applications violate the rules. However,
because they do, Windows XP has to quarantine them from the rest of the system.

The Windows XP System (Kernel Mode) Files

The first thing you need to understand is what the term *operating system kernel* means.
Think of the kernel as the central core of the operating system—the part that binds
everything else together and provides a basic set of features. A programmer accesses the
kernel using a special interface. Most programmers call this interface the Application
Programming Interface (API).

When a developer creates an application for Windows, he makes calls to the API. An API
call asks the operating system to perform a task. It's like asking a friend to pick up a few
groceries for you while he's at the store. The code for the API appears in the system
files. Of course, this is a simplified view of the API. Windows XP actually uses two
Windows APIs—one 16-bit API and one 32-bit API. Each API allows user mode applications to make requests of the operating system, which operates in kernel mode.

No matter which API your Windows application uses, it'll address three basic operating
system core components. The 16-bit versions of these files are GDI.EXE, USER.EXE,
and KRNL386.EXE. The 32-bit versions of these files are GDI32.DLL, USER32.DLL,
and KERNEL32.DLL. Developers call this set of files the *Win32 API.* A developer also
uses other APIs to perform other tasks. In most cases, an API call occurs when an application operating in user mode calls on an operating system component operating in kernel mode to perform a task. The following list describes these three components in detail:

> **Note:** The other operating systems that Windows XP supports do so through the system of drivers, services, and environment DLLs I talked about earlier in this chapter. In other words, the server translates the calls made by the application into a Windows API call. In essence, applications that rely on the other operating systems are using the same components as any Windows application would, even though they're designed for another operating system.

- *Windows Kernel (KRNL386.EXE or KERNEL32.DLL)* This part of Windows XP provides support for the lower-level functions an application needs to run. For example, every time your application needs memory, it runs to the Windows Kernel component to get it. This is the literal core of the operating system, but Windows wouldn't operate at all without the other two components. Think about this file as the "parts that didn't fit anywhere else bin," and you'll have a better idea of what it contains. Obviously, the Windows Kernel component doesn't deal with either the interface or devices; it interacts only with Windows itself.

- *Graphical Device Interface (GDI.EXE or GDI32.DLL)* Every time an application writes to the screen, it's using a graphical device interface (GDI) service. This Windows component takes care of fonts, printer services, the display, color management, and every other artistic aspect of Windows that users can see as they use an application.

- *User (USER.EXE or USER32.DLL)* Windows is all about just that—windows. It needs a manager to keep track of all the windows that applications create to display various types of information. However, User only begins there. Every time your application displays an icon or pushbutton, it's using some type of User component function. It's easier to think of the User component of the Windows API as a work manager; it helps you organize things and keep them straight.

The Plug and Play BIOS

Something we haven't discussed so far is how Windows XP detects your hardware so that it knows to install a driver. The current system uses a feature called *Plug and Play* (PnP) for hardware detection. PnP provides one of the easiest ways to configure the hardware on your machine.

From a historical perspective, PnP is quite old for a computer technology. The first microchannel architecture (MCA) machine produced by IBM contained everything PnP needed—except an operating system. Many Extended Industry Standard Architecture (EISA) machines also used a form of PnP. This technology first made an appearance in an operating system with the introduction of Windows 95.

PnP is actually the work of three system components: hardware, BIOS, and operating system. The BIOS queries all system components during startup. The BIOS activates essential system components, such as the disk drive and the display adapter. Everything else waits on the sidelines until the operating system boots.

During the boot process, the operating system finishes the task of assigning interrupts and port addresses to every system component. Unlike Windows 9x, Windows XP can override interrupt and I/O address settings made by the BIOS. This technique gives Windows XP a hardware configuration advantage.

When looking at a PnP-compatible system, you should see more than just three different entities cooperating to provide automatic system configuration. PnP wouldn't be worth all the hubbub if that were all it provided. The following is a list of the additional features you get as part of a PnP system:

- *Identification of installed devices* Windows XP automatically detects all the Plug and Play components attached to your system. This means you should provide a minimum amount of information during installation and nothing at all during subsequent reboots.

- *Determination of device resource needs* Every device on your computer needs resources in the form of processor cycles, input/output ports, DMA channels, memory, and interrupts. Windows XP works with the BIOS and peripheral devices to meet these needs without any intervention. Don't be surprised if you see PCI devices sharing resources, such as IRQs. The PCI bus identifies the source of an interrupt or the recipient of an I/O request using the PCI slot number in addition to traditional identifiers. This is what makes resource sharing possible.

- *Automatic system configuration updates and resource conflict detection* All this communication between peripheral devices, the BIOS, and the operating system enables Windows XP to create a system configuration without user intervention. This enhanced level of communication also enables Windows XP to poll the peripherals for alternative port and interrupt settings when a conflict with another device occurs.

- *Device driver loading and unloading* Plug and Play compatibility enables Windows XP to dynamically load and unload any device drivers your system needs. That is why you can install most devices under Windows XP without the reboot required under earlier versions of Windows.

- *Configuration change notification* Plug and Play might make system configuration changes automatically, but it doesn't mean Windows XP leaves you in the dark. Every time the system configuration changes, Windows XP notifies you by displaying a dialog box onscreen. Essentially, this dialog box tells you what changed. This capability provides an additional benefit—Windows XP also notifies you whenever your equipment experiences any kind of failure. When a piece of equipment fails, Windows XP notices that it's no longer online. Plug and Play requires two-way communication, and a defective device usually fails to communicate. Rather than find out that you no longer have access to a drive or other device when you need it most, Windows XP notifies you of the change immediately after it takes place.

Windows XP Compatibility Configuration Files

Windows used to require several external configuration files to be able to boot, including AUTOEXEC.BAT, CONFIG.SYS, WIN.INI, and SYSTEM.INI. Windows XP doesn't require any of these files and ignores both CONFIG.SYS and AUTOEXECT.BAT. This means anyone upgrading from Windows 9x will have to find alternatives to these two files if she used them for anything. It also means upgrading older hardware that relied on either file to initialize.

Windows XP supports, but doesn't need, WIN.INI and SYSTEM.INI. In fact, you can run the MSCONFIG utility, shown in Figure 11.3, and disable the processing of these two files. Simply clear the Process SYSTEM.INI File and Process WIN.INI File options. You can also go to the SYSTEM.INI or WIN.INI tabs and disable individual boot elements. However, you can still use the files for older application needs. The following sections discuss how to use these two files.

FIGURE 11.3
Use MSCONFIG to disable compatibility file processing.

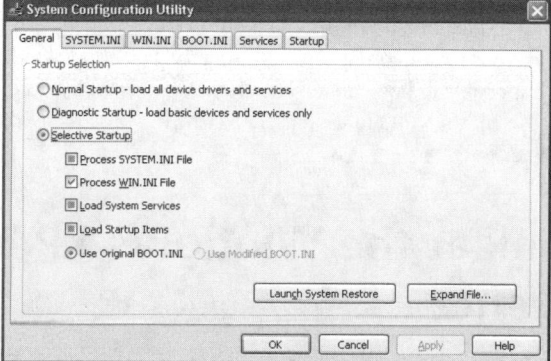

WIN.INI

Windows XP can get along just fine without WIN.INI. However, before you get rid of your file, you might want to check it out first. A few applications, especially screen savers, load themselves by using the LOAD= or RUN= lines of this file. You can get around this limitation by adding the filenames to your Startup folder and changing the application settings as needed. (You may want to get rid of a screen saver that uses these WIN.INI entries if it's a 16-bit application. A 32-bit screen saver will be more responsive and less likely to crash your system.)

Many applications also store their file association information in WIN.INI. Windows XP applications don't need these entries because they already appear in the Registry. Any new 32-bit applications will know to look in the Registry for file association information, but some older 16-bit applications won't. You might want to check for problems by disabling the [Extensions] section using MSCONFIG and then rebooting the system. If all your applications seem to work properly, you might be able to remove this section for good.

> **Note:** Windows XP always checks for new entries in both WIN.INI and SYSTEM.INI. Windows XP automatically adds any new entries it finds to the appropriate section of the Registry. This is the reason that you can get rid of these two files if you have a stable system and none of the 16-bit applications that used to rely on them. Of course, that's a big "if," and you still have to deal with the mysterious Windows XP problem with SYSTEM.INI. In reality, you probably need to wait until you've gotten rid of all of your 16-bit applications before you can get rid of these two files.

SYSTEM.INI

Although WIN.INI contains application settings, such as file associations, SYSTEM.INI contains device driver entries and settings needed to configure them. For example, you'll find both the wave file and windows timer entries in this file.

You're going to find other entries in SYSTEM.INI as well. Microsoft adds entries that older applications need in order to work properly, but Windows XP doesn't use this file itself. It's impossible to know in advance if you'll eventually need these compatibility entries, so use MSCONFIG to disable SYSTEM.INI processing rather than delete it from your machine.

A Look at the Windows XP Boot Sequence

The *boot process* is a series of steps required to get your machine up and running after you turn the power on. The process starts at the time that the Power-On Startup Test (POST) routines begin and continues until you can start to use the machine.

We'll look at the boot process from a user's perspective in the following sections. You won't get a blow-by-blow description of every file loaded and every device initialized— we'll just look at the highlights of the boot process.

> **Tip:** If you ever do want to see a blow-by-blow description of the entire boot process, create a BOOTLOG.TXT file by pressing F8 during the boot process and then selecting the Enable Boot Logging option. Once your machine is booted, you can look at NTBTLOG.TXT in the Windows directory of your machine. (Users of older versions of Windows will remember that this information used to appear in BOOTLOG.TXT in the root directory of the first drive.) This file records
>
> *continues*

every action that Windows XP performs during the boot process. However, it doesn't include a few of the initial actions, such as loading the Windows XP loader (NTLDR.BIN). At most, three or four actions take place before the log starts, though, so your chances of missing anything important are almost nonexistent.

The Windows XP Startup Sequence

Loading the initial system is straightforward. The boot sector on the hard drive points to *NTLDR*—the program the BIOS will call as soon as the POST routine completes, just like it would do with any other operating system loader file. NTLDR calls the NTDE-TECT.COM program. This program displays the Windows XP splash screen.

NTDETECT.COM also begins a search for the installed hardware. Once it gets a complete list, NTDETECT.COM displays the computer's hardware characteristics, such as what kind of hard disk it uses, and passes the information to other applications through the Registry.

After NTDETECT.COM completes its task, it passes control back to NTLDR. The next phase in the operating system boot process is to determine which operating system to load. BOOT.INI contains a list of operating systems installed on your machine. Windows XP displays the screen that allows you to boot any installed operating system. If the countdown timer stops before you select an operating system, Windows XP will then begin to load the default operating system.

Tip: You can always interrupt the countdown timer by pressing the up or down arrow. This allows you as much time as you need to choose an operating system—NTLDR will simply wait until you press the Enter key to begin the loading process.

The next step in the process is to configure Windows XP at a basic level. NTLDR looks in two places for this information. The Registry contains all the hardware information it needs to configure the various devices on your system. In some cases, it also needs to look in BOOT.INI to see which devices to use. The BOOT.INI file also tells Windows XP which services, such as networking or a power monitor, to start.

This whole process works mainly with the Registry. Its function is to load some low-level executable files into memory to handle the rest of the loading process and configure Windows XP for use. It also allows you to choose another operating system before Windows XP begins to load. We're still using NTLDR to get the job done, but now we need to do something with the information we've accumulated.

At this point, you reach the time when Windows XP can begin logging the boot process. The first file it loads is NTOSKRNL.EXE. Because this file depends on HAL.DLL, BOOTVID.DLL, and KDCOM.DLL, these files load as well. NTOSKRNL.EXE contains the basic kernel and system files. HAL.DLL contains the hardware abstraction layer (HAL) used to create communications between the hardware and the operating system. BOOTVID.DLL contains a simple VGA display driver used to display information onscreen during the boot process. Finally, KDCOM.DLL contains a simple hardware debugger in case Windows XP runs into any problems booting the system.

Now that we have some of the basic operating system files loaded, it's time to start scanning the hardware. Windows XP loads PCI.SYS (PnP enumerator), ISAPNP.SYS (ISA bus driver), INTELIDE.SYS (PCI IDE driver), and PCIIDEX (PCI IDE bus driver). The term *enumerator* is a fancy way of saying this file looks for PnP devices and then asks them about their capabilities. The three bus drivers may seem a bit confusing until you consider that many computers have two expansion buses and one or more integrated device electronics (IDE) controllers on the motherboard. The industry standard architecture (ISA) bus is old, so many new computers don't have one. The peripheral component interconnect (PCI) bus is newer and still undergoing change.

Windows XP now loads a series of media support files for your hard drive and other media storage devices. The list of drivers it loads varies by machine because each machine is different. You'll very likely see the MOUNTMGR.SYS (mounts the media for use), DMLOAD.SYS (disk manager), PARTMGR (manages the partition information), and VOLSNAP.SYS (volume management functions) files in the list of drivers. The drivers will also include small computer system interface (SCSI) support, if needed, along with other disk-related device drivers.

Special video drivers come next in the list. For example, depending on the chip set on your motherboard, you might see an accelerated graphics port (AGP) driver load. This is also the point where Windows XP loads the Motion Pictures Experts Group (MPEG) port support. If you have network support enabled, Windows XP will likely load network driver interface specification (NDIS) support.

You now have a barely functional operating system because Windows XP has scanned and loaded all the required hardware driver support. However, the operating system would be featureless without any services. Windows XP begins loading drivers for all of the services your system supports, such as the Remote Access Service (RAS). It also loads secondary hardware drivers, such as the one used to create a connection with the television tuner on your display adapter.

At some point, Windows XP will complete the driver-loading process and begin starting services. Once the services start, you'll see the familiar login screen as Windows XP starts the GUI features, such as Explorer. You log in, and the system is ready to go.

Windows XP Internals

As mentioned earlier in this chapter, Windows XP is a modular operating system. You'll find that each of the files we've discussed so far (and the many others found on your hard drive) fall into several categories or subsystems. The following paragraphs describe the various Windows XP subsystems in enough detail to understand what's going on. This is an overview and doesn't get into all of the details of the Windows XP inner construction.

The New Kernel

Several elements make up the Windows XP architecture, as shown in Figure 11.4. Each element takes care of one part of the Windows environment. For example, the Windows API layer lets applications communicate with Windows internals, such as the file management system. You couldn't write a Windows application without the API layer.

FIGURE 11.4
Windows contains several major elements.

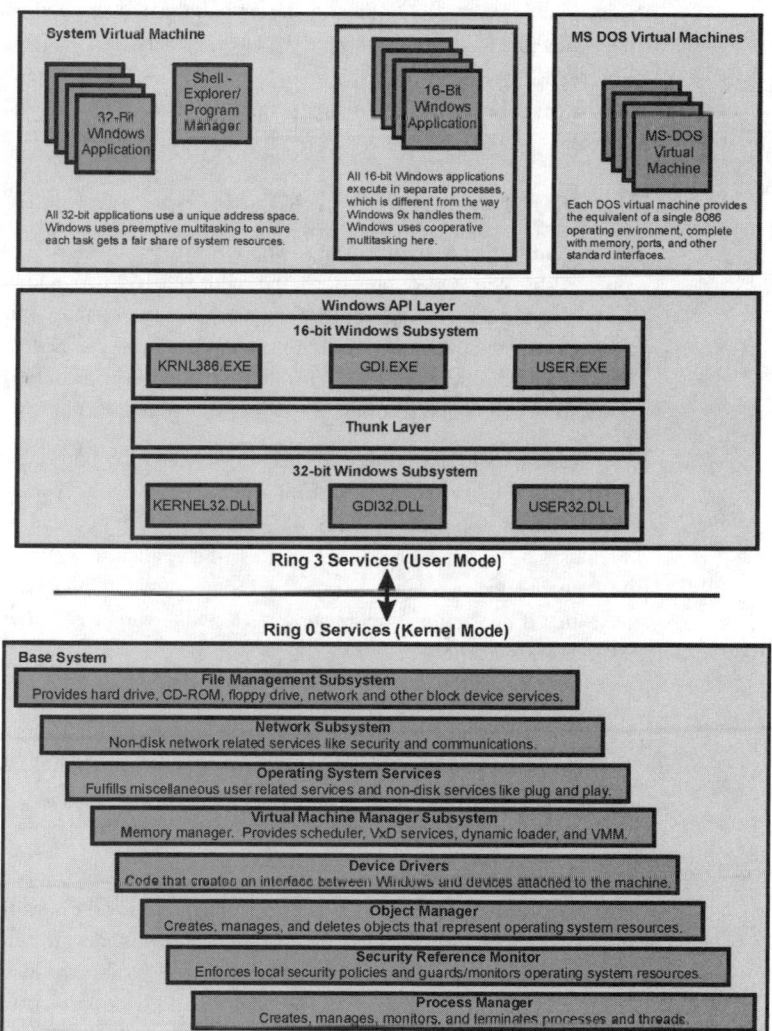

In short, Microsoft built Windows XP on layer after layer of operating system services. Each layer provides a different level of support and adds its particular capabilities into the mix. The interaction between the layers is important to the total operation of the system. It's like ordering from a catalog. The user is on the telephone in his home (the User-mode system). He makes a telephone call to order some item. The catalog center (the Kernel-mode service) answers the telephone. The user must be explicit in his request; otherwise, he'll get the wrong item or nothing at all. The catalog is a published set of instructions for ordering an item. It contains item codes, colors, sizes, and options. The user must define each of these to get what he wants. The catalog center must also pass the information correctly to manufacturing and the delivery company to meet the order. This is how the interaction between the layers occurs. The "catalog" that our little Windows XP operation typically uses is called the API set (Win32 API). The following sections describe each of the main operating system components shown in Figure 11.4 in detail.

The System Virtual Machine

The System Virtual Machine (VM) component of Windows XP contains three main elements: 32-bit Windows applications, the shell, and 16-bit Windows applications. Essentially, the System VM component provides most of the Windows XP user-specific functionality. Without it, you couldn't run any applications. Note that I don't include DOS applications here. The reason is that Windows uses an entirely different set of capabilities to run DOS applications. It even runs them in a different processor mode.

There's another difference between Windows XP and Windows 9x when it comes to 16-bit Windows application support. Unlike Windows 9x, which still contains lots of 16-bit code in some support areas, Windows XP uses all 32-bit code. Unlike Windows 9x, which uses a shared memory area for all 16-bit applications, Windows XP runs each 16-bit application in a separate process. Using a separate process for each application means that if one application crashes, it's less likely to affect other applications executing on the same machine.

The bottom line from a user perspective is that Windows XP provides a higher level of protection for 16-bit Windows applications. You won't see many application-induced crashes. Even if you do, it's unlikely that the system as a whole will crash. The downside of this protection is that Windows XP is also less tolerant of older 16-bit Windows applications that might have broken some of the rules for running properly with other applications.

Theoretically, the System VM also provides support for the various Windows API layer components. However, because these components provide a different sort of service, I chose to discuss them in a separate area. (Needless to say, the distinctions between the client or System VM and server or Windows API Layer parts of Windows XP architecture are much clearer than under Windows 9x.) Even though applications use the API and users interact with applications, you really don't think about the API until it comes time to write an application. Therefore, I always think of the API as a programmer-specific service rather than as something the user really needs to worry about. The following list describes the System VM components in detail:

- *32-bit Windows applications* Windows XP can use a wide variety of fully functional 32-bit applications, some of which won't run under Windows 9x because it uses the Win32 specification (a subset of the Windows XP API). A 32-bit application usually provides better multitasking capabilities than its 16-bit counterpart. In addition, many 32-bit applications support new Windows features, such as long filenames, whereas most 16-bit applications don't. Also, 32-bit applications provide two additional features. The more important one is the use of preemptive versus cooperative multitasking. This makes your work move more smoothly and forces the system to wait for you as necessary rather than the other way around. The second feature is the use of a flat memory address space. This feature really makes a difference in how much memory an application can address and determines how well the application can use it. In addition, an application that uses a flat address space should run slightly faster because it no longer has to spend time working with Intel's memory-segmentation scheme.

- *The shell* Unlike previous versions of Windows, Windows XP comes with only one user shell—Explorer. Explorer provides full 32-bit capabilities. It also sports the new interface we've discussed in many areas of the book. (Of course, you can still use the Windows 2000 interface if you want.)

- *16-bit Windows Applications* Microsoft has made many changes in its 16-bit Windows application support under Windows XP. Generally, you'll find that 16-bit applications run more smoothly because they each reside in a separate session. In addition, the use of compatibility mode "flavors" each session according to application needs, so the application sees its environment in a form it can best use.

Note: One of the most important features in Windows XP is the compatibility mode support we discussed in the "Using Compatibility Mode" section of Chapter 10. The use of separate sessions for applications means that Windows XP can change the appearance of the environment as needed to help it run. For example, if your application doesn't support 16-bit color, a compatibility mode setting will allow it to run in 256-color mode. This makes Windows XP more flexible than Windows 2000, but also changes the way it handles applications.

The Windows API Layer

Two Windows APIs are included with Windows XP. The first API is exactly like the old one supplied with Windows 3.1. The first API provides all the 16-bit services that the old Windows had to provide for applications. An older 16-bit application will use this API when it runs. The other API is the 32-bit Windows API used by Windows XP. The 32-bit API provides a much larger feature set than 16-bit Windows and offers higher reliability.

You can physically see the two Windows APIs if you look in the right place. These two APIs exist side by side in separate files in your SYSTEM (16-bit) and SYSTEM32 (32-bit) folders. For example, all of the common dialog boxes—such as the ones you use to open files and search for text in your document—appear in two files: COMMDLG.DLL (16 bit) and COMDLG32.DLL (32 bit). The 32 in a filename often gives it away as a 32-bit program. Using common dialog boxes gives your applications the consistent look you've come to expect. You'll find other pieces of the API in your SYSTEM folder. Microsoft groups the various API calls and places them in separate files to make it easier to update the operating system later. Using separate files also makes it easier to install upgrades to various operating system components and reduces the amount of hard disk space you lose to unwanted features.

Notice the "thunk layer" between the two APIs. Windows XP doesn't maintain 16-bit code to answer the needs of any 16-bit applications on your system. However, 16-bit calls and data aren't compatible with 32-bit calls and data. Windows XP translates any 16-bit calls to the 32-bit API. Likewise, it translates 16-bit data to a 32-bit form. The 16-bit API files contain code that performs the required translation and passes the call on to the 32-bit API. When the 32-bit API answers the request, it passes the information back to the 16-bit API, which performs a translation back to 16-bit data and returns the result to the client.

The Base System

The Base System component of Windows XP contains all of the internal or low-level operating-system–specific services. Some books call this the operating system kernel. You, as a user, will never interact with the Base System. In fact, few programmers interact with this "hidden" part of Windows. The following list describes each part of the Base System in detail:

- *File Management Subsystem* This part of the Base System provides an interface to all of the block devices—such as hard drives, CDs, DVDs, and floppy drives—connected to your machine. It doesn't matter how the connection is made—physically or through a network. All that matters is that your machine can access the device.

- *Network Subsystem* Windows for Workgroups was the first version of Windows to address the networking needs of the workgroup. It even incorporated networking as part of the operating system rather than as a third-party add-on product. Windows XP extends this capability. Not only can you run a Microsoft peer-to-peer network, but Windows XP also provides protected-mode hooks for most major LAN products. In fact, you can keep more than one network active at a time. The modular nature of the Network Subsystem enables other vendors to add to Windows XP's inherent capabilities.

Up to this point, Windows 9x and Windows XP provide similar features, although Windows XP does provide the superior form of security. Two versions of Windows are based on the NT/2000/XP kernel. Microsoft designed the version we look at in this book for workstation use. On the other hand, Microsoft designed the Windows server version to act as a file server. In this respect, it acts more like the client/server architecture used by Novell NetWare. We'll examine networks in detail in Part VII, "Networking with Windows XP."

• *Operating System Services* This part of the operating system deals with features such as hardware profiles. It also fulfills miscellaneous user and operating system requests. For example, every time the user asks Windows XP for the time of day, she is requesting a service from this Windows XP component. Unlike Windows NT, Windows 2000/XP does provide an equivalent level of user-level services to Windows 9x. In fact, the Windows XP version provides complete support for Plug and Play, which is a nice change from Windows NT. (Windows 2000 came close to providing Plug and Play support, but some users experienced problems in some areas.) Windows XP also provides a more robust hardware profile setup than Windows 9x does, thus allowing you to switch between hardware setups with ease. Except for the relatively steep hardware requirements for Windows XP, you can use it equally well on both desktop and mobile machines.

• *Virtual Machine Manager* This component holds everything else together. The Virtual Machine Manager takes care of task scheduling, and it starts and stops every application on the system (including any DOS applications you might run). This operating system component manages virtual memory on your machine as well. Of course, your application uses the Windows API to make the request rather than talk with this part of the system directly. Because the Virtual Machine Manager handles all memory allocations, it also has to act as a DPMI (DOS Protected Mode Interface) server for DOS applications that run in protected mode. When a DOS application makes a memory request, it's actually calling routines in this component of Windows. As with Windows applications, DOS applications can't directly access this component of Windows. The DOS application uses a DOS extender API to make its call. Finally, the Virtual Machine Manager is responsible for intertask communications. All this means is that all DDE and OLE requests filter through this section of the operating system.

• *Device Drivers* Windows would never know what to do with your system if it weren't for the lowly device driver. This bit of specialty code acts as an interpreter. It takes Windows service requests and sends them to the Hardware Abstraction Layer (HAL) in a format HAL can understand. Note that it doesn't send the request directly to a device because a Windows XP device driver never knows what kind of machine you're using. The device driver thinks that it's talking to a device, but the HAL intercepts the request before the device actually sees it. Windows XP provides support for the Windows Driver Model (WDM) drivers. This driver is the same type that Windows 98 and later uses. However, you can't use a Windows 98 driver directly with Windows XP (and vice versa).

• *Object Manager* This component of Windows XP creates, manages, and deletes objects. Most of these objects represent abstract operating system resources, such as memory, or a physical resource, such as a hard drive. An *object* has properties, events, and methods. Think of a *property* as something you can use your five senses to detect. For example, an apple has red or yellow as a color property. Likewise, every component (such as a dialog box) that you see on your monitor has a color property. A *method* is what you can do with the object or something the object itself knows how to do. For example, you can eat an apple, and the apple knows how to grow. Likewise, you can display a control, and the control can center itself onscreen. *Events* are a reaction of some sort. For example, when you cut an apple in half, the inside turns brown as it reacts to the air. Likewise, buttons generate an event when you click them—some reaction occurs. The Windows XP environment is much more complex and uses more modular components than Windows 9x, so it needs this extra Base System component. (Windows 9x does use some object technology to implement many of the user interface components—Windows XP extends this to the operating system itself.) Using objects allows Windows XP to view its computing environment in much the same way as you view the world, thus making it easier for programmers to manage all of the numerous pieces needed to make this operating system work. Every time you need to create a new system object, such as an icon or dialog box, you call the Object Manager.

- *Security Reference Monitor* Windows XP provides a major feature that you'll never find in Windows 9x—Class C2-level security, which restricts access to computer resources on a need-to-know basis. Implementing this level of security requires lots of work on the part of the operating system in general and this module in particular. You'll find all the qualifications for C2-level security in DoD manual 5200.28-STD. The security levels range from Class D (least secure) to Class A (most secure). In essence, this added level of security allows government agencies to use Windows XP in a secure environment. It probably won't affect you much as a user unless you work for the government. Windows XP also provides support for the new standards in security, such as Kerberos. Part of the System Reference Monitor's job is to monitor system resources. This prevents one process or thread from grabbing all of the system resources, such as memory. The bottom line is that the module prevents the operating system from losing control for too long. An application is forced to work with the operating system in such a way that every process and thread gets a fair share of the computing resources. Finally, the System Reference Monitor provides statistical data that a network administrator can use to monitor system performance.

- *Process Manager* Windows XP also supports a wider range of processing options than Windows 9x does. Multiprocessing environments require the use of heavier-duty process management techniques. The Process Manager creates, manages, and terminates both processes (applications) and threads (streams of execution within an application). It also allows the operating system to suspend and resume processes and threads as needed to keep the overall system stable. Like the System Reference Monitor, the Process Manager provides statistical data that a network administrator can use to monitor system performance.

The DOS Virtual Machine

I've separated the DOS Virtual Machine component of Windows from the other components for several reasons. Users have relied on DOS applications to use the PC for a long time. In fact, for many years, nothing else was available. Yet, developers wrote most of these applications at a time when the standard PC ran only one application. That one application had total control of the entire machine.

Each DOS application you start under Windows XP runs on what Intel calls a *virtual machine*. Essentially, the processor fools the application into thinking that it's the only application running on your machine. Each virtual machine has its own memory space and access to devices on the system. The amazing thing is that you can have many virtual machines running on your one physical machine at a time. Windows XP has to perform back flips to make this whole concept work properly, especially when you consider Windows-hostile applications, such as games.

It may sound like Windows XP would lose control of the system when it runs a DOS application. The truth is that each one of these virtual machines is still under strict control of the processor. If the application makes a request that the processor can't fulfill, the processor raises an exception. Windows XP pays close attention to these exceptions and doesn't allow a DOS application to continue running when it sees one. Windows XP also monitors display memory and every device on your machine. It ends applications that try to access a device improperly.

On Your Own

I always find it interesting to see exactly what my computer is doing. Look through the NTBTLOG.TXT file on your boot drive to see which drivers Windows XP is loading and in what order it loads them. See if you can find all the drivers in your SYSTEM32 folder. You might be surprised to find that they don't all appear there. Which files (if any) does Windows XP place in other locations? Why do you think it places them there?

Spend some time in the SYSTEM and SYSTEM32 folders trying to find various API elements. How do the 32-bit names differ from their 16-bit counterparts? Right-click the API components and select Properties from the context menu. Select the Version tab and look at the Description field and Item Name entries. Do any of the entries help you understand what task the file performs?

Spend some time looking at the SYSTEM.INI and WIN.INI files on your system. What types of entries do these files contain? Can you disable the WIN.INI file without causing any application problems? Does disabling the SYSTEM.INI file by using the MSCONFIG utility create any boot or application problems?

The Windows XP Registry

A *Registry* can evoke many different images in the mind of the person reading the word. The term normally implies the act of formally recording names, items, or actions. The Windows XP Registry is a place for recording all kinds of information. It's a special kind of hierarchical database. As many of you know, a hierarchical database is freeform and relies on a tree-like structure to connect all of the pieces of information.

The Registry first appeared in Windows with Windows NT. All Windows 9x versions include a Registry, and you find it in Windows 2000. The Registry replaced earlier attempts at storing information, such as the INI files found in early versions of Windows. In fact, you still find that older applications use INI files because developers are familiar with using them and a few developers view the Registry as a difficult-to-use black hole in the Windows environment.

Microsoft created something useful and usable with the Registry. It has undergone few changes over the years because it works so well. Using the Registry, you can store complex information in an easy-to-retrieve manner. In addition, the Registry handles several kinds of data, making it easy to store the values you need without converting them into some other format first.

This chapter tells you about the Registry. You learn how the Registry stores information about every part of Windows, including your personalized settings. Although I didn't design this chapter to provide a comprehensive look at every Registry element, you learn enough to perform simple (and safe) edits that help Windows run better.

An Overview of the Hives

As mentioned, the Registry is actually a kind of hierarchical database used to store all kinds of information about Windows XP. The problem is that some data refers to applications, and other data refers to you, Windows, or the machine it runs on. With data coming from this many sources, it would be difficult to create a single file that contains everything you need. However, as we see in "The RegEdit Perspective" section of this chapter, the Registry looks like a single file when you view it in the Registry Editor.

How does Microsoft pull off this trick? It uses a concept called *hives* in creating the Registry. Each hive holds a particular type of information. When you open the Registry in the Registry Editor, the editor combines the data from all of these sources into a single view. The use of multiple files allows Microsoft to place the data in different areas of the hard drive and helps create a secure environment. One user can't view another user's data unless she has permission to do so. The hive containing the user data appears in the same secure directory as the rest of the user's data.

You see the term *HKEY* used frequently in this chapter. Some people confuse an HKEY with a hive. The two terms are different. A *hive* is an individual file containing related data, and an HKEY is short for handle to a *key*. The HKEY is a developer tool that represents the lowest level of the Registry the developer can access directly. Once the developer reaches this level, he has to open the Registry and obtain the proper rights to look further. We study the whole issue of HKEY later, in the "A Detailed Look at the Registry" section of this chapter.

Hives do affect certain Registry keys. We see in the section "The RegEdit Perspective" that a key is a pointer to a value. The Registry links all of the keys in such a way that Windows XP can follow them to a specific value. The value is the information the Registry stores. For example, you might have a Registry key named "Favorite Color" and a value for that key, named "Blue." As you can see, the value describes the Registry key, which is just a general entry in the Registry. Most Registry key/value pairs follow this pattern, although the type of data varies from key to key. In addition, many keys have more than one value associated with them.

Now that you have a better idea of what the Registry is all about, let's discuss some specifics. The following sections tell you about three important aspects of the Registry. You learn about the Registry Editor (REGEDIT.EXE), the system files, and some additions to the Registry that occur when you set a group policy. (The group policy information is most useful when you have larger networks with one or more dedicated servers.)

The RegEdit Perspective

As complex as the Registry is, you need some type of tool for working with it. REGEDIT.EXE (the Registry Editor) is your main tool for viewing and editing the Registry. You won't find this tool in your Start Menu, and I can understand why Microsoft would want to keep such a powerful tool hidden. This tool does appear in the \Windows folder on your machine. You can access the application using Windows Explorer or the Run dialog box, accessible from the Start Menu.

> **Note:** Before proceeding, you should add the Registry Editor to your Start Menu. We looked at the process for working with the Start Menu in the "Start Menu Customization" section of Chapter 3, so I won't cover it again here. I normally place my shortcut to the Registry Editor in the Administrative Tools or in a maintenance directory, where I can protect it with security. It's helpful to look at the Registry entries as you read about them. I also present some exercises that help you better understand the inner workings of the Registry.

Open the Registry Editor, and you see the five HKEY values that contain information about your machine. Each HKEY contains information about a different configuration element. For instance, HKEY_CLASSES_ROOT contains some application information along with the file associations that make double-clicking a reality. Figure 12.1 shows a typical example of the Registry Editor.

FIGURE 12.1
The Registry Editor is your window into the Registry.

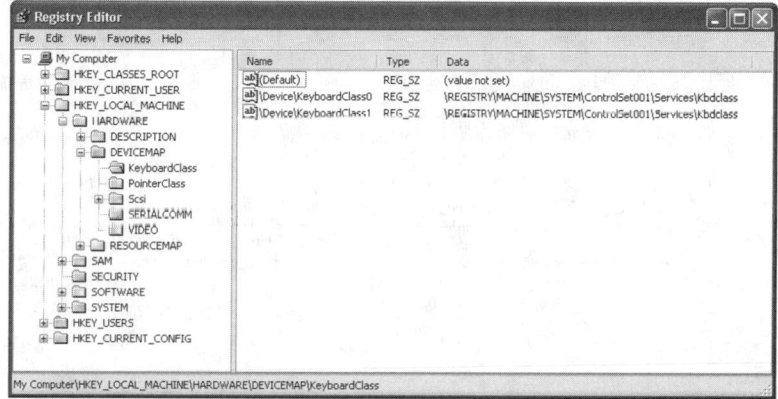

> **Warning:** RegEdit is an application designed to assist experienced users in changing the behavior of Windows XP and associated applications. Although it enables you to enhance system performance and makes applications easier to use, it can have unexpected results when misused. Never edit an entry unless you know what that entry represents. Failure to observe this precaution can result in data loss and can prevent your system from booting the next time you start Windows XP.

Notice the hierarchical structure of the data. You would reference this point in the Registry using the hierarchy as a description. Most people use backslashes, just as you would when working with a path on your location drive. Figure 12.1 shows the HKEY_LOCAL_MACHINE\HARDWARE\DEVICEMAP\KeyboardClass key. However, we refer to it KeyboardClass for short because you know where the key is located in the hierarchy. Because the Registry can contain multiple copies of the same key, you want to use the longer description when talking with someone about changes you want to make. In addition, this is how you see the key referenced when reading articles, such as those found in the Microsoft Knowledge Base (http://search.support.microsoft.com/kb/c.asp).

Figure 12.1 also shows some typical values. Notice that this information is in human-readable form. That's because it's a string value. You can always tell the type of the value by looking at the Type column of the display. The Name field contains the name a developer uses to access the value, and the Data field contains the actual value. Keys always have one default value that has the name "(Default)." The developer can access this value directly through the key. Table 12.1 tells you about the common value types the Registry supports. You can create the values, but you see other specialty types as well.

> **Note:** The term *human readable* in Table 12.1 doesn't mean human understandable. String values contain text of various types. Most people understand a path description, such as C:\TEMP, but few understand the ramifications of a globally unique identifier (GUID), such as {92FA2C24-253C-11d2-90FB-006008A1F441}. A GUID is still contained in a string value, and developers understand it, but most users don't.

Table 12.1 Common Registry Data Types

Name	Registry Type	Description
String	REG_SZ	Contains a string in human-readable format. The end of the string has to have a 0 (null) attached to it. The "SZ" part of this type stands for string zero.
Binary	REG_BINARY	Contains a binary value displayed in bytes using hexadecimal format. You can create binary strings of any length, and they can contain any type of data.
DWORD	REG_DWORD	Contains a double word value, which is any number between 0 and 4,294,967,295.
Multi-String	REG_MULTI_SZ	Contains multiple strings in human-readable format. The developer separates each string with a null character.
Expandable String	REG_EXPAND_SZ	Contains a string that includes expansion values. For example, you could see an expansion value of %ProgramFiles% that equates to the position of the Program Files folder on your machine.

Peter's Principle: Using the REGEDT32 Editor

Most professionals are particular about the tools they use. I know that I have my favorite tools and find using something else cumbersome, to say the least. Windows NT/2000 provided two versions of the Registry Editor. The first is REGEDIT.EXE, the version we use throughout this book. The second is REGEDT32.EXE, found in the \SYSTEM32 folder of your system. Some developers liked the second form of the Registry Editor because it provided an interface consisting of cascading windows, like the one shown in Figure 12.2. In addition, this version of the Registry Editor could open the Registry in read-only mode.

Unfortunately, Microsoft considers REGEDT32.EXE outdated. Windows XP still supplies the REGEDT32.EXE file, but double-clicking it presents the standard REGEDIT.EXE interface shown in Figure 12.1. However, you don't have to use the new interface if you don't want to. The REGEDT32.EXE file found on Windows 2000 machines appears to work fine under Windows XP. I haven't tested it extensively, so you need to use it at your own risk.

The alternative version of Registry Editor does the same things as the version you see in Figure 12.1. The arrangement of some menus is different, and the interface is a little more cryptic. Using a separate window to display each HKEY tends to keep the display a little cleaner. You can also find specific data faster when you have a number of keys displayed onscreen. In short, you don't gain anything by using the old version, but for some people it's like getting rid of an old and comfortable pair of shoes.

FIGURE 12.2

The older form of the Registry Editor provides a windowed interface that many people find convenient to use.

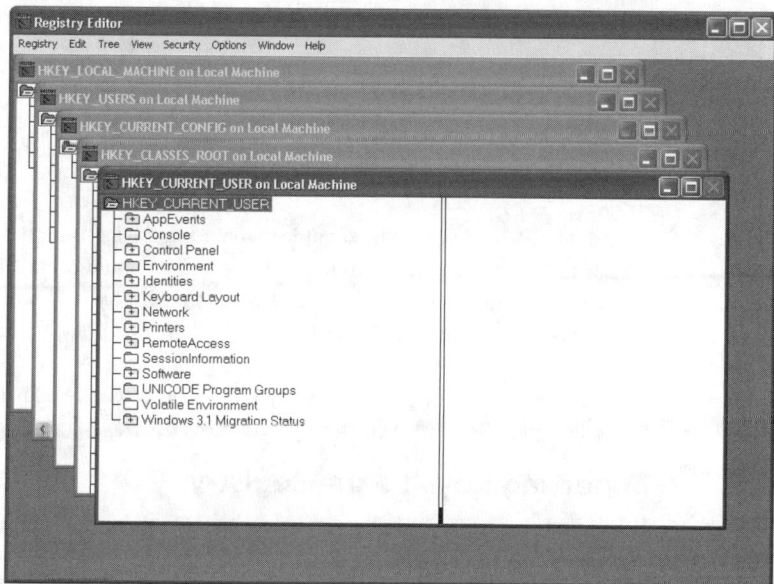

Exporting Keys from the Registry

At some point, you'll want to export keys from the Registry. You may want to make a small change, see the effects, and then have a means to change the settings back if necessary. Some people create backups of their Registry before they do anything. Exporting the Registry to a text file allows you to make a backup that you can also edit as needed. Suffice it to say that you have many reasons to export at least a small part of the Registry.

Exporting a key always copies all subkeys and associated values. The Registry Editor calls this *exporting a branch*. To export a Registry branch or the entire Registry, highlight the branch you want to export. Use the File | Export command to display the Export Registry File dialog box, as shown in Figure 12.3.

FIGURE 12.3

Use the Export Registry to save a copy of your Registry to the hard drive in text format.

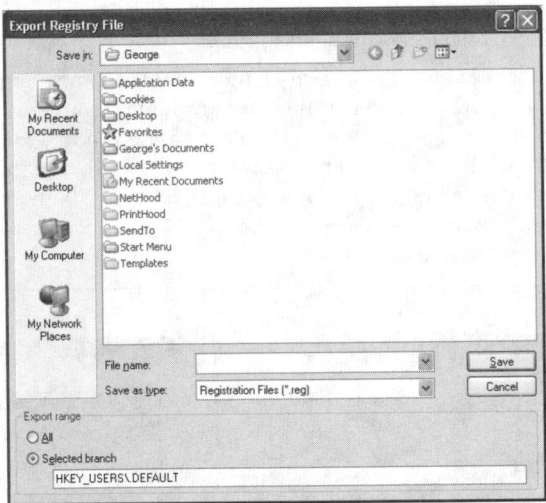

Notice that you can select an output location using the icons on the left side of the display or using the standard technique. Hidden at the bottom of this dialog box is an option to export the entire Registry or just a selected branch. If you choose the Selected Branch option, you can also decide which branch. Selecting the branch you want to export before you get to this dialog box saves some typing time. All you need to do now is type a filename and click Save. The Registry Editor automatically adds a .REG extension to the end of your filename. You can still use a text editor, such as Notepad, to view the file.

Importing Keys to the Registry

You'll find a wealth of .REG files on your hard drive from the applications you've installed. Most applications make some type of changes to the Registry. Some venders supply the .REG file so that you can restore your settings in case of Registry corruption. In some situations, you might download a .REG file from the Internet to correct a problem with your system.

Microsoft doesn't force you to open the Registry Editor to import keys into the Registry. You can double-click the file if desired. Windows XP asks if you want to import the information into the Registry. If you say yes, Windows XP imports the information and then displays a success message.

Of course, you can also use the Registry Editor. Open the Registry Editor and use the File | Import command to display the Import Registry File dialog box. Locate the .REG file you want to import and then click Open. The Registry Editor imports the file and tells you if it was successful.

The System File Perspective

At this point, you may wonder why I even introduced you to hives because it appears that you don't need to know anything about them. The fact is that you do need to know about them in certain cases because you need to access data in those hives. The following sections look at the system files and show how you might access them from within the Registry Editor.

An Overview of the Files

The Registry Editor assumes that you want to edit your data, not the data on another machine or another user's data on the same machine. In addition, you might want to look at the same hive from two different locations for comparison purposes. The list goes on, but the idea is that knowing about hives allows you to use the full capability of the Registry Editor. With this in mind, look at Table 12.2. It shows some common hives, their associated filenames, and the normal paths to those files. We discuss the content of these hives in the "A Detailed Look at the Registry" section of this chapter.

Table 12.2 Locations of Standard Registry Hives

Hive	Filename	Standard Path
HKEY_USERS\.DEFAULT	DEFAULT	\WINDOWS\system32\config
HKEY_CURRENT_USER	NTUSER.DAT	\Documents and Settings\<Username>
HKEY_CURRENT_CONFIG	SYSTEM	\WINDOWS\system32\config
HKEY_LOCAL_MACHINE\SAM	SAM	\WINDOWS\system32\config
HKEY_LOCAL_MACHINE\Security	SECURITY	\WINDOWS\system32\config
HKEY_LOCAL_MACHINE\Software	SOFTWARE	\WINDOWS\system32\config
HKEY_LOCAL_MACHINE\System	SYSTEM	\WINDOWS\system32\config

Note: Windows XP usually stores a repair copy of the current user's hive in the \WINDOWS\repair folder. Never work with this copy of the HKEY_CURRENT_USER hive. Always use instead the copy that appears in the user's folder.

Table 12.2 doesn't contain all of the files associated with the Registry; it contains only those you're likely to work with outside of the normal Registry Editor loading process. Most of these files also have support files. The support files have the same name as the main file, but include a file extension. The following list tells you about each support file:

- *.ALT* Contains a backup copy of the HKEY_LOCAL_MACHINE\System hive. This hive is the only one that uses this file extension. This file is the Windows XP relies on to restore the last good configuration when you boot the machine, so you want to refrain from editing it in any way.

- *.LOG* Contains a list of the changes made to a hive during the current session. Windows XP uses this file to ensure that all changes to the Registry commit successfully or that it rolls partial transactions back so that the hive appears in its original state. The NTUSER.DAT equivalent of this file is NTUSER.DAT.LOG.

- *.SAV* Contains a copy of the hive as it looked at the end of the text portion of the Windows startup sequence. Windows XP can use this file to rebuild the hive if it becomes corrupted during the graphics mode portion of the startup process. Because Windows XP doesn't erase this file after it completes the boot process, you always have at least one backup copy of the Registry. The NTUSER.DAT file doesn't have a .SAV file.

Loading and Unloading Hives

When you start Registry Editor, it assumes that you want to work with only your files. This means that you can't use other user configuration files, machine settings, or anything else, for the matter. Only your settings are available on your local copy of the Registry Editor.

The hive load and unload features of the Registry Editor allow you to look at other parts of the Registry by loading other hive files. The most common way you use this feature is to load the settings for another user to change them—for example, if you're a network administrator and you don't want to exit your account to make the changes.

This feature is actually beneficial from a security perspective. You can disable access to the Registry for every user on the network except those in the administrator group. Many network administrators find that their workload decreases because users can no longer try "neat" Registry changes they read about on the Internet. Those who like to tinker with Windows will find that they're thwarted (at least in this one area) as well.

Windows XP places limits on the hives you can import. You can load only hives that belong to HKEY_USERS or HKEY_LOCAL_MACHINE. This restriction isn't as limiting as you might think. HKEY_CLASSES_ROOT and HKEY_CURRENT_CONFIG are both global to an entire machine. HKEY_CURRENT_USER is specific to the current user, which is you because you logged on to the machine. Generally, you find that there aren't any limitations on the hives you can load.

To load a hive, choose either HKEY_USERS or HKEY_LOCAL_MACHINE in the Registry Editor. Use the File | Load Hive command to display the Load Hive dialog box. Select the hive you want to load and then click Open. Registry Editor asks you for a hive name because it can't use the same hive name you're using for your personal settings. Type a hive name and then click OK. The Registry Editor loads the hive as long as you have the correct permissions.

Unloading a hive is even easier. Highlight the hive you want to unload. Select the File | Unload Hive command. Registry Editor asks if you're sure you want to unload the hive. Click Yes, and you see that the hive is gone.

> **Tip:** Because you can load and unload hives as needed, you can unload a portion of the Registry you don't normally edit in order to clean up the display. Windows XP remembers your Registry settings, so you'll find that you need to do this only once to keep your display clean. If you need to load the hive again later, you can use the File | Load Hive command to do it.

Working with Permissions

The Registry provides the means to assign permissions to specific Registry keys. You can tell Windows XP to allow access to the key by some people, but not by others. In addition, you can also set the permission level. For example, you might give a user permission to read or query a key, but not to write to it. Defining Registry access can help enforce company policies or reduce the chance that a user will make unwanted changes.

> **Warning:** You should exercise care in changing the permissions for a Registry key. The changes you make at one level also appear at lower levels unless you specifically turn off inheritance at those levels. In other words, a change at an upper level flows down to all lower levels in the key. Therefore, a change at an upper level that appears to prevent unauthorized settings to an application could make the application inaccessible to the user. Some Registry interactions produce completely unexpected results.

You assign permissions to a Registry entry by highlighting the key and using the Edit | Permissions command to display the Permissions dialog box shown in Figure 12.4. Notice that this dialog box lists only the users and groups that have access to the key and provides course control over permission assignment. Click Add and you see a Select Users or Groups dialog box you can use to add users or groups to the list. Highlight a user or group and click Remove, and you see that name removed from the list.

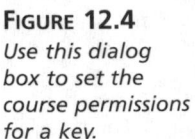

FIGURE 12.4
Use this dialog box to set the course permissions for a key.

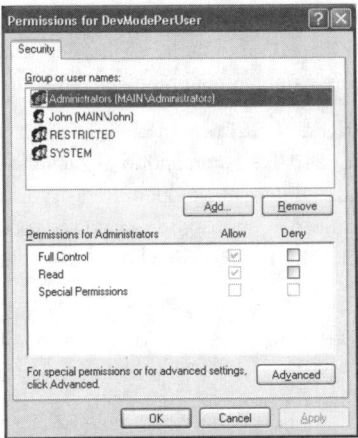

Note: Permissions affect both values and keys. However, you can set permissions only at the key level, not at the value level. This means that you may give permission to use a value you wanted to remain protected because the value exists within a key containing other values the user needs to access. For this reason, you want to coordinate Registry key support with developers of custom applications. Make sure that any custom applications use keys in such a way that you can protect values as needed.

Click Advanced, and you see the Advanced Security Settings dialog box, shown in Figure 12.5. Notice that the settings on the Permissions tab reflect those on the Permissions dialog box, shown in Figure 12.4. However, this tab contains options that permit you to add inheritance to the changes you make at this level. In addition, you can tell Windows XP to pass any changes you make to child objects immediately after you commit them at this level.

FIGURE 12.5
The Advanced Security Settings dialog box contains tabs for more precise control of the Registry settings.

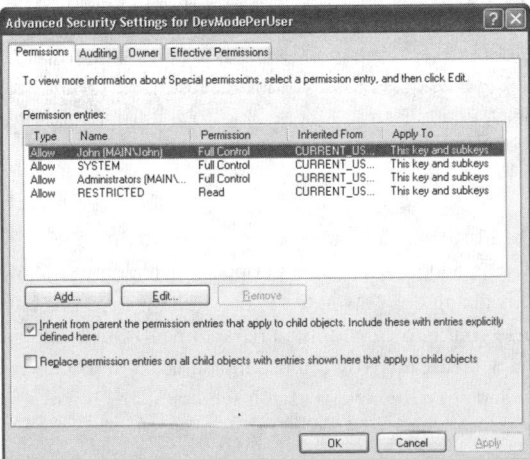

The Permissions tab also allows you to add and remove users with the Add and Remove buttons. The System automatically grays the Remove button for entries you can't remove. For example, you can't remove the owner of a key. You have to change ownership first before you can remove the user entry.

This tab is also where you gain full control over user permissions. Highlight an entry and click Edit, and you see the Permission Entry dialog box, shown in Figure 12.6. Notice that the permissions are explicit and offer fine control over Registry key access.

FIGURE 12.6

The Permission Entry dialog box provides fine control over Registry key permissions.

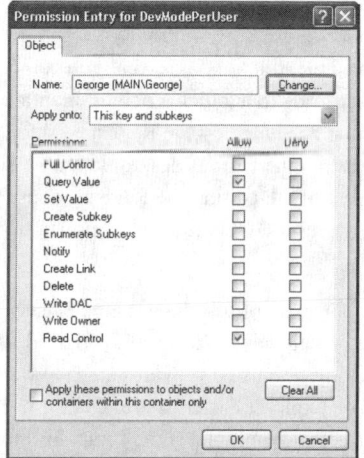

The Permission Entry dialog box also provides control over inheritance of permissions by the user or group. The Apply Onto field contains three settings: This Key and Subkeys, Subkeys Only, and This Key Only. Using this field gives you even better control over the key access. You could set different permissions for the current key and the subkeys it supports.

The Auditing tab of the Advanced Security Settings dialog box acts much the same way as the Auditing tab for disk drives. You click Add to add a name to the list or Remove to remove it. When you add a name, the Registry Editor presents an Auditing Entry dialog box with the same entries as the Permission Entry dialog box, shown in Figure 12.6. The only difference is that you're auditing successful or failed attempts to perform a task, such as querying the target key.

The Owner tab of the Advanced Security Settings dialog box changes the owner name for the selected key. The default owner is the one who originally created the key. The Administrator is a co-owner of all keys in the Registry.

Use the Effective Permissions tab of the Advanced Security Settings dialog box as a means to troubleshoot Registry permission problems. When you select a group or user name in the Group or User Name field, the Registry Editor shows you the rights that user or group has to the current key. To add a user or group entry, click Select. You see the Select User or Group dialog box. Type the user name, or use the find feature to locate it. Click OK, and you see the effective rights of the selected user or group.

A Detailed Look at the Registry

When you look at the Registry, you see a complete definition of Windows XP as it relates to your specific machine. The Registry contains not only hardware and application settings, but also every piece of information you can imagine about your machine. You can learn a great deal about Windows by simply looking at the information presented by this database. For example, did you know that you can use multiple desktops in Windows XP? Of course, that leads to another problem: maintaining those separate desktops. The hierarchical format presented by the Registry Editor helps the administrator compare the differences between the various desktops. It also allows the administrator to configure them with ease. Best of all, editing the Registry doesn't involve a session with a text editor. Windows provides a GUI editor the administrator can use to change the settings in the Registry.

Knowing that the Registry contains lots of information and is easy to edit still doesn't tell you what it can do for you. When was the last time you used Explorer to check out your hard drive? I use it frequently because it provides an easy way to find what I need. The Registry can help you make Explorer easier to use. One of my favorite ways to use it for Explorer modifications is to create multiple associations for the same file type. Suppose that you want to associate a graphics editor with PCX and BMP files. This isn't very difficult. However, what if each file type requires a different set of command-line switches? Now you get into an area when using the Registry can really help. Using the Registry to edit these entries can help you customize file access.

It's time to take a look at how the Registry is organized. To start the Registry Editor, simply open RegEdit as you would open any other application on the Start Menu. You'll probably get much more out of the detailed discussion that follows if you open the Registry Editor now. Using the Registry Editor to see how Windows XP arranges the various entries can make it easier in case of an emergency.

The first thing you need to know about RegEdit is what you see. RegEdit has two panes, just like in Explorer. The entries in the left pane are *keys*. Look at a key as you would see the headings in a book—they divide the Registry into easily understood pieces. Using keys also makes finding a specific piece of configuration information fast.

The entries in the right pane are values. A *value* is Registry content, just like the paragraphs in a book. The Registry has three kinds of values: string, binary, and DWORD. The string type is the only one you can read directly. Binary and DWORD values contain computer-readable data using two different size variables. In most cases, you won't have to worry about what these values contain because your applications and Windows XP takes care of them automatically.

I always step lightly when it comes to the Registry. Before you go much further, you might want to follow the same procedure I use to back up the Registry. The big advantage to this method is that it produces a text file you can view with any text editor. (The file is huge; Notepad won't handle it, but WordPad will.) You can use this backup file to restore the Registry later if you run into difficulty. Unfortunately, this method won't help much if you permanently destroy the Registry and reboot the machine. Windows XP needs a clean Registry to boot.

Let's take that brief overview I talked about. The next few sections acquaint you with the contents of the Registry as a whole. I don't go into much detail, but at least you'll know the general location for specific types of information.

HKEY_CLASSES_ROOT

Precisely what HKEY_CLASSES_ROOT contains depends on your viewpoint. From a developer perspective, HKEY_CLASSES_ROOT is one of the more complex Registry keys. It contains a wealth of component object model (COM) entries used to access and create components on your machine. A component is, in this case, any object that Windows can create—everything from a file to a pushbutton to a low-level system object. From a user perspective, HKEY_CLASSES_ROOT contains the file association information that makes applications work. Yes, you notice the effects of the COM entries, but you seldom need to change them directly.

Two major types of file association keys are under the HKEY_CLASSES_ROOT key. The first key type is a file extension. Think of all the file extensions you've used, such as DOC and TXT. Windows XP still uses them to differentiate one file type from another. (Because Windows XP also provides long-filename support, you can use the Registry to create associations for extensions longer than the usual three letters.) The Registry also uses extensions to associate that file type with a specific action. For example, although you can't do anything with a file that uses the DLL extension, it appears in this list because Windows XP needs to associate the DLL extension with an executable file type.

The second key type is the application designation used to open the file, such as the Access.Database key. The file extension entries usually associate a data file with an application or an executable file with a specific Windows XP function. Figure 12.7 shows the typical HKEY_CLASSES_ROOT organization.

I've highlighted the .ZIP extension in Figure 12.7 because it contains a number of interesting subkeys. File extension keys can include subkeys that perform special tasks, but most don't include anything more than an application designation value as the (Default) entry. For example, if you see a file type on the New context menu, it likely contains shell extension (ShellEx and ShellNew) entries as part of the file extension key.

Notice that the .ZIP extension is associated with the WinZip application. However, what would have happened if I hadn't installed WinZip on my system? Windows XP provides a persistent handler, called *CompressedFolder,* that would have shown me the content of the file as a folder.

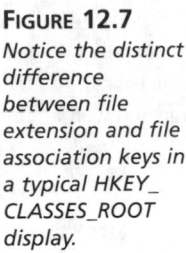

FIGURE 12.7
Notice the distinct difference between file extension and file association keys in a typical HKEY_ CLASSES_ROOT display.

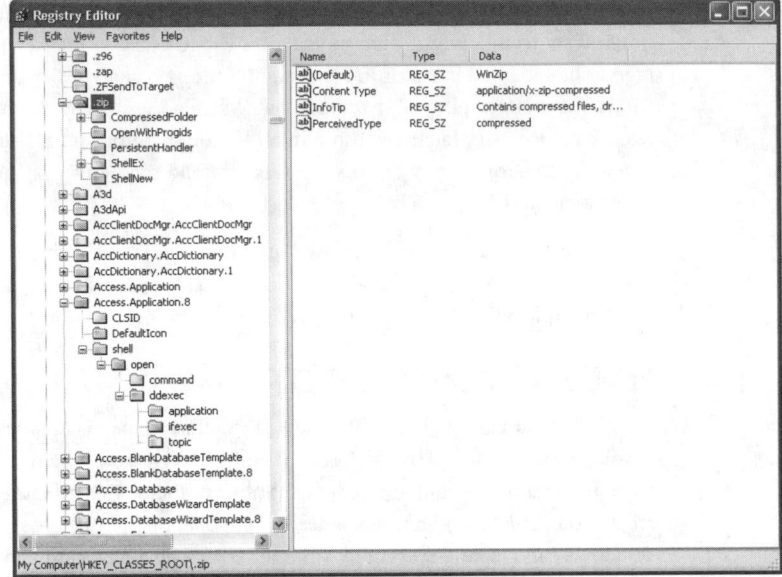

Application designations provide additional information, too. The application designation subkey include entries for the menus you see when you right-click an entry in Explorer. The application designation also contains keys that determine what type of icon to display as well as other parameters associated with a particular file type. The CLSID entry normally contains a pointer to the COM information for the file association. Windows XP needs a bit of information to make the file association work properly and to perform special tasks when needed. Never change the CLSID entry unless you know which CLSID you plan to provide in its place.

HKEY_CURRENT_USER

The HKEY_CURRENT_USER key contains the "soft" settings for your machine. Soft settings tell how to configure the desktop and the keyboard. This key also contains color settings and the configuration of the Start Menu. All user-specific settings appear under this key. In fact, this key contains special user-specific settings that we discuss in the "Saving Individual Application Settings" section of the chapter.

The HKEY_CURRENT_USER key is slaved to the settings of the current user, the one logged in to the machine. This key is different from all the user configuration entries in other parts of the Registry. HKEY_CURRENT_USER is a dynamic-setting key; the other user-related categories contain static information. The Registry copies the contents of one of the user entries in the HKEY_USERS key into this key and updates HKEY_USERS when you shut down. Each user HKEY_USERS appears in a separate hive.

This area is where Windows XP obtains new setting information and places any changes you make. As you can see in Figure 12.8, keys within the HKEY_CURRENT_USER category are self-explanatory in most cases. All the entries adjust a user-specific setting of some type—nothing that affects a global element, such as a device driver.

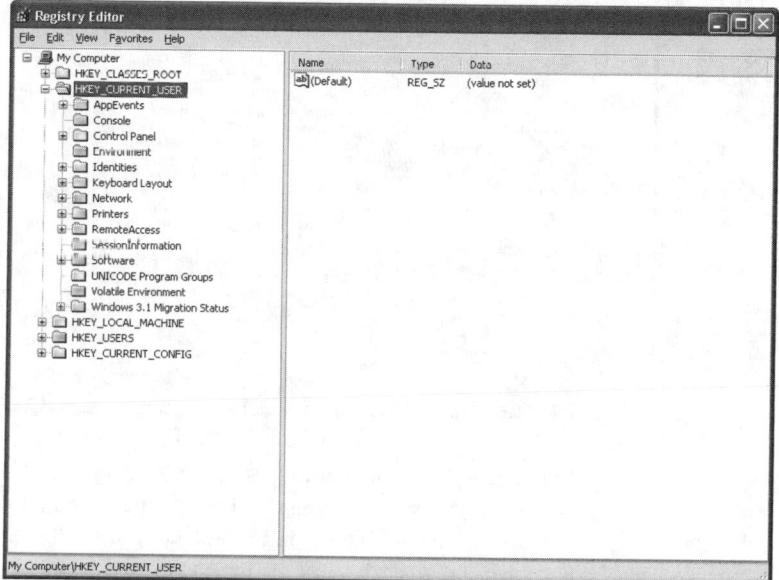

FIGURE 12.8
The HKEY_CURRENT_USER key contains all user-specific settings.

Applications and Control Panel applets maintain most of the HKEY_CURRENT_USER subkeys. However, you may experience situations when you make a change yourself rather than use standard methods. For example, occasionally it's easier to set display colors by using this technique because you can see all of the entries in a list, as shown in Figure 12.9. In fact, if you look through the entries in this list, you find entries such as buttons that you can't change using the options in the Advanced Appearance dialog box. You have direct control over every aspect of button appearance.

Now that you have a better idea of what the HKEY_CURRENT_USER key contains, let's talk about some of the subkeys. A typical HKEY_CURRENT_USER key has several additional subkeys you'll work with less often (if ever). The following list tells you about the more important subkeys, the ones you're likely to work with.

- *AppEvents* Contains a list of the application events for your machine and their associated sounds. This key also contains the schemes you define for your system.
- *Console* Contains the settings for the command prompt. It pays to look at these settings because some of them are difficult to modify in other ways. For example, you can use a nonstandard font, change the cursor size, or alter the color scheme by altering values in this key.

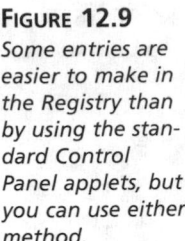

FIGURE 12.9
Some entries are easier to make in the Registry than by using the standard Control Panel applets, but you can use either method.

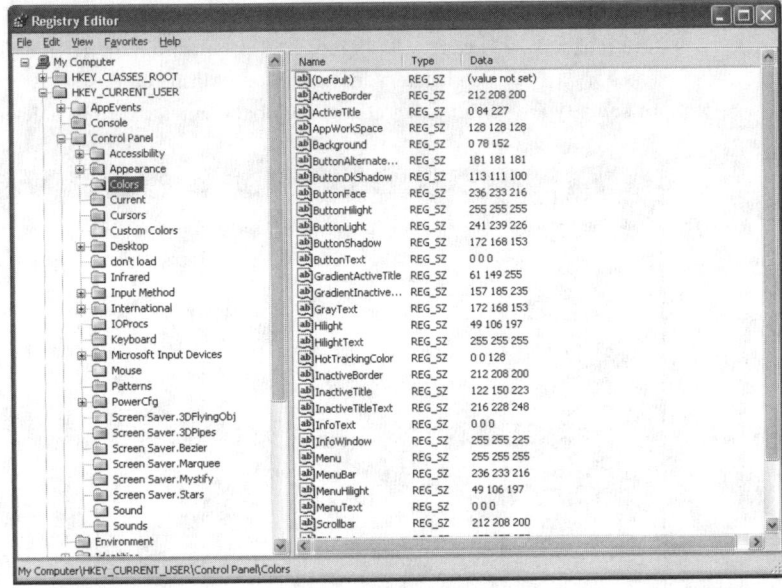

- *ControlPanel* Contains entries for Control Panel applets that make personalized changes to the system environment. For example, you find the international, color, keyboard, and mouse settings in subkeys, but you don't find other settings, such as your Internet options, because the Internet options are associated with a specific application.

- *Identities* Contains a list of all of your Internet identities and their associated data. For example, you find the list of blocked senders for each identity. The subkeys also contain a list of accounts and the account settings.

- *Network* Contains a list of networked drives and their settings.

- *Printers* Contains a list of networked printers and their settings.

- *RemoteAccess* Contains a list of your Internet connections and their settings.

- *Software* Contains a list of all of the software on your machine. This key starts with a list of vendor subkeys. Each vendor key has one or more application subkeys. The application keys contain subkeys that adjust software operation.

HKEY_LOCAL_MACHINE

The HKEY_LOCAL_MACHINE key focuses its attention on machine hardware, including the drivers and configuration information required for using the hardware. Every piece of hardware appears in this section of the Registry. If a piece of hardware doesn't appear here, Windows XP can't use it.

Lots of subtle information about your hardware is stored under this key. For example, this key contains all the Plug and Play information about your machine. It also provides a complete list of device drivers and their revision levels. This section might even contain revision information for the hardware itself. For example, there's a distinct difference between different revisions of the same soundboard. The soundboards may all have the same names, but different revisions tend to have unique driver requirements because vendors change chips or add an additional feature or two. Windows XP stores these differences in the Registry.

HKEY_LOCAL_MACHINE also contains global system settings. For example, if you install an application that sets some configuration items for everyone who uses the machine, those settings appear here.

Some of the software information affects installation information. For example, a 32-bit application stores the location of its Setup and Format Table (SFT) under this key. This file is used by the application during installation. Some applications also use the file during setup modification. Applications such as Microsoft Word store all their setup information in SFT tables. The only application information that appears here is global-configuration-specific, like the SFT.

Finally, you find some security information in HKEY_LOCAL_MACHINE, including the Security Access Manager (SAM) account information. Figure 12.10 shows a typical HKEY_LOCAL_MACHINE category setup.

FIGURE 12.10
The HKEY_LOCAL_MACHINE key contains global hardware, software, and security settings

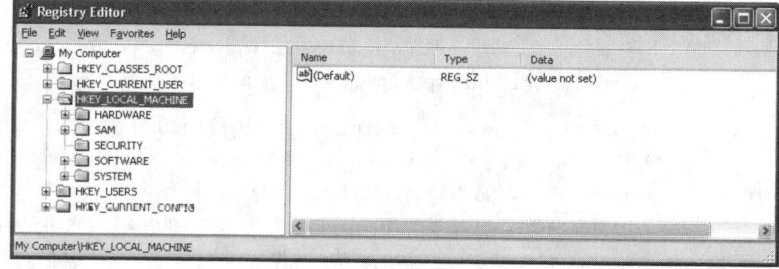

You often find amplifying information that you need to work with Windows in HKEY_LOCAL_MACHINE. For example, if you check HKEY_LOCAL_MACHINE\HARDWARE\DESCRIPTION\System\CentralProcessor, you find additional information about the central processor on your machine. Instead of learning from the General tab of System Properties that you have an Intel Pentium II processor, you can learn that you have an x86 Family 6 Model 5 Stepping 2 processor, a more precise description in anyone's book.

> **Peter's Principle:** Security Settings for Home Users
> The Windows XP Home Edition is somewhat crippled by its lack of security settings. You can't change settings as simple as forcing network logins to use the Guest account. The security settings exist; the problem is that Microsoft doesn't provide access to them.

Fortunately, there's a solution to the problem. Check under the HKEY_LOCAL_MACHINE\SYSTEM\CurrentControlSet\Control\Lsa key and you find a value named "forceguest." Set this value to 0 to disable this feature and 1 to enable it. The Local Security Authority (LSA) key holds all of the security settings for your machine. You have to set the values carefully because setting any value incorrectly could prevent anyone from logging in to your machine.

HKEY_USERS

The HKEY_USERS key contains a static list of all of the users of this Registry file. It never pays to edit any of the information for the current user you find under this key. However, you can use this key for reference purposes. The reason for this hands-off policy is simple: None of the entries here takes effect until the next time the user logs in to Windows XP, so you really don't know what effect they have until you reboot the machine. In addition, changing the settings for the current user is a waste of time because Windows XP overwrites the new data with data contained in HKEY_CURRENT_USER during logout or shutdown.

You can use this key for loading other user information if you need to make edits on another account. Use the information found in the "Loading and Unloading Hives" section, earlier in this chapter, to load other user keys as needed. The setup of these keys is the same as for HKEY_CURRENT_USER. The only difference is that you edit another user's account. Of course, you have to exercise care in editing another account because the other user could experience problems if the account is active.

Figure 12.11 shows a setup that includes the .Default key. The .Default key is used when the user doesn't have a local identity. For example, someone who logged in to the Guest account would use the contents of the .Default key instead of the normal content. Windows also uses this account when it starts creating a new account for a user. For these two reasons, you want to check the contents of the .Default key from time to time to ensure that it matches the current security and setup policies for your organization.

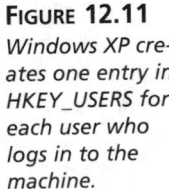

FIGURE 12.11
Windows XP creates one entry in HKEY_USERS for each user who logs in to the machine.

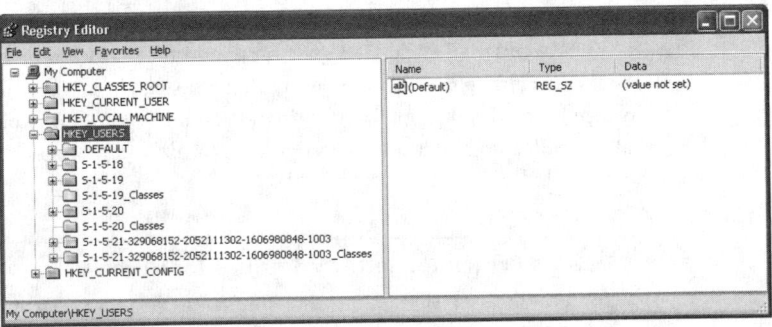

HKEY_CURRENT_CONFIG

The HKEY_CURRENT_CONFIG key is the simplest part of the Registry. It contains two major keys: Software and System. Essentially, these entries are used by the GDI API (described in Chapters 14, "Fonts And Printing," and 16, "Video Configurations") to configure the display and the printer. HKEY_CURRENT_CONFIG also contains some minor Internet settings.

The Software key provides two subkeys: Fonts and Microsoft. The Fonts subkey determines which fonts Windows XP uses for general display purposes. The subkey displays these raster (non-TrueType) fonts when you get a choice of which font to use for icons or other purposes. Raster fonts are essentially bitmaps, or pictures, of the characters. Chapter 14 takes a more detailed look at fonts.

The Microsoft subkey contains some minor Internet settings several layers deep. The first setting determines if Windows XP enables autodial, and the second determines the use of a proxy for Internet connections.

The System key contains printer, sound, and video settings for the most part. For example, this is where you find the display resolution for your display adapter. It's also where you find printer settings for attached (versus networked) printers. You also find some Direct-Sound settings. Some minor settings include the type of Uninterruptible Power Supply (UPS) installed on your system. Figure 12.12 shows the major keys in this category.

FIGURE 12.12
The HKEY_ CURRENT_CONFIG category echoes the settings under the Config key of the HKEY_LOCAL_ MACHINE category.

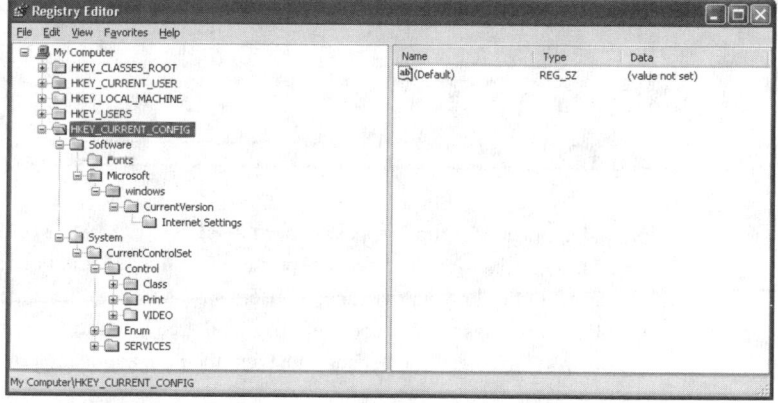

Saving Individual Application Settings

You spend a great deal of time configuring your applications so that they work just as you want them to. New applications use the Registry or a combination of the Registry and external files (such as INI files) to store configuration information. At some point, you want to reformat your drive to get a new start, move to a new machine, or set up multiple copies of your application settings on more than one machine. Administrators may want to create an application setup and then move it to new machines as they set up new users. In short, you have many good reasons to save your applications settings to disk and restore them later.

Fortunately, the Registry makes it easy to find the application settings for your machine. You don't even have to know much about the application to find the settings—just the vendor and application names. The application settings appear in two areas of the Registry. You find personal settings under the HKEY_CURRENT_USER\Software key. Just look for the name of the vendor and then the name of the application. For example, Figure 12.13 shows the user settings for Jasc Paintshop Pro.

FIGURE 12.13

Most applications have a single set of settings under the vendor name and then the application name.

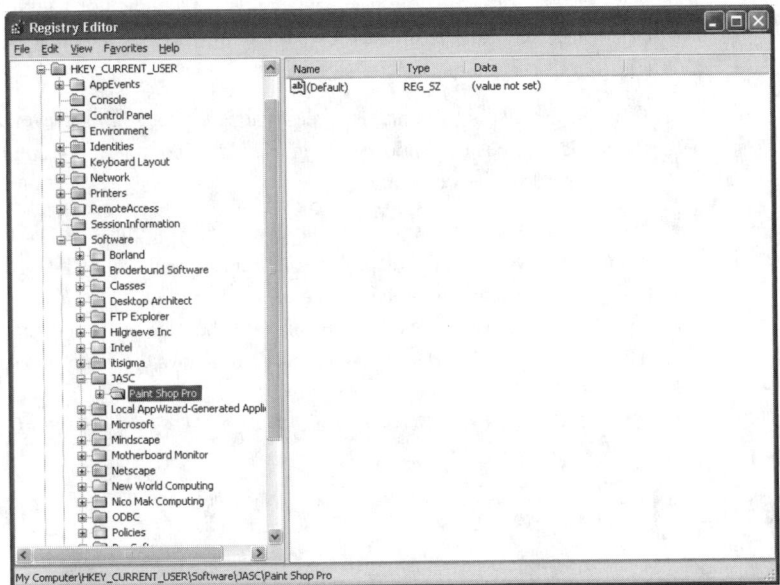

Global application settings appear under the HKEY_LOCAL_MACHINE\SOFTWARE key. These settings tend to affect every user of an application. For example, if you install Microsoft Office on your machine, all users have access to the same components. The installation settings would appear in the global area because a user can't customize them. Again, you look under the vendor name and then the application name to find the settings.

Some complex applications require more than one set of Registry settings. For example, when working with Microsoft Office, you find keys for Office and Microsoft Reference under the personal settings. You might also want to save the Shared Tools key settings, at least those for the Proofing Tools. Under the global settings, you find keys for Microsoft Reference and Microsoft Office. In my case, I also have to save the MS Office 97 Professional settings and the Proofing Tools keys. In short, if you're going to save your application settings, you need to spend a little time in the Registry figuring out the various entries. I keep a notebook of Registry settings I find for each of my applications to make it easier to save them the next time.

Applications do create other entries, but you don't need to save them. For example, most applications create file associations. However, unless you've customized the file associations in some way, you don't have to save them because the application re-creates those settings during installation. In fact, given the complexity of some file association setups, you may want to leave this area alone or at least save the settings with care. A bad path or other discrepancy between your old and new setups can spell disaster.

Restoring your settings is easy if you create a good backup and follow a simple restoration procedure. After you install the new copy of the operating system on your machine, you want to install the applications. Don't open any of the applications—just install them. When you get done installing the applications, double-click each of the REG files you created as part of the setting-saving process. Each REG file contains part of the information needed to restore your application to its former state.

Of course, you may wonder why we don't just save a copy of the whole Registry to disk and restore it as part of the operating system update. Part of the reason to reformat your drive is to clean your system up, which includes cleaning the Registry. By saving just the settings you need for your application, you ensure that none of the unused Registry entries is added back into the Registry, and that your applications still operate as before.

Care and Cleaning of the Registry

Some applications are rude. Installation normally goes without a hitch, but if you decide to remove them, they leave behind bits and pieces of themselves in the Registry. Over time, the added Registry entries not only increase the size of the Registry, but they also affect performance. Of course, the problem is to determine what to do with the extra Registry entries. If you know the location of the Registry entries, you can remove them manually, but removal usually isn't that simple.

If you know the application has problems, you can try to clean up the Registry a little after a failed uninstall. Of course, the first thing you should do is create a backup of your Registry because you want to restore anything you modify by accident. I usually make backups of each key I erase or modify as well to make restoring needed settings easier. The following steps show what I normally check when I notice that an uninstall routine produces less-than-stellar results.

Tip: Some applications provide one or more REG files you can study as part of the setup process. The REG files may not contain every entry the application places in the Registry, but they help. You should also look for INF files associated with the application because these files commonly contain Registry settings. Finally, check for installation logs. These logs often contain a "blow-by-blow" description of the installation process and can help you locate Registry entries (along with files in the Windows and System32 folders).

1. Check for application entries under HKEY_CURRENT_USER\Software and HKEY_LOCAL_MACHINE\SOFTWARE. Look for the vendor name and then the application name. Remove just the application entry because you may have other applications on your machine for that vendor.

2. Check these four keys for entries:

   HKEY_CURRENT_USER\Software\Microsoft\Windows\CurrentVersion\Run

   HKEY_CURRENT_USER\Software\Microsoft\Windows\CurrentVersion\Runonce

   HKEY_LOCAL_MACHINE\SOFTWARE\Microsoft\Windows\CurrentVersion\Run

   HKEY_LOCAL_MACHINE\SOFTWARE\Microsoft\Windows\CurrentVersion\Runone

   (Removing the automatically executing entries reduces errors during the boot process.)

3. Search for the application executable throughout the Registry. You likely find file associations in HKEY_CLASSES_ROOT that you can eliminate. Make modifications very carefully. In this case, make notes on every entry you find for the various keys. You must eliminate the entire file association. This means tracking down all of the associated class entries. In some cases, you need to associate a file extension with a new application. If the application has more than one executable, you need to perform this step for each executable.

4. Remove all INI files for the application from the \Windows folder.

5. Remove all of the application's folders from the hard drive.

6. Remove all application entries from the Start Menu.

7. Restart Windows and verify that it boots cleanly. Look for any lingering trace of the application. Make sure you hold on to all of the REG files for that application until you're sure there are no interactions to consider.

No matter how careful you are, there's a chance that you'll miss some of the application entries. After a while, your Registry begins to fill with useless entries that slow performance and cause other problems. Microsoft provides several tools to maintain and clean your Registry automatically. None of these tools works on the whole Registry—they all concentrate their efforts on HKEY_CLASSES_ROOT. The following list describes these utilities and tells where you can download them:

- *RegClean* (ftp://ftp.microsoft.com/Softlib/mslfiles/) An automated Registry cleaning tool. Just run the application at the command line and RegClean clears out unused entries. RegClean also creates a REG file containing all of the entries it removed, so you can restore your system if the cleaning process is a little too complete. You find this file in the RegClean directory with the name Undo <machine name> <yyyymmdd> <hhmmss> .REG. For example, if your machine name is Main, you might find a file with the name Undo Main 20011020 140122.REG. The advantage of using this utility is that it doesn't require user intervention.

- *RegMaid* (`ftp://ftp.microsoft.com/Softlib/mslfiles/`) A version of RegClean with a user interface. It also checks the Registry for unused entries and creates a backup REG file in the process. However, RegMaid asks you about the entries, making an incorrect choice less likely. It provides a full user interface where you can delete all of the suggested entries or just those you feel certain about deleting.

- *CleanReg* (`http://www.microsoft.com/msj/defaulttop.asp?page=/msj/archive/s358.htm`) A utility that takes a different approach to cleaning the Registry. It looks for filenames in the Registry and then tries to identify the entries associated with the filename. Unfortunately, Microsoft doesn't support this tool. You also need a compiler to compile the source code into an executable for your machine. However, you do get to read an article from a master programmer that explains how Registry cleaning works.

As you can see, the number of tools for cleaning the Registry is small, but you want to choose one of them. My personal favorite is RegClean because it's automatic. However, RegMaid is probably the safer of the two choices. Figure 12.14 shows a typical view of RegMaid.

As you can see, RegMaid provides a list of the Registry entries it wants you to remove. If you want to remove an individual entry, highlight it and then click Delete (the button with the red X). You can also choose multiple entries and delete them at one time. Use the Clean Up | Delete Entries command if you want to remove all of the entries in the list.

FIGURE 12.14
RegMaid provides a display with each Registry entry it thinks you should remove.

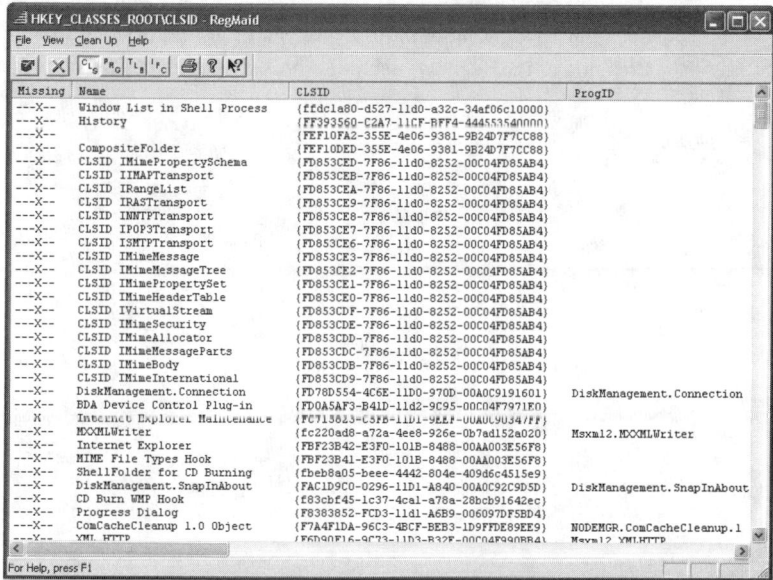

The Refresh button reads the Registry and displays any changes onscreen. RegMaid also provides four Registry views, one each for classes, interfaces, program identifiers, and type libraries. If you delete a class entry, make sure you also delete the associated interface, program identifier, and type library entries. The TypeLib view also contains a list of the filenames associated with this entry. Make sure you record the names of the files and remove them from your system (but save a copy somewhere else) if you no longer need them.

On Your Own

Use the Registry Editor to create a copy of your Registry using the procedure found in this chapter. Make sure that you store this text copy of the Registry in a safe place.

The Registry is a central part of Windows XP. You can't do anything without it. Explore the Registry using the Registry Editor. What do the values associated with each of the keys tell you about your system's configuration? Make sure that you exit the Registry Editor without making any changes to any of the keys.

Create a temporary key in your Registry and use the temporary key to try various techniques listed in this chapter. For example, you can create and delete values or create and delete subkeys. Use the temporary key to learn about security. Make sure you delete the temporary key when you finish using it. There's no need to clutter the Registry with unnecessary information.

If you've been using your Windows XP setup for a while, try cleaning the Registry to maintain good operation. Make sure you follow all of the instructions in the "Care and Cleaning of the Registry" section of this chapter to ensure success.

The Windows XP File System

What precisely is a file system, and why should you care? A *file system* defines how the operating system places data on a drive and then reads the data, erases it, and otherwise moves it around. The reason you need to care about the file system is that it affects the performance, reliability, and stability of the operating system as a whole. In addition, the file system can either make your data easy to access or cause damage to it.

Now that you know what a file system is, you probably have other questions. For example, should you use the NT File System (NTFS) or the older and more widely used File Allocation Table (FAT) for your file system on Windows XP? The first answer that many people give is, "Well, I'm using Windows XP, so I should use NTFS." Let's just say this approach to the question is a little shortsighted, given the advanced capabilities that Windows XP provides.

NTFS is superior in many ways to the old FAT system, but if you divide your hard disks into volumes 1GB or smaller, FAT is actually the better performer. (FAT32, which Windows XP supports, extends the performance advantage to at least 2GB.) In addition, many professionals acknowledge that FAT is superior to NTFS when engaged in random reads of a disk, no matter what the volume size. There are, of course, other issues beyond sheer performance—stability and security prominent among them. However, making the decision between FAT and NTFS is far from clear-cut. Helping you make an informed decision on this issue is one focus of this chapter.

When you look at Windows XP, you're seeing an operating system that offers a choice of two base file systems: FAT/VFAT (Virtual File Allocation Table) and NTFS (originally called the New Technology File System). You can break the FAT support further into FAT16 (16-bit file allocation tables) and FAT32 (32-bit file allocation tables). Likewise, there are several versions of NTFS support: NTFS 4, NTFS 5, and a newer, Windows XP variant. We talk about these varying levels of support as the chapter progresses.

> **Note:** At one time, Windows versions based on Windows NT worked on more than one platform. All versions of Windows work on some form of Intel processor today, so there are fewer multiplatform concerns. However, it's not certain at the time of this writing if Windows XP users will see differences between 32-bit and 64-bit support. Theoretically, you shouldn't see any difference, but the change in processor and supporting code could cause unforeseen problems.

I want to mention a little more about the VFAT support provided by Windows XP. You'll find it interesting to discover that Windows XP supports long filenames as easily on a FAT-formatted drive as it does with any other drive. If Windows XP merely provided a true FAT file system, you couldn't use long filenames. I also found it interesting that these long filenames are as accessible from the command prompt as they are from Explorer. You'll also find that Windows XP uses many of the same dynamic link libraries (DLLs) that Windows 9x does (well, not precisely the same) to provide FAT file system access. Microsoft's documentation doesn't even mention VFAT, but I think that calling the level of Windows XP FAT file system support *VFAT* is more accurate. I get into the details of VFAT later in this chapter, when I talk about the Windows XP architecture.

> **Note:** Some people mistake the Windows XP command prompt for the DOS prompt provided under Windows 9x because it looks and acts like DOS. The command prompt under Windows XP isn't true DOS; instead, it's simulated. That's why you can use long filenames in this "DOS" window. If you want to see true DOS, reboot the machine with a DOS boot disk. You can't use long filenames in that case.

This chapter tells you about the various file systems Windows XP supports. I describe the architecture first and then the individual differences between the various file systems. I think it's important to understand how Windows XP views the file system before you attempt to make changes to it. After I fully discuss the theory, I examine some user-related issues, such as LNK files. I also spend some time looking at the utility end-of-file system support. You learn to perform tasks such as formatting a disk, defragmenting your drive, and creating a backup.

An Overview of the File System

Let's take a tour of the Windows XP file system. The Windows XP file system has to support every method of formatting that Windows XP supports. This means that the file system can become quite complex. The first section that follows tells how Windows XP handles the various file formats that Microsoft has created over the years.

Windows XP also requires a robust file system architecture to handle today's varied media. The second section that follows will tell you about this file system architecture.

We won't get into how the bits and bytes flow through your system, but you'll learn more about those mysterious files in the SYSTEM32 folder. In short, the following sections tell you why the file system is so complicated and show an overview of file system construction.

Windows XP File System Support Concerns

Before you can begin to understand the file-system support provided by Windows XP, you need to understand why there's so much of it. My hard drives have a proliferation of file systems. Right now, I can boot DOS, Windows 2000, and Windows XP. All of these operating systems support the FAT16 file system. All three can at least read the FAT32 file system, but DOS doesn't support long filenames. Windows 2000 and Windows XP also support their own file systems in the form of NTFS. Unfortunately, the version of NTFS for Windows XP is newer than the one for Windows 2000.

> **Note:** According to Microsoft and personal observation, Windows XP automatically upgrades any NTFS partitions it finds on your system to the latest version of NTFS. So far, I haven't seen any compatibility problems using the new version of NTFS under Windows 2000. However, you need to update all of your NTFS utilities. Many third-party products stop working the second you install the new version of NTFS on a system.

Microsoft designed all of these file systems at one time or another to meet various goals. For example, Microsoft based the FAT file system on UNIX. Microsoft had to have a file system when it built DOS—the FAT file system is the result. The following sections will help you understand the various file systems better and show what Microsoft does in Windows XP to support them.

> **Note:** Microsoft dabbled in other formatting schemes that we don't discuss in detail in this chapter because Microsoft doesn't support them any longer. The most notable is the High Performance File System (HPFS), used by OS/2. HPFS provides better speed and reliability than FAT, but isn't as useful as NTFS. Suffice it to say that Microsoft attempted to create a truly useful formatting scheme several times and they're still tweaking it.

FAT Versions

Some people are under the impression there's only one or perhaps two version of the FAT file system. Unfortunately, Microsoft's first attempt wasn't as good as it could have been. It used a 12-bit allocation scheme that seemed quite generous when DOS was young, but soon caused problems when the size of a hard disk exceeded 32MB.

The next version of FAT used 16-bit table entries, thus enabling users to create much larger partitions. Eventually, even the 16-bit table entries provided by FAT16 proved too small, prompting Microsoft to create FAT32 for the Original Equipment Manufacturer (OEM) Service Release 2 (OSR2) version of Windows 95. FAT32 support has become standard in Windows 98 and later. In reality, there are three different FAT formatting schemes (12 bit, 16 bit, and 32 bit). However, from a user's perspective, there's only one.

There's also the matter of FAT-versus-VFAT to consider. When Windows 9x came along, users wanted the capability to use long filenames, but Microsoft needed a method for easily updating these systems, and that meant keeping the FAT file system. The compromise is the VFAT file system. VFAT doesn't require the resources that NTFS does, but it enables users to use long filenames. If you take a hard look at Windows XP, you see that a good deal of the Windows 9x VFAT technology comes from the way Windows XP handles the FAT file system.

NTFS Versions

Windows NT offered yet another opportunity for Microsoft to fiddle with the file system. NTFS is an improvement from a number of technical perspectives that I describe later. The two features that differentiate NTFS from other file system formatting techniques are the capability to use larger files and partitions and the fact that NTFS is more fault tolerant. The bottom line for you as a user is that Microsoft stressed both reliability and efficiency when it created NTFS.

Microsoft keeps tweaking the NTFS file system. Windows NT 4 users received NTFS version 4, and Windows 2000 users began using NTFS version 5. Windows XP has an even higher update that provides more features, better reliability, and better performance. The tweaking will probably continue far into the future because hard drive technology, user needs, and application requirements continue to change.

FAT as a File Formatting Method

What do you do with a system that's literally bogged down with incompatible file systems? You could take the easy way out—the way I originally took—and use FAT for everything. If you stick with the FAT file system, you certainly get all the operating systems talking to each other and run into a minimum of problems. This solution has only one problem. If you stick with the FAT file system, you have compatibility, but you also miss the special features the other file systems offer.

> **Tip:** The primary reason that FAT remains the most popular file system even today is compatibility. For a long time, FAT was the only file system IBM PC users could employ. As a result, no matter which operating systems you now use, they can all access data from a FAT volume. You can have multiple operating systems on your computer, as I do; and, as different as they are, none of them has problems with a FAT volume. (The following list of operating systems can access FAT: MS-DOS, OS/2, Linux, Windows 3.x, Windows 9x, and Windows NT/2000/XP.)

FAT versus NTFS—The Details

You can sum up the weaknesses of the FAT file system in two words: inefficiency and exposure. FAT sets up its allocation table at one location, near the start of the FAT volume. The FAT and the root directory must be located in a particular zone on the drive. There is, therefore, a distance penalty caused by the need to update the FAT (located at the start of the volume) continually. With today's huge hard drives (10 GB to 40GB is now common on new workstations), this back-and-forth travel to the FAT exacts a serious performance hit. It doesn't matter on small drives, but remember that Microsoft designed FAT when hard drives were about $\frac{1}{1000}$ the size they are today.

> **Note:** NTFS locates small files close to the NTFS directory on the drive. This approach to file storage is an intelligent one. A hard drive head has to go to the directory first and then to the file. If a number of small files are gathered around the directory, it's more efficient than placing files anywhere on a volume, willy-nilly, regardless of size or fragmentation, the way FAT does.
>
> Interestingly, NTFS uses what's called a Master File Table (MFT), a table that's a rough equivalent to the FAT. The MFT is divided into records like a database, and each stored file or folder has a series of attributes, including location, name, Access Control Lists (ACLs), and data. NTFS considers data to be just another attribute.
>
> If the data is smaller than 2KB, Windows XP stores it right there in the MFT itself, along with the other attributes of the file or folder. Also, the MFT is copied to several locations on the drive, depending on the size of the drive and the number of files and folders on the drive.

FAT has another weakness: It locates files unintelligently. It just looks for the first available blank space and writes—never mind if this space is too small to hold the entire file and has to be broken into linked chunks scattered here and there on the disk. In other words, write efficiency is the only consideration; how effectively this file is read later isn't even thought about. The result: Severe fragmentation problems and a second major performance hit.

> **Tip:** Third-party products can reduce the problems you encounter in working with more than one operating system on your machine. For example, Partition Magic (http://www.powerquest.com/products/desktop.html) enables you to move partitions of different types around dynamically. Another utility, called System Commander, (http://www.v-com.com/product/sc2_ind.html) manages a multiple-boot situation very nicely. Together, these programs can handle any combination of operating system and file system you can think of. Make absolutely certain that you obtain the latest versions of these products, and verify that they work with Windows XP before you use them.

Both FAT and NTFS define a basic unit of organization called the *cluster*. FAT clusters are, well, too fat. No matter how much information you're storing in a file, that file takes up at least one cluster. If you're storing a Notepad TXT file that contains a single three-letter word, don't expect it to take up three bytes (or six bytes with Unicode) on your hard drive. Amplifying this wasted space problem is the fact that larger hard drives require larger cluster sizes. Table 13.1 provides some idea of just how inefficient FAT16 gets when working with large drives.

Table 13.1 FAT16 Cluster Size in Relation to Volume Size

Default Cluster Size in KB	Volume Size in MB
4	0–15 (12-bit allocation)
2	16–127
4	128–255
8	256–511
16	512–1,023
32	1,024–2,047
64	2,048–4,095
128	4,096–8,191
256	8,192–16,384

As you can see in Table 13.1, the smallest possible file stored under FAT16 requires a minimum of 2,048 bytes on a small, ancient 127MB hard drive and 131,072 bytes on a typical drive today. Compare the FAT cluster sizes to the NTFS cluster sizes shown in Table 13.2

Table 13.2 NTFS Cluster Sizes

Default Cluster Size(KB)	Volume Size(MB)
½ (512 bytes)	0–512
1	513–1,024
2	1,025–2,048
4	2,049 and bigger*

*I say "and bigger" because an NTFS volume can be as large as 2 exabytes. Now, exabytes isn't a word you hear very often because current technology can't offer hard drives smaller than a swimming pool with that much storage. An exabyte is 2^{64} bytes, or 17,179,869,184GB. (NTFS enables you to adjust the cluster size, but the cluster sizes listed in Table 13.1 for FAT volume are fixed and can't be adjusted.)

Finally, there's the fact that even dim-bulb spies have little trouble getting to the data on a FAT disk, which can be a real problem for many businesses. The drive contains personnel information, proprietary designs, business plans, and much more—all of which is exposed to the first person who boots off a floppy and then types C: and presses Enter at the DOS command line. This person might be interested in finding out information or destroying it. In either case, NTFS offers sophisticated security measures, whereas FAT includes only a simple, crude directory security and "hidden" files and "read-only" files that are, to anyone with a little knowledge, neither hidden nor unwritable. NTFS offers improved reliability and a higher access speed than the old FAT file system.

Peter's Principle: A Method of Dealing with Multiple File Systems

After a great deal of thought, I finally came up with a middle-ground solution to the problem of dealing with multiple file systems on one computer. This solution offers the maximum in compatibility, yet allows me to make the most out of what the other file systems have to offer.

The first thing I did was partition my drives. I set aside one partition for each of the operating systems installed on my machine. I had to do that anyway, to get everything to boot correctly. Each operating system's specific partition uses the special file format it provides. This way, the operating system and its utility programs can benefit from the improved performance and reliability the new file system offers. I also stuck any operating-system–specific applications in these partitions.

After I figured out where the operating systems would go, I installed them. Each installation required a bit of time and patience, but I got through it. It's important to test the capability to boot each operating system after you install a new one. Windows NT/2000 and Windows 9x like to overwrite the bootable partition marker. This means that whatever boot manager you've installed doesn't boot until you use a disk editor to set the active partition to its original position. Note that Microsoft suggests you install Windows XP last if you install it with other Windows products.

After I installed the operating systems and tested the boot sequence, I had one large partition left (actually, I had set aside a whole second drive). I labeled the partition on this drive COMMON and placed all my data and common applications there. It uses the FAT file system so that all the operating systems can access it. Obviously, you can use FAT32 if the operating systems you plan to use can read it properly. In some cases, I had to install each application once for each operating system. If you're careful, however, you can determine which files to copy from your Windows SYSTEM directory into each of the other SYSTEM directories. (DLLs and Virtual Anything Drivers (VxDs) need to appear in the SYSTEM directory in most cases; otherwise, Windows can't find them.) Is this a perfect solution? Not by a long shot. However, it's a solution that works.

Why did I go through this entire rundown of my system configuration? I think you might find yourself in the same dilemma. You have to test out all (or at least many) of the solutions available today, which means keeping multiple operating systems on your machine. This solution might be just what the doctor ordered when it comes time to test a Windows 9x or Windows NT/2000/XP solution that your company might adopt. If you don't test the advanced file system that comes with the operating system, can you really say that you tested everything when the time comes to make a decision?

How the File System Works

Now that you have a better idea of what the issues are, let's look at the file system architecture. Windows XP has a great deal to juggle when it comes to file system access. Figure 13.1 shows you how it gets the job done.

Although this looks like lots of ground to cover, the file system architecture isn't too difficult to understand if you break it into smaller pieces. The following sections provide an overview of each of the architectural elements seen in Figure 13.1.

FIGURE 13.1

The Windows XP File System handles multiple file systems and media types.

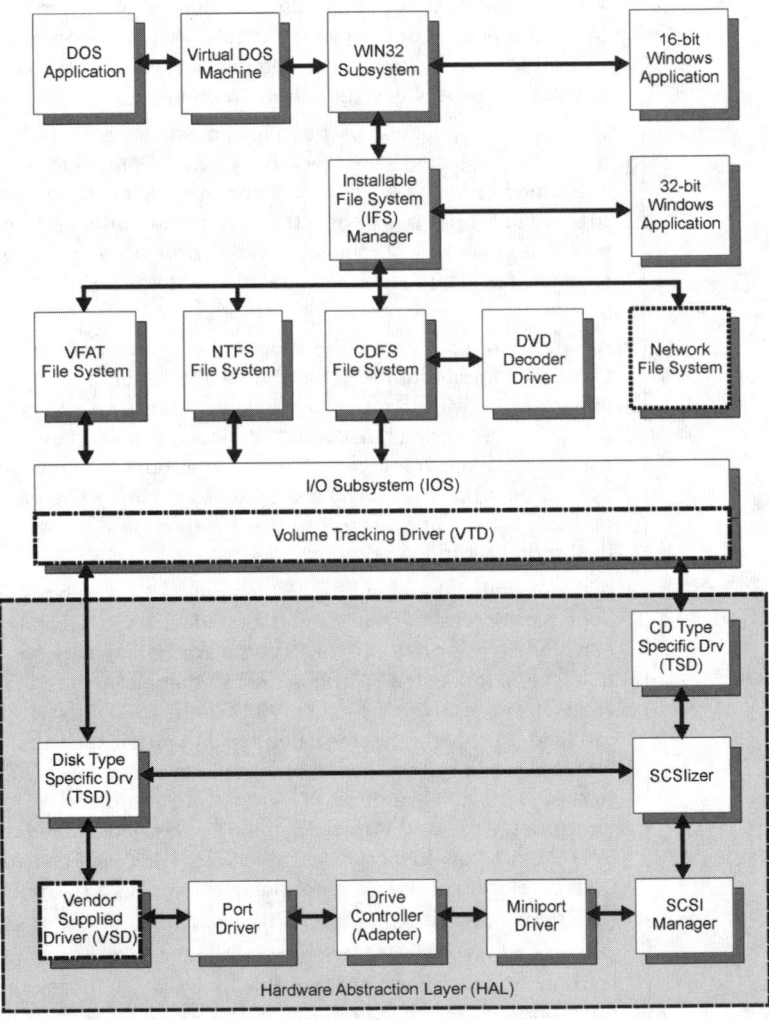

Win32 Subsystem

Remember that Windows XP uses a client/server approach to taking care of the needs of the various applications it supports (see Chapter 21, "Networks" for a full description). It does this through the Win32 subsystem—a buffer layer that translates foreign operating system calls into something Windows XP can understand. In this case, Windows XP supports DOS and 16-bit Windows applications. The translation, in both cases, is from a 16-bit to a 32-bit environment.

Virtual DOS Machine (VDM)

Windows XP places each DOS application in its own Virtual DOS Machine (VDM). To provide the higher level of system reliability that Windows XP users demand, Microsoft had to make sure that each application has its own environment—an environment completely separate from that used by every other application. This effectively adds two layers to every interaction—one for the VDM and another for the Win32 subsystem. As with everything else, this additional layering is transparent to the user. The application still uses the same interfaces as before.

Installable File System (IFS) Manager

The Installable File System Manager is the highest layer in the file system. The IFS is a series of DLLs that provides the interface to applications. It doesn't matter whether the application uses the DOS interrupt 21h interface or the 16- or 32-bit Windows interface; IFS Manager is the component that receives application requests. It's the responsibility of the IFS to transfer control to the appropriate file system driver (FSD). Notice that Windows XP supports four different file system drivers. Chapter 21 discusses the network support.

File System Driver (FSD)

The most common file system driver layer component is the NTFS File System Driver (FSD). However, you can also use any of the other FSDs provided with Windows XP, including VFAT, CDFS, and Network. Except for the Network FSD, these VxDs take care of all local hard drive requests. Besides file system–specific needs, each FSD provides the long filename support and protected-mode stability that make Windows XP better than its predecessors. Your machine might have several other FSDs, depending on the type of equipment you've installed.

> **Note:** I'm using CD and DVD for generic references because there are so many forms of these drives today. I'll use CD-ROM, CD-RW, DVD-ROM, and DVD-RAM as specific references because these are the common types of drives available on machines today. I won't reference any of the other odd assorted permutations of these drives because they are too new, non-standardized, unstable, or unpopular.

Notice that the block diagram shown in Figure 13.1 includes a CDFS driver, for example. This special driver is designed to access a CD or DVD drive. This set of DLLs increased greatly in size under Windows XP because it supports CD-RW and DVD-RAM drives as well as CD burning and other long-awaited drive management features. The CDFS driver actually consists of several files on your system, including CDAUDIO.SYS, CDFS.SYS, CDROM.SYS, REDBOOK.SYS, and STORPROP.DLL. This is just the tip of the iceberg because these files rely on many other files to do their job. Windows XP installs the CDFS driver only when it detects a CD or DVD drive attached to your system. Note that under Windows XP, the main difference from a user perspective for CD or DVD support is that there are additional decoder drivers for the DVD drive that allow it to play DVDs in addition to CDs. All of the FSDs communicate with the IFS manager. They also send requests to the layers that directly communicate with the hardware.

> **Note:** The Windows XP CDFS driver is based on the ISO 13346 standard rather than on the older ISO 9660 standard. The new level of support is required in order to support DVD drives in addition to CD drives.

DVD Decoder Driver

Like CDs, there are three kinds of DVD: static data, erasable data, and multimedia (movie) DVDs, all of which are handled by the DVD decoder driver. This driver is composed of several files on your system. The actual number depends on the DVD decoder hardware you use. As a minimum, you'll find that Windows XP installs DVDPLAY.EXE for multimedia DVDs. This program further relies on new Windows XP features, such as DirectShow, and older features, such as the media control interface (MCI). The DVD Decoder Driver also introduces a new executable file extension: AX. The AX files all work with streaming media, such as the kind found on DVDs, and they provide links to Microsoft's newer ActiveX technologies, such as ActiveMovie.

> **Tip:** The level of support the DVD Decoder Driver provides depends on your system setup. Using a hardware decoder greatly speeds the use of these drives and reduces memory penalties. However, you need a third-party driver for the hardware decoder because Microsoft doesn't provide such a driver for Windows XP. Many users have complained that their DVD vendor provides little support for anything beyond Windows 9x. A third-party alternative is the Sigma Designs Hollywood Plus MPEG Decoder (http://www.sigmadesigns.com/support/download_hollywood_plus_win2000.htm). I've tried this driver with a Creative PC-DVD with the Dxr3 hardware decoder, and it works great. Make sure you use the Hollywood player with the Hollywood decoder for optimum performance.

I/O Subsystem (IOS)

The I/O Subsystem is the highest level of the block device layer. What do I mean by a block device? Any device that sends information in consistent size groups (such as a hard drive) is a *block device*.

A hard drive usually uses some multiple of 512 bytes as its block size. (The block size determines the number of bytes in one disk storage unit.) Other devices might use different block sizes. Network devices, tape drives, and CD/DVD drives all fall into the block device category. The IOS provides general device services to the FSDs. For example, it routes requests from the FSDs to various device-specific drivers and sends status information from the device-specific drivers to the FSDs.

Volume Tracking Driver (VTD)

The Volume Tracking Driver handles any removable devices attached to your system. If you have a floppy disk, CD, or DVD drive, Windows XP installs this component. Windows XP doesn't install this component if you use a diskless workstation or rely on local and network hard drives alone. The VTD performs one, and only one, basic function: It monitors the status of removable media drives and reports any change in media. This is the component that complains if you remove a floppy disk prematurely (usually, in the middle of a write).

Hardware Abstraction Layer (HAL)

The Hardware Abstraction Layer (HAL) is another conceptual element in Windows XP. Microsoft wrote the drivers and other software elements in such a way that it could easily move Windows XP to other platforms. The basic architecture of Windows XP is the same, but the low-level drivers are different. Figure 13.1 shows the elements for a 32-bit Intel processor machine. You might see something slightly different when using a 64-bit machine.

Type-Specific Driver (TSD)

Every device needs a driver that understands its needs. For example, the hard disk drive driver wouldn't understand the needs of a floppy disk drive very well. This layer deals with logical device types rather than specific devices. One Type-Specific Driver (TSD) handles all the hard drives on your system, and another TSD handles all of the floppy disk drives. A third TSD handles all network drives. A data read or write can follow one of two paths after it leaves the TSD. Windows XP provides one level of handling for most standard drives, such as IDE and ESDI. It provides a special level of handling for SCSI drives.

The CD Type-Specific Driver gets a special entry because it has to handle multiple data types. The TSD works in a similar fashion to the one I described for a standard drive. Because a CD or DVD drive has to play multimedia as well as read from (and, in some cases, write to) data media, it requires a special kind of a TSD—one that's more complex than a general drive requires. The fact that CDs and DVDs are removable media also serves to complicate the driver. Unlike a floppy disk drive, where a simple detection of a floppy disk change is needed, a CD has to detect not only the change, but also the media type. Also, think of game and educational programs where the CD may contain both data and music—talk about a complicated situation. I don't want to get into the bits and bytes of CD and DVD data handling here, but it's important to realize that CD and DVD drives are a unique class that require special handling.

Vendor-Supplied Driver (VSD)

This entry in the block diagram (Figure 13.1) is where a vendor would install support for a special device, such as a ZIP drive. Windows XP provides a whole list of standard drivers that it also installs at this level. For example, an IDE drive has its own VSD. Every specific device type needs a driver that can translate its requests for Windows. The VSD knows information about the drive, such as the number of heads a disk has and the amount of time it needs to wait for a floppy disk drive to get up to speed.

Port Driver (PD)

The Port Driver communicates with the device through an adapter. It's the last stage before a message leaves Windows and the first stage when a message arrives from the device. The PD is usually adapter specific. You have one VSD for each hard drive type (such as IDE) and one PD for each hard drive adapter (a *port*, in Windows XP terms), for example. If your system uses an IDE hard drive, Windows would load the IDE PD to talk to the IDE adapter.

A typical example of an IDE PD layer includes an ATAPI driver, the IDE driver, and an IDE extension for the PCI bus. In addition, drivers for each IDE channel provide ATAPI support and display configuration property pages.

SCSI Support

I grouped SCSIizer, SCSI Manager, and Miniport driver together as SCSI support because they represent a driver set. The SCSIizer portion of the file system deals with the SCSI command language. Think of the command language as the method the computer uses to tell a SCSI device to perform a task. Windows XP has one SCSIizer for each SCSI device.

The SCSI Manager is a platform-specific driver that enables you to use Windows XP on many machine types without making wholesale changes to the operating system. It translates commands issued by the SCSIizer to a format the Miniport driver understands.

The *Miniport* driver is a device driver that provides support for a specific SCSI device. Every device has a separate miniport driver. The miniport driver works with the SCSI Manager to perform the same task as a PD. Windows NT/2000/XP and Windows 9x use the same miniport drivers.

Drive Controller (Adapter)

The drive controller (adapter) is the physical device that provides disk services for the machine. Windows XP has to support a variety of controller types. The HAL makes communications between the internal portions of Windows XP and the drive hardware possible.

Using Shortcuts

Pointer is a term familiar to programmers when it's used as a computer term. However, it's familiar to everyone when talking about a directional finder, such as an address on a house. Think of shortcut files in Windows XP as pointers to something. They help you create a link to an object, such as a file or folder located somewhere else.

What good are shortcuts? Suppose that you're a manager and you need to gather files for the group that will eventually put a project together. A graphics illustrator worked to create drawings for the past few weeks. A second group created the figures and statistics with Excel. Another group wrote some text and designed charts to go with the other elements of the project. You're ready to get everything together for a full-fledged presentation.

You could copy all of the files to one directory and print them. After lots of redlining during your meeting, each group could make the required changes. What an inefficient way to spend your week. Many places work this way, but I can't think of anything less productive.

Some groups have become more modern. They place all the files in a directory on the network so that the group can work on them without making red lines. This method works a bit better, but it still isn't the best way because you have two copies of the files lying around. This allows too many chances to make a mistake. Besides, what happens if George finds another change later? Does he try to find the correct file and make the change (or, worse, try to find the correct person to make the change for him)? Using double files is okay, but they can create a version problem.

Windows XP offers an alternative. The manager can create a project folder containing shortcuts to all the project files. The folder is easy to distribute, even if the users aren't in the same building. Shortcuts make it easy for the person using the folder to access a single copy of the real file. You don't need duplicates, so there's no chance of mislaid files or having to figure out which is the file with the latest edit. Everyone can work on all the files as needed, and no one but the manager needs to know the physical location of the files. This is what a shortcut file can do for you.

Look for additional shortcut usage details in the "Working with Desktop Objects" section in Chapter 3. Now that you have a better idea of what a shortcut is, we explore them in detail in the following sections.

Creating Shortcuts

You can create shortcuts using a number of techniques. The easiest method is to right-drag an object from Windows Explorer to a new location. When you release the right mouse button, you see a context menu containing options such as Move and Copy. One context menu option is Create Shortcuts Here. Select this option and you see a new shortcut appear in the desired location. Remember that the shortcut is a mere pointer to the actual file.

Performing General Configuration

Creating a shortcut doesn't mean it's ready to use. In a few cases, you also need to perform some shortcut configuration. Figure 13.2 shows a typical shortcut file for a Windows application. Data files include only the General and Shortcut tabs. The Windows application shortcut is the kind you work with most often. The "Settings" section of Chapter 8 discusses the various shortcut configuration issues for DOS applications. You need to check this section for the contents of the Program, Font, Memory, Screen, and Misc tabs.

FIGURE 13.2

A shortcut file Properties dialog box provides a General tab similar to the one provided by other file types.

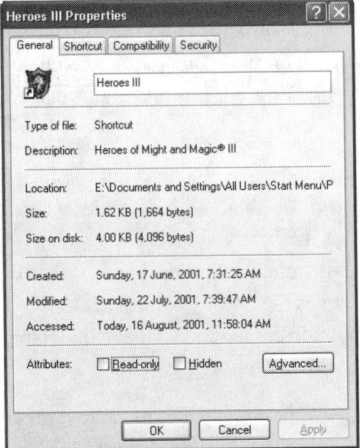

As with the General page of any file Properties dialog box, you can set the file attributes: Hidden and Read-Only. This page also tells you the filename and other statistics, such as when someone last modified the file. This is about all you see for a shortcut on a FAT formatted drive.

Shortcuts on NTFS drives also include an Advanced button. Click this button and you see an Advanced Attributes dialog box. Options in this dialog box determine if the file is indexed, ready for archiving, compressed, and encrypted.

The Shortcut tab appears in Figure 13.3. The following list outlines the four major fields on the Shortcut page along with the function of each entry; of course, the two you use most often are the Target field and the Run drop-down list box:

- *Target* Contains the location of the program you want to run or the data file you want to open. This field can also contain command-line arguments that modify the way an application works. For example, you can include an argument for Windows Explorer that changes its starting directory.

- *Start In* Windows XP assumes that everything the shortcut needs appears in its target directory. This is probably true for data files. However, you might find that some applications need to use a different "working directory" from the directory they start in. The working directory often contains support or data files. For example, when you start your word processor, you may want to assign it your data folder as a working directory.

- *Shortcut Key* The Shortcut Key field enables you to assign a key combination to the particular shortcut file. Using a shortcut key can dramatically speed access to your favorite applications or data files. For more information, refer to the "Shortcut Keys" section in Chapter 6.

- *Run* Windows provides three run modes for applications. You can run them minimized, maximized, or in a window. I find that the Windows default setting works for most of my applications. (In the majority of cases, this is a normal window.) I normally start data files maximized. This is especially true of my word processing files because I like to get a full-screen view of them.

- *Comment* Use this field to make a comment about your shortcut. The contents of the Comment field appear when you hover the mouse over the entry in Windows Explorer or on the Start Menu. Typing a short but informative comment can act as a reminder of why you created the shortcut.

FIGURE 13.3

Use the Shortcut tab options to control the pointer to your data or application file.

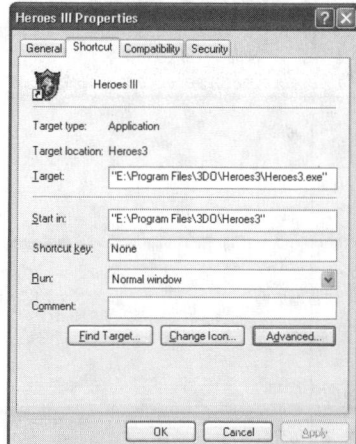

The Shortcut tab can also contain up to three buttons. The Find Target button displays a single-pane view of Windows Explorer that you use to locate the application or data file if the link gets broken. Click Change Icon to modify the icon used to present the application or data file. Windows XP defaults to the application file unless the application file lacks icons. Use the Advanced button to display the Advanced Properties dialog box. Options in this dialog box help you run the application using different credentials or run it in a separate memory space.

The Security tab looks the same as the Security tab for any file in Windows Explorer. You see a list of users and groups that have access to the shortcut. Highlight any of the entries in this list and you see their rights in the Permissions list. Use the Add and Remove buttons to manage the Group or User Name list. The Advanced button displays the Advanced Security Settings dialog box, used to maintain fine control over the security for this shortcut.

Using Compatibility Mode

Windows XP includes the new Compatibility tab, shown in Figure 13.4. There are a few reasons that Microsoft included this tab, including the loss of lower-resolution and lower-color-depth display modes. However, the settings on this tab also correct problems with Windows 2000. Many games and education software wouldn't run in that environment because of the strict environment it provides. These settings ease the Windows XP restrictions slightly and create a robust game-playing environment. If an application breaks the rules too much, Windows XP still stops it, but you find that many games will run.

As you can see from Figure 13.4, the Compatibility tab includes three display-setting modifications. You can change the display to run in 640×480 simulation mode, use 256 simulated colors, and turn off visual themes. The themes setting is especially important for educational software that tends to react badly to screen savers and other display changes.

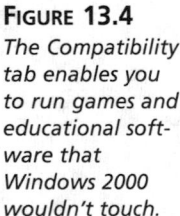

Figure 13.4

The Compatibility tab enables you to run games and educational software that Windows 2000 wouldn't touch.

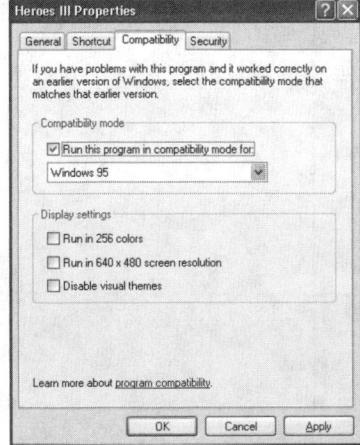

The Run This Program in Compatibility Mode for drop-down list box contains entries for Windows 95, Windows 98/Windows Me, Windows NT 4.0 (Service Pack 5), and Windows 2000. Windows XP will lie to the application by telling it that you're using the compatibility operating system instead of Windows XP. This setting thwarts many applications that search for specific version numbers. Windows XP also makes changes to its environment that help the application run better.

Working with VxDs (Virtual Anything Driver) and DLLs (Dynamic Link Libraries)

You eventually need to know about the DLL and VxD because they're essential parts of Windows. Windows 3.x started the DLL and VxD craze for a good reason: Creating a Windows program is a complex undertaking, and programmers need tools to get the job done quickly.

DLLs and VxDs are both application modules, sort of like Legos for application developers. A developer can create an application more quickly because DLLs and VxDs perform part of the work. Using a modular approach ensures that items such as dialog boxes look the same no matter which application you use.

Using DLLs and VxDs to build applications can also save memory because each module can perform the same task for multiple applications. People already started to complain about the huge memory footprint of Windows during the Windows 3.x days. Even when applications could share some code or data, it still took lots of memory to get anything done. A program calls a DLL or VxD to perform specific tasks. Essentially, both files contain executable code—often in the form of a library of procedures (bits of code that perform a single task). When Windows sees the request, it loads the program (DLL or VxD) into memory. Both DLLs and VxDs contain entry points. Any number of applications can simultaneously access the program file and use whatever parts they need. For example, you might have noticed that the File | Open command in most applications produces the same dialog box. This dialog box is actually part of the COMMDLG.DLL file located in your SYSTEM directory.

Why do you need to know about DLLs and VxDs? It might seem a very unlikely prospect, but data corruption can affect any file on your system. Although Windows XP includes many features for ensuring the integrity of your system files, accidents will happen. Knowing that the File Open dialog box appears in the COMMDLG.DLL file could help you fix the system with just a few minutes' worth of work. All you would need to do is restore a good copy of this DLL file from your backup. In many situations, a support person working for an application or hardware vendor will ask you to perform this task to repair a problem with your system.

What DLLs do for software, VxDs do for hardware. When part of your system needs to access a piece of hardware, it usually calls a VxD. (Drivers don't necessarily use the VXD extension. Some use SYS, others use DLL, and a few use EXE.) Of course, drivers can also work with software components, but from a different perspective from DLLs. Drivers always provide some type of interface to a system component. For example, Windows uses some types of VxD to perform memory allocation. Most users don't worry about this function, but it's very important to your system.

Using Disk Cleanup

Sometimes the best thing you can do for your system is clean up the wealth of useless files that accumulate. For example, many applications generate temporary files while you work on your data. In some situations, those files continue to lurk on your hard drive until you delete them manually.

> **Warning:** In most cases, the Disk Cleanup utility performs safe disk searches, so the chances of deleting or modifying a file by mistake are low. However, you're still deleting files from your data drives, so data loss can occur when using this utility. Always create a backup of your system before you perform any disk maintenance task, especially one that removes "unnecessary" files from the system, like this one does. The data you save is worth the time expended to create the backup.

Fortunately, Microsoft includes the Disk Cleanup utility in the Programs\Accessories\ System Tools folder of the Start Menu. When you start this utility, you see a Select Drive dialog box, which contains a Drives list box. Select the drive you want to clean from the list and then click OK. Disk Cleanup displays a Disk Cleanup dialog box while it performs maintenance tasks, such as compressing old files on your drive. The progress indicator shows how much time Disk Cleanup requires. When Disk Cleanup completes the first part of the process, you see a Disk Cleanup dialog box like the one shown in Figure 13.5.

The Files to Delete field contains options for removing unnecessary files from your system. Each entry contains a checkbox you use to select the item. It also tells you the location of the files and shows how much disk space you can save by using this feature.

You might still have reservations about deleting the files based on location alone. Click View Files, and you see an Explorer view of the files in that location. The view you see depends on the location. For example, when looking at the Downloaded Program Files folder, you see the status of the file along with the date of the last access. If you decide that you don't want to delete all of the files in a particular location, you can delete just those you think are outdated while in Explorer view. Make sure that you clear the option in the Disk Cleanup dialog box when you're finished.

FIGURE 13.5
Disk Cleanup searches your drive for problem areas, performs a few maintenance tasks, and then displays this dialog box.

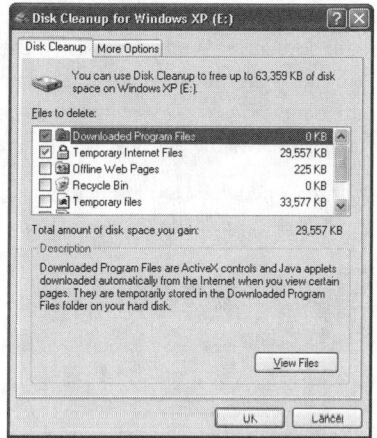

The More Options tab of the Disk Cleanup dialog box contains three areas. You can use the options on this tab to perform additional disk cleanup by removing optional Windows components, installed programs, and restore points from System Restore. When working with System Restore, Disk Cleanup saves the last restore point and removes all of the others.

Defragmenting Your Hard Drive

Defragmenting your hard drive is one of the most important performance-related mainte-nance actions you can do. As you work with a disk drive, Windows XP has to find new places to put files. At some point, all of the spaces available for holding files get too small for the file you want to save and Windows XP has to place it in two sections of the hard drive. Every time the system needs to access that file, it has to move the drive read head to two locations, which is expensive in computer time. Of course, this problem begins affecting more than just one file. After a while, many of the files on your drive experience some level of fragmentation, and you definitely see the performance drop.

The Disk Defragmenter utility reorders the content of your hard drive. It places the files back into one section of the hard drive and frees continuous space by moving all of the files to one end of the hard drive. A defragmented hard drive runs much faster. Unfortunately, this fix doesn't last forever—you have to redo your hard drive on a regular basis.

Note: Disk Defragmenter works only on local drives. In other words, you can't start it on a local drive and hope to defragment your server drives. Disk Defragmenter is also Windows version-specific in many cases. You need to use the version of Disk Defragmenter that comes with your system (or a compatible third-party product).

When you start the Disk Defragmenter utility, it displays a list of the drives on your machine. The statistics include the formatting method, capacity, amount of free space, and percentage of free space. You can perform two tasks: analyze and defragment. Performing analysis first on large hard drives can save time. It pays to defragment drives smaller than 1GB each time you perform maintenance.

To analyze your drive, click Analyze. The Disk Defragmenter display changes, as shown in Figure 13.6. Disk Defragmenter checks each file on the drive for fragmentation.

FIGURE 13.6

Disk Defrag-menter helps you check your drive for frag-mentation.

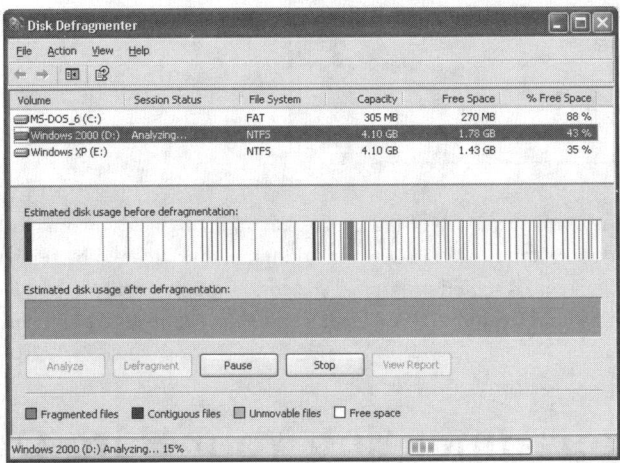

When the analysis process is complete, you see a dialog box that either recommends you defragment your drive or leave it alone for now. If you want to see a detailed report of the analysis, click View Report. You see an Analysis Report dialog box like the one shown in Figure 13.7. This dialog box provides information about the volume and lists the most fragmented files. Even if your drive doesn't require defragmentation, you may want to defragment the drive if one or two files have an exceptional amount of fragmentation.

FIGURE 13.7

The Analysis Report dialog box provides detailed information about the fragmentation state of your hard drive.

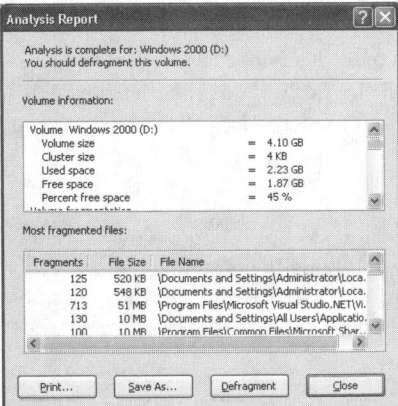

Click Defragment when you want to defragment a drive. Disk Defragmenter performs a quick analysis and then begins the defragmenting process. You see the areas of fragmentation disappear as the program moves files around on your system.

Creating a Backup

Let's take a quick tour of the Backup utility that Microsoft has come up with for Windows XP. The first time you start Backup, it asks if you want to use the Backup Wizard. This is a great choice if you have no experience in creating backups. On the other hand, this selection is cumbersome for advanced users who have experience with Backup. If you choose to use the Backup Wizard, proceed to the "Using the Backup Wizard" section.

Advanced users will want to clear the Always Start in Wizard Mode option and then click the Advanced Mode link. Windows XP displays the Welcome tab of the Backup Utility dialog box. At this point, you can create a backup, restore and manage media, and schedule backup tasks. We discuss these options in the sections that follow the "Using the Backup Wizard" section.

Using the Backup Wizard

The Backup Wizard automatically starts when you start the Backup utility. You can also access it from the Welcome tab of the Backup Utility dialog box. The following steps tell you how to use the Backup Wizard to create a backup:

1. Click Next to get past the Welcome screen. Backup Wizard asks if you want to create a backup or restore previously backed-up files.

2. Select Backup and then click Next. You see a What to Back Up dialog box. Select one of the four options. If you select the Let Me Choose What to Back Up option, Backup Wizard displays an Explorer-like dialog box that lets you choose the backup files. Select the files you want to back up and then click Next. Backup Wizard asks which device you want to use for backup purposes. You can use a dedicated tape drive, a floppy drive, or an area on another hard drive.

3. Select a backup device and then click Next. You see a completion dialog box. Notice the Advanced button at the bottom of the dialog box. This enables you to choose advanced backup features, such as type of backup and the use of verification after the backup.

4. Choose Advanced Features if desired. Follow the prompts to make any changes to the standard setup. Click Finished. Backup performs the backup you created.

Eventually, you'll need the backup you created. That's when you perform a restore using the same Backup Wizard. The following steps show how to restore previously backed up files:

1. Click Next to get past the Welcome screen. Backup Wizard asks if you want to create a backup or restore previously backed up files.

2. Select Restore files and settings and then click Next. You see a What to Restore dialog box that looks similar to a two-pane view of Windows Explorer.

3. Select an entire backup or just a single file in a backup, using the same techniques you've used to choose files in Windows Explorer.

4. Click Next. You see a completion dialog box. Notice the Advanced button at the bottom of the dialog box. This enables you to choose advanced restore features, such as restore location and whether Restore should overwrite existing files.

5. Choose Advanced Features, if desired. Follow the prompts to make any changes to the standard setup. Click Finished. Restore will add or replace any required files on your system.

Creating a Backup

Creating a backup is somewhat time-consuming the first time, but is worth the effort. Always create backup jobs for your system. You perform the same backup process more than once, so saving your settings is always a good idea. Even if you have to modify the default settings, making small changes usually requires less time than creating a new backup. Begin the job creation process on the Backup tab of the Backup Utility. The following steps show how to create a backup job and start it:

1. Use the Explorer-like display to select the files you want to back up. Note that it's better to use My Network Places entries than to use network shares when selecting network files. You never know when a network share will go away or change—making your settings obsolete.

2. Select a backup destination and a backup media or filename. The backup destination can include a backup device or file. You can use any accessible location when working with a file. It's best to use another machine for this purpose so that the data is not stored locally.

3. Use the Tools | Options command to display the Options dialog box. Select a backup type on the Backup tab.

4. Select the Backup Log tab and choose one of the three logging options. You normally want to create a log to ensure Backup can record any backup errors.

5. Select the Exclude Files tab and add or delete file specifications as needed. Backup always includes files and directories that are active during backup. However, you want to add file specifications, such as *.BAK, to reduce backup time.

6. Select the General tab and perform any required configuration. For example, Microsoft assumes you don't want to verify data after the backup completes; yet this is an extremely important feature.

7. Click OK to close the Options dialog box.

8. Use the Job | Save Selections command to display the Save As dialog box. Give your job a name and then click Save.

9. Start the backup by clicking Start Backup. You see a Backup Job Information dialog box.

10. Click Start Backup. You see a Backup Progress dialog box. The Backup Progress dialog box eventually tells you that the backup is complete and allows you to view a report if desired.

11. Click Close to complete the backup process.

Restoring a Backup

Eventually, you need to restore a backup. Unlike with backups, you seldom perform a restore. For this reason, the Backup Utility doesn't allow you to create a job for your restore. To begin the file restore process, select the Restore and Manage Media tab of the Backup Utility dialog box. The following steps show how to restore a backup:

1. Select the backup media you want to use from the Explorer-like display.

2. Choose one or files from within that media. The Backup Utility doesn't allow you to restore files from more than one media at a time, so if you try to choose files from more than one media, it asks if you want to clear the previous selections.

3. Select a restore location. If you choose anything but the Original Location option, you also need to provide a directory name.

4. Use the Tools | Options command to display the Options dialog box. Select a restore option from the Restore and Managed Media tab. Microsoft recommends that you never replace an existing file with one from the backup. You do have the choice of replacing only older files or replacing all files.

5. Click Start Restore. You see a Confirm Restore dialog box. The Advanced button on this dialog box allows you to change additional restore options, such as restoring security. Generally, you want to leave these options alone.

6. Click OK, and you see a Restore Progress dialog box. This dialog box tells you when the restore is complete and provides you with restore statistics. As with the backup, you can view a report containing any restore anomalies.

Testing and Maintaining the Backup System

After you select the hardware and software you intend to use to back up your system, it's important to test and maintain them. Testing ensures that the data you back up today will work when an emergency arises. Maintenance increases the longevity of the equipment you use.

It's important to take a two-phase approach to testing your new backup system—a full test today and a maintenance test tomorrow. After the initial equipment installation, you should test your system to make certain it works. You need to test the hardware, software, automated procedures, macros, and anything else that might stop you from getting a good backup. Test your system in stages, using the procedure in the following section, "Initial Installation."

After you're up and running, you should continue to test your system from time to time to confirm that the software and hardware are still working. Remember that even a little failure is of concern to you. Some breakdowns aren't as obvious as smoking tapes or tape drives and remain undetected by the backup software.

Let's talk about another issue that most people fail to consider—tape drive maintenance. Every drive on the market requires cleaning and physical head inspection. You can use a cotton swab and alcohol (much like the maintenance you perform on your tape system at home) or a specially designed tape cartridge to clean the drive. In addition, the vendor manual that comes with your tape drive should include detailed maintenance procedures. (Most don't include complete instructions, so I've included the set instructions that I use in the following sections.)

Initial Installation

I always perform a visual equipment check before I install the equipment. If the vendor supplies a checklist or picture of the equipment, use it to make sure you have everything. Perform the same check for your software. Perform a virus check on any disk, and then make sure you have the right licenses and that the disks aren't corrupted. Check your tape supply and make sure you have enough on hand to perform a full backup cycle. When you have all the components required to install your tape drive, it's time to do the actual work.

The following steps help you get a great tape drive installation. These are generic instructions, so you need to make some modifications to this procedure to reflect your hardware and software setup:

1. Install the hardware using any vendor-supplied instructions. Make sure you observe the proper static safeguards by grounding yourself before you begin. In addition, attach any required cables, including a grounding cable.

2. Test your initial hardware installation using vendor-supplied diagnostic software. Some drives don't provide any diagnostic software, so you could skip this step and move on to step 3.

3. Check for hardware and software interaction. Begin by performing any software tests the vendor supplies. For example, most backup software provides a speed test to make sure your hardware can perform at a given backup speed.

4. After you complete the vendor-specific check, perform a check of your own. Back up a directory containing nonessential data and then perform a compare of the tape contents to the drive contents. If possible, restore your data to a different directory. Use the FC utility (or any other utility that performs a detailed comparison) to compare the files in the original directory to the new directory. If either of these steps fails, check the setup of your software to make sure all the settings are correct for your machine, tape drive controller, hard disk controller, and tape drive.

5. Create any required macros and setup files. Check each of these setups manually to make sure you set them up correctly. You want to verify that the backup software works by carefully executing the macros using simulated conditions. Resolve any problem areas by reviewing the procedures for setting up the macros and setup files in the vendor-supplied file.

6. Perform any required setups for the scheduling software. Make sure you take power failures and other contingencies into account. Check the scheduling software to make sure it triggers properly. Reset the backup workstation's system clock to see that the software starts at the proper time.

Routine Maintenance

Tape drive maintenance includes cleaning, replacing filters and belts, and physical examination. The following steps show you how to perform generic tape drive maintenance. Make sure you have a flashlight, cotton swabs (the type used to clean tape drives), methyl or isopropyl alcohol, computer-grade compressed air, and any required filters. If you have a digital audiotape (DAT) or other advanced drive, make sure you use the cleaning tapes in place of the cotton swabs and alcohol. Use the cleaning tape before you perform these inspection steps:

1. Carefully open the tape drive door, using a nonconductive material. The plastic screwdrivers included with some computer maintenance toolkits are very useful for this purpose. Use a flashlight to examine the interior of the tape drive. A penlight usually works the best. Figure 13.8 shows the contents of a typical tape drive.

2. You need to examine several pieces of hardware in the drive. To obtain specific details about your drive, refer to the tape diagram in the vendor manual (if the vendor supplied one). Look at the black rubber wheel (the *idler* wheel) on one side of the drive carriage. If the wheel looks shiny and has a brownish cast to it, you need to clean it using alcohol and a cotton swab. It might take a little time to get the wheel clean, but it's essential to do so.

FIGURE 13.8
The interior of a typical tape drive contains several components you need to check.

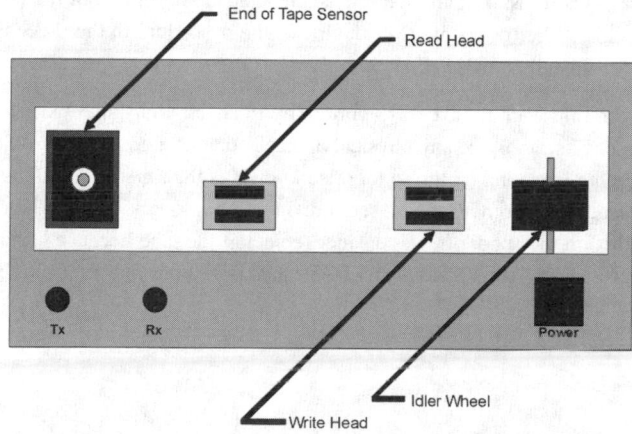

3. Check the read and write heads next. (Some tape drives use a combination read/write head, so you might see only one head.) Clean them with a fresh cotton swab and some alcohol if you haven't used the cleaning tape. Make sure you don't apply lots of pressure because you might scratch the head surface. Polish the heads with a dry cotton swab, using gentle pressure. Check the heads for damage, such as scratches. Both heads should appear brightly polished.

4. Clean the end of the tape sensor if your tape drive has one. This usually looks like a square or rectangular black plastic box with a tiny round light in it. The light is a photo sensor. You must clean the plastic covering on the photo sensor so that light can get through and tell the tape drive when it reaches the end of the tape. Moisten a cotton swab with alcohol and use a rotating motion to clean the sensor if it looks dirty. Most vendors recess the sensor in the black plastic case, so rubbing back and forth only forces dirt further into the recess.

5. Close the tape drive door. If this is an internal tape drive, complete the cleaning sequence by opening your computer and blowing out any dirt inside the case, using computer-grade compressed air. You can proceed to step 9.

6. External tape drive units often come with filters. Look at the back of the tape drive unit to see if it uses a filter. If so, carefully remove the old one. A holder and some screws usually hold the filter in place. Refer to the manual supplied with your tape drive for further details.

7. Replace the old filter with a new one. Some vendors might not supply replacement filters for their systems. If this is the case, carefully wash the filter using clear water. Don't use soap because that clogs the filter. Let the filter dry thoroughly and then replace it.

8. If the tape drive provides some form of external access, open the case and carefully blow the dust out of the inside, using computer-grade compressed air. Never force the case open.

9. Now that you've fully cleaned your tape unit, place a blank tape in the drive and test it. Make sure that this is a test tape and not one of the tapes in your backup set. Perform steps 2 through 4 of the procedure in the preceding section, "Initial Installation."

You might want to take this opportunity to check your tapes using these three quick steps. First, look for any physical damage such as a cracked case. Second, look at how the tape is wound on the spool (also known as the *tape pack*). Does it appear wavy instead of smooth? Can you see individual wraps sticking above the level of the other wraps on the spool? If so, consider replacing the tape because it may have stretched areas. Third, replace old tapes. DAT tapes last about five years, whereas others last about two years.

Tape Rotation

You can rotate tapes in many different ways. The technique you use depends on the requirements of your company, the value of your data, the types of applications you use, and the number of tapes you have on hand. Every tape-rotation method shares the following three things:

- Always store at least one tape offsite. An offsite tape has a better chance of surviving the smaller disasters in life.

- Use at least three tapes to implement what the industry calls a grandfather backup strategy. A *grandfather* strategy ensures that at least three generations of tape are available at all times. Using this strategy usually reduces the probability of virus infection and other forms of data loss.

- Include a plan for retiring old tapes and integrating new ones.

I normally use a three-tape strategy for small businesses. In this scenario, you keep two tapes onsite: this week's and the one from two weeks ago. Last week's tape is always stored in an offsite location. You perform a full backup on Monday and then an incremental backup for other days of the week. This strategy uses a minimum number of tapes (so it's the least expensive), but it provides adequate protection in many cases.

My own setup uses a six-tape strategy. A six-tape full-backup technique uses one dedicated tape for each day of the week. Yesterday's tape is always stored offsite, with the other tapes remaining onsite. This reduces the probability of virus infection and other damage that can occur when you use one tape for both full and incremental backups all week long. This is a good technique for most people who use applications in a nonshared environment.

Offsite Storage

You should never consider offsite storage optional. It's a mandatory part of the backup process. Disasters strike when and where you least expect them. An unexpected electrical fire could wipe out your company tomorrow. Floods, earthquakes, broken pipes, and other disasters can strike at any moment. Placing your data in more than one location helps reduce the probability of tape destruction by a disaster.

Two types of offsite storage are available. The more expensive solution is to use the services of a company that specializes in providing offsite storage. These companies usually provide a fireproof vault for storage. It's unlikely that tapes stored in such a facility would experience damage in an emergency.

The second solution is to select a couple of people from management so that you can use their homes as offsite storage sites. Make sure you obtain the approval of management first. Unless management really trusts these people, you could end up handing company secrets to someone who might try to sell them.

Formatting Disks

Formatting floppy disks is one of those tasks that everyone must perform from time to time. In Windows XP, all you need to do to format a floppy disk is right-click the drive where you want to format from within Windows Explorer. Choose the Format option and you see the Format dialog box.

Windows XP provides the option to create an MS-DOS startup disk. The disk boots as anticipated. However, in the process of creating the startup disk, Windows XP also places an inordinate number of other files on the floppy. When you create a boot floppy using Windows XP, you may have to perform a little cleanup before you can actually use it for something useful, like an emergency boot disk.

> **Tip:** Always use the Quick Erase option to format floppy disks that you know are good. This option formats the floppy disk in a little more than one-tenth the time a full format takes.

All you need to do now is select the options you want and click OK. Windows XP does offer a few nice surprises in addition to the interface. For one thing, it works very well in the background. I didn't experience a single problem working on something else while formatting a floppy disk.

On Your Own

Try using the settings on the Compatibility tab to help an older application run under Windows XP. In many situations, the use of features on this tab permits Windows XP to run older games or educational software programs that require specific settings. Using these settings enabled me to run older educational software on my machine without resetting the Windows display each time. In addition, some older games that didn't run under Windows 2000 now run without problems.

Determine whether you have FAT32 installed on your machine using the various clues we talked about in this chapter. In addition, make certain you know what kind of installation you're getting on a new machine. You don't want to corrupt your hard drive inadvertently using old utilities on an NTFS or FAT32-formatted drive.

Write your own tape rotation plan, based on the examples in this chapter. Make sure you weigh the cost of the time involved in creating the backup versus the cost of replacing lost data after a system crash. Add time to the schedule for replacing your tapes, and don't let an old tape lull you into a false sense of security.

Now that you know a little more about Backup and how to maintain your tape drive, it might be a good idea to create a backup of your hard drive. Make sure you set up a tape rotation scheme while you're at it, and stick to the backup schedule. Get hardware maintenance and tape drive testing schedules put together as well so that you can be sure that you're creating a good backup. Backing up your system may seem like lots of unnecessary work—until your hard drive fails.

Disk maintenance is extremely important. After you complete a backup of your system, it's time to use the Disk Cleanup utility to remove unnecessary files. You'd be amazed at how much space you can save by performing this simple task. Next, you'll want to defragment your drive to return it to peak performance. Sometimes, you'll see a big performance difference after you perform these maintenance steps because the system doesn't have to work nearly as hard to find data on your system.

PART V

Windows and the Underlying Hardware

Fonts and Printing

Printing is one of the fundamental requirements for every computer setup, but, because printers vary widely in capability, it remains one of the most burdensome parts of an installation. Windows XP improves the printing process over what most people were used to seeing with previous versions of Windows. One change over older Windows 9x versions is the use of Windows Driver Model (WDM) drivers, which should improve the robustness and usability of the printer drivers.

Managing fonts is also easier than it was under older versions of Windows. Windows XP places them in a separate directory and provides a utility you can use to manage them. Unfortunately, some vendors have taken advantage of the ease of use that Windows XP provides and started providing special fonts for every application. This, in turn, can use up lots of valuable hard drive space by cluttering it with fonts you don't need. In short, you need to learn how to use the management capabilities Windows XP provides to get rid of the fonts you don't want.

The following sections take you on a tour of the complex world of printers and fonts. I'll show you how to use the printer management features to your benefit and explain some of the more intriguing aspects of the environment Windows XP provides. In addition, we'll talk about the kinds of fonts that are available to use with your printer and show how you can maintain a reasonable number of fonts on your machine.

Installing a Printer

Before you can use a printer, you have to install and configure it. The "Special Printer Installation" section of Chapter 7 showed you how to perform a special file installation. Chapter 9 looked at a few of the most efficient ways to use your printer's capabilities. This is especially true of the "Using Fonts" and "Working with Printers" sections of that chapter. The following sections provide detailed printer installation instructions. The sections also include some productivity tips.

Understanding the Printer and Faxes Folder

Even if you don't have any printers installed on your system, you have a Printers and Faxes folder in the Control Panel. You can also access the Printers and Faxes folder from the Start | Settings menu and from Windows Explorer. At a minimum, this folder contains an applet that enables you to install a new printer. There actually are two types of installation, local and network, and we will look at both.

Local Printer Installation

A *local* printer is attached to your system through a parallel, serial, or USB port. Windows XP can consider a printer local if you attach it directly to your network through a TCP/IP connection local as well. We will see the special requirements for this kind of connection as the section progresses. We also will look at some configuration details. The following steps take you through a local printer installation:

1. Use the Start | Settings | Printers and Faxes command to open the Printers and Faxes folder. You might see one or more printers already in the folder, along with the Add Printer applet.

2. Double-click the Add Printer applet. You see the Add Printer Wizard dialog box.

3. Click Next. The Local or Network Printer dialog box appears. This is the point at which you determine whether this printer will be a network or local printer. Selecting the A network printer, or a printer attached to another computer option enables you to use a printer located on the network. Notice that this dialog box has an option to detect a Plug and Play printer. Some newer printers are Plug and Play. Most printers more than two years old have no Plug and Play capability, so Windows XP doesn't detect them. If you select the Plug and Play detection feature and the Add Printer Wizard doesn't detect your printer, you continue with a manual installation.

Note: You might not see the Local or Network Printer dialog box if your machine doesn't have network support installed. If not, simply bypass step 3 and the first sentence of step 4.

4. Choose Local printer attached to this computer and click Next. The Add Printer Wizard asks you to select a printer port. The Use Following Port List contains all of the local ports for your machine, any special ports you've already configured, and any network ports created for you by Windows XP.

Note: You must select the Create a New Port option if you want to access a printer connected directly to your network using a TCP/IP connection. Choose the Standard TCP/IP Port option from the list and then click Next. The Add

(continues)

Standard TCP/IP Printer Port Wizard dialog box appears. Click Next to get past the Welcome screen. Type the printer name or the IP address of the printer. Type a name for the port. Click Next. The Add Standard TCP/IP Printer Port Wizard attempts to contact the printer. If it makes contact, it creates the new port for you and you can select it from the Use Following Port list. At this point, you'll continue with the second part of step 5, where you select a printer type.

5. Select a port from the list, create a new one, or create a TCP/IP connection. Click Next. The Add Printer Wizard asks you to select a printer, using the Install Printer Software dialog box, shown in Figure 14.1. Notice that there are two lists. The one on the left contains a list of printer vendors. Selecting a vendor changes the list on the right to display printers manufactured by that vendor. Windows enables you to install an unsupported printer by clicking the Have Disk button. Chapter 7 covered this procedure, so I won't talk about it again here.

Figure 14.1
Use the entries in this dialog box to select a printer vendor and model.

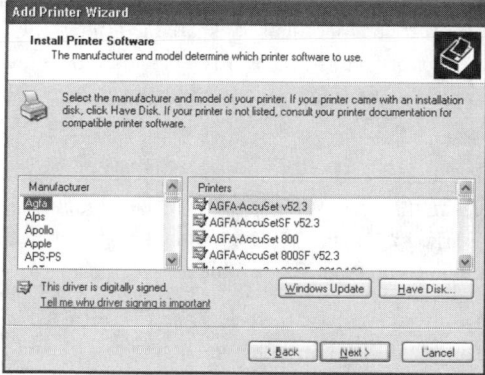

6. After you've selected a printer vendor and model, click Next. The Name Your Printer dialog box asks what name to use for the printer and whether you want to use it as the default printer.

Tip: You can create multiple connections for one printer. I normally add a file connection as a minimum so that I can delay printing until later. A fax connection is also a good idea to support applications that don't provide a fax connection.

7. Type a printer name and indicate whether you want to use it as the default printer. (The Add Printer Wizard suggests an appropriate name you can use to create the first copy of the printer.) Click Next. The Add Printer Wizard asks if you want to share the printer. If you choose to share the printer, you need to provide a share name as a minimum. A second dialog box will ask for optional location information and a comment.

8. Choose whether you want to share the printer. Fill out any additional information for sharing the printer, if necessary. Click Next. The Add Printer Wizard asks whether you want to print a test page. I always send a test page to a local printer connected to an actual port. It makes little sense to print a test page for a file connection. Unless you already have your network connections configured, you need to test them later. Choose to print a test page and click Finish to complete the installation.

9. Choose whether you want to print a test page and then click Next. The Add Printer Wizard displays a completion dialog box.

10. Click Finish. Windows XP displays a status dialog box as it copies all the needed files to your drive. After it completes this task, you see the appropriate icon in the Printers and Faxes folder. Make sure that you check the output of any test pages for errors or other problems.

Network Printer Installation

A *network* printer is one you attach to another machine and share for network use. In the previous section, you had the opportunity to share the printer. (See step 8 in the "Local Printer Installation" section in this chapter.) You can also share it after the fact by right-clicking the printer icon in the Printer and Faxes applet and choosing Sharing from the context menu.

In this section, we discuss the methods for creating a network printer connection. You have several choices in this area. For example, you can double-click on the printer icon in Network Neighborhood. You can also right-drag the printer from Network Neighborhood into the Printer and Faxes folder.

Windows XP also allows you to use the Add Printer Wizard, as we did in the preceding section. You must have a network installed (including drivers and required connections) before installing a network printer. Use the following steps to install a network printer:

1. Use the Start | Settings | Printers and Faxes command to open the Printers and Faxes folder. You might see one or more printers already installed in the folder, along with the Add Printer applet.

2. Double-click the Add Printer applet. You see the Add Printer Wizard dialog box.

3. Click Next. The Local or Network Printer dialog box appears. This is the point at which you indicate whether this will be a network or local printer. If you don't see this dialog box, stop—you don't have the required network support installed.

4. Choose A network printer, or a printer attached to another computer, and click Next. You see a Specify a Printer dialog box where the Add Printer Wizard asks you to provide a network path or queue name. You can use the Browse option to find the required printer in Network Neighborhood. Notice that you can also choose a printer on an Internet site. All you need to do is provide an URL for the Web resource. Unfortunately, the Browse option helps you find only local resources, so you need to know the correct URL if you want to use this option only.

5. Type the network path or queue name for your printer. Click Next. You see the Default Printer dialog box. If you select this printer as the default, any print job you start using automated means uses this printer.

6. Select Yes or No for the default printer option and then click Next. You see a Completion dialog box.

7. Click Finish. If Windows XP finds drivers for this printer on the server, it uses those drivers for the installation on your machine. Otherwise, Windows XP displays an error message stating that the server doesn't include the required files. You need to select the correct printer. Windows XP displays a status dialog box as it copies all the needed files to your drive. After Windows XP completes this task, you see the appropriate icon in the Printers and Faxes folder.

Adding, Deleting, and Configuring Network Ports

Adding a network port is easy under Windows XP. All you need to do is right-click the Printer icon, select Properties, and click the Ports tab. You should see a Printer Properties dialog box, similar to the one shown in Figure 14.2. You use this dialog box exclusively for port configuration needs. This tab contains a complete list of all of the ports on your machine, including network ports Windows XP created for you and custom ports you created in the past. Note that you can't add ports for network printers. You can only add ports for local printers, and you should limit the new ports to printers physically attached to your machine.

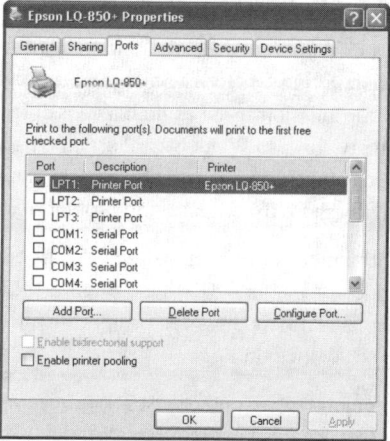

FIGURE 14.2

The Ports tab contains a complete list of ports for your machine.

Clicking the Add Port button displays the Add Port dialog box. You can choose between two types of ports: Local Port and Standard TCP/IP Port. Remember that the Standard TCP/IP Port option works with printers that connect directly to the network without the aid of an intervening server. Unlike in previous versions of Windows, you can't create a new network port, but you can create new port types. A new port type requires you to provide an INF file containing the port monitor description for the port. In most cases, the only time you use this feature is to add a special port supplied by your printer vendor.

To add a new port, click New Port. You see a Port Name dialog box. Type the name of your new port and click OK. Generally, adding a new port without associating it with a device doesn't accomplish much. Nonstandard port names help you create connections with ports that Microsoft may not support. Microsoft suggests using this option with vendor-specific drivers, direct network attached printers, and Macintosh printers.

> **Tip:** It's true that adding a port without associating it with a device doesn't work. However, you can use this feature with a disk location. For example, you could create a port named C:\Temp\MyOutput.TXT, and Windows XP will use it as an output device. Although this technique is similar to using the File port, it's more convenient because Windows XP doesn't ask you for a file name. Note that Windows XP overwrites the file each time you print, so you receive only the latest printout. However, I've used this feature for a variety of needs, such as testing printer output and acting as a quick printer output for long jobs. Printing to disk is extremely fast, and you can run the actual job as a background task once you print it to disk.

Many ports require configuration. For example, when you select an LPT entry and click Configure Port, you see a Configure LPT Port dialog box. The only entry this dialog box contains is the option to change the number of transmission retries until Windows XP registers an error for the printer. Setting this value higher helps slow or heavily loaded printers acknowledge Windows XP requests without generating an error message.

Click Configure Port with a COM port highlighted, and you see the COM Properties dialog box. This dialog box contains options for changing the transmission speed of the printer. You should set the transmission speed as high as possible. Microsoft assumes that all serial printers are extremely slow, so Windows XP sets the transmission speed at a mere 9,600bps. You can also set the data bits, stop bits, parity, and flow control for the port. This area is one to troubleshoot if you're having problems with a serial printer.

A TCP/IP port requires a little more work than the typical port because it contains more settings, many of which are confusing in the extreme. Figure 14.3 shows a typical example of this port. The port name and IP address are straightforward enough; they're the values you entered when you set the port up.

The Protocol setting is extremely important because it can mean the difference between a printer that works and one that ignores your requests. Windows XP assumes you want to use Raw (Port 9100) output. The Raw format is a streaming format in which the printer accepts a data stream containing the information to print. Most printers use port 9100 in this mode, but you can configure the port number as needed. However, many printers use the RFC1179 (http://www.faqs.org/rfcs/rfc1179.html) standard for printing. In this case, you want to set the printer to Line Printer Request (LPR) mode. In this mode, the printer uses a queue to hold the information instead of accepting input directly.

FIGURE 14.3

Use the Configure Standard TCP/IP Port Monitor dialog box to configure the TCP/IP port.

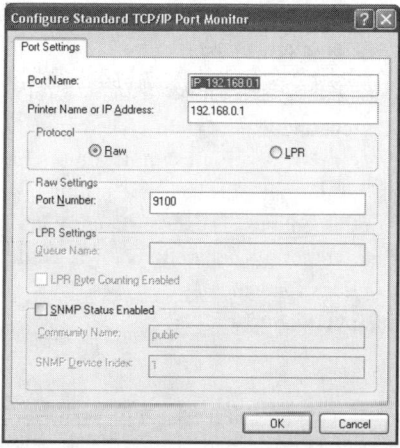

Printers that support their own network connection can also provide Simple Network Management Protocol (SNMP). This standard allows you to perform management tasks over a network connection. For example, you could ask the printer for its status or tell it to use a different printer bin. SNMP relies on an "agent" on the client end that performs the monitoring and communication tasks. You use an application, often embedded in an HTML page, to manage the printer. You can find out more about SNMP at http://www.snmp.com/ and http://www.ibr.cs.tu-bs.de/ietf/snmpv3/.

Deleting a port is the easy part of working with ports. Highlight the port you want to remove and click Delete Port. Windows XP asks if you're sure that you want to delete the port. Click Yes and you see the port disappear from the port list.

Configuring Your Printer

Windows XP provides a default set of printer settings, but, in many cases, those settings don't work. You generally need to consider your printer to gain optimum output from it. For example, Windows XP often assumes you want to use middle-grade printer output when you really need high-quality all of the time. Most settings control the appearance of the output and the features the printer provides to the user. In some cases, a configuration option also affects the speed of printing. I'll let you know what kind of choices you'll be making as we go along.

Opening the printer's Properties dialog box is as simple as right-clicking the printer's icon and selecting the Properties option from the context menu. Every printer provides similar, but slightly different, configuration options. The following sections describe the most common printer tabs and the options you commonly see.

General Tab

The first tab you always see is the General tab, which contains the printer name, location, a comment that identifies the printer, and a feature list. The comment can contain any information you want, such as the days and times the printer is available for use. You'll also see a Print Test Page button at the bottom of the screen. You can use this button to test the capabilities of your printer at any time.

The Printing Preferences button on the General tab displays a Printing Preferences dialog box that contains two tabs: Layout and Paper/Quality. The contents of these two tabs vary by printer and the features it provides. For example, on the Layout tab, a generic printer might provide options for portrait and landscape printing, while a laser printer might also provide duplex printing options. The Paper/Quality tab also contains various options. A standard laser printer might provide options for selecting a paper source. Color printers often include options for switching between black-and-white and color printing, paper quality, and output quality.

Sharing Tab

The Sharing tab enables you to share a local printer with other people when using a Windows peer-to-peer network. (You must have printer sharing enabled to use this option.) The Sharing page contains two radio buttons. Selecting the Share this Printer button enables other people to use the printer. You must provide a share name. After you share a printer, Windows XP adds a hand to the printer's icon.

> **Tip:** Sharing reduces your spooling options. In addition, using a shared printer imposes other speed penalties on the local user. I always create a second printer for myself that I don't share. This way, I get the best of both worlds—a shared printer for other people to use and a nonshared printer configured specifically for my needs.

Advanced Tab

The Advanced tab, shown in Figure 14.4, contains advanced Windows settings that determine how Windows interacts with the printer. You can use this dialog box to set features, such as the availability of the printer. Windows XP assumes that you want to make it available 24 hours a day. You can also use this dialog box to change the printer driver from the Windows XP default to an updated or vendor-specific version.

The middle section of the Advanced tab controls printer performance. Figure 14.4 shows the default setting, which represents the middle ground of performance. If you want to use system resources most efficiently, check the Print Directly to the Printer option. This option makes your system faster, but presents a user delay because the user can't work with the application until it completes printing. If you want to get the user back to work quickly, use the Start Printing After Last Page Is Spooled option.

The bottom portion of the Advanced tab contains special spooling and output features. If you select the Hold Mismatched Documents option, Windows XP compares the configuration of your printer with the configuration requested by the document. If the two don't match, Windows XP holds on to the document. The holding action doesn't prevent other documents from printing.

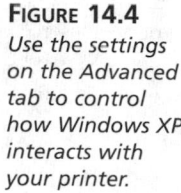

FIGURE 14.4
*Use the settings
on the Advanced
tab to control
how Windows XP
interacts with
your printer.*

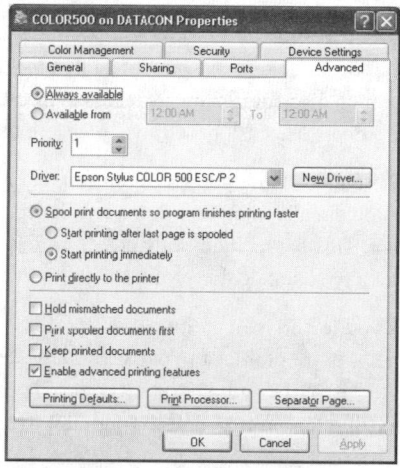

The Print Spooled Documents First option represents another performance consideration. Spooled documents tend to print quickly because the application has performed all required formatting and all of the information is in place. A direct-to-printer job may experience delays waiting for the application to do its work. Selecting the Keep Printed Documents option prevents the spooler from deleting them from the queue once the application prints them. The advantage of this technique is that you can resubmit jobs without using the original application. The disadvantage is that the print job continues to consume disk space.

The final option we discuss, Enable Advanced Printing Features, uses the advanced printing features of your printer and enables the use of Enhanced Metafile Format (EMF) printing. You should keep this option enabled unless you printer experiences compatibility problems with the advanced features.

The three buttons at the bottom of the Advanced tab access other printer features. Click Printing Defaults, and you see the Printing Default dialog box, described earlier in this section. The Print Processor button displays a Print Processor dialog box that enables you to select other forms of printer processing. The default setting is Raw Printing, which relies on the processing capability of the printer for output.

If you enable EMF printing, your machine formats the document before it outputs the data to the printer. This feature can make printing faster, but also increases the processing burden on your local machine.

The final button, Separator Page, displays the Separator Page dialog box, where you can choose a file for each print job. The separator page is a requirement on large networks to ensure that people can find their print job output from a common printer. Make sure you read the "Using the Client Service for NetWare (CSNW) Applet" section of Chapter 21 for additional details about working with separator pages on a NetWare network.

Color Management Tab

Color printers require some form of color management so that the color you see onscreen is the color you see in the output. The color management provided by Windows XP works adequately, but many professionals use custom settings to ensure the best output quality.

The Color Management Tab contains two options: Automatic and Manual. If you choose Automatic, Windows XP automatically chooses a color profile from the list of color profiles supplied for your printer. This list includes only color profiles that the INF file for your driver knows about, not any custom color profiles you might create.

The Manual option enables you to choose a specific color profile. After you select this option, click Add to add one or more profiles to your setup. Use Remove to delete any profiles you no longer need. The Set Default button sets a profile as the default, which means Windows XP ignores all other profiles unless you tell it to use something else at print time.

Security Tab

The Security tab contains the same information as every other device-oriented security tab in Windows XP. The tab displays a list of groups and users who have access in the Group or User Names list at the top of the dialog box. You assign permissions to a group or user by highlighting that entry and then checking or clearing options in the Permissions list. Click Advanced to display the Advanced Security Settings dialog box, to obtain finer control over printer use permissions. The Add and Remove buttons add and remove users from the Group or User Names list.

Device Settings Tab

The final tab of the Printer Properties dialog box is Device Settings. As in so many other cases, the laser printer provides more options than other type of printers you might use, and the printer driver determines the exact options you find on this page. Just about every printer you use includes a Auto Select or Auto Sheet Feeder list box. This list box determines how Windows XP configures output to accommodate the requirements of various paper sizes.

This tab contains three other optional fields. One that's common to most laser printers is the Printer Memory field. The printer usually knows how much memory it has, but the Windows XP driver doesn't. The LaserJet 5 and later versions also include special features, such as page protection and a font substitution table.

Using Point and Print

The point-and-print feature enables you to do a few things you couldn't do with previous versions of Windows, such as simplify remote printer installation. All you need to do to install a remote printer from a Windows 9x, Windows NT/2000/XP, or NetWare network location is drag the icon from Network Neighborhood into the Printers and Faxes folder. Windows XP takes care of the rest. It might ask you to insert the CD-ROM so that it can load the proper drivers on your machine. Each printer requires specific drivers to make it work. Other than that, installation is as close to automatic as you can get.

Discovering Quick Printing Techniques

Remember the context menu I've been talking about throughout this book? Well, you don't escape it in this chapter either. Windows XP takes a proactive approach when it comes to printing. All you need to do is right-click on the document and then choose Print from the context menu. Of course, you still have the usual Windows defaults for sending a document to the printer, including your application's Print menu.

Another method people use to send documents to the printer is to place a shortcut to the printer on the desktop. Then all you need to do to print a document is drag it to the printer you want to use and drop it. Of course, using this technique consumes some valuable desktop real estate, so use it only when required.

Managing Print Jobs

At one time, Microsoft provided different techniques for managing local and remote printing jobs. Windows XP makes this task much easier by providing a consistent interface that you'll find easy to use. No matter where your printer is located, you need to know how to manage the print jobs you create. For example, you might need to delete a print job or give another print job a higher priority.

Whenever you create a new print job, Windows XP displays a printer icon in the notification area of the Taskbar. Double-click this icon, and you see a printer management dialog box (the name varies by printer), like the one shown in Figure 14.5. You can also access this dialog box by double-clicking the printer entry in the Printers and Faxes dialog box.

FIGURE 14.5
Use this dialog box to manage your printer jobs for the printer whose name appears in the title bar.

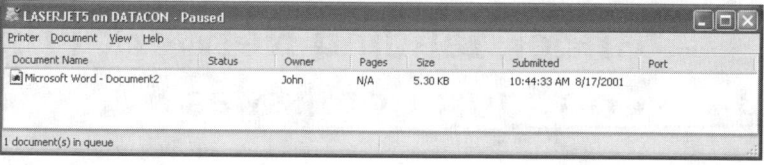

When you open the dialog box, you see a list of print jobs, if you have any printing. Each print job tells you the name of the file, the application that created it, the status (if the print job is paused), the owner name, the number of pages printed, the time the job was submitted, and the port number used to print the job.

This dialog box gives you lots of control over your print jobs and some control over the printer. The following File menu options are the ones you use most often:

- *Printing Preferences*   Changes the way the printer outputs documents. The resulting dialog box contains all of the preferences for your printer, such as printing in landscape or portrait mode, the paper and print quality, and printer options.

- *Pause Printing*   Pauses all print jobs going to the printer. If you want to pause an individual print job, you need to right-click the print job and select Pause from the context menu.

- *Cancel All Documents*   Removes all print jobs from the queue. Use this option if the printer is experiencing problems and you want to clear the print queue.

- *Properties*   Displays the Printer Properties dialog box. This dialog box gives you access to all of the physical printer settings, such as sharing, the printer port, security, and any advanced printer settings.

As mentioned earlier, you also have control over any documents you output to the printer. Right-click the document, and you'll notice that you can pause, cancel, or restart the print job. The restart option comes in handy if you've printed part of a document, had a printer jam, and want to restart the printer to get a clean printout.

If you right-click the document and select Properties, you see a simple Properties dialog box. The first entry in this dialog box allows you to enter the name of a person to notify when the print job is complete. Normally, Windows XP notifies the person who printed the document.

The priority slider gives your document a higher priority than other documents in the list. The base priority for all documents is 0, or the lowest priority.

The Schedule setting changes the time that the printer accepts the document for printing. Normally, the document doesn't have a time restriction, but you can use this setting to ensure that the print job doesn't complete after you leave work for the day.

Understanding Network Printer Configuration Issues

In most cases, local printers are easier to set up than network printers are. For example, you have direct input from a local printer. You can see what the printer is doing and how it responds to commands you send. In addition, the connection is simple; all you have between your machine and the printer is a single cable. If the printer refuses to work, you have only two culprits to consider: Either the printer is bad or the cable is bad. If you replace the printer cable and the problem persists, you know that something is wrong with the printer.

Most users view network printers as a complex mystery they have to deal with to get any work done. The output of their application meanders to the server, where it resides in a queue for some extended amount of time. The printer seems to output the document when it gets around to it rather than when the user needs it. In some cases, the output never appears. It disappears in the black whole known as the print server, never to see the light of day again.

Another problem that makes this situation worse is the way printer vendors view their products. I purchased a color inkjet printer and placed it on my network. Many frustrating hours later, I discovered that any attempt to use the vendor software would result in more frustration. The manual acted as if networks didn't exist, so any attempt to get help from the vendor was clearly useless. In short, I had to discover yet another way to extend the knowledge I already had in order to get this thing to work.

You can fight back; you don't have to feel like a second-class citizen stuck in a world of the vendor's creation. Of course, this may mean a little extra work installing the printer, but you find that the task goes quicker if you follow a logical process when doing it.

First, you want to make sure that your equipment works. It seems like the printer should work right out of the box, but I've found both bad cables and inoperative printers in the past. Install and test the printer as a local printer on the host machine, if possible. If not, install and test it as a local printer on another machine. Make sure that you run all vendor-supplied diagnostics, test the print driver, and use the test-page-printing feature. It's important to verify that everything is operational before you move the printer to the network.

Second, determine if any vendor-supplied software will cause problems on the network. For example, many color printers come with special alignment utilities and other gizmos that make life easier for the local user, but cause problems in a network setting. See if Windows XP provides a generic driver for the printer, and use that driver if nothing else. If you do run into connectivity problems, look at the proprietary software as the major culprit. However, don't discount the effects of using a vendor-supplied driver. Make sure that your system uses drivers and software designed for network use.

Third, after you test the printer, move it to the server (if necessary). In some cases, all you'll do is set the sharing options for the printer. However, when working with servers such as NetWare, you need to configure the printer for network use. I still use the older NetWare method of creating three objects for each printer: server, printer, and queue. However, Novell also provides Novell Distributed Print Services (NDPS), which is an improved system for larger networks. Make sure you check the documentation that comes with your server for any printer and print queue setup instructions.

Fourth, use My Network Places to locate the printer. If you can't see the printer in My Network Places, you can't attach to it using the Add Printer Wizard either. Check the printer sharing settings for problems first. If you shared the printer correctly, check the security settings. Often, Windows XP blocks all views of the printer if you don't set security correctly. Try rebooting the client as well. Sometimes, Windows XP fails to browse the network for new hardware, and a reboot will force the browse to take place.

Finally, verify that the client drivers will work in a network setting. Again, many vendor-supplied drivers work well locally, but don't work in a network setting. If you experience problems using the vendor-supplied drivers, try the Microsoft-supplied generic drivers. You'll likely lose some functionality using this approach, but at least you have access to the printer.

Windows and Fonts

Microsoft Windows provides you with more fonts than you'll ever use. Add a few applications to the mix, and you'll find your hard drive literally swimming with fonts that you never knew existed. The fact that each font consumes disk space means that you're wasting space for something you don't need—or do you? Therein lies the problem. If you don't know what fonts are stored on your system, you're unlikely to ever use them. The following sections tell you about Windows fonts. You learn about the differences between font types, learn how to install new fonts, and delete fonts you really don't want. We also discuss how to view and print fonts. In addition, you learn about the Euro font and see what makes ClearType so special.

Understanding Font Differences

Let's talk about font differences for a moment. Many of you realize that Microsoft has peddled TrueType fonts since the days of Windows 95. TrueType fonts offer the advantage of small file size because it uses vectors to represent the font as an outline. The use of vectors and "hinting" also means that TrueType fonts scale well. The biggest problem with TrueType is that it's proprietary, so you don't find it anywhere but in Windows.

Okay, let's discuss a few of the terms in the preceding paragraph. The first term is vector. Fonts come in two types: vector and raster. A *vector* font uses mathematical equations to describe what it should look like, but there's no physical representation of the font. A *raster* font uses actual bits in the form of a bitmap to create the image. The raster font uses a physical representation to store the font.

In the past, most people considered vector fonts a better choice if you had to represent many difference font sizes because you can't stretch a bitmap without distorting it. On the other hand, raster fonts provide a smooth appearance compared to the output of many older vector fonts.

Today, vector fonts use a technique called hinting to get rid of the display problems they once had. A *hint* is an extra piece of information that tells the vector font how to represent itself at different sizes. It might use one hint at small sizes, such as 6 point, another hint for medium sizes, and still other hints for large sizes. The point is that vector fonts commonly output a smooth display that rivals the hand-drawn raster fonts.

TrueType still has a problem. Although it scales well at different sizes and requires only a modicum of hard drive space, it's still proprietary. With this in mind, Microsoft and Adobe designed the OpenType fonts. These fonts have the same features as TrueType, but they aren't proprietary. You can read a detailed description of OpenType from the Adobe perspective at `http://www.adobe.com/type/opentype/main.html`. You'll find the Microsoft perspective of OpenType at `http://www.microsoft.com/typography/faq/faq9.htm`.

Installing Fonts

Just about everyone needs a new font from time to time. Getting ready for a presentation, introducing a new company policy, differentiating your work from someone else's, or simply needing a change can provide the motivation needed to install a new font. Use the following procedures to install a new font:

1. Open the Control Panel and double-click the Fonts icon. You should see an Explorer-style display, like the one shown in Figure 14.6, that enables you to view all of the fonts installed on your machine.

FIGURE 14.6
Windows XP tells you the name and type of fonts you've installed on your system.

Note: Notice that the fonts displayed in Figure 14.6 use three different icons. (You may see even more, depending on the fonts you've installed on your system.) Any font shown with an "A" icon is a raster font. It offers fixed font sizes, and Windows XP generally disallows any scaling beyond the font capability. Fonts shown with a stylized "TT" are proprietary TrueType fonts. Finally, fonts with an "O" in the center are OpenType fonts. Note that vendors sign many OpenType fonts, which means that a cracker can't hide viruses in them. Any change in the font signature shows up as an error when you attempt to use the font.

2. Choose File | Install New Font to display the Add Fonts dialog box, shown in Figure 14.7. It may take a while to see the files on the file list because Windows XP must read them from the source location you choose. A progress indicator tells how far the font reading has progressed.

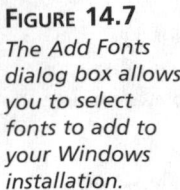

FIGURE 14.7
The Add Fonts dialog box allows you to select fonts to add to your Windows installation.

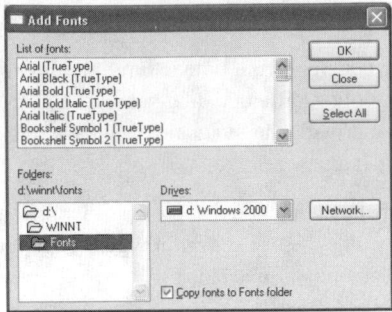

3. Browse your hard disk, floppy disk, or CD-ROM drive until you find the fonts you want to install. You must create a drive mapping to install fonts from a network. Click Network to create new drive mappings as needed. Windows XP normally copies the new fonts to your local Fonts folder. In some cases, you can also choose to create a pointer to the font and save disk space.

4. Highlight the desired fonts and click OK. Windows XP displays a progress indicator as it installs the fonts for you. When the Install Font Progress dialog box disappears, you see the new fonts in your Fonts folder.

Removing Fonts

Removing fonts is easy under Windows XP. All you do is open the Fonts folder (either through Explorer or by double-clicking the Fonts applet in Control Panel), select the fonts you want to remove, and press the Delete key. It's that easy.

You need to observe a few precautions. First and foremost, don't erase any font you're not sure of. Windows XP requires some fonts for system use, and erasing them could cause problems. Second, if you do erase a font, make sure that you don't need it any more or that you have a copy stored somewhere. For example, you won't want to erase Arial because Windows XP uses it for many displays. Likewise, you'll want to exercise care erasing fixed fonts (those with the letter A as an icon) because Windows XP uses them for dialog boxes and the command prompt.

Viewing and Printing Fonts

The interface in the Fonts folder might be Explorer, but the options are different. The View menu contains some unique features that you'll want to use to see your fonts. I'm not talking about the files themselves, but rather the fonts. Let me show you want I mean. Open Control Panel and double-click the Fonts applet. Open the View menu. Notice that Explorer now sports some new View options.

The List Fonts By Similarity option is the one I like. It enables you to see which fonts you could substitute for something else. For example, you might like the font you're using for a particular purpose, but want a slightly different effect. You could use this option to find the closest match in your directory or on a CD-ROM full of fonts. Figure 14.8 shows a typical example. Notice that the Fonts folder shows which fonts match the target font closely; the folder also tells which fonts match only a little. The List Fonts By Similarity to field contains the name of the font you want to match.

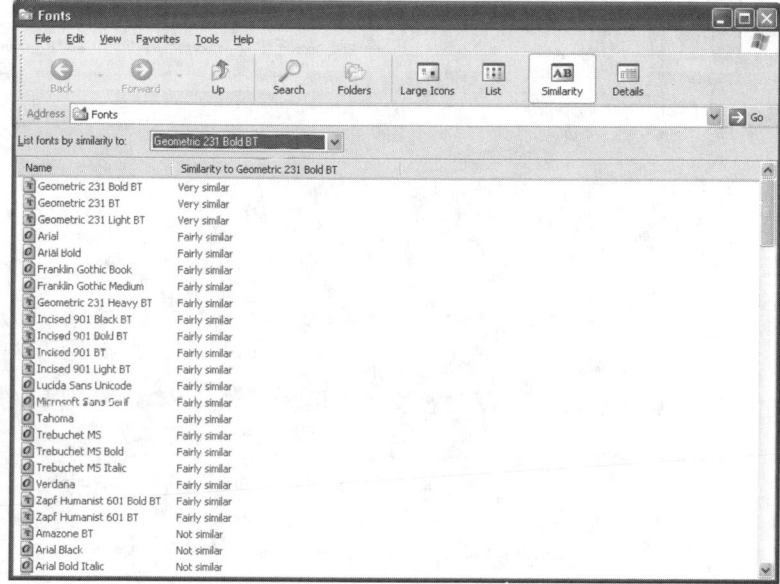

Another handy view selection is the Hide Variations option. You can use it with any of the display formats to hide the different files required to create a complete font family. For example, if you turn on this option, you'll see only one Arial font, even though the directory contains four Arial font files. Variations typically include bold, italic, and bold italic versions of the font.

To display a font, just double-click it. You also can use the Open option on the context menu. Figure 14.9 shows a typical example of a font display. Notice that you can see a sample of most common characters. In addition, this display presents statistics about the font, such as the amount of space it consumes on disk.

> **Tip:** You may not find all of the capabilities you need in the standard Windows font viewer. A wealth of third-party applications help you to do more with a font file than simply view it. For example, Font Impressions (http://www.fontimpressions.8m.com/) allows you to work with fonts using an Explorer-type display. This program also doubles as a Character Map–type program by allowing you to copy special characters to applications like Word. This product works with TrueType and PostScript fonts. Another great shareware utility is Printer's Apprentice. Like Font Impressions, this product works with a variety of font formats. The feature that makes Printer's Apprentice unique is that it can look at uninstalled fonts on CDs. This allows you to see the font before you install it. You can find out more about Printer's Apprentice at: http://www.loseyourmind.com/.

FIGURE 14.9
*The font display
tells you about
the font and
shows how it will
appear onscreen
and in print.*

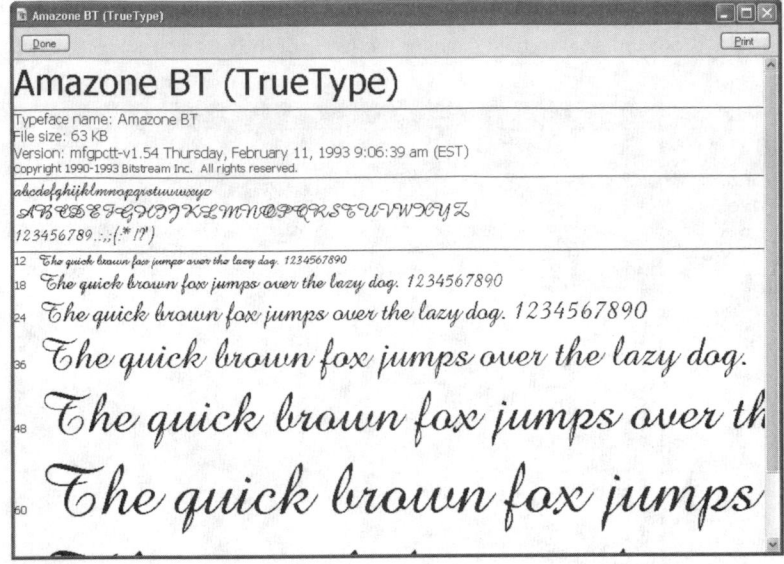

It's easy to print a sample of a font. All you need to do is right-click and select Print from the context menu. As an alternative, you can always click the Print button when viewing the font or use the File | Print command.

Working with the Euro Font

The European Union has created a common currency known as the *euro*. It uses a symbol that looks like this €" (a *C* with two lines through the center). This common currency makes it easier to buy things from Europe because you don't have to worry as much about the currency used by individual countries. However, the creation of the euro also means that we have a new monetary symbol to add to the collection, which means that the font files on your machine have to be changed as well.

> **Tip:** The euro means many changes for businesses, especially those that deal with Europe in some way. You can find out more about these effects and how the euro is being introduced by checking the €uro Web site at `http://europa.eu.int/euro/html/entry.html`. Interestingly enough, this Web site comes in a wealth of languages, making it easy to find the information you need in the language you speak. Microsoft also has support of the euro for older versions of the Windows operating system. Check `http://www.microsoft.com/windows/euro.asp` for details.

Windows XP comes with several font files that contain the euro symbol, including Arial, Courier, Times New Roman, and Tahoma. If you're not lucky enough to own Windows XP or you need more fonts than Windows XP provides, you can download a core set of fonts from `http://www.microsoft.com/typography/fontpack/default.htm`.

Accessing the euro character is relatively easy. All you need to do is press the Alt key and then type **0128** on the numeric keypad. (Don't use the numbers at the top of the keyboard—you must use the keypad.) Remember to include the 0 in the 0128; otherwise, you don't get the euro symbol as anticipated.

You can also use the Character Map application that comes with Windows to find the euro symbol. Just select the euro character in the character list, click Select, and then click Copy. Following this sequence places the euro symbol on the Clipboard, where you can copy it into documents as needed.

Understanding How Windows Matches Fonts

Windows uses something called the font-matching table to find a replacement font if the one you request isn't available. The *font-matching table* isn't actually a table; it's an algorithm that Windows XP uses to match fonts. Windows uses the following criteria to find a matching font: the character set, variable versus fixed pitch, family, typeface name, height, width, weight, slant, underline, and strikethrough.

Windows XP always replaces a TrueType font with another TrueType font or OpenType, even if a raster or vector font is a closer match. This enables your application to maintain the flexibility that TrueType and OpenType provides.

If the font you're trying to use is either a vector or raster font, Windows XP uses some additional sources to obtain a good match. These sources include the printer ROM font, printer cartridge slot font, downloadable soft font, and TrueType font.

Understanding ClearType

Let me tell you up front that ClearType is a great feature if you're using a laptop, but the worst thing you can do to a desktop machine using a CRT. The ClearType technology is another way to smooth fonts so that they look clearer. Microsoft specifically designed this feature for flat-screen monitors because these monitors don't react well to the standard Windows XP smoothing technique. What many people get when they use ClearType on a standard monitor is a headache. The technology appears fuzzy on a CRT, but looks clear on a flat-screen display. The difference is due to the methods the two devices use to present information.

> **Tip:** Technical analysis of ClearType is still a little hard to find as of this writing. However, if you want to see a full-blown Microsoft description of how ClearType works at the pixel level, check out http://research.microsoft.com/~jplatt/cleartype/. You can also find a ClearType demonstration (works well only on a flat-screen display) at http://research.microsoft.com/~jplatt/cleartype/samples.html.
>
> If you want something more than the Microsoft view on this technology, you'll find two good alternative write-ups on the Internet. If you want the plain-
>
> *(continues)*

English description of ClearType, try `http://grc.com/cleartype.htm`. You can find an extremely technical (and somewhat heated) discussion of the technology at `http://www.geocities.com/SiliconValley/Ridge/6664/ClearType.html`.

This second discussion points out that Microsoft is again borrowing well-known technology and calling it new. Whether it's new is up to you, but ClearType is "clearly" built on solid technology.

Adding ClearType to your display is easy. The following steps show you how:

1. Right-click the Desktop and choose Properties.
2. Select the Appearance tab and click Effects. You see the Effects dialog box.
3. Check the Use the Following Method to Smooth Edges of Screen Fonts option.
4. Select the ClearType option from the drop-down list box.
5. Click OK twice to clear both dialog boxes. You should see a difference in display quality. If not, try rebooting your machine.

On Your Own

Try the drag-and-drop method of printing. To begin, place a shortcut to your printer on the Desktop. Drag a file using your mouse pointer to the Printer icon and drop it.

Try creating special ports for your local printer. For example, try using the local file approach. You'll find that applications output to a local file much faster than to a printer port. Using this technique enables you to print the output and then send it to the printer as a background task. You can continue to work undisturbed.

This chapter showed you how to install fonts. Many graphics programs include additional fonts. Use information in the "Windows and Fonts" section of the chapter to install the set of fonts that get the job done for you.

Look in your \FONTS folder to see whether you can identify the various types of fonts that Windows 98 supports. How can you tell them apart? What purpose does each kind of font serve?

Install several versions of your printer, each with different settings. Try these new installations for several weeks to see whether you notice the additional ease of use that several pseudo-printers can provide. Also, try the various Print settings to see whether you notice variations in print speed and output quality that I mentioned earlier.

If you own a laptop machine, try using the new ClearType font smoothing technology. Compare the screen with what you see using standard font smoothing and no font smoothing. Most flat-screen users see a slight but noticeable difference in screen quality that can reduce eye stress.

Mice and Keyboards

The keyboard has been the main tool for data input from the beginning of personal computers. Although the keyboard remains almost unchanged from the early days, the few changes are notable.

The Microsoft Natural Keyboard (and others like it) attempts to prevent the problems people encounter with carpal tunnel syndrome and other types of repetitive-stress injury. In addition, some keyboards attempt to solve accessibility problems. Others use unique layouts, such as the Dvorak layout, used to enhance typing speed and reduce repetitive-stress injuries. (The Dvorak layout uses a key arrangement that reduced repetitive stress injuries and can increase typing speed.)

Some keyboards, such as those from Logitech, try to solve productivity problems. This keyboard contains extra buttons that make your Web surfing experience easier. In addition, some keyboards use a radio frequency (RF) connection to the computer, allowing the user to dispense with the cord. This means a user can sit in any position and continue to type.

The mouse, on the other hand, has changed more drastically in appearance. It started out looking like a bar of soap, but today's versions are all shaped to fit the palm of your hand and some use special materials to reduce fatigue. Every vendor uses a different human for measurement, as reflected in the size and shape variations of this new breed of rodent.

At least manufacturers seem to have settled on two or three mouse buttons. If you've been around long enough, you probably remember the multibutton monstrosities some companies originally introduced. Of course, vendors like Logitech have improved the mouse by adding scroll wheels and thumb buttons. Mice, like keyboards, now employ RF connections, making it easy to work from just about any position.

Some people don't like the mouse, so they use a trackball instead. The trackball stays in a fixed position on your desk. To move the mouse cursor around, you move a little ball on the top of the trackball. The trackball provides two or three buttons, just like the mouse. For many people, the trackball provides an extra measure of flexibility and provides precise cursor movement not available when using a mouse.

Windows XP has joined the new-and-improved input device bandwagon. The following sections provide a tour of the great and not-so-great mouse and keyboard improvements in Windows XP. In addition, we'll look at the old standby features you'll find in most versions of Windows. Make sure you spend some time looking at Microsoft Accessibility information. This new feature is part of Windows XP.

Multilingual Support

Windows is the most popular desktop operating system built today, so it's not surprising that Windows comes with a variety of language options. Microsoft improves multilingual support with every version of Windows. During the early days of Windows, you needed to be a guru and hand-edit your files to add support for more than one language. Today, you'll find that you can add and remove support without much trouble at all.

The following sections discuss multilingual support in Windows XP. Of course, this only affects the way your keyboard works. You also need to know about fonts so that the language features display properly. Although most of the fonts provided with Windows XP work fine in a multilingual environment, you want to verify that the font you use has the required features. See the "Windows and Fonts" section of Chapter 14 for additional details.

Installing a New Language Using the Keyboard Applet

Before you can use a new language, you have to install support for it under Windows XP. This also holds true for keyboard layouts that differ from the one you have installed now. Fortunately, multilingual support in Windows XP is convenient and you don't have to memorize code page numbers. Installing a new keyboard language takes just a few clicks. The following steps explain how to install a new language on your machine:

1. Open the Control Panel. Double-click the Regional and Language Options applet and select the Languages tab. Click Details. You should see a dialog box similar to the one shown in Figure 15.1. Note that English is the only language listed in the Installed Services field. This field also tells you the type of English used (United States) and the keyboard layout (United States). This tab also enables you to select a default language using the Default Input Language field.

2. Click the Add button to display the Add Input Language dialog box. It's important to consider which version of a language to choose. English is a good example. I have United States English installed. Other forms of English might require a different keyboard layout. Pressing Shift+4, for example, could produce a pound symbol rather than a dollar sign. The choice of language affects the default Windows selections for monetary and numeric format.

FIGURE 15.1

The Language tab of the Keyboard Properties dialog box enables you to select one or more languages for your computer.

3. Select a language and a keyboard layout. Click OK. You should see the new language added to the Language field. Completing this process also enables several other options. For example, you can configure the Language Bar and choose control keys for switching between languages. In addition, you can remove one of the languages and set a default language.

4. Select a default language by selecting it in the Default Input Language field. Windows XP will highlight the default language of the keyboard layout in the Installed Services field.

5. Click Language Bar. You'll see a Language Bar Settings dialog box, like the one shown in Figure 15.2. The Language Bar is a new Windows XP feature that enables you to select a language without opening the Regional and Language Settings dialog box. Unlike the International icon of old, the Language Bar usually resides in the upper-right corner of the screen. You can access it from the Desktop or within most applications. (The Language Bar appears in the title bar, near the Minimize button.)

FIGURE 15.2

The Language Bar is a new Windows XP feature that makes selecting a language easy.

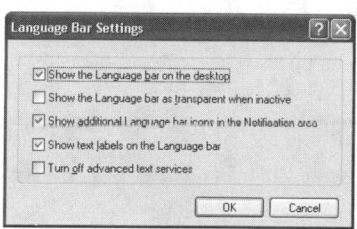

6. Select one or more of the Language Bar options. You must clear the Turn Off Advanced Text Services option before the options are displayed. Click OK. In most cases, you'll see the effects of the changes you made immediately. Sometimes, you need to restart your applications or Windows to see the changes.

7. Click Key Settings. You'll see the Advanced Key Settings dialog box, shown in Figure 15.3. Use this dialog box to change the method used to switch languages. Windows XP defines Left Alt+Shift as the key combination to toggle between languages by default. You need to assign key combinations to the specific languages or layouts (if desired) by clicking Change Key Sequence. Once you enable and set the key combination you want to use, click OK, and it will appear in the Advanced Key Settings dialog box.

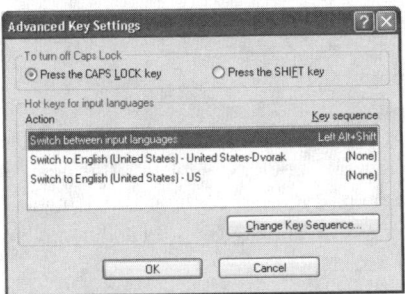

Figure 15.3
The Advanced Key Settings dialog box changes the control-key combinations used to switch languages.

8. Select any required key settings and then click OK. Click OK to close the Text Services and Input Languages dialog box. Click OK again to close the Regional and Language Options dialog box. In most cases, you can access the new language immediately.

Even if you change the keyboard language and layout, Windows XP doesn't display prompts in the language you select. The change only affects how the keyboard reacts and helps Windows XP provide better input for other configuration selections.

Removing a Language

You might need to remove a language from your list at some time. For example, Microsoft could come out with an updated layout that makes using the language easier. The following steps show how to remove a language:

1. Open the Control Panel. Double-click the Regional and Language Options applet and select the Languages tab. Click Details. You should see a dialog box similar to the one shown in Figure 15.1.

2. Highlight the language or keyboard layout you want to remove. Click Remove to delete the language from the Installed Services list.

3. Click OK twice to complete the action.

Accessing a Language from the Taskbar or Language Bar

Windows XP provides two methods for accessing your language. The first is to use the new method of using the Language Bar. A second method is to start the International applet. This applet is found in previous versions of Windows XP and is likely provided for compatibility purposes, which means it may not stay around for much longer.

Using the Language Bar is easy. Just click the displayed language, and you see a list of available options, as shown in Figure 15.4. Choose a language from the list, and it becomes your default language.

FIGURE 15.4

The Language Bar usually appears in the right side of the title bar, but you can move it as needed.

You can also minimize the Language Bar to the Taskbar, display an Options menu, and ask for help. The Options menu contains entries for turning the Help icon on and off, displaying the Text Services and Input Languages dialog box, and resetting Windows XP to its default state.

For many people, using the International icon is an easier and less space-consuming method of changing languages. It appears in the notification area of the Taskbar rather than take space in other areas of the display, as shown in Figure 15.5. Using the International icon means starting INTERNAT.EXE from the Run dialog box. The icon appears in the notification area of the Taskbar. (Note that some people may not find INTERNAT.EXE on their hard drive, but you can use the INTERNAT.EXE found on Windows 2000 systems.)

FIGURE 15.5

Many users prefer the International icon, which is the older method of selecting a language.

You can use the International icon to determine which language is in use. Each language has a two-character abbreviation, as shown in Figure 15.5, that's used in the Taskbar. The icon in the figure shows that I have the English language installed. As with other icons on the Taskbar, you can momentarily hold your mouse cursor over the International icon to display the full name of the language and keyboard layout in use.

Click the International icon to display a list of languages installed on the machine. The list preceded each entry with its two-digit abbreviation. This is one way to determine which language you're using if you forget what the abbreviation on the icon means. To select a new language, just click it as you would with any other menu.

Right-clicking the International icon brings up a context menu containing two entries: What's This? and Properties. In adding the What's This? option, Microsoft apparently thought users would not be able to figure out this icon for themselves. At least the entry helps those who are just beginning to use Windows XP.

The Properties option in the context menu acts just as you would expect. It takes you to the Regional and Language Options dialog box, previously discussed. Although it automatically displays the Regional Options tab, you can switch to other tabs as necessary.

Configuring Your Keyboard

Keyboards come in all shapes and sizes today. You'll find everything from 83- to 109-key keyboards (and beyond). Vendors make keyboards with special features, such as Internet buttons and keyboards that fold up for use with personal digital assistants (PDAs). The connectors used with keyboards vary as well. Some people still use the ancient DIN 5-pin connector, but the two most popular connections now are the PS/2 and USB connectors.

> **Tip:** Many USB keyboards and mice come with a dual adapter for PS/2 use. It pays to get this dual adapter because Windows doesn't always recognize USB input devices, for a number of reasons. The problem was significant enough that Microsoft created a Knowledge Base article to discuss it for Windows 98 (http://support.microsoft.com/support/kb/articles/Q206/0/02.ASP). This same advice works for Windows XP.

Some keyboards vary by feel. I prefer the kind that uses switches because it has a nice solid feel when you type. Some people prefer a keyboard with a "mushy" feel because that's what they're used to using. In some cases, a good keyboard is so important that people go to extremes to use one. For example, I found one Web site that shows how to use a Windows USB keyboard on a Macintosh (http://207.208.148.74/12-27-99.shtml).

The following sections describe keyboard configuration issues. I don't plan to delve into absurd-looking keyboard lookalikes or amaze you with a description of strange keyboard-configuration problems. However, you learn enough to work with all standard keyboards and many keyboards with special features.

Standard Keyboard Configuration

For those of you who have upgraded from previous versions of Windows, Microsoft decided to separate the keyboard from language issues in Windows XP. The Keyboard applet contains only two tabs now. The Speed tab, shown in Figure 15.6, contains the main selections regarding keyboard setup. On this tab, you can specify how the keyboard will react to your key presses.

FIGURE 15.6
The Speed tab contains options to help the keyboard adjust to your typing habits.

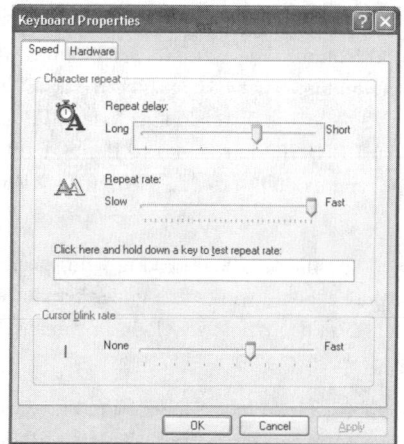

> **Tip:** Make sure that you get the right kind of keyboard plug when you buy a new keyboard. Three kinds of plugs are now in use. The first is a large DIN 5-Pin model that's used on older machines. The second is a smaller, PS/2–style 6-pin plug that's used on many new machines because it requires less space. (Some people also refer to this type as a Mini-DIN 6-Pin.) The third type is the newer USB connection.
>
> The problem of figuring out which plug to use happens frequently enough that many keyboard vendors attach one type of plug to the end of the keyboard cable and then include an adapter for the other kind of plug. This is the best choice if you aren't sure about what kind of connector you have on your machine. The size of the two DIN connectors is different enough that you can't make a mistake once you compare the plug on the end of your keyboard against the connector for the machine you're using. You can see a picture of the two DIN connectors at http://www.mouse.demon.nl/ckp/misc/conchart.htm.

The Repeat Delay setting adjusts how long the keyboard waits before it starts to repeat keys. If this value is too short, you might have to undo excess keystrokes.

The Repeat Rate setting adjusts how fast the characters repeat across the screen. Setting a slower rate helps you to control repeated keys better. Microsoft provides a test area to check the combination of settings. Make sure that you actually try the keyboard settings before you make big changes in them.

Use the Cursor Blink Rate setting to change how many times the edit cursor blinks per second. Some people prefer a fast rate, and others like it a bit slower. Use a slower rate on portable machines rather than on desktop machines because the displays on portable machines take longer to react.

Keyboards with Special Features

Some keyboards have special features. For example, my Logitech Internet Keyboard provides a special set of Internet buttons that make surfing much faster. To make the special features work, you need vendor-specific drivers and software. For example, the Logitech keyboard installs as a standard 101-/102-key keyboard if you don't supply the special driver. Unfortunately, many vendors don't provide a Windows XP version of their product yet.

Many users run into some odd problems when working with special keyboards under Windows XP. Just because the keyboard works fine under Windows 9x or Windows NT/2000 doesn't mean it works under Windows XP. In fact, many of the keyboards with special features don't work properly.

Some problems are nearly impossible to locate unless you know what to look for. If the vendor doesn't sign the driver for whatever reason, Windows XP doesn't install it during a standard setup. You see the management software install, but the driver itself doesn't install. Windows XP doesn't tell you about the problem either. The only way to verify this problem is to check the Hardware tab of the Keyboard Properties dialog box or to check the Keyboard entry in Device Manager.

You can still install the keyboard driver manually by selecting Update Driver from the Driver tab of the <Keyboard Name> Properties dialog box. Access this dialog box by clicking Properties in the Keyboard Properties dialog box. When you see the Hardware Update Wizard, choose the Install from a List or Specific Location (Advanced) option. Click Next. Select the Don't Search, I Will Choose the Driver to Install option. Click Next. Use the Have Disk option to select the driver manually from the vendor-supplied disk. In many cases, the keyboard will work as anticipated once you complete the driver installation.

At least a few people report that installing the special driver doesn't work. The special buttons activate, but the keys don't work as anticipated. For example, you might press one key and see the Calculator utility instead of the anticipated action. This tells you that the keyboard is acting like a Microsoft keyboard. Unfortunately, the best thing you can do is unload the driver and management software and wait for the vendor to release another version of the driver.

Another problem is that the keyboard works properly, but you can't manage it. The management tabs you were expecting to see in the Keyboard applet don't appear after installation. In some cases, rebooting the machine fixes this problem. However, in other cases, you may have to live with the vendor's default settings until the vendor releases another version of the driver and management software.

Configuring Your Mouse

The mouse started out as an optional feature in DOS, and you could navigate early versions of Windows without one. Today, however, a mouse is a required part of Windows. To use Windows, you have to have a mouse because some tasks are difficult or impossible to perform without one. Although you can still move around and control many applications without a mouse, it's important to realize that keyboard shortcuts only go so far.

Like keyboards, mice come in several shapes and sizes. In fact, the shape part is almost staggering. My mouse looks outright strange, yet provides a comfortable grip for long use. You find that vendors use materials other than plastic to allow for longer use. Many mice include a rubber gripping area.

Most vendors have settled on two or three standard buttons for their mice. However, some mice feature a thumb button to replace the Enter key, and others feature a mouse wheel for scrolling through text. A few mice feature both the mouse wheel and the center button, allowing you to perform additional tasks using your rodent.

Mice can use three different connections, and a few vendors provide adapters for all three as part of the package. The serial port connection is the oldest form of mouse connector and usually the most reliable. The PS/2 connection is easier to use and offers nearly the same level of reliability as the serial port. The USB connector is the new kid on the block and suffers from compatibility problems (see the "Working with a USB Mouse" section for details).

Now that you have some idea of what a mouse could look like, let's look at some details. The following sections show you how to configure your mouse. They also discuss special issues that mouse users have to consider. For example, some mice require special configuration when used on a laptop.

Standard Mouse Configuration

Just as you should configure your keyboard for optimum performance, you should do the same for your mouse. (This section assumes that you're using the default Windows XP drivers; some third-party drivers replace all or part of the standard mouse applet.) To configure your mouse, open the Mouse Properties dialog box by double-clicking the Mouse applet in the Control Panel. You see the Mouse Properties dialog box, as shown in Figure 15.7. The following sections tell you what each tab means.

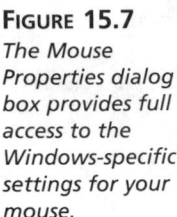

FIGURE 15.7
The Mouse Properties dialog box provides full access to the Windows-specific settings for your mouse.

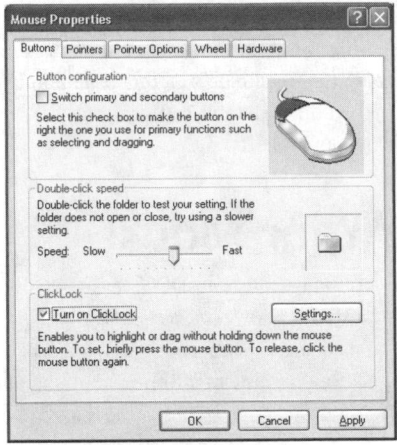

Buttons Tab

The Buttons tab helps you configure the mouse physically. The first group of settings on the Buttons tab enables you to reverse your mouse buttons for left-handed use. (Windows XP defaults to a right-handed installation.)

The second group enables you to change the double-click speed. Your mouse's double-click speed is important. If it's set too slow, you might double-click without intending to. This is especially annoying in graphics programs because you move the mouse and click to select items. Setting this value too fast is an exercise in frustration because Windows doesn't wait long enough for you to double-click things. The test area enables you to practice using this setting. A folder alternately opens and closes when you double-click.

The Turn on ClickLock setting (the third group) is new for Windows XP. Select this option, and you can drag your mouse without holding the left button down (this feature doesn't work with the right mouse button). Simply click for a second or two, and the button "locks" into place. Move the mouse where you want to stop dragging, click again, and the mouse button unlocks. Windows XP highlights or selects the area where you dragged the mouse. Click settings to adjust the length of time you must hold the button down before the mouse button locks.

Pointers Tab

The Pointers tab enables you to change the type of mouse pointer used to indicate a specific event. Windows XP provides a few "fancy" cursors, such as the 3D versions that give the screen a feeling of depth. In addition to static cursors, Windows XP also provides animated cursors that move.

The upper section of this tab enables you to save and load various mouse schemes. Think of a mouse scheme as you would a color scheme in previous versions of Windows. Use the Scheme list box to select a previously saved scheme. Clicking the Save As button displays a dialog box you can use to enter the name of a new scheme.

Tip: Windows XP provides a wealth of mouse pointers, including some extra-large ones. Microsoft designed the extra-large pointers for use with some of the Accessibility options. They also come in handy for laptops (on which seeing the cursor can be a real chore) and presentations (a larger-than-normal cursor helps to make your point). Tired eyes also can benefit from the use of large, easy-to-see cursors.

The bottom section of the Pointers tab displays the actual mouse pointers. The purpose of each pointer is self-explanatory. To change a cursor, highlight it and click Browse. Windows displays the Browse dialog box, which contains a list of cursors in the Cursors folder (found within the main Windows folder). Double-click the cursor you want. Windows replaces the current cursor with the one you double-clicked.

This dialog box also displays a preview of the cursor. Animated cursors appear to move within the Preview box. This shows how they'll look when you use them in an application or on the Windows desktop. If you select a cursor by accident and want to return to the default setting, click the Use Default button at the bottom of the Pointers page.

Pointer Options Tab

The Pointer Options tab appears in Figure 15.8. As you can see, it consists of two sliders and several check boxes, which affect the appearance of your mouse onscreen. The slider at the top of the page enables you to set the pointer speed. Setting the speed too fast can cause jerky cursor movement and can make it difficult to control operations such as drawing. If you set the speed too slow, however, you have to make a large movement with the mouse to see a small movement onscreen.

The Enhanced Pointer Precision option controls the precision of the mouse. Check this option and the mouse will move smaller increments for a given amount of movement on the mouse pad. The mouse also stops faster. Using this option is great if you use a mouse for drawing, but can become a problem for tasks such as word processing.

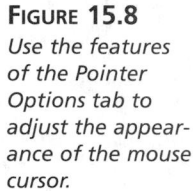

FIGURE 15.8
Use the features of the Pointer Options tab to adjust the appearance of the mouse cursor.

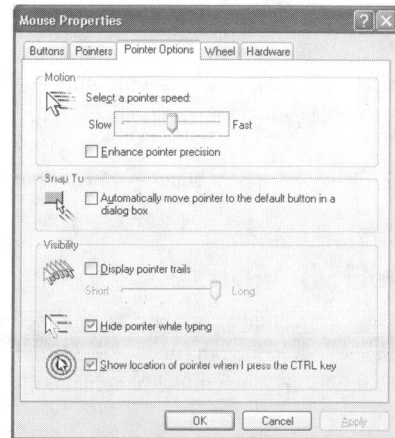

The middle section of the Pointer Options tab contains a single option. Check the Snap To option, and the mouse will automatically move to the default button of any dialog box you open. This comes in handy when using a mouse on a laptop because it's often hard to find the mouse when you need it.

The bottom section of the Pointer Options tab controls the visibility of the mouse. Check the Display Pointer Trails option, and Windows XP provides pointer trails. A pointer trail isn't what most people envision it to be. Windows produces many copies of the pointer to track the movements you make with the mouse. These additional pointers comprise the pointer trail. The slider controls the length of the trail, and the check box turns the option on or off. The Hide Pointer While Typing option is nice because the mouse often gets in the way while word processing. The mouse cursor reappears the second you move the mouse. The final option displays a "bulls-eye" of circles around the mouse cursor when you press the Ctrl key.

Wheel Tab

For those of you who are lucky enough to have a wheel mouse, the Wheel tab helps you control its functionality by enabling you to choose the number of lines to scroll with each "click" of the wheel. You can choose to scroll a single line, multiple lines, or move a whole screen at a time. Most users find that moving a single line at a time is too slow and that moving a screen at a time is too fast. The default setting works well in most cases.

> **Tip:** Many wheel mice include a center button that's part of the wheel. Click this button by pressing down on the wheel. You'll see the mouse cursor change into a double arrow. Move the cursor up and the page will smooth-scroll up. Likewise, move the cursor down and the page will smooth-scroll down. The further you move the mouse from center, the faster the page will smooth-scroll. This feature is especially handy when you want to read something online and don't want to use the wheel constantly.

Hardware Tab

The hardware tab contains information about your mouse and two buttons. Click Troubleshoot, and Windows XP opens the mouse troubleshooting section of the Help and Support Center. This option provides guided instructions for fixing many mouse problems. Click Properties, and you see the <Mouse Name> Properties dialog box of the Device Manager. You can use these settings to change your mouse driver or perform other tasks.

Working with a USB Mouse

The USB mouse is troublesome for a number of reasons. For one thing, the USB specification is still in a state of change. A vendor can follow the 1.0, 1.1, or 2.0 specifications. In addition, the early specifications left much to the imagination, so vendors didn't provide consistent implementations. You'll want to check the "Universal Serial Bus (USB)" section of Chapter 9 for details on USB compatibility problems.

The USB mouse can also cause problems. Some vendors don't follow USB specifications closely enough when designing the mouse. In addition, the special software you get with your mouse often lacks the functionality required by Windows XP. In this case, using the generic Windows XP driver is actually better despite the loss of some mouse features.

Interestingly enough, many mice don't get along with other devices, especially PDAs. Several systems I've worked with have this problem, and I've heard of many other people complaining of the same thing. In this case, the only thing you can do is hope your mouse has an adapter. Fix the problem by plugging it into either a serial or PS/2 port. Generally, you find that the serial or PS/2 port is more stable and less likely to cause installation problems.

Some advocates of the USB solution cite mouse performance as the reason to switch. So far, I haven't seen anyone who is able to move a mouse fast enough to tax the bandwidth of even a serial connection, much less a PS/2 or USB connection. Most users don't see any different using a mouse with a USB, serial, or PS/2 connection.

Special Laptop Configuration Considerations

Laptop computers have special needs when it comes to the mouse. There isn't a good place to put a mouse when using a laptop, especially when you're on an airplane. Some laptop vendors take care of this problem by incorporating a special pointing device into the keyboard area. Other times, you can use a trackball that rides along the side of the case. Whatever mouse you use on the road, it likely requires some special configuration. (The options you see depend on the laptop vendor and the type of mouse you've installed.) As with a desktop machine, you can access the Mouse Properties dialog box on a laptop by double-clicking the Mouse applet in the Control Panel.

The first tab you're likely to see is the Quick Setup tab. (The tab use other names such as TrackPoint—the features also vary by vendor.) This tab helps you make quick transitions between mouse setups. Unlike with a desktop machine, you can't rely on your laptop's environment staying the same. For that matter, you can't even be certain you'll use the same mouse from session to session. You might prefer to use a standard mouse at the office, another standard mouse at home, and the built-in mouse on the road. Configuring a laptop mouse isn't even close to configuring a desktop machine. (Because each mouse configuration is different, you should rely on vendor documentation to set it up.)

Note: Most vendors provide the Orientation tab of the Mouse Properties dialog box in standard laptop installations. Custom pointing-device drivers might not include this tab, but may provide an alternative if you need to be able to change the orientation of your mouse. In addition, Windows XP doesn't appear to provide the Orientation tab, so you need to rely on custom vendor software if the ability to change the orientation of your mouse is important.

The Orientation tab of the Mouse Properties dialog box addresses another problem with laptops. A trackball user, for example, might need to switch the trackball from one side of the laptop to the other during a trip because his seat is next to a window and there isn't room to move. To make this switch, click the Set Orientation button. Windows XP asks you to move the balloon toward the clouds at the top of the screen. Moving the trackball adjusts the orientation as necessary to keep mouse movement the same as it normally is when you use a standard mouse. In other words, moving the mouse up actually moves the cursor toward the top of the screen. If you don't move the mouse cursor in a straight line, Windows displays an error message. Try again and Windows XP will set the orientation for you.

Most people use more than one mouse with their laptops. Unlike other hardware components, Windows XP doesn't automatically register a mouse change—especially if your laptop has a built-in mouse. This is why the Devices tab of the Mouse Properties dialog box is important. It enables you to either add a new mouse device or select an existing one.

To select an existing mouse device, select it from the drop-down list and then click Apply. Make sure that you plug the mouse in before you do this, or you might find yourself without a functional pointer device. (Most laptop software searches for the pointing device before switching over, but you can't be sure that it will.)

To add a new device, click the Add Device button. You'll first see a warning message. As stated in the message, you usually can plug in a serial mouse while the machine is running. If you try to plug in a PS/2 port mouse while the machine is running, however, there's a good chance you'll damage it. Always shut the machine down first, and then plug in the PS/2 mouse. After you see this warning message, you can click OK to start the search for a new pointing device. If Windows XP finds a new mouse, it takes you through the setup and configuration process.

Human Interface Device (HID) Issues

If you use a USB input device of any kind, you see a Human Interface Devices (HID) folder in the Device Manager. The device entries you see add to those that the device normally uses. A USB mouse has an entry in the Mice and other pointing devices folder as well as the Human Interface Devices folder.

The Human Interface Device (HID) is a platform independent way of looking at USB input devices. Most large operating systems, including Linux, support HID today. Microsoft provides HID support in Windows 98, Windows 2000, and Windows XP. HID support in Windows enables both hardware and software developer to create devices and drivers with greater ease and functionality. You can read the detailed description of how HID works at http://www.microsoft.com/hwdev/desinit/WDMINput.HTM.

Access for Users with Disabilities

Windows XP provides special access features for people with disabilities. However, I look at them as tools for everyone. We all get tired and have special needs from time to time. A higher-contrast screen helps everyone with tired eyes, and many people find using the cursor keys more precise than a mouse. It pays for everyone to know about the availability of these tools.

We already discussed the shortcut keys provided for the Accessibility options, in the "Startups from the Keyboard" section in Chapter 6, so I don't discuss them again here. Instead, the following sections discuss how you can use these features to enhance productivity. To look at these features, open the Control Panel and double-click the Accessibility Options applet.

The Accessibility Settings Wizard

You access the Accessibility Wizard in the Start\Programs\Accessories\Accessibility folder. The following procedure takes you through a typical configuration scenario:

1. Click Next to get past the Welcome screen. The second screen of the Accessibility Settings Wizard asks how well you can see the display. You can choose from normal or large text. A third option enables you to combine large text with the Microsoft Magnifier for maximum display size.

2. Click Next, and you'll see a screen that summarizes the changes the Accessibility Settings Wizard will make to your display.

3. Click Next to make those changes and continue with the configuration process. The wizard next asks you to specify which areas of Windows cause problems for you. Figure 15.9 shows this dialog box.

FIGURE 15.9

The Accessibility Settings Wizard enables you to define which areas of Windows are giving you trouble.

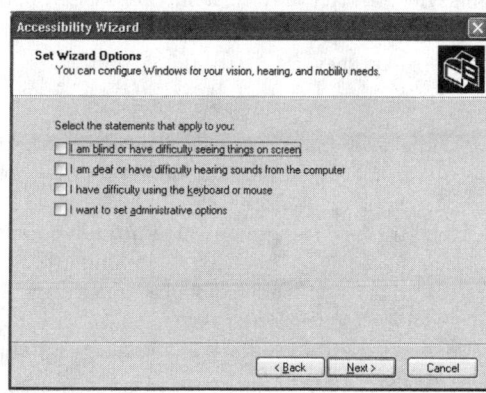

4. Check the appropriate boxes to start the Accessibility option configuration. Click Next. The wizard helps you define a solution. For example, if you select the first check box (I Am Blind or Have Difficulty Seeing Things on Screen), the wizard displays a series of dialog boxes to change scrollbar sizes, icon sizes, the color scheme, and so on.

5. Follow the instructions in the various dialog boxes to adjust Windows to meet your needs. When finished, you'll see a final summary screen that tells what changes you made.

6. Read over the list of changes and click Finish if you want to make them. Otherwise, click Cancel to return your screen to normal.

Using Microsoft Active Accessibility

Microsoft Active Accessibility is a feature that originally appeared in Windows 98, but Microsoft has enhanced it for Windows XP users. From a user perspective, Microsoft Active Accessibility means that the accessibility features Microsoft has built into Windows XP are available all the time. In other words, you no longer need to install the Accessibility option to gain access to accessibility features that vendors have added to a third-party application.

The programmer's view of Microsoft Active Accessibility is slightly different. Microsoft used to implement the accessibility features in the Windows Application Programming Interface (API) as a standard set of functions. An application could call on these functions just as it would any other part of the Windows API.

Now, however, Microsoft implements the accessibility features as COM objects. Using objects means that developers can access and use the accessibility features with greater ease. Essentially, using COM represents a method for creating objects, like buttons and dialog boxes, within Windows. Active Accessibility uses COM interfaces, making it much easier for programmers to add accessibility features to their applications, no matter which programming language they use.

> **Tip:** This chapter only gives you a brief overview of the internal workings of Microsoft Active Accessibility. You can find more details by looking at the Microsoft Active Accessibility Web site (http://www.microsoft.com/Enable/msaa/details.htm). Microsoft used to provide information about its Active Accessibility Java class. However, Windows XP no longer has Java support built in. It appears that Microsoft no longer supports Java in any way. (You can still download and install the old version of Java from Microsoft's Web site or use a third party alternative.) This means that some Web sites that provide Active Accessibility support may not work.

Special Keyboard Features

Windows provides three special keyboard features: StickyKeys, FilterKeys, and ToggleKeys. You can find them on the Keyboard tab of the Accessibility Options dialog box, as shown in Figure 15.10. Double-click the Accessibility Options applet in the Control Panel to display this dialog box. Microsoft provides special key combinations to turn them on.

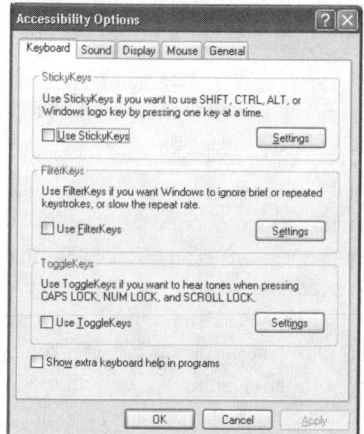

FIGURE 15.10
You can turn on the keyboard accessibility-related functions from the Keyboard page.

These features all have one thing in common: They change the way the keyboard works, independently of the keyboard driver. You must install the Accessibility Options feature to make them work. The Show Extra Keyboard Help in Programs check box at the bottom of the page adds help information to applications that support this feature.

Using StickyKeys

The StickyKeys feature comes in handy for a variety of purposes. It makes the Shift, Ctrl, and Alt keys act as toggle switches. Press one of these keys once, and it becomes active; press it a second time, and it's turned off. I use StickyKeys in graphics programs that require you to hold down the Ctrl key to select a group of items. It can be inconvenient to hold down the Ctrl key while you look around for objects to select. The StickyKeys feature alleviates this problem. Click the Settings button on the Keyboard tab of the Accessibility Properties dialog box to open the Settings for StickyKeys dialog box.

There are three groups of settings for StickyKeys. The first group, Keyboard Shortcut, enables you to turn on StickyKeys using the shortcut key. There's no reason to turn this off. It's very unlikely that another application would use the same control-key sequence.

The Options group contains two settings. The StickyKeys option usually works like a toggle. Checking the first box tells Windows to wait until you press the same control key twice before making the control key active. The second check box enables two people to use the same keyboard if one needs to use StickyKeys and the other doesn't. Pressing a control key and a noncontrol key at the same time turns StickyKeys off.

The Notification group also contains two settings. The first setting tells Windows to play a different sound for each unique control key it activates. This can prevent you from activating a control key by accident. The second option displays an icon on the Taskbar so that you can control StickyKeys more easily. I select this option to make it easier to turn StickyKeys on and off.

Using FilterKeys

FilterKeys helps eliminate extra keystrokes so that you don't get "tthis" instead of "this." As with StickyKeys, you can adjust the way FilterKeys works by clicking the Settings button.

The first option in this dialog box enables you to turn the shortcut key on and off. This works just like the same feature in StickyKeys.

The Filter Options group enables you to select from two ways of filtering keystrokes. The first option filters keys that get pressed in rapid succession. This feature would filter the rapid typing of the extra *t* in the previous example. The Settings button displays a dialog box that enables you to select how long an interval must pass between the first and second times you press the same key. It also provides a field in which you can test the setting. The second option in this group filters accidental key presses. At one time or another, everyone presses a key without meaning to. As with the StickyKeys option, the Settings button displays a dialog box in which you select how long you have to press a key before Windows accepts it.

The Notification group at the bottom of the dialog box should look familiar. The only difference is that FilterKeys beeps rather than playing a sound when you activate it.

Using ToggleKeys

The ToggleKeys feature emits a tone every time you turn the Caps Lock, Scroll Lock, or NumLock key on or off. The ToggleKeys dialog box contains a single option, which enables you to turn the shortcut key on or off.

Special Sound Features

The Sound tab of the Accessibility Options dialog box controls how Windows XP interacts with sound. The Use SoundSentry option tells Windows XP to display a visual warning when a system sound occurs. You can flash the active caption bar, flash the active window, or flash the desktop. (Flashing means changing the colors of the entry so you can see it easier—think of a flashing light.)

The ShowSounds feature tells Windows XP and your applications to display captions for the sounds they make, including speech. The sounds appear in a balloon help dialog box.

Although both of these features sound good in theory, the SoundSentry option works more often in practice. Most applications don't display the sounds they make as text, even if you enable the ShowSounds feature.

Special Display Features

The features on the Display tab are some of the handiest for everyone to know about. High-contrast screens work well when you're tired. High contrast screens also work well if you're on a plane using a laptop in bright sunlight. Sometimes, a high-contrast screen is even the answer for presentations.

The Display tab contains a High Contrast option. Click this option, and your display will use the current high-contrast settings. The Settings button displays the Settings for High Contrast dialog box that you'll use to adjust the high-contrast settings.

At the bottom of the Display tab you'll find two sliders. The Blink Rate slider controls the rate at which the cursor blinks. The Width slider controls the cursor width. I find that setting the cursor for a slow blink rate aids laptop use in many settings. I also use a cursor that's about one character wide in forms and other situations where finding the cursor might become a problem.

Special Mouse Features

Look at the Mouse tab of the Accessibility Options dialog box, and you find a single option for turning MouseKeys on. MouseKeys enables you to use the arrow keys on the numeric keypad as a mouse. Instead of moving the cursor with the mouse, you can move it with the arrow keys. This doesn't disable your mouse; it merely augments it. The Mouse tab of the Accessibility Properties dialog box contains a check box that enables you to turn MouseKeys on or off.

Click the Settings button on this tab to display the Settings for MouseKeys dialog box, shown in Figure 15.11. The first option, Keyboard Shortcut, enables you to turn on MouseKeys using a shortcut key. There's no reason to turn this option off. It's unlikely that another program would use the same control-key sequence.

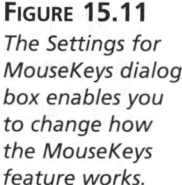

FIGURE 15.11

The Settings for MouseKeys dialog box enables you to change how the MouseKeys feature works.

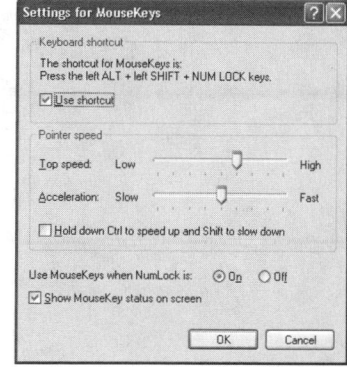

In the second group, Pointer Speed, you can optimize the performance of this particular feature. The first option enables you to set the fastest speed at which you can move the mouse cursor using the arrow keys. The Acceleration setting determines how quickly the cursor reaches full speed after you press it. Windows doesn't start the cursor at full speed; it brings it there gradually. The combination of these two settings determines how much added control MouseKeys gives you over the cursor. The check box in this group provides another option: You can press the Ctrl key to speed up the mouse cursor and press the Shift key to slow it down.

There are two settings at the bottom of the dialog box. The radio buttons control when MouseKeys is active. You must specify whether the NumLock key should be on or off when you use MouseKeys. The second option determines whether the MouseKeys icon appears on the Taskbar.

Microsoft Magnifier

Most of the time, you don't need an entire screen that contains large characters or graphics. You usually just want to magnify a small portion of the screen to see something in better detail. This is what Microsoft Magnifier is all about. Use it when you need to momentarily view something onscreen in a larger format. After you finish, just put it back the way it was.

There are seven settings in the Magnifier Settings dialog box. The first, Magnification Level, determines how much magnification you see. The default setting of 2 should work for most situations. The Follow Mouse Cursor, Follow Keyboard Focus, and Follow Text Editing options determine where the focus of the magnification is. In most cases, you should use the Follow Mouse Cursor option if your sole purpose is to look at a particular area of the screen. The Follow Keyboard Focus and Follow Text Editing options come in handy when you're working with small type in a desktop publishing program.

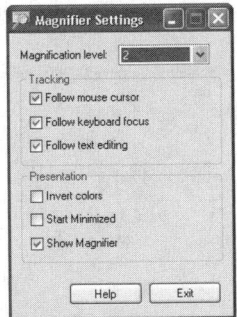

FIGURE 15.12
The Magnifier Settings dialog box helps you adjust the appearance of the magnifier.

The Presentation group controls the appearance of the magnifier display. The Invert Colors option enables you to swap foreground and background colors in the magnified area. The Start Minimized option tells Magnifier to start on the Taskbar rather than in full view. You'll normally check the Show Magnifier option, unless you want to disable it temporarily to perform some other full-screen task.

The Narrator

The Narrator reads everything onscreen to you. I find that it does a relatively good job and use it when I need to "read" documents online. This application also acts as a sanity check for my Web site. I'll see if Narrator stumbles on the content. If it doesn't, I'm sure that no one else will have troubles either. Of course, its main purpose is to help those with low vision make more sense of what they see onscreen.

The Narrator dialog box contains four options. Use the Announce Events Onscreen option to announce when you successfully complete an action, such as changing windows. The Read Typed Characters option tells you which character you typed last, including control characters, such as Backspace. The Move Mouse Pointer to Active Item option moves the mouse cursor so that you can see which item onscreen has the focus. Finally, the Start Narrator Minimized option starts the program with the Narrator dialog box minimized.

Click Voice to display the Voice Settings dialog box. This dialog box allows you to choose a new voice for Narrator. The default setting is Microsoft Sam. Settings on this dialog box also change the speed, volume, and pitch of the voice.

On Your Own

Try the different accessibility options to see whether they provide features you can use. This chapter provides suggestions for how you could use each feature.

Install and try using the Dvorak keyboard layout. After you learn how to use this setup, you can type faster and with less fatigue. This particular setup also can help you fight repetitive stress injuries, such as carpal tunnel syndrome. Nothing provides 100 percent protection. The Dvorak keyboard layout can't reverse years of abuse, but learning this new setup could help prevent current problems from getting worse.

Review earlier chapters and practice using the shortcuts discussed with the Accessibility options turned on. Do the Accessibility options make a difference when using standard shortcuts? Try different combinations to create the fastest keyboard interface possible.

If you need precise mouse cursor movement, try using a trackball. Many users find that it works better than a mouse and seems to provide higher reliability. Of course, input devices are highly personal, so an input device that works for one person may not work for others.

Video Configurations

Video is the most noticeable architectural component of Windows XP. It's the underlying combination of hardware and software that enables you to see the graphics, dialog boxes, icons, and other elements that make Windows XP worth using. It's little wonder, then, that video is also one of the more complex parts of the computing picture.

The problem isn't simply displaying a picture onscreen; that would be easy to manage. The problem is communication between the various elements that create and manage the picture in the first place. The following list illustrates some Windows XP communications problem areas:

- *Compatibility support* Windows XP defaults to an 800×600 resolution and a minimum 16-bit (65,536) color display. Unfortunately, many educational software applications require 256-color support. Older games commonly run on a 640×480 display. This means that Windows XP must simulate these environments to allow the application to run.

- *Application level* Three different kinds of applications use Windows XP. MS-DOS applications usually think they're alone in the world, so they violate just about every imaginable rule for displaying information. Although 16-bit Windows applications are a bit more conscientious than their MS-DOS counterparts, they still use an older interface to draw to the display. Finally, newer, 32-bit Windows applications offer the ultimate in available features, but they're often hampered by other applications running on the machine.

- *Device driver* If the display driver doesn't correctly interpret the commands issued by applications running under Windows, or if those applications use undocumented command features, miscommunication is likely. If the adapter misinterprets the commands an application uses, for example, you get an unreadable screen.

- *Adapter* In the beginning, IBM was responsible for the standard way in which CGA and EGA display adapters worked. By the time VGA adapters arrived, IBM was starting to lose its leadership position. Then came SVGA (super VGA) adapters, and there was no IBM standard to follow. For a while, no standardization existed for the extended modes vendors built into their display adapters. Later in this chapter, you see how this problem was finally resolved.

- *Operating system requirements* The operating system itself is usually the least of your display worries. Sometimes, however, it can actually be the source of your problems. Icons, for example, are taken for granted because they generally work without difficulty. But what happens if a file the operating system needs gets changed by an application or gets corrupted somehow? In most cases, you have to replace this file before things will work again.

Now that you're more aware of Windows communications problems, you might wonder how it works at all. Windows uses an event loop to talk with applications. Think of an event loop as a bulletin board on which Windows and applications can post messages. A message could request a service, such as opening a file, or it could tell an application to perform a maintenance task. Windows notifies an application when it has a message waiting. The application picks up its messages and acts on them. The event loop enables Windows to send "paint" messages to any application that might require them. The application uses the content of the paint message to draw graphics or text on screen. The combination of an event loop and constant redrawing helps Windows keep your display up to date, even if some miscommunication does occur.

This chapter discusses video in Windows XP. More than that, it talks about communication. Without the required level of communication between all system elements, you'd never see anything when using Windows XP. Look for the communication requirements in the following sections.

Graphics Standards

Standards organizations help keep your computer running smoothly by creating rules that everyone follows in designing hardware and software. The standards organization for display adapters and monitors is the Video Electronics Standards Association (VESA).

I first discovered VESA in 1989, but it probably was around before that. IBM had dropped VGA in favor of its proprietary 8514/A display adapter. Without a leader in the field to dictate a standard, the entire display-adapter arena fell into a state of disarray. VESA stepped in to make sense of this chaos. The result of these initial efforts was several VESA standards and some additional software for each display adapter.

VESA continues to release standards. For example, it recently released the Video Signal Standard (VSIS) and Enhanced Extended Display Identification Data Standard (E-EDID) standards. The following list shows many of the common standards VESA has produced. (This selection of standards is by no means complete.)

- *Enhanced Extended Display Identification Data Standard (E-EDID)* If you've ever wondered how Windows XP knows which monitor is attached to your system, this is the standard that helps. Unfortunately, many older monitors don't include the required support. This is why you'll see some monitors identified as "Plug and Play monitor" rather than using a specific name.

- *Video Signal Standard (VSIS)* This standard determines the signals used to control the monitor. It also specifies monitor elements, such as analog video outputs. In addition, it controls the use of test circuits within the monitor. This standard appears to supercede the Monitor Command Control Set (MCCS) standard in many situations and to augment it in others.

- *Digital Flat Panel (DFP)* A monitor normally attaches to the computer through an analog interface. The signal has to be converted from the digital signal the computer understands to an analog signal used by the monitor, a step that obviously takes time and reduces performance. This standard provides a method for a DFP to connect to the computer directly without the use of digital-to-analog conversion.

- *Visual Interface Port (VIP)* Modern computers are filled with an increasing number of specialized video components. This standard defines an interface that components—such as MPEG-2 or HDTV decoders, video digitizers, and video encoders—can use to interact with the display adapter without adding extra traffic to the PCI bus.

- *PC Theater Interconnectivity Standard* This standard defines how consumer electronics vendors can update their products to work with the PC. It appears that most of these products use USB to create the connection.

- *Connector and Signal Standards for Stereoscopic Display Hardware* Gamers and 3D graphics application users will appreciate this standard because it defines a method for connecting stereoscopic devices to a PC.

- *VESA BIOS Extension (VBE)* Use this series of standards to learn about display modes for SVGA and more advanced adapters.

- *Monitor Timing Standards* This series of standards provides a consistent method of producing ergonomically correct displays with a 70Hz refresh rate, which greatly reduces eyestrain.

> **Tip:** VESA can provide detailed specifications for a number of display adapter and monitor standards. You can contact VESA directly:
>
> Video Electronics Standards Association
> 920 Hillview Ct., Suite 140
> Milpitas, CA 95035
> Phone: 408-957-9270
> Internet: http://www.vesa.org/

Windows XP supports several new standards, including DirectX 8 (http://www.microsoft.com/directx/default.asp). This standard enables game vendors to write high-speed graphics routines using a standard interface. DirectX provides the means to write directly to the hardware, yet it keeps Windows in the picture. Windows still tracks the game program's actions, but it does so without the interference a normal application would encounter. The advantages of using DirectX are high speed and maximum flexibility.

Previous versions of DirectX caused more problems than they fixed, in the eyes of many people. A major drawback of older versions was that the vendor had to do more work to get an application up and running. The introduction of higher-quality Software Development Kits (SDKs) and the proliferation of DirectX information has all but eliminated this problem. In addition, many people ran into compatibility problems when using DirectX with nonstandard display adapters in the past. Most display adapters today work fine with DirectX.

The OpenGL standard (`http://www.opengl.org/` and `http://reality.sgi.com/ opengl/`) is still a viable standard, but you see less of it today than in older versions of Windows. It was originally available only to Windows NT users, but most modern versions of Windows contain it. *OpenGL* is a set of graphics library routines. Using these routines can save a programmer a substantial amount of development time and speeds the display of information onscreen.

You can see the effects of OpenGL by using the OpenGL screen savers in Windows XP. Right-click the Desktop, and choose Properties. Select the Screen Saver tab. Choose 3D Pipes in the Screen Saver list. Click Preview and you see a display similar to the one shown in Figure 16.1 (note that I enhanced my display a little). You see a set of high-speed 3D graphics routines in action. The problem with OpenGL is that it isn't quite fast enough or easy enough to use. Most developers today use DirectX games; however, OpenGL is extremely popular for business applications.

FIGURE 16.1
This screen saver gives you a sample of how OpenGL improves the dynamism of 3D animation.

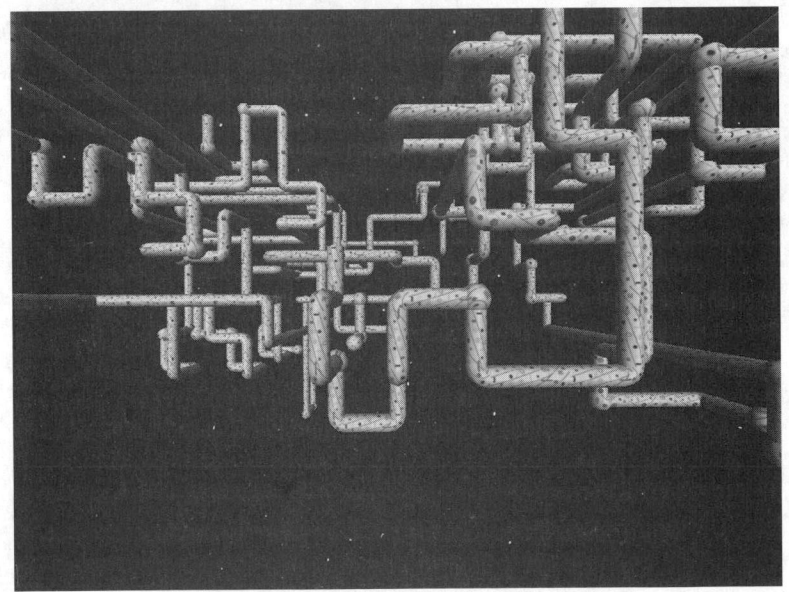

The Windows XP Graphics Architecture

Now that you have some idea of the problems Microsoft (and any other vendor) faces when it comes to providing something for you to look at, it's time to discuss how they do it. Display adapters and monitors have both moved beyond the simpler requirements of the time when IBM was at the helm.

In the interim, we've seen the emergence of even higher resolutions. It used to be that 640×480 resolution and 256 colors were something to whistle about. Today, an adapter is considered almost inadequate at 1024×768 resolution and 24-bit (16.7 million, or true color) colors. In addition, users now are concerned about a video adapter's frame rate (the speed at which it can display animation).. A display adapter must support a minimum of 30 fps (frames per second) to provide decent animation quality. Consequently, display adapters now boast onboard processors and huge amounts of memory.

Windows XP handles this wide range of display adapter capabilities using the same centralized control mechanism it uses for printing—a combination of the minidriver and device-independent bitmap (DIB) engine. One of the main architectural components is the Graphics Device Interface (GDI). Your application interacts with this part of the graphics architecture, which directs the other parts of the architecture.

Microsoft has tuned the GDI throughout the various incarnations of Windows. It's no surprise that Microsoft has spent so much time in this area because many benchmark tests focus on graphics performance. In fact, what users notice most is the way the graphics engine performs. Microsoft did some more tuning of the GDI for Windows XP, but I'd call this tuning more incremental than major. In fact, Microsoft doesn't even say much about the level of tuning in its literature.

> **Note:** The Windows XP GDI has an interesting feature: It's one of the few pieces that Microsoft wrote mostly with C++. (The rest of Windows XP uses a combination of C and C++.) Why would Microsoft take this step? In my opinion, the reason is twofold. First, using C++ allows it to make full use of the Microsoft Foundation Class (MFC) support built-in to C++. Second, using objects rather than procedural code tends to make the GDI easier to maintain (especially in a multiplatform environment like Windows XP).

The Windows XP graphics architecture is very similar to the one found in Windows 2000. It includes some additional code for compatibility mode, such as dual mode support for 16-bit and 32-bit applications. In addition, Microsoft has removed the OS/2 and POSIX elements from the architecture because Windows XP no longer needs them. I don't get into bits and bytes here, but I do tell you about the components used to display your data onscreen. Figure 16.2 is an overview of the Windows XP architecture.

FIGURE **16.2**
The Windows XP graphics architecture displays data onscreen.

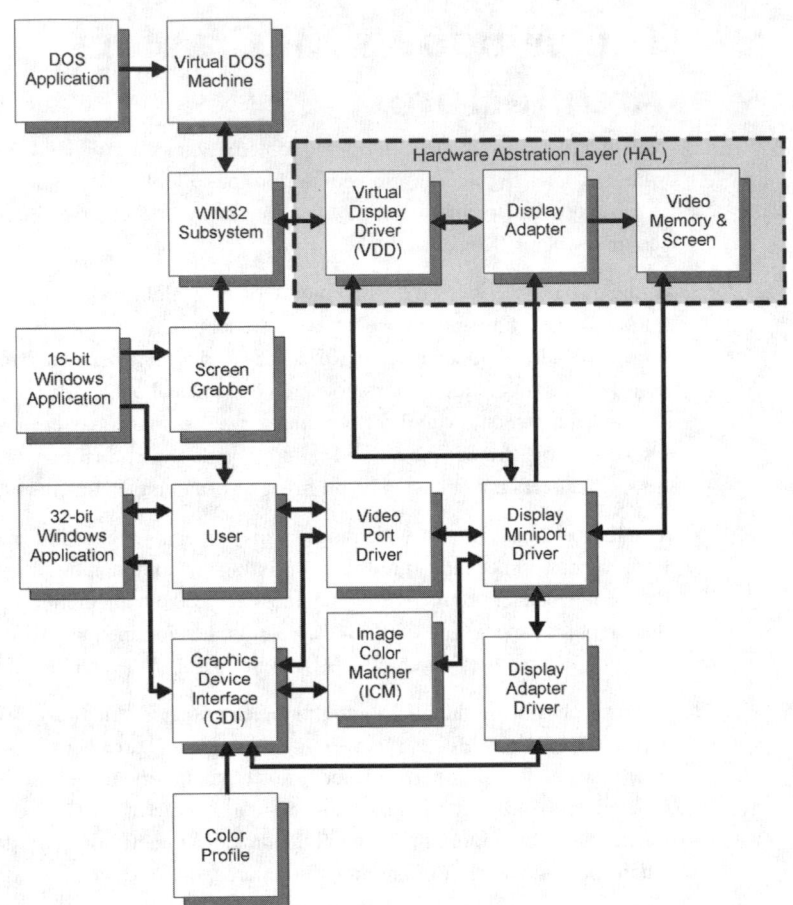

The actual graphics architecture is more complex than Figure 16.2 would suggest. This block diagram shows a simplified view of the Windows XP graphics architecture. I didn't include some redundant elements, such as dual-mode compatibility support, because it looks the same as its 32-bit counterpart. The following list tells you what task each of the components performs:

- *WIN32 subsystem* Remember that Windows XP uses a client/server approach to taking care of the needs of the various applications it supports. The way it does that is through the WIN32 subsystem—a buffer layer that translates foreign operating system calls into something that Windows XP can understand.

- *Virtual DOS machine (VDM)* Windows XP places each DOS application in its own VDM. To provide the higher level of system reliability that Windows XP users demand, Microsoft had to make sure that each application had its own environment, completely separate from that used by every other application.

Also remember that unlike Windows 9x, 16-bit Windows applications use individual VDMs. Windows XP always starts a VDM and then runs a copy of 16-bit Windows in it to service the needs of the 16-bit Windows application. This effectively adds two layers to every interaction: one for the VDM, and another for the WIN32 subsystem. The use of a separate VDM for each application also means that Windows XP can more accurately detect when a DOS application is about to take control of the display area. It notifies the User module and the screen grabber so that they can preserve the graphics system status information. As with everything else, this additional layering is transparent to the user. You still use the same interfaces as before.

- *Screen grabber* I always think of this component as a camera because, in essence, that's what it is. The screen grabber takes a picture of the screen and preserves it for later. This enables Windows to restore the screen to its former appearance after you exit a DOS session.

- *User* I've already discussed the uses for this module extensively. (I talked about the Windows API functionality of User in Chapter 11.)This module tracks the state of all the display elements, such as icons and dialog boxes, in addition to drawing them. That's why it needs to be informed before a DOS session comes to the foreground—so that it can take a snapshot of the current state of these components. As I stated, the disk actually has two User-related files—a 16-bit and a 32-bit version.

- *GDI* This is another module that I've spent a lot of time discussing. (I talked about the Windows API functionality of User in Chapter 11.) Like the User module, the GDI has two physical files—one for 16-bit needs and another for 32-bit needs. The GDI module works with the display driver and the DIB engine to produce the graphics components of a Windows display. The DIB engine used to be a separate component of the display subsystem, but is now included within the GDI.

- *Display Miniport Driver* Every video signal goes through the virtual display driver (VDD). The VDD processes the signal and sends it to the display adapter. Windows XP can use a combination of the display miniport driver and the DIB engine for adapters that can support them. Using this driver combination results in a speed increase from 32-bit code. The name of this file varies, depending on the type of display you're using. On my system, it's named ATIMPAE.SYS. Unlike the VDD, which performs all video processing, the display miniport driver takes care of only device-specific details. The DIB engine takes care of graphics rendering. A miniport driver contains much less code than a full-fledged VDD, reducing the amount of code a vendor must write.

- *Display Adapter Driver* This module supports any special rendering features your display adapter provides. With so many different display adapter processors on the market, it's important to support these special rendering features. The name of the file associated with this module varies by display adapter. On my machine, these functions are contained in the ATIDRAE.DLL file.

- *Video Port Driver* Microsoft is moving toward a system of drivers that are completely generic. This driver represents part of that effort with regard to the display adapter. It contains functions that allow the User and GDI modules to perform general display adapter tasks, like moving data from one point to another in memory. There are also status functions, like one that checks the VGA setup of the display adapter, and others that work with AGP port setups. The functions carried out by this module normally appear in the VIDEOPRT.SYS file.

- *Color profile* This data file contains the color capabilities for your output device. It doesn't matter whether the device is a printer or a display adapter; the type of information is the same. The purpose of a color profile is to provide the ICM with the information it needs to keep the display and other color devices in sync. That way, when you select dark red on the display, you get the same dark red on your printer. I discussed some of the problems with color matching in the "Color Management Tab" section of Chapter 14, so I won't go into them again here. You find all the color profile files in the COLOR folder in the SYSTEM folder. All these files have an .ICM extension. The Properties dialog box associated with each one gives you many more technical details about the actual profile.

- *Image color matcher (ICM)* The whole process of matching the output of your printer to what you see on the display is complex—much too complex to cover here. I discussed the problem of color matching earlier in this chapter. The *ICM* is the module that actually performs the work. It subtly changes the output of your printer and display so that they match. The GDI, display minidriver, and ICM work together to compare the current color set and translate it into something that works on both devices. It's not a perfect solution, but it works for the most part. The results are very close, but not absolutely the same. Most of us wouldn't notice, but a professional artist might. Of course, this solution can't take into account the many details that a professional would, such as temperature, humidity, and other environmental aspects beyond the control of Windows. The files that contain the ICM include ICM32.DLL and ICMUI.DLL; both appear in the SYSTEM folder.

- *Virtual display driver (VDD)* Older, 16-bit applications use this module as their sole source of communication with the display adapter. Windows XP provides it for compatibility purposes and for DOS applications. In most cases, the name of this file contains some part of the name of the display adapter vendor. You'll find it in the SYSTEM folder. This driver converts drawing commands into signals the display adapter can use. It also manages the display adapter and performs a variety of other tasks related to the way that all the applications on your machine share the display adapter. In essence, it's a 16-bit version of the display minidriver and DIB engine combination.

- *Hardware Abstraction Layer (HAL)* This is another conceptual type of element in Windows XP. At one time, you could run Windows NT on various machine platforms, such as the MIPS and Alpha processor. However, that's no longer true. Even so, Microsoft retains the ability to run Windows XP on other platforms. The HAL separates the hardware-specific elements from the rest of Windows XP. If Microsoft wants to move Windows XP to another platform, all it needs to do, in theory, is rewrite the HAL to accommodate the platform.

- *Display adapter* This is the physical hardware in your machine.

- *Video memory and screen* Video memory is where the electronic form of the image you see onscreen is stored. Note that although your display adapter has its own onboard memory, that's not the memory we're talking about here. Windows XP creates a virtual memory area for each application so that one application doesn't interfere with others using the machine. Windows XP combines the content of all the virtual memory areas and sends it to the real memory on your display adapter. In short, this is still a hardware concept.

- *VGA Boot Driver (Not Shown in Figure 16.2)* The VGA Boot Driver is normally used only in safe mode, when the main graphics system has broken down for some reason. This is a generic 32-bit driver that any Windows-friendly display adapter can use to display information at the low resolution of 640×480. Note that this driver no longer uses 256-color mode—you have a choice of 16-bit or 24-bit color display instead. The system uses this driver before it identifies the display adapter in your machine during the installation process. For the most part, Windows XP uses this driver only during installation and troubleshooting, and it usually stays in the background, which is why I chose not to include it in the figure. You'll find this functionality stored in the BOOTVID.DLL file.

Keep in mind that this was a *quick* tour of the video subsystem. The actual inner workings of this part of Windows XP are much more complex than you might think. To give you a better idea of the way things work, think of Windows XP as having three video paths (although it's more complex than that, don't get mired in too much detail at this point):

- 16-bit DOS
- 16-bit Windows
- 32-bit Windows

The path Windows XP uses depends on the applications you're using, the type of adapter you have, and the video performance settings you select in the Display Properties dialog box. The 16-bit DOS path consists of the VDD, display adapter, and video memory. The 16-bit Windows path adds WINOLDAP.MOD, the screen grabber, User, and the GDI. The 32-bit path includes User, the GDI, the display miniport driver, the display adapter driver, the video port driver, the DIB engine, and video memory. Both Windows paths can include the ICM and the associated color profiles. It depends on your setup, the drivers that Microsoft eventually includes, and the capabilities of the devices you're using.

Video Boards

While I have your attention focused on the complexities of the video subsystem, take a quick look at video boards. You might have missed a few performance clues tucked away in the discussion of architecture. Of course, one of the big requirements today is display memory. Notice that Windows XP no longer supports the low-end modes of previous Windows versions. This means you can't get a performance boost any more by resorting to 640×480 mode and 256 colors. Your display adapter has to provide the resources for a higher resolution and color depth display.

The topic of video memory is important, given all of the applications that rely on fast memory usage. You gain from having more video memory in two ways. First, more memory means more colors. A higher number of colors results in improved resolution and makes possible photorealistic-quality images.

The second advantage is that a large video frame buffer can speed up the frame rate of animation because Windows XP can move the image from the display onto the monitor page-by-page rather than in smaller chunks. No matter which way you look at it, however, more colors and high resolution cause a performance hit. With today's special video-acceleration features, such as DirectX version 8 and AGP, however, you probably won't notice the hit. The AGP (Accelerated Graphics Port) is a standard that increases the PCI bus bandwidth.

Note: DirectX version 8 improves your system's multimedia features, particularly video. Vendors optimize the video card drivers for 3D animation and high-resolution color. Microsoft created DirectX technology using several APIs (Application Programming Interfaces). With these APIs, programs can directly access many of your computer's hardware devices. Programs want to do this for precisely the same reason that DOS games were so notorious for directly writing to the screen hardware—added speed and control.

The DirectX Foundation layer detects your computer's hardware abilities and then makes sure that applications' behaviors respond appropriately. This way, various applications can fully exploit any high-performance hardware you might own: 3D graphics acceleration chips, for instance. You'll find a deeper discussion of DirectX 8 in the "Installing and Configuring DirectX" section of Chapter 10.

In spite of all these improvements in video standards, nobody can repeal the laws of physics—moving the video window around takes a little time. Each layer of management you add to the video subsystem chews up processor cycles. How do you get around these problems? Consider these suggestions:

- *Double Data Rate Synchronous Dynamic Access Memory (DDR SDRAM) or Dual-ported Video RAM (VRAM)* Many display adapters come with high-speed memory, but some don't. DDR SDRAM is the latest innovation in high-speed memory. It's essentially a high-speed version of common DRAM. The advantage of DDR SDRAM is that it's inexpensive compared to other solutions, such as VRAM. That's why you find it installed on so many display adapters today. I don't discuss the inner workings of DDR SDRAM in this chapter. However, you can find out about DDR SDRAM at `http://www6.tomshardware.com/main-board/00q4/001030/`.

VRAM is a Texas Instruments innovation. The company first introduced it with its TMS340x0 series of processors. The reason that it's called dual-ported is that it actually makes use of two ports and can thus simultaneously send and receive data. A serial buffer enables the display to read the contents of video memory. A parallel buffer allows Windows to simultaneously write to video memory. Dual-ported memory gets rid of one of the constraints an application had with the display adapter: You could write to video memory during only part of the display cycle. (For more discussion of VRAM and related issues, see the following Peter's Principle.)

Note: Remember that the capabilities of your graphics card can be quite modest if you use the computer for standard business applications. Word processing, for instance, certainly doesn't justify the extra cost of replacing an older card with a new one containing high-speed VRAM memory. For many business applications, you can easily get by with the simplest of the older-style video boards with slower memory, like EDO DRAM (Dynamic RAM). But if you plan to work with graphics in any fashion or expect to need to display multimedia or games or to visit the many visually advanced Internet sites, insist on VRAM memory.

- *Memory* Video memory today is inexpensive compared to even a few years ago. In today's market, more memory is better. Some display adapters I see today contain 32MB or 64MB of display memory, and there are discussions of making display adapters with even more memory.

- *Graphics processor* Quite a few display adapters also come with a graphics processor. Windows XP has graphics processor support built right in. It offloads as much of the display processing as possible to the graphics processor rather than use the DIB engine. This speeds performance in two ways. First, because offloading part of the graphics processing responsibility frees processor cycles, you'll notice an overall improvement in system speed. Second, the display processor is usually a special-purpose state machine. It processes the graphics instructions much faster than the DIB engine could.

- *AGP display adapter* The Accelerated Graphics Port (AGP) helps your display adapter move data quickly. Graphics routines process lots of data. There's no way around it. To display an image, you have to move data, and that requires time. However, you can reduce the amount of time by using a wider data path. Some display adapters come with a 64-bit or 128-bit internal data path. AGP also speeds up the data bus. A typical PCI bus moves data at 133Mbps, and even a slow AGP bus moves data at 266Mbps. (See the "Understanding the Accelerated Graphics Port (AGP)" section, later in this chapter, for more details.)

- *DirectX for Games* Some vendors still produce Windows games that don't use DirectX. There are many problems with these games. For one thing, they may not run, because these games normally have compatibility problems. Using DirectX also speeds games up by allowing them to access the hardware directly.

- *OpenGL, Open Graphics Library for CAD* This API, originally developed by Silicon Graphics (SGI), allows a Windows XP workstation to be as swift and efficient as a dedicated graphics workstation when using business applications. A number of vendors who create high-end CAD, 3D design, animation, multimedia, and other demanding applications have written their software for OpenGL. OpenGL has become the de facto graphics API for two main reasons: It's relatively easy to write hardware drivers for it, and it's scalable—you can see it on the fastest, best, dedicated-graphics workstations, and also on humble, unaccelerated PC cards. (It displays lurching animation, at best, with an unaccelerated display adapter; but at least it works.)

Working with Display Adapters and Monitors

Chapter 9, "Exploiting Your Hardware," described the physical process of installing your display adapter as part of the hardware installation process. The process for installing or upgrading a display adapter driver isn't much different. The following section, however, shows you an alternative to that process. In addition, we'll discuss what you can do when Windows XP fails to recognize your monitor, a common problem for older monitors that don't follow the VESA specifications (or monitors that Microsoft simply chose not to support).

Making General Settings Changes

Windows XP provides two special settings for your display adapter, both of which appear on the General tab of the Advanced Display Properties dialog box. You access the General tab by right-clicking the Desktop and choosing the Properties option. Select the Settings tab and click Advanced. The Advanced Display Properties dialog box appears.

The first setting on the General tab controls the dots-per-inch (dpi) setting of your display. This is the number of dpi used for formatting fonts. If you have trouble reading the screen, set the dpi setting higher and Windows XP will use more dots for all fonts, making them larger. Likewise, you can reduce the dpi and see the fonts in a smaller size. The only problem with this setting is that some utilities only work in the default 96 dpi setting. For example, you can't read all of the text in my motherboard monitor if you set the dpi setting higher than 96 dpi. In short, although this setting helps those with poor eyesight, you'll normally want to use the settings on the Appearance tab of the Display Properties dialog box to control the size of the fonts.

The second setting controls how Windows XP reacts after you change the settings on the Settings tab of the Display Properties dialog box. Unlike previous versions of Windows, Windows XP assumes that your display adapter can handle the change and uses a default setting of Apply New Display Settings Without Restarting. If you find that your system is unstable after the change, then you'll want to select Restart the computer before applying the new display settings.

The third option, Ask Me before Applying the New Display Settings, requests that Windows keep you informed about display settings changes. This option displays a Compatibility Warning dialog box that gives you the option of making the change with or without a reboot. You can also cancel the change.

Installing or Upgrading a Display Adapter

At some point, you'll want to install a new display adapter or upgrade your existing display adapter. Installing a new display adapter isn't difficult. The following procedure shows you how to do it:

1. Right-click the Desktop and choose the Properties option. You should see the Display Properties dialog box.

2. Select the Settings tab. Click Advanced to see the Advanced Display Properties dialog box, which should be similar to the one shown in Figure 16.3. You should notice several features in this dialog box. First, the dialog box tells you which drivers the display adapter requires. This entry is the adapter itself, not the video subsystem as a whole. The video subsystem also contains a number of files that are either generic or specific to certain conditions. Second, this dialog box tells you the current display adapter type and its version number. This can provide important information when troubleshooting. Third, the dialog box provides a list of the display modes your display adapter can produce when you click List All Modes.

FIGURE 16.3

The Advanced Display Properties dialog box enables you to reconfigure your display adapter or monitor.

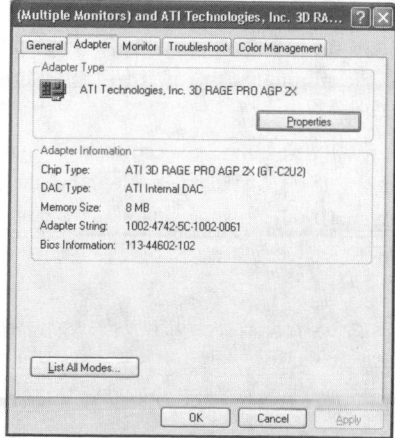

Note: Your display may look different from the one shown in Figure 16.3. That's because some vendors add features that make their display adapters easier to use or more flexible in some way. Always refer to your vendor documentation when you encounter differences between the standard Windows XP setup and the one on your machine.

3. Click Properties on the Adapter tab. You see the Display Adapter Properties dialog box.

4. Select the Driver tab and then click Update Driver. You'll see the first screen of the Hardware Update Wizard. This wizard helps you either choose a new driver or upgrade your existing driver.

5. Click Next. The Hardware Update Wizard will ask if you want to perform an automatic install or install the display adapter driver manually. You don't need this procedure if Windows XP can recognize your driver automatically because Windows XP will ask if you want to install the driver as part of the startup process. In most cases, you need this procedure because your display adapter is so old, new, or specialized that Windows XP can't recognize it.

6. Select the Install from a List or Specific Location (Advanced) option and then click Next. Windows XP will ask where you want to search for a driver. If you have a disk, choose the location for that disk from the list. Most modern display adapters use a CD, so you'll choose the Search for Removable Media option. However, if you downloaded the driver, choose the Include This Location in the Search option and specify the driver download directory. You'll use the Don't Search, I Will Select the Driver to Install option only if you know that Windows XP won't recognize the driver disk or you know that Windows XP supports the device, but doesn't recognize it correctly. If you choose this option, skip to step 8.

7. Select one or more search locations and then click Next. Windows XP will search the locations you specified. If Windows XP finds the driver, you'll see the information onscreen. Follow the remaining prompts (vendor specific) to install your device. If Windows XP can't find the driver, it will tell you that it can't continue the installation. Click Back.

8. Select Don't Search, I Will Select the Driver to Install. Click Next. The dialog box displays a list of compatible display adapters. Note that the dialog box only lists one display adapter type. (If other display adapters are compatible with this one, the list box will contain those as well.)

Note: If you have a vendor disk containing drivers for your display adapter, click the Have Disk button. The Have Disk dialog box works just like any other file browser in Windows XP.

9. Clear the Show Compatible Hardware option. Windows changes the list to show all the display adapters it supports, in alphabetic order by vendor (see Figure 16.4). You can use this screen when selecting a new display adapter. Clicking Cancel takes you back to the initial screen without changing your display adapter type.

FIGURE 16.4

Click the Show All Hardware check-box to show every display adapter supported by Windows XP.

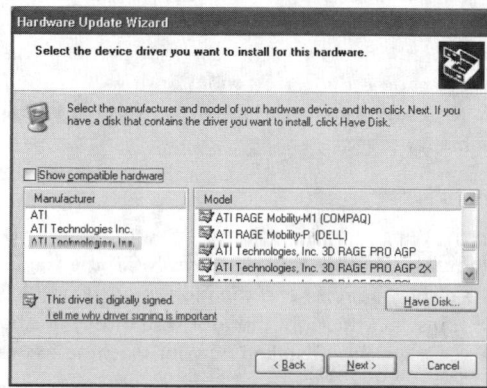

> **Tip:** If your display adapter vendor doesn't appear in this list and you don't have a vendor disk containing drivers, you can always use the Standard Display Adapter category at the beginning of the Manufacturers list. You don't get the same number of features as with the special disk, but using the standard drivers will provide a performance boost. Once you have your machine up and running, you can always check the vendor Web site to see if they provide a 32-bit driver. In addition, you can use Windows Update to see if Microsoft has an updated version of the driver for your display adapter.

10. After you select the manufacturer and display adapter model from the lists, click Next. Windows XP will install the driver software. Windows might ask you to insert disks as it installs the new adapter. You'll see a completion dialog box.

11. Click Finish. You'll return to the Display Adapter Properties dialog box.

12. Click Close to close the Display Adapter Properties dialog box, click OK to close the Advanced Display Properties dialog box, and then click OK to close the Display Properties dialog box. Windows XP may ask you to reboot your machine at some time during this process.

Upgrading a Monitor

Windows XP often chooses a "generic" monitor during installation when it doesn't recognize the monitor attached to your machine. In many situations, this means performing an upgrade to ensure you have the correct monitor installed. It might not seem important to tell Windows XP which monitor you're using, especially if that monitor doesn't provide any special capabilities. The monitor you select, however, determines which display adapter features you can use. Selecting the right monitor type helps Windows XP provide you with better information regarding your display choices.

> **Note:** When using previous versions of Windows, you could check the Monitor Is Energy Star Compliant checkbox if that feature was provided. Windows XP no longer has this checkbox and implements Energy Star compliance only when the settings for the monitor driver you choose includes them. This makes it even more important to choose the correct monitor driver for your system. Otherwise, Windows XP assumes that your monitor isn't Energy Star compliant and refuses to support those features.

Previous versions of Windows also included an Automatically Detect Plug & Play Monitors checkbox. This feature told Windows XP to use the Plug and Play features of both the display adapter and the monitor. Again, this feature is still present, but only if you select the right monitor. You must have both a Plug and Play display adapter and a monitor installed on your machine to use this feature.

A Plug and Play monitor tells Windows XP about itself and reduces the amount of configuration you have to do. It also can tailor some of the options you have to choose from in the Display Properties dialog box. Some monitors offer both a suspend (standby) mode and a power-down mode. Power-down mode works about the same as shutting off the monitor. Some monitors have to go through a restart cycle to work properly after the system powers them down.

Now that you have a better idea of why you might want to upgrade your monitor, let's look at the procedure you'll need to follow. The following steps discuss a typical monitor upgrade:

1. Right-click the Desktop and choose the Properties option. You should see the Display Properties dialog box.

2. Select the Settings page. Click the Advanced button to see the Advanced Display Properties dialog box. Select the Monitor tab. You'll see an Advanced Display Properties dialog box, similar to the one shown in Figure 16.5.

    The Monitor Type group shows you which monitors you have installed. As you can see in Figure 16.5, Windows XP allows more than one monitor. The Screen Refresh Rate field enables you to set the refresh rate of the display. Using a higher refresh rate usually results in less eye fatigue. Unfortunately, a high refresh rate also produces more heat. In some situations, one refresh rate will interact with the lighting in your office and another doesn't. Always check this setting to make sure that Windows selections really work in your situation. Another option, Hide Modes That This Monitor Cannot Display, affects the content of the List All Modes dialog box, accessed from the Adapter tab. If you clear this checkbox, you can see all of the modes your display adapter can display. Comparing the results of the two displays (checked and cleared) tells you how many modes your monitor doesn't support that your display adapter can provide.

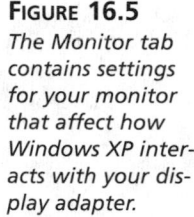

Figure 16.5
The Monitor tab contains settings for your monitor that affect how Windows XP interacts with your display adapter.

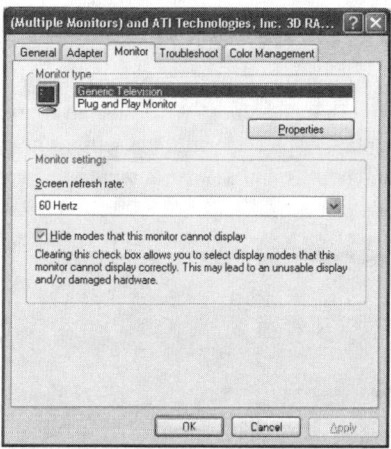

Note: Previous versions of Windows included a Reset Display on Suspend/Resume checkbox, which told Windows XP to send the monitor a reset signal when you resumed a session. Unfortunately, this feature is no longer in place and Windows XP doesn't appear to support it. This may mean shutting your monitor off and starting it again if it doesn't work within the confines of settings that Windows XP does provide.

3. Choose the monitor you want to upgrade in the Monitor Type list and then click the Properties button on the Monitor page. You'll see the Monitor Properties dialog box.

4. Follow steps 4 through 12 in the "Installing or Upgrading a Display Adapter" section, earlier in this chapter, to upgrade your monitor.

Monitors are especially troublesome in Windows in general, and Windows XP is no exception. A monitor can last for years, but the Microsoft mentality is seconds. Consequently, I often find myself working directly with INF files in order to restore settings for monitors that Microsoft deems too old. We've discussed how to modify INF files in the "Creating Your Own INF Files" section of Chapter 4.

Because monitors are such a big headache and Windows XP has wiped out so many helpful features, I show you specifically how to create an INF file for a monitor in Chapter 4. If you can find monitor settings in an earlier version of Windows, you can generally move them to Windows XP with care. Otherwise, all you need is the manual that came with your monitor to create the INF file. Make sure you do install the correct monitor for your system so that you don't miss any features.

Using the Troubleshoot Tab

The Troubleshoot tab of the Advanced Display Properties dialog box (see Figure 16.6) doesn't really help you troubleshoot anything. What this tab contains is hardware acceleration features for your display adapter. In short, the settings help you select a level of acceleration that works with your display adapter, monitor, and applications.

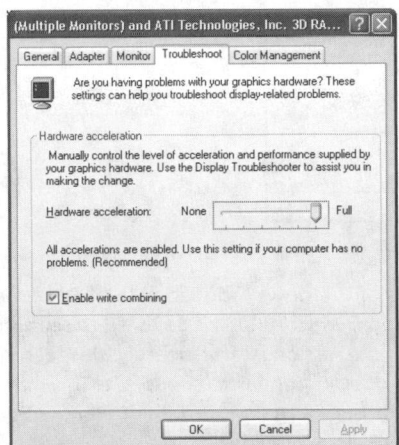

FIGURE 16.6
Use the Trouble-shoot tab settings to adjust the hardware acceleration for your machine.

The first setting you should check if you're experiencing any form of display corruption with Windows XP is Enable Write Combining. This is a new feature for Windows XP that seems to work well with new high-speed display adapters, but drives older adapters crazy. For example, one display adapter I worked with is an ATI All-in-Wonder Pro. With 8MB of video RAM, it still does the job for my client's needs, but the adapter experienced problems with Windows XP. Turning this setting off solved the problem.

The second setting you should check on the Troubleshoot tab is the Hardware Acceleration slider. Most modern display adapters can use the Full setting. In fact, you need that setting if you want to play games successfully under Windows XP. Business applications run just fine with lower acceleration rates. If you find that the system is locking up or you still have display corruption after disabling write combining, try setting the slider one notch lower. Keep trying the setting at each successive notch until you find one that works.

> **Tip:** You may wonder how the changes you make on the Troubleshoot tab affect your system because the tab doesn't tell you. Choose Start | Run to open the Run dialog box. Type **DXDIAG** in the Open field and click OK. You'll see the DirectX Diagnostic Tool. Select the Display tab to obtain a better idea of how the changes you make in the Troubleshoot tab affect your system. You can learn more about the DirectX Diagnostic Tool in the "Testing Your Hardware" section of Chapter 10.

Color management is an important part of your computing environment if you output what you see onscreen in color through a printer or other device. We've already discussed the printer end of color management in the "Color Management Tab" section of Chapter 14. Color management for monitors works essentially the same way: You select one or more color profiles on the Color Management tab by clicking Add and then choose the profile you want to use. The Remove button deletes any old color profiles. You select a default profile by highlighting the profile you want to use and clicking Set As Default.

Using More Than One Display

One of the features provided by Windows XP is the capability to use more than one display. It might seem like an unnecessary feature to people used to working with one display; multiple displays, however, can provide quite a bit of added functionality when used the right way.

The most obvious place this feature helps is in programming. Programmers can view the code they're working on in one display and view its output in another. This has the potential to increase programmer productivity, and it also makes it easier for programmers to find some types of bugs.

Game programs will probably use this feature soon as well. Consider being able to see the countryside on one display, uninterrupted by everything that takes up display space now. You could, for example, place your character statistics and inventory on a second display. Another way this technology could be used is to provide a display everywhere you'd find one in a real airplane. Rather than switch views with a joystick control, you could turn your head and look around. There are many other ways you'll see this technology used in games. It just depends on what game vendors can think up and whether users want to buy more than one display.

Imagine how useful multiple displays could be for stockbrokers who need to track more than one item at a time. In fact, multiple displays could help anyone who's looking for a little relief from a crowded Desktop.

How do you control multiple displays? Just use the Settings tab of the Display Properties dialog box. (Right-click the Desktop and select Properties from the context menu to display this dialog box.) At the top of the dialog box, you'll see a monitor. In the center of the monitor is a number that indicates the display adapter you're working with. (When using lower-resolution displays, you might have to click the monitor to see the number.)

If you want to use a different monitor—or just see the settings it's using—choose it from the Monitor drop-down list box. Click the Want to Use This Monitor checkbox when you see the monitor you want. Don't worry—Windows XP will continue to update applications that appear in other monitors as you work with the foreground monitor.

Understanding the Accelerated Graphics Port (AGP)

Display adapter vendors are working harder each year to get the last ounce of power from various graphics technologies. Just looking at a game such as Quake or an application such as CorelDRAW tells you that graphics have become more than just a nice bonus feature. The Internet itself is rife with various presentations. You even can watch full-motion video on many sites, especially those using Microsoft's NetShow or RealAudio.

The Accelerated Graphics Port (AGP) is the latest technology in the display adapter arsenal. Rather than keep graphics on the extension bus—where they've been all these years—AGP places them on the high-speed memory bus. The result is improved drawing speed, especially for 3D graphics, such as those used in many CAD programs, and games, such as Doom. The AGP provides vendors with lots of bandwidth—66MHz at 32 bits wide. You can find the following levels of AGP support:

- 1X (266MB/s)
- 2X (533MB/s)
- 4X (1.07GB/s)

To put this into perspective, a typical 3D PCI display adapter used today has a 33MHz bus speed and a data transfer rate of 133MB/sec. A PCI display adapter can maintain somewhere between 15 and 30 frames per second (fps) when drawing on a 640×480, 24-bit color display. An AGP display adapter can conceivably maintain a 75fps rate. Rather than provide graphics that look somewhat jumpy at times, an AGP display adapter provides smooth animation without any jumpiness.

AGP solves another problem. Currently, your display adapter uses memory that's totally separate from main memory. This means that you can only use whatever memory you have installed on the display adapter, even if you have free memory elsewhere on the computer. In most cases, this limits a programmer to between 4MB and 64MB of VRAM for storing graphics images, texture maps, and sprites. An AGP display adapter continues to provide high-speed DDR SDRAM or VRAM storage. However, it also has access to system memory. This means graphics programmers have access to up to 4GB of RAM under Windows XP in addition to the VRAM used for fast graphics storage. (Intel recommends that programmers use video memory for display purposes but move other video objects, such as textures, to system memory.)

Another feature AGP provides is *sideband addressing*. This feature enables the graphics processor to talk with the system over multiple channels, which enables it to hold several conversations at once. One channel, for example, could be transferring data from main memory to VRAM while another channel is getting instructions from the CPU on what to draw next. Sideband addressing can provide a large gain in performance after programmers learn how to use it. Developers will have to rewrite software to use this feature before you'll see any performance gain. (Programmers can access AGP through the DirectDraw API while Windows manages details, such as mapping from system memory to video memory, in the background.)

> **Tip:** Two of the better sites on the Internet for additional information about AGP are `http://www.asus.com/Products/Techref/Misc/Agp/agpqa.html` and `http://www.agpforum.org/`. Both sites contain links that offer information about AGP. You also can download a copy of the Intel specification at `http://www.intel.com/technology/agp/agp_index.htm`. If you want up-to-the-minute information about AGP from Microsoft, go to `http://www.microsoft.com/hwdev/`.

On Your Own

An underpowered machine might not provide the speed people need to get their work done fast. Try a variety of display resolutions and color-level settings to find a compromise between system performance and the aesthetic value of the display. Also, try various font size settings. Perhaps a custom setting will provide that perfect balance between readability and the number of icons you can fit on the Desktop or within an Explorer pane.

Check your System folder to see if you can find all the files that make up the video subsystem. Use the video subsystem discussion in this chapter as the basis for your search.

Look through the documentation for your monitor and video adapter. Which graphics standards does your equipment follow? It always helps to know where to find this kind of information before you go to a store to buy new equipment. Never take the salesperson's word for what a piece of equipment can do; verify that it meets the standards required to get the job done.

If you haven't updated a 3D graphics card that contains a minimum of 8MB (32MB or 64MB is much better), now is the time to do it. The performance of your machine will suffer when using an older display adapter. In addition, now might be the time to upgrade to AGP if your motherboard provides the required slot. In most cases, you see an instant improvement in your display capabilities when using AGP rather than an older PCI display adapter.

Spend some time looking at the various settings on the Advanced Display Properties dialog box. Most people don't realize how much of an impact these settings have on your system. If you have a hard time seeing them, try using a higher dpi value for your monitor. Make sure your system uses an appropriate refresh rate as well. Finally, check the monitor setting for your system. If you don't have the right monitor installed, you're missing many features your display adapter might be able to provide.

17

Mobile Computing

Few business travelers can get by without their constant companion, a notebook (laptop or portable) computer. No longer do people regard notebooks as second computers. Notebooks contain most, if not all, of the same features as desktop computers. The only differences are the display, mouse, and keyboard, all of which you can replace with better third-party substitutes.

> **Note:** This chapter uses the term *notebook computer* in a generic way to refer to all mobile computers. Computers in this category vary in size and capability. Many members of the media use *notebook* to refer to the smallest and least-capable class of mobile computer. They apply *laptop* to mobile computers of medium size and capability. Some people still use the term *portable computer* to refer to those mobile computers that are mobile in name only. This chapter avoids the confusion of introducing multiple names for mobile computers by referring to them as *notebooks*.

For most road warriors, the notebook has replaced the desktop machine of old for a number of reasons. The notebook is small and portable. Vendors also design notebooks for ease of maintenance. In fact, most users who spend any time on the road use docking stations to gain the benefits of a desktop machine from their notebook. Unfortunately, the docking stations don't always work as anticipated (an issue we'll discuss in the "Hot Docking" section of this chapter).

This chapter helps you better understand the link between Windows XP and your notebook computer. A *notebook* computer is the smallest computer that will run Windows XP. In fact, Microsoft spent a great deal of time trying to beef up the support for notebook computers in Windows XP. You'll find that you have fewer problems than ever before in using Windows XP with your notebook and that the new features actually make notebook use pleasurable.

The notebook is actually too large for some business users today, so we'll also discuss the handheld device. We'll concentrate on the Personal Digital Assistant (PDA) in this chapter. Yes, some companies are touting their cellular telephone solutions, but this technology isn't ready for prime time in most cases. The best you can hope to achieve is voice mail and e-mail support.

Many of the trade press articles you read discuss how some companies are lowering their total cost of ownership (TCO) numbers by giving some users a PDA in place of a notebook. The PDA is an extremely useful tool in a small package. If you have a Palm computer, you can read your e-mail and manage your contact list. PocketPC users have access to even more in the form of an Internet Explorer clone, miniature version of Word, Excel, and even Access. In short, you really could replace your notebook with a PDA in some situations.

Of course, the big difference between a notebook computer and a PDA for this chapter is that the notebook computer runs Windows XP. PDAs run a variety of operating systems. The closest you get to Windows is using Windows CE on a PocketPC system. Even so, PDAs use a different processor than their notebook and desktop kin, making any direct comparisons difficult. Because of the Windows XP support issue, I'm limiting the PDA discussion in this chapter to creating a connection between your Windows XP machine and your PDA.

> **Note:** You'll notice a difference in the screen shots for this chapter. I'm using the Windows 2000 interface and have turned off all of the extra "gizmos" that Microsoft includes to conserve power. You'll find that the extra pizzazz of the Windows XP interface burns considerable power, especially when you're using the battery. We discuss this problem further as this chapter progresses. The bottom line is that a Spartan interface is one of the best things you can do for your notebook computer battery.

PCMCIA Devices on Your Notebook Computer

The Personal Computer Memory Card International Association (PCMCIA) bus is a "little" bus, specially designed to meet the needs of the notebook computer market. However, you'll also find it in a growing number of desktop machines. The PCMCIA bus uses credit-card–size cards that connect to external slots on the machine. This is perfect for notebooks because they're notorious for providing few, if any, expansion slots. A PCMCIA bus makes it easy for the user to change a machine hardware configuration without opening the computer up. For example, you could take out a memory card to make room for a modem card.

This bus also supports solid-state disk drives in the form of flash ROM or SRAM boards. Flash ROM boards are especially interesting because they provide the same access speeds as regular memory but with the permanence of other long-term storage media, such as hard drives. Unlike SRAM boards, flash ROM boards don't require battery backup. Many people use solid-state drives to store applications or databases that change infrequently.

Windows XP provides more levels of PCMCIA support than previous versions of Windows. For example, it supports the PC Card 32 (Cardbus) bridges. You also can use 3.3-volt cards in addition to the older 5-volt models. Windows XP also supports multi-function PCMCIA cards and specialty devices, such as Global Positioning Satellite (GPS) cards.

The capability to change cards on the fly means Windows XP needs to adjust dynamically. You wouldn't want Windows XP to try to access a card that's no longer in place. Plug and Play enables Windows XP to detect and compensate for changes in the PCM-CIA bus configuration. This means users don't need to reconfigure their systems when a component changes. Microsoft designed Windows XP to detect system changes and to make the appropriate modifications to its setup.

Windows XP does provide a PC Card (PCMCIA) Properties dialog box for managing your PC Cards. You access it by double-clicking the PC Card (PCMCIA) applet in the Control Panel or by double-clicking the PC Card (PCMCIA) Status icon in the Notification Area. (Some vendors call this a Safely Remove Hardware icon—you might see other names depending on your machine vendor.)

Using Windows XP drivers enables the PCMCIA enhanced mode. What does enhanced support give you? The following list is an overview of enhanced support features:

- *Friendly device names* Provides users with device names they can recognize. It also helps users determine which devices are present and which are disconnected.

- *Automatic installation* Enables the user to hot-swap various devices in and out of the PCMCIA slot without worrying about reconfiguring the machine.

- *Drive-change detection* Detects RAM drive device changes. If enhanced support is disabled, the user sometimes has to unmount and then mount a PCMCIA drive before Windows XP recognizes the change.

- *Other device-specific mode and configuration information* Displays additional information about PCMCIA or the cards it supports. Check the documentation that accompanies the specific device for further details about special features.

The PC Card (PCMCIA) Properties dialog box contains a few options for managing PCMCIA cards. The first checkbox, Show Control on Taskbar, displays an icon in the Notification Area. (Some vendors fail to include this option, which means you'll always see the icon in the Notification Area of the Taskbar.) You can use this icon to obtain a list of installed cards, to stop a card that's installed, or to display a context menu containing the Properties option. The second checkbox instructs Windows to display a message if you try to remove a card before you stop its operation. (Some vendors have also eliminated this option in an effort to automate PCMCIA usage.)

Just what does "stopping" a card mean? Stopping a card tells Windows XP to remove support for that feature. Windows XP usually detects changes in your PCMCIA setup.

You can help it along, however, by stopping the card before you remove it. Just highlight the card you want to stop and then click the Stop button.

Next, take a look at the Global Settings tab of the PC Card (PCMCIA) Properties dialog box. (Some newer laptops such as the IBM Thinkpad T21 lack this tab.) There are only a few options on this tab. You usually keep the Automatic Selection option checked. Clearing this option enables you to set the card-service memory area manually—a task you usually need to perform for troubleshooting purposes only. The second checkbox, Disable PC Card Sound Effects, tells Windows that you don't want to hear sound effects every time the status of the PCMCIA bus changes.

Generally, the PCMCIA support under Windows XP runs without a hitch. That's because you aren't fighting with real mode drivers that some vendors insist on installing on older systems. In a few cases, you might run into trouble, just as you would with any other device. The following list provide additional troubleshooting tips you can use when experiencing PCMCIA problems:

- Windows XP usually tells you when there's an I/O port address or interrupt conflict. To make sure, however, you should check the settings in the Resources tab of the PCIC or Compatible PCMCIA Controller Properties dialog box. (PCIC stands for peripheral connect interface card.) To open this dialog box, right-click My Computer and select Properties from the context menu. Select the Hardware tab and click Device Manager. Any nonfunctional devices have a yellow question mark on their icon.

- Always make sure that you have a card installed in at least one of the slots while booting. Failure to do so can prevent Windows XP from detecting the PCMCIA card slot.

- Make sure Windows XP supports your card by checking it with the Hardware Installation Wizard in the Control Panel.

Microsoft's support of PCMCIA has increased dramatically as users have purchased more notebooks. If your machine works with Windows XP at all, it's likely that Windows XP will also support your PCMCIA card slot. However, it always pays to check with your notebook vendor to ensure that your notebook will work with Windows XP. In some cases, you might require an upgrade.

Hot Docking

At the beginning of this chapter, I mentioned that Windows XP has a solution to your docking problems. A Plug and Play feature called hot docking enables you to remove a portable computer from its docking station without turning it off. The portable automatically reconfigures itself to reflect the loss of docking station capability. If you plug that portable back into the original docking station, or into a new one somewhere else, it automatically reconfigures itself to take advantage of the new capabilities the docking station provides.

Hot docking isn't a new feature. Windows 9x and Windows 2000 both provided hot docking support (Windows NT doesn't have this support, nor do early versions of Windows 9x). The news for Windows XP is that hot docking support seems stable. You'll find that the configuration changes occur automatically and you don't need to check them as you did in the past. I've also found that some annoying glitches, such as odd networking behavior, are gone.

> **Tip:** It isn't always a good idea to move your computer with the power on. Sure, it can save you a little time when you perform a setup. Unless you're in the middle of something you spent hours setting up, however, it's usually better to shut down and turn the power off before you remove the computer from its docking station. Moving a computer with the power on can create surges or other electrical interference that shorten the life of your machine. You could accidentally short something out, for example, when removing the notebook from its docking station. Moving your machine from place to place without turning it off is a supported option, but you need to consider the cost of exercising it.

I'm still finding a few oddities in hot docking that you need to know about. Some of you may also see these problems as you work with Windows XP. The biggest problem appears when you remove the machine after working with a server that uses another operating system, such as NetWare or Linux. In some cases, I found that the other operating system didn't log me out for several hours, making it impossible to log back in if I put the notebook computer back into the docking station. The only way around this problem is to log the affected user out manually at the server console (or using something like RConsole to do it from your desk).

Another hot docking problem relates to the first. Some people experience problems with phantom computers on their system. The computer is no longer hot docked or connected to the network, but Windows refuses to recognize the loss. This problem is especially prevalent when working with a mix of older and newer computers on the same system. Generally, using View | Refresh cures the problem. However, in some cases, you simply have to wait until the system realizes that the notebook computer is gone and removes it from the list.

Windows XP does fix some of the more interesting hot docking problems that Windows 2000 users experienced. For example, some Windows 2000 users couldn't get the notebook computer display to work after undocking their system. Fortunately, this problem had an easy fix, but most users didn't know about the "secret handshake" for implementing it. If you're interested in history, you can learn more about this problem at http://support.microsoft.com/support/kb/articles/Q228/3/36.ASP.

Hot Swapping

Another problem I talked about earlier in this chapter is the need for a capability to take one card out of the PCMCIA slot and plug another into its place. Plug and Play answers the call here as well. A Plug and Play–compatible system reconfigures itself dynamically. You might have seen advertisements for portables that provide hot swapping, a component of the Plug and Play specification. *Hot swapping* enables you to remove components from a machine without rebooting it.

> **Warning:** Never touch the contacts of your PCMCIA cards when you remove them from the bus. Doing so could give the card a static-electric shock that might damage it or shorten its life.

Hot swapping enables you to change cards without turning the machine off. The computer automatically recognizes that it can no longer communicate with the Internet, for example, and that network lines are now open. The Plug and Play component of Windows XP even installs the required drivers and configures them in the background. This means users no longer need to worry about how a device works; they can now focus on the work they need the device to perform. (The only exception to this rule is when Windows XP can't find the required drivers on your hard disk. It then asks you to supply a disk containing the required drivers.)

You can run into some interesting problems with hot swapping as well. For example, you normally don't want to hot-swap a hard drive. It's possible, but some users experience problems when they try to do it with Windows XP. The problem occurs most often with Ultra Direct Memory Addressing (UDMA) Integrated Device Electronics (IDE) drives. What you'll generally see is that the notebook computer enters a sleep state or freezes completely. Fortunately, this problem is rarer than it was under Windows 2000.

Another problem you'll run into is that the system will display two devices when you replace one device with another. In this case, it appears that Windows XP doesn't enumerate the devices correctly after the swap. This problem also appeared when using Windows 2000, and Microsoft produced a partial fix for it. You can always get rid of this problem by rebooting your machine (or you can simply ignore the extra device).

Multifunction PC Cards

Most notebooks are limited to two PC card slots. This means you can either do lots of swapping to get added functionality from your notebook or make use of a new feature offered by Windows XP—the capability to use multifunction PC cards.

Multifunction PC cards provide the functionality of multiple cards in one slot. You might see a PC card, for example, that provides both modem and network card functionality. Multifunction PC cards enable you to extend your notebook even further and reduce wear and tear on your machine by making the need for card swaps less frequent than before.

Advanced Configuration and Power Interface (ACPI)

One major goal for most notebook vendors is getting more out of a single battery. Achieving that goal, however, has been difficult. Users have lacked the capability to set up their machines to use battery power completely and still use the notebook as a desktop replacement.

Windows XP provides an improved power-management scheme that gives users full flexibility in configuring how the power-saving features in any computer are used. You access this configuration capability through the Power Options applet in the Control Panel or by double-clicking the battery icon in the Notification Area.

Figure 17.1 shows a typical Power Options Properties dialog box for a Toshiba laptop. Your display might vary from the one shown. For example, the IBM laptops use a somewhat different dialog box arrangement. The first section of the Settings for Portable/Laptop power scheme area contains two items: Turn Off Monitor and Turn Off Hard Disks. The second section contains System Standby and System Hibernate items. All four items have two columns of settings: one for plugged in and a second for on batteries.

FIGURE 17.1

Use the Power Options Properties dialog box to configure the power-management scheme for your computer.

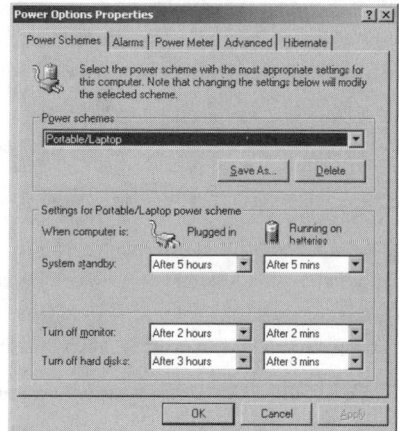

Vendors often include other tabs in the Power Options Properties dialog box. For example, Figure 17.1 includes an Alarms tab and a Power Meter tab. I'll describe both later in this section. You should also note the Hibernate tab, which is a new Windows XP feature. This feature also appears on desktop machines, even if the desktop doesn't support other power-management features.

Look at the Power Schemes tab of the Power Options Properties dialog box. The settings in this dialog box affect three major subsystems: system standby, monitor, and hard disk. Notebook computers usually provide individual settings for wall power and battery power. Using two sets of settings enables you to define different power strategies for the two environments without having to open the Power Options Properties dialog box all the time. You can also save various power-management schemes, just as you're able to do with sound schemes. You can create a power-management scheme for regular use, another for travel, and still another for when you perform machine maintenance.

> **Tip:** Windows XP's power-management features monitor keyboard and mouse activity and automatically shut down the machine after a specified period of inactivity, even if you're performing an unattended task, such as downloading a file. That's why you should set up schemes for downloading and maintenance that don't shut down the machine for a long time (or at all). You can always shut down just the monitor and save power when not viewing it.

Most laptop vendors provide alarms so that you know when battery power is running out. I'm assuming that most laptop vendors provide something equivalent to the Alarms tab because it's such a useful feature. Look at the Alarms tab in the Power Options Properties dialog box. There are two alarms—one for a low battery and another for a critical battery. You can use the slider for either alarm to set the amount of power left in the battery when the alarm goes off.

Clicking Alarm Action displays a Critical Battery Alarm Actions dialog box. You can set the type of alarm you want to receive, and you can specify other actions for the computer to perform automatically, such as going into either standby or shutdown mode. The alarm can display a message, play a sound, or both. When you choose to place the machine in shutdown or standby mode, you can also decide whether to force the mode change. In some applications, forcing the machine to shut down or to go into standby mode could cause data loss. In most situations, however, shutting the system down saves the data.

The Power Meter tab shows you the current power status of your machine. A checkbox enables you to display the specifics for each battery installed. This tab also shows you the amount of power left in the battery and the estimated time it'll last. You can even click the battery icon to see specifics about your battery, such as the manufacturer.

The Advanced tab enables you to set two power-management options. The first option is to display the power meter in the Notification Area. Selecting this option enables you to set various battery options without opening the Control Panel. The second option is to prompt for a password whenever the machine goes from standby mode to full power. This feature closes a security hole in which someone could wake your sleeping notebook and gain access to company secrets.

As mentioned earlier, the Hibernate tab is a new feature for Windows XP. It contains a single option, Enable Hibernate. Check this option if you want the machine to hibernate after a period of inactivity. For example, you might want to use this option if you plan to leave the machine on overnight. The tab also tells you how much free space your hard drive has and the amount of disk space required by Hibernate. You must have enough disk space to store the contents of RAM or else Hibernate will fail.

Windows XP Mobile Computing Services

Microsoft provides more of the same computing services in Windows XP. You'll find that Briefcase is still your best friend when going on the road because it helps you store data locally and synchronize it with your main copy later. This feature isn't exclusive to mobile computer users, though. I've used it to send files to people across a network. Experiment to see where it works best for you.

> **Tip:** The rumors of the demise of Briefcase are greatly exaggerated; Microsoft simply hid the feature to make life more interesting for average users. Unlike previous versions of Windows, Windows XP installs Briefcase by default. Unfortunately, Windows XP doesn't create a Briefcase for you, so many users assume that the feature is missing. To create a new Briefcase, right-click the Desktop and choose New | Briefcase from the context menu. Windows XP will create a new Briefcase that you can name anything. In fact, you can create multiple Briefcases on your Desktop, one for each project.

This section also looks at Dial-Up Networking from a notebook user's perspective. You can get around potential problems by using this feature to communicate on the road. Windows XP uses a different method than previous versions of Windows to create a remote access connection. You'll learn about the desktop computer end of Dial-Up Networking in the "Making Software Attachments" section of Chapter 18.

Briefcase

One of my favorite Notebook features for Windows XP (and all previous versions of Windows) is Briefcase. As its name suggests, you use the Windows Briefcase to store files you need to move from place to place. The Briefcase is an application stored on the Desktop, like the Recycle Bin and My Computer.

Setting up your Briefcase is easy. It installs with the Windows software automatically. Just stuff the Briefcase with files you plan to move from place to place. This should be a centralized storage location for all the files you work on, even if those files appear in different areas of your hard drive.

Working with Briefcase files is no different from working with any other files. Windows XP monitors the status of the files and presents a display when you open the Briefcase icon, as shown in Figure 17.2. This display informs you when you need to update or synchronize the Briefcase to match the files on your desktop machine. Select the Briefcase | Update All command if files are out-of-date. When the files are up-to-date, you can move the Briefcase from your machine to a network drive or floppy disk.

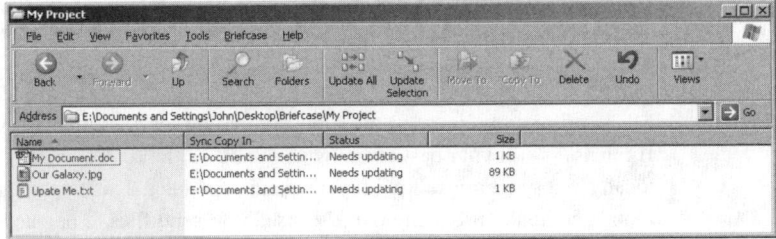

FIGURE 17.2
Briefcase offers a fast and convenient method of centralizing your files.

Briefcase provides a context menu for each of its files, just like the context menus in Explorer. The one special feature on this context menu is an Update option. Select this option when you want to synchronize the copy on your notebook computer with the one on your desktop machine. Briefcase also provides a Properties dialog box for each document. The General, Summary, and Security tabs all look like those for a standard document. However, the special Update Status tab, shown in Figure 17.3, enables you to perform Briefcase-specific tasks with the document.

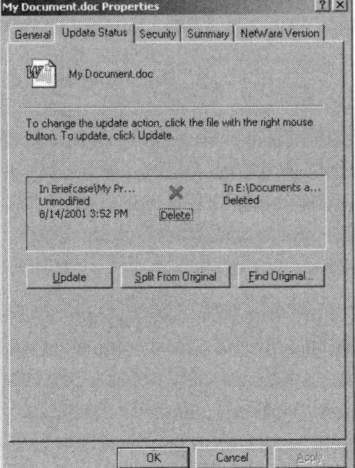

FIGURE 17.3
The Update Status tab helps you perform Briefcase-specific tasks with your document.

As you can see, the Update Status tab provides information about the document in your Briefcase. The status information tells you how this document compares to the one on your desktop machine (when known). For example, you can determine if the original file exists or if the document on your desktop machine is newer.

There's an interesting feature in the central field that contains the status information. All that this area tells you is the comparison information between the Briefcase and the original file. However, if you right-click this area, you'll see a context menu that enables you to perform tasks with the file, such as create a new copy or remove it from Briefcase. In this case, I purposely deleted the file on my desktop machine. With a simple right-click, I can choose to create a duplicate copy of that file on my Desktop using the Briefcase copy as a template.

How many times have you wished you had a copy of your original file? Wouldn't it be nice to restore a document to its original form without resorting to a backup tape? If you keep your Briefcase up-to-date, you always can restore an original copy of a document after you change it. This safety feature comes in handy when a few hours of editing don't turn out as you anticipated. This list has a third entry that enables you to skip an update. Just select the skip option (it might say Don't Update or Don't Delete) and close the dialog box. This option enables you to retain the original version of this particular file even if you choose to update all your other files.

> **Tip:** You can use the Briefcase as a rudimentary version-control system. Here's how it works. Create an additional Briefcase as you reach each new milestone in a project. Change the name of the new Briefcase to match the milestone's name or date. Place a copy of all the files in the Briefcase, but never update it. You should end up with a bunch of Briefcases, each one representing a stage of your project. Although this technique consumes lots of hard drive space, it also saves you lots of rework time later.

Three buttons in the Update Status tab of a document's Properties dialog box enable you to manipulate the link you've created. The Update button updates your linked copy to match the original document (or does just the opposite). The direction of the Replace arrow determines the direction of the update. The Briefcase default is to update whichever document is older. The Split From Original button enables you to separate the copy from the original. This button comes in handy if you decide to make a new document from the copy in your Briefcase. The Find Original button opens a copy of Explorer with the original document highlighted. You can use this button to find a document in the Briefcase quickly.

Using your Briefcase is simple. Right-drag the files you want to take home from your desktop machine to the Briefcase on your laptop. When you let go of the mouse, you'll see a context menu containing a Make Sync Copy option. Choose this option and Windows XP will place a copy of the file in your Briefcase. The original file and the copy in the Briefcase now have a link. Any change you make in the Briefcase file will appear in the original when you synchronize the files.

Synchronizing Files

Keeping the files on your notebook computer in sync with your desktop system isn't just a nicety—it's a necessity. Taking work home is one thing; making sure those changes get into the final document is something else. The easiest way to keep your files in sync is to use the same machine as both notebook and desktop. This isn't always practical, though.

Before Windows XP, notebook users had only two choices for keeping files from two or more machines in sync. One method was to keep all the mobile data on a floppy. Then you just passed the floppy around as necessary to keep the files in sync. This easy solution also had a significant problem: A floppy's access speed isn't very good, and its storage capacity is much more limited than a hard drive.

The other solution was to copy files from your hard drive to a floppy and then back again. This had the advantage of using the best possible speed for opening and using files. Its main disadvantage was that it relied on a person's memory to make sure files were kept in sync.

Using the Briefcase option in Windows XP is a big step forward for notebook users. It has the speed advantage of creating a copy, without any of the memory problems. Synchronization is easy: Just right-click on the Briefcase and choose Update All from the context menu. You can also update individual files by right-clicking on them inside Briefcase and choosing Update from the context menu.

Is Briefcase the only Windows XP solution to the problem of keeping files synchronized? Probably not. I've also used the folder concept that I've discussed in various places in this book. It helps a group to keep one set of files on a central machine in sync. However, how do you use this feature if you're working on a document at home? That's where Dial-Up Networking comes into play. Instead of simply moving a Briefcase around, you can use Dial-Up Networking to call into the network and edit the files from a remote location. That way, even though you're working on the file from another location, your team can continue updating it as well.

> **Tip:** If you're a team supervisor, using the combination of folders and Dial-Up Networking is ideal. It enables you to continue your work while on the road without resorting to the Briefcase. Even if you're the only one currently working on the documents, there might be an occasion when a team member needs them as well. If you use the Briefcase, however, people working in the office don't know whether they're using the current versions of the documents. Using this combination also enables you to monitor the team's progress. Checking in each day to see the work they've accomplished helps you keep an eye on things back home while you're on the road.

Remote Dial-Up (Dial-Up Networking)

A remote connection to your server can be a lifeline while on the road. Instead of working with static data, you can work with the same data everyone else from the company uses. As mentioned earlier, you'll find the desktop view of creating a remote access connection in the "Making Software Attachments" section of Chapter 18. However, once you get the software installed and configured, where do you go from there? If you're a notebook user, there are plenty of reasons to use Dial-Up Networking:

- *Document access* I've already mentioned how you can use Dial-Up Networking to enable an entire group of people to work together. All you need to do is place a folder with shortcuts to the team's documents in a network folder. When a person calls into the network, he can open the folder and see all the pieces of the project without looking very hard for them. I often place this folder in the user's home directory on the network. That way, I can personalize each folder as required and the user doesn't need to memorize yet another location on the network.

- *Application access* You probably don't need to access applications (such as word processors or spreadsheets) from a remote location very often. However, what do you do about the custom database your company uses as a contact manager? Unless you plan to either print the entire database or create a copy of it on your notebook hard drive, you need to access it remotely. In fact, this is probably the only way you could use this centralized application if it contains sales or inventory information you'll need to update later. (We'll also discuss the benefits of using disconnected applications in the "Understanding Disconnected Applications (COM+)" section of this chapter.)

- *E-mail* It's amazing how much a company depends on e-mail to keep employees apprised of events. Think about the e-mail messages you receive, such as getting a new access code for the security system or updating your W-2 form. Losing this method of communication means you'll be out of touch when you return from your trip. A few minutes of online time can keep you up-to-date on current situations in your company and can reduce the "vacation" syndrome many people feel after a road trip.

- *Emergency decisions* What if you're traveling in Europe and your company is in California? How do you find a good time to call the company and make a decision that requires a 24-hour turnaround? Using e-mail to leave a message and then checking for responses later can provide a few extra hours of sleep at night. After all, who wants to fight company politics and sleepiness at the same time?

- *Missing-file syndrome* Notebooks almost always need at least twice as much hard disk space as they have. How often have you cleared a bunch of files off your notebook only to find that you needed them after all? A remote connection enables you to grab files you didn't think you'd need. Placing a copy of your desktop machine's hard drive—or, at least, the data—where you can access it with a remote connection can save you trouble later. Be sure to ask the network administrator's permission before you do this.

You'll find that these are the most common ways to use Dial-Up Networking with a notebook. It's important to determine the techniques that apply to your specific situation. For example, in my particular case, I find it handy to use Dial-Up Networking to grab presentations. I have room for only one or two on my notebook, but I might need several during the time I'm on the road. This feature enables me to call in and grab the next presentation I need. The result is that each presentation is then fresh and specifically designed for the group I'm talking with, yet I don't have to lug around a monster-size hard drive or other storage medium.

Remote Network Users

Networking is an essential part of any business today. I've already talked about Dial-Up Networking to an extent, but let's look at some of the communication and other considerations you need to make. Using Dial-Up Networking is one thing; using it efficiently is another.

I'd like to begin by providing a little insight into one of the problems with using Dial-Up Networking. Most people know that the telephone company charges more for the first three minutes of a long-distance call than for the time that follows. People try to keep their long-distance calls short and to the point. The telephone company capitalizes on this by charging you more when you make several short calls instead of one long one.

Given this set of circumstances, imagine the difference in cost between making one long computer call and a bunch of short ones. It's easy to get into the habit of dialing your company every time you need information. Consolidating your information needs into one call is better than making several short ones. You can also save money by delivering all your mail during off-peak hours.

There are times when it's impossible to take care of all your communication needs in one call. You'll still find the need to make a few short calls during the day to gather information. You don't have to do that for message delivery. Delivering e-mail responses and performing other chores always can wait until off-peak hours, especially when you're overseas and the recipient won't see it until after you're in bed anyway.

The following sections describe other methods you can use to reduce the cost of Dial-Up Networking. Although these techniques don't work when your need for data exchange with another party is immediate, they work in the majority of cases.

Local Communications

There are many forms of long-distance communication, and some of them are local. Here's one scenario: You're in Detroit and your company is in Los Angeles. It's important that you send a file containing new information about your client to an assistant for processing. You also need additional information about another client that's stored in your company database. You have access to both Dial-Up Networking and the Internet. Which do you use? Some people would use Dial-Up Networking because it's faster and more convenient. In this case, however, the low-cost solution would be the Internet.

Sometimes, the obvious choice isn't the one you should use. Suppose that you need to transfer the aforementioned files and retrieve the same information. This time, however, you're in another part of the state instead of in another part of the country. You could call your ISP, but that would entail a toll call and potentially some long wait times if you experience the usual Internet lag. If you make the toll call directly to your company, however, it costs only about 40 cents and you gain access to a high-speed modem with little or no lag time. In this case, using Dial-Up Networking is the right choice.

If your company has its own Internet address, you might be able to access it to transfer information over a local call. You still need an account with a local provider to make this work, however. As with the other suggestions in this section, you should compare the cost of using an Internet solution against that of making a long-distance call.

Dynamic Networking

Despite your best efforts, sometimes you need to work "live" with the company database or applications. You can't solve every problem with e-mail or a file upload. At times, working with live applications or data is the only way to get the job done. You should keep these times to a minimum, but keeping a local database management system (DBMS) current might override other cost considerations. Even if your company is in this situation, you don't need to pay through the nose to get the kind of service you want. Your notebook still has a few tricks up its sleeve to help solve the problem. The following is a list of the ideas I've come up with, but you can probably think of others based on your unique set of circumstances.

> **Tip:** If you're using a custom DBMS, it might be possible to add batch-updating capabilities to it. This would enable you to use a smaller version of the application on the road to create new records, modify existing ones, and make changes in batch mode when you return from your trip. You could also make the update as part of an upload to the company database. In many cases, this is a less-expensive solution for inventory control or other types of sales databases than making the changes live. There are two criteria for using a batch system. First, you need a large outside sales force to make the change cost-efficient. Second, the company must be able to get by with daily or weekly database updates instead of real-time data. This works in most situations, but you couldn't use it for, say, an airline ticket database. COM+ provides a third solution, which we'll discuss later in this chapter.

- *Internet access* Using the Internet still might provide the best means of working with live data. You need to overcome two problems, however. The first is gaining access to a local server that allows live connections. The second is that you have to make a TCP/IP connection and use a special modem to make this work. You can solve both problems given enough resources. In the past, this solution might have seemed more like a dream than reality. Today, intranets (private versions of the Internet) abound. Even small businesses can occasionally write off the cost of using an intranet solution because it's less expensive than anything else.
- *Virtual Private Networking (VPN)* A VPN enables you to create the equivalent of a wide area network (WAN) using the Internet. You have to install VPN support to gain access to this feature. One of the problems with using VPN is a lack of security. Although it's theoretically possible to create a secure connection, many analysts worry that the connection isn't secure enough. In addition, you might

experience reliability problems with this technique. Make sure the developer designs your database manager to recover from partial transactions before you commit to using this method. New technologies, such as eXtensible Markup Language (XML) and Simple Object Access Protocol (SOAP), offer viable solutions in this area.

- *Using a local office's PBX connection* Sometimes, a local office provides the long-distance call solution you need. It might mean a little wrangling with the local boss and, perhaps, a short drive, but this solution could save your company some money.

- *Keeping notes* Even if your database doesn't support batch-mode processing, you still could keep notes and make all the updates at one time. This enables you to make one telephone call instead of many to record the required information. This solution still doesn't work with "live" data, such as ticket sales.

- *Off-hour calling* This is probably the least likely solution. If your data needs are so time-critical that you can't afford to wait even a few minutes, off-hour calling won't work. You could combine this technique, however, with batch-mode or note-taking methods to work with live data on the network. You could even use this off-hour calling technique when using a local office's PBX connection. This might reduce the local boss's objection to tying up the line in order to service your needs.

Offline Printing

Chapter 14 discusses two techniques for offline printing that notebook users will love. The first method is to create a printer for every purpose. You can create printers for all the local offices you'll visit during a trip. That way, you can print whatever you need without worrying about whether you have the proper print driver installed. You also can use this technique to print at client sites that are amenable to your doing so.

This isn't the only way you can print, however. You can also print to your hard drive using the offline printing technique discussed in Chapter 14. Just set the printer to work offline. Everything you send to disk waits on the hard drive until you send it to the printer.

Whenever you disconnect your notebook from the network printer or docking station, Windows XP detects the loss of printing capability and automatically sets the printer to work offline. Unfortunately, this doesn't work all the time. Sometimes, Windows XP doesn't detect the printer disconnection. Check your printer the first time and you should be able to rely on the connection being consistent from that point on.

Understanding Disconnected Applications (COM+)

The term *disconnected application* sounds like some sort of weird science that only a programmer could love. However, you'll find examples of disconnected applications in daily use right now. E-mail is a perfect example of an application you often work with in a disconnected state. Getting e-mail ready offline and then getting online just long enough to transmit the data to a server is one of the common tasks we've all performed.

What makes a disconnected application special? The disconnected applications that Microsoft is talking about rely on Queued Components. It's a programmer-sounding term with a simple meaning. When an application works in the disconnected state, it sends messages to a local mailbox. When you create a connection to your local network, Queued Components automatically sends the messages in the mailbox to the server for processing. As far as you're concerned, the application works the same as it does normally. If you create an order with your database application, it ends up in the local mailbox, rather than on the server, until you connect. You don't have to do anything special to get the order from your machine to the server. Submitting an order is the same in connected and disconnected modes—only the timing of the actual submission changes.

Disconnected applications do have some limitations. For example, if you request the status of an order, you don't receive a reply until you make a connection to the server. The request will remain in your mailbox, but you won't see the result immediately. In some cases, this isn't a problem. You can call a local client later with status information when you upload all of your requests to the server. However, it does mean that disconnected applications aren't quite as convenient as applications with a connection.

Developers are considering a wealth of uses for the disconnected application model. For example, a network administrator may want to track the status of all of the machines under his or her control. This is a relatively easy task to perform on the local network. All you need to do is load an agent on the client machine and then use some type of server-based product to query the agents for status information. Monitoring packages today can tell an administrator everything from what applications a user is working with to the speed of the cooling fan. The laptop version of the agent can make entries in a local mailbox instead of send them to the server immediately. When the user connects to the server, Queued Components sends all of the agent data to the server.

It's easy to misuse any technology. Disconnected applications mean freedom when used correctly. You can go on the road, take orders, and work with clients, all without any need for a connection to the company. It isn't a perfect solution, but at least you can get your work done. However, if you try to use disconnected application technology for an application that requires a live connection (such as monitoring your stock portfolio), you'll be disappointed.

Working with an Infrared Data Access (IrDA) Port

The Infrared Data Association (IrDA) port is a major feature in personal computers. You'll find it on every notebook; even some desktop models are beginning to sport them. Peripheral devices, such as laser printers, offer infrared ports as an option, and it won't be long before IrDA ports become a standard feature on networks. Infrared data ports are becoming popular for good reasons. They're more convenient when you don't need a permanent connection to something.

Let's examine the Windows XP infrared support. Chapter 9 discussed standard hardware installation techniques, so I won't repeat them here. After you install the software for your infrared port, you'll see an Infrared applet in the Control Panel. Double-clicking this applet displays the Infrared Monitor dialog box.

> **Note:** Most notebook computer vendors provide some means for controlling the infrared data port. This section looks at one of the common methods you'll find. However, if your vendor installs special software, you might see dialog boxes and controls that I haven't discussed in this section.

The Status tab of the Infrared Monitor dialog box contains connection information. If there aren't any ports to connect to, a message will tell you so. The tab also shows the status of any existing connections. You can find out how well each connection is working. This information comes in handy when you need to transfer a large amount of data and it seems to be taking too long. Sometimes, you can improve the connection by moving your machine to be more in line with the other infrared data port.

The Options tab of the Infrared Monitor contains settings that control IrDA port operation and configuration. The Enable Infrared Communication option enables infrared communication using a specific serial and parallel port. Windows XP selects a port you haven't associated with another device on your machine.

The second checkbox on the Options tab enables an automatic search for other infrared ports. Scanning for other ports uses processor cycles you might want to devote to other activities. Turning off the scan feature while you're on the road doesn't just make your computer run faster—it saves power too. There's also a field for defining how often you scan for another port. The default value of three seconds works fine in most cases. You might find, however, that a smaller value helps you fine-tune a connection faster. A longer increment could save precious processing cycles after you have a connection established.

The third checkbox on this tab enables you to limit connection speed. That might not seem like a good idea at first, but you might find it helpful in a few situations. The first occasion is when the receiving device can't handle the full-speed connection. You might try to establish a connection with a serial device, for example, and find that it doesn't work properly. Data overruns are the first symptom of this problem. The second occasion occurs when you have a good connection but keep getting data errors. For whatever reason, you're spending more time transmitting old data than new data. Slowing the connection down could reduce data errors and might actually improve the data rate of the connection.

The Enable Software Install for Plug and Play Devices in Range option of this dialog box is simultaneously helpful and annoying. I find it most helpful when visiting locations that I don't visit on a regular basis. This option automatically configures your machine to use any Plug and Play infrared devices that happen to be in the area—making life much more automatic. On the other hand, my machine keeps configuring devices I don't want. You should probably keep this option unchecked unless you're planning to visit a new location.

The Preferences tab of the Infrared Monitor dialog box enables you to set the features of your infrared port. The first checkbox on this tab enables you to display an Infrared icon on the taskbar. As with most icons you can display on the Taskbar, you can perform one of three actions. Holding the mouse pointer over the icon gives you the current port status, a double-click performs a default action (opening the Infrared Monitor dialog box), and a right-click displays a context menu. The context menu contains four entries. The first opens the Infrared Monitor dialog box. The second enables infrared communication. The third option enables automatic searches for other devices in range. The fourth option enables automatic installation for Plug and Play devices.

The next two checkboxes on the Preferences tab work together. The middle checkbox enables you to open the infrared port for interrupted connections. This comes in handy when someone passing by could interrupt the line of sight to the other port. You also should enable it when you have a less-than-ideal connection to the other device. The third checkbox on the Preferences tab tells Windows XP to sound an alarm whenever it finds a device in range or if it loses a connection to another device. It would have been more convenient if Microsoft had used two separate sounds for these events, but at least you get an alert of some kind. You should turn off this option in an office if you're sharing the same space with other people. Some people find the constant noise coming from the computer a little distracting.

The last tab in this dialog box, Identification, contains two edit fields. The first field tells who you are. The second field provides a description of your computer. You should come up with something unique, yet generic, for a portable computer. There isn't any way to know exactly who'll be using your computer, so a generic name is best. On the other hand, you don't want the name you choose to interfere with others on the network.

Power-Management Strategies

Chapters 4 through 6 discussed many useful tips for getting the most out of your computer. You might want to review them when setting up your notebook.

After you get past these basic strategies for making your computer do more with fewer resources, you can start working with special strategies for notebook computers. The following list provides ideas of what to look for on your notebook. Not all notebooks provide every feature listed here, and you certainly might find some features unique to your system. The first tip, then, is to explore the vendor documentation with your notebook. You'll be amazed at the little tips you'll find there.

- *Forget fancy software* Screen savers eat more power on a notebook than most people imagine. Because most notebook computers come with a feature that turns off the monitor automatically, there's no reason for you to install a fancy screen saver. In fact, you might actually cause more harm than good because most notebooks use flat-screen displays. A screen saver could inadvertently interfere with the automatic shutdown software and could end up reducing the life of your screen, not extending it. In addition to interfering with the way your notebook runs, some screen savers constantly access the hard disk, causing further drain on the battery. There are other culprits in this area as well. For instance, try getting by with a subset of your word processing software. I installed the full version of my word processor the first time around, and one of the features kept hard disk activity at a frantic pace. In an effort to provide the latest information on my files, the software was just eating power. I don't keep many files on my notebook, so I always know exactly what I have available. Kill the fancy features of your software, and a battery that usually lasts 3 hours will probably last $3\frac{1}{2}$.

- *Use the classic Windows 2000 features* Windows XP comes with a wealth of gizmos that make it look sharp on a desktop machine. However, these special effects consume lots of battery power that you could use for other purposes on a laptop. Begin by choosing the Windows Classic theme on the Themes tab of the Display Properties dialog box. Select the Appearance tab and you'll see an Effects button. Click it and you'll see an Effects dialog box. Disable all of the features you don't need to use your computer comfortably. To access another set of options, right-click My Computer, choose Properties, and then select the Advanced tab of the System Properties dialog box. Click Settings in the Performance area and you see a Performance Options dialog box. Select the Adjust for Best Performance option, and then click OK twice to make the change permanent. Using this changes could increase your battery life by as much as 15 or 20 minutes.

- *Look for power-saving features* Many notebooks come with a function key (FN on my system) that's poorly understood by users. In my case, there's a faucet at the top of the screen. Pressing FN+faucet reduces power consumption on my machine considerably—yet I wouldn't have found this feature by looking at the documentation. The vendor hid it in the screen section of the text, not in the power-management section, where you'd expect to find it. If you're in doubt about a button on your notebook, keep searching the documentation until you find it. Most notebooks now come with a power-saving mode you can use while on the battery. In some cases, programs run a little slower and the backlight doesn't work as well, but you get much more life out of your battery.

- *Change power-wasting habits and software configurations* Occasionally I develop a habit that's long on intent but short on true usefulness. When I start thinking about what I want to write, I save my document. It sounds like a good habit. After all, if you save during think time, power outages and other types of hardware failure are less likely to affect you. It's fairly unlikely, however, that you'll experience a power outage when working with a notebook—unless you totally ignore the battery level. In addition, the more rugged hardware now used in notebook construction is much less prone to failure than the hardware of days past. Consider looking at your software configuration as well. I used to set the automatic save for my word processor to 10 minutes. That was just enough time for the drive to start spinning down. Consequently, I wasted a huge amount of power starting and stopping the drive. Setting the automatic save to 20 minutes proved much more efficient from a power perspective, and I haven't lost a single bit of data because of the change.

- *Turn off your sound* At times, it's great to have sound effects. Sound boards consume quite a bit of power, though, and you have to ask whether you really need to hear sounds while working on a document at 30,000 feet. In most cases, you can turn off your sound board with a setting in the Control Panel. Making this small change in configuration not only saves power, but it also makes you more popular with the person sitting next to you. You also should avoid playing your latest music CD while using the battery. A CD keeps the disk running almost continuously, which greatly reduces battery life.

- *Give it a break* More than a few people try to eat lunch and work on their notebook at the same time. In addition to the risk of spilling something on the keyboard, trying to work and eat at the same time probably isn't the most efficient way to use notebook battery power. Suspend your notebook for the duration of your meal. You'll not only use battery power more efficiently, but you'll also get to enjoy your food hot for once.

- *Plug in at lunch and breaks* You may not have a plug near you when you're in a conference, but there are likely to be places that have plugs when you take a break. Take advantage of every opportunity to recharge your machine. While you're recharging with a good lunch, allow your machine to recharge as well. Even if you have to make a trip back to your room, it's a good idea to recharge your notebook whenever possible.

Working with Handheld Devices

The use of handheld devices of all types is on the rise. You see ads for them on television, they grab your attention in books and magazines, and you even get inundated with information at the store. The type of handheld device you buy is as much a matter of personal choice as it is features and flexibility. For example, my Casio Cassiopeia comes in a number of colors. The color does affect the features of the device, but they do add aesthetic appeal. I prefer blue or green in devices, but that's a personal choice.

Some devices on the market offer limited functionality and even less in the way of connectivity. For example, a cellular telephone works well for checking telephone messages and e-mail. I wouldn't try to use it to run a spreadsheet. Windows XP doesn't have much to offer devices in this class now, but you may see connectivity options develop in the future.

The main event for handheld devices from a Windows XP viewpoint is the PDA. A PDA offers a larger screen and more capabilities than a cellular telephone. In some cases, you can even perform simple computing chores using a PDA. For example, I've used my PDA to edit (not write) documents in the past. It's not as convenient as my laptop, but it works.

No matter how many features a PDA provides, it's somewhat useless without some means of data exchange. Windows XP provides several connectivity options for PDAs. The one you choose depends on the capabilities of the PDA and the money you have to spend for gizmos. Most people find that a serial or wireless connection works best for PDAs. Some people are brave enough to use parallel or USB connections to communicate with their device. In even fewer cases, you can also rely on a direct network connection by purchasing a network interface card (NIC) for your PDA.

We'll also discuss Microsoft ActiveSync in this section. People have more than a few problems getting this product to work, yet it's the main application for PocketPC users. I show you how to circumvent a few of the major communication problems.

Making a Connection

Before you can do anything with your PDA, you have to create a connection for it. The following sections discuss the common methods for creating a connection for your PDA. This probably doesn't represent every potential connection method (I've seen some that are strange, to say the least), but you learn about those that are in common use.

Serial

The serial connection is the most reliable way that you'll find to connect your PDA to a desktop machine. The advantage to using a serial connection is that vendors understand it, and the standards for using a serial connection are stable. Few people ever complain that their serial port connection failed to work as anticipated.

Serial ports are also universal. The oldest machine in your company probably has two serial ports on it as a minimum. A PDA that has a serial port interface can literally connect anywhere that has software to support the connection. The universal appeal of the serial port is one of the biggest reasons that vendors still use this option.

The disadvantages of a serial connection are many. The biggest problem is speed. You'll find that serial connections are brain-numbingly slow. Depending on the size of files you need to transfer, you might have time to eat lunch while waiting for the transfer to complete. (Of course, if you forget to configure the port for maximum speed, you'll find that the transfer is even slower.)

Another disadvantage of using a serial connection is convenience. Your desktop machine will never discover the PDA attached to your serial port by itself. A serial connection requires manual configuration. If you don't mark the ports on your machine, you might find that the configuration process takes even longer as you attempt to decipher the ports by trial and error.

IrDA

Using an Infrared Data Association (IrDA) connection is about the fastest way to connect two machines. However, this connection is problematic at best when using a PDA. For one thing, some vendors place the IrDA port in the worst possible position on the device. You find yourself performing finger gymnastics in an attempt to use the PDA and keep the port free of interference.

However, let's say you decide to create the connection in the other direction, from the notebook or desktop machine to the PDA. This solution works better because you can easily reach the keys on the notebook or desktop machine to perform any data transfer tasks. The problem now is one of alignment. I've actually ended up looking for things like decks of cards, *TV Guide*s, and memo pads in an effort to get the PDA IrDA port at the same height as the notebook IrDA port. In short, alignment is everything when working with IrDA, and vendors don't make it easy to keep the ports aligned.

Does this make IrDA a poor choice for making PDA connections? In many cases, you'll want to use one of the other connection types discussed in this section in situations where you'd need to work with the PDA directly. However, many vendors already have plans for using the IrDA port for quick data downloads and in situations where other connection types don't work. For example, some airlines consider IrDA the optimum choice for onboard networks because they don't radiate energy as a wireless network does.

Some vendors also talk about the possible uses for IrDA as an information distribution technology. Consider the schedules you normally have to track for airlines, buses, and trains. All of these places could download current schedules to your PDA using an IrDA port placed in convenient locations. In some respects, this technique would allow the airport to make better use of wireless bandwidth. Users could use wireless to contact the Internet and IrDA for airline- or airport-specific information.

You do need to consider a few technical problems with IrDA. The first consideration is that IrDA normally appears to the PDA or notebook as a serial or parallel port. In some cases, the IrDA port appears as both a serial and parallel port; Windows XP chooses the configuration that matches the remote computer setup. If possible, use the parallel port for your IrDA port. The serial port configuration limits you to 128 Kbps transfer rates, far below the real transfer rate of an IrDA port. (At least Windows XP raises the serial transfer speed from the 115.2 Kbps that Windows 9x/NT/2000 supports.)

Another problem is that IrDA support on desktop machines is far from universal. Many desktop machine motherboards actually support an IrDA port, but the case doesn't include a place to put an IrDA port, so the vendor doesn't install the support. If you can live with a modified case, you can generally obtain the required port from the motherboard vendor, install it, and then configure it within Windows XP. For those machines that lack an IrDA port, you can always buy one as an add-on board.

Now that you know the pros and cons of using an infrared connection, let's look at some connectivity issues. Windows XP provides two configuration dialog boxes for infrared data association (IrDA) connections. The first is the IrDA Protocol Properties dialog box, which you'll see when you open the device found in the Infrared Devices folder in Device Manager.

The IrDA Protocol Properties dialog box has the standard General and Driver tabs. You'll also find an IrDA Settings tab. Depending on the vendor that created your IrDA port, you may see any number of settings on this tab. However, all IrDA ports support two entries. The first is Maximum Connection Rate. Windows assumes that you want to use the 115,200 bps transfer rate, but you get a performance boost setting this option to 128,000 bps. If you find that you have connection problems, you'll need to use a lower rate. The second is the Communications Port field. You select the port you want to use for communications purposes with IrDA.

After you install an IrDA port on your machine, you'll also see a new Control Panel applet named Wireless Link, as shown in Figure 17.4. As you can see, this applet helps you configure wireless communications for your system. It works with other types of wireless communication, not just IrDA ports.

FIGURE 17.4
Use the Wireless Link applet to configure IrDA communications for your machine.

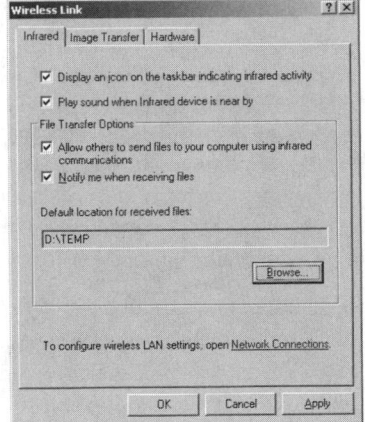

The Infrared tab contains all of the settings for your IrDA port. You can use this tab to control the appearance of an IrDA icon in the Notification Area that shows current port activity. You can also set options such as when to play sounds for port activity. In most cases, the use of sound is important because of the need to point the IrDA-enabled device in the right direction. The Infrared tab also has a Default Location for Received Files field. This field is blank by default, but you'll want to provide a default download location. This ensures that file transfers will work smoothly and the user won't have to worry about where the files will end up on the drive.

The Image Transfer tab defined the IrDA interface with devices such as cameras. The options on this tab enable image downloads from alternative devices. Again, you'll want to set a default download directory for image information. A special feature on this tab automatically opens a copy of Windows Explorer so that you can see the pictures after the download completes.

The final tab, Hardware, shows all of the wireless hardware on your system. The tab also includes Properties and Troubleshoot buttons you can use with the highlighted device. The Properties button takes you to the device Properties dialog box in Device Manager. Troubleshoot opens a copy of Help and Support Center to assist in finding problems with your setup.

USB

Many new handheld devices, especially PDAs, use a USB port to create a connection to the desktop computer because this connection offers advantages over other connection methods. The two biggest advantages are data transfer speed and automatic configuration. We've already discussed USB ports extensively in the "Universal Serial Bus (USB)" section of Chapter 9, so I won't discuss USB basics again.

From a handheld device perspective, the USB port is both a blessing and a curse. Yes, you do get higher performance from a USB port, and device recognition is a breeze. In addition, you can unplug a USB device without shutting the computer down. However, USB ports tend to have problems with some handheld devices, especially PDAs.

You can convince Windows XP to recognize the PDA, but the vendor software often has problems seeing the PDA and transferring data with it. Of all the PDA software out there, Microsoft ActiveSync is the most renowned for USB compatibility problems. ActiveSync often declares there's no USB port on your machine, much less a device attached to that port. I show you how to circumvent this problem in the following section.

Fortunately, as more vendors learn to work with USB, the problems you see will become less severe. Microsoft recently released a new version of ActiveSync that fixes some of the problems with the old version. In addition, Windows XP offers operating system support that you didn't see in the past. Eventually, USB will become the port of choice for handheld device users everywhere.

Using Microsoft ActiveSync

Microsoft ActiveSync is one of the most common applications used to create a connection between a PDA and a desktop machine. It has a reputation of causing more than a few problems. However, you can take a few steps to avoid problems. The first step is to ensure that your system can actually see the PDA. Open the Device Manager and then locate the USB Root Hub entry and open it. Look at the Power tab. If you don't see the PDA listed, you need to check your connections before you attempt to install the ActiveSync software.

After you verify that Windows XP can see the PDA, it's time to install ActiveSync. The following steps take you through the process I normally use to install ActiveSync:

1. Start the ActiveSync Setup program. You see a Welcome screen.

2. Click Next. You'll see a Select Installation Folder dialog box. The default folder normally works well.

3. Choose an installation folder (if necessary), and then click Next. Windows XP will copy the files to the hard drive. At this point, the setup program will disappear. You still need to configure ActiveSync to use your PDA.

4. Double-click the ActiveSync icon on the desktop. You'll see the ActiveSync dialog box.

5. Remove the PDA from its cradle. Windows XP should make a sound signifying that it noticed the PDA is unplugged.

6. Place the PDA in its cradle. Windows XP should make another sound signifying that it sees the PDA. Microsoft ActiveSync will display a New Partnership dialog box.

7. Select Yes when asked if you want to create a partnership, and then click Next. If you already have a partnership with another computer, ActiveSync will ask if you want to maintain it. Choose Yes or No, and then click Next. You'll see a Select Synchronization Settings dialog box, like the one shown in Figure 17.5. Notice the highlighted Files entry. Having a synchronization folder can prevent many problems with your desktop-to-PDA communication. Place a file in this folder and ActiveSync will copy it to the PDA during the next synchronization. This is a "must have" feature for all PDA users.

8. Select the synchronization settings you want, and then click next. You'll see a Setup Complete dialog box.

9. Click Finish. ActiveSync will begin the synchronization process with your PDA. When the process is complete, your dialog box will look like the one in Figure 17.6.

FIGURE 17.5

Make sure you include a synchronization folder in your synchronization settings.

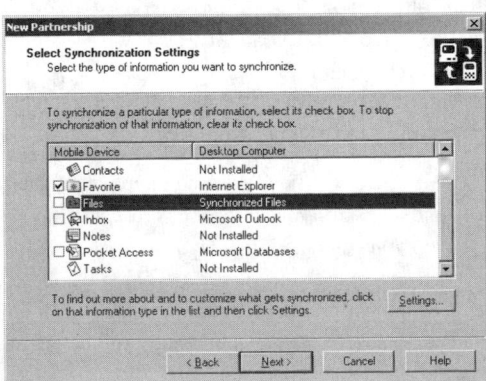

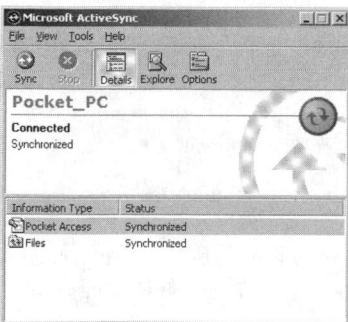

FIGURE 17.6
The completed ActiveSync installation process leaves your PDA in a synchronized state.

Adding a NIC

Many PDAs, especially of the PocketPC variety (`http://www.microsoft.com/mobile/pocketpc/default.asp`), provide a slot in the top or the side that will accept a special NIC. In general, you have to buy the NIC as a third-party product. For example, Kingston produces the EtheRx Compact I/O Ethernet Adapter (`http://www.kingston.com/compactio/CIO10T.asp`). The adapter includes special software that enables you to connect the PDA directly to the network.

Because the PocketPC includes Internet Explorer and software for browsing network drives, you can gain a level of network interaction that you wouldn't get otherwise. You can even set the PDA to use a live Internet connection hosted on your server. It does require additional work, but you'll save time in the end. The two big problem areas are getting the PDA to talk to the network initially and recognizing the server as a proxy.

One caveat to direct network connection is that the NICs I found online all come with one port type: twisted pair. In addition, they all run at the same speed: 10 Mbps. However, that's much better than the speeds you achieve using any other method. I find that using a PDA in this mode makes data transfers almost terrifyingly fast—don't blink or you'll miss it.

Networks normally imply two-way communication. Placing your PDA on the network does create a two-way communication environment, but one that's tenuous. It's important to remember that the operating system on your PDA is different from the one on your desktop, even if it does say Windows CE. The version of Word you'll use is compatible with the desktop version, but nothing else seems to provide full compatibility. In the end, you need to exercise extreme care with this option. Other people on the network can see your PDA, you have no way to secure it, and the PDA uses incompatible data formats. Consider the NIC solution a temporary high-speed data connection.

On Your Own

Power is king for mobile computers. Use the information in this chapter to create one or more power-management strategies for your notebook. You'll find these schemes on the

Power Schemes tab of the Power Options Properties dialog box. Make sure you include schemes for activities such as maintenance and file downloads. Trying to restart a download can be frustrating, especially if the site you're trying to access is busy. You should also include some personal schemes in the list. For example, you might want to create a special power scheme for when you go to lunch.

You can also enhance productivity by combining the Briefcase and Dial-Up Networking. Try splitting your projects into two categories: those you're working on alone, and those you're working on with a group. Try using the Briefcase method with projects you're working on alone. Use the folder and Dial-Up Networking combination for projects you're working on in a group.

Make a list of the ways you can use Dial-Up Networking to improve your productivity. This chapter mentioned the most common ways, but your company might have special needs that weren't covered. It's important to use creativity when thinking about the ways Windows XP can help you. Keep the list handy and refer to it when you're looking for ways to solve a particular mobile-computing problem.

If you have a handheld device, consider some of the connection strategies found in this chapter. Most handheld devices provide more than one connection method, so finding the most efficient connection method for your handheld device is important. Make sure you try using a NIC to connect your PDA directly to the network if you own a PocketPC or other compatible device. Remember to exercise caution when using this option to prevent accidental disclosure of sensitive data or damage of the data on the PDA.

PART VI

Making the Right Connections

Hardware and Software Connections

Making hardware and software connections is one of the more difficult parts of working with any operating system. Windows XP provides several different types of connections, and each of them helps you communicate in some way.

I'm not going to tell you that every type of connection works well under Windows XP. You'll need to address some real problem areas to make the port, the connection, and the attached device work properly. For example, communication isn't always as clear as it could be. This chapter takes you through the process of managing connections and helps you avoid the pitfalls you could experience when creating a connection.

This chapter has three main sections. All of them build on information discussed in previous chapters. The first part spends some time with physical details I haven't covered yet. Network connection is a necessary step in getting your machine ready for information exchange of all types.

The second main topic I talk about is software connections. After you have a network connection, you need a software connection to do things such as send files to a remote site or read your e-mail.

The third main topic is advanced connections. You won't require these connections to get started with Windows XP, but they do come in handy down the road. It's important to understand all three connection types before we spend much time working with networks.

Making Network Connections

Network connections aren't the same as they were when I started computing. In days gone by, you placed a network interface card (NIC) in every piece of equipment set aside for network use and then connected the whole thing with cables. Today, cables are optional. Vendors no longer tie you to using cables to create a connection because computers can use other media, such as light (infrared) and radio waves (wireless).

The proliferation of other connection types has changed the face of computing. It's now possible for someone to walk into an airport and have an instant connection with everyone else in the airport. You can also grab an Internet connection while waiting for your plane. This has become a major selling point for some of the larger airports.

Because networking is so much easier today, you also have new problems to solve. Networks I worked with during the early years of the PC were inherently secure and risk-free. They had no outside connections to worry about and the technology was relatively new, so no one had security holes to exploit, and proprietary networks made it unlikely that someone could use any data they did find.

The following sections discuss the two sides of the networking coin. On one side, you have the advantages of standardized networking technologies with advanced functionality. On the other side, you have the security and the advanced application usage problems that plague network administrators today. You won't learn enough in one chapter to become a networking guru, but you'll know enough to avoid the major pitfalls of modern technology.

Would I go back to the old days? Not a chance. Having a network that operates correctly most of the time is worth too much to me. Anyone who has worked with that old equipment can tell you that the technology today is much better. All you need to do is exercise care in implementation and maintenance.

Understanding IrDA Connectivity

The Infrared Data Association (IrDA) connection is commonly associated with laptop computers. We discussed this technology as part of the mobile computing discussion in the "Making a Connection" section of Chapter 17. In this scenario, you point your laptop or other mobile device at a machine with a compatible port. After you make a connection with a device, such as a printer, you can use the device. The problem with this form of IrDA connection is that it uses line of sight: If you move your laptop even a little, you'll find that you can no longer communicate with the device.

However, IrDA connectivity comes in more than one flavor. The current data transfer speed of IrDA 1.1 is 4 Mbps with a packet size of 2,048 bytes, which is on par with many wireless technologies and some alternative wired technologies, but far below even an old Ethernet network. Some types of IR communication enable you to transfer data up to 16 Mbps at a range of 1.5 miles. However, you'd normally associate this type of communication with network connections between buildings, not the type you'd use in the building itself.

Unfortunately, the speed you actually get from Windows XP depends on your hardware configuration. If you configure the IrDA port as a serial port, the maximum speed you get is 115 Kbps. Using a parallel port configuration is much better.

> **Tip:** You can find out more about IrDA on many Web sites. One of the best places to look first is the IrDA Web site at `http://www.irda.org/`. If you have an interest in IrDA details, check out the specification at `http://www.irda.org/standards/specifications.asp`. You can read about future uses for IrDA connections at `http://www.ettm.com/news/irda_group.html`. The Links2Go Web site (`http://www.l2g.com/topic/Infrared_Data_Association`) includes a wealth of IrDA links you can use to find out additional information. This site also includes a link for an IrDA chat area.

The IrDA community is looking at ways to expand your use of the technology. For example, IrDA is a good solution in places where wireless doesn't work. You may eventually see IrDA connections on planes because using wireless could interfere with the operation of the plane. These future uses of IrDA are still on the drawing board, but are important considerations and are one of the reasons that vendor's place IrDA ports on an increasing number of devices.

One interesting dilemma for IrDA users is desktop computer support. You find IrDA ports on most laptops and handheld devices. Most printers and other peripherals devices offer an IrDA port as an option, if not standard equipment. The problem is connecting your desktop machine to a laptop through an IrDA port. Interestingly enough, many desktop motherboards include an IrDA port. For example, many of those from Asus include the required connector. The problem for the desktop vendor is finding a case with the proper opening. Normally, you can detect whether your motherboard supports an IrDA port by looking at the advanced features in the CMOS setup (accessed during the boot process). If you find that your motherboard supports an IrDA port, all you may need is the sensor and a means to expose it for laptop use.

Understanding Ethernet Connectivity

Ethernet connections come in several speeds and types. The first issue to consider is the type of connection to create. Most networks today use a twisted pair cable connection to an RJ45 connector on the back of the system. Each cable also plugs into a central hub or switch that connects every computer to every other computer on the network.

A second option that's still popular, but less so than it once was, is thinnet. This kind of connection uses coaxial cable, which is very resistant to noise. The cable also tends to provide better resistance to damage than twisted pair. However, many network administrators find the cable stiff and difficult to install. A thinnet setup is also harder to troubleshoot because it lacks the central connection of twisted pair. You "daisy chain" machines together using tee connectors. A third option that has become quite unpopular is thicknet. You use a thick cable that's extremely resistant to noise. The cable is hard to find, expensive, and much more difficult to install than either thinnet or twisted pair. Generally, you should avoid a thicknet Ethernet connection unless you have it installed.

The data transfer speed issue boils down to one of how much you can afford. An entry-level Ethernet setup runs at 10 Mbps and supports small networks with up to 10 nodes. Of course, if you're running large graphics applications or transferring video over the network, 10 Mbps isn't enough bandwidth. Some small-business networks have moved to 100 Mbps networks today. Larger businesses use progressively larger "pipes" by installing gigabit- or even higher-speed networks. In the end, the larger the pipe you need, the more it costs to install.

If you do decide to go the twisted pair route, you'll need to choose between a hub and a switch to connect the machines on your network. Some people don't realize there's a big difference between the two.

A *hub* is a simple connection device and costs little. It's reliable because there are few parts inside to break. Many small businesses use a hub for these reasons.

A *switch* has intelligence. It can create multiple connections simultaneously, whereas a hub can make only one connection at a time. For this reason, a switch provides better efficiency for networks that might otherwise provide marginal performance. In addition, switches often use their intelligence to provide other features, such as advanced diagnostics. A switch does cost more, but you also gain a great deal by using one.

Understanding Alternative Connection Options

In at least a few cases, people spend far more on their network than they should because they fail to realize they don't need a full network. If you have a home system or a two-node business network, it's unlikely that you'll generate enough network traffic to warrant the cost of even a low-end Ethernet network.

I'm not telling you to save money today, only to find out that you don't have enough capacity tomorrow. However, many businesses require a small network today and will never grow beyond their current size. Such a network doesn't require a top-of-the-line cabling system and expensive NICs.

Sometimes, the major cost of a network is in the installation. An older building might present challenges you never even considered. I know of one building where the residents spent nearly double the originally quoted installation price because of poured plaster walls and voids in odd places. In another situation, a metallic ceiling prevented a wireless network from working at full capacity. Removing the ceiling was out of the question because the tenant didn't own the building. In short, you can run into some odd problems (perhaps not as odd as these, but odd nonetheless).

You'll find a myriad of alternative networking solutions available. For example, some systems use the existing building wiring. You have a connection to the network wherever you have an open outlet. Just plug a special adapter into the outlet, connect your computer to the adapter, and you're ready to go. Another existing wiring scenario relies on the telephone cable already installed in your house. Of course, you can also use radio frequency (RF) systems. Both FireWire (IEEE 1394) and USB also offer networking solutions. You can find out more about these alternatives at the following Web sites:

- 3Com Residential – HomeConnect (http://www.3com.com/solutions/personal/)
- ActionTec (http://www.actiontec.com/products/)
- Anchor Chips EZ-Link USB (http://www.ezlinkusb.com/)
- BreezeCOM BreezeNET and BreezeACCESS (http://www.alvarion.com/HomePage.asp)
- Computer Networking (http://compnetworking.about.com/)
- Diamond HomeFree (http://www.diamondmm.com/)
- D-Link DHN910 Phoneline and DHN-920 USB Phoneline (http://www.dlink.com/products/kits/)
- Home Networking News (http://www.homenetnews.com/)
- Home Phoneline Networking Alliance (http://www.homepna.org/)
- HomeRF Web Site (http://www.homerf.org/)
- IEEE (http://www.ieee.org/)
- InnoMedia InfoAccess (http://www.innomedia.com/)
- Intel AnyPoint (http://www.intel.com/anypoint/)
- Linksys HomeLink Phoneline (http://www.linksys.com/products/)
- SOHOware CableFREE (http://www.sohoware.com/)
- The Home PC Network Site (http://www.homepcnetwork.com/)
- Tut Systems HomeRun (http://www.tutsys.com/products/expressomdu/)
- Wireless LAN.com Answer Page (http://www.proxim.com/)
- X-10 ActiveHome (http://www.x10.com/products/)
- ZDNet Family PC Home (http://familypc.zdnet.com/)

Using Direct Peripheral Connections

Part of a network setup involves creating connections to the peripheral devices that provide resources to you and those that work with you on the network. The three devices used most often by everyone on the network are printers, modems, and disk drives. We've already discussed the common hard disk drive in several sections of this book, but haven't discussed DVD and CD drive in detail. The following sections discuss connectivity issues for all three device classes.

Printers

Chapter 14 covers the topic of printers in detail. I cover printer connections in this chapter. Some people think there's only one way to connect a printer—through a parallel port. For some printers, that's correct. A few older printers used only a serial port connection. Some other, newer printers provide two or three connection types. These printers might have a serial port connector in addition to the standard parallel port connector, and they might have a network connector (AppleTalk or Ethernet) in addition to the serial or parallel port connectors.

> **Tip:** Some printers don't provide a serial port as standard equipment; you have to buy it as a separate piece. Your vendor manual should provide details about buying the serial port option. Look to see if the vendor also supports other connection options that might help in some situations.
>
> Many vendors now support a network connection as standard equipment; others support it as an optional module. If your printer doesn't provide a network connection, you might want to look at print server solutions, such as Intel's NetportExpress. This small box connects to the side of your printer. It provides three printer connections (one serial and two parallel) and connects to the network through an Ethernet port. The setup software enables you to install and manage the printer server from the administrator workstation.

Choosing between these two connections isn't always easy, even if it seems like a no-brainer. A parallel port delivers the data eight bits at a time and at a faster rate than a serial port. Choosing the parallel port doesn't take too much thought if your machine has only one printer attached to it. However, what happens if your machine acts as a print server for many different printers? You could easily run out of parallel ports in this situation.

Just about everyone resorts to an A/B switch to increase the number of available connections (which may void the printer warranty in some cases), but there might be a better solution. Connecting your printer to the machine through an unused serial port provides better access to it. No one has to flip an A/B switch to use it. (Some electronic A/B switches provide automatic switching when you send certain commands through the printer cable, but this means training users to send those commands and a great deal of frustration when the user forgets to do so.) The problem is that the access is slower when using a serial port than with a parallel port.

Categorizing how people will use the printers attached to your machine is the next step. Placing a printer that the user is less likely to use or a printer that usually has a lower level of activity on a serial port shouldn't cause any problems. Just make sure you warn people that their print jobs could take a little longer in the new configuration.

> **Tip:** There's a point at which it becomes difficult to support too many printers on a low-end peer-to-peer network. I start to look at other solutions when the number of workstations exceeds 10 or the number of printers exceeds 4. After this limit, the performance of a low-end peer-to-peer setup diminishes to the point where it's doubtful you can get any useful work accomplished.

Some printers come with a built-in network interface card (NIC). You can attach such printers directly to the network without a workstation connection. The two most popular connection types are Ethernet and AppleTalk. Whether this solution works for you depends not on the NIC so much as on the software included with the printer. The printer actually boots as a workstation or a self-contained print server on the network. You see it just as you would any other workstation. The only difference is that this workstation is dedicated to a single task—printing. You need to find out which networks the vendor supports. This solution is great for a peer-to-peer network because it allows you to use the printer without overloading the workstation. Adding a printer this way also preserves precious workstation resources, such as interrupts and I/O port addresses.

Printers also support some of the more exotic network connections these days, but it might be difficult to find them. One solution I see gaining popularity is the wireless LAN. Just think: Using this type of connection, you can unwrap the printer, plug it in, and perform a few configuration steps to get it up and running. In the future, adding a printer to the network might be even easier than adding it to your local workstation.

Modems

Modems are an essential part of networks because they provide everyone with a view of the outside world. Admittedly, some people view modems as passé in a world where cable, DSL, and satellite communications rule. However, many of these solutions rely on modems—they're simply special versions of the traditional modem. In addition, despite what the media would have you believe, many people find the high-speed solutions inaccessible, too expensive, or too cumbersome. Computers still rely heavily on modems to create external connections.

There are two kinds of traditional modems: internal and external. I prefer an external modem for several reasons, one of which is portability. I can move an external modem in a matter of minutes by disconnecting it from the current machine, moving it, and reconnecting it to the new machine. Another advantage is that even though most software displays the indicators you usually see on the modem, an external modem has an edge when it comes to troubleshooting because the software light indicators might not always reflect reality. In addition, some software doesn't accurately report the modem's connection speed, an important piece of troubleshooting information.

Another advantage of the external modem is that you can turn it off without turning off your computer. This can come in handy when you must reset the modem manually and you don't want to reboot your computer. It also provides some people with added peace of mind because when you turn the modem off, no one can call into the computer. (You can keep people from calling into a computer with an internal modem by setting up the modem so that it doesn't answer the telephone line.)

Once you get past the physical location of a modem, you get to the connections. The first connection is the telephone cable required to contact the outside world. Most offices don't have the RJ-11 jacks that a modem uses as standard equipment (they might have a six-wire jack that looks like a larger version of the RJ-11, but it won't work for your modem). Normally, you have to get an office wired for a modem before you can actually use it. Some recent telephone instruments in offices and increasingly in hotel rooms sport a standard RJ-11 jack labeled a "data port." This is a fine place to plug in the cable from your modem. Of course, home users don't run into this problem because a modem uses a standard home telephone jack. (The second RJ-11 jack on your modem is normally reserved for a telephone so that you can use the same telephone number for both.)

Another connection for external modems is between the modem and the computer. You'll normally use a standard serial port cable that has either a 9- or 25-wire connector at each end. A few external modems differ in that they connect to your computer's parallel port. You can also find a number of good USB modems on the market that rely on a connection to your USB port. The biggest advantage of a USB modem is that it configures itself automatically.

Vendors also rate modems by speed and capability. The speed at which modems can communicate has stabilized. You won't find a traditional modem that communicates at any speed other than 56 Kbps. The special modems used for cable, DSL, and satellite access communicate at much higher speeds that depend on the technology in use. For example, DSL connection speeds range from 192 Kbps to 2.31 Mbps.

There are a ton of modem standards, most of which don't matter to you as a user. However, you should know about some standards to ensure that you buy a modem that works properly. Vendors who design inexpensive modems still take shortcuts in the standards department, which means you face obstacles when creating a connection. A great deal of standardization has to do with the modem's speed, the way it corrects errors, or the method it uses to compress data. Knowing about these standards can mean the difference between getting a good buy on a modem and getting one that's almost useless. The following list shows the more common modem standards, but you also should be aware of any new standards that develop for higher-speed modems:

- *CCITT V.32* Defines the 4800 bps, 9600 bps, 14.4 Kbps, 19.2 Kbps, and 28.8 Kbps standards.
- *CCITT V.34* Defines the data-compression specifics for the 28.8Kbps standard. It also defines the 33.6Kbps standard.
- *CCITT V.42* Defines a data compression method for modems that enables modems to transfer data at apparent rates of up to 19.2Kbps (also requires the modem to provide MNP levels 2 through 4—see the last item in the list for details).
- *CCITT V.42bis* The second revision of the modem data-compression standard. It enables a compression factor up to four, an apparent transfer rate of 38.4Kbps from a 9600bps modem.
- *CCITT V.FAST* This is a proprietary method of defining data compression for the 28.8Kbps standard. It has been replaced by the CCITT V.34 standard.
- *CCITT X.25* Some asynchronous modems also support this synchronous data-transfer standard. You don't need it if your only goal is to communicate with online services.
- *MNP 2-4, 5, 10* This is a Microm Networking Protocol, a standard method of error correcting for modems. The precise differences between levels aren't important from a user perspective. A higher level is generally better.

Knowing about these standards should help you choose a modem. It's vitally important that your modem adhere to all the standards for speed and other capabilities. Otherwise, the modem might not be able to make a good connection at a lower speed. Also, make sure that the modem manual outlines just how the modem adheres to the standards. The manual should include information on FCC rules Parts 15 and 68 or the equivalent for the country you're in. The manual also should state the connection type. For example, the current standard for serial ports is RS-232C. Some modems require that standard; others can use older ports. In most cases, you don't need to worry unless you have an older machine.

CD and DVD Players

CD and DVD drives usually have two connections you need to consider. The first is the bus connector, which allows data transfer between the computer and the device. Generally, this is a SCSI connector or an IDE or EIDE connection. The principle is the same: The data transfer rate might be much slower, depending on the method of connection. SCSI always beats IDE hands-down, but SCSI and EIDE offer comparable performance. The bus connector for a CD or DVD serves the same purpose as the equivalent connector for your hard drive. It enables you to transfer data from the CD or DVD to your machine.

Some people don't really think about the second connection. They try to use a CD drive with a game or another application that plays sound right off the CD—just as with a music CD—and discover that the game doesn't appear to work with their machine.

You could say the same thing about playing movies from a DVD drive. The problem is that they don't have the RCA plugs in the back of the CD drive connected to anything. External drives use RCA connectors, like the speaker outputs on your stereo. Internal drives usually require some type of special connector for your sound card. This is a proprietary connector in some cases; in other cases, the vendor tries to make you believe that its common cable really is proprietary. Check with your local computer store to see whether it has an inexpensive alternative to the expensive cable the vendors normally offer.

In addition to the other connections on your CD or DVD drive, you'll find a headphone connector on the front. Imagine my surprise when I plugged some headphones in and heard sound out of my speakers and headset at the same time. Some vendors disable the speaker output when you plug in the headset; others don't. You want to check out this feature if this is an important consideration for your application.

Making Software Attachments

After your hardware is up and running, you have to get some software to talk to it to do any useful work. The following sections describe several utilities included Direct Cable Connection, Dial-up Connection, and Phone Dialer that come with Windows XP. They don't help you surf the Net or download the latest industry gossip, but they do help you make the necessary connections.

Peter's Principle: The Right Kind of Connection

It might be very tempting to use a single type of connection to meet all your computing needs, but that wouldn't be the most efficient way to do things. You might view a direct cable connection as the panacea for all your portable-data transfer woes, but the direct cable connection works best for occasional rather than daily use. A direct cable connection works fine for quick transfers from one machine to another when you have a large amount of data to move. For example, it works well when you initially set up the portable.

If you use a portable on a daily basis, using such an Interlink-style connection is a waste of time. You'll want to find some other method of creating your connection to the Desktop. If you have a docking station that can accept a standard network card or if you plug in a PCMCIA network card, you can use this Ethernet connection to make your data transfers much faster. However, this works only if you have a network and a PCMCIA card. Alternatively, you could get an external Ethernet adapter that plugs into your portable's parallel port. This solution works well, but it isn't quite as speedy as the standard network interface cards that plug into the computer's bus or the PCMCIA network adapters.

Briefcase isn't a physical connection to your desktop machine, but it does the job for smaller amounts of data. In fact, you'll find out that Briefcase can hold a substantial amount of data if you use it correctly.

Okay, so the network and Briefcase options are out of the question because you're out of town. You can still make a connection to your desktop by using Dial-Up Networking. It won't be as fast as some other techniques, but it enables you to get the data you need while on the road or when you work from home.

Windows XP provides many different connections. You need to use the right one for the job, and that means taking the time to learn about the various options available to you. A connection that works well in one instance could be a time killer in another. Don't succumb to the one-connection way of computing; use every tool that Windows XP provides.

Making a Direct Cable Connection

Those who use portables will love the direct cable-connection feature that Windows XP provides. You can make a direct connection using the serial, infrared, or parallel port. However, unlike previous versions of Windows, Windows XP doesn't rely on a special utility to create a direct cable connection. You create such a connection using the New Connection Wizard.

Direct cable connections rely on three elements. First, you must have some means to connect the two computers. Second, one computer must provide host services. Normally, the desktop machine is the host if you're connecting a laptop. However, it doesn't matter which machine acts as the host. Third, one of the machines must act as a client. It doesn't matter which computer is the client, but you must have one host and one client.

I assume that you've made a connection between the host and the client machines. Remember that you can use a serial, parallel, or infrared connection. If you choose either the serial or parallel options, you'll need a special cable that has a NULL modem built into it. Sometimes, you can get a separate adapter for the purpose and use a standard cable.

Now that you have a connection between the two machines, you need to set the host computer up for use. The host is the machine that will accept the incoming "call" from the client machine. Starting on the host machine, use the following steps to create a host direct cable connection:

Note: Exercise care when using this feature. I lost my connection to my NetWare server every time I performed the following procedure. At least one person reported that Linux has the same problem. In short, you might give up your file server connection to use this feature.

1. Start the New Connection Wizard found in the Network Connections dialog box. Select Next to get past the Welcome screen and you'll see the Network Connection Type dialog box.

2. Select Set Up an Advanced Connection and then click Next. You'll see an Advanced Connection Options dialog box.

3. Select Connect directly to another computer and then click Next. You'll see a Host or Guest dialog box.

4. Select the Host option for the first connection and then click Next. You'll see a Connection Device dialog box.

5. Choose a connection device from the Device for This Connection field. Make sure you verify the connection device so you don't use a device that's already in use for another purpose. Click Properties if you want to verify the properties for the connection device. Click Next. You'll see a User Permissions dialog box that lists all of the users on the current machine. Windows XP doesn't list domain users in most cases.

6. Check the user entries you want to access this connection. Use the Add, Remove, and Properties buttons to manage user accounts. Click Next. You'll see a Completion dialog box.

7. Click Finish. Windows XP will create the connection for you.

At this point, your host computer is ready to receive connections from a client. If you want to change the incoming connection settings, open the Incoming Connection entry in the Network Connections dialog box. You see an Incoming Connections Properties dialog box, like the one shown in Figure 18.1. Notice that this dialog box automatically contains an entry for dial-up connections. All you need to do is select the modem as an incoming call source. This dialog box also contains a setting that enables the use of your connection over the Internet using Virtual Private Networking (VPN). (You can learn more about VPN in the "Remote Network Users" section of Chapter 17.)

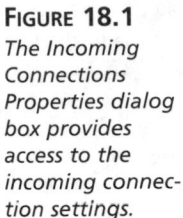

FIGURE 18.1

The Incoming Connections Properties dialog box provides access to the incoming connection settings.

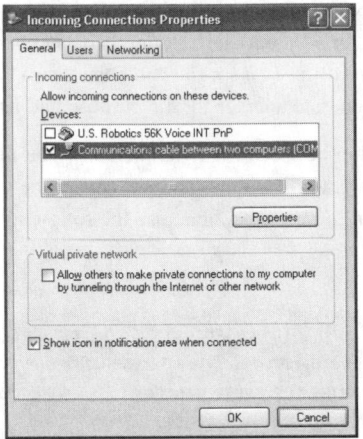

The Users tab of the Incoming Connections Properties dialog box contains the same list of local users you saw when creating the connection. You can use the New, Delete, and Properties buttons to change the list entries. Checking a user entry enables that user to make a connection to your machine. One difference you'll notice is that the Users tab contains an option that allows palmtop users to access your machine without entering a password. Windows XP turns this option off by default.

The Networking tab contains a list of the protocols, clients, and services installed on your machine. The checkboxes next to each entry determine if that entry is available for incoming calls. If you clear an entry, the incoming call can't use it. However, making a change here doesn't affect the entries for general networking purposes.

Now that you have a host setup, it's time to create the client. You must perform this task on the client machine. Use the following steps to create a client connection:

1. Start the New Connection Wizard found in the Network Connections dialog box. Select Next to get past the Welcome screen and you'll see the Network Connection Type dialog box.

2. Select Set Up an Advanced Connection and then click Next. You'll see an Advanced Connection Options dialog box.

3. Select Connect Directly to Another Computer and then click Next. You'll see a Host or Guest dialog box.

4. Select the Guest option. Click Next. You'll see a Connection Name dialog box. You'll see this name in the Network Connections dialog box after you complete the wizard.

5. Type a name for your connection. The New Connection Wizard suggests using the computer name, but you can use any name you wish. Click Next. You'll see a Select a Device dialog box. (The wizard might prompt you at this point to provide a list of users who can access this connection. Follow the prompts to add users to the list.)

6. Choose a connection device from the Device for this Connection field. Make sure that you verify the connection device so you don't use a device that's already in use for another purpose. Click Next. You'll see a Completion dialog box.

7. Click Finish. Windows XP will create the connection for you and then display the Connect dialog box, shown in Figure 18.2. This dialog box enables you to save the name and password used for the direct connection. You can use the same name and password for all sessions or require each user to enter a password individually.

8. Type your name and password. Choose whether you want to save the name and password for future use. Click Properties if you want to change any of the connection properties. Click Connect. Windows XP will create the connection for you.

FIGURE 18.2
The Connect dialog box contains fields for your name and password.

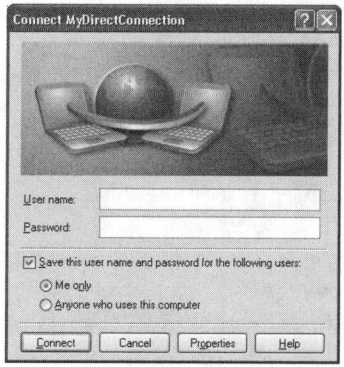

At this point, the two computers are connected and you can perform any required tasks. You can adjust settings for the client portion of the connection by clicking Properties on the Connect dialog box. The General tab of the Connection Properties dialog box contains a Select a Device field, where you can change the port used to make the connection.

The Options tab of the Connection Properties dialog box contains the settings shown in Figure 18.3. Notice that the dialing options include features like displaying a prompt for a user name and password. Windows enables the Include Windows Logon Domain option only if you also choose to provide a name and password. The only time you need to provide a domain is if you want to sign on to a server that's part of a domain and you need to access domain resources. You can also use the settings on this tab to control the redial interval and the number of times Windows XP will redial the connection.

The Security tab contains two main settings. You can choose between the Typical (recommended settings) and Advanced (custom settings) options. The Typical options include validation type, automatic use of Windows user name and password, and a requirement for data encryption. The Advanced options enable you to choose the protocols Windows XP uses to make the connection. Click Settings and you'll see the Advanced Security Settings dialog box, shown in Figure 18.4.

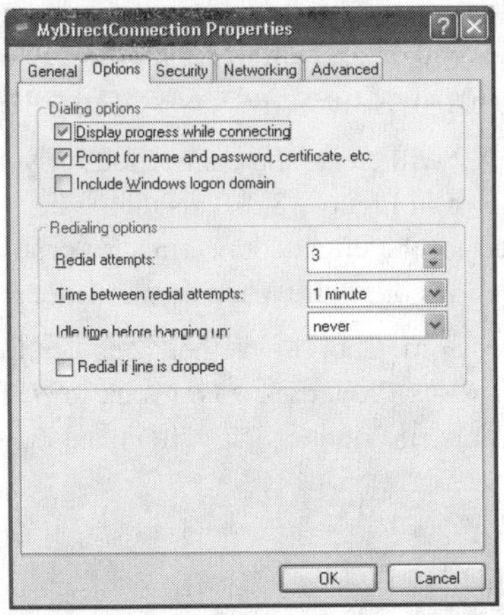

FIGURE 18.3
*Use the entries in
the Options tab to
control the con-
nection settings.*

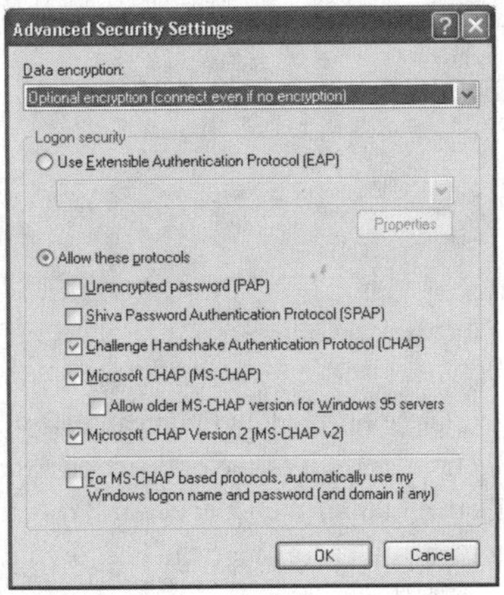

FIGURE 18.4
*Use the Advanced
Security Settings
dialog box to con-
trol connection
security at the
protocol level.*

It's interesting to note that the options you see checked in this dialog box initially reflect the options you've checked for the Typical options, so you can see the interactions between the two settings. You can choose between two basic types of advanced security settings. Normally, you use the Extensible Authentication Protocol (EAP) for high-security scenarios that require the use of smart cards and/or certificates. The other protocol selections provide various levels of security. You can choose everything from unencrypted passwords for local connections to the Challenge Handshake Authentication Protocol (CHAP), used for secure LAN connections.

The Networking tab contains the same network protocols, services, and clients I described earlier for the host. You use them in the same way the host computer uses them. The only difference is that you can choose a connection protocol, which includes Point-to-Point Protocol (PPP) and Serial Line Internet Protocol (SLIP).

The Advanced tab contains settings for using the new firewall feature of Windows XP and Internet Connection Sharing (ICS). You can share a direct connection as you would any other connection on your machine. Of course, you need to determine if sharing such a connection is worthwhile because this type of connection is temporary. Microsoft designed it to provide a means of transferring data between machines and nothing more.

Making a Dial-Up Connection

Windows XP also makes it possible to share your machine using a dial-up connection. This comes in handy if you want to call into your machine from home. As with the direct connection described in the previous section, you create a host and a client setup. You don't need a cable because the connection occurs through the telephone line using a modem. The settings and properties for this connection type are the same as for a direct connection, so I won't describe them again. However, the process for creating a host connection differs, so we'll discuss how you create one using the following steps:

1. Start the New Connection Wizard found in the Network Connections dialog box. Select Next to get past the Welcome screen and you'll see the Network Connection Type dialog box.

2. Select Set up an advanced connection and then click Next. You'll see an Advanced Connection Options dialog box.

3. Select Accept incoming connections and then click Next. You'll see a Devices for Incoming Connections dialog box containing a list of communication devices for your machine.

4. Check one of the device entries in the list. Make sure the device can actually create an external connection. The list may include direct connection devices. Click Next. You'll see an Incoming Virtual Private Network (VPN) Connection dialog box.

5. Choose a VPN option and then click Next. You'll see a User Permissions dialog box. This dialog box contains a list of users for the local machine. Use it to determine which users can access your machine.

6. Check one or more user entries. Use the Add, Remove, and Properties buttons to manage the user entries as needed. Click Next. You'll see a Networking Software dialog box. This list helps you determine which clients, services, and protocols the incoming connection can use. The Install, Uninstall, and Properties buttons help you manage the networking software entry list.

7. Verify the network entries. Make any required changes. Click Next. You'll see a Completion dialog box.

8. Click Finish. Windows XP will create the connection for you.

At this point, a client can call into your system using any program that allows such communication. You can also set Windows Explorer up to access remote services. If Explorer can't find the remote resource, it will ask if you want to create a dial-up connection to access it. In short, this new connection enables users to see resources on your machine from a remote connection.

Creating Scripts for Dial-Up Networking

The connections provided by older versions of Windows worked fine if you had a straight connection. However, the connection feature could also become a bit cumbersome if you wanted to create a connection for something like a Windows NT/2000 server. Because a standard connection still works for the vast majority of users, Microsoft wisely chose to leave it alone. To supplement the standard connection, Windows XP also provides a scripting capability. If you create a script and then add it to a connection, Windows XP uses the script instead of the standard connection setup to make your dial-up connection to a server work.

> **Note:** This section assumes at least a modicum of programming experience. You need to know what a variable is and have at least a little experience creating macros. Obviously, the more programming experience you have, the faster you learn the material in this section.

To add a script to a connection, you'll need to open the Connection Properties dialog box. Select the Security tab, as shown in Figure 18.5, and you'll see an Interaction Logon and Scripting section.

FIGURE 18.5

The Interaction Logon and Scripting options enable you to run a script during the logon process.

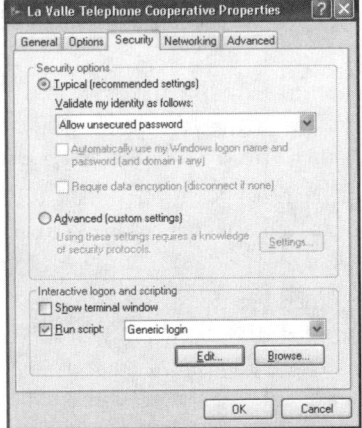

The File Name field contains the name of the script file you want to use. You can type in a name or select the name of an existing script from the list. Notice the two buttons directly below this field:

* *Edit* Enables you to modify your script.
* *Browse* Displays a File Open dialog box you can use to find a script file.

The Show Terminal Window option displays a window that helps you monitor the script activity. You can clear this option when you're certain the script works as anticipated; but clear it only if you won't need to enter any information. However, you'll want to keep this option checked until you're certain that the script works as intended.

> **Tip:** Microsoft provides a set of default scripts with Windows XP in the \WINDOWS\SYSTEM32\RAS folder. You can use these scripts as templates for creating your own scripts. They show how to use many of the programming constructions we'll discuss in the sections that follow.

Starting a Script

You'll always create a script by using a text editor, such as Notepad. A script can't contain any fancy formatting or other additions you normally associate with a word processing document. Script files should also have an SCP extension to make them easy to find. If you want the script to appear in the script list box shown in Figure 18.5, you'll need to place it in the \WINDOWS\SYSTEM32\RAS folder.

How do you start the scripting process? If you've programmed in any scripting language or a language such as Visual Basic, some of the following will sound familiar. Scripts use procedures. You enclose all your scripting code with a pair of statements: proc and endproc. Every script has to have a main procedure, and you should add some comments to tell other people (or simply remind yourself) how it works. These are the first lines of text you add to your script file:

```
; This is a comment telling about the script.
proc main
endproc
```

Now that you have a main procedure, Windows XP recognizes this file as a script. It doesn't do anything, however, until you add some code to it.

Using Variables

You must declare all the variables you use, and these declarations have to appear at the beginning of the procedure. A declaration always contains the variable type and the variable name. You also can assign the variable a value. Dial-Up Networking doesn't allow you to declare variables outside a procedure. Variable names always begin with a letter or an underscore, and you can't use reserved names for a variable. Here are the types of variables you can use within a script:

- *Integer* Any number, either positive or negative.
- *String* A collection of characters, such as "Hello World". Strings can contain numbers.
- *Boolean* Variables that are either true or false.

Let's look at variables in action. Here's a script with some variables:

```
; This script shows some variables.
proc main
; This is an integer variable.
integer    iValue
; This is a string variable with an assigned value.
string     sMyString = "Hello"
; This is a Boolean variable.
boolean    lAmICorrect
endproc
```

You'll also find some predefined variables used with Dial-Up Networking scripts. Table 18.1 provides a list of these predefined variables and their purposes.

Table 18.1 Predefined Script Variables

Name	Type	Description
$USERID	String	The name of the user as it appears in the User Name field of the Connect To dialog box.
$PASSWORD	String	The user's password as it appears in the Password field of the Connect To dialog box.
$SUCCESS	Boolean	A variable set by certain commands. You can use this variable to determine whether a command succeeded.
$FAILURE	Boolean	A variable set by certain commands. You can use this variable to determine whether a command failed.

Special Considerations for Strings

Trying to get a string to do everything you need it to do could prove frustrating if the scripting language didn't provide a few additional features. For example, how do you send a control character to the server? Many servers require you to send a Ctrl+Break character before they'll respond. The caret translation feature takes care of this. Simply place a caret (^) in front of one of the first 26 characters. For example, "^C" sends a Ctrl+Break.

> **Tip:** Make sure you always use quotes when defining a string in a script, even if that string represents a control character. Otherwise, the script engine will report an error and the error text may not provide a straightforward, "you forgot a quote" type of response.

There are also text substitutions for control characters. For example, "<cr>" is a carriage return and "<lf>" is a line feed. Using a "<cr>" in your code is much less cryptic than "^M".

Finally, you find that Dial-Up Networking scripts support several escape character sequences that C programmers are familiar with. For example, using "\"" in your code produces a double quote. You also need a way to display the caret. You do it like this: "\^". Likewise, you need a way to display the backslash—"\\"—and the less-than sign—"\<".

Using Commands

The scripting language provided with Dial-Up Networking supports certain commands right out of the box. You also can create other commands (simple ones) by using the proc and endproc keywords to create a procedure. Let's look at the commands you get as part of the product. Table 18.2 lists the built-in commands you can use within a script.

Table 18.2 Built-in Script Commands

Command	Description
delay <iSeconds>	This command enables you to pause the script for iSeconds. You'd normally use this command to wait for the hardware to complete a task. For example, when dialing out from the company PBX, you might have to wait for it to make a connection to an outside line.
getip [<iIP>]	Use this command to retrieve the IP from the host. If your ISP sends the IP in the string, you can use the optional iIP variable to specify which IP you want.
goto <Label>	This command tells the script to go to the label you've defined. A *label* is a piece of standalone text followed by a colon. For example, MyLabel: is a label.
halt	This command tells the script to stop. You'd normally use it as part of your error control or in response to an unexpected event. This command doesn't remove the terminal window, which enables you to see what kind of error condition halted the script.
if <lValue> then	The if command checks for a specific condition (a Boolean value) specified by lValue. If the condition is true, the script commands between then and endif are executed. If not, program execution continues with the first command after then.

(continues)

Table 18.2 Continued

Command	Description
set port databits <iValue>	Use this command to set the number of data bits used for communication purposes. It enables you to set up the communications port automatically instead of relying on the user to do so manually. You have a choice of 5, 6, 7, or 8 data bits.
set port parity <sValue>	This command enables you to set up the communications port parity. Choose between none, odd, even, mark, and space.
set port stopbits <iValue>	Use this command to set the number of stop bits to 1 or 2.
set screen keyboard <lValue>	Use this command with a value of Off to turn the keyboard off in the terminal window. You can turn the keyboard back on by using this command with a value of On.
set ipaddr <sValue>	Use this command to set the workstation's IP address for the session. sValue must contain a string in IP format, such as "200.100.100.1".
transmit <sValue> [raw]	Use the transmit command to send data to the host computer. sValue can contain any string of characters you choose. Dial-Up Networking usually interprets the string as previously shown in the section "Special Considerations for Strings." You can send the string without any interpretation by adding the raw argument to this command.
waitfor	This is the most complex command provided by the script language. Its basic function is to receive input from the host and act on it. I discuss this command in the text that follows this table.
while <lValue> do ... enddo	The while loop tells Dial-Up Networking to continue performing the commands between do and enddo until lValue returns a value of false. You can use any conditional statement for lValue. The only criterion is that it return a value of true or false.

Now that we've looked at all of the available commands, let's take a closer look at the waitfor command. Let's look at a simple example first:

```
waitfor "Login:"
```

All this command says is to wait until you get a Login: string from the host computer. After you get it, start executing the statement immediately following this one. But what if you don't want to proceed with the very next statement? This form of the command shows what to do in that case:

```
waitfor "error" then FixError
```

In this case, we wait for a string from the host containing error, and then we go to a label called FixError. Obviously, this form of the command is a bit limited, so you might want to add other labels.

In addition, this form of the command tells Dial-Up Networking to wait 15 seconds and then proceed with the next command after the until argument:

```
waitfor
    "Go For It"     DoGoForIt
    "Logged In"     DoLogInStuff
    "Error"     FixError
until 15
```

As you can see, you can keep building on this command until it directs every kind of traffic possible for you. Place this command within a while do ... enddo command, and you have a program loop for handing the entire communications session.

Using Phone Dialer

The Phone Dialer for Windows XP is completely different from the one found in previous versions of the product. You'll find it in the \Program Files\Windows NT\ directory as DIALER.EXE. Gone is the cute-looking telephone keypad you used in the past. This version of the Phone Dialer is more functional and designed to work in both the Internet and corporate environment. Figure 18.6 shows the conference display.

All of the high-end features of this product require a centralized server that you can use a domain controller. Phone Dialer queries the server for information, such as the user names and other information found in the domain database. In short, the corporate features, such as conferencing, require a centralized server, normally a Windows Server setup of some type. These corporate features work much like the same features in NetMeeting.

You can still enter telephone numbers in Phone Dialer, which is one of the main purposes for this utility. To enter a new number, right-click Speed Dial and then choose New Speed Dial from the context menu. Type a display name and telephone number for the speed-dial entry. You can choose between three types of contacts: telephone call, Internet call, and Internet conference.

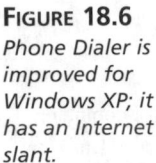

FIGURE 18.6
Phone Dialer is improved for Windows XP; it has an Internet slant.

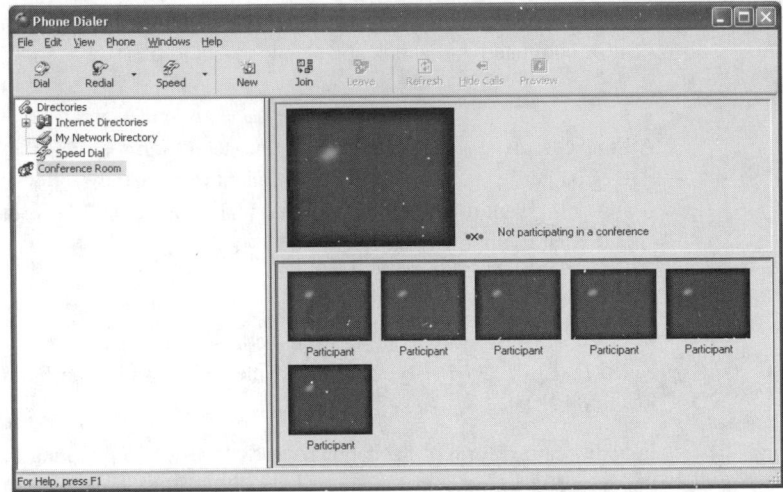

After you create an entry, you can highlight it and click Dial. You see two dialog boxes. The first contains the settings for your machine. The second contains the remote machine settings. The second dialog box shows some activity as it makes the call for you. When the recipient answers, both dialog boxes become active and you can continue your call. Use the microphone and speaker sliders as needed to make conversation easy.

On Your Own

If you've thought about setting a network up in the past, but have found the price too high, check out some of the alternative options found in this chapter. Most small businesses and home users find these alternatives perfectly acceptable for low-bandwidth tasks, such as word processing.

If you have a notebook computer—and both a network and direct cable connection are available for it—try both methods of transferring a file. Most people have a serial connection available, so try that first. You should find the network connection to be much faster, but it's interesting to see how much faster. Try the same thing with a parallel connection (if possible).

Try creating a script program for a Dial-Up Networking connection. You might want to try this with a local setup first to get a feel for the capabilities of the scripting language.

Install and set up Phone Dialer. Try it for a few days to see whether its additional features make phone calling a little easier for your harder-to-reach numbers. Also try the log feature to see how well it meets your needs.

Network Connections with an Internet Appeal

The Internet is a major focus of most communication today. It represents a nexus for people from all over the world. Most companies have an Internet plan in place right now, and many have implemented an Internet plan (dot-com crash not withstanding).

The preceding chapter looked at some of the intricacies of making connections within Windows XP. However, we looked at internal connections for the most part, not outside of your machine. Even the Dial-Up Networking section focused on personal communication needs. This chapter looks at some of the things you can do with those connections after you make them. This is the worldview of networking connections.

Once you open yourself up to the world at large, you also open possibilities for others to contact you. Sometimes, this experience is positive. For example, when you get help from another user, even one you've never met, it always makes your day because that's one less problem you have to worry about. On the other hand, a cracker attack on your machine can prove devastating.

This chapter also finishes some networking odds and ends. For example, you'll learn about the Home Networking Wizard and Universal Plug and Play (UPnP). Both of these additions to Windows XP help make networking easier for you. Of course, both work to varying degrees because they're new technology and their machine configurations differ.

An Overview of the Communications Architecture

Before we get into the communications packages, let's look at the communications subsystem architecture. Actually, we don't get the total picture in this chapter. Figure 19.1 reflects only the local part of the communications structure. Chapter 17 covers the remote network architecture. However, if you look carefully, you'll see all three of the main connections discussed in Chapter 18, including Dial-Up Networking, Phone Dialer, and Direct Cable Connection.

FIGURE 19.1
*An overview of
the Windows XP
local communica-
tions architecture.*

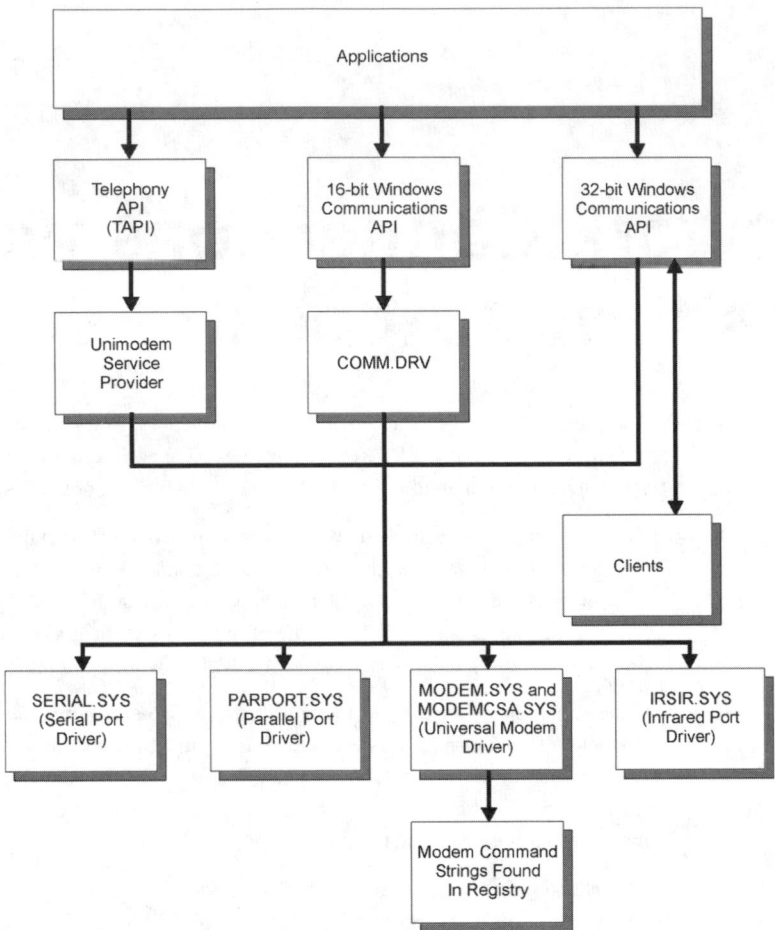

Now that you've seen the communications architecture, let's discuss it in detail. The following list provides details about all the components of the communications subsystem:

- *Telephony API (TAPI)* All the modem-specific services are clustered under this API. It provides command translation for the new Windows XP applications that use it. When an application asks about the modem's setup or status, this module provides the information translation required for a seamless interface. TAPI might configure the modem from a virtual point of view, but VCOMM still manages the actual port. Modem commands flow through the port from TAPI. A good analogy of this arrangement is that VCOMM provides the pipe, but TAPI provides the water. TAPI encompasses multiple DLLs on your hard drive. For example, TAPIUI.DLL contains all of the user interface elements, while TAPISNAP.DLL provides the MMC snap-in you use to configure TAPI options. A special TAPIPERF.DLL contains the counters that help you monitor TAPI performance.

- *Windows 16-bit communications API* This API is the module that accepts instructions from a 16-bit application and translates them into 32-bit instructions that Windows XP can understand. One API instruction might require an entire module's worth of detailed instructions in order to perform a specific task. Windows XP doesn't use the 16-bit version of the Windows communications instructions; it uses the 32-bit API, described in the next bullet. The old 16-bit instructions didn't provide the robust environment that the rest of Windows XP provides. However, instead of writing a new 16-bit module for older applications to use, Microsoft provides access to the new 32-bit interface through these instructions and the COMM.DRV module, which I'll describe in a moment.

- *Windows 32-bit communications API* This is the enhanced 32-bit instruction set for Windows XP. Like its 16-bit counterpart, the 32-bit API translates application requests into commands that Windows can actually implement. Windows XP also got rid of the VCOMM.386 file by placing all of its components within the 32-bit communications API. VCOMM.386 was a static device VxD that previous versions of Windows always loaded during the boot process. Part of the job that VCOMM.386 performed was to load all the port drivers shown in Figure 19.1. Other parts of Windows also called VCOMM.386 through their respective APIs to perform a variety of port-specific services. KERNEL32.DLL now handles all these services. The net effect of this change is to speed communication by reducing the number of calls the communications subsystem has to make.

- *Unimodem service provider* This is the specific driver for your modem. It translates the generic commands provided by the TAPI module into something your modem understands. Unimodem support existed within a single module in previous versions of Windows. It requires two primary modules in Windows XP: MODEM.SYS and MODEMCSA.SYS.

- *COMM.DRV* This is the oldest module in the communications system. In fact, you'll find that even the copyright date is old (the file date, however, is new). Under Windows 3.x, this module carried out the communications tasks ordered by the API. The Windows XP version is a thunk layer to the 32-bit instructions held in the 32-bit communications API and VCOMM.386. The positive aspect of this is that you'll see a definite boost in the speed of communications programs, even if you use an older 16-bit application. The negative aspect is that Microsoft decided to maintain the old 16-bit instruction set rather than upgrade it to the fuller 32-bit set.

- *Clients* VCOMM.386 (which was incorporated into the 32-bit communications API) provides services to more than just the communications subsystem. Every time any other Windows subsystem requires port access, it must go through VCOMM.386 as well. APIs that act as clients field these requests to this module. This is an internal Windows XP function that you'll never really notice, but you should know that there are interactions between subsystems. A port failure might not always be the result of a communications- or print-specific problem; it could be related to some interaction from another, unrelated subsystem.

- *SERIAL.SYS* This is the serial port driver. It's the actual serial port engine. Another driver is associated with the serial port as well: SERIALUI.DLL provides the interface you use while setting up the serial ports.

- *PARPORT.SYS* This is the parallel port driver. Unlike the serial port, the printer subsystem normally managed the parallel port. Consequently, it relies on MSPRINT.DLL for user interface services.

- *IRSIR.SYS* This is the infrared-communication port driver. You usually see it on a laptop machine, but any machine with an IR port can use it. In most cases, an IR port is also associated with either a parallel or serial port (in some cases, both). A communications program might end up transferring data through the serial or parallel port routines before it gets to the infrared-data port drivers. This driver also works with the IRDA.SYS (protocol driver) and IRENUM.SYS (bus enumerator) to provide a complete infrared communication package.

- *MODEM.SYS* The modem setup is a little more complex than the other port drivers supported by VCOMM.386. This one actually works with either a serial or parallel port to provide modem services for the rest of Windows. It's also responsible for making any modem-specific Registry changes. Every time you change the modem strings, this module records them in the Registry. As with the serial port driver, the VxD doesn't provide any interface elements. It relies on MODEMUI.DLL to provide these services. There's also a Control Panel element to worry about in this case. You'll find that MODEM.CPL manages this aspect of the interface. MODMEMCSA.SYS actually provides the Unimodem filtering required by the driver.

- *Modem command strings found in the Registry* Actually, this is the completion of a circle. Many of the upper modules rely on the Registry entries to know how to interact with the modem. These strings provide those instructions. Each string defines some aspect of modem behavior. In most cases, it affects the modem's setup or the way it communicates with another machine. Refer to your modem manual to get a better idea of exactly how these strings work.

Unlike many other subsystems, the communications subsystem looks fairly straightforward, and it is—to a point. There's a risk of underestimating the effect of this subsystem on the rest of Windows if you don't account for the number of ways in which it interacts with other subsystems. The centerpiece of this whole subsystem is KERNEL32.DLL. This module loads the port drivers, provides access to them during system operation, and generally manages the way Windows interacts with the outside world. You might take this important role for granted until it stops working. Chapter 25 looks at some things that can go wrong with this subsystem.

Understanding Virtual Private Networking (VPN)

Most of you are aware of how Dial-Up Networking allows you to make contact with the Internet. You're also aware that the initial connection you make with the Internet isn't very secure. Anyone with the proper equipment can track your communication with the server and determine precisely what you're doing. More than that, they can change the content of your messages to the server and affect the outcome of your communication with the server.

> **Note:** Virtual Private Networking (VPN) is a standard feature of Windows XP. If you're using an older version of Windows, you probably won't see this feature offered on the Windows Setup tab of the Add/Remove Programs dialog box. By the time you read this, Microsoft may have made VPN a Windows feature that you can download from the Internet. See the Microsoft Web site at http://www.microsoft.com/ for more details.

Modern communication methods can add a great deal of communication security by encrypting and digitally signing every packet of information that passes between the client and the server. There are a number of methods available to do this, but most of them rely on some form of certificate for identification purposes. Of course, these communication methods also impose a heavy performance penalty on both client and server, and there's still a chance that someone could decode the data you've exchanged, given sufficient time. This lack of security is one of the problems with trying to create a secure communication link between two parties who don't really know each other.

A VPN creates a second connection between a client and a server, one that's totally secure and that relies on the two parties who are creating the connection having some knowledge of each other. A VPN normally relies on an underlying protocol, like point-to-point tunneling protocol (PPTP), to create the second connection. In sum, you'd begin the session by dialing your ISP to gain access to the Internet using TCP/IP and then use VPN to create a second connection using PPTP.

Installing VPN Support and Creating a VPN Connection

We've already discussed how to create many different hardware, software, and network connections in this book. The process for creating a VPN is the same as for creating a direct cable connection. You need to change only one setting. This part of the setup process appears in the "Making a Direct Cable Connection" section in Chapter 18. When you want to make a VPN connection, use the procedure found in the "Making a Dial-Up Connection" section of Chapter 18.

An Overview of VPN Security Requirements

When you create a VPN, you need more than a connection at both ends; you also need a security plan. Every time you open a new method of communication for your company, someone else is equally willing to make use of that hole to cause problems. Crackers make it their business to search for holes in your security. A VPN is as good as any other hole the cracker might exploit.

Chapter 22 contains all of the procedures you need to secure your system. However, you need to know what to secure and from whom. When you create a VPN connection to your system, you need to ensure that only those who require access can actually do so. This means spending time educating users in proper password use. It also means setting local policies on your machine that require complex passwords. The harder you make the password to break, the longer the cracker will require to gain access.

You also need to understand that the best security in the world won't deter someone who really wants to break into your system. A determined cracker will find some chink in your security armor, so the best thing to do is monitor your system for signs of illegal entry. Crackers often erase files or falsify logs to hide their tracks. You need to question log entries that show abnormal usage habits. For example, if Jane suddenly decides to work at home at midnight, you need to ask her if she's really working or if someone is using her account. Many people are unaware that someone else is using their account and you'll find out only if you ask.

Another security measure is keeping your VPN turned off when you don't need it. If you run a small company and plan to take off for a four-day weekend, turn the VPN off. Crackers love to attack systems when no one is home, so you can partially thwart their efforts by making sure the hole is sealed before you leave.

Internet Connection Sharing (ICS)

Windows XP has a feature that I think has already revolutionized Internet access for home and small-business users with more than one computer, called Internet Connection Sharing (ICS). In the past, if I wanted to get online, I had to check with the other computer users in my office first because we have only three lines. I had to make sure that the line we set aside for modem use was free. With ICS, you don't have this problem. Everyone can use the same connection to get online.

> **Warning:** It's not safe to use ICS on networks that have a Windows NT/2000 Server installed. Nothing terrible will happen to your equipment, but you may find that your network no longer works properly. For one thing, ICS automatically attempts to set your IP address to 192.168.0.1. This is a safe IP address to use, but your network might not use it. As a result, you'll more than likely see error messages at the ICS server that say you can't log on to the Windows NT/2000 domain
>
> *(continues)*

and that the ICS server won't start. ICS could affect other computers as well, bringing communication on the network to a complete standstill. Even if you do manage to get the ICS server running and all of the computers can communicate, ICS may still not work properly. ICS is a solution designed to help the home or small-business user who has a peer-to-peer network to get more from his system.

The way that ICS works is that one computer acts as a communications server. Every time someone wants to dial out, he uses the modem or other communication device attached to that machine. ICS routes the Internet connection request through the network from the client machine to the server and then through the server machine modem to the Internet. In sum, you're using one machine as the source of contact between the computers on your network and the Internet.

Before you can use ICS, you have to set up a few things on your computer. First, all of the computers that'll use an ICS connection need to have a network connection and have TCP/IP installed. Second, you need to have a browser installed. You can use any version of Internet Explorer version 3.*x* or above or Netscape Communicator version 3.*x* or above. The ICS server also needs a connection to the Internet.

At this point, you may be wondering how much of an effect this new method of making an Internet connection has on the server, the network, and the connection as a whole. Let's talk about the server first. You'll see a slight performance drop on the server because it has to take care of communication concerns in the background. However, even with three computers performing simultaneous communications, I didn't notice much of a performance drop. Obviously, you'll want to use the least-loaded machine in your office for this task so that the performance drop is least noticeable.

The effect on your network depends on three things. First, you need to consider the current capacity of your network. If you're using a 100 Mbps network, it's unlikely that you'll notice any difference at all. On the other hand, if you're using a 1 Mbps home network, you'll definitely notice some performance degradation. The amount of performance degradation you'll notice depends on your current network load, the second factor you'll need to consider. If your network normally uses nearly all of the available bandwidth, chances are that you'll notice at least some degradation in performance. A 10 Mbps Ethernet network used for word processing in a small business office isn't even close to using all of the available bandwidth. On the other hand, the same network used for multimedia will be using most of its bandwidth. Finally, you need to consider the kind of Internet connection you have and the number of people using it. One person connected to a 56 Kbps modem connection won't make a big difference. On the other hand, three people connected to a digital subscriber line (DSL) or cable modem connection will make a difference.

Even if there weren't any performance problems for either the server or the network, some people might question the effect of multiple users on the Internet connection itself. Many people complain that the Internet is already too slow, so they think adding multiple people to the connection will only make things worse. The truth is that the effect of ICS on the connection varies. If you're performing normal research, you might not notice any difference at all. That's because you normally download a Web page and look at it for a while. Someone else could be downloading another Web page while you're reading. In other words, they'd be using the connection when you aren't really using it. Obviously, if someone is downloading a large file while you're trying to perform research, you'll notice a definite performance difference. You'll notice a little performance degradation if two people are trying to download Web sites at the same time.

Now that you have a better idea of what ICS can do and how it will affect your computer, let's look at what you need to know to use it. The following sections discuss how to install, configure, use, and remove ICS.

ICS Installation and Configuration

I remember when ICS first came out in Windows 9x. It was a monster to install and terrifying to configure, and it sometimes didn't work. ICS is still a little touchy. It can cause problems that hide as something completely different on your network. Perhaps Microsoft will make ICS detection and configuration easier the next time. However, it has made ICS easier to install and configure. The following steps show how to install ICS:

1. Create a connection to the Internet. It doesn't matter what type of connection. You can use anything from a dial-up connection to the fastest DSL or satellite. I'll tell you how to create a connection with the Internet in the "Using Dial-Up Networking" section of Chapter 20.

2. Test your connection to be sure it works. Make sure the connection works well with a single user attached. If the connection is too slow, you might want to look into another connection type before using ICS. A shared dial-up connection for research purposes is fine; using the same connection for multimedia won't work.

3. Open the Network Connections dialog box by right-clicking My Network Places and choosing Properties from the context menu. Right-click the connection in Network Connections and choose Properties from the context menu. Select the Advanced tab, and you'll see a Connection Properties dialog box, similar to the one shown in Figure 19.2.

4. Check the first Internet Connection Sharing option. Windows XP will enable the second and third options when you do this. Check the second option if you want ICS to dial automatically every time someone needs an Internet connection. This feature is a good one to have; otherwise, someone will constantly bug the person using the server to create a connection. The third option allows users on your network to control the connection. This feature is helpful only if the users on your network have advanced skills and you don't mind providing them with control over an important network feature.

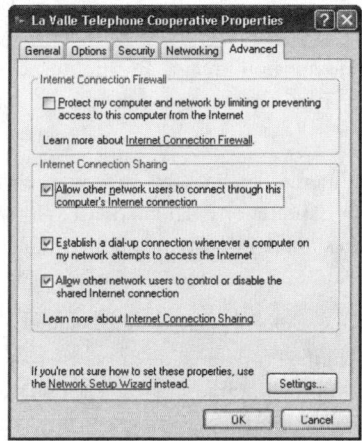

Figure 19.2
The Advanced tab provides options for both a firewall and ICS.

That's all there is to it. You have an ICS setup that can accept requests from other computers on the network. Of course, you have to configure the other computers to use this connection. However, before we leave the Connection Properties dialog box, shown in Figure 19.2, click Settings and you'll see the Advanced Settings dialog box, shown in Figure 19.3. You need to use the options on this dialog box to make any services your system might provide available to Internet users.

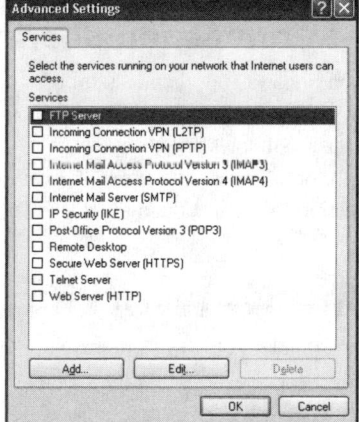

Figure 19.3
The Advanced Settings dialog box enables you to make services available to Internet users.

The only time you need to use the Advanced Settings dialog box is if you install a Web server, FTP server, or mail server on your system. These options tell ICS to open additional "ports" for your setup. Ports are doorways into your system and allow Internet users to access the servers. If you don't check these options, Internet users can't access the associated service even if you have it installed, configured, and running on your machine.

Using Internet Connection Sharing

If your machine is the ICS server, you won't notice any difference in the way you access the Internet after you install ICS. That's because your machine makes the connection to the Internet in the same way.

Client machines also access the Internet in about the same way as they did before. All you need to do is enter a URL in Explorer or open Internet Explorer or Netscape Communicator to get the process started, just as you did in the past. There are few very slight differences once you've requested a resource on the Internet.

The first difference is that you may notice a message in the Internet Explorer status bar (at the bottom of the browser) that the browser is looking for a proxy server. Don't worry—this message is perfectly normal. In most cases, you don't even see it because Internet Explorer will usually find the proxy server immediately. The proxy server is the ICS server—which means that you have yet another term to remember for the same device.

The time delay in creating the connection may seem longer. In reality, it probably won't be any longer, but it will seem so because you're no longer getting the same aural cues that you used to get. You don't see the Connect To dialog box, you don't hear the modem pick up the receiver and dial, and you don't see any of the connection messages. Consequently, your first clue that a connection exists is that you'll see the requested Web page appear within your browser.

Removing Internet Connection Sharing

Removing ICS used to be an even bigger chore than installing it because the removal process left stray DLLs on your system. The DLLs would occasionally cause interesting side effects for some users. Because Windows XP always installs ICS on every system, you don't actually remove it any more. You can disable it. All you need to do is clear the first ICS checkbox in the Connection Properties dialog box, shown in Figure 19.2.

Using the Home Networking Wizard

Let me say at the outset of this section that creating any form of automated network installation is difficult because the vendor can't guess the specifics of your network while designing the wizard. Even if the vendor writes software that correctly determines the capabilities of every device on your machine (something Windows XP does well), a network isn't about one machine. Networks consist of several machines connected using cable. Many networks require add-on devices, such as hubs or switches, for even basic network functionality. In short, attempting to guess the specifics of your network from the clues left in the machinery is nearly impossible.

The Network Setup Wizard does a reasonably good job at setting up small (two- or three-machine) networks where your computing needs are light. Microsoft designed it to meet the needs of the home network, not the corporate environment or even the small-business environment in many cases. In fact, Microsoft originally called this tool the Home Networking Wizard.

> **Warning:** Use the Network Setup Wizard with care. The Network Setup Wizard doesn't work if you are attached to a domain. In addition, it can cause odd problems to occur on a machine that is already configured with network support. For example, you could lose contact with your server or the machine might require additional configuration after the wizard completes. In short, this tool has a lot of potential, but requires more work to use successfully.

You'll find the Network Setup Wizard in the Start\Programs\Accessories\ Communications folder. When you start the application, you'll see a Welcome screen that tells you the tasks the wizard can perform. It pays to read this list so that you know precisely how Network Setup Wizard can help you. The following steps tell you how to complete the process:

1. Click Next. You'll see a list of tasks you need to perform before you use the wizard. Make sure that you perform all of these tasks before proceeding. Otherwise, the wizard doesn't perform as expected.

> **Tip:** Some of the bullets on the Before You Continue dialog box are unclear. When Microsoft says you need an Internet connection, it means you must have a live connection. If you're using Dial-Up Networking, make sure you can interact with the Internet (the telephone is connected) before you begin this wizard. In addition, you need to verify that all printers and other peripherals have a connection to the network and are turned on and active. Windows XP seems to have a problem detecting printers and other peripherals in power-saving mode. The printer will still accept print jobs, but it doesn't always provide a response to Windows XP queries for information.

2. Complete the preparatory steps requested by the wizard and then click Next. You'll see a Select a Connection Method dialog box. This dialog box contains options for three types of Internet connection. Essentially, you need to decide if your computer connects directly to the Internet or if you use another machine to make the connection. If you select the Direct Internet Connection option, the wizard assumes you want to install Internet Connection Sharing (ICS). The Other option takes you to another screen with three more options, including using a hub, a direct connection without any network support, or no connection.

3. Choose an Internet connection option and then click Next. You'll see a Give This Computer a Description and Name dialog box.

You must provide a name for your computer. However, the description is optional, and some people find the description more trouble than it's worth on a small network. Older versions of Windows would display the actual name of the machine and you could obtain the machine description if desired. Windows XP provides the machine description first, with the machine name in parentheses afterward, as shown in Figure 19.4 for the Aux machine. If the network administrator uses an inconsistent description or leaves the description out on some machines, you get the flawed network setup shown in the figure.

FIGURE 19.4
Windows XP displays computer descriptions differently from older versions of Windows.

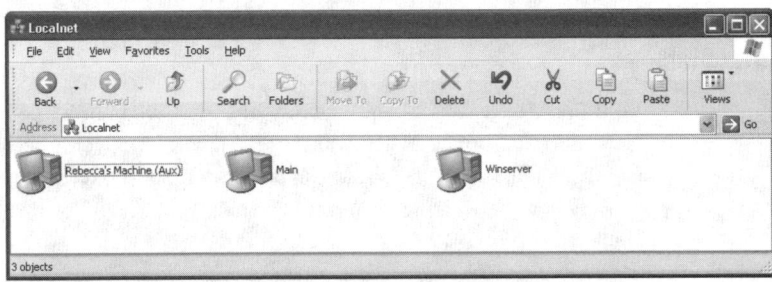

4. Type a name for your computer in the Computer Name field. Type a description in the Description field if desired. Click Next. You'll see a Name your network dialog box. Every computer on your network has to use the same network name. Otherwise, the computers will act as if they're on different networks and don't talk with each other. Make sure you select a name you'll remember to use for all computers on your network.

5. Type a network name and then click Next. You'll see a Ready to Apply Network Settings dialog box, like the one shown in Figure 19.5. This is your last chance to verify the network settings before you begin the network installation. Make sure you check every entry on the list before proceeding.

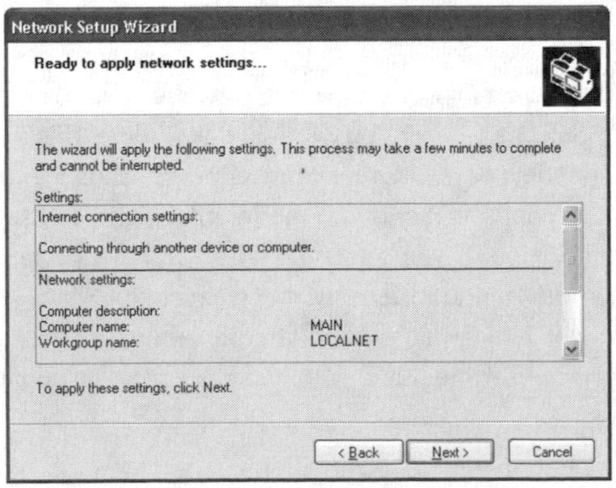

FIGURE 19.5
Make sure that you check your network settings before proceeding.

6. Check the network settings and then click Next. The Network Setup Wizard will perform some analysis and setup on your system. This process can take a long time. Be patient and wait for it to complete. A small two-machine network requires about 5 minutes for this step to complete; larger networks will require more time. When the configuration process is complete, you'll see a You're Almost Done dialog box. This dialog box contains four options for saving your network settings. Generally, using the floppy works best.

7. Select one of the setup disk options. The procedure assumes you'll select the Create a Network Setup Disk option. Click Next. You'll see an Insert the Disk You Want to Use dialog box.

8. Insert the floppy disk in the drive. Click Format Disk to format the floppy, if required. Click Next. The Network Setup Wizard will copy the setup information to the floppy and then display a dialog box containing instructions for using the floppy.

9. Write or type the instructions in a safe place so that you can find them later. Click Next. You'll see a completion dialog box.

10. Click Finish. At this point, your network setup should be ready to go, at least on this machine.

Using Web-Based Enterprise Management (WBEM)

WBEM is a tool that's designed to make managing computers for large companies much easier. Essentially, it's a set of technologies that allows remote administrators to work with your computer over the Internet or through an intranet. You don't see any noticeable changes to your machine when you install WBEM; everything happens in the background. The WBEM components you install act as agents (some people would say spies) that look at your system and report its condition to the network administrator on request.

WBEM was originally created by a group of companies that form the Desktop Management Task Force (DMTF)—it's not a Microsoft-specific technology. Microsoft is implementing WBEM as part of the Windows Management Infrastructure (WMI) that appears in Windows 2000. This technology makes it easier to manage network resources as objects. The object technology used, in this case, isn't COM, but rather the DMTF's Common Information Model (CIM). CIM allows the network administrator to look at the various features of your machine as standardized objects that don't rely on a specific operating system implementation. In fact, this technology is designed to work with other non-operating-system–specific technologies, such as simple network management protocol (SNMP), which has been around for many years now.

The whole point of using WBEM is to reduce the total cost of ownership (TCO) for large companies. Imagine the cost of having a network administrator go to each of a thousand machines to make a single change in the network setup. The cost of doing this if the network administrator physically had to be present at each machine would be astronomical. Reducing TCO means getting rid of this kind of network administrator task. Remote administration is much less expensive.

HyperTerminal

Many people have used HyperTerminal to promote communications between computers over the years. This is one of the older products available for Windows XP. You can use it for a variety of communications needs, including file transfers.

When used for server communications, HyperTerminal is the graphical version of the text mode Telnet application. In fact, HyperTerminal will ask if you want to make it your default Telnet program when you start it the first time. HyperTerminal also has the capability of creating peer connections between two computers.

The following sections discuss ways you can use HyperTerminal to transfer data between your laptop and your desktop machine. In many cases, you're limited to simple file transfers, which may be all you actually need. These sections concentrate on how to perform common data transfer tasks using HyperTerminal.

Creating a Telnet Connection

One of the prerequisites for using HyperTerminal for a server connection is an operational Telnet server on the host machine. Microsoft turns the Telnet server service off by default because many people don't require Telnet and it represents a hole in your security if it's left open to crackers.

Windows NT/2000 Server includes an actual Telnet Administration entry in the Administrative Tools folder. Select this option and you'll see a command prompt open with a menu. One of the options on the menu will start the service. When using Windows XP Professional Edition, you need to open a command prompt. Type **TLNTADMIN START** and press Enter to start the service. Make sure you stop the Telnet server when you finish using it by typing TLNTADMIN STOP and pressing Enter.

Before you can use HyperTerminal to create a server connection, you need to create a connection with it. If HyperTerminal detects that you don't have any connections defined, it will ask you to create one as part of the startup process. You can also use the File | New Connection command to display the Connection Description dialog box. The following steps tell how to create a new connection:

1. Type a name for your new connection and select an icon to associate with it. Click OK. You'll see the Connect To dialog box.

2. Select the TCP/IP (Winsock) option in the Connect Using field of the Connect To dialog box. The Connect To dialog box fields will change to include entries for the host address and port number.

Tip: One way to enhance Telnet security is to use a nonstandard port. The Telnet Server Administration utility allows you to change this port number to something else. Make sure you avoid other common ports, such as port 80, which most servers use for the Web server.

3. Type the required connection information. Click OK. HyperTerminal will attempt to make the connection. If HyperTerminal is successful, you'll see a login screen, like the one shown in Figure 19.6. Otherwise, you'll see an error message and will need to try again.

4. Use the File | Save command to save the connection to disk.

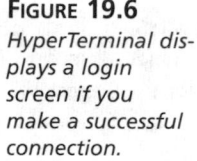

FIGURE 19.6
HyperTerminal displays a login screen if you make a successful connection.

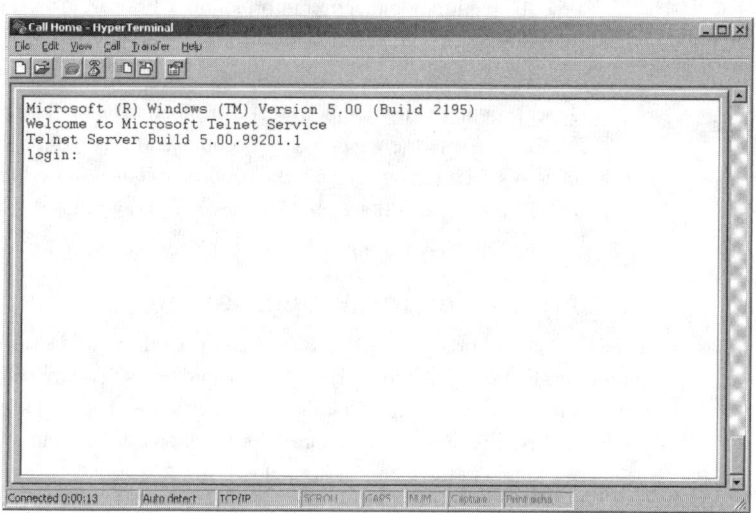

The Telnet connection limits you to tasks you can perform with Telnet. For example, you have full access to the command prompt using the default server settings. Unless the administrator changes the default shell, you can access any character mode utility you have permission to access. However, you can't upload or download files using HyperTerminal because no server allows this capability.

Creating a Peer Connection

The Telnet server option for HyperTerminal offers an automated interface as the server end. If you want to use HyperTerminal in peer mode, you need two people working at the computers, one at each end.

A peer session begins when one person sets his machine up to receive a call. To ensure the previously loaded settings don't contaminate the environment, use the File | New Connection command to display the Connection Description dialog box. Click Cancel to clear all of the settings. Use Call | Wait for Call to begin waiting for the call. You'll see the Connection Description dialog box again. Type any name and click OK. The dialog box will go away and your system will begin waiting for the call.

Now that we have someone waiting for a call, it's time to create a connection to it. The following steps show you how:

1. Use the File | New Connection dialog box to display the Connection Description dialog box.

2. Type a name for your new connection and select an icon to associate with it. Click OK. You'll see the Connect To dialog box. This dialog box contains the country, area code, and telephone number used to make the call. You can also choose a device to use for the connection.

3. Type the required connection information. Click OK. You'll see a Connect dialog box with the current location settings for your system.

4. Change the location settings, if required. Click Dial on the Connect dialog box. HyperTerminal will attempt to make the connection. If HyperTerminal is successful, the cursor in the window will become active. Anything you type will appear on both systems. You'll also see a connected indicator on the left side of the status bar. Otherwise, you'll see an error message and will need to try again.

5. Use the File | Save command to save the connection to disk.

Setting Connection Properties

The initial connection properties you see on the Connection Description dialog box don't fully describe the connection. HyperTerminal assumes that you want to use certain defaults for the connection. Click the Properties button and you see a Call Properties dialog box. The properties on the Connect To tab should look familiar because they're the ones you entered in the Connect To dialog box.

Select the Settings tab and you'll see a dialog box like the one shown in Figure 19.7. The figure shows the default settings that HyperTerminal uses. For example, HyperTerminal assumes you want to send function, arrow, and Ctrl keys to the server for control purposes. If you select the Windows Keys option, HyperTerminal will use the function keys locally.

The Emulation field determines which terminal type to emulate when making a connection to the server. This setting hails back to the days when the only connection was one made to a mainframe. HyperTerminal still has to emulate a terminal to create the connection to the host machine. The Auto Detect setting is the safest selection, unless the host machine is looking for something specific and doesn't provide the proper "handshaking" to allow auto detection.

Use the Backscroll Buffer Lines field to determine the number of lines of text that HyperTerminal saves during the session. Using fewer lines saves memory, and more lines permit you to scroll back further in the session. The 500-line default works for most situations, but you might want to increase this number if you need to capture the screen buffer for a long session. Capturing the screen buffer creates a record of the session that you can store in a text file for later analysis.

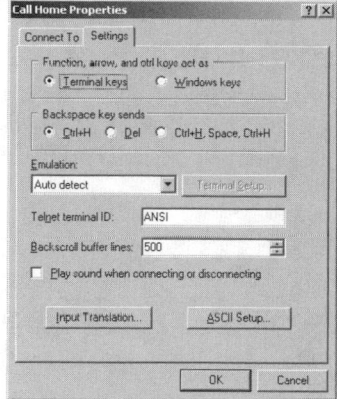

FIGURE 19.7
The Settings tab enables you to select various terminal settings.

Click ASCII Setup and you'll see the ASCII Setup dialog box, shown in Figure 19.8. As you can see, this dialog box controls the manner in which HyperTerminal handles ASCII communication between client and server. The ASCII Setup dialog box includes separate settings for sending and receiving data.

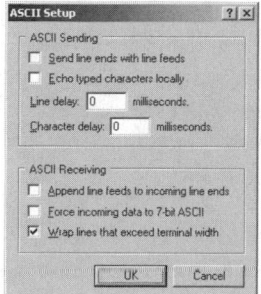

FIGURE 19.8
Use the ASCII Setup dialog box to set special ASCII communication parameters.

Each of these settings helps communication with older systems. For example, some systems don't acknowledge input unless HyperTerminal sends both a carriage return and a linefeed as part of the end-of-line communication (when you press Enter). Selecting the Send Line Ends with Line Feeds option resolves this problem.

Sending and Receiving Files

When using HyperTerminal in peer mode, you can send and receive files using the Transfer | Send File and Transfer | Receive File commands. The normal sequence is for the receiving computer to use the Transfer | Receive File command to display the Receive File dialog box, select a location for the file, and then click OK. The system will enter a wait state.

The sending computer uses the Transfer | Send File command to display the Send File dialog box. The user locates the file to transfer using the Browse button (or typing it directly into the dialog box). Both users can choose from a number of send and receive protocols, but the Zmodem with Crash Recovery option is the best in most situations.

After the two machines complete their setups, the sending machine clicks Send in the Send File dialog box. Both the sending and receiving machines will see the dialog box shown in Figure 19.9. This dialog box will disappear as soon as the file transfer is complete.

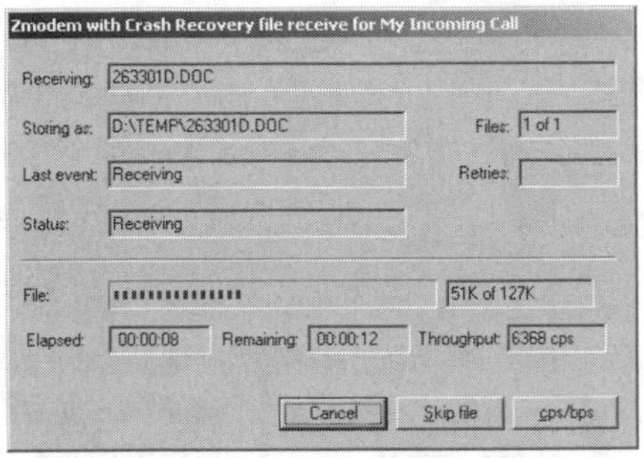

FIGURE 19.9
The sending and receiving computer will see this transfer dialog box.

Capturing a Session

You can capture a session to a text file using the Transfer | Capture Text File command. You'll see a Capture Text dialog box. Type the name of the text file you want to use to store the session information and then click Start. When you complete capturing the session, use the Transfer | Capture Text | Stop command. HyperTerminal will save the file to disk so that you can review the session later.

Sending Text

You can send files back and forth between computers. However, you might want to display a large block of text onscreen at certain times. You can use the Transfer | Send Text File command to transfer the text onscreen. You'll see a Send Text File dialog box. Select the file you want to send and then click Open. The text will appear on both screens.

Testing Your Modem

Windows XP provides a number of obscure methods for testing the condition of your modem. For example, you can use the options on the Diagnostics tab of the Modem properties dialog box. HyperTerminal is another option. Instead of running predefined tests, you can run vendor-specific tests that appear in your modem manual.

> **Tip:** If you can't see what you're typing at the HyperTerminal window, you need to enable the "echo" feature of your modem. Type ATE1 at the HyperTerminal window and press Enter. You'll begin to see everything you type.

To begin testing, type the **"AT"** command you want to run in the HyperTerminal window. For example, if I type **"ATI4"** and press Enter in HyperTerminal, my modem responds with a list of modem settings. If you've somehow lost your manual, you can always type **AT$H** and press Enter to see a display of the various AT commands supported by your modem. A modem usually provides multiple pages of help, and you may have to execute other commands to see a test command menu.

Universal Plug and Play (UPNP)

Windows XP includes support for Universal Plug and Play (http://www.upnp.org/), which is actually a step up from a network-ready device. You still need a network connection, and the device is usually of the general-purpose printer, disk drive, or scanner type. Some vendors even plan to create Universal Plug and Play versions of CD jukeboxes.

You can sum up the difference between Universal Plug and Play and network-ready devices in one word: automation. Instead of actively looking for the device, the device actively looks for you. All your workstation needs is the ability to detect the Universal Plug and Play device. As soon as the operating system and the device make contact, Windows XP presents a message in the Notification Area of the Taskbar, telling you that the device is available. In addition, Windows XP displays any Universal Plug and Play devices that it finds in My Network Places.

Some of the same problems that plague network-ready devices also plague Universal Plug and Play devices. For example, broken network cables or odd configuration software cause problems because you still need the connectivity they provide. However, you don't have as many problems finding the device because it actively searches for your machine. In addition, because these devices are newer, you run into fewer problems finding Windows XP–specific drivers.

Universal Plug and Play devices have several advantages for mobile users as well. When using a network-ready device, the mobile user needs to install support by locating the device, just as any desktop user would. However, when using Universal Plug and Play, the devices are automatically available to the mobile user with sufficient rights to use them. This means a guest using your network doesn't have to reconfigure their entire system just to access a network printer.

Windows XP doesn't come with Universal Plug and Play support installed. You find it in the Networking Services folder of the Windows Component Wizard. You don't have to perform any special installation steps; just use the procedure found in the "Using the Add/Remove Programs Utility" section of Chapter 8. Universal Plug and Play doesn't require any configuration beyond that needed for the device.

When you install Universal Plug and Play, you notice that Windows XP doesn't start the Universal Plug and Play Device Host service right away. That's because this technology relies on the Simple Service Discovery Protocol (SSDP) Discovery Service (`http://www.globecom.net/ietf/draft/draft-cai-ssdp-v1-01.html`) to search for new devices. *SSDP* is a multicast protocol that provides two message types: OPTIONS and ANNOUNCE. The client issues the OPTIONS message to ask all of the servers on the network if they provide a certain service. The server uses the ANNOUNCE message to tell all of the clients that it provides a given service. Between the two message types, your machine will locate a service it needs in the form of a Universal Plug and Play device. When the SSDP Discovery Service sees a Universal Plug and Play device, it starts the Universal Plug and Play device host.

Using Body Language in Your Messages

Body language is a missing element in online conversations. You can't use a wry smile to tell someone that a comment is tongue-in-cheek because he won't see the smile. To help avoid conflict, whenever possible, people have come up with something called emoticons. An *emoticon* is a little text icon that tells the other person what you mean by a certain comment. Just look sideways to see a facial expression, in most cases, or a text version of a picture in others. Table 19.1 lists common emoticons you can use to dress up any written communication. In fact, you could even use them in your company e-mail.

Table 19.1 Standard Emoticons

Emoticon	Description
:-)	A happy face
:->	An alternative happy face
:-D	Said with a smile
:<)	Humor for those with hairy lips
:<)=	Humor for those with beards too
B-)	Smiling and wearing glasses or sunglasses, or a message from Batman
8-)	Smiling and wearing glasses or sunglasses; also used to denote a wide-eyed look
:-1 or :-,	A smirk
'-)	A wink
:-(	Unhappy
:-c or (:-(	Very unhappy
:/)	Not funny (The receiver of a message sends this emoticon to show that a particular comment wasn't received as the sender intended.)
(:-&	Angry

Emoticon	Description
:-))-:	Theatrical comments (Use this for comments that are either theatrical in nature or are used for emphasis.)
;-)	Sardonic incredulity
(@ @)	You're kidding!
:-"	Pursed lips
:-C	Incredulous, jaw dropped
:-<	Forlorn
:-B	Drooling or overbite
:-|	Disgusted
:-V	Shouting
:-o or :-0	More versions of shouting
:-w	Speaking with a forked tongue (You're lying to the other person in a whimsical sort of way. In other words, you're making a point sarcastically.)
:-W	Shouting with a forked tongue
:-r	Tongue sticking out: Bleahhh!
<:-0	Eek! (You can use this for a number of purposes. You can even use it to tell the network administrator that your equipment is down and you can't do anything without it.)
:-*	Oops! (covering mouth with hand)
:-T	Keeping a straight face, tight-lipped (Use this emoticon when you mean something in a serious way that the receiver could interpret as a humorous comment.)
:-#	Censored (You'd love to use a little profanity but resisted the urge.)
:-x	Kiss, kiss
:-?	Licking your lips
:~i	Smoking
:~j	Smoking and smiling
:/i	No smoking
:-) :-) :-)	A guffaw
:-J	A tongue-in-cheek comment
:*)	Clowning around
:-8	Talking out of both sides of your mouth
<:-)	For dumb questions (Everyone knows the only dumb question is the one you failed to ask before trashing the network. However, some people might feel that they have a dumb question they want someone to answer.)

(continues)

Table 19.1 Continued

Emoticon	Description
oo	Headlights on (Use this emoticon to show someone that you want him to pay special attention to a comment.)
:-o or #:-o	"Oh, nooooooo!" (à la Mr. Bill)
|-(	A late-night message
(:-$	Ill
#:-)	Matted hair
:^)	A big nose
:-{#}	Braces
(:^(	A broken nose
:-(=)	Big teeth
&:-)	Curly hair
@:-)	Wavy hair
?-(	A black eye
%-)	Broken glasses
:	A fuzzy person
*:**	A fuzzy person with a fuzzy mustache
(:<)	A blabbermouth
+<:-|	A monk or nun
(:-|K-	A formal message
||*(	A handshake is offered
||*)	A handshake is accepted
<:>==	A turkey
@>--->----	A rose
(-_-)	A secret smile
<{:-)}	A message in a bottle
<:-)<<|	A message from a spaceship
(:-...	A heartbreaking message
(:>-<	A message from a thief (Hands up!)
...--...	SOS
:-I	It's something, but I don't know what.... (You can't figure out what the other person is trying to say or reference.)
@%&$%&	Profanity

Tip: If Table 19.1 doesn't contain enough emoticons for you, entire Web sites contain entries devoted to this topic. Two of the better Web sites are Recommended Emoticons and Smileys for E-mail Communication (http://www.windweaver.com/emoticon.htm) and The Original Emoticon Site (http://www.angelfire.com/hi/hahakiam/emoticon.html).

On Your Own

Check your SYSTEM folder to see whether you can identify the various pieces of the communications subsystem. This chapter provides you with a list of the major files and many hints on how you can find the other special files that pertain to your system.

Spend some time working with the material in the VPN section of this chapter if you normally spend a great deal of time on the road. It's a good idea to try out this technology at your business before you get on the road so that you can work out any potential problems when technical assistance is easy to get. If VPN doesn't look like the right choice, you can always try using Dial-Up Networking Server (discussed in the "Using Dial-Up Networking" section of Chapter 20). Dial-Up Networking Server is a great alternative when other technologies don't work.

If you're a home or small-business user with a peer-to-peer network, see if ICS will work for you. I've found that it allows everyone using my network to work more productively and that we don't spend as much time interrupting each other to ask about the modem. Not only that, but imagine the cost savings you'll experience by having one phone line for all Internet connections rather than a phone line for each computer with a modem.

Administrators are often unaware of all of the resources at their disposal. WBEM is still a work in progress, but it's already a good tool for managing your network. If you have a combination of machine types on your network, now might be a good time to see if WBEM can solve some of the network administration problems you've experienced in the past.

I provided you with a list of standard emoticons in this chapter. One of the fun elements of online computing is coming up with your own set of special emoticons (of course, this means that you have to explain them to everyone). Try creating a few emoticons of your own. For example, one person recently created an emoticon that resembles Bill the Cat.

Internet Connections

In the minds of some people, the Internet has become a virtual singles bar—a place to meet new people and exchange ideas. I don't go more than a day or two without receiving some type of lonely-hearts advertisement in my e-mail. Other people view the Internet as just another source of information for their favorite hobby or form of entertainment. For example, during one evening, a friend and I saw that no less than 90 percent of the new television shows include an Internet address as part of their programming. An equally interesting idea is that the Internet is some kind of a communications magic carpet. Of course, problems with making this "magic carpet" fly in business applications still exist, but companies are working hard to make the idea viable. Consider all the other uses for the Internet. One magazine I recently looked at suggested that artists use the Internet in place of a gallery to show previews of their art for sale. I've also seen some articles that talk about how the fashion industry uses the Internet to tell people about new trends. Obviously, you'll see uses that are more mundane as well. You'll find a large number of newsgroups on the Internet, and more than a few people use it for research purposes. In fact, the Internet started as a means for government and educational organizations to exchange information.

Of course, not everything is rosy in the world of the Internet. The recent fall of the dot-com companies is just one sign that the Internet is still a volatile place. However, the long-term outlook for the Internet is great because it does provide so much of value. Whether business has anything to offer you as a user depends on the way you use the Internet.

E-commerce has changed the way just about everyone shops. In the past, you had to dread crowds at the mall whenever you made a purchase. Today, the mall is a nice place to visit if you have the time, but the Internet is available if you're in a rush. Today, if a vendor wants to stay in business, it has to offer competitive prices because the next store is a mere click away. You also use time more efficiently because shopping doesn't include any driving time, poor parking conditions, or other time-wasting activities. Finally, an online store is never out of stock. Even if the item you order isn't in the warehouse, the vendor can normally order it and send to you in a minimum length of time. Of course, getting your purchase delivered is a nice perk, too. In short, although online shopping doesn't offer the natural feel of a bricks-and-mortar store, it does offer many advantages that make it the store of choice for most users.

The Internet certainly fulfills some part of all these ideas. You can use it as an extremely valuable research tool, to exchange ideas with other people, or create a Web site for your employees at remote sites. However, none of these uses for the Internet really tells you what the Internet is all about and how you can use it to your best advantage. That's what this chapter's all about. I'm going to spend some time telling you about the foundations of the Internet and the tools you can use to explore it. Surfing the Net should be an experience that helps you meet specific goals and broaden your horizons. The problem is that with such a large number of items on the menu, you could easily get lost.

Using Dial-Up Networking

We've already discussed Dial-Up Networking in some detail. You've learned how to create a direct cable connection and how to share a connection with other people. You can create new Internet connections in several ways. The standard approach is to use the New Connection Wizard shown in Figure 20.1, which you'll access using the New Connection Wizard icon in the Network Connections applet of the Control Panel.

FIGURE 20.1

The New Connection Wizard consolidates connection techniques and provides a new interface to the Internet Connection Wizard.

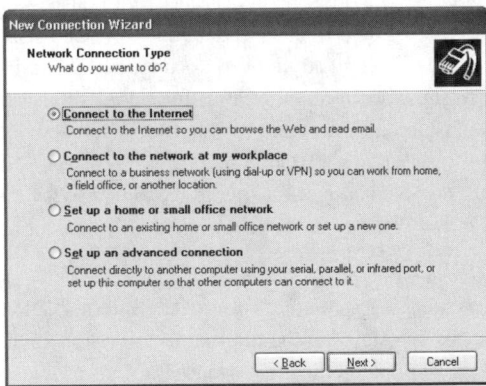

In most cases, however, you can save time and effort using the Internet Connection Wizard directly. For example, if you decide to create an entirely new connection, it requires four additional steps to use the New Connection Wizard. Part of the reason Microsoft made this change is to ensure you can access an MSN connection with relative ease. However, the New Connection Wizard also places a needless burden on those who don't want to use MSN. With this in mind, we'll use the Internet Connection Wizard throughout the chapter.

Tip: Using the MSN connection necessitates using Passport, a technology that stores your personal information on Microsoft's server. Many industry specialists consider Passport unsafe for a number of reasons. You can read more in Brian Livingston's column for InfoWorld (`http://www.infoworld.com/articles/op/xml/01/09/10/010910oplivingston.xml`). Even if Passport keeps your data safe, there are privacy issues to consider. More than a few privacy organizations also feel that Passport is too invasive. In short, use the MSN option with care.

You access the Internet Connection Wizard by opening the Run dialog (Start | Run), typing **ICWCONN1** in the Open field, and clicking OK. The following steps show you how to create a basic Internet connection; use this process only if you need a new account:

1. Ensure that you select the Create a New Internet Account option. Click Next. You'll see a dialog box containing one or more Microsoft ISP referral telephone numbers.

2. Select a telephone number and click Next. The Internet Connection Wizard will dial the selected number. If there are any service providers in your area, Internet Connection Wizard will show you a list.

3. Choose one of the ISPs and then click Next. At this point, you'll see one of two screens. If you choose one of the vendors that normally appears in the Online Services folder, you'll see a completion dialog box. Otherwise, you'll see a sign-up dialog box. This dialog box allows you to provide your personal information to the ISP.

4. Fill in the required information and then click Next. You'll see a list of billing options that vary by vendor.

5. Choose a billing option and then click Next. You'll see another personal-information dialog box that includes credit card information.

6. Fill in the required credit card information and then click Next. At this point, the Internet Connection Wizard will dial the ISP and complete your setup. Because this part of the procedure varies by ISP, you'll need to follow the instructions provided by the ISP to complete the process. Once you complete this setup process, you're ready to set up your Internet mail account. Proceed to the "Creating an E-mail and Newsgroup Account" section of this chapter. Of course, you could always exit the Internet Connection Wizard now and create your e-mail and newsgroup accounts later.

Many of you have existing accounts or special needs. In some cases, you need to make a connection manually. When working with a modem connection, you need the ISP telephone number and any special connection information. Your ISP should supply all the required information. The following steps discuss the manual methods for creating a Dial-Up Networking account:

1. Start the Internet Connection Wizard by opening the Run dialog (Start | Run), typing **ICWCONN1** in the Open field, and clicking OK. Choose the Manually Configure My Telephone or Network Internet Connection option on the initial Internet Connection Wizard dialog box, and then click Next. The Internet Connection Wizard asks whether you want to create a connection using your LAN or modem.

2. Choose the I Connect Through a Phone Line and a Modem option and then click Next. The Internet Connection Wizard will ask you to enter the telephone number used to access your ISP. This dialog box also allows you to choose whether to use the area code in dialing the ISP. An area code might be necessary in rural areas where the ISP is outside of your normal dialing area. In addition, you need an area code when dialing into the ISP from outside an area code's service zone.

> **Note:** Your ISP may provide you with some special configuration options for your connection. Click Advanced to display the Advanced Connection Properties dialog box. These configuration parameters include the kind of connection the ISP offers: point-to-point protocol (PPP), Serial Line Internet Protocol (SLIP), or Compressed Serial Line Internet Protocol (C-SLIP). You can also change the logon procedure (besides logon name and password) and both the IP and DNS address for the connection. In most cases, the default settings for these advanced options work just fine. The only time you need to adjust them is if the ISP tells you to do so in the instruction sheet you receive when you sign up for service.

3. Fill in the required information, make any required changes to the settings, and then click Next. Internet Connection Wizard will display a dialog box that asks for your user name and password.

4. Type the required information and then click Next. Internet Connection Wizard will ask for a name for your new connection.

5. Type a descriptive name for the connection and then click next. It's time to set up your Internet e-mail account.

Protocols and URLS

This section discusses two very important Internet topics: uniform resource locators (URLs) and protocols. A URL defines a particular Web server resource, such as a Web page or a file. Protocols define how you communicate with the server after you find the URL.

Understanding Uniform Resource Locators (URLs)

The URL is the basis for movement on the Internet, so it's important to understand how it works. Let's start by looking at the Microsoft home page address—that's where you check in before exploring the rest of the Internet:

```
http://www.microsoft.com/
```

Note: The automatic completion features offered by some browsers may make it appear that you no longer need to use complete URLs. However, all that these features do is complete the URL for you—the whole URL is still required in order to access the site. With this in mind, it's still important for you to know how URLs work on those few occasions when you need to troubleshoot your setup. Adding to the confusion is the fact that some administrators no longer add the www in front of their company name. In some cases, this means that a complete URL could consist of only a protocol, a company name, and a domain identifier, as explained in the sections that follow.

This typical URL identifies a particular server and clues you in to its capabilities. The first portion of the URL—in this case, http://—tells you what kind of data exchange protocol to use when accessing the server. Here you are using Hypertext Transfer Protocol. The data transfer protocol tells you what to expect from the server. An FTP site (accessed using ftp://), for example, doesn't provide much in the way of user-friendly graphics. You commonly use FTP sites for downloading files instead of providing content.

The next section contains the domain name system (DNS) address for the site you want to visit—in this case, www.microsoft.com/. DNS addresses normally have three sections. However, this is changing as the Internet grows. Some DNS addresses have a fourth, or even fifth, section that contains the computer, state, or country name. A few DNS addresses that I've seen reflect the school grade level or other pertinent information about the site. In most cases, you'll still see DNS addresses containing three sections.

The first section of the DNS address tells you about the service (or, as some books call it, the subdomain). In this example, you visit the World Wide Web (WWW). WWW sites usually provide some type of graphical presentation. The DNS address doesn't have to start with WWW; for example, the address http://home.microsoft.com/ takes you to the home page for Microsoft Network, where you can personalize your settings when visiting this Microsoft site. Another common subdomain is support. For example, http://support.novell.com/ takes you to the Novell support pages. Many sites use WWW, however, because everyone expects to find their Web site on the World Wide Web.

Note: Adding to the confusion of DNS addresses, some vendors use a process called *redirection*. A vendor might redirect several addresses to a single physical location on its Web server. This enables users to find the Web site with greater ease. The underlying principle is still the same from the user perspective—just the underlying implementation has changed.

The second section of the DNS address contains the domain name itself. In this case, it's microsoft. If you want to visit the Microsoft Network, however, you use MSN as a domain name. Most domain names are either full names or acronyms for the organization—some of which can be quite convoluted. The Internet site must register the domain name with InterNIC. (*InterNIC* is an Internet regulatory organization that takes care of a variety of Internet housekeeping chores, like issuing domain names so that each Web site has a unique name.)

The third section of the DNS address is the domain identifier. Table 20.1 shows some sample domain identifiers. The Internet provides a great number of other domain identifiers, and some third parties provide even more. The vendor that a company registers with usually suggests a domain identifier that fits the organization best. Note that this table doesn't contain every identifier you'll ever see, but it does contain the more common identifiers.

Table 20.1 Common Internet Domain Identifiers

Identifier	Description
.com	Commercial companies, such as Microsoft or CompuServe use this domain identifier. Most online service Internet access providers have a .com domain identifier.
.edu	Not-for-profit educational (4-year post-secondary) institutions use this domain identifier. (There's some discussion about whether the school really has to be not-for-profit; but, in most cases, you find that they are.)
	Technical and secondary schools use a different method of identification. It includes the school name, grade levels, state or province, and country, as in `MySchool.k12.wi.us`. This example describes a primary or secondary school named MySchool located in the state of Wisconsin in the United States.
.gov	All government agencies use this domain identifier. If you see it, you know you're dealing with someone from the United States government.
.mil	The United States military uses this special domain identifier, which keeps it separate from the rest of the government.
.net	This domain identifier usually is reserved for Internet access providers. The exception is when the access provider is a commercial company. In that case, it uses the .com domain identifier. As with every rule, this identifier has some crossover between access providers and commercial companies. A telephone company might have a .net identifier, for example, even though it's a commercial company, because its main focus is providing Internet access.
.org	Some sites fall outside these other designations and, therefore, use the .org domain identifier.

That's the makeup of a basic URL. Some URLs, however, are much longer than the preceding example. What does the rest of the information mean? The URL for my Web page is `http://www.mwt.net/~jmueller/welcome.html`. You should be able to recognize the protocol and domain name of `http://www.mwt.net` within this address. Now let's decipher the sections after the domain name.

I rent space on someone else's server. My Web site—`/~jmueller`—actually exists within a subdirectory on the Midwest Tel Net (mwt) server. Think of the forward slashes as you would subdirectories in a DOS path.

In this example, you're in a particular area of my Web page—the `/welcome` page, which contains my home page information. Notice the `.html` extension here. Some Web servers shorten this to `.htm`, but my particular Web server uses the longer form. HTML, which stands for Hypertext Markup Language, is discussed more in the "A Quick View of Protocols" section. For now, you just need to know that this extension signifies a page that your browser formats graphically.

Another type of URL has to do with e-mail addresses. These addresses aren't difficult if you understand a basic URL. You normally see an address like this: `JMueller@mwt.net`. The first part of the address is the person you want to contact (in this case, `JMueller`). The `@` (at) sign separates the recipient's name from the DNS address of the server used to hold the message. You've already learned how to decipher the DNS address, so I don't repeat it here.

A Quick View of Protocols

Protocols are the basis for conversation on the Internet. Just as its name implies, a *protocol* is a formal set of rules. Protocols, both formal and informal, define the way people conduct business. A formal rule might state that you must be in the office by a certain time to begin work. An informal rule could be as simple as not making disparaging remarks about someone's new haircut or clothes.

Computers also need rules. You won't run into some of them because they affect esoteric things, such as the distance between nodes on a network. Others, such as those used for Internet communication, might become very important to you. Literally thousands of rules affect Internet communications in one way or another. Table 20.2, however, concentrates on some of the protocols you'll actually encounter while performing a typical user activity, such as surfing the Net.

This doesn't begin to scratch the surface of everything you see on the Internet. Think of Table 20.2 as a small sampling of the technologies you use on a regular basis.

Table 20.2 Common Internet Protocols

Acronym	Full Name	Description
CGI	Common Gateway Interface	A special method for accessing an application from a Web page. When a vendor asks you to enter information on a form, for example, you're probably using CGI. The most common use for CGI is in database applications. This is the only Web-server-to-background-application standard currently supported by the IETF. Two other proposed methods are ISAPI and NSAPI.
FTP	File Transfer Protocol	Represents one of the earliest forms of communication recognized by the Internet. There are no graphics at an FTP site, just files to download. This is the only file download protocol currently supported by the IETF. The limitations of this particular protocol have prompted other standards, such as CORBA and DCOM.
HTTP	Hypertext Transfer Protocol	Defines the standard Web page. Whenever you go to a Web site that begins with http:, you're using this protocol. It's the technology that enables you to download an HTML (Hypertext Markup Language) document—the kind that includes fancy graphics and buttons. Essentially, HTTP enables you to download an HTML script—a document containing commands rather than actual graphics. Your browser reads these script commands and displays buttons, text, graphics, or other objects accordingly. That's why the capabilities of your browser are so important (and why you need a new browser if you want to use any of the new protocols mentioned in this table). However, some vendors are already complaining that the IETF standard versions of both HTTP and HTML are old and are less than optimal for tomorrow's needs. That's why there's such a proliferation of other protocol standards and of associated HTML script commands on the Internet today. People are looking for better ways to make information accessible.

Working with Internet Explorer

Let's discuss what you need to do to get going on the Internet. The next six sections cover basic usage for Internet Explorer 6.*x* (the version shipped with Windows XP) and its companion program, Outlook Express. If you happen to have an older version on your machine, you should download the newer version. (Microsoft will also send you a CD containing the current version for the price of shipping and handling.) You'll find the updated version of at `http://www.microsoft.com/windows/ie/`.

Getting on the Internet

All you need to do to get on the Internet is double-click the Internet icon on your desktop. When you do, you see a Dial-up Connection dialog box. (The "Using Dial-Up Networking" section in this chapter talks about this dialog box.) Enter your user name and password (if necessary) and click Connect to get started.

At this point, a number of things could happen, depending on how you created your Internet connection (you can also change the configuration of Internet Explorer to get a variety of results). In most cases, you start at a Welcome to Microsoft Internet Explorer Web page or a Microsoft Network (MSN) Web page, similar to the one shown in Figure 20.2. Microsoft changes this page all the time, so your page won't look exactly like mine.

FIGURE 20.2
You normally start your Internet session at the Internet Explorer or MSN home page.

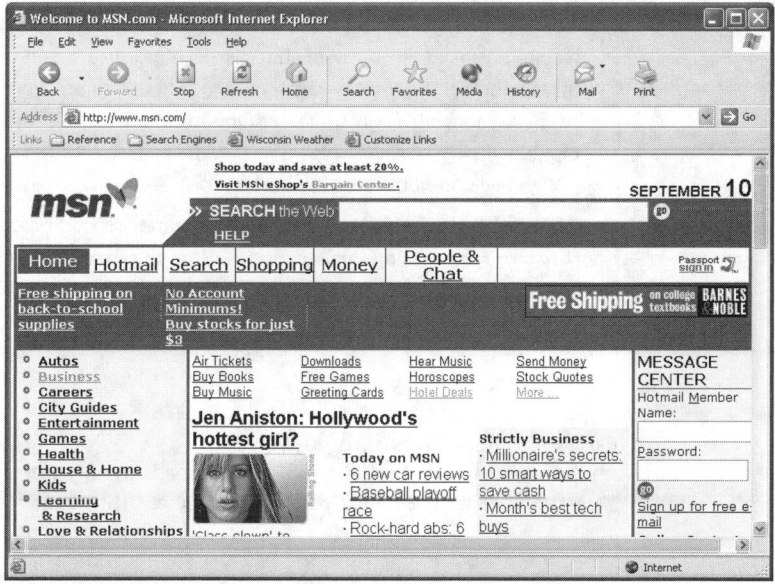

Now that you're online, let's look at some of your controls in more detail. Everything you need is on the toolbar. I don't think I've ever used the menu system in Internet Explorer except to see what it contained. (There's always an exception to the rule. In this case, it's the Favorites menu, described in the next section.) The following list gives you a quick overview of the various controls on the menu; I cover some of them in detail as this chapter progresses:

- *Back/Forward* These two buttons come in handy when you want to move quickly between several areas you've already visited.

- *Stop* Some Internet sites seem to provide more than the usual number of graphics, so they take a long time to download. This button tells the browser to stop downloading content from the Web site. If the browser stops after a few seconds of loading, it typically displays the text contained on the page with few or no graphics, which can save time if you're in a rush. The disadvantage is that you don't see all the neat graphics and buttons the Web page designer placed on the site. The advantage is that you can get back to work faster.

- *Refresh* Explorer, like most browsers, uses a cache to store images. Sometimes the Internet page changes without your knowledge because your browser is looking at the cached page instead of the live page on the Internet. Use this button to update the current page contents. (This button also comes in handy if part of the page became garbled during transmission and the browser didn't catch the error.)

- *Home* Some browsers use the term *start page* for the default page that opens when you start your browser; Internet Explorer uses the term *home page*. Clicking this button always takes you back to your home page. (You can change your home page by choosing Tools | Internet Options and then selecting the General tab of the Options dialog box. Just type a new address in the Address field (you can even use a Web page on your local hard drive).

- *Search* I'll cover this button (and other search-related procedures) in the "Finding What You're Looking For" section, so I don't cover it again here.

- *Favorites* Internet Explorer allows you to maintain a list of favorite places. This button displays the Favorites Explorer Bar, which contains a list of your favorite places.

Tip: You can save your favorite Web pages on disk for future reference by choosing File | Save As. The default save area is the My Documents folder on the Desktop, making it easy for you to just double-click a favorite Web page the next time you need to access it. Clicking one of the hypertext links opens a connection. I use this feature to store the top-level page of places I visit on a regular basis, making it easier for me to find what I want in a pinch. If you don't want to clutter your Desktop with many Internet site locations, stick them in a folder on the desktop. You can still find them quickly by opening the folder when needed.

- *Media* Clicking this button displays the Media Explorer bar, which contains the media player and a list of default links to media locations on the Internet. The Media Explorer bar concentrates its time on popular music, movies, and radio. You'll also see a link for MSN Music, a feature that helps you look for new titles. A link called Today tells you about current music videos, movies, and other forms of media entertainment.

- *History* Clicking this button displays the names of the pages you visited in the past. You can choose to look at past weeks or at previous days of the week. The listings appear in an Explorer-like format.

- *Mail* Clicking this button displays a menu containing five options: Read Mail, New Message, Send a Link, Send Page, and Read News. The Read Mail option displays the Outlook Express program or Windows Messaging (depending on which you chose for your mail reader). Internet Explorer requests any new mail from your ISP's mail server and displays it in the window. The New Message option brings up a new message dialog box using the capabilities of Outlook Express. I'll cover the messaging capabilities of Outlook Express further in the "Using Outlook Express" section of this chapter. The Send a Link option works much like creating a new message. However, in this case, you send someone a link to your current Internet site in addition to the message. This capability allows you to have a discussion with someone else concerning the particulars of an Internet site. The Send Page option lets you send the Internet page instead of a link for the page. Finally, the Read News option brings up the Outlook Express program, discussed in the "Using Outlook Express" section of this chapter.

- *Print* Use this option to send the current page content to the printer.

Now that you've read an overview of the Internet Explorer connection features, let's take a more detailed view of specific features. The following sections will provide you with more information about what I consider essentials.

Using the Favorites Folder

Getting on the Internet is only part of the battle for obtaining information. Finding the right Web site is another part. However, after you find the information you need, how do you ensure that you can find it later? The Favorites folder comes into play at this point. It helps you keep track of various forms of content important to your business and personal life by tracking the Web sites that contain the required information.

Actually, you can track two different kinds of information with the Favorites folder: Web sites and documents. Web sites contain URLs that take you to a specific Web site on the Internet or an intranet. It's like the shortcuts you use in the Start menu to access applications, but, in this case, the link takes you to a Web site instead of to an application.

Documents can contain pointers to your personal data or content in another source, such as a help file. Internet Explorer is no longer limited to just the Internet or a local intranet.

You can also use it to view folders and documents on your local hard drive. If Internet Explorer doesn't provide direct support for a particular type of file, it uses OLE to call on an application that does provide the required support. In some cases, the application simply takes over the Internet Explorer menus and toolbar, allowing you to view and edit your document without ever leaving the Internet Explorer environment.

Using the Favorites folder is easy. All you need to do is click the Favorites menu entry in Explorer and then choose a destination. This list includes all the URLs you've saved, any help or other document links, and anything in the My Documents directory as a default. The following sections look at how you can add new entries to the Favorites folder and then organize them in a way that's easy to use.

Adding to the Favorites Folder

Adding a new favorite to your Favorites folder is easy. Choose Favorites | Add to Favorites in Explorer to display the Add Favorite dialog box. In many cases, you can just click the OK button, at this point, to add the favorite to your Favorites menu. You can perform quite a bit of customization as well.

The Name field of this dialog box contains the title of the Web site you're visiting. Sometimes the Webmaster of the site you're visiting doesn't provide a distinctive name, so you need to change this value to something you'll recognize later. You'll see the contents of the Name field in the Favorites menu when you look for this favorite later. A name such as Home Page (one of the more common titles I see) doesn't tell you much when you're looking for a specific favorite later. Make sure you choose something distinctive but not too long. I find around 40 characters is a good limit to observe.

Click the Create In button and your Add Favorite dialog box expands. The directory list at the bottom of the dialog box works just like the one in Explorer. Highlighting a specific folder places your new favorite in that folder. You can also click the New Folder button to add a new folder to the list.

Organizing the Favorites Folder

Even if you organize your favorites as you add them to the Favorites folder, you'll still find the need for an occasional "housecleaning" of your folder contents. Choose Favorites | Organize Favorites to display the Organize Favorites dialog box, shown in Figure 20.3.

> **Note:** This section assumes that you're using the version of Internet Explorer 6 that comes with Windows XP. If you're using any other version, your dialog box will likely look different from the one shown in Figure 20.3. The functionality is the same; just the method of organizing them is different.

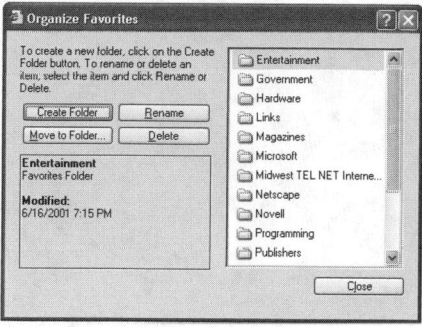

FIGURE 20.3
The Organize Favorites dialog box allows you to manipulate the contents of the Favorites folder.

The buttons you'll find in the Organize Folders dialog box depend on what version of Internet Explorer you're using. The following list explains the buttons found in Internet Explorer 6.x:

- *Move to Folder* You may want to move a favorite to a new location, like a sub-folder within the menu. To do so, highlight the favorite you want to move and click the Move button. You then see a Browse for Folder dialog box, which allows you to select a new location for the favorite. Highlighting this new location and clicking OK moves the favorite.

- *Rename* This button allows you to change the name of a favorite so that it better matches the content and purpose of a Web site or other content in your Favorites folder.

- *Delete* This button allows you to remove a favorite when you no longer need it.

- *Create Folder* This button allows you to add a new folder to the list of folders that currently appear in Favorites.

- *Close* Use this button to close the Organize Favorites dialog box.

Showing Related Links

The Tools | Show Related Links can be either the best thing ever happened to you or a complete waste of time, depending on the Web page you're looking at. The purpose of this command is to show you Web sites related to the one you're viewing now. Selecting this option displays an Explorer Bar similar to the one shown in Figure 20.4. This particular Explorer Bar shows the results for the Internet Explorer Web site (http://www.microsoft.com/windows/ie/). (Note that Web site content changes all the time, so your screen may not precisely match the one in the figure.)

You use this option by clicking entries in this Explorer Bar. The entries remain in place as you explore other Web sites. In short, you can view everything that the Search Companion thinks will relate to the topic at hand.

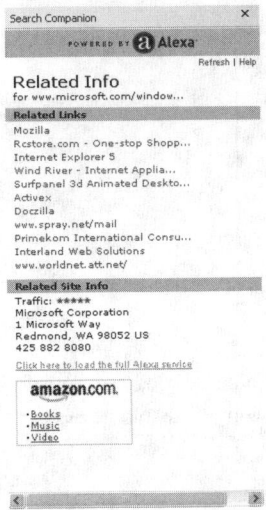

FIGURE 20.4
Show Related Links shows you Web sites related to the one you're looking at now.

The only problem is that this feature works well, in some situations, but mainly provides you with less-than-accurate results. For example, there isn't any way you can link the RCStore site (listed in Figure 20.4) with Internet Explorer, yet that's one of the links you get. What I had expected to see is a list of third-party add-on products or other resources for Internet Explorer. This option appears to work best on sites where the site designer provides an extremely accurate description and the Web site topic is somewhat narrow.

Finding What You're Looking For

If you do much research on the Internet, you realize the benefits of finding what you need quickly. Internet Explorer provides some handy tools for this purpose. First let's look at the most basic tool. Click the Search button in the Internet Explorer toolbar, and you'll see a Search Companion display, similar to the one shown in Figure 20.5. You'll always see Search Companion, even if you turn it off for Windows Explorer.

Depending on how you configure Internet Explorer, the first site you'll see when you begin a search is MSN Search. This is a perfectly acceptable search engine, but many people prefer alternatives. To search other engines, click Automatically Send Your Search to Other Search Engines. You'll see additional search options appear, including DirectHit, Google, and Excite. A third page provides links to About.com and Ask Jeeves. Unlike previous versions of Internet Explorer, you can't configure this option for your personal-favorite search engines.

One of the best ways around this problem is to set up a folder named Search Engines in the Favorites\Links folder. Add all of the search engines you like to use to the list and the list will appear on the Internet Explorer toolbar, like the one shown in Figure 20.6 for my system. Using this technique enables me to get past what Microsoft thinks I need and into what I know I need.

FIGURE 20.5
Internet Explorer provides access to 10 search sites on the Internet.

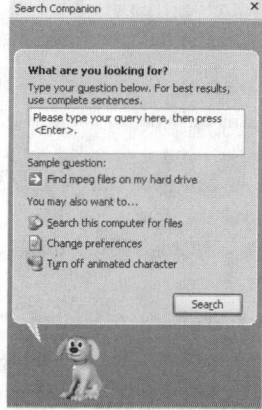

FIGURE 20.6
Create your own Search Engines menu in place of the Microsoft offering.

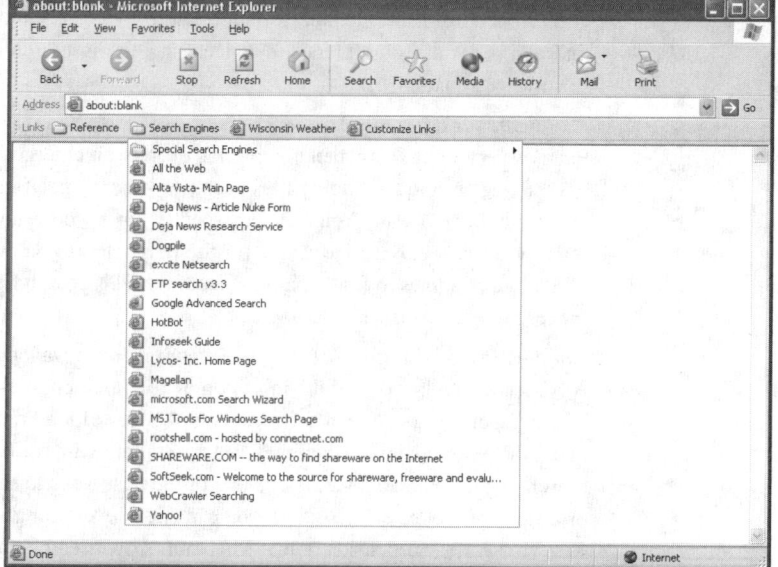

You might think one search engine is enough to fulfill your needs, but that usually isn't true. It's difficult to come up with a "best fit" for search engines because they all work differently. A search engine that works well for one person might not work at all for another. It's important, therefore, to learn about the most common search engines with a quick overview of how they work. You should try them all to see what works best for you in different situations.

The following is a list of common search engines. I've provided URLs so that you can access them directly. To access the search engine page, click the Open button on the tool bar and enter the URL. When you find a search engine you like, you might want to add it to your Favorites list so that you can find it easier the next time:

- *AltaVista (http://www.altavista.com/)* A benefit of using this search engine is a lack of information overload. It returns only the amount of information you want about each hit. The service tends to focus on Web pages containing articles, which means you get some narrow hits when using it. AltaVista's descriptions use excerpts from articles or other sources of information that are accessed. This service uses a somewhat esoteric Boolean search engine, making it difficult to narrow your search criteria.

- *Excite (http://www.excite.com/)* This service focuses on Web sites rather on than pages within a particular site. In other words, you can get to a general area of interest, but then Excite leaves it to you to find the specific information you're looking for. This can be an advantage when you're not really sure about the specifics of a search. A wide view can help you see everything available, and then you can make some refinements. Excite also provides a summary of what you'll find at a particular site. It tends to concentrate on discussion groups and vendor-specific information.

- *FTP Search (http://archie.is.co.za/ftpsearch)* You might not need to search for files very often, but when you do, it's usually an emergency. FTP Search is the best engine around for finding files because you can specify so many specifics about the file you want. You can even specify when you want to perform a case-sensitive or case-insensitive search for the filename. If you ever need an array of FTP search engines to find what you need, try FTP Search Engines (http://www.ftpsearchengines.com/).

- *Google Advanced Search (http://www.google.com/advanced_search)* Google Advanced Search is one of the most complete search engines today on the Internet, but it's also one of the most complex. I've found many items of interest using this search engine when they were completely unavailable on any other search engine. For example, this is one of the best ways to search for information on Microsoft's Web sites because you can check everything at once. I often find Knowledge Base articles here that Microsoft's own search engine doesn't reveal. This site is also adding new search features, such as the ability to look for images.

- *Google Groups(http://groups.google.com/)* For those of you who remember Deja News, this is the new version of that search engine. You can use this search engine when you need to find information in news and chat groups (among others). The only problem with this particular engine is that you might find yourself doing a search more than once to get everything it provides. The engine enables you to search by a specific group or subgroup or by all of the newsgroups on the Internet. In fact, this is the most complete engine you'll ever find for newsgroup work—a real must for some types of research.

- *HotBot (http://www.hotbot.com/)* This service provides a fairly broad range of site-search options and a very clean interface. Consider this site a halfway point between complexity and the ability to search for what you need without having to delve through several levels of menus. The search results normally contain links organized by the number of words that match. HotBot provides one or two sentences that describe the Web site, making it easier to determine if the site contains what you want.

- *Infoseek (http://infoseek.go.com/)* The strength of this particular service is that it provides just the facts. It uses excerpts from articles or other sources of information it finds. The hits are much narrower than some search engines provide because Infoseek concentrates on specific Web pages rather than on general sites. The only problem with this particular service is that it severely limits your capability to narrow search criteria.

- *Lycos (http://www.lycos.com/)* Of the common search engines, Lycos tends to provide the most diverse information. It catalogs both Web sites and pages, but it concentrates on pages whenever possible. Lycos provides a combination of summaries and excerpts to describe the content of a particular hit. Its capability to narrow a search is superior to most search engines available right now. The downside to using this particular search engine is that there's almost too much detail. If you aren't sure what you're looking for, you might find yourself searching false leads and ending up with totally unusable information.

- *Yahoo (http://www.yahoo.com/)* This search engine provides the best organization of all the engines listed here. It categorizes every hit in a variety of ways, which increases your chances of finding information. This service, however, doesn't provide the broad range of information you find with other search engines. It also relies on very short summaries to explain the contents of a particular hit. Yahoo works well as a first-look type of search engine—something that gives you the broad perspective of a single keyword.

- *Web Crawler (http://www.Webcrawler.com/)* This search engine requires a bit more work than most to use because it doesn't provide much in the way of excerpts or summaries. On the other hand, it provides a full Boolean search engine and an extremely broad base of information. The only search engine in this list that provides a broader base is Lycos.

All of these search engines have one thing in common: They look for information using only their search databases. The problem with this approach is that it's possible the user won't find what he needs. Some "super" search sites on the Internet allow you to make a single search that covers more than a single search engine. One of the more interesting entries in the category is Dogpile (http://www.dogpile.com). This super search site allows you to look through up to 24 standard search engines at one time. The only problem with conducting such an intensive search is that it takes time and the large number of hits may be difficult to search through. In most cases, you'll want to save super search sites like Dogpile for obscure information searches.

Changing the Internet Properties

Microsoft tries to make Internet Explorer extremely flexible. You can change many Internet Explorer features by accessing the Internet Options dialog box, shown in Figure 20.7, using the Tools | Internet Options command.

FIGURE 20.7

You configure Internet Explorer using the Internet Options dialog box.

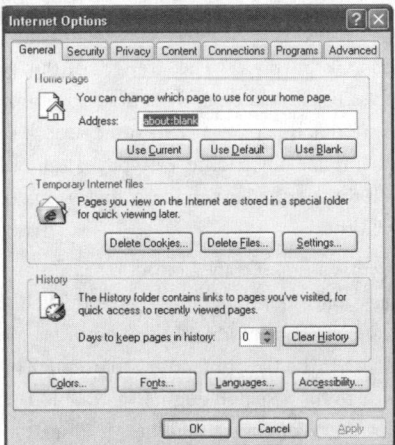

The following sections discuss each of the tabs within this dialog box. We don't discuss every option on every tab. However, you'll walk away with enough information to make Internet Explorer a truly flexible environment for your Internet browsing needs.

General

The first option on the General tab, shown in Figure 20.6, allows you to change how Internet Explorer starts. You can type any address you want in the Address field. For example, if your company has an intranet site, you can tell Internet Explorer to start every session by checking that page. Internet Explorer also provides three default destinations. Use Current changes the address to whatever site you're viewing. Use Default takes you to the MSN Web site. Finally, Use Blank starts Internet Explore, but leaves the choice of initial destination to you. This option is the one to use if you start from a different location every day. Otherwise, you have to waste time stopping the default page from downloading.

The General tab allows you to change the way Internet Explorer interacts with Web sites. Every Web site you visit creates temporary files. Eventually, the number of temporary files increases until you've used up the hard drive space on your system. Of course, this is a less-than-optimal way to browse the Internet, so you need some method for clearing the old temporary files quickly. Delete Cookies and Delete Files removes of the majority of the temporary files for you. Click Settings if you want to tell Internet Explorer how to delete the files automatically. Internet Explorer watches the amount of disk space you set aside and deletes the oldest files as needed.

Internet Explorer also tracks the sites you've visited. This feature works with the History Explorer Bar to allow you to find places you looked at, but didn't put into Favorites. The problem is that these links also consume space (albeit a small amount of space). Many people don't use the History Explorer Bar, so this space is still wasted. You can clean up the history files by clicking Clear History. Keeping the history files clean is a matter of setting the Days to Keep Pages in History option to 0.

The final four buttons—Colors, Fonts, Languages, and Accessibility—control the Internet Explorer environment. You can choose how Web pages appear in your browser, at least to a certain extent. The Web page designer may set specific options, so the view you see is the one the designer wants you to see. You can override the color choices the designer makes by using the options on the Accessibility dialog box. In fact, if you take the extra time to create a style sheet, you'll find that you can control almost every aspect of the Web page appearance.

Security

Internet Explorer uses a zone security setup. For example, when you get online, that's one zone. Working on a local intranet is another zone. You can also add individual URLs to either a Trusted Sites or a Restricted Sites zone. Internet Explorer assumes that any address that doesn't go through the proxy server is an intranet address, but you can also add addresses to the Local Intranet zone.

Adding sites to any of the zones is easy. Select the zone you want to modify and click Sites. You'll see a properties dialog box for that zone. To add sites to the Trusted Sites or Restricted Sites zone, type the URL for the site and click Add. Highlight a site and click Remove to delete it from a particular zone. The Local Intranet zone requires a little more work. Open the Local Intranet dialog box by clicking Sites and then clicking Advanced. The resulting dialog box looks and acts the same as the one for the Trusted Sites and Restricted Sites zones.

Each zone maintains separate security settings, so you need to adjust each one separately if you want to make a general change to all of them. You can use either custom-level or default-level security. Click Default Level and you'll see a slider bar that goes from High to Low. The Low setting is almost the same as not setting security at all.

Using the Custom Level option allows you to adjust each security setting individually. Click Custom Level and you'll see a Security Settings dialog box containing entries such as Download Signed ActiveX Controls and Installation of Desktop Items. Most of these entries allow three values: Enable, Disable, and Prompt. The Prompt setting is the best one to use if you're unsure about the effect of a security setting. Internet Explorer will ask for verification every time it runs into a situation where the security rule will take effect. After you see how the security setting will affect your browsing, you can choose to enable or disable it.

Privacy

Most people who used pre-6.0 versions of Internet Explorer remember that the privacy settings used to appear in the Security Settings dialog box. Internet Explorer 6.0 attempts to simplify the security settings by placing privacy settings on a separate tab. The Privacy tab contains five controls: a Privacy Preferences slider, an Import button, an Advanced button, a Default button, and an Edit button.

The Privacy Preferences slider moves from Accept all Cookies to Low to High to Block All Cookies. Medium is the default setting. At the High security level, most Web sites can't store cookies on your system. This means you can't shop online or use many of the Microsoft Web sites (to name a few). Most online shopping systems rely on cookies to keep track of your purchases along with other information.

The Medium security level allows more flexibility. For example, Web sites can now store cookies on your system as long as they have an acceptable privacy policy. Both the medium and high security levels report when a site doesn't have an acceptable privacy policy in place. Just look at the status bar and you'll see an eye with either a yellow or red circle if the policy isn't satisfactory. Double-click the eye and you'll see a Privacy Report dialog box, which tells about the privacy problems for the Web site.

Note that, in many cases, the Web site has an acceptable security policy, but the banner ads have privacy problems. In fact, since I started using this feature, I've found that many Web sites try to follow the rules. The banner ad sites are the ones that flood me with cookies and try other odd things when I visit the main site. For this reason, I keep my privacy policy set to high until I go to the checkout of a Web site that I trust for purchasing goods or when need technical information from a responsible vendor.

Content

The Content tab helps you control the information viewed by Internet Explorer users. The tab controls three main areas of Internet Explorer functionality. The first section is the Content Advisor. Web sites supposedly provide input, similar to that used by the movie industry, that tells Internet Explorer what type of content the site contains. If the site has content that the Content Advisor settings disallow, the user can't view the information. In reality, the system doesn't work. Pornography sites seldom advertise that they contain R-rated material.

The second section controls your certificates. Click Clear SSL State if you want to clear the certificates from Web sites from your local cache, which forces Internet Explorer to download a new copy of the certificate the next time you visit the site. At first, this feature may not seem important, but it's essential if you shop online regularly. By forcing a new download of the certificate, you can flush out crackers posing as the site in question. The Certificates button allows you to check any certificates issued to you for identification to other parties. You use certificates to exchange information with secure Web sites and to encrypt personal e-mail. Finally, click Publishers if you want to view the people, publishers, and certification authorities your system trusts. Normally, you don't have to worry about this setting unless someone issues a false certificate (as happened with Microsoft recently) or you no longer want to trust an individual.

The third section controls the storing and distribution of personal information. Internet Explorer allows you to create a profile that helps identify you to other people. Consider it a form of electronic business card. You also have access to an AutoComplete feature. This feature allows you to fill in forms without retyping the information. For example, you can use it to add your name and address to a form with a simple click.

Connections

The Connections tab contains information about the connections you have with the Internet. Click Setup and you'll start the New Connection Wizard, which we discussed in the "Using Dial-Up Networking" section of this chapter.

The middle of the Connections tab contains a list of network connections for your machine. Normally, this section contains dial-up connections, but it could contain other connection types, depending on how you set up your system. You can add new connections using Add, or remove old connections using Remove. If you have more than one connection, you can use Set Default to decide which connection to use automatically. Click Settings if you want to reconfigure a connection. For example, you may want to change the name and password information or set the connection up to use a proxy.

This part of the Connections tab also contains three options. Select Never Dial a Connection if you have a LAN connection set up (such as when you're using ICS) and never want to use a dial-up connection. Select Always Dial My Default Connection if you have a single workstation setup or this is the host machine for an ICS setup. Finally, Dial Whenever a Network Connection Is Not Present tells Internet Explorer to check for a network connection first and then dial if the connection isn't present. In theory, this option should provide you with the best of both the LAN and dial-up connection worlds. In practice, Internet Explorer often makes the wrong choice, which makes creating a connection frustrating at best.

Click LAN Settings to display the Local Area Network (LAN) Settings dialog box. This dialog box contains the same settings we created in the "Using Dial-Up Networking" section of this chapter for a LAN connection. The dialog box allows you to change your selections about automatically detecting the server and the address to use for a proxy.

Programs

Like most browsers, Internet Explorer relies on "helper" applications to perform certain tasks. The Programs tab contains entries for task-oriented applications such as HTML editor, e-mail, newsgroups, and calendar. These helper applications are important because they allow you to open links and perform other tasks with Internet Explorer. The drop-down list boxes on this tab allow you to change the programs used for helper tasks from the defaults normally associated with Internet Explorer to other applications you may have installed on your system.

Advanced Options

The entries on the Advanced Options tab are a hodgepodge of settings that don't appear within other dialog boxes or that Microsoft considered too dangerous for the average user. You can modify everything from accessibility features to security settings using the options on this tab.

The biggest piece of advice I can offer when using these options is to think twice before checking many of them. In some cases, it might be a good idea to maintain a log of the changes you make because some settings can have unintended results. For example, you may choose to disable script debugging in the interest of security, only to find later that you have to reboot your machine after visiting some Web pages because you can't break out of errant script code.

You'll want to spend time reviewing all of these options. In some cases, Microsoft made some dubious decisions regarding the default settings. For example, you'll find a Check for Publisher's Certificate Revocation option in the Security section that's cleared by default. This means someone can offer you a revoked certification (one that's bad) and Internet Explorer will never know the difference. I always check this option, even though it slows online access when using secure Web pages.

This tab is also the one to check when it comes to types of encryption technology you want to use. For example, Internet Explorer assumes that either SSL 2.0 or SSL 3.0 is an acceptable encryption technology. You may want to ensure that Internet Explorer uses only SSL 3.0 to protect your system better. Although this is a less frequently used technology, it's also simpler and a little more secure than some SSL implementations.

One of the more interesting sections on this tab for laptop users is Multimedia. Internet Explorer assumes you want to play everything. You can keep these options selected, but you'll find that your battery lasts longer and those around you are less irritated if you turn the multimedia options off. This is especially true in close quarters, such as in an airplane, or areas where electricity may not be available, such as in a car.

Using Outlook Express

Outlook Express is Microsoft's Internet e-mail reader and newsreader. You configure Outlook Express as part of the Internet Explorer configuration process (Internet Mail and Internet News require separate configuration). This section begins with everything you need to know to use the e-mail portion of Outlook Express. This includes creating e-mail and newsgroup accounts for your system. E-mail helps you to send private messages to one or more people. You'll learn how to maintain your address book, how to retrieve messages, and how to send messages to other people.

The next section of this chapter will look at the newsgroup portion of Outlook Express. I'll tell you how to join a newsgroup, how to read messages, and how to send two kinds of messages (private e-mail and public newsgroup messages) to people on a newsgroup.

A *newsgroup* is a public forum for discussing issues or asking questions about a specific topic. One person begins the whole process by making a comment or asking a question. He uploads this information as a message. After you read the message, you can reply to it. A third person may see what you've written and respond to your message. Well, you get the idea. A series of messages form a message *thread*. By reading the messages in a message thread in order, you can see a conversation.

Creating an E-mail and Newsgroup Account

Before you can use Outlook Express, you need to create a connection to the Internet. See the "Using Dial-Up Networking" section for details. After you create a connection to the Internet, the Internet Connection Wizard will automatically start the e-mail and news-group account configuration process. It's important to understand that your connection is already operational. You can use Internet Explorer to access the Internet before you con-figure anything else. This procedure simply makes Outlook Express functional.

If you decide to skip the e-mail and newsgroup configuration process for now, Outlook Express will ask you to perform it the first time you start the application. When you start this procedure from Outlook Express, you'll start at step 3. The following procedure assumes that you're completing the process from the Internet Connection Wizard; the process may vary slightly if you begin by opening Outlook Express after completing the Internet Connection Wizard.

1. You should see the Internet Mail Account dialog box. This dialog allows you to choose between creating an e-mail account immediately and waiting until later. If you choose No at this dialog, you'll see a completion dialog. Just click Finish to complete the process. The completion dialog allows you to dial your new connec-tion immediately, if so desired. The steps that follow assume that you want to set up an e-mail account.

2. Choose Yes and then click Next. If you have one or more existing e-mail accounts, Internet Connection Wizard will ask if you want to use one of the existing accounts or create a new one. If you choose an existing account, the Internet Connection Wizard will ask you to accept the settings for that account and then show you the completion dialog. The steps that follow assume that you want to create a new account.

3. Select the Create a New Internet Mail Account option, and then click Next. The Internet Connection Wizard will ask you for a display name. This is the name that other people will see when you send them e-mail messages.

4. Type the display name that you want to use, and then click Next. Internet Connection Wizard will ask for your e-mail address. This is normally your login name, followed by an at (@) sign, followed by your simple mail transfer protocol (SMTP) server name. It looks something like this: Jmueller@nowhere.net.

5. Type your e-mail address, and then click Next. The next dialog will ask you what kind of server you have: HTTP, Internet message access protocol (IMAP), or SMTP. In addition, you'll have to provide both incoming and outgoing server names. In the case of an HTTP connection, both servers will have the same name, so you'll just have to enter this information once.

6. Configure your Internet mail settings as needed, and then click Next. The next dialog will ask for your username and password. Use the username for your e-mail, not the one used to log onto the Internet.

7. Type your name and password, and then click Next. You'll see the completion dialog.

8. Click Finish; you're ready to go online.

Basic Outlook Express Usage

Let's begin looking at how Outlook Express works. The first thing you'll notice as you begin using Outlook Express are the buttons on the toolbar. The default setup includes nine buttons. However, you can add more buttons as needed. These buttons are available when you use e-mail. Click a newsgroup, and you'll see 11 buttons for newsgroup purposes. Many of these buttons overlap in function, so I'll discuss them only once. The following list describes the purpose of the buttons you'll generally use with Outlook Express:

- *New Post or Create Mail* This button enables you to create a new message. Outlook Express provides options to include files and an electronic business card with your message. You can also set priorities, digitally sign, and encrypt your messages. You can even find options for inserting HTML code for elements such as horizontal lines and graphics. A standard message uses plain text to keep things simple, but Outlook Express also includes a feature for using stationery with your messages. Stationery has become quite popular. In fact, you can find some great additions to the Microsoft offerings at Cloud Eight Stationery (http://thunder-cloud.net/stationery/). Finally, you can use the Compose Message button for creating new messages in a newsgroup.

- *Reply Group* Use this option to send a reply for the current message to the entire group. In other words, you can make a public response to a message that someone else left. You can use this option to ask for clarification of the previous sender's message, ask a similar question of your own, provide an answer to the initial message, or simply make a pertinent comment about the subject under discussion.

- *Reply* This button appears when you're looking at either an e-mail or newsgroup message. When used in e-mail, it allows you to respond to an incoming message. This option sends the response only to the message author—not to anyone else who may have been on the message as a recipient. The author's name appears in the From section of the message. If multiple e-mail addresses are listed in the From section of the message, your response is sent to all those recipients. The Reply to Author button serves a slightly different purpose when used in a newsgroup. Use it when a public response to a question in a newsgroup isn't ideal. For example, you may want to use this option when providing personal information, answering a personal question, or providing information that the rest of the group really wouldn't interested in hearing.

- *Reply All* This button sends a response to everyone who received a copy of the original message, along with the message author. You see this button only when working with e-mail.

- *Forward* This button sends a copy of the current message to someone else. What you see is a standard e-mail message dialog box with the forwarded message at the bottom. You can add your own message to the beginning of the forwarded message. This option also allows you to provide a CC list.

- *Print* This button sends a copy of the message to the printer. You can use it from your e-mail or a newsgroup reader. The message formatting reflects the formatting used by the message author. However, backgrounds might not print unless you choose this option as part of your Internet Explorer setup.

- *Delete* This button places the selected e-mail messages into the Deleted Items folder. Because you can't delete newsgroup messages directly using Outlook Express, you find this button only on the e-mail toolbar. If you're in the Deleted Items folder, this option permanently removes these items from Outlook Express.

- *Stop* This newsgroup toolbar button serves the same purpose as it does within Internet Explorer: It allows you to stop downloading a message or message heading from the news server.

- *Send/Receive* You use this option to send any messages in your Outbox folder. You also use it to receive any new messages from your ISP's mail server. Any new messages appear in your Inbox folder. (See the next section for a discussion of folders.) This option automatically checks all your accounts. Choose Tools | Send and Receive | <Account Name> if you want to send or receive messages for a single account.

- *Addresses* This e-mail toolbar button allows you to display the address book. I'll tell you more about the address book in the "Managing Your Address Book" section of this chapter.

- *Find* Use this button to locate information in your e-mail or on a newsgroup. The arrow next to the button enables you to choose a specific type of search. For example, you can find a message in all available folders or just the current folder. One option enables you to search for people as well.

- *Newsgroups* This button displays the Newsgroup dialog box, which allows you to choose which newsgroups you want to work with. Obviously, it's available only on the newsgroup toolbar. I'll talk more about this feature in the "Adding Newsgroups to Outlook Express" section of this chapter.

- *Headers* Use this button to download the next set of messages from a newsgroup. Windows XP defaults to downloading 300 messages at a time. However, you can set it to download all of the messages in one pass for offline reading.

Every Outlook Express window (beside the toolbar) contains a minimum of three main sections. On the left side, you see the first section that contains a listing of your e-mail and newsgroup folders. The second contains a list of headings for the e-mail folder or newsgroup. *Headings* are a list of the message subjects you find in your e-mail or the newsgroup. Outlook Express uses a variety of symbols to show whether you've read an e-mail or newsgroup message. E-mail messages usually use a closed envelope to show unread messages and an open envelope to show the ones you've read. Newsgroup messages use a colored sheaf of paper for unread messages, a full sheaf of paper for the messages you've looked at during this session, and a half-sheaf of paper for the messages you've read during other sessions. The third section contains the high-lighted message. You see the message subject and its author's name at the top of this area. The message text follows.

You may optionally display a list of contacts in a fourth window. This feature enables you to see your address book without having to open a separate window. For example, you might need to look up a telephone number and not want to open the Address Book separately.

You also need to know one additional piece of information. If you look at the status line, you may notice that Outlook Express tells you the number of messages in the current folder when you're looking at e-mail. Newsgroups include three statistics: the number of messages in the newsgroup, the number of messages you've downloaded but haven't read, and the number of messages remaining to download.

Working with Folders

Now, we're ready to talk about folders—one of the items you use to organize your mail. Outlook Express comes with the five basic mail folders. The Inbox receives all your new mail. The Outbox holds messages you want to send to someone else. The Sent Items folder holds copies of the e-mail messages you send to other people so that you can refer to them later. The Deleted Items folder holds any messages you deleted from other folders. Finally, the Drafts folder contains the messages you're working on right now and intend to send to someone in the future. In other words, you can use this folder to hold work in progress.

You can access six folder-related commands by choosing File | Folder. The following list tells you the purpose of each command:

- *New* This option allows you to create new folders.
- *Move* Use this command to move a folder from one location to another. This option allows you to create a hierarchical folder format if you want to organize your e-mail by project or content type.
- *Rename* This option allows you to change the name of an existing folder.
- *Delete* This option allows you to delete folders you no longer need. Outlook Express doesn't allow you to delete the four default folders.
- *Compact* Outlook Express doesn't actually recover the space used by old messages until you compact the associated folder. This option allows you to compact just the selected file. You'd use it if you just deleted a number of messages and didn't want to spend time compacting all the other folders.
- *Compact All Folders* This option allows you to compress all the folders using a single command.

I usually organize my messages by project. Each project gets its own folder. This way, cleaning up is easy when I complete a project; I just delete the associated folder.

Now, let's look at the process for creating a new folder. Choose File | Folder | New to display the Create Folder dialog box. Type the name of the new folder, highlight the place in the folder hierarchy where you want to place the new folder, and then click OK to create the folder. You then see a new folder in the Outlook Express window.

To Move a message from the Inbox folder to a specialty folder, choose Edit | Copy To Folder or Edit | Move To Folder. Selecting either of these menu options displays a list of the folders on your machine. The big difference between the Move To and Copy To options is that the Copy To command leaves the selected message in the current folder and copies it to the new folder. You can also move or copy messages using the same drag-and-drop techniques you use in Explorer.

Sending an E-mail Message

After you have Outlook Express installed and configured for use, you can use it to send some messages. Click Create Mail and you'll see a New Message dialog box. Let's look at the buttons along the toolbar first because they provide the features you'll use most often:

- *Send* This button sends the message you've just created using the default account. You must define a recipient in the To field before sending a message. In addition, Outlook Express checks the Subject field to make sure it's not blank. You can bypass this requirement by clicking Yes when Outlook Express asks whether you want to send the message without a subject.

- *Cut/Copy/Paste* These three buttons work much like they would with any Windows application. You can cut or copy information to the Clipboard or paste information from the Clipboard into your message.

- *Undo* Outlook Express provides one level of undo. Therefore, you can undo only your last action. A second click redoes the last undone action.

- *Check* Say you don't want to try to remember numerous esoteric e-mail addresses when writing a message. All you need to do is type the person's name and then click the Check Names button. When you do, you see a Check Names dialog box, which lists the names Outlook Express found in your address book that match the one you typed. (If only one name matches the one you typed, Outlook Express automatically inserts it for you.) Highlight the recipient you want to use and click OK, and Outlook Express adds the full form to your message heading. If Outlook Express doesn't find the name in the To field, it gives you the option of adding the name to your address book.

- *Spelling* You can set Outlook Express to check your spelling automatically, or you can click this button before you send the message to the recipients you've chosen. In either case, Outlook Express will check your spelling, but not your grammar.

- *Attach* Use this button to insert a file into your message. Outlook Express opens a standard File Open dialog box, which you can use to select the file.

- *Priority* Allows you to set the priority of your message to low, normal, or high. All messages default to a normal priority. High-priority messages appear in the recipient's inbox with a red exclamation mark. Low-priority messages appear with a blue down arrow.

- *Sign* One of the problems with using the Internet to send e-mail is that no one can be absolutely certain that you sent the message using normal messaging methods. Outlook Express provides new features that allow you to digitally sign your messages, ensuring that you are who you say you are. You need to get a digital ID from a third party, such as VeriSign, before you can use this button.

- *Encrypt* Digitally signing your message may tell the other person that the message is indeed from you, but it doesn't prevent someone else from intercepting and reading the message. The encryption feature that Outlook Express uses depends on both parties having the digital ID of the person they want to communicate with. In essence, you encrypt the message in such a way that only someone with the right key can read it. You must have the required digital IDs installed on your machine before this feature will work. You can get a digital ID from a third-party vendor, such as VeriSign.

- *Offline/Online* Determines if you're working online or offline. When working online, you can send messages immediately. On the other hand, if you work offline, Outlook Express holds the messages until you decide to get online and send them.

After you've added a name or two to your recipient list, you need to type a subject for it. The first thing to notice is that the title for the New Message dialog box changes to match the message subject. You can also define the priority level for your message, although not all browsers and mail readers support this feature. After you add some content to your message, click the Send button to send it. You then see a Send Mail dialog box, telling you that Outlook Express added your message to your Outbox folder. Outlook Express automatically sends the message the next time you click the Send and Receive button in the main Outlook Express window.

Managing Your Address Book

You can gain access to your address book in several ways, but the most common method is to choose Tools | Address Book. You use the Address Book dialog box to maintain your address book.

You can create three kinds of e-mail address entries in the Address Book dialog box. The first is a *contact*—someone you want to send e-mail later. This entry type uses a Rolodex page as an icon. The second is a group, which uses two people as an icon. *Groups* contain one or more of the contacts you create. You can also create folders, which help you to organize contacts by project or other means. Clicking a folder shows you all of the people associated with that project.

To create a contact, click New and select New Contact from the drop down list. You then see a contact Properties dialog box. This dialog box has seven tabs:

- The Name tab contains all the personal contact information for the new entry, such as name and e-mail address. You can even add more than one e-mail address to the list. Notice that Outlook Express designates one e-mail address as the default. Outlook Express uses this address unless you specify an alternative address. You can specify a new default e-mail address by highlighting it and clicking the Set Default button. To add a new e-mail address, type it into the E-mail Addresses field and click Add. If you need to change an existing entry, highlight the e-mail address and click Edit.

- The Home tab contains all the personal information for your contact. It contains personal contact numbers. You can also enter the URL for a personal Web page. Notice the Go button, next to the Personal Web Page field. Clicking this button opens your favorite browser and then takes you to that person's personal Web page.

- The Business tab looks much like the Home page. It contains entries for business phone numbers, including office phone, office fax, and pager. On this page, you also find a Business Web Page field that works just like the Personal Web Page field on the Home page. Clicking the Go button on this page takes you to the client's business Web page.

- The Personal tab contains information about the person's family, including spouse and children's names. You can also enter gender, birthday, and anniversary.

- The Other tab contains notes about your contact. It also contains a list of the groups the person belongs to, but you can't edit this information from this tab. You may want to reserve this tab for long-lasting notes and use a contact manager to keep track of current business information.

- The NetMeeting tab contains settings to define a Web address for contacting a person using a conferencing application, like NetMeeting. In addition, you can set up one or more servers as a meeting place. Outlook Express automatically selects a default and backup server for you if you provide more than one server address. Adding a new server is easy: Just type its name and then click Add. The other four buttons on this page allow you to remove an entry, edit an entry, set an entry as the default server, or set an entry as the backup server.

- The Digital IDs tab contains digital IDs for the e-mail address for the purpose of secure communication. All you need to do is select an e-mail address (or none, for entries without an e-mail address) and then click the Import button to import the digital ID sent to you by the other person. If the person has more than one digital ID, you can choose a default digital ID to use. You can also remove old digital IDs or export an existing one.

Let's get back to the main Address Book window. You can edit a group or single contact by highlighting the desired entry and clicking the Properties button on the toolbar. Getting rid of an unneeded entry is just as easy: Simply highlight the entries you no longer need and click Delete.

So, how do you create a group? Click New Group, and you'll see a group Properties dialog box. The entries for a group include a group name, a list of members, and some notes. Outlook Express provides a separate Group Details tab that contains information like a group meeting address and telephone number in addition to the notes. When you send an e-mail message to a group, every member gets a copy.

There are four buttons along the side of the Group tab. Click New Contact to create a new contact and add it to the address book. If you want to remove a member entry, simply highlight the member name and click Remove. Highlight a member name and click Properties to open a contact Properties dialog box like the one you used to add the contact in the first place. Finally, the Select Members button displays a Select Group Members dialog box, which contains a list of addressees in your address book. Just select the contact or group you want to add to your member list, and then click the Select button. Click OK and you return to the group Properties dialog box. Notice that you can also add or edit entries from within this dialog box.

Adding Newsgroups to Outlook Express

You have to subscribe to a newsgroup before you can read the messages it contains. Outlook Express helps you create connections for multiple news servers—just like you can have multiple e-mail accounts. You need to select a news server in the folder list to place Outlook Express in the proper mode. The news server you connect to has a list of newsgroups for you to choose from. Normally, you can click Newsgroups to display the Newsgroups dialog box, where you can select the newsgroups you want to participate in. As your needs change, you can use this dialog box to change the newsgroups you frequent.

The All tab of the Newsgroups dialog box displays all the newsgroups you can join. If you're worried about finding a specific newsgroup in the thousands that Outlook Express downloaded, don't panic. Using a few strategies, you can quickly find what you need. Finding the Microsoft-specific newsgroups in a section starting with *microsoft* shouldn't be too surprising. In many cases, all you need is a vendor name, or perhaps a good idea of what you're looking for.

After you find a newsgroup that you think sounds interesting, click Subscribe to subscribe to it. As soon as you do, you see a little newspaper icon appear next to the entry. If you later decide that you don't need this newsgroup, highlight it again and click Unsubscribe. Click Reset List to download a new list of newsgroups from the ISP's news server.

You don't have to subscribe to a newsgroup without looking at it first. Just highlight something that looks interesting, and then click Go To. Outlook Express displays the requested newsgroup in the newsgroup viewing panes (described in the "Writing a Newsgroup Message" section).

Let's talk about the two additional tabs listed in the Newsgroup dialog box. The second page, Subscribed, looks just like the All tab. The only difference is that it shows only the newsgroups to which you've subscribed. This way, you can find a newsgroup quickly, in case you don't want to subscribe to it any longer. The New tab helps you to find new newsgroups quickly. Outlook Express normally fills this page automatically when it sees new newsgroups on your server.

Downloading and Reading Newsgroup Messages

Before you can do anything with newsgroups on the Internet, you need to know how to download and read the messages they contain. After you've selected a new server and subscribed to one or more newsgroups, you can download the messages.

Reading messages online is a three-step process. First, select a news server and click the plus sign next to it to display the newsgroups. Second, select a newsgroup by clicking its entry. Outlook Express begins downloading the headers for that newsgroup and displays them in the headers pane of the newsgroup window. Third, select the message you want to read. At this point, you see the text of the message appear in the message pane of the newsgroup window.

Outlook Express provides a second method of downloading messages. You can give one or more newsgroups a synchronization setting. Once you do, click Synchronize Account to download the messages for those newsgroups according to the synchronization settings you choose. The three settings that produce a result when you click Synchronize are All Messages, New Messages Only, and Headers Only.

Writing a Newsgroup Message

Getting a message uploaded to the Internet is much like writing a message for your mailbox. There are some differences, of course. For one thing, you're addressing a public forum. You don't need to specify a recipient for your message because the entire group will look at it. I find it interesting that some people act as though they're addressing a specific person in a newsgroup, when in reality they can't. Always keep the idea of public versus private communication in mind when you're working in a newsgroup.

Let's look at a basic newsgroup message. Click New Post on the Outlook Express toolbar, and you'll see a New Message dialog box. The following list tells you about the functions of the various toolbar buttons:

- *Send* Use this option to post your message on the news server. You probably won't see the message appear right away. Some Webmasters (moderators) monitor the messages they allow to appear on the newsgroup.

- *Cut/Copy/Paste* These three buttons cut or copy information to the Clipboard and paste information from the Clipboard into your message.

- *Undo* Outlook Express provides one level of undo that undoes your last action. A second click of this button redoes your last action.

- *Check Names* Works just the same as it does for an e-mail.

- *Spelling* You can set Outlook Express to check your spelling automatically, or you can click this button before you send the message to the newsgroup you've chosen.

- *Attach File to Message* Inserts a file into your message. Outlook Express opens a standard File Open dialog box, which you use to select the file.

- *Digitally Sign Message* You can use this button only after you define a signature by choosing Tools | Options within the main Outlook Express dialog box. You can find the signature options on the Signatures tab.

- Work *Offline/Work Online* Determines if you're working online or offline. When working online, you can send messages immediately.

The New Message dialog box contains a few special features. Click the newspaper icon next to the Newsgroups field, and you'll see a dialog box for sending your message to more than one newsgroup. Highlight one of the newsgroups in the left list, and then click Add to place it in the right. Notice that this dialog box defaults to showing only the newsgroups to which you've subscribed. Click the newspaper in the lower-left corner of the dialog box, and you see all the available newsgroups.

The Select Recipients dialog box appears when you click the index card next to the CC field of the New Message dialog box. You can use this dialog box to select people who will receive a copy of the message through e-mail. Highlight a user or group name and then click the Reply To or CC button. The section "Using Outlook Express," earlier in this chapter, describes the features of this dialog box, so I won't describe them again here.

> **Note:** One thing you should avoid on the Internet is sending messages to people you meet on a newsgroup because you think they might be interested in some new product or Web site. This practice is *spamming*, and most people react negatively to it. You can find out about other things to avoid doing online by looking at the RFC1855 Netiquette Guidelines, available at `http://www.faqs.org/rfcs/rfc1855.html`.

On Your Own

Create an Internet connection and then explore the Internet using Internet Explorer. Try going online and looking around. The MSN home page is usually a good place to start, but don't limit your choices. Work with some of the search engines mentioned in this chapter so that you know how to find information when you need it.

Spend some time discovering e-mail. Learn to send and receive messages with friends. After you master e-mail, try working with the newsgroups.

PART VII

Networking with Windows XP

21

Networks

This chapter describes the networking capabilities Windows XP provides. For the most part, I purposely avoid talking about networks in general or even comparing the various options you have. The reason is simple: A single chapter can't possibly contain everything you'll ever need to know about networking. You can find volumes of information about this topic—and some people think that those books are just barely adequate. In this chapter, I'll provide you with some insights into the way Windows XP provides network services.

The discussion in this chapter also assumes a certain level of knowledge on your part. I strongly suggest that you spend some time learning about networks in general before you install one. You don't need to be a networking guru to understand this chapter, but you need to know what logging in is all about and know some of the easier terms, such as network interface card (NIC).

The Client Module

This section of the chapter looks at the *how* of network support under Windows XP. It answers questions such as "What can you expect?" and "Why do things work the way they do?" Of course, these are just some of the questions I answer here. Before we become too embroiled in some of the details of actually using Windows XP's networking capabilities, I'd like to spend a little time looking at its architecture.

You need to understand a few things about Windows XP before you look at its architecture. The first thing you need to understand is that Windows NT/2000/XP always has had a strong peer-to-peer networking component. I'm talking from an architectural and usage point of view here (something called the network model), not the media point of view that often equates peer-to-peer to lack of power. (The media perspective has changed since Napster, but the effects of the past still linger and will continue to linger as long as the usefulness of the peer-to-peer model remains in question.) Windows XP provides more than sufficient power to compete even with some of the client/server model networks on the market.

The second thing you need to understand is that Microsoft added the networking support for Windows XP to its I/O subsystem. In essence, the operating system views networking as extended I/O. This really makes sense when you think about it: A connection is still a connection, no matter how long the wire. Keep these two points in mind as you read the description of the architectural components. Figure 21.1 shows the Windows XP network architecture.

FIGURE 21.1

An overview of the Windows XP network architecture.

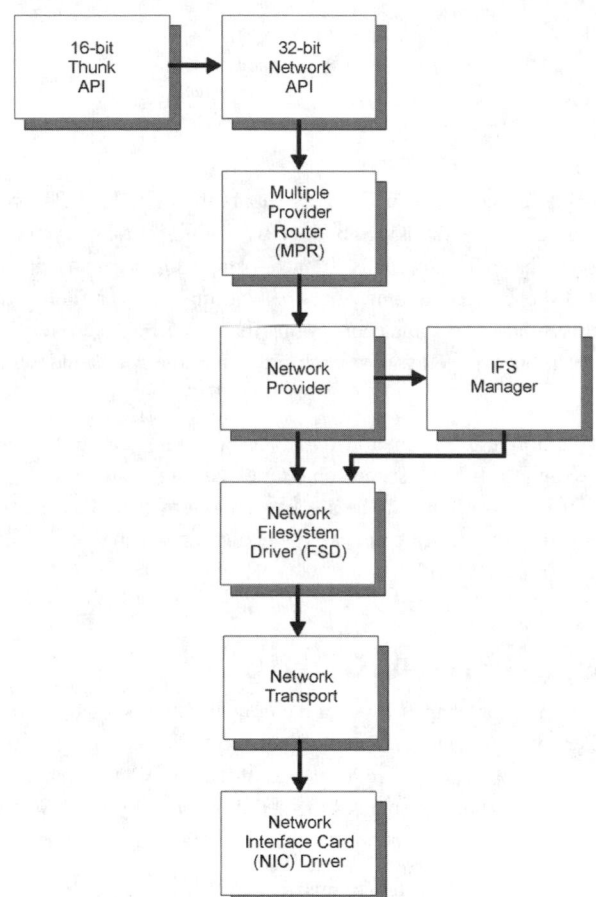

Now that you've seen the architecture, let's discuss it. The following list describes each architectural element:

- *16-bit Thunk API* Windows XP provides full network support using 32-bit code. However, there are still some 16-bit applications to support out there as well. This module replaces the Windows 3.x 16-bit API (known as Winnet16) with calls to the 32-bit API. It has to provide thunk support to do this. We looked at the thunk process in "The Windows API Layer" the section of Chapter 11.

- *32-bit API* All application requests start at this module. I don't go into details about the API, but Microsoft has gone to great lengths to reorganize and simplify it. A user doesn't notice these details, except in the way they affect network performance, but they have a definite impact on programmers—a positive impact. The API translates one application request into one or more standardized network requests. Quite a few files are involved in creating the network API under Windows XP. Exactly which files get loaded depends on your network setup. The two most prominent files are NETAPI.DLL and NETAPI32.DLL. Loading NETAPI32.DLL also loads SECUR32.DLL (security), NETRAP.DLL (remote administration), SAMLIB.DLL (security account manager), WS2_32.DLL and WSOCK32.DLL (32-bit Windows socket), WLDAP32.DLL (lightweight directory access protocol), and DNSAPI.DLL (domain name server). These files provide most of the low-level functionality the API requires.

- *Multiple Provider Router (MPR)* You'll likely use more than one protocol with Windows XP. In fact (theoretically, at least), you should be able to mix and match protected-mode drivers on the same network. You can mix NetBIOS and IPX/SPX on the same network, for example. In addition, some protocols automatically load when you request a specific service. The Microsoft data link control (DLC) falls into this category. It provides connections to mainframes and network printers.

  All network protocols require a network provider. The whole function of the MPR is to accept network requests from the network APIs and send them to the appropriate network provider (NP). Part of each request states which NP to use. Some requests are generic, however. A request for the status of the entire network, for example, falls into this category. In that case, the MPR calls each NP in turn to fulfill the application request. In still other cases, a request might not include enough information for the MPR to know which NP to use to fulfill the application requirement. In this case, the MPR "polls" the NPs to see whether one of them can fulfill the request. If none of the installed NPs can, the MPR returns an error message.

  You'll find that the MPR functions are located in the \SYSTEM32 folder in MPR.DLL. MPNOTIFY.EXE loads this DLL during startup. An intermediate file, MPRUI.DLL, provides a user interface. This DLL contains the dialog boxes you see when you want to map or disconnect from a network drive.

- *Network Provider (NP)* The network provider performs all the protocol-specific functions an application requires. It makes or breaks connections, returns network status information, and provides a consistent interface for the MPR to use. An application never calls the NP; only the MPR performs this function. Although the internal structure of NPs varies, the interface they provide doesn't. This mechanism helps Windows XP to provide support for more than a single protocol. The code used by the MPR can remain small and fast because none of the NPs requires special calls. If a NP can't fulfill a request because of a limitation in the network protocol, it just tells the MPR that the required service is unavailable. The NP also keeps the Installable File System (IFS) Manager updated on the connection status. This is how Explorer knows when you've made a new drive connection.

- *IFS Manager*   When the IFS Manager obtains new status information from the NP, it calls the network file system driver (FSD) to update file and other resource information. When the NP tells the IFS Manager that it has made a new drive connection, for example, the IFS Manager calls on the network FSD to provide a directory listing. The same holds true for other resource types, such as printers. Besides this function, the IFS Manager performs its normal duties of opening files and making other file-system requests. The MPR doesn't know what to do with a path name, so it passes such requests through the NP to the IFS Manager to fulfill. Of course, applications also access the IFS Manager in other ways. The only time the MPR becomes involved is if a network-specific request also requires its intervention.

- *Network Filesystem Driver (FSD)*   Each server on the network could use a unique file system. NetWare and other client/server networks all use special file systems that the vendor thinks will enhance performance, security, reliability, and storage capacity. Windows XP doesn't inherently know about the special requirements of such storage systems. To access these other file systems, it needs a translator; to maintain consistency of access, it uses a translator for all network calls. The network FSD performs this task. It translates the intricacies of a foreign file system into something Windows XP can understand. A network FSD is usually composed of a file-system-specific driver and a redirection driver. The second file provides the Windows XP interpretation of the file system specifics. Normally, there's only one network FSD for each NP. There's nothing to enforce this limit, however. A NP might require access to both FAT and NTFS network FSDs for a Windows XP Server. If so, Windows XP installs both drivers when you install network support. The IFS Manager also calls on the Network FSD for support. Although the NP usually makes requests for network status or connection information, the IFS Manager takes care of application needs, such as opening files and reading their contents. These two modules, NP and IFS Manager, work in tandem, each fulfilling completely different roles.

> **Note:** You might wonder why Microsoft didn't combine the NP and the IFS Manager into one module. After all, from my previous comments, it would appear that the IFS Manager is just part of an access strategy for network drives. However, remember that the IFS Manager works with local drives as well as network drives. For each of these drives, a different file system might be in place. The whole point of the IFS is to allow for new and unknown file systems communicating with Windows XP. Consequently, this two-part structure makes sense. The IFS provides access to any installed file system driver. Windows XP can then communicate with any file system for which there's a driver. Uniting the IFS with a single FSD would eliminate this flexibility by marrying Windows XP to a single file system. It's also worth pointing out that the system applies several networking components as file system drivers. This way, the system achieves access to local and remote resources through the same common component.

- *Network transport* I placed a single module, called network transport, in Figure 21.1. Actually, this module combines many smaller modules and drivers. The complexity of your setup and the requirements of the protocol determine the number of pieces in a network transport installation. There are four elements within the network transport: the transport driver interface (TDI), the transport protocol, the network device interface specification (NDIS) interface, and the NIC driver. The smallest network transport could consist of a mere four drivers.

- *Network Interface Card (NIC) driver* I make special mention of this part of Windows XP for a reason. This particular driver is hardware-specific. It has to communicate with the NIC on a level the NIC can understand. You have one driver per NIC, and this requirement can lead to problems, especially when you change the NIC. I've run into situations when I thought I had completely removed an old driver and installed a new one to support a new NIC, only to find that a piece of the old driver was hanging around. If the new driver attempts to access the file because of a similarity in name or a misdirected Registry setting, network calls can fail. The solution, of course, is always to make sure that the old driver is gone. Remove it from the Network Connections Control Panel applet, and then reboot to make sure that the Registry reinitializes completely.

All these files might seem like a great deal of effort just to create a networked workstation, but that's only half the picture on many peer-to-peer installations. After your workstation gets past being a workstation, it has to take care of network requests as well. In the next section, I show you how Windows XP provides peer-to-peer network services. We look at Windows XP's peer-to-peer support from a server level. We also look at many of the implementation details. For example, I answer the question "How do you share your printer or local hard drive with someone?"

Peer-to-Peer Support

Peer-to-peer networking represents the easiest and least expensive way to get started in networking. Everyone starts with a workstation, the same requirement for using computers in any business environment. You can't share resources on standalone workstations, however; you need to connect them to do that.

In the past, the standard method for sharing resources was to buy additional machines (called servers) and place the common components there. The investment in hardware and software for a full-fledged network can run into tens of thousands of dollars—prohibitively expensive for many companies.

Peer-to-peer networks take a different route: One or more workstations simultaneously act as workstation and server. In fact, if you work things right and the network is small enough, everyone will probably have access to everyone else's machine in some form. This means that, except for the NICs, hubs (in some cases), and cabling, a peer-to-peer solution under Windows XP is free for the asking.

Windows XP (both Home Edition and Professional Edition) provides peer-to-peer networking capabilities right out of the package. All you need to do is install an NIC on each machine, run some twisted pair (or other network) cable, and add a few drivers to your setup. In some cases, you may also need to add a hub or a switch, depending on the kind of network support you install. (A hub provides a passive means for connecting machines on a network together, while a switch has a processor that provides an intelligent means to connect the computers together. The switch is more expensive, but provides better performance.) In fact, the Setup program is designed in such a way that adding network support requires almost no effort at all on the part of the installer. Of course, after you get everyone set up, you'll want to install a few extra utilities, such as a centralized calendar and e-mail.

Peter's Principle: Building a Straight-through Cable for a Two-node Network

If you're using twisted pair cabling for your network, you might think that you have to have a hub to support it. However, if you have only two computers you want to connect, you can often use just a cable to connect them. In fact, you might find such a cable at your local electronics store.

Fortunately, building your own cable isn't difficult. All you need is a few simple tools, a soldering iron, and a little shrink-wrap. The principle is simple. Pins 1 (white/orange wire) and 2 (orange wire) of your cable always have the transmitted data, and pins 3 (white/green wire) and 6 (green wire) have the received data. Two computers can't communicate if you connect the transmit pin on one computer to the transmit pin on the other computer. The first computer must transmit data to the receive pin of the second computer, and vice versa. A hub normally switches transmit and receive lines for you, but you can simulate this action for a two-node setup.

To build a straight-through cable for your system, begin by cutting a twisted pair cable in half. Expose about $1\frac{1}{2}$ inches of the wires on both ends. Be careful not to cut through the sheathing (plastic) covering the individual wires. Tie the blue and brown wires back toward the cable covering so that they don't interfere with your work. Remove a half-inch of the sheathing on all of the orange and green writes on both cables. Place a piece of shrink-wrap on the four remaining wires on the first cable. Make sure you don't cover the ends of the wire. Connect the green wire from the first cable half to the orange wire of the second cable half. Repeat for the green/white wire and the orange/white wire. Now, connect the orange wire from the first cable half to the green wire of the second cable half. Repeat for the orange/white and green/white wire. Solder the connections so they remain tight. Place the shrink-wrap over the connections to cover them and insulate the connection. Generally, a high-wattage blow drier shrinks the shrink-wrap around the connections. Connection your new cable; the two machine should be able to communicate.

We've already taken a detailed look at what it takes to provide workstation support under Windows XP. What happens if you also want your machine to act as a server, however? Providing server support means that your machine must accept requests from other workstations, process those requests, and return the requested information. Figure 21.2 shows the Windows XP peer-to-peer network server support.

FIGURE 21.2
An overview of the Windows XP Server architecture.

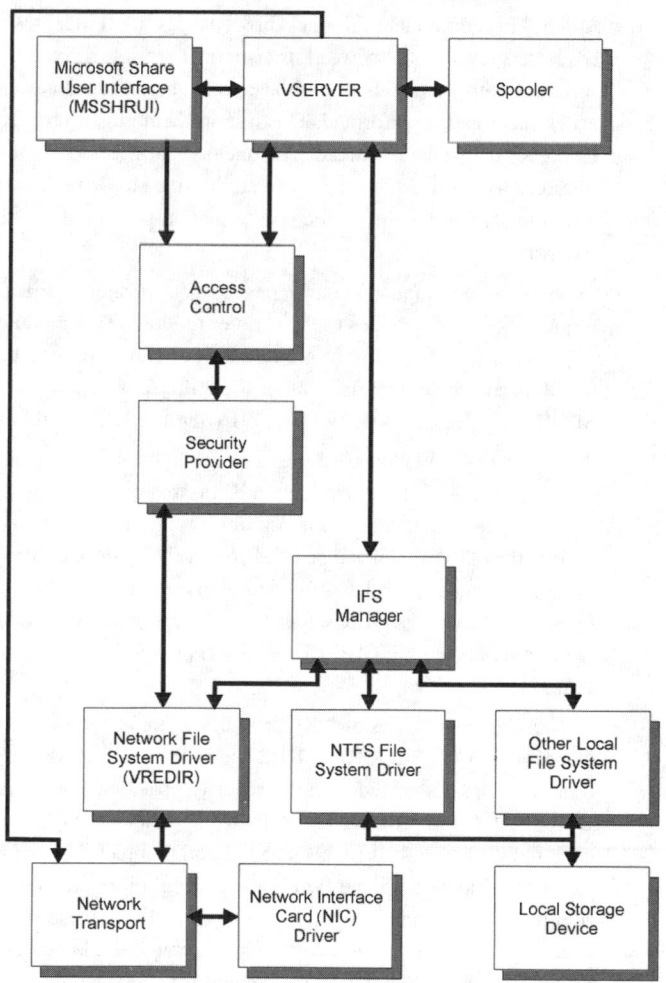

Now that you've seen the pictorial view of Windows XP peer-to-peer networking, let's talk about the various elements (refer to Figure 21.2) in detail. The following list describes each component:

- *Microsoft Share User Interface (MSSHRUI)* This module responds to external requests from users for network resource configuration. Every time you right-click on a resource and tell Windows XP that you want to share it, this module fields that request. It works with the Access Control module to set password protection. An interface to the MPR and ADVAPI32.DLL enables the MSSHRUI to set the proper entries in the Registry. You find MSSHRUI in the NTSHRUI.DLL file in your \SYSTEM32 folder.

- *VSERVER* The central point of all activity for the server is the virtual server driver. As with all the other drivers in this chapter, you find it in your \SYSTEM32 folder. This component provides direct access to all local resources for network requesters through the network transport. It works with the IFS Manager and Access Control modules to limit access to shared resources and to ensure that any access is properly performed. The system maintains each access to shared system resources in a separate thread. This means that access by one requester need not interfere with any other request. In addition, a single requester can make multiple requests. Of course, the protocol settings you provide limits the number of actual requests.

- *Spooler* If you grant someone access to your printer, VSERVER sends any requests for print services to the spooler module. This module treats a network request just like a local print request. As far as it's concerned, the request originated locally. There are four spooler-specific files in your \SYSTEM32 folder: SPOOLSS.DLL, SPOOLSV.EXE, WINSPOOL.EXE, and WINSPOOL.DRV.

- *Access control* Windows XP uses this module for a variety of purposes, not just network access control. Windows calls on this module to verify your initial logon password, for example, even if you don't request access to a network afterward. Unlike the other modules discussed so far, the Access Control module makes use of Registry entries (or data provided by a domain controller using Active Directory) to verify and set security. You find access control in several files. The two main files are NETAPI.DLL (16-bit) and NETAPI32.DLL (32-bit) in the \SYSTEM32 folder.

- *Security provider* Windows XP provides a single centralized security provider. You find it in the SECURITY.DLL file in the \SYSTEM32 folder. Obviously, other files are associated with the security provider. For example, the KERBEROS.DLL file provides the Kerberos security package. The security provider calls the Kerberos security package when an object requests Kerberos security. You can always access the Windows XP Login module even if the network isn't running. The advantage to using it is that the Login module is always available, even if you change the network setup or remove it altogether. The security provider performs two tasks: It asks you for a password and combines the user's logon name and password to verify any network requests.

- *NTFS File System Driver (FSD) and other local file system drivers* I covered both these modules in detail in the "Understanding How the File System Works" section of Chapter 13.

- *IFS Manager, network FSD, network transport, and NIC driver* I talked about these modules earlier in this chapter.

Understanding the server capabilities Windows XP provides is straightforward from a conceptual point of view. After you get past theory, however, implementation becomes another story altogether. The problem isn't due to a poor plan, but rather to all the compatibility issues that come into play. Fortunately for users, the design of the server capabilities makes all these details easy to manage.

Sharing Files and Printers

Sharing resources is the main reason to install a network. The very concept of networks came from the need to share expensive peripheral devices and files. Windows XP provides an easy-to-use interface that enables you to share just about everything on your network using a few clicks of the mouse. Let's take a look at what you need to do to share files and other resources located on your machine.

The first thing I like to do before I start trying to share files is to make sure I actually have the required support loaded. This is a no-brainer under Windows XP because you really don't have a choice about loading the support during setup. Someone could come along and remove the support later, however, so it's always best to check. Just open the Network Connections dialog box by right-clicking the My Network Places icon and choosing Properties from the context menu. Right-click the Local Area Connection icon in the Network Connections dialog box and choose Properties from the context menu. Look for the File and Printer Sharing for Microsoft Networks entry, as shown in Figure 21.3. Make sure that this entry is both present and checked, as shown in the figure.

After you make sure that the File and Printer Sharing for Microsoft Networks service is enabled, you need to select the items to share. Right-clicking any of your drive or printer icons and choosing Sharing and Security from the context menu displays an additional Sharing tab, similar to the one shown in Figure 21.4.

FIGURE 21.3
File and Printer Sharing for Microsoft Networks service enables you to share files and other resources under Windows XP.

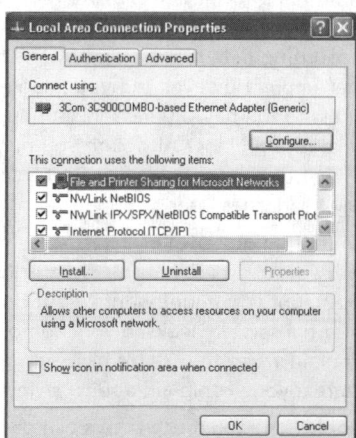

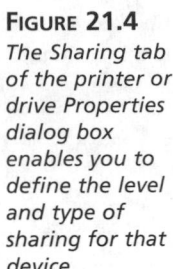

FIGURE 21.4
The Sharing tab of the printer or drive Properties dialog box enables you to define the level and type of sharing for that device.

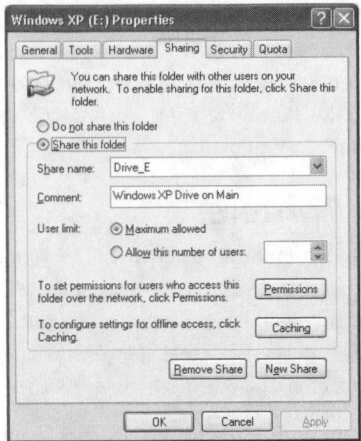

The first two radio buttons on this page enable you to share the resource. By selecting Do Not Share This Folder (Not shared for printers), no one can see the resource, even if he or she has other types of access to your machine. If you do select Share This Folder (Shared as for printers), some additional options become available. The following paragraphs provide the details on how to manage a drive under Windows XP.

Peter's Principle: Maintaining Control of Your System

Sharing doesn't always mean that you allow everyone to access every resource on your machine. It's easier to provide access to an entire drive than it is to set the required level of security folder by folder. However, the drive strategy might not be the best way to go when it comes to your company's health.

Many of us work with confidential information that we must keep safe, but we also work with other people who need to see some of this information. Someone working in the accounting department might need to share analysis files with a workgroup, for example. However, can you imagine what would happen if he also shared access to the payroll files? What happens if someone shares the company's new marketing plans? Although you need to share access to the current project, you want to keep that new project a secret. A little bit of discretion can save you many headaches later.

It's important that you provide the right level of access to everyone in your workgroup. I don't cover every bit of security in this chapter (we look at this subject in detail in Chapter 22), but you might want to put on your thinking cap now. Where are the potential security leaks in your company? It's a well-known fact that people complain when they don't have enough access to the network. Have you ever heard anyone complain about having too much access?

Finding the areas where people have too much access will give you the most trouble. Audits and other forms of security checking are just as important as the sharing itself on your network. Performing an audit takes time and resources that might be very difficult to defend when management asks for an accounting. Of course, having a security breach is even more difficult to defend. Allow others to use the resources you have available, but don't allow the misuse of those resources. It's up to you to do your part in maintaining the proper level of security on your network.

Creating a New Share

You can create more than one share name for a particular resource under Windows XP. Each share name can have more than one group or user account associated with it and a variety of restrictions for that set of groups and users. To create a new share, just click the New Share button. You see the New Share dialog box.

> **Tip:** Windows XP doesn't limit you to providing access to an entire drive or printer. You can define access to an individual folder as well. In addition, you can modify the permissions that individual users have to a file or folder, which means that some users may be able to write to the file or filer, while others may only be able to read it. I find it very convenient to set aside a temporary directory on my machine for file sharing. People can upload their files to a specific directory and avoid changing the contents of the rest of my drive. You can use the same principle for other resources. The key is to maintain control of your system.

You need to provide a resource name in the Share Name field. This is how Windows XP will present the resource in dialog boxes, such as with the Drives field of the File Open dialog box. The optional Comment field enables you to provide a little more information to someone who wants to share the resource. I normally include the precise resource name and my name as part of the comment. This reduces the chance that someone will accidentally try to use a resource on my system.

After you define a resource name and assign it a comment, click the Permissions button to display the Permissions for Resource dialog box, shown in Figure 21.5. The top list box shows who can access this resource. Highlighting an entry in this top list will show the kind of access the user or group has to the resource in the lower list box.

You can use the Add and Remove buttons to add or remove users or groups from the top list. Just check or uncheck rights as needed to give the user or group the proper access to the resource. You can provide four actual levels of access:

- No access (all check boxes unchecked)
- Read
- Change
- Full Control

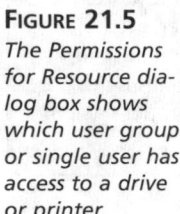

FIGURE 21.5
The Permissions for Resource dialog box shows which user group or single user has access to a drive or printer.

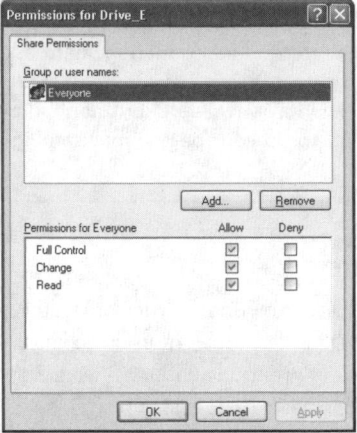

Read access enables someone to read from a resource but not modify it in any way. *Change* access enables someone to read and write to a resource, but not to create or delete anything. Use change access to set up a group of shared files where users can edit a file but not delete it. Obviously, *Full Control* access enables users or groups to do anything you can do with the resource. Use this option with discretion because someone can damage your drive or other resource if you give him or her full access. When you click the Add button to add a new user or group, you see the Select Users or Groups dialog box, shown in Figure 21.6.

FIGURE 21.6
The Select Users or Groups dialog box enables you to define who can access a particular resource.

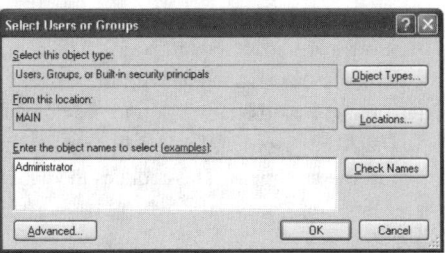

Click Object Types, and you'll see an Object Types dialog box, which contains the object types associated with this object. For example, when working with a drive, you'll see the Built-in Security Principals, Users, and Groups object types. Clearing dialog boxes for object types you don't need limits the scope of any searches you perform. This makes the search faster and reduces the time for finding the user, group, or other object you need.

The Locations button displays a Locations dialog box. If you're on a peer-to-peer network, you see just the local machine. On the other hand, if you're working with a domain controller, you see domain and local entries. Choose a location to determine the source of users, groups, or objects.

Adding names is easy. Just type the name you want in the supplied list box. Check your entry by clicking Check Names. If you don't know the name you want to add, click Advanced. You'll see a larger version of the Select Users or Groups dialog box. Adjust the object types and locations as necessary and then click Find Now. Windows XP will display a list of users and groups you can select for resource access.

> **Note:** Some products, such as Microsoft Word and most other word processors, require full access to a drive. That's because they create a backup file before writing any changes to the original word processing file. You might have to limit word processing files to one or two directories. That way, you can still limit overall drive access and provide better security.

After you select the people you want to give a particular level of access, click OK. You'll see the new users and groups added to the top list box of the Permissions for Resource dialog box. At this point, you might wonder how to add password protection to your resource. Users normally have to log on to your system before they can use a resource. That password acts as their key to gaining access to the resource, so Windows XP doesn't assign any added password to the resource here. In Chapter 22, I'll show you some techniques for adding more security to your system. To complete the action, click OK in the Permissions for Resource dialog box and then click OK in the Drive Properties dialog box.

Removing a Shared Resource Name

A single resource can have more than one share name. You might need to remove one of those share names when a particular user or group no longer needs it. To remove a shared resource name, open the Sharing tab of the Drive Properties dialog box (refer to Figure 21.4). Select the shared resource name you want to remove from the Share Name drop-down list box. Make sure that it's the one you actually want to remove because Windows XP doesn't provide much feedback in the way of an Are You Sure? confirmation box. Click Remove Share. Windows XP will mark the permissions associated with a particular shared name for deleting. At this point, you can still recover them by clicking Cancel. If you click Apply or OK, the change becomes permanent.

Removing or Changing a User or Group Share

You'll eventually need to modify some details associated with a shared resource. If a user leaves the company, for example, it's important to remove their access to your machine. To start the process, open the Sharing tab of the Drive Properties dialog box. Select the name of the shared resource you want to change from the Share Name drop-down list box. Click Permissions to display the Permissions for Resource dialog box (refer to Figure 21.5).

Removing a share is simple. Just highlight the share you want to remove in the Permissions for Resource dialog box and then click Remove. I wish, in some respects, that Microsoft had made this process a little more difficult or at least provided some additional feedback. Right now, you don't get any kind of feedback except for a missing line in the Name box. With this in mind, I always double-check a share before I remove it.

Changing a share is easy too. Just select the user or group you want to change, and then select a new level of access from lower list box. I described these various access levels in the "Creating a New Share" section, so I won't do it again here.

Click OK to close the Permissions for Resource dialog box. You can still change your mind, at this point, by clicking the Cancel button in the Drive Properties dialog box. If you decide to make the change permanent, just click Apply or OK.

Understanding TCP/IP

Windows XP provides a complex and complete set of Transmission Control Protocol/ Internet Protocol (TCP/IP) related features. A *network protocol* establishes rules that allow two nodes—whether they're workstations, mainframes, minicomputers, or other network elements, like a printer—to talk to each other. TCP/IP is one of the more popular sets of network communications rules.

In almost all cases, the TCP/IP support that Windows XP provides is for remote communications. However, there are exceptions. For example, the monitoring capability provided by SNMP could work in a local server setup. It's important to include this support as part of the operating system, for two reasons. First, adding TCP/IP to the operating system makes it easier for software developers to write *agents* (special applications that use the rules these protocols establish to perform useful work). If you added either protocol as a third-party product, there wouldn't be any standardization, making it nearly impossible for other third-party vendors to write standard agents. Second, adding this level of protocol support to the operating system means that Microsoft can incorporate an additional level of support as part of its utility program offerings.

SNMP Support

Windows XP provides remote monitoring agent support for agents that use the Simple Network Management Protocol (SNMP). SNMP originally existed on the Internet. It allows an application to manage devices from a variety of vendors remotely, even if a device doesn't normally work with the managing device. For example, a mainframe can use SNMP to send updated sales statistics to a group of satellite offices in a large company. You can use an SNMP console to monitor a Windows XP workstation after this support is installed. SNMP support under Windows XP conforms to the version 1 specification. Microsoft implements SNMP support for both TCP/IP and IPX/SPX using WinSock (which I'll describe later). The following procedure enables you to install SNMP support under Windows XP:

1. Right-click My Network Places and choose the Properties option. You'll see the Network Connections dialog box.

2. Use the Advanced | Optional Networking Components command to display the Windows Optional Networking Components Wizard.

3. Highlight the Management and Monitoring Tools option and then click Details. You'll see a Management and Monitoring Tools dialog box.

4. Scroll through the list of services, highlight Simple Network Management Protocol, and click OK. Click Next. Windows XP may ask you to insert the installation CD if you don't already have it in the CD-ROM drive. It will then copy some files to the drive.

At this point, the SNMP service is installed and running. However, before you can use it, you'll need to configure the service. The way you do that is to double-click on the Services applet found in the Administrative Tools folder of the Control Panel. Scroll through the list of services and find the SNMP Service. Right-click this entry and then choose Properties from the context menu. You'll see the SNMP Service Properties dialog box shown in Figure 21.7. The first configuration tab we'll talk about is the Agent tab.

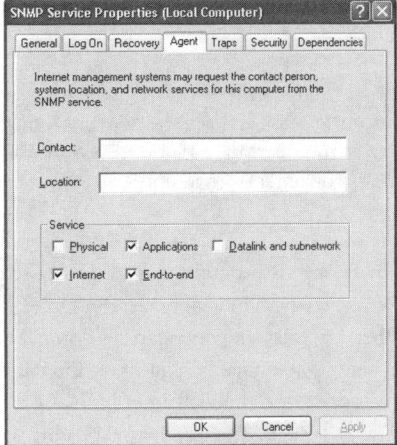

FIGURE 21.7
The Agent tab contains contact information and a list of services provided by SNMP.

As you can see, the SNMP Service Properties dialog box contains all of the usual entries, plus the Agent tab. The following list talks about the items on the Agent tab:

• *Contact and Location fields* These two fields tell whom to contact if you're using an Internet-based service. Someone calling into your workstation from the Internet gets this message, enabling him to contact you if he has any problems.

• *Service* You can offer a variety of services using SNMP. Figure 21.7 shows the default settings. There are five services you can offer: Physical, Applications, Datalink and Subnetwork, Internet, and End-to-End. You need to enable the Physical check box if your Windows XP workstation manages any physical

TCP/IP device, such as a repeater. The Applications check box refers specifically to TCP/IP-enabled applications, such as e-mail. In most cases, you'll want to leave this check box enabled. Enable the Datalink/Subnetwork check box if your Windows XP workstation manages a TCP/IP datalink or subnetwork, such as a bridge. The Internet check box tells other computers that your workstation acts as an Internet IP gateway. Finally, the End-to-End check box infers that your work-station acts as an Internet IP host (an Internet server, in most cases). As with the Application option, you want to keep the End-to-End check box enabled in most cases.

On to the second tab of our configuration, Traps. So what precisely is a trap? A few of you programmers should have a good idea. What happens on a remote communication if someone wants to access a community (the hosts your computer can connect to) that doesn't exist? Let me put this in easier-to-understand terms. Suppose that you want to open a file, so you choose the File | Open command. Now, instead of typing the name of a file that exists, you either leave the filename blank or type the name of a file that doesn't appear on the drive. In a program, this produces an error condition. You'll see a message from Windows or the application saying that the file doesn't exist; some well-rounded applications even give you a chance to create a new file with that name to get around the error condition.

> **Tip:** You're going to look at many definitions for traps in a variety of books. Here's my short definition—the least complex way of looking at this complex topic. A *trap* is an automatic monitoring method. It automatically updates the host when specific events occur on your machine.

In SNMP terms, a *trap* (or *error trap*) is programming code that reacts to errors, perhaps fixing the problem or merely displaying a message describing the problem. The process is a bit more complex than that, but this is a good starting point. There's also a certain amount of security involved here. If someone is requesting the name of a community that doesn't exist, you can assume one of two things: Either he made a mistake or he's a cracker trying to break in to your system. The trap has to be able to deal with both conditions. Now that we're all talking about the same thing, let's look at the fields in this dialog box:

- *Community Name* This drop-down list box specifies the name of a community you want to set a trap for. You see in the next section that you can set a variety of trap types. For right now, all you need to know is that this is a community name. After you enter the name of a community, click the Add to List button to add it to the list. Similarly, if you want to remove a community from the list, highlight it in the Community Name drop-down list box and click Remove from List.

- *Trap Destinations* Use this box to define a list of host IP or IPX addresses you want to send SNMP traps to. The IP or IPX address must be one of the machines in that community. All you need to do is click Add to add a new address. You'll see a Service Configuration dialog box, which asks for the IP or IPX address of the computer. This box also provides Edit and Remove buttons that enable you to change or delete IP or IPX addresses from the list.

If you've been reading the trade press (or even the local newspaper) for the past few years, you'll know that security is a major issue. The next page in the Microsoft SNMP Properties dialog box should come as no surprise then. This tab enables you to change the security for your SNMP configuration. More than that, it provides the means for creating connections to your computer—certainly a part of the security process. The following list provides a description of each option in this dialog box:

- *Send Authentication Trap* Enabling this check box tells Windows XP to send an authentication trap whenever an authentication fails.

- *Accepted Community Names* This section defines the hosts from which your computer accepts requests. The default community name is Public. You can enhance security by deleting the Public entry and adding unique names of your own. Although they aren't the same, you could look at a community as a NetWare group or a Windows XP domain. Three buttons are associated with this field: Add, Edit, and Remove.

- *Accept SNMP Packets from Any Host* This radio button enables your computer to accept packets from any SNMP host. This option provides a maximum of flexibility but a minimum of security.

- *Accept SNMP Packets from These Hosts* Selecting this option reduces the number of hosts that can access your machine to the list in the box below it. You need to click the Add button to add some hosts to this list, or else no one can access your computer. Providing specific host names provides maximum security, but it does tend to reduce the flexibility of your configuration. As with the Accepted Community Names section, you'll find an Edit and Remove buttons here for managing your host list.

Once you've finished configuring the SNMP service, you can click OK to make the changes permanent and close the SNMP Service Properties dialog box. You can then close the Services dialog box and open the Administrative Tools folder. Even though Windows XP doesn't force you to restart the machine, at this point it's usually a good idea to do so to ensure that the changes get implemented during the current Windows session.

Using the FTP Utility

Using the Internet requires some form of browser support if you want to download files or upload messages. FTP is actually a utility program that Windows XP installs for you along with TCP/IP support. It's a DOS application that uses a standard character-mode interface. The syntax for FTP follows:

```
FTP [-v] [-n] [-i] [-d] [-g] [-s:<Filename>] [-a] [-w:<Buffer Size> [-A] [-?]
[<Host>]
```

> **Note:** FTP uses case-sensitive switches. For example, -A isn't the same as -a.
> In addition, you must use the - (minus) sign and not the / (slash) when typing
> command-line arguments. You need to type the command with these require-
> ments in mind.

As you can see, you can start the FTP application using command-line switches to change its behavior. Most of these switches also appear in the interface, so you can modify the behavior after you start the application. The following list defines each FTP switch:

- **-v** This switch disables the display of remote server responses. It comes in handy if you want the download to progress in the background without disturbing your foreground task.

- **-n** Use this switch to disable auto-logon on initial connection.

- **-i** You can use this switch to remove interactive prompting during multiple file transfers. This enables you to automate the file-transfer process.

- **-d** Use this switch to display all FTP commands passed between the client and server. This enables you to debug script files.

- **-g** This switch disables filename globbing, which permits the use of wildcard characters in local filenames and pathnames.

- **-s:<Filename>** Replace <Filename> with the name of a text file containing FTP commands. In essence, this switch enables you to create a script for your FTP download. Use this switch instead of redirection (>).

- **-a** This switch tells FTP to use any available interface when creating a connection to the host.

- **-w:<Buffer Size>** Use this switch to change the data transfer buffer size. The default size of 4,096 bytes normally works well. However, you might want to decrease the buffer size if you experience errors on a connection or use a larger buffer size for local connections. A large buffer is more efficient, but you lose less data for each damaged packet when working with a small buffer.

- **-A** Use this switch to log in as an anonymous user. Note that this is the only switch typed in uppercase.

- **-?** Use this switch to display online help. Note that, at the time of this writing, there are typos in both the Help and Support Center document and the application-supplied help.

- **<Host>** Replace this parameter with the name or address of the host you want to connect to for a file download.

The FTP utility provides a surprising array of commands you can use after you run it. There really are too many to list here, but you can get a list easily enough. All you need to remember is one command: the question mark (?). If you type a question mark, you see a list of all the things you can do with FTP.

Remote Procedure Call (RPC) Support

Remember near the beginning of this chapter when I discussed network transports and the way Microsoft implements them? I mentioned then just how complex network transports could become if you added a few features. Remote procedure calls (RPCs) are an established concept for Windows XP; Microsoft added them to Windows NT 4. Window XP implements them as a network-transport mechanism using named pipes, NetBIOS, or WinSock to create a connection between a client and a server. RPCs are compatible with the Open Software Foundation (OSF) Data Communication Exchange (DCE) specification.

So what do RPCs do for you? OLE uses them, for one. Actually, OLE uses a subset of RPCs called light RPCs (LRPCs) to enable you to make connections you couldn't normally make. OLE is only the tip of the iceberg, however. There are other ways that RPCs can help you as a user.

The best way to think about RPCs is as a means of running code on other machines. Without RPC, all that code has to appear on your machine or in a place where Windows will find it. This means that every time a network administrator wants to update software, he or she has to search every machine on the network to complete the job. However, what if you could "borrow" the DLL from someone else's machine? That's what RPCs allow you to do. An RPC lets your application grab what it needs in the form of executable code from wherever it happens to be.

Windows Sockets (WinSock) Support

Windows sockets (WinSock) started out as an effort by a group of vendors to make sense of the conglomeration of TCP/IP protocol-based socket interfaces. Various vendors had originally ported their implementations of this protocol to Windows. The result was that nothing worked with anything else. The socket interface was originally implemented as a networked interprocess communication mechanism for version 4.2 of the Berkeley UNIX system. Windows XP requires all non-NetBIOS applications to use WinSock if they need to access any TCP/IP services. Vendors may optionally write IPX/SPX applications to this standard as well. Microsoft includes two WinSock applications with Windows XP: SNMP and FTP.

Before I go much further, let me quickly define a couple of terms used in the preceding paragraph. You looked at what a protocol was earlier. It's a set of rules. TCP/IP is one common implementation of a set of rules. Think of a socket as you would the tube holder that you might find in an old television or radio. An application can plug a request (a tube) for some type of service into a socket and send it to a host of some kind. That host could be a file server, a minicomputer, a mainframe, or even another PC. An application can also use a socket to query a database server. It can ask for last year's sales statistics, for example. If every host uses a different-size socket, every application will require a different set of tubes to fit those sockets. WinSock gets rid of this problem by standardizing the socket used to request services and make queries.

Besides making the interface easier to use, WinSock provides another advantage. Normally, an application has to add a NetBIOS header to every packet that leaves the workstation. The workstation at the other end doesn't really need the header, but it's there anyway. This additional processing overhead reduces network efficiency. Using WinSock eliminates the need for the header, and users see better performance.

Sockets are an age-old principle (at least in the computer world), but they're far from out-of-date. The WinSock project proved so successful that Microsoft began to move it to other transports. For example, Windows XP includes a WinSock module for the IPX/SPX transport.

Of course, WinSock is really a stopgap measure for today. In the end, companies will want to move from the client/server model for some applications and use a distributed approach. Technologies such as eXtensible Markup Language (XML) and Simple Object Access Protocol (SOAP) are only the beginning of a deluge of new technologies based on Internet communications. Distributed applications require the use of an RPC-like interface rather than WinSock. You already looked at the implications of RPC in this chapter.

Configuring TCP/IP—The Short Form

The same flexibility that makes Windows XP so easy to use with TCP/IP makes it nearly impossible for an inexperienced user to configure it. With this point in mind, I decided to provide a very fast and easy method for you to configure TCP/IP for a local intranet. I assume that you're going to use Personal Web Server on a LAN in this section, but the principles apply equally well to other kinds of setups.

The first step is to modify the TCP/IP properties of your computer so that other computers can see you. Right-click My Network Places and choose Properties from the context menu. Right-click Local Area Connection and choose Properties from the context menu. Select the Internet Protocol (TCP/IP) option on the General tab of the Local Area Connection dialog box. Click Properties and select the General tab, and you see the Internet Protocol (TCP/IP) Properties dialog box shown, in Figure 21.8.

Look at how I've configured the General tab in my dialog box. You need to worry about only two fields in a pure peer-to-peer network setup: the IP Address field and the Subnet Mask field. These two fields work together. An IP address is composed of two parts. The first part defines your organization, and the second part defines your individual computer.

FIGURE 21.8

Use the General tab of the Internet Protocol (TCP/IP) Properties dialog box to configure your computer's network settings.

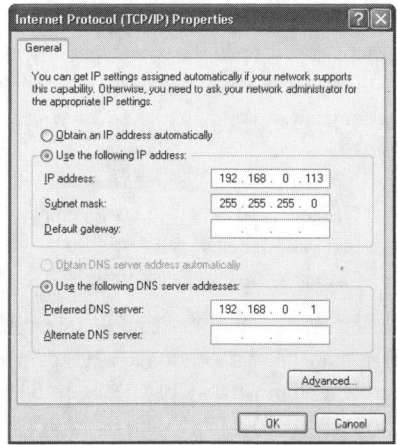

Notice that the IP address is actually composed of four numbers separated by periods. You can choose one to three of those numbers to represent your organization. The remaining numbers represent your computer. A single entry can contain any value from 0 to 255. All four entries combined make up the IP address. If you were on the Internet, you'd have to apply to InterNIC to get an IP address. On a local intranet, however, you're not really talking to anyone but your own organization. You just have to make sure that each machine has a unique IP address and uses the same subnet address.

When working in an intranet scenario, make sure you use the standard recommended numbers for your network. Windows XP normally selects these numbers for you automatically, but you may run into a situation where you need to configure them manually. A Windows XP network uses either 192.168.0.XXX or 169.254.XXX.XXX as an IP address. (Replace the XXX with individual computer numbers.) Networks that use Internet Connection Sharing (ICS) always use the 192.168.0.XXX series of numbers because this address range is "hard wired" into the ICS service. There's nothing to stop you from using other numbers, but using the standard numbers ensures compatibility with the Internet.

Now comes the question of how the computer knows how to read this address. At this point, the subnet mask shown in Figure 21.8 comes in. Like the IP address, the subnet mask contains four numbers separated by periods, where each number is either 0 or 255. As you can see from the figure, I placed a value of 255 for the first three numbers because I've used those numbers to represent my organization. I placed a 0 in the last position because it represents my workstation.

The final step is getting one computer to talk to another. Every computer on your network must use the same organization number; otherwise, it can't hear the other computers. In addition, every computer must have a unique node number. Because 113 is already in use by the machine shown in Figure 21.8, I'll use 114 for the next node. You must configure all the computers on your network before they can talk to the Internet server on your workstation.

Checking these connections is relatively easy as well. Windows XP provides a DOS utility called PING (Packet Internet Groper) to check your capability to communicate with other TCP/IP workstations. All you need to do is type **PING <Workstation Name>** or **PING <IP Address>** at the command prompt. To make sure your own workstation is configured properly, use the PING command; for example, type **PING 192.168.0.113,** where 192.168.0.113 identifies your own workstation. You could also type **PING LocalHost** because LocalHost (IP address 127.0.0.1) is the special name for your computer. PING transmits three packets and listens for a response. If you see three responses from a particular workstation, you know that you've configured it properly.

Another handy utility is TraceRT (trace route). You can use this utility to determine the precise route a packet takes from the current location to a destination. Knowing the route a packet takes can help you troubleshoot network problems, such as finding a router that's not working properly. TraceRT can also help you figure out why accessing a location on the Internet takes so long. Packets that go through many routers take much longer to reach their destination than those that go through just a few do. (Each router that a packet passes through is a *hop*.) All you need to do to use the TraceRT utility is type **TraceRT <Workstation Name>** or **TraceRT <IP Address>** at the command prompt.

Working with User Accounts

Before anyone can use your network, you need to add some user accounts. You can add accounts during the installation process, but many of the changes you make happen after you install Windows XP. You'll add new users to your system and remove accounts when users move on to other jobs. In short, working with user accounts is a never-ending task.

Windows XP provides two methods for working with user accounts. The User Accounts applet provides a simplified interface that works well for small networks, but doesn't provide full access to all user account settings. The Local Users and Groups snap-in for the Computer Management console is more complex than the User Accounts applet, but provides full access to user account information. You use this approach for small- to medium-size business networks and workgroups within the enterprise.

You'll also want to monitor logon policies for user accounts. For example, you'll want to ensure that users have to reset their password at specific intervals and use complex passwords. It's important to provide policies that help users maintain the security of your network.

Using the User Accounts Applet

When you open the User Accounts applet, you'll see a User Accounts dialog box, similar to the one shown in Figure 21.9. As you can see, the dialog box contains a list of user accounts on the local machine. Note that I've disabled the Guest account for security reasons. This is a built-in account that you can't delete, so disabling it is your only option. Notice that each account specifies an account type and password-protection level. If you don't enable password protection on an account, that account is open for anyone to use.

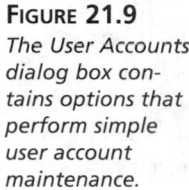

FIGURE 21.9
The User Accounts dialog box contains options that perform simple user account maintenance.

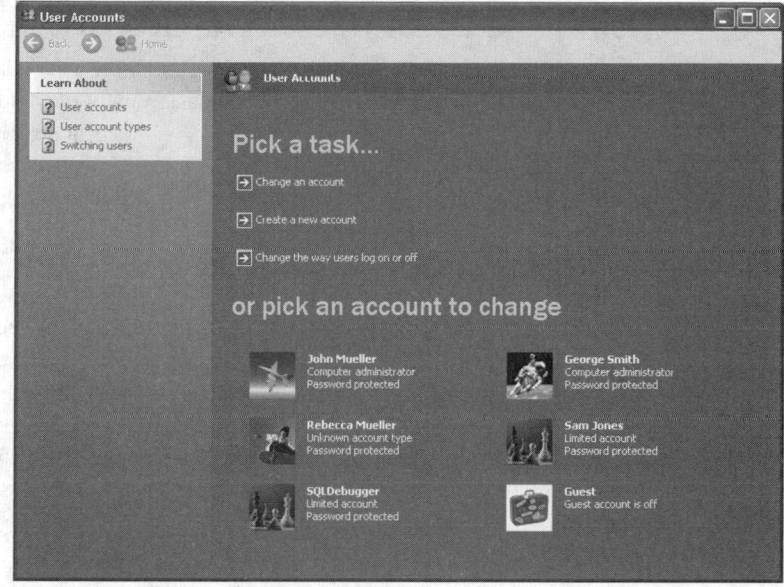

As mentioned earlier, you can perform three essential tasks using the User Accounts dialog box. The following list provides a quick overview of each task:

- *Change an Account* Click this link and you see a list of user accounts on the local machine. Select an account and you see a list of actions you can perform on the account. This feature enables you to change the user name, password, picture, and account type. You can also remove password protection or delete the account. A final option enables you to set up Passport for the account. The number of features a user sees varies by their access to account information. For example, a standard user might not see the option to remove password protection if the local security policy requires each account to use password protection. You can also reach this dialog box by clicking a user account in the initial User Accounts dialog box.

- *Create a New Account* When you select this link, Windows XP asks you a series of questions about the new user account. You begin by providing a username. The applet also asks you to provide an account type. Once you create the account, you have to click on it to add password protection and change account characteristics, such as the user picture.

- *Change the Way Users Log On or Off* Click this link and you see a Select Logon and Logoff Options dialog box containing two options. The first controls the Welcome Screen, which helps users log on to the system by displaying their user icon. The second controls Fast User Switching, which is a feature that allows one user to stay logged in while another uses the system.

Using the Local Users and Groups Snap-in

The Local Users and Groups snap-in has many similarities with other MMC snap-ins we've discussed. It uses a hierarchical format consisting of two folders: Users and Groups. The Users folder contains a list of users on the local machine (if you want to see domain users, you need to connect to the server). The Groups folder contains a list of groups on the local machine. It's always better to use groups to help organize users and make security configuration easier.

Working with Users

User accounts are the basis for all user-related access to your system. To create a new user account, right-click the Users folder and then choose New User from the context menu. You'll see a New User dialog box, where you can type the user name, full name, description, and password. This dialog box also contains options that force users to change their password during the next logon. You may optionally disable the account, set the password so that it never expires, or disable the user's ability to change his or her password.

If you want to modify an exiting user account, double-click the user account. You see a User Properties dialog box, containing four tabs. Note that the Dial-in Tab is useless unless you have Windows Server installed. Even so, the tab is useless unless you connect to the server. The following list tells you about the other tabs:

- *General* Contains the same information as the New User dialog box. However, this tab contains an additional entry for Account Is Locked Out. Windows XP enables this option only if the user violates a policy that results in a lockout condition, such as entering a password incorrectly more than a predefined number of times.
- *Member Of* Contains a list of groups to which the user belongs. You can add new groups using the Add button or remove existing groups by highlighting the group and clicking Remove.
- *Profile* Contains entries for the user's profile, login script, and home directory or mapped drive. The *user profile* is a set of configuration options on the server that enables users to log in to any machine and restore their settings on that machine. The login script contains configuration options. Finally, the home directory or mapped drive contains the user's data and other personal information.

Deleting a user account is easy: Highlight the user name in the Users folder and press Delete. Windows XP will ask if you're sure that you want to remove the account. Click Yes to complete the action.

Working with Groups

As mentioned earlier, groups save the network administrator time by organizing users and by reducing the number of individual settings the network administrator must make. A user gains any right you assign to a group. If you have 10 users assigned to a group, assigning a right to the group is the same as making the change in all 10 user accounts. The only difference is that you don't have to make the change to each account separately.

To create a new group, right-click the Groups folder and choose New Group from the context menu. You'll see a New Group dialog box containing the group name, description, and Members field. Type the name of the group and a description. Click Add to add new members, or highlight an existing member and click Remove. After you finish configuring the group, click Create.

If you need to change a group, double-click the entry in the Groups folder. You'll see a Group Properties dialog box containing a single tab. The tab contains the same entries as the New Group dialog box. You can use the Add and Remove buttons to add and remove members.

Deleting a group is easy. Highlight the group entry in the Groups folder and then Press Delete. Windows XP will ask if you're sure that you want to delete the group. Click Yes and Windows XP will remove the group from the list.

Setting Logon Policies

Windows XP provides the Local Security Policy snap-in. This snap-in enables you to set policies that affect all users on a machine. Using policies helps maintain system security by enforcing specific rules. They also reduce management time because you don't spend as much time tracking down inconsistent behavior. Finally, using a policy helps you treat all users equally.

It's important to set logon policies as part of your account setup. You find all of these settings in the Account Policies folder. We discuss this folder in the "Account Policies" section of Chapter 22.

Using the Novell Client

You can choose between one of two NetWare Directory Services (NDS) clients for a Windows XP computer. The Microsoft version of this client comes as part of the Windows XP package. You need to download the Novell version of the client (I'll tell you where in the "Installing the Client" section of this chapter). You must install the NetWare client if your server uses IP instead of IPX. The Microsoft client supports only IPX.

What are the differences between the two NDS clients? Microsoft's client is very lean. It consumes very few system resources when compared to the Novell offering, but it doesn't offer many of the features you need, either. For example, the "Using Explorer with the Novell Client" section of this chapter explains that the Novell client modifies the way Explorer works. It permits you to view and assign user rights to directories and files (provided you have the proper rights).

My Network Places is enhanced as well, as explained in the "Differences in My Neighborhood Places" section of this chapter. The Novell offering also provides configuration flexibility—something you really need if you want to get the most out of your network. The added flexibility also comes in handy when you start experiencing compatibility or other network-related configuration problems. Finally, you absolutely have to have the Novell client if you want to use the NetWare Administrator utility.

Obviously, all these added features come with a price. Although the Novell client helps you locate data faster and provides a faster interface, you pay a heavy penalty in memory usage. Finally, even though I find that the Novell client is more reliable than the Microsoft offering, you may find that all the features this client offers can get confusing. At a minimum, you find that users have more, not fewer, questions when it comes to My Network Places after you get this client installed. Be prepared to spend a little more time holding users' hands after you install the Novell client.

> **Tip:** There isn't any rule that says you have to use only one client on your network. In most cases, I use the Microsoft client on the vast majority of machines. It's small and easy to use, so users feel more comfortable using it. I install the Novell client if a machine has problems accessing the network or needs added flexibility. Every network administrator machine also gets the Novell client, as do manager machines where the manager needs to have some kind of access to NDS.

Installing the Windows XP Client on Windows XP

It's unlikely that you'll find a Novell client for Windows XP immediately after the Windows XP release. In addition, if you try to use the existing Windows 2000 client, you'll receive an error message stating that Windows XP can't install it. Fortunately, you can install the Windows 2000 client on many machines without problem. However, you do need to exercise care because you could run into compatibility issues.

The following procedure enables you to install the current Windows NT/2000 client version 4.8 or higher. You must have an installed copy of Windows 2000 to make this procedure work because it relies on one of the Windows 2000 files. Don't try to use this procedure with an older client. In addition, this procedure doesn't come with any guarantees; it could fail. Make sure that you test it on a clean system. To install the current Windows NT/2000 client version 4.8 or higher, follow these steps:

1. Open the User Accounts applet in the Control Panel. Click Change the Way Users Log On or Off.

2. Clear the Use the Welcome screen option (if selected) and then click Apply Options. The default NetWare client doesn't work with the Welcome screen. If you leave this option checked, you'll still install the NetWare client, but the Desktop

will be blank when you start the system. To recover from this problem, start the system in Safe mode, clear the Welcome screen option, and then restart the system.

3. Create a NetWare client directory that has all of the setup files. The client file you download from the Internet will ask for an installation directory. I used the root directory of my Windows XP drive, but you can use any convenient location.

4. Copy the SETUPDLL.DLL file from Windows XP \SYSTEM32 folder or the source CD (expand it if necessary) to the \NOVELL\ENGLISH\WINNT\I386 folder. Make sure this is the folder with the SETUPNW.EXE file.

5. Rename SETUPNW.EXE to SETUP.EXE.

6. Follow the steps in the "Installing the Client" section to complete the process.

Installing the Client

Installing the Novell client on your machine is about as easy as software installation gets. You download the required software from http://download.novell.com/sdMain.jsp. The current client version at the time of this writing is version 4.8. If you're using a different version, some features may change and some screen shots may change from what you're seeing. The following procedure gets you started using the Novell NDS Client:

1. After you download and unpack the software, double-click the Setup icon. You then see a Client License Agreement dialog box.

2. Read the license agreement and then click Yes if you agree with it. You'll see a Select an Installation Option dialog box. Generally, most people can use the Typical Installation option if they need only the client services. However, most administrators or those using special NetWare features will want to use the Custom Installation option. The remainder of the procedure assumes that you're using the Custom Installation option.

3. Select Custom Installation and then click Next. You'll see a list of custom options. The options you see checked in the list are the options the Setup program installs for a typical installation.

4. Select one or more custom installation options, depending on your networking needs. Make certain that you select the Novell IP Gateway if your server has IP installed in place of IPX. Click Next. You'll see a Protocol Preference dialog box. This dialog box determines how the client accesses NetWare. If your server has only IPX installed, it's best to use the IPX option. However, if you have IP installed, always use the IP with IPX Compatibility or the IP and IPX option to ensure that you have a backup protocol when working in mixed environments.

5. Select a protocol and then click Next. You'll see a Login Authenticator dialog box. The two options on this dialog box help you select between NDS and Bindery operation. In most cases, newer systems use NDS, but verify this setting before you make a choice.

6. Select an authenticator and then click Next. You'll see a Workstation Manager dialog box. This dialog box contains a single field that contains the same tree information you would enter in the CSNW applet, discussed later in this chapter.

7. Type the tree information for your network and then click Next. You'll see a completion dialog box.

8. Click Finish. Setup will begin copying files to your system. If it sees the Microsoft client installed, Setup will ask if you want to remove it. Click Yes. The installation process takes some time, so be patient as Setup copies the files. You'll see an Installation Complete dialog box.

9. Click Reboot. The client is ready to use.

Differences in My Network Places

The Novell client works differently from Microsoft's client when it comes to My Network Places. The first thing you'll want to look at is the NetWare Connections option on the My Network Places context menu. Selecting this option displays a NetWare Connections dialog box, which tells you all about your connection. It tells you about the server connection and your context, including the NDS tree name.

My Network Places also includes other Novell client-specific entries on the context menu. You can log in to the system, map a network drive, and begin and end printer port captures. You'll also find all of these entries on the Novell icon (the big, red N), found in the Notification Area of the Taskbar.

Using Explorer with the Novell Client

The Novell Client affects the way Windows Explorer displays the Properties dialog box for a network drive by adding several new tabs, including the NetWare Volume Statistics tab, shown in Figure 21.10. This tab provides statistics on current disk usage and the amount of resources left.

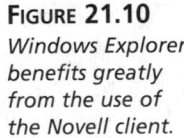

FIGURE 21.10
Windows Explorer benefits greatly from the use of the Novell client.

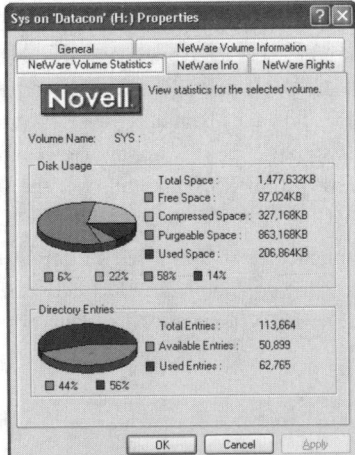

The NetWare Info tab provides access to the volume attributes. (Files provide a similar page with file-specific rights, such as Transactional, so I won't discuss it in this section.) You can also change NetWare-specific attributes, such as Don't Compress and Immediate Compression. Normally, you'd have to open the NetWare Administrator utility to change these settings. This tab also tells who owns the folder (or file).

The NetWare Volume Information tab includes Name Space, Volume Number, Block Size, and Installed Features fields. You can use this information to determine which directories a change in name-space support would affect. This tab also includes your personal statistics. For example, you can determine the amount of data storage space you have left on the volume.

The NetWare Rights tab contains three sections. The first section helps view and assign the trustee rights for users of a folder or file. To change the rights for a particular individual or group, just check or uncheck one or more of the rights check boxes. Removing a trustee is equally easy. Just highlight the trustee you want to remove and click the Remove button.

The second section of the NetWare Rights tab provides a list of groups and users in the current context. (You need to change your context if you want to see users and groups in other parts of the NDS tree.) To add a user to the Trustee list, just highlight his name and then click the Add button. The user automatically has a default set of rights assigned, but you can just as easily change those rights. You need to click Apply or OK to make the changes permanent.

The final section of the NetWare Rights tab shows effective rights. At first, you might think that it shows the effective rights of the highlighted trustee. The fact is that it shows your effective rights to the folder or file. Even if a user can't change trustee rights, he can use this page of the dialog box to see what his rights to the folder are.

Using the Client Service for NetWare (CSNW) Applet

Installing NetWare support on your workstation also adds a new applet to the Control Panel: CSNW. The Client Service for NetWare dialog box (see Figure 21.11) appears when you open this applet. You've probably seen it before; Windows XP displays it during the client installation process.

This dialog box contains three sections. The first section defines the way you log on to the network. You can choose to look for a specific server or to use the NDS-specific method of tree and context. The second section defines your print options. You decide whether to process a logon script in the third section. I cover the first two issues in this section of the chapter.

FIGURE 21.11

The Client Service for NetWare dialog box. After installing CSNW, you see a new Control Panel applet.

Selecting a Logon Method

Let's spend a few moments discussing server logon options. You see two methods in the CSNW applet. Use the Preferred Server option for systems that use the user database called the *bindery*. All NetWare 3.x servers use bindery emulation. You have a choice between bindery emulation and NDS when you install NetWare 4.x and later. To exercise this option, specify a preferred server in the Logon dialog box. All Windows XP does is request the nearest server with the name you specify.

If your NetWare 4.x or later server is set up for NDS, select the Default Tree and Context option. In this case, you need to enter the name of a tree and context in the Logon dialog box. The simple view for right now is that the Tree entry defines the server's position in the organization's hierarchy, whereas the Context entry defines your position on that server.

Defining Your Print Options

Now that we've gotten the logon process out of the way, let's discuss the simple print options that the Client Service for NetWare dialog box provides. You need to consider three options: using form feeds, getting print-job-completion notification, and printing a banner.

In most cases, you want to clear the Add Form Feed check box. This option sends an extra form feed after a print job completes. Because most applications already do this, you just waste paper if you choose it.

The Notify When Printed check box is pretty handy. Unlike days of old, when your workstation had a printer attached, networks tend to keep printers in one room. You no longer get auditory or visual cues when your print job finishes. This option enables you to continue working until the print job is complete. Then you can go to the printer area to pick it up. This is one of those personal preference options. I normally enable it unless I don't want to be disturbed about a low-priority print job. You need to decide whether the interruption is worth it for you.

Network printers also share one other feature you didn't have in the world of non-networked machines: Everyone on the network shares one or more printers, which means that you're bound to have confusion about print jobs from time to time.

The third print option, Print Banner, helps alleviate this problem. It sends a banner with your name to the printer. Because each print job starts with a banner page, you can figure out who owns which print job. I always enable this option because there isn't any other good way to sort through the chaos otherwise.

On Your Own

Use the information in this chapter to determine which of your system resources are shared and which aren't. You might want to create a written list of who has access, and where, for future reference. That way, you can plug any security leaks whenever someone leaves the company.

After you determine who has access to your machine, look for any security leaks. Be sure to change passwords on a regular basis, especially after someone leaves the company. Check to see how the use of your system resources by others affects system performance and overall usability.

I discussed the network subsystem architecture in this chapter. Go through your \SYSTEM32 folder and see whether you can identify the components that comprise it. See whether your network needs any specialty components because it uses a different protocol than normal. You might also want to take this opportunity to look for any real-mode drivers that are still lurking around your hard drive.

Setting Up Security

Network security is a major thorn in most network administrators' sides. Even a small network requires some level of planning, and many managers fail to see the value of implementing the type of security they really need. Of course, I've seen the opposite side of the coin as well. Some administrators wrap the people who use the network in a tight cocoon of regulations and passwords. The chokehold these people create inhibits any kind of creative resource management and often impedes work as well.

It's difficult to create a bulletproof network setup that offers the level of flexibility most users require. Adding a bit of flexibility normally means that you also open a security hole. A network administrator must reach an important balance. Users require a flexible work environment, yet data requires protection. Security seems like a simple problem to solve, but it isn't because you often have contradictory needs to consider.

Added to this problem is cracker tenacity. You need to realize that someone else can breach any security system you design. So, what do you do—leave the network open to whoever might want to access it? That's not the way to go either. The real goal is to put reasonable security restraints in place. After you create a great security plan, you must monitor the system for potential cracker attacks. Sometimes, this means asking a hacker consultant to check your system for leaks. You must also change your security plan and setup as the threats to your network change.

> **Note:** For the purposes of this book, the term *cracker* always refers to an individual who breaks into a system on an unauthorized basis. This includes any illegal activity on the system. On the other hand, a *hacker* refers to someone who performs low-level system activities, such as testing system security. Hackers also develop low-level software, such as device drivers, and perform other tasks that help users. This book uses the term *hacker* to refer to someone who performs services that are both legal and authorized.

More important than physical security and password protection is the cooperation of those around you. I recently went into a client's office to check on his network setup. He let me use one of his employees' desks to get the work done. Right in front of me was one of those yellow reminder pads. It contained not only the employee's password, but also the superior's password. Usernames were all over the desk. Anyone could have simply walked into the office and gained access to the network because of this security breach. Don't get the idea that a clean desk means great security. Some crackers simply call your office and convince an employee to give them their name and password.

This incident reminded me of the importance of the human factor in any security plan. To implement a good security system, you need to consider the following elements:

- *Physical security* Place your file server in a locked room. I can break the security of most networks if I have access to a running file server. If you lock up the file server, I can't access it unless I have a key.

- *Software protection* Using passwords and other forms of software protection is your next line of defense. Make sure that all the right kinds of security measures are in place. I cover this topic in detail later, but Windows XP can really help in this area. It contains all the right features; all you need to do is implement them.

- *Cooperative security* You can't secure the network by yourself. The larger your network, the more you need every user's cooperation. If you expect the user to cooperate with you, you need to talk to him and find out what's reasonable. No one uses an unreasonable security plan. This cooperative strategy also extends to management. If you don't talk to people in management and tell them what your security problems are, they won't be able to help. You also need to make sure that management knows what kinds of security risks are present in the current setup. This reduces the chance of someone being surprised later.

- *Training* It's never a good idea to assume that users know how to use the security features Windows XP provides. You can implement much of the physical security, but the user uses the software part of the equation. An untrained user might not use a particular security feature correctly or might not even know that it exists. In addition, untrained users often resist using security features because they don't understand their purpose.

- *Timing* It's easier to set up your security plan at the beginning of a network installation. Setting up a security plan once you've gotten all the pieces in place might mean taking some things apart and redoing them. Worse, it might mean compromising the safety of your network because you can't redo a portion of the network setup.

- *A written security plan* As your network becomes larger, it becomes vitally important to get the rules put down in writing. Otherwise, how will a user know what's expected or how to react in a crisis? Writing everything down also makes management aware of the security you have put in place.

This might seem like a great deal of work to implement security, but when you consider the loss that a single security breach can cause, these steps actually seem minor. A cracker doesn't steal last week's letter to the public; he steals something valuable. The more secret something is, the better the pirate likes it. Even if a cracker doesn't take anything, he could leave something behind. What would a virus do to your network? It doesn't take too much thought to imagine your entire setup crumbling as a virus infects it.

This chapter helps you understand the three major areas of security that Windows XP helps you implement: local, network, and Internet. By looking at these three rings of security as separate issues, you ensure that there are no holes in your security plan.

Setting Local Security Policies

Great security begins at the local machine. The second that someone gains access to your machine, your security plan is in jeopardy. A Trojan horse virus can infect your machine and provide a backdoor (secret entrance) to your machine. The machine might look secure, but the cracker can access it at will over an Internet or other connection. The best crackers can do all this without alerting you. After all, if you know there's a problem, you'll do something to fix it. Great crackers are secretive and perform their deeds long before you realize there's a problem; and then, of course, it's too late.

Peter's Principle: When Will a Cracker Break In to Your Machine?

When I visit a site to offer advice on security, the first sign of trouble I see is the level of confidence. If someone is confident that a cracker can't break into his system, I'm almost positive that the cracker will find a way to do so. In fact, based on the level of confidence, I can also predict that the network administrator won't even be aware of the break-in until someone else brings it to his attention.

Think about the very concept of security software for a second. A programmer, who wants to provide you with the best protection he can, developed the software you're using. An equally competent cracker thinking along the same lines can overcome any software designed by this programmer. All the cracker really needs to do is figure out what line of reasoning the programmer followed when creating the security software and then think of a way around it.
The idea that anyone can overcome your security is an important concept to remember.

So, if you can't count on your security software to prevent a break-in, what good is it? There are three ways that security software can help. First, it does act as a direct deterrent to people who are essentially honest and really don't want to cause problems. Second, it can slow even a good cracker, which gives you time to react and prevent any major problems. Finally, good security software admits that it didn't stop the cracker and alerts you to the problem. The

---

one way that security software doesn't help is to deter a cracker from breaking in at all.

The number-one way to stop a cracker in his tracks is to start out by thinking that he's going to get past your security software. Once you get that idea in mind, you can start looking for breaches in your security. A good piece of security software works with you to help you locate holes or unauthorized entry (which could be as simple as a break in someone's normal pattern of system access or an unusual number of password retries). Unfortunately, looking for holes is the only way you keep someone from damaging your system.

Windows XP does more than any previous version of Windows to make your machine safe. Windows 9x users have the most to gain, but even Windows 2000 users benefit from improved local security. One of the most important features is improved local security settings. A local security setting determines how Windows XP reacts in a given situation. If you tell Windows XP that every user must provide a password that's five characters or longer in length, Windows XP enforces that policy. I discuss the settings in detail in the sections that follow, but even Windows 2000 users will note some new policies they can use to secure their system.

Note: Unlike Windows 9x, users can't easily bypass security policies. I won't go so far as to say that they can't bypass them at all, but it would require a concerted effort. If a user breaks a policy, you can be certain that they meant to do so. You couldn't say that with Windows 9x because the security was too flimsy. For example, simply leaving the logon screen blank or providing a different name doesn't allow users to bypass security. Windows XP only accepts input from bona fide users.

Another major win in the security department is improved NTFS security. Windows XP has a newer version of NTFS than Windows 2000 does. This new version includes extended functionality in the form of enhanced encryption. For example, when you encrypted a file under Windows 2000, only one person could open that file. The version of NTFS provided with Windows XP allows multiple people to share the encrypted file, which encourages encrypted file use. The basic NTFS operation hasn't changed, but some underlying security features have, making policies and auditing more extensive and complete. (See Chapter 13 for details on the Windows XP file system.)

Unfortunately, many of these benefits are only available to Professional Edition users. Home Edition users will find that they have access to some features, such as reliable password security, but can't set other features, such as file encryption. The bottom line is that if you want complete security for your system, you need to get the Professional Edition of Windows XP.

> **Note:** It's important to consider the ramifications of giving information to anyone. For example, many people have questioned the viability of Passport, Microsoft's online user data storage. Recent articles say that those who use Passport are at risk because crackers have already discovered methods of gaining access to your Passport data. You can read more about this problem at http://www.infoworld.com/articles/op/xml/01/09/10/010910oplivingston.xml. The bottom line is that storing data where you can't physically protect it from discovery is a risk. Make sure that you take steps to protect your personal information.

Now that you have a better idea of what local security features Windows XP has to offer, let's discuss the tool used to manage them. The Local Security Settings MMC snap-in contains a wealth of security settings that change the way users access your machine and any attached network. Figure 22.1 shows what this tool looks like. You'll find it in the Administrator Tools folder of the Control Panel (double-click the Local Security Policy icon).

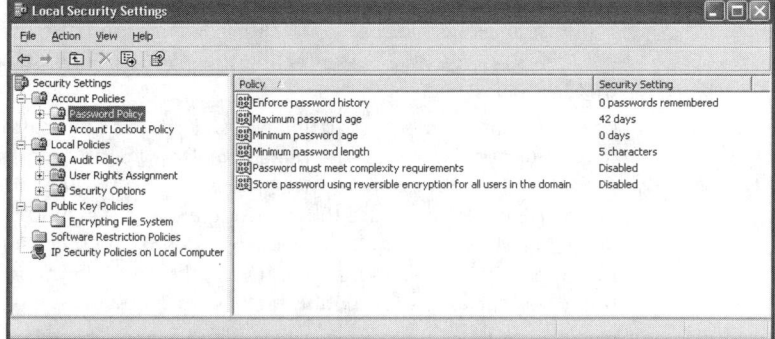

FIGURE 22.1
The Local Security Settings snap-in enables you to change both machine and network settings.

As you can see, the Local Security Settings snap-in divides the security policy settings into functional areas. The combination of all settings determines your local security policy. Windows XP also supports group security policies. An administrator implements these policies on a domain controller (a centralized server). Group policy settings override local policy settings, so a local setting change doesn't guarantee a change in policy for larger networks.

Account Policies

The Account Policies folder affects everyone's ability to log in to the system. It consists of the Password Policy folder, shown in Figure 22.1, and the Account Lockout Policy folder. You can view the Password Policy folder as granting access and the Account Lockout Policy folder as denying access. Of all the folders you can modify, this is the most essential. Remember: The best way to prevent damage to your system is to keep crackers out in the first place.

The Password Policy folder contains entries that affect the way that users log in to the system. A password policy grants access to the system. Figure 22.1 shows the default settings for this folder. As you can see, the settings aren't very challenging. To make these settings a little tougher for a cracker to break, enforce the Password History option to ensure that users have to change their password. In addition, I recommend a maximum of 30 days between password changes. However, even a weekly change isn't too much if you're working with secure data. (Daily changes might become annoying after a while.)

One setting in the Password Policy folder is more important than any other setting you can make. Notice the Password Must Meet Complexity Requirements option. Select this option and users will need to select unique passwords that contain three categories of characters (out of the four available categories), including numbers, uppercase letters, lowercase letters, and special symbols. When you add this requirement to a minimum password length of at least six characters, the passwords are much harder to break.

> **Tip:** Some people's idea of a hard-to-break password is something long and difficult to remember, such as xyz@2aBC$928. I'm sure that most users would just roll their eyes at such a password and then write it down somewhere—I know that I would.
>
> Of course, the problem is creating a password that's difficult for the cracker to guess, but easy for the user to remember. How about using two words and a special symbol? For example, My$Password uses all of the criteria for a complex password, is relatively hard to figure out, and yet is easy to remember. If you don't want users to write their password down, give them something they can remember. Of course, it also helps if you add something to your security plan that details penalties for writing the password down.

Windows XP provides three account-lockout policies for your system. An *account-lockout* policy denies access to your system after certain events occur. The account lockout threshold policy is the key to these settings. The default setting of 0 means that users can enter the wrong password all day long and you would never know about it. A policy setting of 3 or 4 incorrect logins usually ensures that the system can handle typos, but leaves crackers with little room for invading your system. The other two policies set the lockout duration and the amount of time that must pass between incorrect logins before the lockout counter resets. The default of 30 minutes really isn't long enough to discourage crackers. In addition, it might tempt employees to wait before reporting problems. I normally set both counters to a minimum of 1,440 minutes, which is 24 hours.

An account lockout occurs when a user types his or her password incorrectly a given number of times. When this occurs, Windows XP will display a message telling the user that the system has locked him or her out and he or she needs to contact the network administrator. Figure 22.2 shows the results of a lockout. You enable the account by removing the check next to the Account Is Locked Out option. Whether you clear the User Must Change Password at Next Login option depends on the reason for lock out. In most cases, you'll want the user to create a new password for his or her account.

FIGURE 22.2
One of the effects of the account-lockout policy is that the user must change their password afterward.

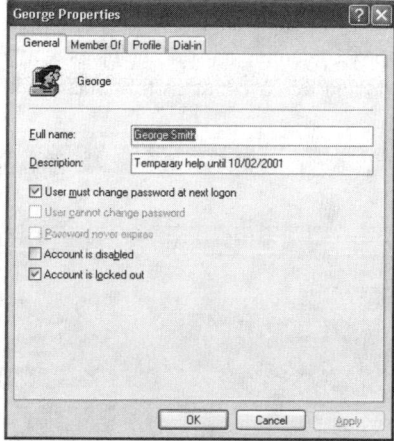

The Account Lockout Threshold setting also shows another part of the Local Security Settings console. Whenever you change a policy that affects other policies, you see a Suggested Value Changes dialog box, like the one shown in Figure 22.3. This dialog box tells you what Microsoft suggests as minimum policy settings to go with the change you want to make. You can always set the policy settings higher than suggested.

FIGURE 22.3
The Suggested Value Changes dialog box tells you Microsoft's recommendations for additional security settings.

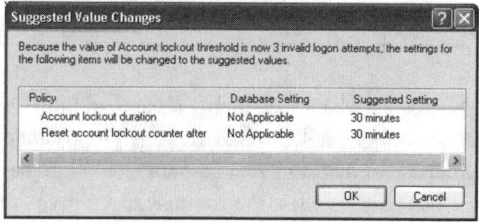

Local Policies

The Local Policies folder contains three major folders: Audit Policy, User Rights Assignment, and Security Options. This is the heart of the local security policy for your system because it contains the settings the user relies on while working with Windows XP.

The Audit Policy folder contains the main audit settings for your system. Windows XP doesn't cover the entries in this list in other areas. For example, you see options to audit account logon events. Double-clicking these entries displays a dialog box that contains Success and Failure options. You can audit none, either, or both of the options.

The User Rights Assignment folder is basically misnamed. It actually contains settings that control the access provided to every object in the system. Figure 22.4 shows an example of the entries in this window. Notice that you can change settings, such as the user's right to change the priority of applications. When you double-click any of these settings, you'll see a dialog box containing a list of the users who have the right in question. It contains the usual Add and Remove buttons for management purposes.

FIGURE 22.4
The User Rights Assignment folder affects the rights of every object on your system, not just the user.

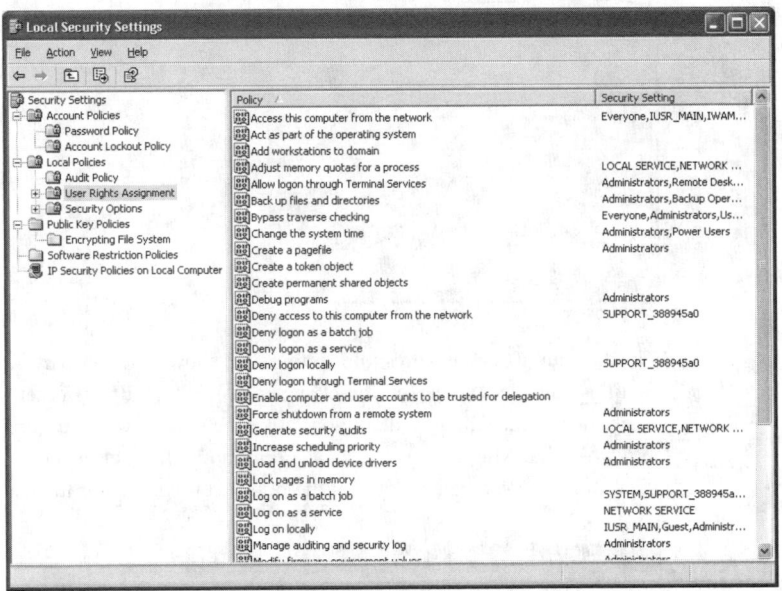

You'll want to observe the user additions in this folder carefully because changes could indicate cracker activity. For example, if the Everyone group suddenly has the power to deny local logins, you can bet that someone has tampered with the settings. You'll also want to modify a few standard settings. For example, even if you disable the Guest account, the Log On Locally policy still contains Guest as one of the people who can log on. Removing Guest from the list adds a little more security to your system.

The Security Options folder, shown in Figure 22.5, contains policies that affect system processes. For example, you can restrict access of the CD-ROM drive on your machine to users who log on locally. No matter what you change in Windows Explorer, this policy can't change (unless you change it with a global policy or modify the local policy).

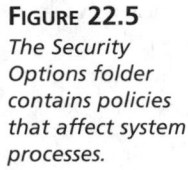

FIGURE 22.5
The Security Options folder contains policies that affect system processes.

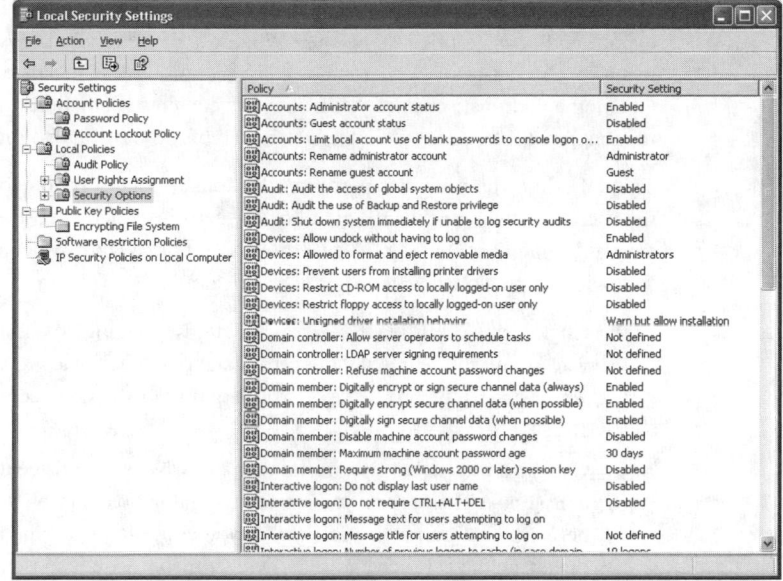

Some of the more important security settings reside in the Security Options folder. For example, you find the Interactive Logon settings in this folder. Use the Do Not Require Ctrl+Alt+Del setting to determine if users go directly to the logon screen when they start the machine. Other settings change the logon message and title. You can also delete the name of the last user who logged in with an Interactive Logon setting.

Notice that this folder contains even more audit options. It's important to realize just how much auditing you can perform on a Windows XP system. Windows XP provides the means to monitor just about every form of system activity.

Public Key Policies

The Public Key folder normally contains just one folder, Encrypting File System. The Encrypting File System folder contains all of the certificates for your system. (See the "Understanding Certificates section for details.) This listing tells you the following information:

- Who owns the certificate
- Who issued the certificate
- The date the certificate expires
- How the system uses the certificate
- The certificate's friendly name
- The certificate status
- The template used to create the certificate

Generally, you don't need to do anything with the certificates on this tab. You can delete, export, and open certificates. Because Windows XP generally keeps certificates even when they're out-of-date, your major housekeeping task is to delete the certificate. Opening a certificate enables you to view its contents. Sometimes, you find useful information about the issuer within the Details tab of the Certificate Properties dialog box.

The only time you need to export a certificate is to send it to someone else or to move the user to another machine. Right-click the certificate and choose All Tasks | Export from the context menu. You see a Certificate Export Wizard Welcome screen. The following steps show how to export a certificate:

1. Click Next. You'll see the Export Private Key dialog box. Always export the private key if you're moving the certificate to another machine or create a backup. Never export the private key if you're going to share the certificate with someone else.

2. Choose a private key option and then click Next. You'll see an Export File Format dialog box. The options you see in this dialog box vary by your machine setup, the network configuration, and whether you chose to export the private key. If you're exporting the certificate to share with someone else, choose a file format that's compatible with his or her machine setup.

3. Choose an export file format and then click Next. You'll see a File to Export dialog box.

4. Type or choose a filename and then click Next. You'll see a Completion dialog box. Notice that the dialog box contains all of the settings for the file export.

5. Verify the certificate output settings and then click Next. The Certificate Export Wizard will create the file for you.

IP Security Policies

Windows XP provides the means for creating a secure IP computing environment. The IP Security Policies on Local Computer folder contains the following three entries:

- *Client* Describes how the client reacts to requests from the server and what type of information the client supplies to the server. The standard settings allow the client to communicate in unsecured (plain text) mode. If the server requests a secure connection, the client negotiates the type of security used.

- *Secure Server* Defines the settings for a secure server environment. The default setting requires secure communication with the client, preferably using Kerberos. The server doesn't allow any form of unsecured communication.

- *Server* Defines the settings for a normal server environment. The standard settings ask the client to use Kerberos for a secure environment. If the client doesn't respond, Windows XP will use clear text communication.

If you double-click on any of these entries, you'll see a Policy Properties dialog box. The General tab contains the name and description of the policy. It also contains a setting that determines how often Windows XP checks for new security policies. You can also click Advanced if you want to change the key exchange settings.

The Rules tab contains the rules used to administer the policy. If you want to add a new rule, click Add. You can also edit and remove rules using the associated buttons. Whenever you add a new rule, you have a choice of creating the rule using the New Rule Properties dialog box or using the Security Rule Wizard. Both methods produce the same results, and most people find the Security Rule Wizard (the default setting) easier to use. The following steps tell you how to create a new security rule using the Security Rule Wizard:

1. Click Next. You'll see a Tunnel Endpoint dialog box. This dialog box contains the address of an endpoint (the remote machine) for a communication. If this is a general rule, you don't want to provide an endpoint value.

2. Enter an endpoint value if necessary, and then click Next. You'll see a Network Type dialog box. Windows XP divides the rules into three types: those that affect all networks, those that affect the local network, and those that affect remote communications of any type.

3. Select a network type option and then click Next. You'll see an Authentication Method dialog box. Windows XP doesn't support Kerberos without a domain controller (Windows Server) that has Active Directory installed. If you have a smaller network without the required support, you need to choose one of the other authentication methods.

4. Choose an authentication method. Type any required information. Click Next. You'll see an IP Filter List dialog box. Unless you want to install a new file, Windows XP provides you with a choice of standard IP or Internet Control Message Protocol (ICMP) filtering. Even if you choose one of the standard filtering choices, you can highlight the option and then click Edit to change the settings. Never remove a default filtering option.

5. Select or create an IP filtering option and then click Next. You'll see a Filter Action dialog box. The filter normally allows three actions. The first is to allow unsecured transactions. The second requests a secure transaction, but allows an unsecured transaction if the client or server doesn't provide the required support. The third requires secured transactions. You can add other actions as necessary using the Add button.

6. Select or create an IP filtering action and then click Next. You'll see a Completion dialog box.

7. Click Finish. The Security Rule Wizard creates the rule for you.

Network Security

Securing your machine is indeed the first stop in creating a secure environment. However, you can't ignore the network because a cracker will eventually break in. The network is also more vulnerable to attack because servers, by their very nature, answer requests for information—something the cracker is very interested in obtaining. In fact, network attacks appear most often in the news. Some cracker attacks, such as Code Red and Code Blue, are devastating on a major scale. They affect not only your network, but also every network with which your network interacts.

Some companies have complex security policies because they're large or do something special such as work with the government. If you work for a company like this, you probably use one or more security companies to help you set up your system. You might even employ hackers to make simulated attacks on your network.

Most companies, however, have simpler network security requirements. You can normally break these requirements down into three areas:

- *Workgroup* Determines the security of the people you work with. You might even have a workgroup server or group polices that affect the workgroup. The workgroup level is where internal security threats occur.

- *Domain* Determines security at a company or subsidiary level. A domain is the combination of all workgroups and individual users who don't belong to a workgroup. Large companies can (and typically do) have more than one domain. Domain security is essential because it affects everyone at the company or subsidiary level. Most external security threats occur at the domain level.

- *Other Servers* Determines security for special needs, such as back-end, database, Web, file, and print servers. For example, you might have a Linux server in use for Web services or a NetWare server for file and print services. Most special security threats—those made by advanced crackers—occur at this level. Most administrators find that crackers attack Windows machines first because they can find information about Windows security holes more easily than other operating systems.

Now that you have an idea of where your security threats lie, let's look at workgroups, domains, and other servers in detail. The following section tells you more about the three levels of network security you need to consider when creating a security plan.

Workgroup

A workgroup is a small organizational unit. It normally consists of a single department within a company, such as accounting, or a group with a single purpose, such as a research and development team. In many cases, a workgroup relies on peer-to-peer connections and shared folders. In other cases, a workgroup relies on a small server to store data and provide print capability. Generally, a workgroup doesn't rely on a domain controller even if the server does use Windows Server as an operating system. We'll discuss what constitutes a domain controller in the "Domain" section that follows.

It wouldn't seem that a small group would require much security, but you can't afford to skimp at this level. Most security experts agree that disgruntled employees are actually a greater source of problems than your local cracker. Good workgroup security includes three elements:

- *User Accounts* The first place security begins in a workgroup is with user accounts. Use groups as needed to make setting security easy. Make sure that every user sets a password and changes it. Ensure that every password is complex enough to thwart crackers. We discussed many of these issues in this chapter. You can find additional information in the "Using the Local Users and Groups Snap-in" section of Chapter 21.

- *Shared Resources* Some resources on your network are always shared. For example, it's likely that you'll share any printers with the entire workgroup. However, other resources require limited sharing. For example, disk drives usually require discretionary sharing. We discussed both sharing issues in the "Sharing Files and Printers" section of Chapter 21.

- *Secured Resource* "It's easier to grant access to a resource than to take it away." Every network administrator should probably have that statement posted on his desk somewhere. A network begins with everything secured during installation, so a user can't miss what he doesn't know about. However, once the user knows a resource exists, removing access to it is difficult. Even if the user has no need for the resource and never uses it, the fact that the resource is unavailable causes a sense of loss. In most cases, it's better not to grant access to a resource until you know for sure that the user actually needs it.

After you accomplish these three tasks, you can truthfully say that your network is secure. You've ensured that everyone has what they need (but only just what they need) and that access by others is difficult. As mentioned earlier, setting security is only part of the picture. You must continue to monitor the network and change security settings as needed to reflect new threats. Security, even for a workgroup, is an ongoing process.

Domain

As a network becomes larger, it requires a larger server and better management. In fact, you might find that you need several servers to manage the network. The point is that the network increases in complexity as it gains in size. The security setup you have when working with a workgroup just doesn't work with a larger system. It's at this point that you need a domain controller for your network.

A domain controller is a special kind of a Windows (or other) server setup. You can promote a standard Windows server to a domain controller using the DCPROMO command in most cases. It doesn't matter which server you're using—the act of promoting it to a domain controller changes your network relationship. The server works in the same way as the client/server configuration used by other operating systems, although the actual configuration is more like a peer-to-peer connection.

In a client/server setup, a workstation makes a request of the server and the server either grants or denies it. All security, machine, and user information comes from a central location. The system is easier to manage when you have a large number of machines. In addition, multiple domain controllers can share information, which means a change on one server propagates (appears) on all other servers on the network.

Security becomes more complex as well. Generally, you set group policies, not local policies. The group policies affect the network as a whole. You use them for items such as password length and type. Group polices also affect logon procedures, such as a requirement to press Ctrl+Alt+Del before logging on to the system. Local policies act to restrict access to special machines. For example, you might add audit policies to a certain computer to ensure that Windows XP records all access.

Other Servers

Most medium-to-large networks today have more than one server, at least one of which uses an operating system other than Windows. A vast majority use NetWare or Linux as a secondary operating system. Of course, many other operating systems exist, and companies can use non-PC solutions, such as mainframes or minicomputers as ell. The point is that your company might have to integrate several network operating systems into a cohesive whole.

From a security standpoint, using other operating systems involves some risk and an increased training requirement for network administrators. For example, we saw in the "Using Explorer with the Novell Client" section of Chapter 21 that using the NetWare client changes the appearance of Windows Explorer, but that this change is a requirement for network administrators. If you read this section, you'll learn that the Microsoft client doesn't provide full access to all NetWare features, potentially opening a security hole.

Using a mixed network adds flexibility to your system, but you also need to consider the requirements for the other network operating system. For example, when using Linux, you need to make settings directly at the server to set up and configure access properly. Windows XP contains nothing in the way of built-in features for Linux, so everything has to appear on the Linux server itself. In most cases, this means working with Samba to make the connection.

Note: *Samba* is a tool that enables Linux resource sharing with a Windows computer. This sharing works between both computers. You can use Samba to provide shares on a Linux server; and you can access Windows from Linux using the client portion of Samba. You can learn more about Samba at http://www.samba.org/.

From a Windows perspective, Linux looks just like another Windows machine. The secret is in the Linux machine configuration. Of course, you can say the same of NetWare. Until you add long filename support to NetWare, it looks like a DOS drive. After you add support at the server, the system looks more like a Windows drive. In short, mixing operating systems on a network means added complexity in your security plan.

Internet Security

The question of Internet security has gotten lots of press lately, and I imagine that it'll get much more press before anything is resolved. In many respects, it's not even a matter of security we're talking about here—it's a matter of access. Security implies that you're locking something up, and that's clearly in opposition to how people actually use the Internet. Shared information, but shared with only the people you want to share with, is what Internet security is really about. In short, it comes down to a matter of access.

What kinds of access are we discussing? There are a number of ways to look at information exchange. You can exchange information willingly, or someone can steal it from you. Consider just one form of information exchange that people consider stealing. You register your software electronically rather than use the mail-in card as usual. Getting online is easy, but it seems to take a long time. Only after you actually look at what was transferred do you realize that the vendor not only received the information you provided, but also conducted a complete survey of the contents of your machine.

Some people also question the information that a vendor requests in the open. Some experts view Internet security requirements and privacy as two sides of the same coin. Consider all of the forms you fill out online. The registration form for a site might include your name, address, telephone number, and e-mail address. You've just given the Web site owner everything needed to contact you using several means in a situation where you might not want contact. A cracker comes along and steals this information from the vendor Web site and then posts that information online. Your privacy is at risk because of security issues.

Peter's Principle: Privacy at a Price

What would you spend to ensure that your Internet session is completely secure and anonymous? Privacy is a major concern for most users of the Internet. Several recent surveys by large consulting companies show that about 86 percent of users consider privacy a major concern and one of the reasons they don't trust Internet commerce.

A few companies, such as Anonymizer.com (http://www.anonymizer.com), have set up secure servers you can use to surf the Web in privacy. You must click a button on your Internet Explorer toolbar to enable the service and can disable it at any time. The way the service works is that you send the URL you want to surf to Anonymizer, which then obtains the data for you and sends it back to your machine. As a result, it's impossible for anyone to track you, your personal information, or your IP address or to send cookies to your machine. (See "The Cookie Monster" section of the chapter for more information about cookies.) This also means that you can't use Anonymizer to access a financial institution or to shop online.

Anonymizer and other, similar sites are grappling with the issue of keeping their sites safe from use by crackers to hide their activities. In addition, these privacy services plan to provide secure services to financial institutions. You'd use a high-encryption method to access the financial institution with Anonymizer in the middle to ensure that nothing unexpected happens during the communication.

The question for Windows XP users is whether services such as Anonymizer serve a useful purpose given the new privacy features provided by Internet Explorer 6. The privacy features of Internet Explorer 6, when set high enough, do protect you from cookies. They can also hide your identity to an extent. However, the third-party Web site can still see your IP address and identify you in that manner if you have a permanent address assignment. So, yes, Anonymizer does fulfill a purpose, but whether you need the service depends on how anonymous you want to remain.

There are other forms of unintentional access. For example, a user may decide to visit an Internet site. During the process of downloading the Web page, he might also download a destructive ActiveX control that wipes out his hard drive. An investigation by authorities shows that there wasn't any malicious intent on the part of the control's author—the control simply conflicted with a disk utility running in the background. Damage to both hardware and software becomes a very real issue when you start running those cute-looking controls that are springing up on Web pages all over the world.

The effect of unrestricted access on your machine's hardware and software isn't the only consideration. Many people are beginning to shop online—I'm one of them. How do you know that the vendor is using your credit card information correctly? For that matter, how do you know that someone isn't monitoring your "conversation" with the vendor and copying that number? You could end up paying for someone's new car or clothing with your credit card.

Tip: One person recently told me an interesting way to keep your risks low when shopping online. Simply obtain a credit card with a low limit. She uses a credit card with a $1,000 limit, but I've seen some companies offer credit cards with $500 and $750 limits as well. When the bill arrives, pay it off, and you're ready to shop online again.

The need to restrict access doesn't affect just the user. What happens to companies that lose their competitive edge when someone snoops through their supposedly secret files? It happens. Just look at all the news in the trade press regarding updated firewalls and other security items. Much of the security software that people depended on the most ended up having some flaw that rendered the security features useless. (Fortunately, firewall and other security software is becoming much more secure because of the hard work of both vendors and users.)

It doesn't take too long to realize that creating a secure environment on the Internet can be more difficult than you first thought. I'm not going to spend a lot of time telling you horror stories of companies that lost millions of dollars because of the seemingly petty crimes committed by crackers. Nor do we explore the test cases of home users who let their guard down for a few moments only to discover that those were the most important few moments of their computer's history. What we'll concentrate on instead are the security measures you can take to protect yourself when using a standard browser under Windows XP.

Understanding Certificates

There are efforts under way right now to make downloading ActiveX controls, Java applets, or anything else from the Internet just a little safer. In fact, many of these measures are already in place in a preliminary form, and the companies involved are working on making them safer. Some of the trade press calls this new technology a *certificate*, and others use the term *digital signature*. I view *certificate* as a friendly but imprecise term, so I use *digital signature* throughout this section.

Figuring out the precise technology behind digital signatures right now is a little like nailing Jell-O to the wall—you might be able to do it, but who would want to try? There's a simple way to look at a digital signature from a user's perspective. Think of it as you would a driver's license or an identification card because it has the same function. A *digital signature* identifies who created an Internet object—such as a Java applet or an ActiveX control—and potentially could provide a wealth of other information. For example, if the object happens to be a client or a server, a digital signature shows the current owner. In other words, you know the identity of the person or company you're dealing with.

Giving someone a digital certificate for the life of an object leaves a few things in doubt. For example, what happens if the company sells the rights to its ActiveX control to another company? To alleviate this problem, the digital signature, like a driver's license, also expires—forcing the vendor to keep proving that it is who it says it is. The expiration date also gives crackers less time to figure out how to steal the certificate. (Because each certificate is a separate item, learning how to steal an individual certificate doesn't necessarily buy the cracker anything.) Using a digital signature helps to keep everyone honest because it forces everyone to go through a central verification point.

Looking for Digital Signatures

How do you identify someone who has a digital signature versus someone who doesn't? As long as you tell your browser to warn you (the default setting with most products), you see some kind of warning dialog box when accessing an insecure site. Likewise, you'll see a Security Warning dialog box, like the one shown in Figure 22.6, when accessing a secure site.

FIGURE 22.6

The first time you visit a site that has a digital signature, your browser should display it in a dialog box.

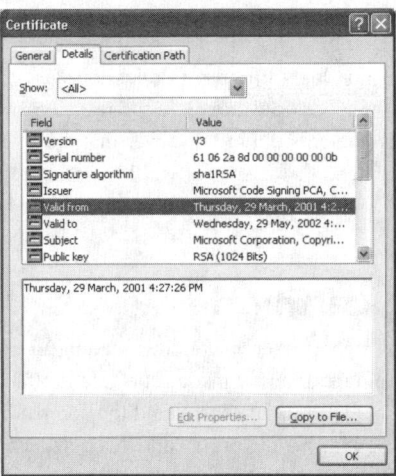

Make certain that the date is current and the digital signature belongs to the person or company you thought it belonged to. If you want additional information, you can click the link associated with the certificate (Microsoft, in the figure) to display the Certificate Properties dialog box, also shown in Figure 22.6. This dialog box provides detailed information about the certificate holder as well as the authority that issued the certificate.

Notice that the Security Warning dialog box gives you the option to always trust this certificate holder. Checking this check box adds a particular company to the list checked by WinVerifyTrust—this is a special API function designed to check the security of the certificate. If you check this box, your browser doesn't ask you about the certificate each time you request a download from that particular vendor.

Obtaining a Digital Signature

Just as you want to know with whom you're dealing, people will want to know who you are. For that reason, VeriSign and other digital signature providers offer a way for you to get a digital signature as well. All you need to do is visit its Web site (you'll find VeriSign at https://digitalid.verisign.com/).

If you choose VeriSign, begin at its Web site. You'll see a Security Information dialog box saying that you're about to request a secure document when you visit the site—don't worry about clicking Yes. Choose the Personal IDs option. You see another warning about leaving a secure connection.

> **Tip:** You can always tell when you're making a secure transmission by looking for special icons provided by your browser. Internet Explorer shows a lock near the center of the status bar. Navigator shows a key on the left side of the status bar. The more teeth in the key, the higher the security level. A missing lock or broken key usually signifies a non-secure connection—you'll want to exercise extra caution when transmitting data if you see a missing lock or broken key.
>
> Unfortunately, the presence of a lock or key only means that the connection between your machine and the server is secure. A cracker could redirect a form that you send using a secure method from the first server to a second server using a nonsecure transmission. In sum, the lock or key represents a secure connection only on one leg of the data's journey. It pays to review the Web site security policy before you place any trust in a secure connection that may be only partially secure.

Digital signatures cost a small amount per year, anywhere from $15 to $20 at the time of this writing. However, VeriSign also provides a 60-day digital ID you can try out. Click this option if you want to see how a digital ID works before you buy one.

Choose the Class 1 Digital ID option and you'll see a registration form for your digital ID. The form isn't all that difficult to figure out. All you need to do is type in a first and a last name. You must supply an e-mail address—that's how your certificate is issued. After you fill in this information, you need to decide whether to include additional information—such as your ZIP or postal code, age, and gender—as part of the certificate.

The final blank is a challenge phrase. I prefer to look at this as a password. You definitely want to choose something out of the ordinary because VeriSign uses the challenge phrase when you need assistance with your certificate. If you choose to get a full certificate, you need to provide some payment information. Only the 60-day demonstration version of the certificate is free. You also see an agreement for using the certificate on the bottom half of the page.

There's an Accept button at the bottom of the page. Click it and you see a Check Your E-mail page. This page tells you that you provided all of the requested information. The e-mail you receive contains a link to the Web site where you download your digital signature. It also contains a special PIN (personal identification number) you have to use at the download site.

After you have your PIN, follow the link to the Web page. Simply copy the PIN you received in your e-mail, and then paste it into the blank provided. Click Submit. After a few minutes, you get a success page. Make certain that you don't disturb the browser during this time. Simply wait for the transaction to finish. Click the Install button at the bottom of the page to complete the process. You see a simple message stating that your browser has installed the digital signature.

The Cookie Monster

If you spend very much time in some of the browser-oriented newsgroups on the Internet, you hear some talk about cookies. What precisely is a *cookie*? It's a small file on your local hard drive with configuration information that a Web site can use to store configuration of other information.

Normally, you find this file in a special directory you can monitor, and the Web site uses it for data such as your name and site preferences. However, your browser can't place any limitations on what kind of information a Web site can write to the cookie, and that can create problems. For example, what would prevent a Web site from writing executable code to the cookie and then fooling the operating system into executing it? This particular problem has actually occurred; but, fortunately, the results were more along the lines of a bad joke than actual damage to the system. It could have been different, though, and that's why people are concerned about cookies.

Internet Explorer stores cookies in separate files in the \Documents and Settings\<User Name>\Cookies folder. Each cookie is represented by a username, followed by an at symbol (@), followed by the site name. Internet Explorer adds a TXT extension so that you can open the cookie file in Notepad to see what it contains. For example, if a person named Ted visits the http://www.msn.com site, MSN downloads a cookie to his machine; then he has a cookie file named Ted@MSN.TXT in his Cookies folder.

The main advantage of this approach is that each user can have individual configuration settings for the same site, even if they all use the same machine to visit it. In addition, getting rid of the settings for a site you no longer use is as easy as erasing a single cookie file. The disadvantages include inefficient disk use and the fact that some users find it difficult to figure out which cookies to get rid of (if they even know that the Cookies folder exists). Obviously, neither the Internet Explorer nor the Navigator approach is perfect.

The point is that you know where the cookies are stored and how to reject them if you want. Internet Explorer provides the means to reject cookies you don't want. In Internet Explorer, you use the View | Internet Options command to display the Internet Options dialog box. Select the Privacy tab and you'll see a dialog box similar to the one shown in Figure 22.7.

As you can see from the figure, this dialog box contains a slider with different options, from Low to High. You can also choose a Block All Cookies option that prevents your system from accepting cookies at all. The various levels represent privacy settings. For example, the High setting blocks any cookie that lacks a compact privacy policy. In addition, this setting blocks cookies that contain personally identifiable information. The Low setting restricts third-party cookies that lack a privacy policy (for example, banner ads). It also restricts cookies that contain personally identifiable information. The last setting on this slider is Accept All Cookies. You shouldn't ever use this setting because it opens your system to cookies of any type.

FIGURE 22.7

The Privacy tab contains settings that determine which cookies your browser accepts.

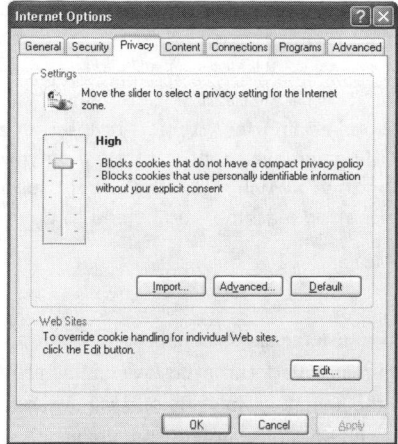

So, if accepting cookies is a normal part of surfing the Internet, but accepting them could be dangerous, how do you work with cookies on a daily basis? I normally keep cookies set somewhere between Medium and High when I'm visiting sites that are business oriented. I disable cookies when I visit a small site that I'm not sure of or perhaps a nonbusiness site that I haven't looked at before.

Normally, cookies from reputable sites are reasonably safe, though, so you'll probably want to give them wide latitude concerning security. Because this is the only file a standard Web page can write to, you'll find that most cookies do just what they're supposed to do—store configuration settings. Because the advent of ActiveX controls and Java applets gives more power to crackers who really want to harm your system, I'd spend more time worrying about these potential breaches in your security.

Sandbox Approach Versus Open Access

Security is more complex than it really needs to be right now because the Internet is going through many changes concerning capability and flexibility. The two main players in all this are ActiveX controls and Java applets. Scripting languages also play a role. However, given the problems with scripts, I normally ask the system to prompt me when they're used. That way, I can disable their use on sites I don't trust and enable them on sites I do trust.

Java applets take what's known as the sandbox approach to security—they don't do anything outside the purview of the applet. For example, Java applets don't allow hard drive access because the applet would have to use the operating system to do so. Some developers complain that the sandbox approach hinders them from writing fully functional applications; and, to a certain point, they're right. If an applet can't access system resources, it can't really do much more for you from a system level than standard HTML can. On the other hand, many users feel safer knowing that the Java applet they just downloaded won't erase the contents of their hard drive or do something else equally devious.

> **Note:** Microsoft has stopped adding Java support to Internet Explorer 6 and Windows XP. If you already have Java support installed on your machine, Internet Explorer and Windows XP will retain the current support. However, if you're using a freshly formatted machine, you'll need to download Java support from a third party.

There's another good reason to use the sandbox approach. It allows a developer to write a single applet that works on many platforms. The Java engine provides everything a Java applet needs to run, so the applet doesn't rely on system services. In other words, a Java applet is self-contained and doesn't really rely on anyone else. (The Java engine is obviously platform specific.)

Microsoft has taken a different approach with ActiveX. It's actually an extension of OLE technology. Unlike Java applets, ActiveX controls can interact with applications on your machine, access the hard drive, and look into the Registry. This makes ActiveX controls much more flexible from the developer perspective. It makes them more useful from the user perspective as well.

The problem lies in the level of access that they obtain. An ActiveX control has the same level of access as any other application on your machine. This means that an ill-behaved control could cause more than a little damage. In addition, it means that the user can't simply download a control without thinking about its origins first.

At first glance, it would seem that the division between ActiveX controls and Java applets is clear. You would accept Java applets if security were foremost on your mind. ActiveX controls would provide added capability, but only if you were willing to accept the consequences of a reduced security net. Let's look at that dividing line, though; it's not as clear as you might think. People have had Java applets use back doors to access the system. There have been a few documented cases where they've actually caused damage. Java supporters have stated that the Java engine seals these security holes. However, you can't be certain because nothing is as secure as the vendor says that it is.

ActiveX supporters further muddy the water by stating that an ActiveX control falls under the same guidelines as any OLE control. In addition, the author has to sign the control, which shows the downloader who created the control. (You can still download the control if the author doesn't sign it, but both Internet Explorer and Navigator display warnings against this practice.) The use of digital signatures means that you always know who created an ActiveX control and can make a reasonable decision about downloading and using it. Java controls are downloaded automatically—you don't get a chance to review a digital signature for them in advance and very often don't even know who created them.

The only thing you can say about the sandbox versus the open approach right now is that neither one offers a clear-cut advantage. About the only thing you can do is watch where you download controls. If you're uncertain about a site, don't take the risk of using it. Security is a user matter right now. Look before you leap. Make sure that you know who created that Java applet or ActiveX control before letting it run on your machine.

On Your Own

Spend some time training the users on your network about security. It's also very important that you take the time to explain what types of passwords are acceptable. Spend a little time with each user who has problems understanding the security plan.

If you're a home user, try setting up a variety of security options on your machine. For example, you might want to create a security profile for young users that gives them access to programs they can use but removes access to programs that could damage your machine. Use the Local Security Policy snap-in and other tools described in this chapter to make the process of creating a home security plan easy.

Anyone who uses the Internet for more than just casual browsing should have his or her own digital signature. Use the procedure in the "Obtaining a Digital Signature" section of this chapter to get your own digital signature. Be sure to reread the rest of the section as well. It's always good to know when you can trust the party at the other end of the connection.

If you're using a peer-to-peer network, try installing the Net Watcher utility to see how it works. This utility is very easy to use and understand and helps you check your machine for attached users before shutting it down at the end of the day.

PART VIII

Troubleshooting Windows XP

Now That DOS Is Gone

It's important to look at an issue that will definitely change the world of computing for many people. If you're a Windows 2000 user, the transition to Windows XP is relatively easy. Except for some differences in hardware requirements, you're already used to the type of environment that Windows XP provides. If anything, Windows XP provides a freer environment where you can run more applications than before. Windows NT users have an extremely large transition to make, but it's from the perspective of user interface and security. Windows 9x/Me users, however, have a long and difficult transition to make from an environmental perspective. DOS is gone, and it's not coming back.

DOS has been an important part of computing for users for many years. The media has reported the death of DOS so many times that everyone has lost count. Yet, beneath the surface, DOS has always remained a factor for Windows 3.x and 9x users. When you see Windows XP, you're seeing an operating system without any form of DOS available, yet Windows XP is able to run most DOS applications as well as Windows 9x (and possibly better than Windows Me).

The purpose of this chapter is to discuss what the loss of DOS means to you. We'll look at issues that include the loss of the AUTOEXEC.BAT and CONFIG.SYS configuration files. In many cases, this means that you'll have to find new drivers for your hardware. Some of your hardware and software won't work, so it's important to make this decision with a minimum of effort. I'll help you understand the conditions under which hardware and software don't work under Windows XP.

The final issue is one of creating a DOS boot disk. It's still important to have a means to boot your system to DOS for diagnostics or to play certain types of games. Unfortunately, the default DOS disk you obtain with Windows XP isn't ready for either task. We'll discuss the techniques for creating DOS disks for specific purposes.

Windows XP Boot Problems

Windows XP provides high reliability and flexibility. This includes the boot process. However, Windows XP isn't Windows 9x, nor is it Windows 2000. Windows XP introduces some differences in the boot process that mean a few of the techniques you used to configure your system in the past won't work today.

Obviously, Windows XP is much closer to Windows NT/2000 than it is to Windows 9x, so Windows 9x users will experience the greatest number of problems during the boot process. In addition, the hardware requirements for Windows XP and Windows NT/2000 are similar. Windows 9x users might have older hardware that provides enough capacity, but not the right kind of drivers. In short, most boot configuration problems will occur for Windows 9x users who upgrade to Windows XP.

The following sections discuss various boot elements. We'll look at problems you'll experience due to missing file support. You'll also learn how to overcome those problems using new Windows XP techniques. Finally, we'll discuss Windows XP options that matter to users upgrading from Windows 9x and Windows NT/2000.

AUTOEXEC.BAT and CONFIG.SYS Don't Count Any More

You might find an AUTOEXEC.BAT or CONFIG.SYS file on your hard drive, but Windows XP doesn't need it. These two files are leftovers from the days of DOS. The interesting thing is that many applications—even new applications—still make entries to these files. It's interesting to note that even the Novell client installation process creates entries for these two files, and it's a Windows application. In short, many applications don't understand that DOS is missing, although they should.

One of the problems you'll run into is that applications need to have settings in AUTOEXEC.BAT and CONFIG.SYS for configuration purposes. We'll see in the "Setting Paths the New Way" section, later in this chapter, that you can overcome some of these problems by making changes to the Windows XP configuration.

Unfortunately, you can make only so many changes using Windows XP environmental settings. For example, you can't load a DOS driver using Windows XP, no matter how many tricks you use to try to do it. Of course, you can create a special configuration file and use it to start the application. We'll see how this works in the "DOS Application Configuration Techniques" section of this chapter.

What happens if you can't load a driver or executable file or make a change to the Windows XP environment? You can still create a DOS boot disk to solve the problem. We'll discuss how to do this in the "Creating a DOS Boot Disk" section of this chapter.

If you still have entries in your CONFIG.SYS or AUTOEXEC.BAT files that you can't use in some way, it's probably time to retire the associated hardware or software. The bottom line is that you have to determine if the benefits of Windows XP outweigh the cost of an upgrade. Of course, you'll want to make this determination before you buy Windows XP and install it on your machine. Once it's installed, you're committed to making a change.

Setting Paths the New Way

Windows XP provides a means for using environmental settings. The most common setting is the file path, but you'll find plenty of other settings to consider. Amazingly, many of the settings you would find in an AUTOEXEC.BAT file also work under Windows XP. Not all of them do, but many do.

To change your environmental settings, right-click My Computer and choose Properties from the context menu. Select the Advanced tab and click Environment Variables. You'll see an Environment Variables dialog box, similar to the one shown in Figure 23.1.

FIGURE 23.1

The Environment Variables dialog box contains entries for all the environment settings for your machine.

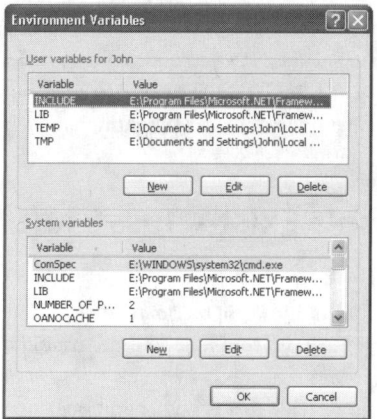

Notice that there are two kinds of settings in this dialog box. The User Variables field contains your personal environment settings. In many cases, you'll find individual application settings in this field. For example, Figure 23.1 shows the settings for a compiler on my machine. I use the compiler, but no one else who uses the machine needs it.

The System Variables field contains the settings for the machine as a whole. Everyone uses these settings, so you need to exercise care in setting them. You'll find entries such as the system path in this field. Applications that everyone uses should also place their settings in this field. You'll also find some interesting environment variables in this field. For example, the ThemesDir entry contains the path to your themes. If you want to move your themes to another location, change this environment variable setting first.

Notice in Figure 23.1 that the dialog box contains three buttons for each field. Click New if you want to create a new environment variable. Type the name of the variable in the Variable Name field; type the value in the Variable Value field. Click OK to add the entry to the Environment Variable dialog box. One thing you should note is that some environment variables don't take effect immediately. You might have to restart your machine to load them into memory.

> **Tip:** Sometimes, performance problems hide in small packages. Every time you start a command prompt, it inherits a complete copy of the Windows XP environment. Many other applications also inherit this environment when you start them, so they know where to find specific items, such as the temporary directory. The more you stuff into the user and system fields, the more memory the environment variables consume and the longer it takes applications to find what they need. Mind you, the memory requirements are small, and the time saved even smaller, but every little bit counts. Keeping your Environment Variable dialog box free of excess entries may not turn your machine into a speed demon, but the smaller size might prevent subtle, yet noticeable problems.

The Edit button works the same as the New button. The only difference is that the Variable Name and Variable Value fields contain values when you open the Edit User Variable or Edit System Variable dialog box. Highlighting an environment variable and clicking Delete removes it from the list.

Real Mode Doesn't Exist—Toss That Old Hardware

I admit it: I have a junk box full of old computer parts that I might use someday. In fact, I've used some of the parts in this box from time to time. An old display adapter might fill in on a machine until I get to the store to buy a new one. An old hard drive might not be useful by itself, but it could provide just enough additional storage to help me complete a project.

The problem with old hardware is that it's usually underpowered, always ready to die at the worst possible moment, and can cause you many headaches with Windows XP. To Microsoft's credit, Windows XP does contain generic drivers you can use for a number of purposes, even old hardware. However, the chances of the generic driver producing acceptable results are somewhat slim. You'll normally get better results if you buy a new piece of hardware as soon as possible.

This leads me to the old hardware still sitting in your system. If you have anything that requires a real mode driver to use, you can't use it under Windows XP. In fact, older hardware that lacks Windows XP–specific drivers should go into the parts box for possible use as temporary spare parts if you need them. In all cases, you're ahead of the game if you buy a new piece of hardware when you need it rather than keeping something old and cantankerous around.

One other possibility exists: You have a piece of hardware that does provide a driver for Windows XP, but Microsoft hasn't signed the driver. Does this mean that the driver is ready for the junk heap? Probably not.

Many smaller companies lack the funds to certify their drivers. In addition, even large vendors don't spend the money to certify drivers for older pieces of hardware. The practical solution is to try the hardware with the Windows XP driver and see how well it works. Sometimes, it doesn't work very well. If you contact the vendor and find there isn't any chance for an upgrade, try to find a third-party driver that works better. Failing that, it's time for an upgrade. Don't keep unreliable hardware in your system.

Windows XP Boot Options

Most versions of Windows have offered boot options. You press a special key during startup and Windows shows a menu you can use to select the startup mode. Windows 9x users have long enjoyed a robust boot options menu that offered several forms for safe mode setup. Windows 2000 users haven't been quite as lucky, which means the right boot option is often missing. Windows XP corrects this problem by offering a robust set of boot options. The following list describes these options:

- *Safe Mode* Starts your system with the minimum number of drivers and uses the simplest possible display driver. You don't have access to most of your hardware and even lack some operating system features. The purpose of this mode is to enable you to uninstall, disable, or otherwise remove software that prevents your system from booting normally. You can also perform a minimal amount of troubleshooting in this mode. However, the main purpose of this mode is to repair your system.

- *Safe Mode with Networking* Starts your system in Safe mode, but adds network drivers to the list of installed features. The only advantage of this configuration is that you can locate drivers and other resources on a network drive.

- *Safe Mode with Command Prompt* Starts your system without benefit of a GUI. You see a command prompt that enables you to run any character mode applications that Windows XP has to offer. This is an extreme repair mode you should use only as a last resort.

- *Enable Boot Logging* Creates a text file containing a list of every drive that Windows XP loads during the process. You can use this option to find drivers you no longer need or to diagnose where the boot process fails. This is also a good feature to use to document your system setup. Knowing which drivers Windows XP loads and when it loads them can help you reconstruct a system after a massive failure.

- *Enable VGA Mode* Performs a normal system start, but loads a generic VGA driver in place of the normal display driver. This option enables you to check for display problems. It also helps you perform certain maintenance tasks, such as updating a display driver with greater ease. You'll want to avoid using this mode for normal operation because many Windows XP utilities won't run.

- *Last Known Good Configuration* Restores a previously stored system configuration. Windows XP uses this existing configuration for boot purposes. Use this option when you install a new driver that doesn't work well on your system and the normal uninstall process doesn't work. The only problem with this option is that it leaves drivers on your system that you don't need.

- *Directory Services Restore Mode* Restores a system configuration stored on a domain controller. You can use this option only with Active Directory. Your system must be part of the domain, and you must have access to the network. This option works well for quick restores when the Last Known Good Configuration option fails to work. In many cases, you'll want to try restoring a backup if this option doesn't work the first time. (A failure means that the Active Directory copy is also corrupted.)

- *Start Windows Normally* Starts the system normally, as if you had selected an operating system option from the boot menu.

- *Reboot* Reboots your system. You don't need to use this option unless you selected one of the other options and decide that you'd prefer to do something else.

- *Return to the OS Choices Menu* Returns you to the boot menu, where you can select an operating system to boot.

As you can see, Windows XP provides a menu option for most occasions. You access this menu by pressing F8 at the boot menu. The Boot Manager will display a message near the bottom of the screen telling you to press F8 to access the boot menu.

Some of the odd uses for this menu include testing software for compatibility problems. For example, I've used Enable VGA Mode to ensure that Windows XP is in a true VGA mode when it starts. In some cases, this enables some software to run. When this happens, I know it's worth my time to try various software configuration options to make the application work under Windows XP.

Diagnosing Application Support Problems

You'll find that certain classes of older Windows applications actually rely on DOS to perform certain tasks. Both educational and game software fall into this category. Windows didn't provide a very robust environment during its early days, so game and educational software vendors often found ways to get around Windows limitations so that they could create applications that ran quickly.

Windows XP does provide the compatibility settings we discussed in the "Using Compatibility Mode" section of Chapter 10. You can use these settings to overcome problems in the vast majority of software. After spending hours testing educational and game software for compatibility, I can truthfully say the compatibility settings work most of the time (a whopping 93.4 percent in my informal test of 46 pieces of software three years old and older—the oldest test application was nine years old).

However, you'll still find some misbehaved software. Windows 9x handles this problem with MS-DOS mode, a solution that Windows XP users don't have. This means you have to make a choice. You can get a new version of the software, or you can diagnose the existing product. Diagnosing software problems can get time consuming. Here are the areas I check most often:

- *Verify Settings* Some older pieces of software include a separate configuration routine. Make sure you run this configuration software. For example, you might have to provide soundboard settings. Also verify that the INI or other files ended up in the correct place. It also pays to check the environmental settings, as mentioned in the "Setting Paths the New Way" section, earlier in this chapter.

- *DOS Drive* Running some older software on an NTFS drive doesn't work. I've found that placing older software on a DOS drive seems to help. It shouldn't make a difference, but an analysis shows that this software is looking for a drive with DOS characteristics and often doesn't understand an NTFS drive.

- *Partial Use* Sometimes you have to settle for partial functionality. For example, convincing game applications that your 3D soundboard is really an ancient Sound Blaster soundboard probably won't work. Configuring the software repeatedly to make it work probably won't help. In many cases, you have to adjust the software to provide the services it can provide and leave it at that.

- *Odd Requirements* Several pieces of educational software I tested checked the COM port. I never did figure out why because they didn't need the COM port for either a modem or a mouse. The fact that Windows XP configured the COM port for an impossible IRQ number caused problems. A reconfiguration of the system enabled the software to work.

- *Skip the Introduction* A few of the games I tested included an introduction. The application would freeze immediately after the introduction completed. Most applications have some special key you can press to get past the introduction. The Spacebar and the Escape key seem to be the most common, but I've seen other keys used. If you find that your program freezes immediately after the introduction completes, try skipping the introduction.

- *Patches* The Internet contains a wealth of patches for older software, and many gamers contribute software they design to make the Windows environment compatible with the game. For example, older Microprose games require a special patch to run on a Pentium system. Some games and educational software run on timing loops that require you to slow their environment. However, I'd consider these measures extreme unless you have no other alternatives.

DOS Application Configuration Techniques

One of my favorite games of all times was Darklands, but I could never get it to run properly under Windows 9x. Windows 2000 wouldn't even start the game. Amazingly, Windows XP runs this 9-year-old game extremely well. The only problem area seems to be sound, a problem for many older games. Note that I used the DOS disk technique for running Darklands; it wouldn't run on an NTFS drive.

Configuring Darklands required creating a Program Information File (PIF) for it. This file is akin to the configuration file for Windows applications that we discussed in the "Using Compatibility Mode" section of Chapter 10. Figure 23.2 shows what a PIF looks like.

FIGURE 23.2
DOS applications use PIFs for configuration purposes.

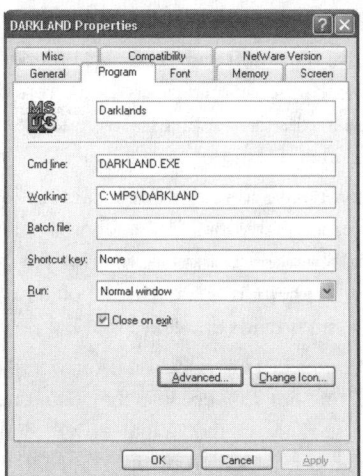

As you can see, PIF files provide quite a few more tabs than Windows applications do. The following sections describe each tab in detail. Note that because we've already discussed the Compatibility tab in Chapter 10, I don't discuss it again in this chapter.

Program

The Program tab enables you to change the way Windows executes a program. At the top of the tab are an icon and a field containing the application's name. The Application Name field is the name you see in Explorer.

The next three fields determine which application to run. The Cmd Line field contains the name of an application, which must end with an .exe, .com, or .bat extension. The example in Figure 23.2 is running a copy of Darklands. The Working field tells Windows XP what directory to use to start the application. In most cases, you start the application from its home directory or its data directory. The choice depends on what kind of information the application needs to start. In the example, Darklands will run from the C:\MPS\DARKLAND directory. The third field, Batch File, enables you to designate a batch file to run with the application. You could include a batch file to set up the path, for example, and to prompt and load any Terminate-and-Stay-Resident (TSR) programs you might need after starting the command processor.

> **Note:** Exercise care in what applications you run using a batch file. Windows XP tolerates an extremely limited number of TSRs. For example, it wouldn't run the Sound Blaster emulator for my soundboard. You might find that you have to do without the services of the TSR in order to run the application.

The Shortcut Key field enables you to assign a shortcut key to the program. We talked about shortcut keys in several areas of this book, including Chapter 10. Generally, you don't want to waste a shortcut key on a DOS application, unless you use the application daily.

Use the Run field to specify how Windows XP should run the application. There are three choices: Normal Window, Minimized, and Maximized. The first two choices affect both windowed and full-screen sessions. The third choice starts windowed sessions maximized. You normally receive the best performance from game and educational software if you run it using the Normal Window option.

It's a good idea to close a DOS session as soon as you finish with it. If you check the Close on Exit option, Windows XP closes it automatically. Otherwise, you see a command prompt after the application completes that doesn't have any purpose.

Clicking the Change Icon button displays the Change Icon dialog box. There, you can select the icon used to identify the application within Explorer and the Start Menu. Windows XP provides the same default choices as other versions of Windows. You also can click the Browse button to select from custom icon sets.

Using the Windows PIF Settings Dialog Box

Click Advanced on the Program tab, and you'll see a Windows PIF Settings dialog box, similar to the one shown in Figure 23.3. The settings on this dialog box might not seem very interesting, but they're the most interesting of all the settings you can make because they help you create a compatible environment for your application.

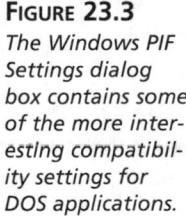

Figure 23.3
The Windows PIF Settings dialog box contains some of the more interesting compatibility settings for DOS applications.

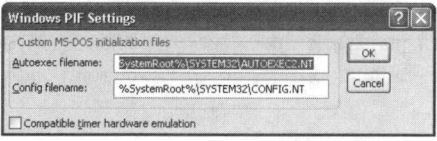

The Autoexec Filename and Config Filename fields contain entries for the Windows XP version of AUTOEXEC.BAT and CONFIG.SYS. You find both of these files in the \WINDOWS\SYSTEM32 as AUTOEXEC.NT and CONFIG.NT. These files don't work precisely the same as their DOS counterparts. For one thing, you'll find that they already contain some entries. Most of these entries provide support that DOS applications require. If you find that your DOS application requires something other than the default settings provided in these files, make a copy of the file and change the settings in the copy. Change the name of the file in the Autoexec Filename or Config Filename fields.

The CONFIG.NT file contains a special setting you need to know about. Remove the REM from the DOSONLY setting if you plan to run TSRs of any type. Use this setting to purify the environment and ensure that the environment runs only DOS applications. The presence of Windows XP applications in the DOS environment can cause problems with some applications.

The AUTOEXEC.NT file also contains a special setting in the form of the Set Blaster=A220 I5 D1 P330 line. This line contains the virtual Sound Blaster line. The virtualized form of this device driver doesn't work for some systems and some games. When working with DOS games, try several settings to see if you can find one that the DOS game likes. Failing that, use the instructions in the AUTOEXEC.NT file to disable the virtualized driver, and then attempt to use the Sound Blaster emulation driver that comes with your soundboard. You'll find that this technique still doesn't work in many situations.

Notice the Compatible Timer Hardware Emulation option on the Windows PIF Settings dialog box. This option can save you more grief than any other setting I tell you about in this chapter. Check this option if it appears that your game is having timing problems caused by newer systems with high clock speeds. Older games use timing loops that don't react well to high-speed clocks. This setting enables Windows XP to detect and correct the problem in many situations.

Font

The Font tab, shown in Figure 23.4, enables you to change the appearance of fonts used to display data in a windowed DOS application. These settings don't affect a full-screen session. This dialog box contains four main sections. The first section controls the type of fonts you see in the Font Size list box. You'll usually want to use the fullest set of fonts available, so select Both Font Types. The only time to switch to one font type or another is when your display has problems with a specific font type. Note that some educational software has definite problems with True Type fonts and you'll need to use bitmapped fonts alone.

The Font Size list box in the second section contains a list of font sizes available for the DOS window. The numbers represent the number of pixels used for each character. A higher number of pixels makes the display more readable. A smaller number of pixels makes the window smaller.

The Window Preview section shows how big the window will be in the display. The Font Preview section shows the size of the print. Combine the output from these two displays to determine the font size to use. It's important to balance the need to see what you're doing with the need to display the entire DOS box at one time.

FIGURE 23.4
Use the Font tab to adjust the fonts used to display information in the command window.

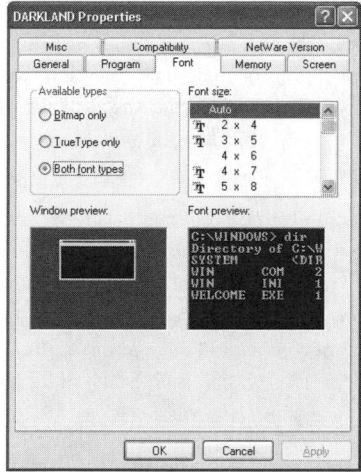

Memory

The Memory tab, shown in Figure 23.5, is the most important tab in the Properties dialog box from a tuning perspective. It contains only five list boxes and two check boxes, but the decisions you make there affect how the application runs. For example, a game like Darklands doesn't run without sufficient conventional or EMS memory. More importantly, these settings affect the way Windows runs.

FIGURE 23.5
The Memory tab enables you to modify the way Windows allocates and manages memory for your DOS application.

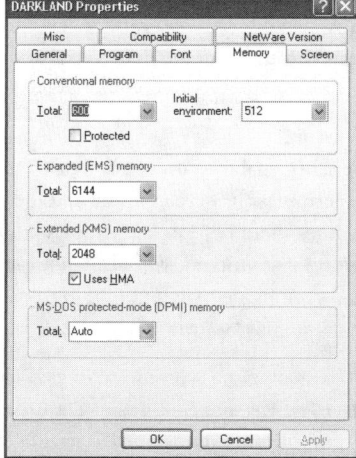

The first group of settings affects conventional memory. The Total field enables you to select any value up to 640KB. Windows usually allocates a 1024-byte environment for your DOS application. This should be enough to handle most situations. I usually set mine to 4096, however, to provide space for all the environment strings required by real-mode compilers. The Protected checkbox is another diagnostic aid. Checking it tells Windows XP to monitor the application for memory-protection errors. The only disadvantage is the performance loss you'll suffer when using it. If your application tends to corrupt memory, check this box to keep your environment stable. Otherwise, consider leaving it unchecked for better performance.

The second section contains a single list box that controls how much expanded memory Windows XP allocates for your application. If you leave expanded memory on Auto, MEM reports expanded memory up to the amount of memory your machine has installed. Windows XP makes only 16 MB of expanded memory usable, even if you have more RAM installed. The only time you should change this setting is when the application grabs every bit of expanded memory it can find. Some older DOS applications get a little greedy, so you need to provide some controls.

The third group of settings controls the amount of extended memory available to your application. The default setting allocates the full amount of RAM installed on your system. This isn't an unlimited amount of memory, but it could be fairly high—much higher than the automatic Expanded Memory setting. As with the Expanded Memory setting, I change this setting from Auto to a specific number only if the application gets greedy or if it has problems coping with the full amount of extended memory available on my machine. I usually leave the Uses HMA check box blank because I usually load DOS in the high-memory area (HMA). If you don't use the HMA, however, you can still choose to load all or part of an application there by checking this box.

The final setting enables you to determine the amount of DPMI memory available to applications. Windows XP usually sets this value to reflect the current system conditions. There's little reason to change this setting from the default.

Screen

The Screen tab, shown in Figure 23.6, enables you to configure the screen settings. The first group of settings, Usage, determines the screen mode and the number of display lines. Set the number of display lines there before you set the options on the Font tab of this dialog box. Otherwise, a setting that worked well at 25 lines might not work at 50. Many games have to run in full-screen mode. Any attempt to run some games in a window results in corruption or the game may not run at all.

The second section enables you to change the window settings. (This doesn't come into play if you use full-screen mode.) The Restore Settings at Startup check box tells Windows XP to update the program information file (PIF) to reflect any changes made in the toolbar. The entries usually are good for only that session. I want Windows to remember my settings from session to session, so I check this box.

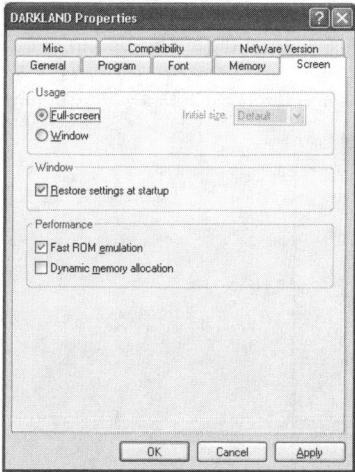

Figure 23.6

The Screen tab enables you to adjust the size and type of display and the method Windows uses to display it.

Note: For those of you who are looking for the Display Toolbar option, Windows XP discontinued the use of this option. However, you can still configure the command window without opening the PIF again. Simply click in the upper-left corner (the icon in the title bar) and you'll see a context menu. Select Properties to configure the window settings. You'll also find menu entries to copy information from Windows to the command window or from the command window to Windows.

The third group of settings on this tab affects your application's performance. The first setting, Fast ROM Emulation, acts just like shadow RAM. It enables your application to use a RAM version of your display ROM. If an application has trouble with shadow RAM under DOS, it also will have trouble with this setting. Otherwise, you should leave this option checked for maximum performance from your application.

The second setting in the Performance section helps Windows more than the application. This setting enables Windows to retrieve memory the DOS application uses for graphics mode when it goes into character mode. This modicum of memory isn't much, but it adds up if you run many DOS sessions. The only time to remove the checkmark from this setting is when your application spends all or most of its time in graphics mode.

Misc

The Misc (miscellaneous) tab, shown in Figure 23.7, provides settings that determine how Windows interacts with your application from a functional point of view. These settings also affect the compatibility of your game or educational software. For example, many people find they have to set the mouse for Exclusive mode before it will run. The settings on this tab also change according to the compatibility settings. For example, you can't use Quick Edit mode unless you set the application to run in Windows 95 compatibility mode.

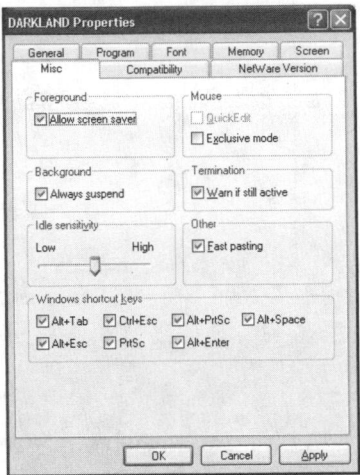

FIGURE 23.7
The Misc tab enables you to control a variety of settings that don't fit into the other categories.

The Allow Screen Saver setting doesn't have much effect when using windowed applications. It determines whether Windows can interrupt a full-screen session to run a screen saver. Some full-screen applications, such as graphics applications, get confused if the screen saver operates.

The Mouse group contains two settings. The QuickEdit check box enables you to use a mouse within a DOS window, just as with any Windows application. The Exclusive Mode check box gives a windowed application exclusive control over the mouse. This means you can't use the mouse with your regular Windows applications while this application is active. You should probably run this application in a full-screen session if it has this much trouble sharing the mouse.

Some of the settings on this tab—such as Background and Idle Sensitivity—provide subtle performance control over your application. Checking the Always Suspend option frees up resources for Windows XP to use with other applications. If you're using a DOS application for something that requires continuous input (such as data entry), it pays to check this box and use the resources for other applications. Idle Sensitivity also changes how Windows allocates resources. Windows tracks the amount of activity from an application to see whether it sits idle while waiting for input from you. If it does, Windows XP reduces the application's CPU resources. This usually works fine, but sometimes Windows doesn't leave the application enough resources to complete the task it's performing. When this happens, lowering the Idle Sensitivity setting gives the application the resources it needs, but it does so at the expense of other applications running on the system at the time.

The Warn If Still Active option in the Termination section displays a message if you try to terminate the DOS application window without ending the program first. You should usually keep this option checked to prevent potential data loss from a premature application termination.

Another performance enhancement is the Fast Pasting option. Always check this option whenever possible so that Windows can use a high-speed method of pasting information into your DOS application. You should change this setting only if you see data damage when using the fast-paste mode.

The final group on the tab regulates the use of control-key combinations in Windows XP. Checking a box in the Windows Shortcut Keys group enables Windows to use that key combination. Clearing an option enables the application to use the key combination. You should change these settings only when the application needs them and you can't change the application's settings.

Creating a DOS Boot Disk

Sometimes, the only way to get an application to run is to create a DOS disk, boot it, and run the application from a DOS partition on your hard drive. If you use this technique, you must have a DOS partition because DOS doesn't understand NTFS, not even the DOS you get from Windows XP. Of course, DOS disks come in handy for other purposes. For example, if you have one of the few diagnostic programs that doesn't self-boot, you probably want a DOS partition on your machine; or, at least, a floppy diskette from which to boot the software. You might also need a DOS disk to perform other maintenance tasks, such as running a vendor-supplied diagnostic.

The following sections discuss several DOS boot disk creation techniques. Generally, you'll find yourself creating a variation on a theme. In other words, these sections provide guidelines, but you might have to modify a suggestion to meet a particular need. Consider these sections the starting point for your DOS disk creation process.

Starting from Scratch

Creating the initial DOS boot disk isn't difficult. Right-click the floppy drive in Windows Explorer or My Computer and then choose Format from the content menu. You'll see the Format Floppy dialog box, shown in Figure 23.8. Notice that the dialog box tells you the detected size of the floppy as part of the title bar.

This dialog box contains several configuration options. Windows XP normally chooses the maximum available disk size in the Capacity field, but you can choose a smaller size if necessary. The only choice in the File System field for a floppy is FAT (File Allocation Table). You also have a single option in the Allocation Unit Size field of Default Allocation Size. You use the File System and Allocation Unit Size options only when working with hard drives or other large media. You must select the Create an MS-DOS Startup Disk option to create a bootable disk.

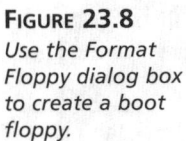

Figure 23.8
Use the Format Floppy dialog box to create a boot floppy.

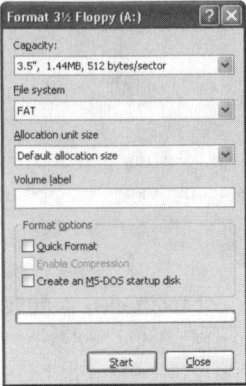

Click Start. Windows XP will warn you that formatting the disk will erase all of the data it contains. Click OK. The progress bar at the bottom of the dialog box tracks the format progress. After a minute or two, you'll see a Format Complete message. Click OK. You now have a bootable floppy disk.

Tricks for Making a Boot Disk Do More

Windows XP indeed creates a bootable floppy disk for you, but this floppy contains so much data that you might find it impossible to add the software you need in order to use the floppy. A typical floppy diskette contains 555KB of data after Windows XP formats it, which leaves only 868KB for other uses. The first thing you need to do is clean off the extra files. Of course, that begs that question of what's extra on the floppy. You can remove any of the extra files and still have a bootable floppy when you're done:

- AUTOEXEC.BAT
- CONFIG.SYS
- DISPLAY.SYS
- EGA.CPI
- EGA2.CPI
- EGA3.CPI
- KEYB.COM
- KEYBOARD.SYS
- KEYBRD2.SYS
- KEYBRD3.SYS
- KEYBRD4.SYS
- MODE.COM

Remove these files and you'll free 347KB of precious disk space. In most cases, you won't miss any of the files or (as in the case of AUTOEXEC.BAT and CONFIG.SYS) you'll need to add new versions to the disk.

This brings me to what I normally add to a DOS disk. If I'm creating a general disk for maintenance purposes, I include the drivers required to enable the mouse and the CD-ROM drive (including MSCDEX.EXE). The disk also includes EDIT.COM, FORMAT.COM, and FDISK.COM. The new AUTOEXEC.BAT and CONFIG.SYS files contain the commands required to initialize any boot devices, such as the CD-ROM and mouse. EXPAND.EXE is another good choice for a maintenance disk option.

Boot Disks and Games

One of the biggest reasons to create a boot disk today is that you have a game that doesn't run under Windows XP. Try as you might, you couldn't get the game to run at all. That's when you create an empty boot disk using the procedures in the previous sections. Remember to remove the files you don't need. Add any drivers you need to the floppy. For example, if you need a soundboard driver, you'll need to include it as part of the floppy disk. Create AUTOEXEC.BAT and CONFIG.SYS files that install and configure the drivers as needed for your game.

After you create the boot floppy, install the game on a DOS partition on your hard drive. You must use a DOS partition because the boot floppy doesn't understand NTFS. Configure the game as needed for the driver settings on the boot floppy. It might take a few tries to get the boot floppy and the game to work together, but generally you can do it in a few tries.

On Your Own

If you're having problems getting a piece of hardware or software to work, check your hard drive for an AUTOEXEC.BAT or CONFIG.SYS file. More often than not, the problem with an older piece of software is that it can't find what it needs in the operating system environment. The settings in an AUTOEXEC.BAT or CONFIG.SYS file are important to the application, so you need to find a way to satisfy that need. The "AUTOEXEC.BAT and CONFIG.SYS Don't Count Any More" section, earlier in this chapter, provides plenty of ideas you can use to resolve problems.

Open the Environment Variable dialog box. See which entries the user and system fields contain. Are there any interesting entries? Do you see any entries you need to change to make your system operate better? Are there any old entries you don't need any longer?

If you have older games or educational software you've been wanting to run, but haven't been able to use under other versions of Windows, give Windows XP a try. We've discussed a number of ways to create a compatible environment for even the oldest software in this chapter. Although none of these techniques comes with a guarantee of success, there's a high probability that one of them will provide the key to gaining access to that older software on your machine.

DOS disks are important because they enable you to run older software or to access diagnostic programs. You also need a DOS disk to perform certain tasks, such as flashing the Flash ROM on your machine during an update. *Flashing* is the process of copying the new BIOS code from your floppy to the Flash ROM. It's a delicate task you must perform in the simple environment provided by DOS in most cases.

Software Problems

It would be nice to say that Windows XP takes care of every problem and that you'll never experience any kind of software error ever again—but that wouldn't be reality. Windows XP does provide a level of safety you've probably never seen. From a security standpoint, it's much better than Windows 9x. If an application is so misbehaved that Windows XP can't find a compatibility mode for it, Windows XP kills it immediately. In four months of extensive application testing, I didn't encounter a single general protection fault (GPF) or system crash under Windows XP—either the application would run or it wouldn't.

Let's take a quick look again at Windows XP versus Windows 9x. When you look at Windows 9x, you're seeing the middle ground of reliability, not the best there is. Microsoft had to make some concessions to allow any legacy programs you used under Windows 3.x to run under Windows 9x as well. In addition, there was a problem getting enough security built into a package that must run in 8MB to 16MB of RAM. Space constraints make it difficult to take care of every kind of software-integrity problem. Windows XP requires more resources than Windows 9x. However, Windows XP uses much of the extra RAM to keep your machine from crashing when running marginal software.

> **Note:** Windows XP does do a much better job of running marginal software than Windows NT/2000 did. I was surprised at the number of games I was able to run. However, there are still many limitations to what you can expect to run under Windows XP, for the reasons discussed in the preceding paragraphs.

I tested Windows XP thoroughly while writing this book. I've changed the Registry and tested what will and won't work. Setup also got a good workout as I added and removed applications. I even changed the network setup quite a few times to test different configurations. If Windows XP ever had a good reason to crash, it was while I kept changing its configuration. During this time, I didn't experience a single application-related crash (contrasted with about one per day with Windows 9x when I did a similar level of testing on it).

However, I did experience several device-driver-related crashes, one of which made my machine unusable. The culprits were old device drivers that Windows XP isn't equipped to run. It definitely pays to get hardware that includes device drivers designed to run under this new operating system. Fortunately, device driver problems are normally a one-time issue. Installing a new device driver usually fixes the problem permanently, unlike the myriad of application-specific crashes you experience when using Windows 9x.

The bottom line is that Windows XP is a better operating system than previous versions of Windows, but it isn't a perfect operating system. Somewhere along the way, you'll run into an application, device driver, or service that causes problems with Windows XP. In fact, that's one of the reasons that Microsoft has increased the requirements for both device driver signing and the Windows XP logo program—to ensure that you run into fewer compatibility problems.

The next few sections cover some of the problems you'll experience from a software perspective. I'll also tell you about some of the fixes that Microsoft provides to solve them. Will those fixes always work? Probably not. Fortunately, the fixes in this chapter always work. I can't say the same thing for Windows 9x. During one incident, I had to reinstall Windows 9x and all my applications because an application trashed the Registry beyond recognition. The application decided to overwrite some files that would have been fine under Windows 3.x but not under Windows 9x. Suffice it to say you'll experience fewer problems under Windows XP. The cures Microsoft provides work most of the time, but thinking they'll cure every problem isn't realistic.

Startup and Configuration Errors

Configuration problems normally manifest themselves in several ways. The most devastating problems occur during system startup. Have you ever seen the infamous blue screen that appears when something strange happens to the machine? (You may see a black screen instead of the infamous blue screen, in some cases, but the effect is the same.) If you reconfigure your machine as often as I do, you'll definitely see it. Fortunately, Windows XP is much less prone to this problem than Windows 9x. During similar periods of the same types of configuration changes (those required to write a book), Windows XP displayed the blue screen of death only one time. Windows 9x displayed it four times. (Still, even that's an admirable record, considering what I put it through.)

> **Tip:** The blue-screen problem relates to errors in Kernel mode. Applications don't cause blue screens; drivers, OS components, and system services cause them. Applications tend to cause Dr. Watson errors, commonly called general protection faults (GPFs). If you see a blue screen, it's time to look carefully in the event logs and other areas mentioned in this chapter in search of a driver problem.

The other types of configuration problems are much more devious. They usually rob your system of its flexibility or make some of its components unusable. You'll find yourself running in circles trying to identify the culprit, only to find that the problem wasn't any of the things you suspected.

One of the problems I found in this category was my soundboard. I couldn't figure out what was wrong. The MIDI Balance setting kept getting out of whack. I looked at the driver—no luck. The same held true with the hardware itself. I thought there might be a problem in the way the CD software was working, so I disabled it. No luck there, either. After several days of searching, I found that the problem occurred only when I ran a particular multimedia program. Problems such as these can really make you want to pull your hair out.

Don't get the idea that configuration problems are always obvious. It's pretty easy to figure out when your soundboard isn't working correctly especially with my previous problems. Even my neighbors knew I had a problem with my soundboard. In some cases, you'll run into a problem like the one I ran into with another application. It would work just fine—at least, just fine on most days. What would happen on the other days is almost indescribable. My machine would make a strange noise, the screen would look funny, and then one or more of my applications would just disappear. (The same problem under Windows 9x caused the system to reboot; disappearing applications are better than a reboot and are a testimony to Windows XP's power to maintain control of the system even during serious perturbation.) I couldn't figure out what was going on. The solution to this problem turned out to be a Control Panel setup problem. One of my applications had overwritten the standard ODBC files. The new files were incompatible with this application in certain low-memory situations. I discovered that the problem always occurred when I had my word processor or any other large application open.

> **Tip:** I could have experienced much less grief fixing the ODBC file problem if I had recorded the time stamp for the files in that section or, at least, made note of the time stamp for my Windows XP files. You can do the same thing. Throughout this book, I've made every effort to tell you the files that affect specific functions. You can use this information when you're troubleshooting. It also comes in handy when you're recording information for a setup that works. When you get into a situation in which the setup no longer works properly, one of the things you can do is go back to your notes to find a potential source of trouble.

As you can tell, I've had lots of fun digging up these real-life problems for you to learn about. The next few sections describe some of the types of problems you'll run into when your machine runs into configuration problems. I'll also provide you with some ideas on how to fix these problems.

Startup Problems

We've already looked at one method for solving startup problems in the "Windows XP Boot Options" section of Chapter 23. Using the boot options enables you to start your machine in such a way that it's easier to locate startup problems. For example, you could use Safe mode to start your machine with just the basic drivers to see if the problem relates to a specific area of your machine.

A second approach that's more efficient, in some situations, is to look at the Event Viewer, shown in Figure 24.1. Any warning or error message is suspect, and you should check it out. You find the Event Viewer in the Administrative Tools folder of the Control Panel (Start | Settings | Control Panel). If there's a device conflict, Windows XP will report it in the Event Viewer's System log during the boot process.

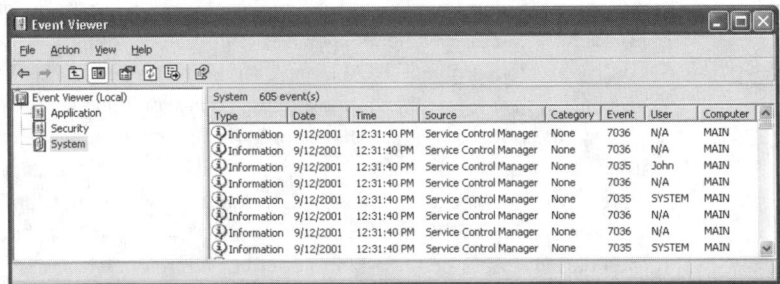

FIGURE 24.1

Use the Event Viewer to find boot problems on your machine.

Event Viewer watches the memory allocation of the drivers and services at startup. Of course, you could do this even before entering fail-safe mode, as long as the system doesn't "go blue screen." In addition, if a blue screen appears, the first and most direct method of determining the problem is to read the blue screen. It can be a bit cryptic, but you can at least figure out which driver caused the problem. After that, search Microsoft's TechNet (http://www.microsoft.com/technet/default.asp) to figure out who owns the driver.

As a final note, remember that SYSTEM.INI, WIN.INI, AUTOEXEC.BAT, and CONFIG.SYS have almost nothing to do with Windows XP. Windows XP leaves the two INI files and the other two startup files for compatibility, but most of their settings are translated by Windows XP into Registry settings. You can look at these four startup files using Start | Run and then typing SYSEDIT or MSCONFIG.

Hardware Configuration Problems

Hardware-specific configuration problems can become an extremely complex issue under Windows XP, but you can do a few things to make life a bit easier. The first thing you should do is to view the logs in the Event Viewer. Normally, it displays a message for each device that doesn't start. If you see two devices that didn't start, it's certain that you have a conflict between them, not a failure of one of them.

Figure 24.2 shows a typical log entry from the Event Viewer display (you can see Event Viewer in Figure 24.1). The Event Properties dialog box shows the detailed description of one of the entries—normally, this text tells you what went wrong with the device's initialization and gives you a starting place for troubleshooting. I discussed the mechanics of using the Event Viewer in the "Using Event Viewer" section of Chapter 7, so I don't cover them again here.

FIGURE 24.2

Hardware conflicts can become a thorny issue under Windows XP; Event Viewer at least gives you a place to look.

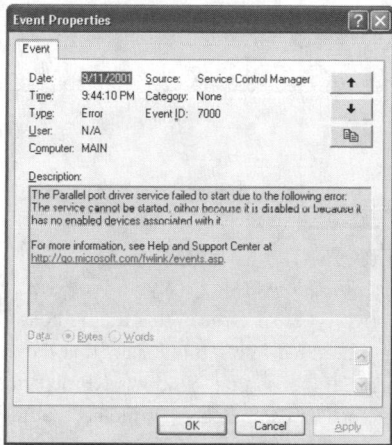

Note: Although Event Viewer does an exceptionally good job of recording events during normal Windows XP operation and a good job of recording startup events, it does a terrible job of recording shutdown events. The reason is that Windows XP normally stops recording events soon after you shut the system down. This action enables Windows XP to ensure the event logs are closed. If you see a blue screen during the shutdown process, it's likely that you won't see an associated entry in the Event Viewer. In this case, make detailed notes of the problem from the blue screen and attempt to contact the vendor about the problem. Theoretically, blue-screen problems are less important during shutdown, but you still don't want to ignore them. Every problem on your machine is important enough to check, even those that seem unlikely to cause problems later.

The Event log normally records every kind of hardware failure that's the result of an actual failure or some kind of conflict. In some situations, however, Windows XP doesn't record a problem. What happens if you've installed a new device, for example, but it doesn't actually get started? Double-click the System applet in the Control Panel, choose the Hardware tab, and click the Device Manager button. You'll see a dialog box similar to the one shown in Figure 24.3.

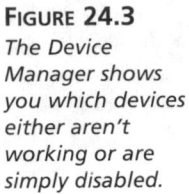

FIGURE 24.3
The Device Manager shows you which devices either aren't working or are simply disabled.

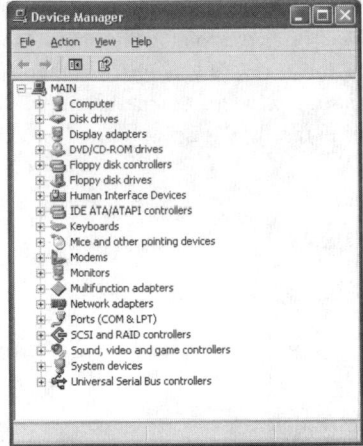

All of the devices on my machine are working, so you don't see any errors in Figure 24.3. However, you can see two types of error in this dialog box. The first has a question mark with an exclamation point added to it—this means that the device isn't working for some reason. In most cases, it means that Windows XP detected the device, but was incapable of finding a driver for it. In some cases, it means that the driver you provided doesn't work with Windows XP. In still other cases, it means that the device failed.

Whatever the cause of failure, you can double-click the device entry to get further information about fixing the problem. The Device Status field on the General tab of the Device Properties dialog box contains a message describing the problem. It also contains an error code that might help technical support staff. Finally, this dialog box contains a Troubleshoot button you can click if you want to try Microsoft's Help and Support diagnostics to fix the problem.

The second error entry type has a question mark with a red X on it—this means that the device is disabled. You must manually disable a device because Windows XP never automatically disables it for you. Enabling a device is as simple as changing the Device Usage field on the General tab of the Device Properties dialog box.

Windows NT/2000 users are familiar with the Services applet found in the Administrative Tools folder of the Control Panel. In the past, this applet would have listed all drivers for your machine; now it lists only the services your machine provides, as shown in Figure 24.4. However, the lack or inclusion of a service on your machine can affect how the hardware runs. For example, the Print Spooler service provides background printing support for any printers attached to your machine.

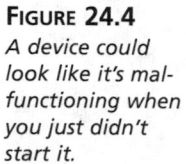

Figure 24.4
A device could look like it's malfunctioning when you just didn't start it.

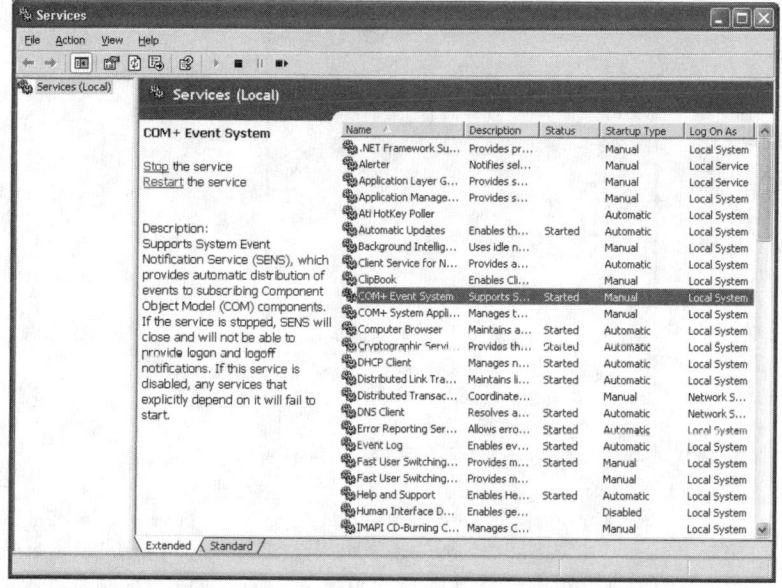

The information in Figure 24.4 might look a little complex at first, but it's relatively easy to understand. Obviously, the first entry you look for is the service name and associated description. The next thing you should look for is a Started entry in the Status column. A blank tells you that the device is stopped, paused, or otherwise unusable. This is where you figure out whether a service will start. Just highlight the device you want to test and then click the Start the Service link. If the device doesn't start, look in the Event Viewer for a potential cause of the problem. On the other hand, if it does start, you might have to look at the device starting mode, which is listed in the Startup Type column of the Service dialog box.

Changing the Startup Type setting for a service is easy. Just double-click the service entry, and you'll see a Service Properties dialog box, like the one shown in Figure 24.5. The Startup Type field of this dialog box enables you to modify the way the service gets started during the Windows XP boot process.

As previously mentioned, Windows NT provided both device and service support through this one utility. Windows 2000/XP needs to provide only service support, so there are fewer startup modes than before. You need to select one of the three starting modes described here for the various services installed on your machine:

- *Automatic* These are services, such as the print spooler, that you need every time you start your machine. Set any service that the system will use every time you start your machine to Automatic. This includes services attached to a specific class of hardware. For example, if you have a smart card attached to your machine, you'll want to set the Smart Card and Smart Card Helper services to automatic. The default setting is manual.

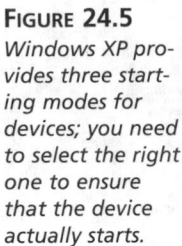

FIGURE 24.5
Windows XP provides three starting modes for devices; you need to select the right one to ensure that the device actually starts.

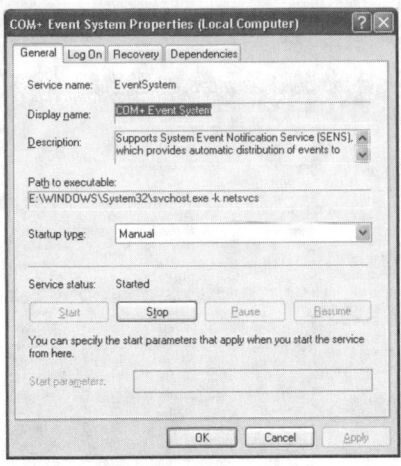

- *Manual* Some services don't get started every time Windows XP starts. This is especially true of services, such as Windows Installer, that you don't use every time you start the machine. Some hardware-related services fall into this category (although they're admittedly fewer than other service types). For example, you might have some special data-gathering device on your machine or a special hardware feature that's not essential to system operation. You can place either one of these devices (and the services that support them) in the Manual category. Dependent devices—those that rely on another device to start them—also fall into this category.

- *Disabled* This is a special setting for services that are installed on your machine but that you don't use. Windows XP can't start a disabled service, even if you try to start it from the Services dialog box. In most cases, you never disable a service unless you're tuning your system and are certain that you won't need the service. Windows XP does use this setting for services it installed, but didn't implement. For example, it always installs the Routing and Remote Access service, but leaves the service in the disabled state until you need routing or remote access services.

Windows Software Configuration Problems

A Windows application configuration can go wrong in many ways. I recently installed an older, 16-bit application that required Program Manager in order to install properly. For whatever reason, the setup application didn't signal its need for Program Manager, and I thought that the installation was a success.

Quite the contrary, the setup program had actually quit before it completed the installation, so I was missing an important INI file. The result was a piece of software that kept freezing; fortunately, Windows XP continued running. I fixed the problem by manually creating and installing the required INI file. The moral of the story is to install any old 16-bit Windows applications with the assumption that they may not work because of simple installation problems rather than application incompatibility with Windows XP. That way, you avoid any problems.

Other Windows application problems can arise as well. Have you ever noticed how many applications want to modify your path statement in AUTOEXEC.BAT? Unfortunately, if the application actually does modify AUTOEXEC.BAT, the settings it needs don't appear under Windows XP. You must set up the path in the System Environment Variables section of the System Properties dialog box (you access it by right-clicking My Computer and choosing Properties from the context menu). Of course, even intercepting these settings and making them by hand in place of the program can cause problems. If you let every application have its way, you'll probably have a mile-long path. Many applications run just fine without a path statement. However, an application can fail in two ways.

Typically, if an application is adjusting AUTOEXEC.BAT, it's a DOS or Windows 3.1 application. In these cases, when the application starts, Windows XP runs AUTOEXEC.BAT as part of creating the DOS session, and it adds application-specific path information to the PATH statement for that session. You can also configure the system to allow for individual paths based on the shortcuts. You can have Windows XP run a batch file ahead of the application to ensure that all those DOS settings get made ahead of the application starting.

I ran across the first problem area by accident: I added the file association required for a new application I installed. Whenever I double-clicked a data file, however, I got a message that the application couldn't find the data file. The application started just fine, but didn't load the data file. After a few hours of troubleshooting, I found that I could get rid of the problem by adding the application's location to my path.

Some applications fail in a big way if you don't add them to the path statement. CA-Visual Objects and some other large applications fall into this category. They usually provide some nebulous error message and quit before you can get them going—either that, or the application loads and then refuses to load any add-ons because it can't find them. You might see symptoms of this problem when an application can't remember any customizations or options you specify. Whenever you're in doubt, try adding the application to your path statement to see whether the problem goes away.

Shared-file (such as DLL) corruption is another problem area. The DLL might not actually contain any bad data—it might work just fine with several other applications. One application might require an older version of the DLL, however, because it uses an undocumented feature of that DLL or uses some bug to its advantage. Sometimes, you need to keep the old version of a DLL on disk to satisfy the needs of a particular application.

However, what happens if one application needs the new version of the DLL and another application requires the old version? In that case, you must decide which of these two applications to keep. In most cases, I use this situation as an excuse to upgrade my software. There usually isn't any reason to keep an old application around if it refuses to work with all your newer applications. In fact, an incompatibility of this type usually means that it really is time to retire that old application and get the newer version.

> **Tip:** A few applications look for the DLLs they need in their home directory before they look in the Windows XP system directory. If you have an application that needs an old DLL to run, try placing the DLL in the home directory of the program. The problem with this approach is that Windows loads only one copy of a DLL at a time into memory. This means that you have to reboot the machine after using the old application in order to clear the old DLL from memory.

I ran into a strange problem with one application on my machine. This was a communications program, but I imagine that the same thing could happen with any application. Every time I tried to open this application, it filled the screen—and then some. No matter what I did, as soon as the main application window appeared, the machine froze and I had to reboot. As it turned out, I discovered that the problem happened after lowering the screen resolution to capture some screen shots for this book. This is yet another example of an application that failed because its environment wasn't set up correctly.

The point I'm trying to make is that the cause of failure isn't always obvious. You usually need to spend some time looking for the potential cause of a problem. Some of these causes can lead you down blind alleys into places you thought would never fail. You can also deal with this kind of problem by pressing Ctrl+Alt+Delete, choosing Task Manager, and then clicking End Task after selecting the offending program from the list of running applications.

Memory-Related Problems

You can face quite a few memory-related problems under Windows XP, and these fall into several categories. It's important to know which one you're dealing with before you attempt to fix the problem. The following list categorizes the various memory-related problems you could have when using Windows XP. Go through the list to see whether you can find the symptoms that match your particular problem:

- *Memory leaks*   A few Windows applications don't manage memory properly. They grab lots of memory from Windows and then don't release all of it when they terminate. The result is a gradual loss of memory capacity that you can actually track by using the Memory field of the application's Help About dialog box. You'll also notice that your other applications start to slow down after a while as the system starts using a larger swap file to make up for the memory loss. If you have an application that shows a gradual loss of memory, the best way to use it is to start it once and then leave it open the entire time you need to use it. Such an application still gradually bleeds memory from the system, but the loss is more gradual if you don't open and close it very much. Eventually, you need to reboot the machine to regain the memory; just restarting Windows doesn't do the trick. You actually need to restart the system from scratch (a cold reboot, so-called because you must turn off the power and then turn it back on). Logging data to the

Performance console is an alternative approach. See the "Checking Performance" section of Chapter 5 for more information on how to using the Performance console. Also, try looking at the Task Manager's Performance tab, which shows you an overall picture of memory usage graphically, although the change in memory usage might be quite gradual.

Note: Microsoft is working on a solution for the memory-leak problem. The .NET Framework helps eliminate memory leaks by providing a centralized method for managing memory. Memory management is no longer in the hands of the programmer, but rather in the hands of the .NET Framework. You'll start seeing applications that use the .NET Framework shortly after the release of Windows XP. However, developers will work on custom applications using this technology first. Eventually, everyone will have .NET applications on their system. Given the amount of time that old Windows 3.x applications have stuck around, I have no doubt that you'll also continue seeing applications with memory leaks well into the future.

- *Too many frills*   Some types of memory problems are created when you have too many frills on your machine. You might find that Microsoft Access or another large application is running very slowly or could even produce GPFs more often after you add a screen saver or another frill to the system. Most people think that utilities have small memory requirements, but this isn't necessarily true. A utility generally accomplishes a more limited, narrowly defined set of tasks than a full-fledged application. However, you shouldn't assume that, because the utility is more limited in its focus, it's necessarily limited in its memory requirements. DOS utilities had to stay small to keep their conventional-memory requirements to a minimum, but Windows utilities have no such limitation. Their designers have fewer reasons to keep their applications small because Microsoft designed Windows to allow for better memory management. In addition, machines generally have much more memory these days.

- *Windows system space corruption*   I find it incredible that some vendors put so little effort into testing their products that this type of problem could actually go unnoticed. The situation that usually happens is that an errant pointer in the application starts overwriting the Windows system memory area. Most of the time, Windows XP detects this problem and displays an appropriate warning dialog box. In fact, I've never actually seen this problem myself, but a few people have reported seeing it. Windows XP always recovers by terminating the application. On a few occasions, Windows XP doesn't detect the problem until it's too late and half its "brain" is gone; then it just freezes. In most cases, you want to contact the vendor about this kind of problem and see whether a workaround or fix is available.

- *Disk thrashing*   If you try to use an application your system can't really support, you might experience something called *disk thrashing*. You know that your system is thrashing if the hard disk light stays on for abnormally long periods and an application runs slowly. Probably the best way to fix this problem is to add more memory (remember that memory is now relatively inexpensive). Of course, you can also look at some of the memory-saving techniques discussed in Chapter 5.

- *Display memory corruption*   Some older Windows applications might experience problems when writing to the display. Although Windows applications use a different method to display data than DOS applications, they can cause problems with the entire display in some situations. The big problem occurs when an application leaves the display in this state even after it exits. You might see other forms of display corruption as well. It's possible for an application to corrupt the icon cache, for example. You'll see some icons on the display that no longer match the functions associated with them, or your icons might disappear altogether. The fix for this condition is to exit the application and reboot the system.

Note: You may have noticed that Windows XP uses a 16-bit minimum color display. A big reason for this is that it enables Microsoft to show off some of the new multimedia features of Windows XP. However, the change also has a basis for fixing problems with the Windows XP display system. One of these situations is when an application changes the palette (the display colors if you're using a 256-color setting or less) without regard for any other applications running on the system. A user can't do much about this problem. The application window will probably look fine, but everything around it will use strange color combinations that might produce unreadable text. Using a 16-bit color display reduces or eliminates this problem.

After you identify and clean up a memory-corruption problem, it's usually a good idea to find the application responsible. Most memory-corruption problems don't just go away. You'll find that the corruption occurs repeatedly at the worst possible moment. After you identify the culprit, you usually must contact the vendor to find out whether a fix is available. If one isn't, you need to decide whether to live with the corruption problem or get a new application, one that hopefully doesn't exhibit the same memory-corruption problem you're trying to get rid of.

So, how do you find the culprit? You can't just assume that the culprit is the foreground application; it could be a background application. For that matter, it doesn't have to be an application at all. A device driver could be causing the memory corruption as you use a specific device. A third class of problem is some type of interaction between two applications or between an application and a device driver. You have to start somewhere, however, and looking at the applications you have running is a good place to start. You can follow this simple procedure to find many, but not all, of the memory-corruption problems on your system:

1. Start a list of potential problem applications. I usually make note of all the applications I had running when a memory-corruption problem occurred. It's also important to make notes on any devices you had running. Of course, some devices are always running, so it doesn't pay to list those.

2. Run the suspected applications one at a time to see whether you can get the problem to repeat.

3. If you still don't find the culprit, go back to your normal setup and try various combinations of applications. You could be seeing some type of interaction problem.

4. Take a look at the Application Log in the Event Viewer to see whether there were any problems in loading the drivers or any conflicts in resource usage. Windows XP is very particular about who can access memory and where.

5. Keep a running list of active applications each time the memory problem appears. Eventually, you'll see a pattern of one or more applications that always seem to be around when the problem occurs. You can try loading just this group of applications and see whether you can get the problem to happen again. Keep whittling down the list until you end up with one or two applications that don't work together. The solution is to avoid running them at the same time.

This kind of testing by a process of elimination is time consuming; if you do it right, however, you can usually track down a stubborn problem without enormous difficulty. Unfortunately, memory problems are inherently difficult to locate in an environment such as Windows XP because so many things are happening simultaneously. Each application and device driver interacts. You'll find that the hardest problems to find are those that result from three or four applications or device drivers working against each other. It always pays to take your time and do a thorough job of testing each potential problem area.

Of course, when you come to a conclusion, finding a permanent fix could prove to be the most difficult part of the journey. You've probably gone through this before: the waiting on the telephone as each vendor points the finger at someone else. In reality, there might not be an easy fix for some types of memory problems; you might just have to avoid the situations that cause them in the first place. Get a newer version of the same application or even go as far as to update your hardware.

Driver-Related Problems

Microsoft is trying to fix a problem on your machine: drivers. In past versions of Windows, drivers could be the worst problem that occurred on the system. Few people understand how drivers work and certainly don't know the inner workings of the specific drivers on a machine. An errant driver could cause endless problems that technical support personnel couldn't fix. A driver problem can quickly spiral out of control and begin affecting other systems. In addition, because a driver runs at the highest privilege level, it can freeze Windows without too much effort.

We discussed earlier in this book that Microsoft uses signed drivers now to ensure that the drivers meet the highest level of quality. A signed driver is your best chance for a trouble-free system. Using all signed drivers on your machine might not ensure absolutely trouble-free operation, but it's a step in the right direction. The first solution to driver-related problems then is to find a signed copy of the appropriate Windows XP–specific driver, if possible.

I can guarantee that someone will try using a Windows 9x or Windows NT driver with Windows XP. It's almost certain that none of these drivers will work. Generally, you need to find a Windows XP–specific driver for your machine. If you can't find a Windows XP driver, some Windows 2000 drivers work, but they don't come with any guarantees.

The easiest way to tell if you have an older driver is to right-click My Computer and then choose Properties. Select Hardware in the System Properties dialog box and click Device Manager. Double-click the device in question and choose the Driver tab. Click Driver Details. You see a Driver File Details dialog box, similar to the one shown in Figure 24.6. Microsoft has signed the highlighted driver in this case. However, you'll also notice that the driver entry includes copyright, provider, and version information. You can use these statistics to determine the age of the driver.

FIGURE 24.6

Avoid using older drivers, and don't use any from Windows 9x or Windows NT.

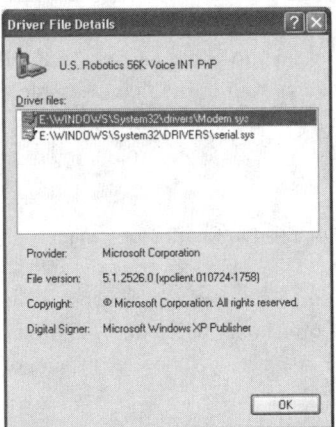

Drivers don't have an interface, in most cases, so, like many other parts of the operating system, they rely on the Event Log to tell you about problems. In most cases, a look at the Event Log will tell you which device driver is experiencing problems. In some cases, the vendor will provide you with enough details about the problem that you can fix it. In at least a few cases, the problem is a simple configuration error or a missing file. You can fix the problem easily once you know what it is.

Another problem to look for with drivers is the Device Properties dialog box. For example, your modem includes both settings and diagnostics tabs. As a fist step, make sure all of the settings for your modem are correct. After you check the settings, run the diagnostics. Vendors often attach these diagnostics to the device driver so that they can help you locate problems.

Try the non-obvious solutions too. For example, the problem might exist in the hardware. We discuss this issue in Chapter 25. In many cases, the driver simply installed incorrectly or the installer didn't follow directions properly. Try uninstalling the driver and then reinstalling it. I've never seen a vendor manual that suggested this solution, yet uninstalling and reinstalling the driver often works miracles.

Using the System Restore Utility

Windows XP includes a feature that helps you fix many of the problems we've discussed in this chapter. You can use the System Restore utility to create a snapshot of your system. The snapshot acts as a log of what you had installed at a certain point. Windows XP can use this snapshot to restore your system to a known good state.

System Restore is one of the better features of Windows XP. It provides a real benefit to anyone who has ever installed the wrong software for all of the right reasons and had it corrupt their system. The following sections tell you the details of this unique utility.

An Overview of How System Restore Works

System Restore is simple in concept, but difficult in implementation. The concept is that you create a picture or snapshot of the system at a certain point in its life by collecting every pertinent piece of data you can. This includes Registry settings, application installation lists, and a wealth of other information. In fact, knowing what to collect is one of the difficulties because you can't grab the entire hard drive in an effort to save the system. Microsoft calls the stored system snapshot a *restore point*. You can create multiple restore points to enable you to move back to a previous version of the system.

The system also creates restore points when certain events occur. For example, every time you install a new driver, Windows XP creates a snapshot of the system before it installs any new files. The restore point enables you to remove the new device if something unexpected happens. The system also creates a restore point when you install low-level software, such as a new network driver.

Windows XP will automatically use the restore point if you can't start the system and choose to use the last known good system configuration for booting the system. You can manually use restore points to reconfigure the system as well. The System Restore utility enables you to create new restore points as well as to use existing restore points. As I said, the entire concept is simple, but the implementation details can become quite difficult.

Some people expect System Restore to perform miracles. The first rule you have to remember is that System Restore can create a snapshot of your system, but it can't re-create every aspect of your system. Snapshots record only what the camera can see. Likewise, restore points contain only the information that Windows XP deemed important at the time.

The second rule to remember is that System Restore corrects only settings. In other words, if an application creates new Registry keys, System Restore might not remove them. You might also see files lingering after System Restore completes its tasks. However, System Restore will return your system to a previous state, which means that it will be successful in restoring system operation in almost every case.

Creating a Restore Point

When you start System Restore, you'll see a wizard with two options. The first enables you to restore your system to a known good state, while the second helps you create a restore point. This section discusses the method of creating a restore point for future use. The following steps show you how. I assume that you've already started System Restore:

1. Select Create a Restore Point and then click Next. You'll see a dialog box that asks you to enter a restore point description. It's important to say something about the restore point so that you can identify it later. For example, "Restore point created before installing the XYZ Widget driver." is an example of a great comment. Using "This is my restore point." is an example of a useless comment.

2. Type a description and then click Create. System Restore will grind away for a few moments. After a while, it will display a success message that includes all of the information about your restore point.

3. Click Close.

That's all there is to creating a restore point. It takes only a few seconds to use this utility, and you'll be glad you did when an installation goes wrong.

Restoring the System Normally

At some point, you'll need to use the insurance policy you created using restore points. System Restore helps you restore the system to a known good shape by asking a few questions and then using the contents of a restore point to make the required changes. In many cases, you'll be ahead of the game if you can uninstall the software that has caused problems before you use System Restore. However, System Restore will work under most conditions. The following steps assume that you've already started System Restore:

1. Select Restore My Computer to an Earlier Time. Click Next. You'll see a Select a Restore Point dialog box, like the one shown in Figure 24.7. The calendar on the left contains a date in bold for every restore point created by the system. The entries on the right contain restore points created on the selected date. To choose a restore point, you need to select both the date and the proper entry for that date.

Note: System-generated restore points have a plain entry entitled System Checkpoint. This is one of the reasons you want to maintain a log of system activity. The descriptions provided by the system are useless, so you need a secondary source of information to use these restore points.

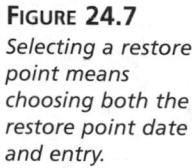

FIGURE 24.7
Selecting a restore point means choosing both the restore point date and entry.

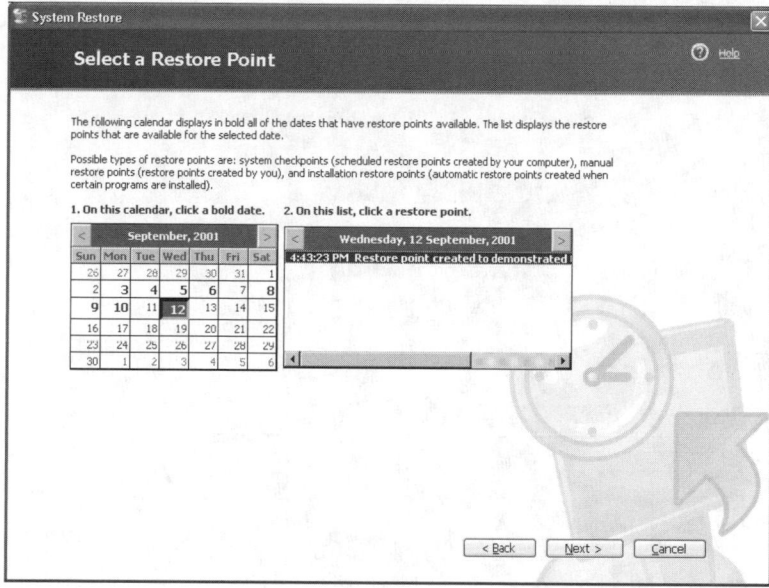

2. Select one of the restore point entries from the list and then click Next. You'll see a Confirm Restore Point Selection dialog box. Make sure that you double-check the entry because this is your last chance to change your mind before the restore takes place. You must close all applications before you begin the restore process. It also helps to close as many icons in the Notification Area of the Taskbar before you begin.

3. Click Next. System Restore will require a few seconds to gather information about your machine. You'll see the system shut down. A System Restore dialog box will appear with a progress indicator that shows the restoration progress. The system will reboot.

4. Start the logon process as normal. Your system may require additional boot time. After your system reboots and you log on, you'll see a Restoration Complete dialog box, which contains details about the restoration process. It also contains additional instructions about other options you might have.

5. Click OK to complete the restoration process. Your system will finish booting. If you didn't choose the correct restore point, you can always make another selection.

Changing the BOOT.INI Options

BOOT.INI contains the boot options for your system. Normally, you'll configure this file from within Windows XP. However, because this is a text file, you can also configure it using a text editor. Exercise caution if you use the manual technique because it's easy to damage this file and make your system unbootable.

To edit your BOOT.INI file from within Windows XP, right-click My Computer and choose Properties. Select Advanced on the System Properties dialog box and click Settings in the Startup and Recover section of the Advanced tab. You'll see a Startup and Recover dialog box, similar to the one shown in Figure 24.8.

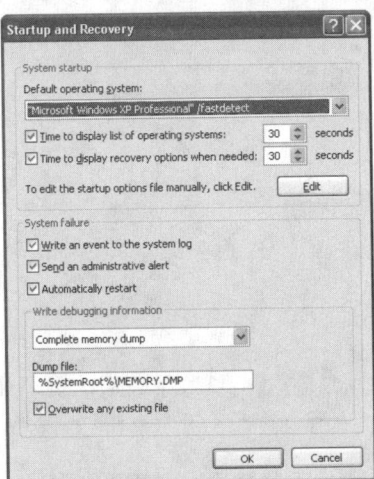

FIGURE 24.8
The Startup and Recovery dialog box enables you to make changes to BOOT.INI.

The settings you want to use appear in the System Startup section. The Default Operating System field contains a list of bootable operating systems on your machine; at least, the ones that Windows XP recognizes. For example, you don't see your Linux installation in this field. The operating system you see in this field is the one that Boot Manager will start automatically if you don't select an operating system within the specified time.

The next option determines whether Boot Manager assigns a time interval to make an operating selection and tells how long it will wait. Generally, it's a good idea to select this option so that the system doesn't wait too long to get started while you get a cup of coffee in the morning.

The third option determines whether Boot Manager displays recovery options for a set amount of time and tells how long Boot Manager will wait for a selection. Again, you want to choose a value so that the system isn't waiting to make a decision. However, you might want to make this setting longer so that the user has time to make a selection. In many cases, the user requires a longer period because the system is down and the user is nervous.

If you click Edit, you'll see the text settings displayed in Notepad or another text editor. Figure 24.9 shows a typical view of the BOOT.INI settings. As you can see, it's easier to change these settings using the options in the Startup and Recovery dialog box.

FIGURE 24.9

*The text form of
the BOOT.INI file.*

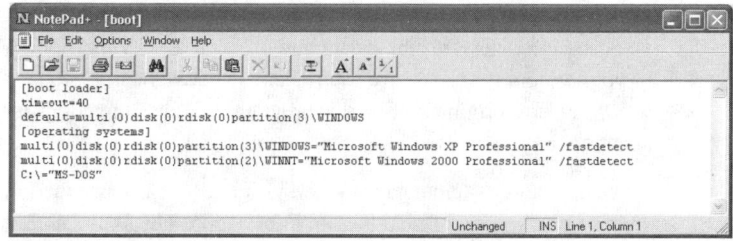

Microsoft System Information Utility

System Information has been around in one form or another for many years. Originally, Microsoft called the product Microsoft Diagnostics (MSD). Microsoft then renamed it WinMSD to reflect a change to a graphical interface. Today, we call an updated form of the same utility System Information. The System Information moniker is actually more accurate than calling this utility a diagnostic. It tells you details about your system, but doesn't tell you that anything is wrong with it.

When you first start System Information, it displays a summary of you system configuration. Figure 24.10 shows the initial display for this application for my machine. Notice that you receive detailed information about your system from the very beginning. However, the utility can provide details at an even greater level. All you need to do is select one of the four categories of information that System Information can provide.

FIGURE 24.10

*System Infor-
mation provides
in-depth informa-
tion about your
computer.*

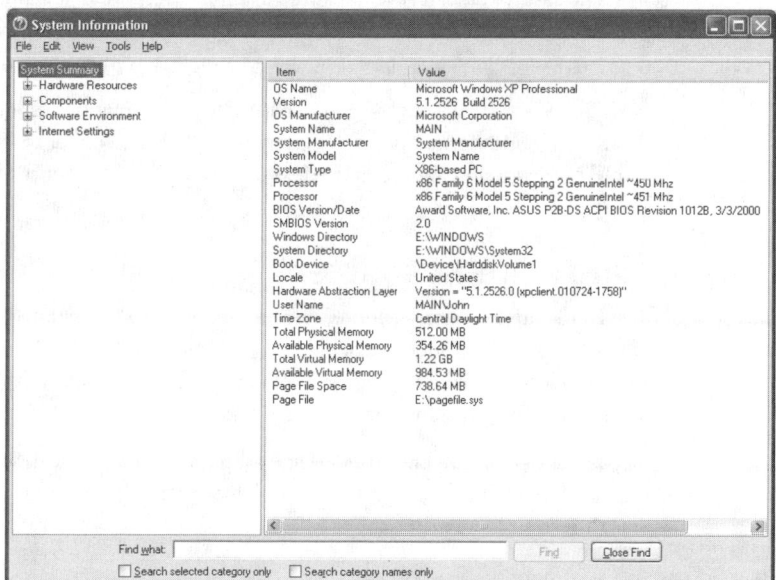

Generally, you'll use System Information to view the status of your machine. However, you can also export this information to a file on disk. This is one way to take a snapshot of your system state and save it for later use in diagnosing problems. In fact, this is the way Microsoft originally used this program. It allows the company to collect information about your system to aid in problem resolution.

You can export system data in two ways. First, you can use the File | Export command to create a text version of your system information. This is the most convenient way to transfer the information to a database for later analysis. Second, you can use the File | Save command to create a file on disk. This file has an NFO extension that permits you to view the file within System Information later. This is the best way to store data if you simply want a snapshot of your system for later use.

> **Tip:** The NFO files that System Information creates use XML. In some cases, this format might be better for importing the data into your database. Of course, the database has to know how to interpret the XML file. Many new database managers and associated languages use XML as a common form of data exchange, so you'll find that this method works better than straight text.

Like many other Windows XP utilities, System Information has a command-line interface. Type MSINFO /? to display a complete list of the current switches. The switches you commonly want to use within a script include those that output system data to disk in silent mode. You can save a text file using the /Report <Filename> switch. Likewise, you can produce an NFO file using the /Info <Filename> switch. You can even switch to a remote computer using the /Computer <Computer Name> switch.

Now that you have a better idea of what System Information can do, let's discus a few details. System Information uses a hierarchical format, similar to the one in Windows Explorer. The following sections tell you about each of the entries in the display shown in Figure 24.10.

Hardware Resources

The Hardware Resource section, shown in Figure 24.11, contains a complete list of hardware resources for your machine. You can use these lists to look for missing or misconfigured hardware. This list also tells you about hardware conflicts (two devices using the same resource) and shows free resources that aren't used by any hardware.

The Forced Hardware entry is especially important because it shows hardware that someone has forced to nonstandard settings on the system. This could point to a problem that wasn't resolved—just sidestepped.

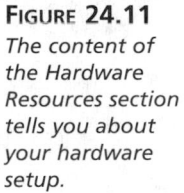

FIGURE 24.11
The content of the Hardware Resources section tells you about your hardware setup.

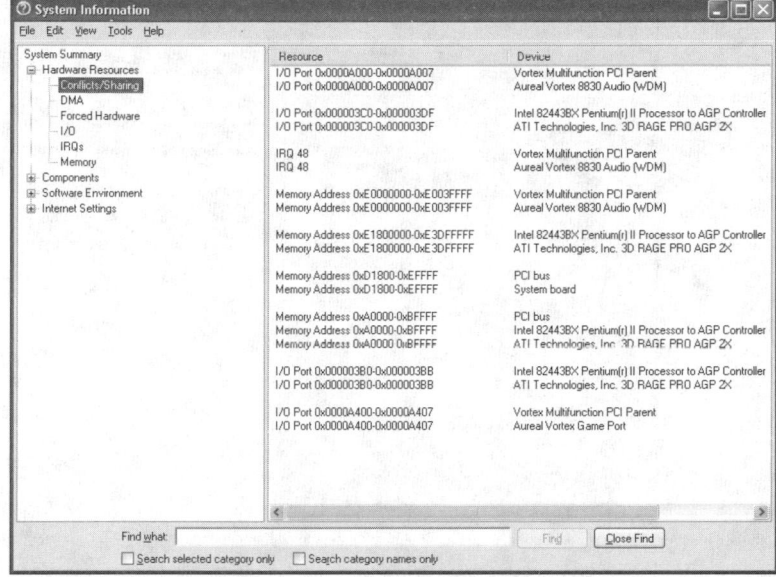

Components

The Components folder, shown in Figure 24.12, describes the individual components of your system. For example, if you select the CD-ROM option, System Information will query your CD and DVD drives for vendor specifics. It will also test the drives and tell you about device characteristics, such as data-transfer rates. Some of the entries shown in Figure 24.12 have additional subentries. For example, you'll generally find two selections under the Input entry: Keyboard and Mouse.

Software Environment

The Software Environment folder, shown in Figure 24.13, contains entries describing every running application on your machine. You'll find entries for applications, services, and drivers.

Notice from Figure 24.13 that System Information differentiates between signed and system drivers. The System Driver entry lists all drivers on your machine, signed or not. The information you receive varies. For example, if you select Services, System Information will tell you if the service is started or stopped, the Start mode, and the kind of service you're viewing.

Internet Settings

The Internet Settings folder, shown in Figure 24.14, contains a list of Internet settings for your machine. More specifically, you'll find information about Internet Explorer under this entry, unless you have another browser installed.

FIGURE 24.12
The Components folder provides detailed information about each device installed on your machine.

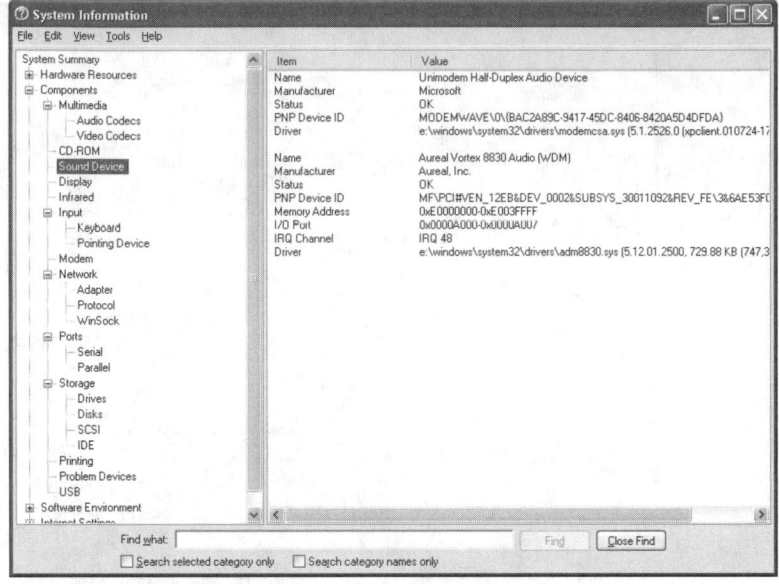

FIGURE 24.13
Use the Software Environment folder contents to learn about the software running on your machine.

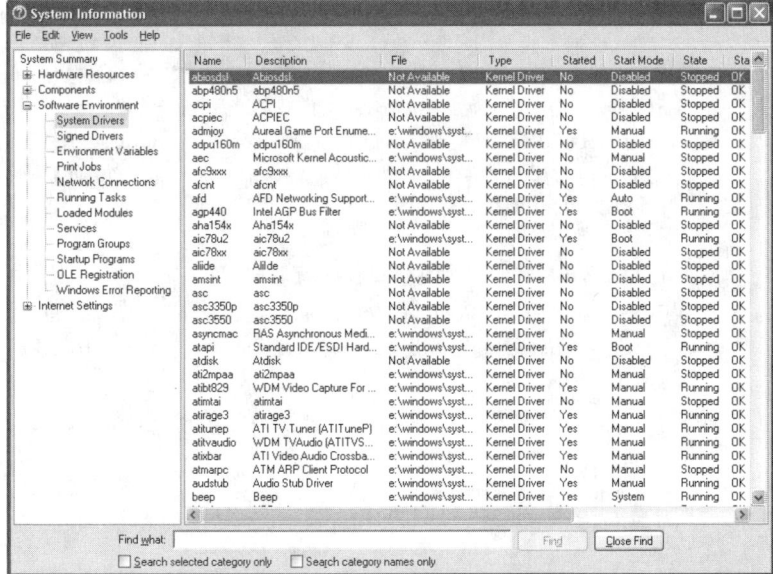

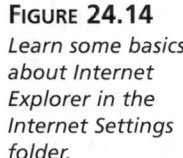

FIGURE 24.14

Learn some basics about Internet Explorer in the Internet Settings folder.

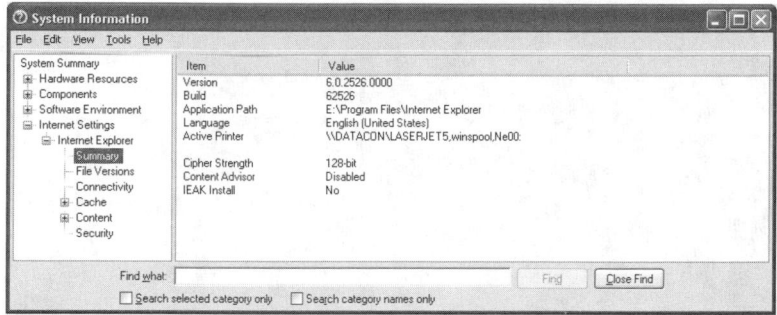

The Internet Explorer information includes facts such as driver version numbers and a few of the settings. System Information seems most interested in security levels, not in the kind of rules you set for discarding junk mail or the last place you visited online.

On Your Own

Check out the contents of the Administrative Tools folder and the System applet in the Control Panel. These two Control Panel entries contain most of the tools you need to troubleshoot your system.

Use the Device Manager, found on the Hardware tab of the System Properties dialog box, to make a list of the devices installed on your machine. (Make note of any devices that aren't operational, and do what you can to make them functional.) You can use this list as a troubleshooting aid when you experience some kind of problem. Comparing the items on your list to those that start during a crisis could help you pinpoint the source of the problem. You'll also want to note the startup mode for the device, just in case an application you install decides to change it.

Devise a recovery strategy for your machine. If you're a network administrator, devise a strategy for all the machines on the network. Keep track of this strategy, and change it as necessary to meet changing user and machine needs.

Use the solutions in the "Memory-Related Problems" section as a basis for a preemptive check of memory problems on your system. In many cases, a search for potential problems now will save you lots of time and effort later. Look at it this way: Right now you have time to perform a thorough check and take care of the problem as time permits. If your system goes offline, you have to locate and fix the problem immediate during a crisis when you don't have time to think about a solution.

Use the Microsoft System Information utility to learn more about your system. Spend time looking in the various folders to learn about the hardware and software installed on your machine. Use the file-export features of this program to create a snapshot of your system for later use.

Hardware Problems

Hardware is the physical part of your computer and includes anything you can touch. For many people, this is the forgotten part of the computer. Hardware is generally the most reliable part of your system. Although hardware problems are generally less of an issue than software problems under Windows XP (or any operating system, for that matter), they do exist. These problems usually fall into two easily recognized categories:

- *Catastrophic* You can quickly determine that a catastrophic failure has occurred because the device in question no longer works. For example, you try to access a hard or floppy drive and nothing happens, or your modem picks up the phone line but refuses to dial. Figuring out the sources of these problems is easy; fixing them is even easier (albeit expensive).

- *Compatibility* A common symptom of compatibility problems is that the device appears to have failed, but later testing shows that it hasn't. You've seen some fixes for this type of problem in Chapter 10. You'll find that these problems are easy to trace and fix under Windows XP.

In this chapter, we begin by looking at one of the tools Microsoft provides to help you fix hardware-related problems with Windows XP—*Help and Support*. Obviously, Microsoft can't anticipate every problem you'll ever have with your hardware, so we'll also look at both catastrophic and compatibility problems. This chapter will show you some of the aids at your disposal for finding and fixing these problems on your own without having to rely on technical support.

A Look at Help and Support

Help and Support contains a wealth of information, much of it hidden away. What you see in the contents isn't what you get from Help and Support as a whole. For example, when you need help troubleshooting a hardware problem, Help and Support is there to provide support. However, rather than access help through the normal Help and Support entry on the Start Menu, you access it through the Troubleshoot button in the Device Properties dialog box. (We'll learn more on this topic in the "Troubleshooting" section, later in this chapter).

The following sections contain ideas on how you can combine the information in Help and Support with other sources of information, such as the Internet. We begin with some ideas for creating a self-help strategy and move on to other areas that Help and Support contains. The final three sections look at ways to augment what you find in Help and Support. For example, many people rely on online help now to get the answers they need. In many cases, someone who has been where you are can help you solve a problem because that person understands it better.

Creating Self-Help Strategies

Sometimes, the best help strategy is the one you create for yourself. When you open Help and Support, you'll see a dialog box similar to the one shown in Figure 25.1. Although this display is friendly, you'll end up wading through layer upon layer of information in trying to find the one topic of information you really need. Using the Search field does help, but only if you know precisely what you're looking for, which isn't the case in most situations. However, one way to shorten the search time is to use the Search option.

FIGURE 25.1
Help and Support provides a friendly interface, but offers too many layers between you and the answer you need.

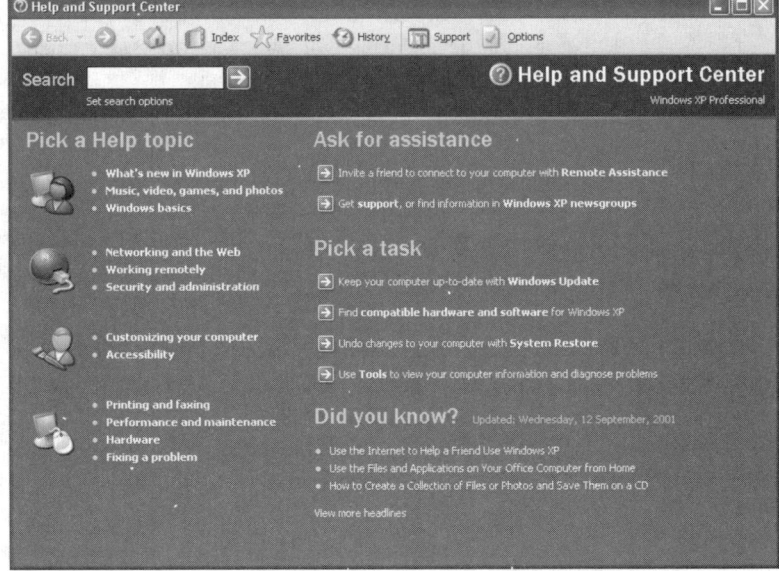

One of the features you should use is Favorites. Unlike previous versions of Windows, Windows XP offers the means to store previous locations in the Help File. The first thing you want to do, though, is create a Help folder under Favorites. Otherwise, you'll mix the Help File entries with your Web site and other entries, making everything difficult to find. Creating a Favorite for the Help File is just like creating a Favorite for Internet Explorer. You can learn more in the "Using the Favorites Folder" section of Chapter 20.

Another form of self-help is creating links to all of the Web sites you find that contain helpful Windows information. Again, you'll want to set aside a folder for all of the help information you find. In this case, I normally create a Windows folder that contains other folders to organize the information. Using a Windows folder keeps the online sites separate from the help file links. The idea is to keep the sources separate so that you know where you found a piece of information.

Newsgroups are another helpful source of information. In this case, you can't create a series of links to helpful advice in Favorites; at least, not without taking a few additional steps. You can handle this situation in two ways, both of which work great. First, you can create a new folder in Outlook Express. Now all you need to do is drag any newsgroup information you obtain into your Windows folder in Outlook Express. As with everything else in Windows XP, you can create as many levels of folders as you like. Second, you can save the newsgroup items you find to your hard drive. Once they're on your hard drive, you can open the file in Windows Explorer and add that location to your Favorites list. I suggest creating a separate area for newsgroup information downloaded to your hard drive.

It would be impossible to keep every source of information you find for Windows because Windows is a large operating system that many people use. Concentrate on the issues you need to understand most. As you learn about Windows, get rid of older information to make room for new materials. One of the folders in my filing cabinet contains clippings from trade journals and magazines. When the clippings reach a certain age, I either discard them or place the information in a permanent file. It's important to keep the information about Windows current and relevant.

Learning Through Tours and Tutorials

Everyone has to begin learning about Windows somewhere. You can use Windows for a long time without really knowing much about it, and many people work this way. As long as they can find the data or application they need, there isn't any requirement to learn more about Windows. However, the time will come when you need to know more. If nothing else, a hardware or software failure means learning something about the operating system to fix it.

Help and Support provides a tour and tutorial for Windows XP, but you might not see it right away on the main Help and Support screen, shown in Figure 25.1. Click Windows Basics. You'll see a list of Windows Basics tasks in the upper-left pane. Click Core Windows Tasks and then Customizing Your Desktop. Notice that the right pane now contains some content. Notice the Walkthrough entry at the bottom of the right pane. Click Walkthrough: Personalize Your PC and you see an image like the one shown in Figure 25.2. Help and Support has several tours and tutorials of this sort; sometimes, finding them isn't all that easy because they're buried, which is why you want to add them to your Favorites when you do find them.

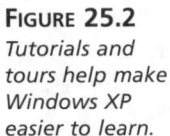

FIGURE 25.2
Tutorials and tours help make Windows XP easier to learn.

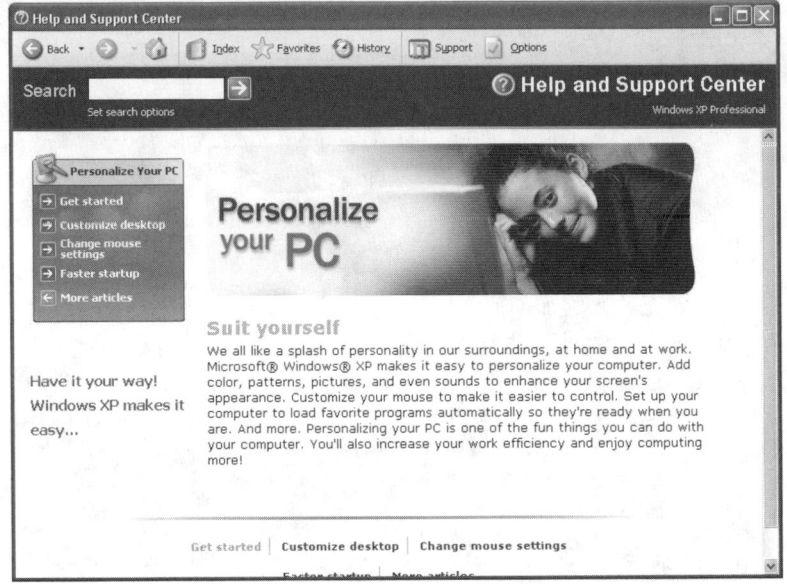

Troubleshooting

The General tab for every device on your system has a Troubleshoot button. Click that button and you'll see a copy of Help and Support open. Sometimes, the help you get is generic. For example, when I clicked Troubleshoot for my soundboard, I saw the Generic Hardware Device Troubleshooter. In short, you can't expect Help and Support to know about every device ever made. However, you can receive excellent help on some common types of hardware.

Modems are one type of hardware you can usually count on getting some help with from Windows XP. Click Troubleshoot in the Modem Properties dialog box and you'll see a dialog box like the one shown in Figure 25.3.

As you can see, Help and Support asks questions about your problems. You select the choice that best matches your situation and then click Next. After you answer enough questions (sometimes as few as one), you'll see an answer to your question, such as the one shown in Figure 25.4.

Notice that this isn't the end of the line. If this suggestion doesn't work, you can select No and click Next. You can also choose to skip the remedy if you know that it won't work. When you click Yes and press Next, Help and Support will thank you for using its services. The process does work for common problems, but it doesn't work if your device has special features or you run into an uncommon problem. Consider the troubleshooter your first choice when finding a hardware problem, but perhaps not your last. You might find that you need other forms of help.

FIGURE 25.3
You can use Help and Support to troubleshoot common hardware problems, but nothing exotic.

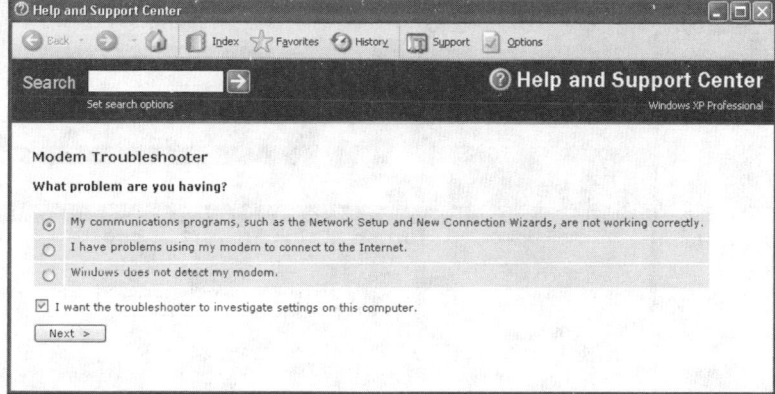

FIGURE 25.4
After you answer enough questions, Help and Support begins providing answers.

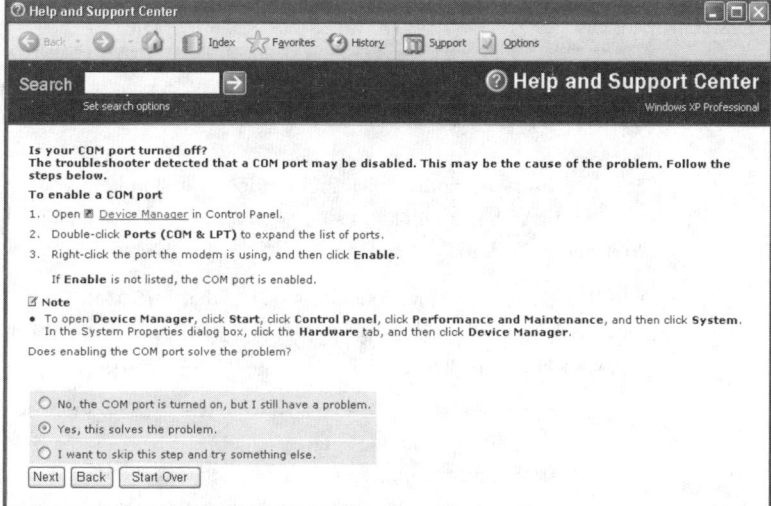

Using Web Resources

The Help and Support utility in Windows XP is only one way to find information from Microsoft. In fact, Microsoft provides a number of ways to find information. If you go to its Product Support Services Web page (`http://support.microsoft.com/directory/`), you'll see that it offers quite a few methods for gaining help. Figure 25.5 shows some of the methods available at the time of this writing. It's important to note that Microsoft is continually experimenting with other ways of providing support, so you might see something slightly different when you get online. Most of the resources we discuss in this section are constant sources of help that Microsoft always provides because they work well.

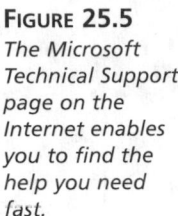

FIGURE 25.5

The Microsoft Technical Support page on the Internet enables you to find the help you need fast.

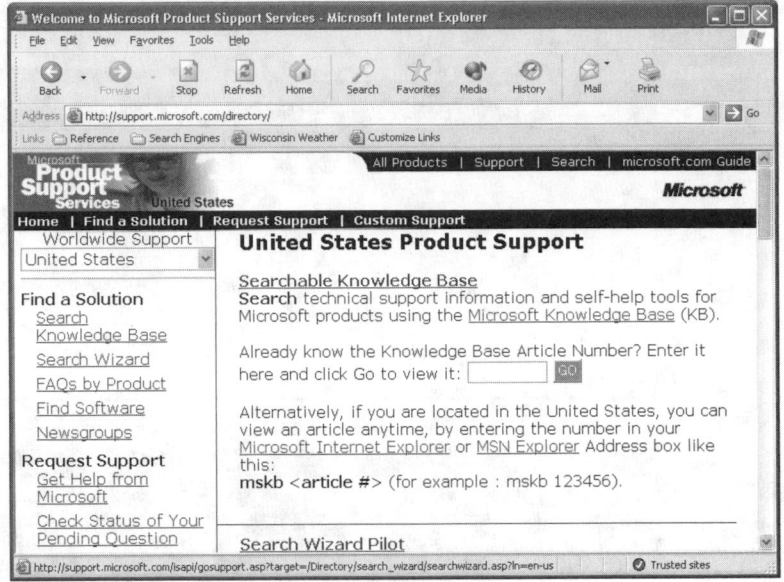

The first thing you notice is a search engine geared to help you find information on Microsoft's Web site quickly. Just type in a keyword and then click the Go button. If you do want to check the entire support site, check the Search Entire Support Site check box.

You'll also see links to various support sites that Microsoft wants to highlight for a specific reason. The following list provides you with a generalized list of some of the support sites for which you see links on a regular basis:

- *Knowledge Base* With so many Windows users in the world, the chance of finding something truly unique is fairly small. The Knowledge Base is Microsoft's method of storing all the information it has gathered about problems in the past. In many cases, you can find a solution to your problem just by searching the Knowledge Base.

- *Frequently Asked Questions* Some problems are so common that Microsoft has written a special FAQ (Frequently Asked Questions) sheet about them. In many cases, you find a solution to common problems here. If you don't find what you need, you can always look through the Knowledge Base for help.

- *Help Files* There really isn't any way to keep your local help files up-to-date because of the fast pace of change in the computer industry. However, Microsoft can at least keep pace with the change. Downloading the latest help files is one way you can ensure that you have the latest information at your fingertips and on your local hard drive.

- *Service Packs* There may or may not be a service pack available for Windows XP when you read this. You can be sure, though, that sometime in the near future

Microsoft will have to release one. A service pack could contain something as simple as new drivers for your hardware, as critical as a patch for a security problem that someone found, or as necessary as a bug fix for the operating system itself. Whatever the reason, you want to check here for the latest service packs.

- *Newsgroups* There are many experts out there who willingly share their knowledge with others through newsgroups. Going to a newsgroup and asking a question could net you the solution to a hard problem. You might also find that you could help a fellow user with a solution to his problem.

- *Telephone Numbers* Some situations call for human contact. Microsoft wants you to find the person you need to talk with as quickly as possible. This link takes you to a list of common Microsoft phone numbers.

Using Assisted Support

Sometimes, you can't solve a problem on your own. No matter what you try in the Microsoft Knowledge Base, a particular problem might prove too difficult to solve (or it may be that no one has encountered the problem before and you need special help to get it resolved). That's when you need to contact a support engineer.

Clicking the Get Help From Microsoft link in the main Product Support Service Web site, shown in Figure 25.5, takes you to an intermediate Web page where Microsoft will ask about your location. Select a location and then click Go. You'll see the Web site shown in Figure 25.6. As you can see, you can use this site to make a request, find telephone numbers for calling Microsoft, or report a bug.

FIGURE 25.6
You can use these entries to get support from Microsoft or to report a bug in a product.

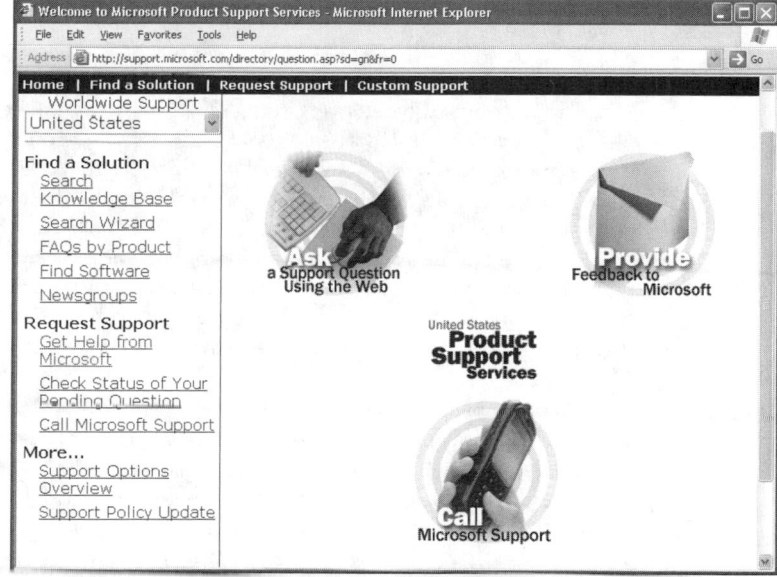

If you select the Ask a Support Question Using the Web option, the Product Support Services Web site will ask you a series of questions about your needs. Make sure you provide the support engineer with everything needed to solve your problem. You need to include a list of running applications, what you were doing at the time the problem occurred, the version of the hardware you need help with, and any drivers you've loaded. The more information you can provide, the faster you'll get accurate help.

When you click the Provide Feedback to Microsoft option, you'll see a somewhat confusing Web site. This Web site has two purposes. First, Microsoft wants to encourage you to look through lists of existing answers to questions and suggestions. For example, the Microsoft Knowledge Base is packed with information, and Microsoft adds more to it on a daily basis. You also find answers in places like Frequently Asked Question (FAQ) lists. The second purpose of this site is to determine what kind of feedback you want to provide. For example, there are separate entries for Web sites and products.

After you get past this confusing screen, you'll see a simple form that asks basic questions. Microsoft will ask for your e-mail address and specifics about the product in question. The product support person who receives your input might need to contact you for additional information.

A Quick Look at Catastrophic Failures

Figuring out a catastrophic error usually takes a little time and a few hardware and software tools. Here's a typical scenario: You start your machine in the morning and Windows XP comes up fine, but you can't use the mouse. If there aren't any conflicts and you haven't installed anything new recently, the most probable cause is some type of hardware failure.

> **Tip:** Faulty or out-of-date drivers cause lots of hardware-related problems. Installing a new piece of software could cause a driver problem to surface the next time you boot your machine, making it appear that the hardware has failed. Of course, part of the problem in diagnosing the failure is to figure out what version of the driver you have installed. That's where Driver Detective comes into play. This program snoops around on your machine and figures out what versions of each driver you have installed. That way, you know if you have the most current version of a driver installed. You can find out more about Driver Detective at `http://www.drivershq.com/dd/indexdd.html`.

All kinds of problems fall into the catastrophic category. For example, severely crimping a cable (putting an obvious dent in it) normally causes some type of hardware failure. It might be as simple as a device that doesn't respond or a network connection that works intermittently. Port failures don't happen often, but they do happen. You'll also find that NICs fail from time to time. And everyone knows that hard drives fail.

Part of the problem for a network administrator or a home user is locating the source of the problem. You could try replacing one component at a time until you locate the problem. However, using diagnostic aids and other troubleshooting tools saves you much more time than they cost. It's also much less expensive to find the right component the first time and replace it.

> **Tip:** Most soundboard and display adapter vendors include a complete diagnostic for their products as part of the package. Some hardware vendors are starting to include this feature as well. I even found one motherboard vendor—Hauppauge—that provides a diagnostic disk with its products. The diagnostic tests basic motherboard functionality and any installed memory.

The following sections aren't designed to be an inclusive list of every tool you'll ever need, but you might find that they provide just enough help so that you can get through a repair with a minimum of effort.

Peter's Principle: Using a Self-booting or DOS-based Versus a Windows-based Diagnostic Program

You can rely on most Windows diagnostics to provide very useful and easy-to-read information. They also find a great majority of the hardware problems you could experience.

However, there isn't any reliable way to test your hardware completely from within Windows. The multitasking nature of the operating system makes this impossible. Some diagnostic programs need total access to the hardware as well, and Windows doesn't allow this kind of access. Many diagnostic tools don't require Windows at all; others run from the DOS prompt, where they have better control over the hardware.

There's another problem with Windows diagnostic programs—something that doesn't occur to most people until it's too late. What happens if you can get DOS up and running, but a hardware conflict or failure prevents Windows from starting? I've had this particular problem more than a few times. Using a DOS diagnostic means that if the system boots at all, you can at least figure out what's going on.

Self-booting is another category of diagnostic program. In this case, you don't need an operating system at all. Just stick the diagnostic disk in your machine, boot the system, and you're ready to perform diagnostics.

Of the three categories of diagnostic programs, the self booting type is the best because it doesn't rely on anything. It has complete access to your system and nothing is masked. DOS diagnostic programs come next. At least you have complete access to the system. However, loading drivers and TSRs can block some diagnostic functions. Finally, Windows diagnostic programs are great at providing information, but are not much good for anything else.

TuffTest

The #1-TuffTest Pro diagnostic program (http://tufftest.pcdiag.com/tufftest.htm) is the least expensive that you'll find on the market today (unless the diagnostic is free). This is the no-frills solution for someone who wants to test just the basics and absolutely nothing else.

You'll want to avoid TuffTest when working with certain types of hardware. For example, it doesn't include anything for working with SCSI drives. You'll also find that its port support is minimal and that you can't test any of your buses. TuffTest doesn't provide any configuration utilities or any of the other add-ons that other diagnostic tools provide. In short, this is the Spartan configuration.

You'll also find some benefits when using this program. The diagnostic is extremely small and fast. The menu system is easy to understand, and the vendor didn't clutter it with many features you'll never use. Unlike with many large diagnostic programs, you can test all of your memory using this product.

One of the features that doesn't stick out at first is the product support you get with TuffTest. The author maintains a newsletter where you can find out more about the product. In addition, there's a mailing list where you can exchange information with other users. Overall, this is one of the better product-support packages.

PC-Technician

PC-Technician (http://www.windsortech.com/pctech.html) is a basic diagnostic program at a reasonable cost. It emphasizes the essentials of your system. You can use it to test main components, such as memory, the hard drive, and your ports. One of the advantages of using this product is portability. PC-Technician is small and executes within about 200KB of RAM. This enables PC-Technician to test all of main memory and perform a few other tricks that larger diagnostic programs can't perform.

What you don't find with PC-Technician is the capability to test some of the newer hardware on the market. For example, this program doesn't test the expansion bus on your machine. If you have a problem with your PCI or AGP setup, PC-Technician doesn't find it. Generally, PC-Technician doesn't work with newer ports. For example, you can't use it to test your USB port.

This program does have similarities to other offerings on the market, but the simple interface makes the features easy to use. For example, you can use PC-Technician to perform burn-in and certification testing. You can also perform certain types of performance tests.

Finally, PC-Technician helps you perform system configuration, as long as the configuration is within the range of PC-Technician capabilities. You can perform all of the essentials, including CMOS configuration. However, PC-Technician lacks a flash ROM utility, so you can't use it to upgrade the BIOS on your machine. Fortunately, most motherboard vendors provide this utility for you.

CheckIt

CheckIt Professional Edition (http://www.smithmicro.com/checkit/) is the Cadillac of diagnostic programs. Of the three diagnostic programs, this one is the most expensive and complex. It does everything the other products do, only better. (Complete memory testing could be problematic because of the size of this diagnostic program.)

You'll also find that CheckIt tests all of the current bus technologies, including PCI, PCMCIA, and AGP. CheckIt analyzes the PCI cards in your system and provides complete information about them. It includes many burn-in and certification tests that the other products don't support. For example, you can run a power cycling test on your system.

Space doesn't allow me to describe the entire feature set of this product, but CheckIt is an example of getting what you pay for. Of course, the price is the major negative of this product. Only those who need the ultimate in diagnostic utilities need to consider this one.

Serial and Parallel Port Loopback Plugs

You can't fully test the serial and parallel ports in a workstation without loopback plugs. These plugs pass the signal from the port's output and then back to its input. To create a loopback plug, you use a blank connector without wires and then connect wires between specific pins. Most of the high-end diagnostic programs you buy (such as PC-Technician, AMI Diags, or the Norton Utilities) provide these plugs. Others, such as CheckIt, don't provide them. (Some packages from TouchStone do include loopback plugs now, but you need to purchase their higher-end products to get them.) TouchStone tells you how to build your own loopback plugs and sells them to you as a separate product.

> **Tip:** The list of modems supported by Windows XP grows with every release. However, you won't find a NULL modem driver for Windows XP in the standard list of hardware options. This makes it impossible to create a Dial-Up Networking connection that requires a NULL modem setup. Don't worry, though—you can download a NULL modem driver from http://www.kevin-wells.com/net/ that works up to 115 Kbps.

Table 25.1 provides the pin connections for a parallel port. Every parallel port uses a 25-pin male connector. Another designation for this type of connector is DB25P. You need to create two connectors to test serial ports. There are 9-pin and 25-pin serial ports. Every serial port uses a female connector. The designation for a 9-pin serial port is DB9S. Table 25.2 lists the pin connections for a 9-pin serial port. The designation for a 25-pin serial port is DB25S. Table 25.3 gives the pin connections for a 25-pin serial port. You can find the blank connectors and wire you need at most electronics stores.

Table 25.1 Parallel Port (DB25P) Loopback Plug Connections

First Pin	Connected to Second Pin
11 (Busy +)	17 (Select Input -)
10 (Acknowledge -)	16 (Initialize Printer -)
12 (Paper Out +)	14 (Autofeed -)
13 (Select +)	01 (Strobe -)
02 (Data 0 +)	15 (Error -)

Table 25.2 9-Pin Serial Port (DB9S) Loopback Plug Connections

First Pin	Connected to Second Pin
02 (RD: Received Data)	03 (TD: Transmitted Data)
07 (RTS: Request to Send)	08 (CTS: Clear to Send)
06 (DSR: Data Set Ready)	01 (CD: Carrier Direct)
01 (CD: Carrier Detect)	04 (DTR: Data Terminal Ready)
04 (DTR: Data Terminal Ready)	09 (RI: Ring Indicator)

Table 25.3 25-Pin Serial Port (DB25S) Loopback Plug Connections

First Pin	Connected to Second Pin
03 (RD: Received Data)	02 (TD: Transmitted Data)
04 (RTS: Request to Send)	05 (CTS: Clear to Send)
06 (DSR: Data Set Ready)	08 (CD: Carrier Direct)
08 (CD: Carrier Detect)	20 (DTR: Data Terminal Ready)
20 (DTR: Data Terminal Ready)	22 (RI: Ring Indicator)

As you can see, the pin connections are relatively easy to make. Whether you buy pre-made loopback plugs or make your own, this tool is essential for your toolkit. Without loopback plugs, you'll never know whether the serial or parallel port you tested really works.

Cable Scanner

Network administrators, especially those managing large networks, can spend lots of time tracing cables. An average cable scanner costs about $1,000, although you can usually find them a little cheaper. Alternatively, you could build your own cable scanner for about $200, using plans in some electronics magazines. For example, the *Circuit Cellar INK* October/November 1992 issue contains a set of plans on page 22. You can order a reprint of the article at `http://www.circuitcellar.com/backissues.html`. The source code for the cable scanner appears at `http://www.dtweed.com/circuitcellar/caj00029.htm`.

One of the better cable scanners on the market is the Cable Scanner from Microtest. (Microtest provides many other cable scanners with more features, but the Cable Scanner model provides the minimum feature set you need in order to maintain a network.) This product tests for opens, shorts, and improper terminations. It tells you the distance from your current location to the cable fault. In most cases, all you need to do is track the cable for the required distance and you'll find the problem. To help you trace the signal, the main unit outputs a signal that you can pick up on a remote unit. Instead of taking down every ceiling tile in your office, you simply use the remote unit to trace the cable.

You can send the data collected by the Cable Scanner to a serial printer. The unit collects the data, stores it, and enables you to output it later. The Cable Scanner provides both text and graphic output. This feature is handy for maintaining records on your system. All you need to do is print the results of the cable check and add it to the network documentation.

The Cable Scanner provides a few other unique functions you might not use very often. For example, it can detect the noise level of the cable on your system. This means that you can reduce the number of packet errors by simply reducing the noise the packet signal must overcome. You can also interface the Cable Scanner with an oscilloscope. This enables you to monitor the signal that flows across the network. An experienced network administrator could use this information to troubleshoot problem installations.

Incompatible Hardware

Windows XP will likely require you to buy updated hardware; there's no easier way to state it. The fact that Microsoft tries to ease the purchase of this new hardware by defining a Windows PC specification doesn't really solve anything—all it means is that the machine you buy to use Windows XP should work out of the package if it meets all of the specifications. In some respects, it's easier to buy hardware for Windows XP than Windows 2000. You'll find that Windows XP places stringent requirements on driver development and provides more flexibility in the application environment. In other respects, you have a harder time getting hardware to work because Microsoft removed many old devices from the Windows XP compatibility list. Devices that still run with Windows XP were removed from the list because the vendor didn't want to support them any more or the device had caused problems in the past.

Windows 95/98 is the hardware-compatibility king when compared to any version of Windows. For the most part, any hardware you used under the DOS or earlier Windows environments also runs under Windows 95/98. Even if you have to use a real-mode driver, you should be able to use that old device under Windows 95/98 if you really want to. The same can't be said of Windows XP. If you want the added reliability and security that any version of Windows XP provides, you need to pay for it. This means that any device you use has to provide a Windows driver—preferably, a Windows XP–specific driver. Old hardware just doesn't provide this kind of support in some cases.

Obviously, the issue of compatibility runs even deeper than simply having a workable driver. Windows XP has to be able to find the device ROM routines in some cases. It always has to have access to the device's ports and interrupts. Windows XP really does try its best to figure out which interrupts and port addresses are in use, but it doesn't always succeed—especially if you have an eclectic mix of old and new hardware (and mixed 16-bit and 32-bit drivers). Fortunately, Windows XP does support Plug and Play, which eases matters considerably.

The best way to avoid hardware compatibility problems today is to purchase Plug and Play hardware designed to work on a newer bus, such as the PCI bus. If you can't get a PCI bus card, a Plug and Play card designed to work on an ISA bus is the second-best choice. Windows still can detect the settings of such a card. If you really must use an older, non–Plug and Play device, you may need to perform some troubleshooting to get it to work properly under Windows XP. The following sections are devoted to helping you achieve this goal.

Understanding the Problem with Older Hardware

When using older, non–Plug and Play hardware and drivers, no automatic checking of actual device settings takes place; every setup is a manual process on the part of the installer. Adding to this problem is the fact that some of these device drivers don't register themselves properly when you load them. A device driver is supposed to register itself in a device chain and provide certain types of information as part of that registration process. If it doesn't provide the right level of information, Windows XP can't fully detect it. (Yes, it knows that the driver is present, but it can't use the driver to access the hardware.) What happens next is inevitable, given such circumstances. If Windows XP doesn't see the device driver or it thinks that the device is using different settings than it really is, Windows XP might assume that the interrupts and port addresses the device uses are free. The result is that you might find two devices trying to share the same interrupt or port address.

> **Tip:** Microsoft has found that signed drivers prevent many more problems than they cause. Windows 2000 provides the initial signed device driver platform. A *signed* driver is one that has met Microsoft testing criteria and contains a special signature that Windows checks. Using a signed driver means that you experience fewer problems in getting your system up and running. However, you can still use older drivers if you really need to. The system warns you that Microsoft hasn't signed these older drivers and that they may not work reliably. Take my advice: Unlike in Windows 2000, where the drivers might work, they normally don't work under Windows XP. You need signed drivers.

One of the best ways to eliminate some of the problems of using older, non–Plug and Play hardware is to make a checklist of all the hardware and settings each device uses. You need to include the port address, interrupts, and the DMA address. Physically check the settings on cards that use jumpers. You might want to use this opportunity to check the BIOS revision of your card physically; an undocumented update could make a big difference in the settings you need to use with Windows XP. A software-configurable device usually includes the current settings as part of the setup dialog box in the Control Panel. (If not, you'll want to contact the vendor and ask how to determine the current settings.) All you really need to do is get out the vendor manual and determine what the settings mean.

After you get all the settings written down, check your list for potential conflicts. Windows XP might tell you that there aren't any, but it's possible that you'll find some anyway. Someone I know recently tried to install Windows XP but found that he couldn't do it. The machine he was using included two SCSI adapters. Windows XP recognized one adapter but not the other. The result: Windows XP didn't recognize the CD-ROM drive attached to the second adapter and therefore couldn't install itself properly. Removing the second SCSI adapter and connecting the CD-ROM drive to the first adapter solved part of the problem.

Fixing the Windows XP installation problem by moving the CD-ROM drive to the first adapter didn't solve all of the problems on this machine. Performance on the network was very slow. A check with Windows didn't show any device conflicts. However, a physical check of the remaining SCSI adapter showed that it was using the same interrupt as the NIC. (Windows XP had claimed that the NIC was using interrupt 5; and the SCSI adapter, interrupt 3.) Physically changing the SCSI adapter's interrupt setting solved the remaining problem. Note that Windows XP does a better job than Windows 2000 or Windows 9x at sharing device resources, but even it can't solve every problem.

At times, you might not be sure that you got all the settings right during the first check. You can also determine the equipment settings by viewing the port and interrupt addresses a device uses. Simply use the MSD utility discussed earlier in this chapter or a diagnostic program, such as #1-TuffTest. In fact, using this technique, along with physical inspection of your hardware, ensures that you have all the settings for each device. Even if there aren't any conflicts, you should still maintain a complete record of your hardware.

Make sure you check with vendors to obtain all of the patches for a device. Some older devices include their own BIOS. Sometimes, the BIOS routines conflict with Windows XP and cause various types of system failures. Most vendors upgrade their BIOS as time goes on. They fix bugs and perform some types of optimizations. I've never been able to understand why, but hardware vendors are notoriously reluctant to tell anyone about these fixes. If you have an older piece of hardware with a BIOS that's causing problems with Windows XP, see whether the vendor has some type of BIOS upgrade that might fix the problem. Installing a new chip is usually cheaper than buying a new peripheral.

Tracking Down Non–Plug and Play Hardware Problems

By now, it should be apparent that hardware incompatibility can cover lots of ground. Everything from misinterpreted settings to a poorly designed device driver can make it appear that your hardware is incompatible with Windows XP. Let's look at the hardware-compatibility problem from a procedural point of view. To do so, follow these steps:

1. Use a DOS or self-booting diagnostic program to test the hardware to ensure that there's no problem with the device itself. As I stated earlier, Windows XP has a bad habit of hiding problems because you can't really access the device. Using a real-mode driver and a vendor-supplied or third-party diagnostic program to check the hardware under DOS might seem archaic, but it's probably the easiest way to go.

2. Check the device settings to see whether there's a conflict with any other device. This is especially important when you try to mix older and newer hardware. After you compile a list of device settings, first manually configure the drivers for the hardware that uses jumpers and then complete the setup for hardware that uses a software-configuration technique.

3. After you determine that the hardware is working and doesn't conflict with anything, see whether the vendor documentation provides any insights into the requirements for using the device driver. In at least a few cases, I found valuable instructions in the box on a separate piece of paper, in README files on the driver disk, or on the vendor Web site.

4. Check your BIOS revision level. Vendors provide a variety of ways to detect this information, so you'll have to check your documentation for details about your particular device. A display adapter I own has a program I run to display the BIOS and setup information. Check with the vendor to see whether a newer version of the BIOS is available. You might have to send the device to the vendor's repair facility to get the BIOS replaced. It depends on the vendor's policy concerning sending BIOS updates to customers.

5. If all else fails, see whether replacing the board with a similar board from another vendor helps. You might find that a software or other conflict is disguising itself as a hardware problem this way. Recall that a problem with a serial port can disguise itself as a faulty mouse, for example. You might find that other types of problems disguise themselves as well.

Incompatible hardware rarely is, in itself, incompatible (except when you don't have the proper driver for it). You'll usually have a problem you can define, given enough time and resources. The question you have to ask yourself is whether that old hardware is really worth the effort. In my case, I replaced the hardware that was giving me problems, which probably saved me time and frustration. Some types of expensive, specialized hardware might be worth the effort involved in looking for the cause of incompatibility, but make sure that you'll get some type of payback.

BIOS Update Requirements

Something that most people don't think about is the BIOS for their motherboards. Actually, it's something I didn't think about until a few years ago. Older systems had a BIOS installed when you bought them, and you seldom thought about it. The BIOS never required replacement, and it wasn't easy to replace the BIOS even if you needed to do so.

Today computers use a new type of BIOS, called a *flash ROM*. You can use a simple program to upload data from a floppy disk or your hard drive to the flash ROM. The next time you start your machine, it uses the new code you uploaded.

The flash ROM can actually contain several kinds of applications, not just the BIOS. Machines have more features now, which means that they require additional code in order to do their work. For example, my motherboard provides complete monitoring capabilities for devices such as the fans in the system. This additional monitoring requires additional software.

You can often trace problems with Windows XP to a problem with your system BIOS. For example, some motherboards refused to provide Advanced Configuration and Power Interface support when a user installed Windows XP. The problem turned out to be a difference of opinion. Sometimes, specifications don't spell out requirements as well as they should. The people drafting the specification can spend hours poring over every detail, yet two people might walk away with two different opinions on how to implement a feature. That's what happened in this case. A repair to the flash ROM of the afflicted motherboards fixed the ACPI problem.

> **Note:** Not every motherboard problem requires a quick update of the BIOS. Some problems require a trip to the vendor's repair facility. Other people having ACPI problems with Windows weren't as lucky as the group I just mentioned. The motherboards required a physical change to make them work. The problem is that you wouldn't know about the fix unless you visited the vendor Web site. In this case, Asus motherboards required a change to the system configuration. You can read about it on the Asus site (`http://www.asus.com.tw/Products/Techref/Acpi/solution.html`). The point is that you need to check the vendor Web site for updates on your hardware as often as possible.

The method used to update a flash ROM varies by vendor. However, you'll normally copy a file to a floppy diskette, along with a special application that reads and writes the flash ROM. When you boot the system, you'll use the special application to read and save the current flash ROM contents. You'll then upload the new flash ROM content using the special application and reboot the machine. When you the machine reboots, you'll have a new (and hopefully fixed) BIOS to use.

What to Do When the Vendor's Instructions Don't Work

Vendor instructions don't always work. Users think that the instructions should always work, but they don't. A vendor does receive hundreds (perhaps thousands) of calls each day. Every call builds the vendor's knowledge base of information about problems with a specific product. However, the knowledge base isn't infinite; it has limitations, so the help you can receive from the vendor is limited.

When it comes to computers, there's no one source of unlimited universe. Finding a fix for a problem often becomes a scavenger hunt. You pick up a piece of information here and another piece there. Eventually, you'll end up with a complete answer to your question. Of course, this method requires time, and most of you don't have time to waste.

> **Tip:** Microsoft provides a vast array of newsgroups you can use to gather information about any hardware or software problems. Peer support is probably the best technique for getting support. Not only is it free, but you're also likely talking with someone who had the same problem as you do now. Unfortunately, you can't always access every Microsoft newsgroup from an ISP. I know that my ISP doesn't provide access to every Microsoft newsgroup. You can add an account for Microsoft's news server to Outlook Express. Simply create an account for `news.microsoft.com`. This news server does provide access to all public Microsoft newsgroups.

If you're in a hurry and you find that none of the Microsoft resources we've discussed in this chapter even comes close to helping, you have three other choices:

- *Peer Support* I've already mentioned this as something you can get from Microsoft newsgroups, but there are many other newsgroups from which to choose. These other newsgroups are available from your local ISP, and they often provide better help than the Microsoft newsgroups do. The point is that you don't have to stick with a Microsoft solution. There are other places to get peer support.

- *Web Sites* Peer support is fine for most problems, but a newsgroup doesn't lend itself to detailed answers to questions. You'll normally receive short answers. Web sites provide a venue for a budding author to express ideas in detail. Using a search engine, such as Google, (`http://www.google.com/advanced_search`) can help you find detailed information quickly.

- *Trade Press Articles* Most large trade press journals have their entire library of articles online. For example, *InfoWorld* (`http://www.infoworld.com`) and *eWeek* (`http://www.zdnet.com/eweek/`) have columns and detailed research center information about important Windows issues. Sometimes, I think the journalists take special delight in reporting a fix for an especially embarrassing Windows problem, but I won't go so far as to say they do. In short, you have someone with a good reason to provide you with great answers to common questions. All you need to do is search on the Web site for the answer you need.

On Your Own

Spend time working with the Help and Support. Try some of the tours and tutorials it provides. Begin building a list of help file locations in your Favorites folder. In addition, create some other self-help files. Look for Windows XP–specific sites online and add them to your favorites. Finally, set up places to store information from newsgroups and any trade journals you read.

Buy a diagnostic program and completely test your system, especially the hard drives. Make sure you get an easy-to-use diagnostic and one that tests everything on your machine. Use the loopback plugs provided with the diagnostic program to test your ports, or create your own loopback plugs by using the procedure in this chapter.

Don't wait until you have a problem to make this detailed checklist of all the device drivers in your system. This can be much easier to do when your PC is working normally. Then, if it fails, you'll already be a good way down the path toward a solution to the problem.

Glossary

Introduction

This book includes a Glossary so that you can find terms and acronyms easily. It has several important features you need to know about. First, every acronym in the entire book is listed here—even if there's a better-than-even chance that you already know what the acronym means. This way, there isn't any doubt that you'll always find everything you need to use the book properly.

Second, these definitions are specific to the book. In other words, when you look through this glossary, you're seeing the words defined in the context in which the book uses them. This might or might not always coincide with current industry usage because the computer industry changes the meaning of words so often.

Finally, the definitions here use a conversational tone in most cases. This means that they might sacrifice a bit of puritanical accuracy for the sake of better understanding. The purpose of this glossary is to define the terms in such a way that there's less room for misunderstanding the intent of this book as a whole.

Although this Glossary is a complete view of the words and acronyms in the book, you'll run into situations when you need to know more. No matter how closely I look at terms throughout the book, there's always a chance that I'll miss the one acronym or term you really need to know. In addition, I've directed your attention to numerous online sources of information, and few of the terms the Web site owners use will appear here unless I also chose to use them in the book. Fortunately, many sites on the Internet provide partial or complete glossaries to fill in the gaps:

- Acronym Finder (http://www.acronymfinder.com/)
- Microsoft Encarta (http://encarta.msn.com/)
- University of Texas Acronyms and Abbreviations
  (http://www-hep.uta.edu/~variable/e_comm/pages/r_dic-en.htm)
- Webopedia (http://webopedia.internet.com/)
- yourDictionary.com (formerly A Web of Online Dictionaries)
  (http://www.yourdictionary.com/)

Let's talk about these Web sites a little more. Web sites normally provide acronyms or glossary entries—not both. An acronym site provides only the definition for the acronym you want to learn about; it doesn't provide an explanation of what the acronym means concerning everyday computer use. The two extremes in this list are Acronym Finder (acronyms only) and Webopedia (full-fledged glossary entries).

The owner of Acronym Finder doesn't update the site as often as the University of Texas updates its site, but Acronym Finder does have the advantage of providing an extremely large list of acronyms from which to choose. At the time of this writing, the Acronym Finder sported 164,000 acronyms. The University of Texas site receives updates often and provides only acronyms (another page at the same site includes a glossary).

Most of the Web sites you find for computer terms are free. In some cases, such as Microsoft Encarta, you have to pay for the support provided. However, these locations are still worth the effort because they ensure that you understand the terms used in the jargon-filled world of computing.

Webopedia has become one of my favorite places to visit because it provides encyclopedic coverage of many computer terms and includes links to other Web sites. I like the fact that if I don't find a word I need, I can submit it to the Webopedia staff for addition to their dictionary, making Webopedia a community-supported dictionary of the highest quality.

One of the interesting features of the yourDictionary.com Web site is that it provides access to more than one dictionary and in more than one language. If English isn't your native tongue, this is the Web site of choice.

Terms

Accelerated Graphics Port (AGP) A special PC bus used specifically for display adapters. An AGP-based display adapter can operate at much higher speeds than the normal ISA or PCI bus will allow. What this means to the user is that display speeds are much higher. In addition to making the display adapter faster, AGP allows the adapter to directly access main memory as if it were part of the adapter's private memory storage. This in turn allows the display adapter to store more complex objects, such as textures, that are used to improve display appearance.

access control list (ACL) Part of the Windows NT security API used to determine both access and monitoring properties for an object. Each ACL contains one or more ACEs (access control entries) that define the security properties for an individual or group. There are two major ACL groups: SACL (security access control list) and DACL (discretionary access control list). The SACL controls the Windows NT auditing feature. The DACL controls access to the object.

ACL See Access Control List.

ACPI See Advanced Configuration and Power Interface.

Active Directory (AD) A method of storing machine, server, and user configuration within Windows 2000 and supports full data replication so that every domain controller has a copy of the data. This is essentially a special purpose database that contains information formatted according to a specific schema. Active Directory is designed to make Windows 2000 more reliable and secure, while reducing the work required by both the developer and network administrator for application support and distribution. The user benefits as well since Active Directory fully supports roving users and maintains a full record of user information, which reduces the effects of local workstation down time.

AD See Active Directory.

Advanced Configuration and Power Interface (ACPI) A specification that defines specific behaviors for the way PCs manage power and configure devices. This includes things like enumerating the boards installed on the motherboard and providing a power-management timer. The specification also provides for optional features, like supporting fan control and a number of CPU power states.

AGP See Accelerated Graphics Port.

American Standard Code for Information Interchange See ASCII.

API (application programming interface) A method of defining a standard set of function calls and other interface elements. It usually defines the interface between a high-level language and the lower-level elements used by a device driver or operating system. The ultimate goal is to provide some type of service to an application that requires access to the operating system or device feature set.

applet Normally, a Control Panel application in Windows. Most applets allow you to perform some type of system configuration or monitoring. For example, the ODBC applet allows you to define sources of data. Specific applications, like Microsoft Mail, also place applets in the Control Panel for configuration purposes.

application independence A method of writing applications so that they don't depend on the specific features of an operating system or hardware interface. It normally requires the use of a high-level language and an API. The programmer also needs to write the application in such a way as to avoid specific hardware or operating system references. All user and device interface elements must use the generic functions provided by the API.

application programming interface See API.

ASCII (American Standard Code for Information Interchange) A standard method of equating the numeric representations available in a computer to human-readable form. For example, the number 32 represents a space. There are 128 characters (7 bits) in the standard ASCII code. The extended ASCII code uses 8 bits for 256 characters. Display adapters from the same machine type normally use the same upper 128 characters. Printers, however, might reserve these upper 128 characters for nonstandard characters. For example, many Epson printers use them for the italic representations of the lower 128 characters.

bidirectional support A printer's capability to transfer information in both directions on a printer cable. Input usually contains data or printer control codes. Output usually contains printer status information or error codes.

binary value A base 2 data representation in the Windows Registry. Normally, used to hold status flags or other information that lends itself to a binary format.

BMP files The Windows standard bitmap graphics data format. This raster graphic data format doesn't include any form of compression.

Boolean A method of determining whether a statement is true or false using rules of logic. Boolean values are often used to help a computer determine whether it needs to take a certain course of action based on current system or application conditions.

browser A special application normally used to display data downloaded from the Internet. The most common form of Internet data is the HTML (Hypertext Markup Language) page. However, modern browsers can also display various types of graphics and even standard desktop application files, such as Word for Windows documents, directly. The actual capabilities provided by a browser vary widely, depending on the software vendor and platform.

cache buffers The smallest storage elements in a cache (an area of RAM devoted to storing commonly used pieces of information normally stored on the hard drive). Think of each buffer as a box that can store a single piece of information. The more buffers (boxes) you have, the greater the storage capacity of the cache.

CAD See Computer-Aided Drafting.

cascading style sheets See CSS.

CDFS (compact disk file system) The portion of the file subsystem specifically designed to interact with compact disc drives. It also provides the user interface elements required to tune this part of the subsystem. The CDFS takes the place of an FSD for CD-ROM drives.

CD-ROM See Compact Disk Read-Only Memory.

CD-RW See Compact Disk-Rewriteable.

CGA See Color Graphics Adapter.

class ID See CLSID.

client The recipient of data, services, or resources from a file or other server. This term can refer to a workstation or an application. The server can be another PC or an application.

CLSID (Class ID) A method of assigning a unique identifier to each object in the Registry. Also refers to various high-level language constructs.

CMOS (Complementary Metal-Oxide Semiconductor) Normally, refers to a construction method for low-power, battery-backed memory. When used in the context of a PC, this term usually refers to the memory used to store system configuration information and the real-time clock status. The configuration information normally includes the amount of system memory, the type and size of floppy drives, the hard drive parameters, and the video display type. Some vendors include other configuration information as part of this chip as well.

Color Graphics Adapter (CGA) A display adapter providing several character and graphics modes. It outputs a digital signal that can produce a maximum of 16 colors in character mode or 4 colors in graphics mode. The high-resolution character mode outputs a display of 80-by-25 characters. The high-graphics mode outputs 640-by-200 pixels by 2 colors.

COM See Component Object Model.

Common UNIX Printing System (CUPS) The default printing system used on a SAMBA server. (SAMBA is the common application used to interface UNIX and Linux machines from Windows.)

compact disk file system See CDFS.

Compact Disk Read-Only Memory (CD-ROM) A device used to store up to 650MB of permanent data. You can't use a CD-ROM the same as a hard or floppy disk because you can't write to it. The disks look much like audio CDs, but require a special drive to interface the drive with a computer.

Compact Disk-Rewriteable (CD-RW) A form of CD-ROM drive that allows both reading and writing. In addition to standard CD-ROM disks, this drive accepts CD-R and CD-RW disks. You can write to a CD-R disk only one time. A CD-RW disk allows multiple rewrites and functions similarly to a hard drive or floppy disk.

Complementary Metal-Oxide Semiconductor See CMOS

Component Object Model (COM) A Microsoft specification for an object-oriented code and data encapsulation method and transference technique. It's the basis for technologies such as OLE (object linking and embedding) and ActiveX (the replacement name for OCX—an object-oriented code library technology). COM is limited to local connections. DCOM (Distributed Component Object Model) is the technology used to allow data transfers and the use of OCXs within the Internet environment.

Compressed Serial Line Interface Protocol See CSLIP

computer-aided drafting (CAD) A special type of graphics program used for creating, printing, storing, and editing architectural, electrical, mechanical, or other forms of engineering drawings. CAD programs normally provide precise measuring capabilities and libraries of predefined objects, such as sinks, desks, resistors, and gears.

cracker A hacker (computer expert) who uses their skills for misdeeds on computer systems where they have little or no authorized access. A cracker normally possesses specialty software that allows easier access to the target network. In most cases, crackers require extensive amounts of time to break the security for a system before they can enter it.

CSLIP (Compressed Serial Line Interface Protocol) An IETF-approved method for transferring data by using a serial port. This particular data transmission method uses compression to improve performance.

CSS (cascading style sheets) A method for defining a standard Web page template. This may include headings, standard icons, backgrounds, and other features that would tend to give each page at a particular Web site the same appearance. The reasons for using CSS include the speed of creating a Web site (it takes less time if you don't have to create an overall design for each page) and consistency. Changing the overall appearance of a Web site also becomes as easy as changing the style sheet rather than each page individually.

CUPS See Common UNIX Printing System.

DAT (digital audiotape) drive A tape drive that uses a cassette to store data. The cassette and the drive use the same technology as the audio version of the DAT drive. However, the internal circuitry of the drive formats the tape for use with a computer system. The vendor must also design the interface circuitry with computer needs in mind. DAT tapes allow you to store large amounts of information in a relatively small amount of space. Typical drive capacities range from 1.2GB to 8GB. DDS-3–formatted drives have even higher capacities.

Data Link Control (DLC) Normally, a protocol used to establish communications with a remote server. For example, the Microsoft DLC provides connections to mainframes and network printers.

data-centric The method used by modern operating systems to view the user interface from a data perspective rather than from the perspective of the applications used to create the data. Using this view allows users to worry more about manipulating the data on their machines than the applications required to perform a specific task.

DCOM See Distributed Component Object Model.

DDE (dynamic data exchange) The ability to cut data from one application and paste it into another application. For example, you could cut a graphical image created with a paint program and paste the image into a word processing document. Once pasted, the data doesn't reflect changes made to it by the originating application. DDE also provides a method of communicating with an application that supports DDE and requesting data. For example, you could use an Excel macro to call Microsoft Word and request the contents of a document file. Some applications also use DDE to implement file-association strategies. For example, Microsoft Word uses DDE in place of command-line switches to gain added flexibility when a user needs to open or print a file.

DDR SDRAM See Double Data Rate Synchronous Dynamic Random Access Memory.

device-independent bitmap See DIB.

dial-up networking (DUN) The ability of Windows machines to connect to a remote server using a modem or other long-distance connection. DUN is used to connect a client to a private server that's running the DUN server, or it can be used to access public networks, like the Internet. From the Windows client perspective, the connection that is created looks just like any other network connection; the main difference is that the DUN connection is slower than a local connection.

DIB (device-independent bitmap) A method of representing graphical information that doesn't reflect a particular device's requirements. This has the advantage of allowing the same graphic to appear on any device in precisely the same way, despite differences in resolution or other factors that normally change the graphic's appearance.

digital audiotape drive See DAT.

Digital Subscriber Line (DSL) A term used to refer to any of a number of technologies that allow higher communication rates over standard telephone lines than normally allowed using standard modems. DSL is normally used between a remote location, such as a home or office, and the switching station or ISP. It isn't used between switching stations. Types of DSL include asynchronous DSL (ADSL), symmetric DSL (SDSL), and high bit-rate DSL (HDSL). The technologies vary by their ability to pack data onto the copper line, their distance from the switching station, and other characteristics. ADSL allows communication from 1.5Mbps to 9Mbps downstream (to the remote connection) and 16Kbps to 640Kbps upstream (from the remote connection). SDSL allows communication up to 3Mbps in both directions. HDSL allows communication up to 1.544Mbps in both directions.

Digital Video Disk (DVD) A high-capacity optical storage media with capacities of 4.7GB to 17GB and data transfer rates of 600KBps to 1.3GBps. A single DVD can hold the contents of an entire movie, or approximately 7.4 CD-ROMs. DVDs come in several formats that allow read-only or read-write access. All DVD drives include a second laser assembly, used to read existing CD-ROMs. Some magazines also use the term digital versatile disk for this storage media.

Digital Video Disk Random Access Memory (DVD-RAM) A form of DVD drive that allows both reading and writing of data. It functions in a manner similar to the CD-RW drive. The DVD Consortium sponsors this drive. A competitor to the DVD-RAM drive is the DVD+RW drive, sponsored by Hewlett-Packard, Philips, and Sony.

direct memory access See DMA.

Disk Defragmenter An application used to reorder the data on a long-term storage device, such as a hard disk or floppy disk. Reordering the data so that it appears in sequential order—file by file—reduces the time required to access and read the data. Sequential order allows you to read an entire file without moving the disk head, in some cases, and only a little in others. This results in a reduction in access time, which normally improves overall system throughput and therefore enhances system efficiency.

Distributed Component Object Model (DCOM) The advanced form of the Component Object Model (COM) used by the Internet. This particular format enables data transfers across the Internet or other remote sources. It adds the capability to perform asynchronous, as well as synchronous, data transfers—which prevents the client application from becoming blocked as it waits for the server to respond. See COM for more details.

DLC See Data Link Control.

DLL (dynamic link library) A special form of application code loaded into memory by request. It isn't executable by itself. A DLL contains one or more discrete routines that an application can use to provide specific features. For example, a DLL could provide a common set of file dialog boxes used to access information on the hard drive. More than one application can use the functions provided by a DLL, reducing overall memory requirements when more than one application is running.

DMA (direct memory access) A memory-addressing technique in which the processor doesn't perform the actual data transfer. This method of memory access is faster than any other technique.

DNS See domain name system.

domain name system (DNS) An Internet technology that allows a user to refer to a host computer by name rather than use its unique IP address.

DOS Protected-Mode Interface (DPMI) A method of accessing extended memory from a DOS application using the extended memory manager.

Double Data Rate Synchronous Dynamic Random Access Memory (DDR SDRAM) A memory technology built on the data-storage techniques used by SDRAM. The only difference is that this type of RAM transfers data on both the up and the down clock. In essence, it transfers data at twice the speed because it transfers data twice per clock cycle.

DPMI See DOS Protected-Mode Interface.

drag-and-drop A technique used in object-oriented operating systems to access data without actually opening the file by conventional methods. For example, this system allows the user to pick up a document file, drag it to the printer, and drop it. The printer prints the document, using the printer's default settings.

driver A special operating system file that allows some presentation graphics programs to send data to an output device.

DSL See Digital Subscriber Line.

dual-ported video RAM See VRAM.

DUN Scc Dial-Up Networking.

DVD See Digital Video Disk.

DVD-RAM See Digital Video Disk Random Access Memory.

Dvorak layout An alternative method of laying out the keyboard so that stress is reduced and typing speed is increased. It's different from the more familiar QWERTY layout, used by most keyboards and typewriters.

dynamic data exchange See DDE.

dynamic link library See DLL.

EDO DRAM See Extended Data Out Dynamic Random Access Memory.

EGA See Enhanced Graphics Adapter.

EIA (Electronics Industry Association) The standards body responsible for creating many hardware-related PC standards. For example, the EIA was responsible for the serial port interface used on most PCs. The EIA also participates in other standards efforts.

Electronics Industry Association See EIA.

EMF (enhanced metafile) Used as an alternative storage format by some graphics applications. EMF is a vector graphic format, so it provides a certain level of device independence and other features that a vector graphic normally provides.

EMM See Expanded Memory Manager.

EMS (expanded memory specification) Several versions of this specification are in use. The most popular version is 3.2, even though a newer 4.0 specification is available. This specification defines one method of extending the amount of memory a processor can address from the conventional memory area. It uses an area outside of system memory to store information. An Expanded Memory Manager (EMM) provides a window view into this larger data area. The old 3.2 specification requires a 64 KB window in the UMB. The newer 4.0 specification can create this window anywhere in conventional or UMB memory.

encryption The act of making data unreadable unless the reader provides a password or other key value. Encryption makes data safe for transport in unsecured environments, like the Internet.

Enhanced Graphics Adapter (EGA) A display adapter providing several character and graphics modes. It outputs a digital signal that can produce a maximum of 16 colors from a palette of 256 colors in character or graphics mode. The high-resolution character mode outputs a display of 80 by 43 characters. The high-resolution graphics mode outputs 640 by 350 pixels by 16 colors.

enhanced metafile See EMF.

Expanded Memory Manager (EMM) A device driver like EMM386.EXE that provides expanded memory services on an 80386 and above machine (there are special
drivers that work with 80286 and a few 8088/8086 machines). An application accesses
expanded memory using a page frame or other memory-mapping techniques from within
the conventional or upper memory area (0 to 1024K). The EMM usually emulates
expanded memory using extended memory managed by an extended memory manager
(XMM) like HIMEM.SYS. An application must change the processor's mode to protected mode to use XMS. Some products like 386MAX.SYS and QEMM.SYS provide
both EMM and XMM services in one driver.

expanded memory specification See EMS.

Extended Data Out Dynamic Random Access Memory (EDO DRAM) A type of
DRAM that buffers the address data and the output data. This change represents a major
reduction in circuitry and still enhances performance. EDO DRAM works by loading the
column address data in a buffer. The entire page of RAM is read into a buffer and the
correct column selected, and the data is then output while the next incoming address is
buffered.

FAT (file allocation table) The method used by DOS and other operating systems
to format a hard disk drive. This technique is one of the oldest formatting methods
available.

file allocation table disk format See FAT.

file system driver See FSD.

file transfer protocol See FTP.

firewall A system designed to prevent unauthorized access to or from a network.
Firewalls are normally associated with Web sites connected to the Internet. A network
administrator can create a firewall using either hardware or software.

folder When used in context of Windows, a specialized area for storing files on the
hard drive. Folders help you manage both data and applications by breaking them up
into smaller and easier-to-recognize groups. The DOS-equivalent term for folders is
directories—the same term used by many other operating systems.

FSD (file system driver) A file subsystem component responsible for defining the interface between Windows and long-term storage. The FSD also defines features such as
long filenames and what types of interaction the device supports. For example, the
CD-ROM FSD wouldn't support file writes unless you provided a device that could
perform that sort of task.

FTP (file transfer protocol) One of several standard data-transfer protocols originated by
the Internet Engineering Task Force. This protocol is designed for efficient file transfer.

GDI (graphics device interface) One of the main Windows root components. It controls the way graphical elements are presented onscreen. Every application must use the API provided by this component to draw or perform other graphics-related tasks.

general protection fault See GPF.

GIF See Graphical Interchange Format.

GPF (general protection fault) A processor or memory error that occurs when an application makes a request the system can't honor. This type of error results in some type of severe action on the part of the operating system. Normally, the operating system terminates the offending application.

Graphical Interchange Format (GIF) The standard file format used to transfer data over the Internet. There are several different standards for this file format, the latest of which is the GIF89a standard, used on most Internet sites. The GIF standard was originally introduced by CompuServe as a method of reducing the time required to download a graphic and the impact of any single-bit errors that might occur. A secondary form of the GIF is the animated GIF. It allows the developer to store several images within one file. Between each file is one or more control block that determines block boundaries, the display location of the next image in relation to the display area, and other display features. To create animation effects, a browser or other specially designed application displays the graphical images one at a time in the order in which they appear within the file.

graphical user interface See GUI.

graphics device interface See GDI.

GUI (graphical user interface) A system of icons and graphical images that replaces the character-mode menu system used by many machines. The GUI can ride on top of another operating system (such as DOS or UNIX) or reside as part of the operating system itself (such as Windows or OS/2). Advantages of a GUI are ease of use and high-resolution graphics. Disadvantages are higher workstation hardware requirements and lower performance, compared to a similar system using a character-mode interface.

hacker An individual who works with computers at a low level, especially in the area of security. A hacker normally possesses specialty software that allows easier access to the target application or network. In most cases, hackers require extensive amounts of time to break the security for a system before they can enter it. The two types of hackers include those who break into systems for ethical purposes and those who do it to damage the system in some way. The proper term for the second group is crackers. Some people have started to call the first group "ethical hackers" to prevent confusion. Ethical hackers normally work for security firms that specialize in finding holes in a company's security. However, hackers work in a wide range of computer arenas. For example, a person who writes low-level code (like that found in a device driver) after reverse engineering an existing driver is technically a hacker.

HAL See Hardware Abstraction Layer.

Hardware Abstraction Layer (HAL) A conceptual element of the Windows NT architecture. Microsoft wrote the drivers and other software elements in such a way that they could easily move Windows NT to other platforms. That's how they moved Windows NT to the MIPS and Alpha machines. The basic architecture of Windows NT is the same, but the low-level drivers—the ones that directly interface with the hardware—are different. The important thing to remember is that as far as your application is concerned, it's still running on an Intel machine. The only time you run into trouble is if your application bypasses the Windows API and goes directly to the hardware.

HDTV See High-Definition Television.

high-definition television (HDTV) A new, higher-resolution television that will eventually replace current National Television Standards Committee (NTSC)–based television sets.

hive The physical storage area on disk used to hold Windows Registry settings. Each hive is associated with a particular set of related keys. For example, all user settings appear in one hive, and application settings reside in another. Some hives contain specific types of data, such as the security access manager (SAM) information used to secure Windows.

HTML (Hypertext Markup Language) A special language that relies on a series of tag words to define character and paragraph formatting. In some cases, HTML has been extended to provide graphical information as well as access to ActiveX controls and Java applets. In essence, HTML defines all the characteristics of a Web page.

HTTP (Hypertext Transfer Protocol) The IETF-supported protocol used to transfer an HTML-formatted document from a Web server to the client browser.

hub A device used to connect two or more nodes on a network. A hub normally provides other features, such as automatic detection of connection loss.

Hypertext Markup Language See HTML.

Hypertext Transfer Protocol See HTTP.

ICM (image color matcher) A special component of the graphics subsystem that allows Windows to match the colors produced by one device with those available on another device. The result is that the output of both devices doesn't show the normal variations in color that Windows applications produce.

icon A symbol used to represent graphically the purpose or function of an application or file. For example, a text file might appear as a sheet of paper with the filename below the icon. Applications designed for the environment or operating system usually appear with a special icon depicting the vendor or product's logo. Icons normally are part of a GUI environment or operating system, such as Windows.

ICS See Internet Connection Sharing.

IETF See Internet Engineering Task Force.

IFS (installable file system) manager The API component of the file system. It provides a consistent interface that applications can use to access a variety of devices—local and remote. This component also provides a standard interface that device drivers can use to provide services such as file opening and drive status.

IIS See Internet Information Server.

ILS See Internet Locator Service.

image color matcher See ICM.

INF file A special form of device or application configuration file. It contains all the parameters that Windows requires to install or configure the device or application. For example, an application INF file might contain the location of data files and the interdependencies of DLLs. Both application and device INF files contain the Registry and INI file entries required to make Windows recognize the application or device.

Infrared Data Association See IrDA.

installable file system helper (IFSHLP) A special real-mode component of the IFS manager used to allow access to Windows drive functions by DOS applications. It uses the same DOS interface as before, but all processing is performed by the protected-mode manager.

installable file system manager See IFS manager.

Internet Connection Sharing (ICS) A special type of proxy server that allows more than one workstation on a peer-to-peer network to share a single Internet connection. ICS requires that one workstation act as the server and have a connection to the Internet through dial-up or other means. All other workstations act as clients and access the Internet through the connection provided by the server.

Internet Engineering Task Force (IETF) The standards group devoted to finding solutions to technology problems on the Internet. This group can approve standards created both within the organization itself and outside the organization as part of other group efforts. For example, Microsoft has requested the approval of several new Internet technologies through this group. If approved, the technologies would become Internet-wide standards, performing data transfer and other specific kinds of tasks.

Internet Information Server (IIS) Microsoft's full-fledged Web server that normally runs under the Windows Server operating system. (Windows XP includes a less capable version of IIS you can use for testing purposes.) IIS includes all the features you'd normally expect with a Web server: FTP, HTTP, and Gopher protocols along with both mail and news services.

Internet Locator Service (ILS) A phonebook of people who are currently using NetMeeting. You can use this feature to see who is using the product and, optionally, join their conversation (if it's open).

Internet Packet Exchange (IPX) A Novell-specific, peer-to-peer communication protocol based on the internet protocol (IP) portion of the TCP/IP pair. Think of this as the language used on the network. If everyone speaks the same language, all the nodes can understand each other. Messages are exchanged in the form of packets on a network. Think of a packet as one sheet of a letter. The letterhead says who sent the letter, an introduction says who the letter is for, and a message tells the receiving party what the sending party wants to say.

Internet Protocol (IP) The information exchange portion of the TCP/IP protocol used by the Internet. IP is an actual data transfer protocol that defines how the sender places information into packets and transmits from one place to another. TCP (transmission control protocol) is the protocol that defines how the actual data transfer takes place. One of the problems with IP that standards groups are addressing right now is that it doesn't encrypt the data packets—anyone can read a packet traveling on the Internet. Future versions of IP will address this need by using some form of encryption technology. In the meantime, some companies have coupled TCP with other technologies to provide encryption technology for the short term.

Internet service provider See ISP.

interrupt request See IRQ.

IP See Internet Protocol.

IPX See Internet Packet Exchange.

IrDA (Infrared Data Association) The standards association responsible for creating infrared data port standards. These ports are normally used to create a connection between a laptop and a device or network. Devices include printers, PCs, modems, and mice.

IRQ (interrupt request) The set of special address lines that connect a peripheral to the processor. Think of an IRQ as an office telephone with multiple incoming lines. Every time a device calls, its entry lights up on the front of the phone. The processor selects the desired line and picks up the receiver to find out what the device wants. Everything works fine as long as there's one line for each device that needs to call the processor. If more than one device tries to call in on the same line, the processor doesn't know who's at the other end. This is the source of IRQ conflicts. Older PC-class machines provided 8 interrupt lines. The newer, AT-class machines provide 16. However, only 15 of those are usable because 1 line is used for internal purposes.

ISP (Internet service provider) A vendor that provides one or more Internet-related services through a dial-up, ISDN, or other outside connection. Normal services include email, newsgroup access, and full Internet Web site access.

Joint Pictures Entertainment Group File Format (JPEG) One of two graphics file formats used on the Internet. This vector file format is normally used to render high-resolution images or pictures.

JPEG See Joint Pictures Entertainment Group file format.

kernel The set of drivers, low-level functions, executables, and other constructs required to create the core of an operating system. The kernel is responsible for honoring application requests for device and data access. It also provides security and system level functionality.

LAN (local area network) A combination of hardware and software used to connect a group of PCs to each other or to a minicomputer or mainframe computer. There are two main networking models in use: peer-to-peer and client-server. The peer-to-peer model doesn't require a dedicated server. In addition, all the workstations in the group can share resources. The client-server model uses a central server for resource sharing, but some special methods are provided for using local resources in a limited fashion.

local area network See LAN.

macro One of several methods for performing automated tasks on a computer. Macros normally include a simple programming language that's executed by an interpreter within an application. In some cases, the application automatically records a macro, based on user keystrokes. The user can later modify this file as needed to complete a task.

MAN See Metropolitan Area Network.

MAPI (Messaging Application Programming Interface) The set of functions and other resources that Windows provides to communications programs. It allows the application to access a variety of communications channels using a single set of calls and without regard to media. This Windows component allows Microsoft Exchange to process information from email and online services using the same interface.

Messaging Application Programming Interface See MAPI.

metropolitan area network (MAN) A partial extension and redefinition of the WAN, a MAN connects two or more LANs using a variety of methods. A MAN usually encompasses more than one physical location within a limited geographical area, usually within the same city or state. (A WAN can cover a larger geographical area and sometimes includes country-to-country communications.) Most MANs rely on microwave communications, fiber optic connections, or leased telephone lines to provide the internetwork connections required to keep all nodes in the network talking with each other.

MFC files See Microsoft Foundation Class files.

Microsoft Foundation Class files (MFC files) The set of DLLs required to make many Microsoft applications work. These files contain the shared classes used as a basis for creating the application. For example, a pushbutton is a separate class within these files. Normally, you find the MFC files in the Windows SYSTEM folder. The files use MFC as the starting letters of the filename.

Microsoft Management Console (MMC) A special application that acts as an object container for Windows management objects, like Component Services and Computer Management. The management objects are actually special components that provide interfaces that allow the user to access them within MMC to maintain and control the operation of Windows. A developer can create special versions of these objects for application management or other tasks. Using a single application like MMC helps maintain the same user interface across all management applications.

MIDI See Musical Instrument Digital Interface.

MIME See multipurpose Internet mail extensions.

miniport driver A specialized Windows component that provides access to a resource, normally a peripheral device of some type. It's also used to access pseudo-devices and network resources.

MMC See Microsoft Management Console.

Motion Picture Experts Group See MPEG.

MPEG (Motion Picture Experts Group) A standards group that provides file formats and other specifications in regard to full-motion video and other types of graphics displays.

multipurpose Internet mail extensions (MIME) The standard method for defining the content of Internet messages. This standard allows computers to exchange objects, character sets, and multimedia using email, without regard to either the sending or receiving computer's underlying operating system. MIME is defined in the IETF RFC1521 standard.

multitasking The ability of some processor and environment/system combinations to perform more than one task at a time. The applications appear to run simultaneously. For example, you can download messages from an online service, print from a word processor, and recalculate a spreadsheet, all at the same time. Each application receives a slice of time before the processor moves to the next application. Because the time slices are fairly small, it appears to the user that these actions are occurring simultaneously.

multithreading The capability of an application to perform more than one task at once. For example, a word processing application could print in the background while you type in the foreground. Multithreading techniques allow an application to make maximum use of processor cycles. In most cases, it does this by processing data in the background while the foreground task waits for user input.

musical instrument digital interface (MIDI) A method for allowing musical instruments to interact with a computer system. There are two components to MIDI. The hardware component provides a physical connection between a computer and a musical instrument. The software component provides the means to represent music in digital format. This includes storage of the information in a file with either an RMI or MID extension.

NDS See Novell Directory Service.

NetBIOS See network basic input/output system.

network basic input/output system (NetBIOS) This is an application programming interface (API) originally developed for IBM's PC LAN. It's a network communication protocol that resides at the session and transport layers of the OSI model for applications that use it.

network interface card See NIC.

network provider See NP.

NIC (network interface card) The device responsible for allowing a workstation to communicate with the file server and other workstations. It provides the physical means of creating the connection. The card plugs into an expansion slot in the computer. A cable that attaches to the back of the card completes the communication path.

Novell Directory Service (NDS) An object-oriented approach to managing network resources. (This technology was originally called NetWare Directory Services, but was subsequently renamed.) It includes a set of graphical utilities that allows the network administrator to view the entire network at once, even if it includes more than one server or more than one location. There are a variety of object types, including servers, printers, users, and files. NDS not only allows the administrator to manage the resource, but also provides security. As with any object-oriented management approach, NDS gives each object a unique set of properties that the administrator can change as needed.

NP (network provider) The software responsible for performing all the network protocol–specific functions that an application requires. It makes or breaks connections, returns network status information, and provides a consistent interface for the multiple provider router (MPR) to use. An application never calls the NP; only the MPR performs this function.

NTFS (Windows NT File System) The method used by Windows NT/2000/XP to format a hard disk drive. Although it provides significant speed advantages over other formatting techniques, only the Windows NT/2000/XP operating system and applications designed to work with that operating system can access a drive formatted using this technique. Windows 2000 uses NTFS5, a version of this file system designed to provide additional features, like enhanced security. Windows XP uses a newer version of NTFS than Windows 2000 that provides other improvements such as encrypted file sharing.

object When used in the OLE sense of the word, a representation of all or part of a graphic, text, sound, or other data file within a compound document. An object retains its original format and properties. The client application must call on the server application to change or manipulate the object. When used in the component object model (COM) sense of the word, it's the encapsulation of data and code into one file. COM objects don't allow direct manipulation of the data they contain. Data is manipulated through the use of methods that the object contains. In most cases, data manipulation is limited to a list of properties exposed by the object that define the object's operation and other characteristics. Some objects generate events in response to certain types of stimulus by either the system or user. Objects can also receive event notifications through the use of sinks. See COM for additional details.

object conversion A method of changing the format and properties of an object created by one application to the format and properties used by another. Conversion moves the data from one application to another, usually without a loss in formatting, but always without a loss of content.

object linking and embedding See OLE.

ODBC (open database connectivity) A Microsoft-supported standard method for accessing databases. In most cases, this involves three steps: installing an appropriate driver, adding a source to the ODBC applet in the Control Panel, and using SQL statements to access the database.

OEM (original equipment manufacturer) One term used to identify hardware vendors that produce some type of PC hardware. For example, a vendor that designs and builds display adapters is considered an OEM. An OEM is normally responsible for writing drivers and other software required to use the hardware it sells. In some cases, a vendor that puts PCs together using off-the-shelf parts is also considered an OEM, but only with regard to higher-level software, such as an operating system. For example, someone who sells turnkey systems that have all the software installed and configured is considered an OEM.

OLE (object linking and embedding) The process of packaging a filename and any required parameters into an object and then pasting this object into a file created by another application. For example, you could place a graphical object within a word processing document or spreadsheet. When you look at the object, it appears as if you simply pasted the data from the originating application into the current application (similar to DDE). When linked, the data provided by the object automatically changes as you change the data in the original object. When embedded, the data doesn't change unless you specifically edit it, but the data still retains its original format, and you still use the original application to edit the data. Often, you can start the originating application and automatically load the required data by double-clicking the object. The newer OLE 2 specification allows for in-place data editing as well as editing in a separate application window.

open database connectivity See ODBC.

operating system (OS) The software that forms the computer interface between the user and the hardware. The operating system normally provides some type of command processor along with low-level functions used by applications. The user sees these low-level services as the ability to send data to the printer or receive information about a file on the hard drive. The operating system also schedules tasks, maintains the file system, and provides many vital security features.

original equipment manufacturer See OEM.

OS See Operating System.

packet Internet groper See ping.

password caching A method of saving the passwords for resources a user might need to access. The user still needs to enter the main password required to access Windows, but Windows remembers the passwords required in order to access other resources, such as a network or an online service that directly supports the Windows password-caching capability.

PCI See Peripheral Component Interconnect.

PCMCIA (Personal Computer Memory Card International Association) A standards group responsible for the creation of credit card–size devices originally used in laptop PCs. A PCMCIA card could contain devices such as a modem or network card. Some of the more esoteric uses for this card include solid-state hard drives and added system memory. Some people refer to a PCMCIA card as a PC Card. The typical bus speed of PCMCIA is 8.33MHz.

PCX file A raster graphic data format originally used by ZSoft Paintbrush. This format has gone through many nonstandard transitions and occasionally presents problems when accessed by applications other than the original. It provides for various levels of color and includes data compression.

PD (port driver) Performs the task of communicating with a device through an adapter. It's the last stage before a message leaves Windows and the first stage when a message arrives from the device. The PD is usually adapter specific. For example, you would have one VxD for each hard drive and one PD for each hard drive adapter.

PDA (personal digital assistant) A very small PC normally used for personal tasks, such as taking notes and maintaining an itinerary during business trips. PDAs normally rely on special operating systems and lack any standard application support.

Peripheral Component Interconnect (PCI) A type of computer system bus that has relatively high access speeds and a minimum of 32-bit access to the system's memory and processor. Older forms of the bus provided a 33MHz bus speed. A newer form of the PCI bus allows 64-bit data access and a 66MHz or higher bus speed; although the older 32-bit data path is normally used for compatibility purposes.

Personal Computer Memory Card International Association See PCMCIA.

personal digital assistant See PDA.

personal identification number (PIN) A special sequence of numbers that identifies someone as the legitimate user of a security card. A security card can take many forms, the most common of which are ATM and credit cards. In the computer world, security cards are used to grant access to various types of information and to resources like computers and printers.

PIF (program information file) A special configuration file that Windows and OS/2 use to define the environment for a DOS application. A PIF usually includes various memory settings along with the application's command path and working directory.

PIN See Personal Identification Number.

ping (packet Internet groper) A special utility program used to determine whether a TCP/IP connection exists between a workstation and a server. This utility is normally used in conjunction with the Internet, but it can be used to test any TCP/IP connection.

Plug and Play The combination of BIOS, operating system, and peripheral device components that provides a self-configuring environment. This self-configuring feature allows the operating system to avoid potential hardware conflicts by polling the peripheral devices, assessing their requirements, and determining and implementing optimal settings for each device.

port driver See PD.

POST (power-on self test) The set of diagnostic and configuration routines that the BIOS runs during system initialization. For example, the memory counter you see during the boot sequence is part of this process.

power-on self test See POST.

program information file See PIF.

quoting The practice of including all or part of an original message within a response. Quoting allows the viewer to see what the original question was without looking up the original message.

RAID See redundant array of inexpensive disks.

redundant array of inexpensive disks (RAID) A set of interconnected drives that resides outside the file server in most cases. There are several levels of RAID. Each level defines precisely how the data is placed on each of the drives. In all cases, all the drives in a group share responsibility for storing the data. They act in parallel to both read and write the data. In addition, a special drive in most of these systems is devoted to helping the network recover when one drive fails. In most cases, the user never even knows that anything happened; the "spare drive" takes over for the failed drive without any noticeable degradation in network operation. RAID systems increase network reliability and throughput.

REG file A special file used by the Windows Registry to hold a text version of the keys and values it contains. Some applications provide REG files you can use to incorporate their file associations and OLE capabilities into Windows.

Registry key A Registry heading that provides the structure required to hold configuration values and other information required by both Windows and the applications it runs.

Registry value An individual record within the Windows registry database. Each value provides some type of Windows configuration information. There are three types of Registry values: string, DWORD, and binary. Of the three, the only human-readable form is string.

remote access The ability to use a remote resource as you would a local resource. In some cases, this also means downloading the remote resource to use as a local resource.

remote procedure call See RPC.

RPC (remote procedure call) The capacity to use code or data on a remote machine as if it were local. This advanced capability will eventually pave the way for decentralized applications.

SAM See Security Access Manager.

SCSI manager Windows NT introduced the miniport driver. With Windows XP, you can use the Windows NT/2000 miniport binaries. However, before you can actually do that, Windows XP must translate its commands to a format that the miniport driver understands. The SCSI manager performs this service.

SCSIzer A file subsystem component that deals with the SCSI command language. Think of the command language as the method the computer uses to tell a SCSI device to perform a task. The command language isn't the data the SCSI device handles; rather, it's the act that the SCSI device will perform. There's one SCSIzer for each SCSI device.

Security Access Manager (SAM) A database containing information about the user and their security settings. Some texts also call this the Security Accounts Manager. In either case, the information appears within a special hive of the Registry. Windows secures this hive to make it difficult to access using the Registry Editor.

Sequential Packet Exchange (SPX) This is the part of the IPX/SPX protocol pair that guarantees delivery of a message sent from one node to another. Think of SPX as the postal clerk who delivers a certified letter from one place to another. In network terms, each page of the letter is called a packet. SPX delivers the letter one page at a time to the intended party.

serial line interface protocol See SLIP.

server message block (SMB) A network messaging format used on DOS and Windows machines to gain access to resources such as devices, files, and directories. NetBIOS uses SMB as a basis for communication.

server An application or workstation that provides services, resources, or data to a client application or workstation. The client usually makes requests in the form of OLE, DDE, or other command formats.

Setup and Format Table (SFT) A file used by an application during installation. Some applications also use it during setup modification. Applications such as Word for Windows store all their setup information in SFT tables. The SFT tells Word for Windows which features are installed so that it can set up menus accordingly and allow the user to remove or install features later.

SFT See Setup and Format Table.

shell extension A special application that gives some type of added value to the operating system interface. In most cases, the application must register itself with the Registry before the operating system will recognize it.

simple network management protocol See SNMP.

SLIP (Serial Line Interface Protocol) An IETF-approved method for transferring data by using a serial port. One of the problems with this method is that it doesn't compress the data and therefore suffers from poor performance. *CSLIP* is a newer form of this protocol that provides improved performance.

smart card A type of user identification used in place of passwords. The use of a smart card makes it much harder for a third party to break into a computer system using stolen identification. However, a lost or stolen smart card still provides user access. The most secure method of user identification is biometrics.

SMB See Server Message Block.

SNA (Systems Network Architecture) A standard IBM mainframe networking protocol. A PC user would normally use this protocol to access the mainframe using a dial-up connection.

snap-ins Component technologies allow one application to serve as a container for multiple subapplications. A snap-in refers to a component designed to reside within another application. The snap-in performs one specific task, out of all of the tasks the application as a whole can perform. The Microsoft Management Console (MMC) is an example of a host application. Network administrators perform all Windows 2000 management tasks using snap-ins designed to work with MMC.

SNMP (Simple Network Management Protocol) A network protocol, originally designed for the Internet, to manage devices from different vendors.

SPX See Sequential Packet Exchange.

SRAM See Static Random Access Memory.

static random access memory (SRAM) One of several types of basic memory. SRAM uses transistors in place of capacitors to record data. The transistors don't need to be refreshed, making SRAM much faster than its dynamic random access memory (DRAM) counterpart. Because of the higher component count, however, SRAM tends to be bulkier and more expensive than DRAM.

Super Video Graphics Array (SVGA) A display adapter providing several character and graphics modes. It outputs an analog signal that can produce a maximum of 256 colors from a palette of 256,000 colors in graphics and text modes. The high-resolution character mode outputs a display of 80-by-50 characters. The high-resolution graphics mode outputs 1024-by-768 pixels by 16 colors or 800-by-600 pixels by 256 colors.

SVGA See Super Video Graphics Array.

system resource Data, peripheral devices, or other system components used to create, delete, or manipulate documents and produce output.

system virtual machine The component of the Windows operating system responsible for creating virtual machines and managing DOS applications.

Systems Network Architecture See SNA.

tagged image file format (TIFF) A bit-mapped (raster) graphics file format used on the PC and Macintosh. The TIFF file format offers a broad range of color formats, including black-and-white, gray-scale, and color. One of the advantages of using TIF is that it provides a variety of compression methods and offers a smaller storage form factor. Files on the PC often use a TIF extension.

TAPI (Telephony Application Programming Interface) An interface used by applications to interface with various types of communication equipment. This currently includes both modems and fax devices.

task-switching The capacity of an operating system to support more than one application or thread of execution at a time. The foreground application or task is the only one that executes. All other threads of execution are suspended in the background. Contrast this with multitasking, in which all threads—background and foreground—execute.

TCP/IP See Transmission Control Protocol/Internet Protocol.

Telephony API See TAPI.

telephony service provider See TSP.

terminate and stay resident program (TSR) An application that loads itself into memory and stays there once you execute it. The program usually returns you directly to the DOS prompt after loading. Pressing a hot key combination activates the application, allowing you to use the application. In most cases, TSRs provide some type of utility, print spooling, or other short-term function.

thunk The programming interface that translates 32-bit data and system calls to their 16-bit counterparts. The opposite translation takes place, going from a 16-bit application to its 32-bit counterpart.

TIFF See Tagged Image File Format.

Transmission Control Protocol/Internet Protocol (TCP/IP) A standard communication-line protocol developed by the United States Department of Defense. The protocol defines how two devices communicate with each other. Think of the protocol as a type of language used by the two devices.

TrueType A special form of vector font originally provided with Windows but used with other operating systems as well. This vector font provides hinting and other features that give it a smoother appearance onscreen.

TSD See Type-Specific Driver.

TSP (Telephony service provider) A special Windows 95 driver that handles program requests, such as dialing and answering the phone line. It's normally associated with voice modems.

TSR See Terminate and Stay Resident Program.

type-specific driver (TSD) Part of the file subsystem, this layer deals with logical device types rather than specific devices. For example, one TSD handles all the hard drives on your system, and another TSD handles all the floppy drives. A third TSD would handle all network drives.

UAE (unrecoverable application error) A processor or memory error that occurs when an application makes a request the system can't honor. The operating system normally doesn't detect an error of this type. The result is that the system freezes or becomes unstable to the point of being unusable. See also GPF.

UART (universal asynchronous receiver transmission) The chip that allows a serial port to communicate with the outside world. Serial-type devices, such as internal modems, also rely on this chip for communications purposes. Newer versions of this chip include special features, such as a buffer that stores incoming and outgoing characters until the CPU can process them.

UDF See Universal Disk Format.

uniform resource locator (URL) A text representation of a specific location on the Internet. URLs normally include the protocol (`http://` for example), the target location (such as `www` for the World Wide Web), the domain or server name (`mycompany`), and a domain type (`com` for commercial). It can also include a hierarchical location within that Web site. The URL usually specifies a particular file on the Web server, although in some situations a default filename is assumed. For example, asking the browser to find `http://www.mycompany.com` would probably display the default.htm file at that location.

uninterruptible power source (UPS) Usually a combination of an inverter and a battery used to provide power to one or more electrical devices during a power outage. A UPS normally contains power-sensing circuitry and surge-suppression modules. Some UPSs provide standby power and a direct connection between the power source and the protected equipment. Other UPSs use the power source to charge the battery constantly. The protected equipment always derives its power from the inverter, effectively isolating the equipment from the power source.

universal asynchronous receiver transmission See UART.

Universal Disk Format (UDF) A method of accessing compact disk read-only memory (CD-ROM) and digital video disk (DVD) drives that is based on the International Standards Organization (ISO) 13346 standard. This file system replaces the older Compact Disk File System (CDFS), which is based on ISO 9660. There are lots of low-level differences between these two standards. However, from a user perspective, the difference is very easy to understand. UDF supports both CD-ROM drives and DVD-ROM drives. This additional support allows you to gain the advantages that DVDs provide when it comes to choice of media and density of data storage.

universal serial bus See USB.

unrecoverable application error See UAE.

UPS See Uninterruptible Power Source.

URL See uniform resource locator.

USB (universal serial bus) A new form of serial bus that allows multiple external devices to share a single port. This technique reduces the number of interrupts and port addresses required to service the needs of devices such as mice and modems.

VBA (Visual Basic for Applications) A true subset of the Visual Basic language. This form of Visual Basic is normally used within applications in place of a standard macro language. Normally, you can't create standalone applications using this language in its native environment; however, you could move a VBA program to Visual Basic and compile it there.

VBE See Visual Basic Editor.

VDD (virtual display driver) Translates application requests into graphics commands and draws the result in video memory. Windows 3.x used this module as its sole source of communications with the display adapter. Windows XP provides it for compatibility purposes and for DOS applications.

VDM See Virtual DOS Machine.

vector font A type of font that uses mathematical expressions instead of a bitmap to define its characteristics.

VESA (Video Electronics Standards Association) A standards group responsible for creating display adapter and monitor specifications. This group has also worked on other standards, such as the Video Signal Standard (VSIS) and Enhanced Extended Display Identification Data Standard (E-EDID).

VFAT (virtual file allocation table) An enhanced method of disk formatting based on the FAT system. It allows for additional functionality, such as long filenames.

VGA See Video Graphics Array.

Video Electronics Standards Association See VESA.

Video Graphics Array (VGA) A display adapter providing several character and graphics modes. It outputs an analog signal that can produce a maximum of 256 colors from a palette of 256,000 colors in graphics mode. It can also output 16 colors from a pallet of 256,000 colors in text mode. The high-resolution character mode outputs a display of 80-by-50 characters. The high-resolution graphics mode outputs 640-by-480 pixels by 16 colors.

video random access memory See VRAM.

virtual display driver See VDD.

Virtual DOS Machine (VDM) Essentially a single copy of a DOS machine created in memory. This machine provides all the access features of the real thing, but it doesn't physically exist. Windows NT places each DOS application in its own VDM. The reason is simple: To provide the higher-level of system reliability that Windows NT users demand, Microsoft had to make sure that each application had its own environment, an environment completely separate from that used by every other application. It's also important to remember that 16-bit Windows applications share one VDM. You need to remember that Windows NT always starts a VDM and then runs a copy of 16-bit Windows in it to service the needs of 16-bit Windows applications. This effectively adds two layers to every interaction—one for the VDM and another for the WIN32 Subsystem. As with everything else, this additional layering is transparent to the programmer. You still use the same interfaces as before.

virtual file allocation table See VFAT.

Virtual Private Network (VPN) A special setup that newer versions of Windows provide for allowing someone on the road to use the server at work. This is where the virtual part comes in: The connection isn't permanent, and you're using it for a short time. The reason this connection has to be private is that you don't want anyone else to have access to your company's network. You call into your ISP using Dial-Up Networking, which gives you access to the Internet. Then you can use Dial-Up Networking to make a second connection to the server using the Point-to-Point Tunneling Protocol (PPTP). The setup is very secure because it uses two levels of data encryption: digital signing of packets and encrypted passwords.

Visual Basic Editor (VBE) A development environment normally used to create and edit Visual Basic for Applications (VBA) code. VBE is also the extension used for many modern script files. The VBE extension the Visual Basic Script (VBS) extension used in the past.

Visual Basic for Applications See VBA.

volume tracking driver See VTD.

VPN See Virtual Private Network.

VRAM (dual-ported video random access memory) A special form of memory that allows simultaneous reads and writes. It provides a serial read interface and a parallel write interface. The advantage of using VRAM is that it's much faster and doesn't require as much detection code on the part of the application or device driver.

VTD (volume tracking driver) This file subsystem component handles any removable devices attached to your system.

WAN See wide area network.

WDM See Windows Driver Model.

wide area network (WAN) An extension of the LAN. A WAN connects two or more LANs using a variety of methods. A WAN usually encompasses more than one physical site, such as a building. Most WANs rely on microwave communications, fiber optic connections, or leased telephone lines to provide the internetwork connections required to keep all nodes in the network communicating with each other.

Windows Driver Model (WDM) A new method of creating software interfaces to system hardware for Windows. In the past, Windows NT and Windows 9.x used separate driver systems. WDM unites the two operating systems and allows both of them to use the same drivers.

Windows NT File System See NTFS.

Windows Scripting Host (WSH) The Windows capability to write and execute scripts at the system level. This means you no longer have to go through repetitive tasks to get your applications to work together. You can use a script, for example, that scans your hard drive for errors, backs it up, and then optimizes it—all without any work on your part (unless the script encounters an error). Scripts can use one of two default languages: JavaScript or VBScript. They can also be created using script languages, like REXX and Perl, if you have a third-party add-in product that allows their use with WSH.

wizard A specialized application that reduces the complexity of using or configuring your system. For example, the Printer Wizard makes it easier to install a new printer.

WSH See Windows Scripting Host.

Index

G